RUSSIA AND THE RUSSIANS

Russia and the Russians

A History

GEOFFREY HOSKING

THE BELKNAP PRESS OF
HARVARD UNIVERSITY PRESS
Cambridge, Massachusetts

First Harvard University Press paperback edition, 2003

Library of Congress Cataloging-in-Publication Data

Hosking, Geoffrey A.
  Russia and the Russians : a history / Geoffrey Hosking.
    p. cm.
  Includes index.
  ISBN 0-674-00473-6 (cloth)
  ISBN 0-674-01114-7 (paper)
  1. Russia—History. 2. Soviet Union—History. 3. Russia (Federation)—History—1991– I. Title.

DK40.H66 2001
947—dc21
00-065085

CONTENTS

	Preface	*xi*
	Introduction: Geopolitics, Ecology, and National Character	*1*
I	PRE-IMPERIAL RUS AND THE BEGINNINGS OF EMPIRE	*27*
1	Kievan Rus, the Mongols, and the Rise of Muscovy	*29*
2	Ivan IV and the Expansion of Muscovy	*83*
II	THE TROUBLED BUILDING OF EMPIRE	*129*
3	The Turbulent Seventeenth Century	*131*
4	Peter the Great and Europeanization	*175*
III	RUSSIA AS EUROPEAN EMPIRE	*211*
5	State and Society in the Eighteenth Century	*213*
6	The Reigns of Paul, Alexander I, and Nicholas I	*245*
IV	IMPERIAL CRISIS	*283*
7	Alexander II's Uncertain Reforms	*285*
8	The Rise of Nationalism	*320*

V REVOLUTION AND UTOPIA   353

9   Social Change and Revolution   355
10 War and Revolution   386
11 Social Transformation and Terror   427
12 Soviet Society Takes Shape   470

VI THE DECLINE AND FALL OF UTOPIA   507

13 Recovery and Cold War   509
14 Soviet Society under "Developed Socialism"   541
15 From Perestroika to Russian Federation   569

    Chronology   615
    Notes   635
    Index   697

vi

MAPS

1. Kievan Rus, 880–1054   *32*
2. Rivers and trade in 1000 A.D.   *43*
3. The Mongol Empire by 1300   *56*
4. The Republic of Novgorod, 1136–1478   *64*
5. The rise of Moscow, 1261–1533   *84*
6. Muscovy, 1533–1598   *118*
7. The expansion of Muscovy, 1550–1700   *144*
8. The expansion of the Russian Empire, 1700–1800   *188*
9. Western Russia under Catherine the Great   *232*
10. Kazakh steppes and central Asia before the revolution of 1917   *323*
11. Russia at its greatest extent   *330*
12. The Caucasus and Transcaucasian region   *429*
13. Soviet central Asia   *430*
14. The Republics and Autonomous Regions of the Soviet Union in 1970   *560*

Credits: Maps 1–6, 14 from Martin Gilbert, *Russian History Atlas* (London: Weidenfeld & Nicolson, 1972), courtesy A. P. Watt Ltd.; maps 7–9, 11 from Geoffrey Hosking, *Russia: People and Empire* (Cambridge, Mass.: Harvard University Press, 1997), courtesy HarperCollins; map 10 from Serge A. Zenkovsky, *Pan-Turkism and Islam in Russia* (Cambridge, Mass.: Harvard University Press, 1960); map 12 from Anna Matveeva, *The North Caucasus: Russia's Fragile Borderland,* Central Asian and Caucasian Prospects Key Paper (London: Royal Institute of International Affairs, 1999), courtesy Royal Institute of International Affairs; map 13 from Shirin Akiner, "Islam, the State and Ethnicity in Central Asia in Historical Perspective," *Religion, State and Society* 24, no. 2 (1996), courtesy Shirin Akiner.

ILLUSTRATIONS

Following page 128:

1. St. Sophia's Cathedral, Novgorod
2. Andrei Rublev's icon of the Holy Trinity
3. Sixteenth-century Novgorod icon of St. George and the dragon
4. Late sixteenth-century German print of Ivan IV
5. A street in seventeenth-century Moscow, from Adam Olearius, *Description of a Journey to Moscovy*, 1663
6. Engraving after the portrait of Peter I by Karl Moor, 1717
7. Popular print: *The Mice Bury the Cat*
8. Admiralty Wharf: the construction of the Russian navy
9. Nevskii Prospekt, St. Petersburg, in winter
10. Merchants of Nizhnii Novgorod at tea, ca. 1850
11. Old Believers from Semonovskii uezd, Nizhnii Novgorod guberniia, late nineteenth century
12. A peasant ploughing his field, late nineteenth century
13. Peasant officials with land commandant, late nineteenth century
14. Monument to General M. D. Skobelev, Moscow, ca. 1890
15. A Tatar encampment, ca. 1900
16. A village Sunday-school class, addressed by a Baptist preacher

Following page 352:

17. Barricades in the Arbat, Moscow, December 1905
18. A steam train crossing a bridge on the Trans-Siberian Railway, 1911
19. Nicholas II blessing troops in the First World War
20. Army deserters making for home, 1917
21. Lenin and his colleagues in Red Square, October 1918
22. Bagmen at a railway station, ca. 1919
23. Caucasian Muslim women listening to a Communist propagandist, ca. 1920
24. An aristocratic mansion converted into a workers' rest home, 1923
25. Tractor agitators in Samara Province, mid-1920s
26. Queues outside Lenin's Mausoleum, 1928
27. Kirov, Stalin, Kuibyshev, Ordjonikidze, Kalinin, and Voroshilov at the Sixteenth Party Congress, 1930
28. Workers on the building site of a blast furnace at Magnitogorsk, ca. 1930
29. Construction of the opera house, Novosibirsk, late 1930s
30. Architectural model of Moscow University, early 1950s
31. Hungarian uprising, 1956: the decapitated bust of Stalin
32. Khrushchev and U.S. Vice-President Nixon in frank debate, Moscow, 1959

Credits: Figures 1, 7–9 courtesy of Victoria & Albert Museum, London; figures 2–6 courtesy of Professor Lindsey Hughes; figures 10, 15, 16, 18–20, 23, 24, 26, 31, 32 courtesy of Hulton Getty Picture Library; figure 11 courtesy of Nizhnii Novgorod Regional Archive; figures 12, 13, 17, 22, 27, 28 courtesy of State Museum of Contemporary History, Moscow; figures 14, 21, 25 courtesy of Toogood Archive, School of Slavonic and East European Studies, University College London; figure 29 courtesy of Local History Museum, Novosibirsk; figure 30 courtesy of Soviet Fund Archive, School of Slavonic and East European Studies, University College London.

PREFACE

Russia is one of history's great survivors. In one form or another it has existed for more than a thousand years, and for part of that time it has been the largest territorial power on our planet. Today it is one of the most formidable powers in Eurasia, and it will remain so.

It is worth insisting on these facts, since in recent years there has been a tendency among Western policymakers to assume that Russia need no longer be taken seriously, that, as threat or as potential ally, it does not merit concentrated attention any more. In this respect our views have been highly volatile even during the last decade. Ten years ago Russia—then in the form of the Soviet Union—was the toast of Western leaders, the partner who was about to adopt democracy and the market economy and join in a great alliance to build global peace and harmony. Nowadays, since these hopes have not been swiftly realized, and Russia has in the process become weaker, we assume that the country can be largely ignored in our thinking about international affairs.

Both today's attitude and that of ten years ago are illusions, and they rest on ignorance about the nature of Russia—an ignorance which this book attempts to do something to dispel. Russia will not go away; it will continue to play a major part in shaping the twenty-first-century world, and by no means a negative part.

There is another motive for studying Russia closely. For most Europeans and North Americans, Russia is the great Other, understood yet not understood, the culture in whose mirror we better appreciate our own. It is sufficiently near to us and sufficiently like us for its fate to be important to all of us. When we talk to Russian colleagues, when we read Tolstoi or listen to Chaikovskii, we know we are in touch with part of our own civilization, the more illuminating because it is of such high quality and because it comes from a society which is in many ways so different from our own. Russian literature and music continue to be very popular in most Western countries, for very good reason, and we are discovering the richness of its visual arts in the nineteenth and twentieth centuries.

This combined distance and closeness means that we do not have about Russia the stable illusions which Edward Said accuses us of harboring toward the Orient. There are good historical reasons for our ambivalence. Over the centuries, Russia has changed its nature and its boundaries many times. Its peoples have differed sharply among themselves about what they mean by "Russia." In July 1998 the last emperor, Nicholas II, and his family were buried in the Peter-Paul Fortress in St. Petersburg—an occasion, one might have assumed, when Russians of all persuasions might have come together both to mourn and to celebrate their own history. On the contrary, politicians of most parties stayed away, as did the patriarch of the Russian Orthodox Church; even the president decided only at the last moment to attend. The past still divides Russians as much as the present. Even today there is no final agreement about the national flag, the words of the national anthem, or even the name of the country: most Russians would not identify the present Russian Federation as being what they understand by "Russia."

This book is an attempt to seek the roots of our ambivalence toward Russia and of Russians' ambivalence toward their own country. It focuses on the variety of identities which Russia has assumed over the centuries. It contains a basic narrative, which should make it suitable for readers coming to the subject for the first time. At the same time, it is laid out thematically, so that readers wishing to pursue particular subjects can readily do so.

The School of Slavonic and East European Studies at University College London, particularly the History Department and the Centre for Russian Studies, has provided a supportive environment and congenial colleagues for my work on this book, while the contribution of its library cannot be overstated. I thank HarperCollins for permission to reproduce text from *A History of the Soviet Union* (third edition, 1992) and from *Russia: People and Empire, 1552–1917*; and to the *Slavonic & East European Review* for permission to reproduce material from my article "Patronage and the Russian State," in

I thank HarperCollins for permission to reproduce text from *A History of the Soviet Union* (third edition, 1992) and from *Russia: People and Empire, 1552– 1917;* and to the *Slavonic & East European Review* for permission to reproduce material from my article "Patronage and the Russian State," in volume 78 (April 2000). I am especially grateful to Bob Service for reading and commenting on the whole of an earlier draft, and to Roger Bartlett, Pete Duncan, Susan Morrissey, and my daughter Katya for their comments on part of it. Any mistakes and misconceptions which remain are due to my stubbornness. My heartfelt thanks also to Murray Pollinger and Bruce Hunter, assiduous literary agents; to Aida Donald and Stuart Proffitt, dedicated, expert, and caring editors; to Caroline Newlove, departmental administrator, who cheerfully shouldered routine jobs which authors hate but normally have to do themselves; and above all to my wife, Anne, and my daughter Janet, who tolerated for years a grumpy, preoccupied, and frequently absent husband/father. I am much indebted to the Leverhulme Foundation, whose award of a personal research professorship greatly speeded the final writing-up of this text.

xiii

University College London
March 2000

RUSSIA AND THE RUSSIANS

INTRODUCTION: GEOPOLITICS, ECOLOGY, AND NATIONAL CHARACTER

The north Eurasian plain is not only Russia's geographical setting, but also her fate. From the Carpathians in the west to the Greater Khingan range in the east, a huge expanse of flat, open territory dominates the Eurasian continent. It divides into four bands of terrain, running from west to east. In the south is desert, broken only by oases along the rivers which run off the mountains along the southern and eastern rims. Then comes steppe, lightly watered country with a thin and variable covering of grasses and scrub, again broken intermittently by oases, gullies, and river valleys. Farther north is a belt of coniferous forest, interspersed toward its southern edge with deciduous trees; only to the west of the Urals does this deciduous belt broaden to become a large and independent ecological zone. Finally comes the tundra: frozen wastelands and swamp, with broad rivers flowing through them to the Arctic Ocean, itself frozen for much of the year.

This is the area which one may refer to as "Inner Eurasia": it consists of the territory ruled over by the Soviet Union in 1990 plus Xinjiang and Mongolia. Bounded by mountains to east and south, and by usually frozen ocean to the north, this territory lies open to the west. The Ural Mountains, situated toward its western end and conventionally marking the border between Europe and Asia, are too low and easily penetrable to form a serious barrier to movement. Besides, the rivers, with brief portages here and there, offer a relatively easy means of movement throughout the area. It is very unusual to find such broad, long rivers in open flat country. Asian traders who entered the Volga from the Caspian Sea thought that such a majestic river must flow from a high mountain range, whereas actually its source lies in the modest, low-lying Valdai Hills, south of Novgorod.

The southern two ecological bands, and especially the steppe, were classic nomadic country. The sparse vegetation, low precipitation, and open terrain rendered these regions difficult to exploit for settled agriculture, even though much of the soil was very fertile. Agriculturalists without elaborate irrigation systems could expect only meager returns, and they were permanently vulnerable to the raids of their more mobile neighbors. However, herds of cattle, sheep, goats, and in places camels could feed on the foliage, moving on when they exhausted it in any particular locality. The human beings who tended those herds lived largely on hides, meat, and dairy products but—and this is crucial for the history of Eurasia—could not depend on them for all their needs, and hence were compelled to seek some kind of interaction with the oasis dwellers in their midst and with the civilizations around the periphery of their pastoral lands. Inner Eurasia, in short, had to interact with Outer Eurasia. Yet in trade the pastoralists were always at a disadvantage, since they had little to offer except the products of their animals, which settled peoples could also produce for themselves. Hence the tendency for the relationship to become violent: only by honing their military skills and raiding adjacent civilizations could pastoral nomads provide properly for their own way of life.

Kinship groups of fifty to one hundred formed the most convenient way of exploiting this ecology. To defend their terrain and herds, clans would form confederations and devote much attention to the training of horses and riders. Cavalry warfare became much more fearsome after the invention of the stirrup about 500 A.D., which allowed a skilled horseman to use both hands to manipulate weapons, whether lance or bow and arrow.[1]

However, though nomads were supremely skilled warriors, they were inept state-builders. (The history of their most successful empire, the Mongol one, demonstrates this: in its full form it was short-lived, and began to break up almost before it was put together.) Hence in a way it was natural that the most enduring empire of Inner Eurasia should be formed at its extreme western end—in a terrain, moreover, not typical of it, in the broad belt of deciduous woodland found mainly to the west of the river Volga. The first major East Slavic polity was founded at the southern edge of this belt, in Kiev, the second toward its northern edge, in Moscow. Both sites afforded some protection from nomadic raids, Moscow more effectively than Kiev, which probably explains its ultimate ascendancy.

The first East Slavic state was able to establish itself thanks above all to trade, standing as it did athwart north–south routes from Scandinavia to Byzantium intersecting with east–west routes from Persia, India, and China to western Europe. These routes were precarious, for they depended on the nomads' willingness to keep them open. Their decline explains in part why the center of gravity of East Slav civilization shifted northeastward, from the eleventh through the thirteenth centuries, to a region where a rather marginal agriculture combined with fishing, beekeeping, logging, and the fur trade to afford a tolerably stable basis for wealth.

However, once a major state, as distinct from a tribal confederation, was established in Inner Eurasia, there were many reasons why it should prove durable. Such a state commanded a zone so extensive, so strategically placed, and so abundantly endowed with resources that its rulers and subjects could survive almost indefinitely. They could retreat virtually without end, recover from devastating setbacks and reverses, bide their time almost limitlessly, and probe the weaknesses of their neighbors without being fatally undermined by their own.

At the same time, that heartland had its own grave drawbacks. Most of it was relatively infertile, cut off from the sea and thus from easy contact with the outside world, and hampered by very difficult internal communications. These handicaps made the mobilization of people and resources extremely cumbersome. Unless the whole of the heartland and all its major approaches could be occupied, its frontiers were open and vulnerable. Its expanses were settled by numerous peoples with diverse languages, customs, laws, and religions: building and maintaining a state which could assimilate all of them proved to be a complex, costly, and at times apparently vain enterprise.

This paradoxical combination of colossal strength and almost crippling weakness has imparted to the Russian Empire its most salient characteristics.

1. Territorially, Russia has been the most extensive and by far the most labile of the world's major empires. Its boundaries have shifted thousands of miles over the plains in one direction and another. It can readily both invade and be invaded—and over the centuries has both inflicted and suffered aggression repeatedly. With one exception, though (the Mongols in the thirteenth century), the really destructive invasions have come from the west, while the more continuous nagging threats have been from east and south, through the broad "open gates" which stretch from the Caspian Sea to the Urals. Over the centuries Russia has had to divert huge resources to defending extensive vulnerable borders: from the sixteenth to the eighteenth centuries it placed at least half of its armed manpower on the *zasechnaia cherta*, its fortified steppe frontier in the south.

4

It dealt with threatening vacuums on its frontiers by exploiting the relative weakness of disorganized nomadic clans and tribes, and even of larger ethnic groups, to invade and absorb their territories—only to go through periods of overreach, when it imploded, leaving its borderlands vulnerable and once again in the hands of others. In that respect the period since 1989 is not unprecedented. At all times the peoples along the frontier, from the Bashkirs and the Cossacks to the Poles, have proved volatile in their attitude to the empire: at times loyal subjects, at times wary allies, at times bitter foes. In this respect also, the period since 1989 is not an aberration, but a resumption of a historically typical pattern.

2. Russia has usually been a multiethnic empire without a dominant nation, ruled by a dynasty and a heterogeneous aristocracy—at least until nineteenth-century attempts to make the Russians dominant. Unparalleled (except perhaps for the British Empire) in its ethnic and religious diversity, it has normally kept order by means of a multiethnic ruling class drawn from many, though not all, of its subject nationalities. This approach has rendered the distinction between internal and foreign affairs much less well-defined than in most polities. This lack of discrimination applied even to the Soviet Union, which until 1943 dealt with foreign countries partly through the Commissariat of External Affairs and partly through the Comintern, a branch of the Communist Party. One historian has called Stalin the "last of the steppe politicians."[2]

3. It has been an economically underdeveloped empire, situated in a region of extreme temperatures, and after the fifteenth century remote from the world's major trade routes. The sheer size of the country frustrated efforts to mobilize its uniquely diverse and abundant resources. The really important feature of its relative backwardness, however, is that it is due not only to natural handicaps (otherwise Canada would be equally backward), but also to its tendency at each stage of historical evolution to replicate itself. At all stages, vulnerability and poverty have required devoting a large proportion of the wealth of land and population to the provision of armed forces and to the creation of a cumbersome official class for administration and the mobilization of resources. Economic growth was generated more by expanding territory than by capital accumulation or technological innovation, much of which in any case came from abroad.

4. The Russian Empire has been permanently situated between two or, arguably, three ecumenes. In its administrative structures it has been an Asian empire, building upon or adapting the practices of China and the ancient steppe empires. In its culture it has been European for at least three centuries, borrowing heavily from both Protestant and Catholic countries.

In its religion it is Byzantine, derived from an East Roman or Greek Christian ecumene which no longer has a separate existence with its own heartland, but which has left enduring marks on the landscape of Europe. Muscovite tsars were cautious and eclectic in choosing which aspects of this heritage to claim: in the sixteenth century, for example, Ivan IV was both Khan (Asiatic ruler) and Basileus (Christian emperor), and resisted the temptation to come down on one side by taking the concept of the "Third Rome" as a basis for his foreign policy. Russia could not simply be a crusading Christian power, since such an ambiguous stance would provoke violent resistance among its considerable Muslim population.

In combining these legacies Russia has frequently offended the sensibilities of its neighbors. Muscovy was described by at least one European visitor in the sixteenth century as a "rude and barbarous kingdom," and it was omitted from the published register of Christian powers maintained by the Vatican. In the late eighteenth century it was widely condemned for deliberately interfering in Polish internal affairs with the aim of undermining and destroying the Polish state—a technique it had frequently employed to overcome its steppe neighbors, from the khanate of Kazan onward. (Such sensibilities did not restrain Prussia and Austria from joining in the carve-up, so the outrage was partly hypocritical.)[3]

Internally, because of its size and vulnerability, Russia needed the structure of an authoritarian state, but in practice, because of the extent of the territory and backwardness of the economy, that state could not directly control the lives of most of the population. Having to improvise structures often urgently and in adversity, it has tended, therefore, not to create enduring laws or institutions, but rather to give official backing to existing personal power relationships. In this respect it partially resembled ancient Rome, which also had to hold together a diverse and extensive land-based empire by military means, and which did so by cultivating binding patron-client relationships (though the sense of law and citizenship was much stronger in the Roman Empire).[4] Such relationships were articulated in the *druzhina* system and *kormlenie* in Kievan Rus and Muscovy, in the landlord-serf relationship in imperial Russia, and in the *nomenklatura* (personnel appointment) system in the Soviet Union. Often the main function of the grand prince/tsar/general secretary has been to mediate and adjudicate between cliques centering upon powerful personalities; both Ivan IV and Stalin tried through terror either to extirpate them or to gain complete control over them, but failed.[5]

The result has been strong, cohesive structures at the apex and the base of society, but in between them weak and labile institutions which have depended largely on personalities. This is the absence of "civil society" which so many observers have noted. The structures the state has needed for recruitment and taxation have tended to perpetuate this intermediate weakness, by exhausting the resources needed for anything more than mere survival and by enfeebling potentially autonomous institutions. Even today, when Russia's strategic vulnerability is much less serious, the structures and mentalities associated with its past needs have survived to obstruct the creation of a market economy, a civil society, and a functioning democracy. Politically, socially, and economically, Russia is still best understood as a network of interlocking patron-client relationships. This is one reason why post-Soviet Russia has such difficulty in generating its own sense of civic community.

Russia has been surrounded by other, usually smaller but still often formidable heartlands or core areas (to use the terminology of Halford McKinder): (1) the Scandinavian world, dominated first by the Vikings, then by Denmark, then by Sweden; (2) Poland; (3) Turkey/the Ottoman Empire; (4) Persia; and (5) China. As the Slav tribes and the peoples of Rus and Russia migrated and expanded, they fetched up against the outliers of these other heartlands, with their own dominant states and peoples. Because of its unique capacity for endurance, Russia was able to wait till each of them went through a period of weakness, for whatever reason, and then move to occupy the peripheral zone between them, or in the case of Poland the core as well. She suffered the same fate herself at the hands of the Mongols in the thirteenth to fifteenth centuries, and much more briefly from the Swedes and Poles in the early seventeenth century. But Rus/Russia recovered from both setbacks and reasserted itself each time with greater force. She proved able to survive even the catastrophic collapse of empire in the early twentieth century.

Against a strong power, Russia has tended to adopt a closed-border policy, intended to keep the other side out and to make possible stable and peaceful trading and diplomatic relations. A weak power on the borders, on the other hand, is both a threat and an opportunity: a threat because it creates a potential vacuum or center of turbulence which can easily degrade or even destroy the border, but also an opportunity because it offers the possibility of expansion. To repel the threat and grasp the opportunity, Russia has tended to deal closely with tribal or ethnic leaders in the zone of turbulence, first to gain information from them, then to influence them or cause divisions between them, then to gain some or all of them as allies, and finally if possible to annex them. In this way the expansion of Russia has led to the strengthening of patron-client nexuses in the borderlands.[6]

AGRICULTURE, HABITATION, AND DIET

One requirement of a heartland is that it afford a strong economic base with good internal communications. As we have seen, the Eurasian heartland is not ideal in this respect. It has always been an unpromising, though not quite hopeless, environment for human development. Its southern, more fertile zones were liable to aridity, which meant that in bad years the harvest could fail totally. Besides, precisely these regions were vulnerable to nomadic devastation. The northern zones, on the other hand, though protected from attack by dense woodland, were cold, waterlogged, and infertile. Only the broad deciduous belt of woodland west of the Urals enabled Rus to become the cradle of a civilization at all. Here the woodland could be relatively easily cleared, and, although the podzol soils were thin, the annual deposit of leaves built up a humus. The first East Slav state, Kiev, was toward the southern edge of this belt, already wooded steppeland, but proved in the long run too vulnerable to nomad attack, and so the focus of Rus moved northeastward to the Opolie region, between the Kliazma and Volga Rivers, an area of unusually north-lying fertile soil, where Vladimir, Rostov, and Suzdal are situated. Moscow, the eventual heartland, lies between the two, but closer to the northern extremity of the belt.

Until the eighteenth century, then, nearly all Russian peasants lived in the forest or at least close to an abundant source of timber. For that reason most of their artifacts were wooden, the only major exception being the ax, which as a result was a specially treasured implement. Ploughs and harrows were wooden, though they might be tipped with iron. All furniture was made of wood, without screws or nails, by precise measuring and joining. Likewise cooking utensils, storage vessels, plates, bowls, and dishes. Carts, sledges, and boats, the main modes of transport and carrying, were all wooden. Most important of all, the peasant hut, the *izba*, was constructed of tree trunks, carefully selected, arranged, and hewed, trimmed and dovetailed at the corners, and often hung with decorated bargeboards or window frames *(nalichniki)*. Even after peasants settled in the treeless steppes in the eighteenth century, the mainframe of the hut remained wooden, though its infill would be of a straw-filled clay daub whitewashed on the outside; this structure was known as a *khata*.[7]

The only nonwooden part of the peasant hut was also its single most important component, the stove. Whereas the rest of the dwelling was normally built by the family, the stove would always be constructed by a specialist, for its malfunctioning could be fatal. It was normally made of brick or clay and could occupy a good deal of the internal living space—reasonably enough, when one considers that it was used for both cooking and sleeping. An early eighteenth-century visitor to Russia described the scene:

> The Peasants Houses are wholly built of Wood, without Stonework, Iron, or Glass-Windows: They have extraordinary large Stoves, which take up one fourth Part of the Room. Such a Stove being well heated, and then shut up towards Evening, the whole Family go to lie promiscuously on the Top of it, and bake themselves thoroughly. If the Stove cannot hold them all, there are Shelves made under the Ceiling, on which the rest stow themselves, for no body lies on the Ground.[8]

Even towns were almost entirely constructed of wood till the eighteenth century. Anthony Jenkinson, the English merchant who visited northern Russia in 1557, reported that in Vologda, "a great Citie . . . the houses are builded with wood of Firre, joined one with another . . . without any iron or stone worke, covered with Birch barkes, and wood all over the same." Even many nobles' townhouses and palaces were made of wood, and as a result none of them has survived. Important churches were built of brick or, better still, stone, but even so some old wooden churches have come down to us, notably the fantastically decorated Church of the Transfiguration at Kizhi, on Lake Onega, with its twenty-two small onion domes set back one above the other, climaxing in a larger dome at the apex.

One compensation for the poor quality of the land was its relative abundance. It was natural, then, that cultivation should be extensive rather than intensive: cultivators would clear woodland as needed by slash-and-burn methods and then extract the maximum from the soil in a short time, before exhausting it and moving on to repeat the process nearby. The natural implement to use in tillage was the *sokha*, the wooden plough (though it might have metal tips), which scratched the soil rather than turning it up, but enabled a large acreage to be covered each day. Yields with this method of ploughing were modest—typically three ears of corn to each one sown—and they were the minimum needed for survival. There was little or no surplus left over for error, misfortune, or the vagaries of the short, unpredictable Russian summer. In Vologda Province it was reckoned in the nineteenth century that reliable summer, during which grass and corn would definitely grow and ripen, lasted only from 8 June to 20 July (20 June to 1 August by the Gregorian calendar). The season might extend a little either way, but equally there might be frosts at either end of it to damage or kill growing plants. Given such marginality, harvest failures tended to be cumulative, since the meager reserves consumed to make up one year's shortfall were no longer available to sow for the following year's harvest.[9]

Epidemics went together with famine and were intensified by population movement on the open Eurasian plain. Bubonic plague remained a serious problem till the late eighteenth century, with particularly savage outbreaks in 1654–1656 and 1770–71. The last of these may have killed as many as 20 percent of the population of Moscow and its district. After the plague eased off, cholera made its appearance, killing perhaps a quarter of a million people in 1830–31 and a million in 1847–1851, while typhus, tuberculosis, pneumonia, and dysentery all claimed numerous victims. These epidemics were especially severe in the cities, where extreme congestion combined with poor sewage facilities and a partially contaminated water supply. The Russian state attempted to implement public health measures from the 1770s onward but was constrained both by lack of resources and by peasants' suspicion of hygienic measures, which violated their traditional norms and which they regarded as actually exacerbating disease.[10]

All this amounted to a highly risk-prone environment, especially if one also considers the constant hazard of fire in villages and towns built almost entirely of wood. It is scarcely surprising, then, that Russian peasants have tended to arrange their social and economic life in such a way as to minimize risk and provide mutual re-insurance. That is why they adopted *krugovaia poruka,* or "joint responsibility," consensus decisionmaking in a communal assembly, a strip system of land tenure, and the practice, which grew commoner in the seventeenth and eighteenth centuries as the state's tax demands grew, of periodically redistributing land among the households of a given village. Thus many of the practices which obstructed economic development were the result of a harsh and risk-filled environment, which encouraged risk minimization and short-term economic horizons.[11]

The mainstay of the peasant diet was grain, above all rye (known in some regions as *zhito,* from the word meaning "life"), which grows reliably in cool and damp soils, even if its yields are not high. It makes a tasty and nutritious, if rather heavy, bread, which has become the characteristic accompaniment to Russian food of all kinds. Wheat and its outcome, white bread, were considered a luxury even after the southern steppes became available for regular cultivation in the late eighteenth century, but buckwheat was often grown and became the basis of a form of gruel *(kasha)* still often used to accompany meat dishes. Oats were grown for animal feed and for *kasha.* All kinds of grain were widely used to make dumplings and pancakes *(bliny)* and to thicken soups and stews. Flax and hemp, which also flourish in northern soils, were crushed to provide oil, as well as being used for textiles.

10

Considering the importance of grain to the people's diet, the Russian state did remarkably little, compared with the Chinese Empire or some west European states, to regulate its quality or price. It is true that in the late sixteenth and early seventeenth centuries, when famine constantly threatened, there were efforts to do both, in the interests of maintaining public order. The landowners' duty to assist their serfs in case of a poor harvest was laid down by decree in 1734 but was not often put into practice. Furthermore, in the mid-eighteenth century, P. I. Shuvalov proposed that the state establish grain stores, to provision the army, to provide for the needy in case of famine, and to moderate fluctuations in bread prices by releasing grain at times of shortage. Nothing was done, perhaps because storage was a problem, perhaps because the great landowners favored high grain prices. As a result, after poor harvests in 1785 and 1786, people were reported to be eating leaves, hay, and moss. More effective measures were taken from the 1820s, but even so, serious famines occurred as late as 1891, 1932–33, and 1946–47. The latter two were aggravated by perverse state policies, but a persistent problem even before then was the shortage of livestock, which rendered Russian peasants overdependent on grain crops for both subsistence and marketing and kept the soil they cultivated deficient in manure.[12]

The overdependence on grain can be clearly seen in the patterns of dearth and abundance. There was a very marked seasonal fluctuation, which would have been less obvious if dairy and meat products had played a larger role. Each year, as autumn turned to winter, berries and mushrooms could no longer be found, fresh vegetables became scarce, and peasants turned more and more to grain and preserved foods.[13]

At one stage the government did hope to improve the people's diet by introducing potatoes, whose advantage was that they provided a higher level of nutrition by acreage than grain. On the other hand, they required a greater and more continuous input of labor, and for most Russian peasants until well into the nineteenth century shortage of land was not a problem. The peasants objected to the compulsory disruption of their well-tried routines, and in some cases rioted when efforts were made to compel them to plant potatoes.[14]

Yet, curiously enough, over the following decades, peasants in most parts of Russia, especially the center and north, peacefully introduced potatoes into their agricultural cycle and their diets, without any compulsion. It may be that by the second half of the nineteenth century the pressure of land shortage was beginning to make the potato's advantages more obvious: significantly, many of the riots had taken place in the north and east, where there was plenty of land.[15]

The main vegetable crop for many centuries was the turnip, which was the functional equivalent of potatoes till the latter eventually took hold. Beetroot and cabbage were also common, both being used to make soups. Cabbage was pickled to preserve it, giving it the distinctive taste which we associate with sauerkraut, and the same was done with cucumbers. Garlic and onion were often used to flavor dishes, to an extent which some foreigners found distasteful. Adam Olearius reported in the seventeenth century: "They generally prepare their food with garlic and onion, so all their rooms and houses, including the sumptuous chambers of the Grand Prince's palace in the Kremlin, give off an odor offensive to us Germans."[16]

Apples, pears, and plums were grown from early times, while cherries were a speciality of the Vladimir region. Berries were plentiful in the forests, as were mushrooms; many Russians pride themselves on an expert knowledge of fungi even today—though they have more or less disappeared from the woods around large towns, wiped out by air pollution.

The abundance of rivers and lakes ensured that Russians could usually rely on a good supply of freshwater fish, which could be salted and preserved for long periods. They could catch fish even in winter by carving a hole in the ice and letting a line dangle through it. Fish is the main component of *zakuski,* the hors d'oeuvre, and is often the basis of soup and main dish as well. The widespread consumption of meat, however, is a fairly recent custom for ordinary people; in any case Orthodox fasting laws forbade consumption of meat for roughly half the year, while permitting fish at any time. Over the centuries Russian peasants have kept few cows, and then (along with goats) mainly for their milk, which was used to create an impressive variety of fermented or semifermented drinks: *smetana* (sour cream), *tvorog* (roughly: cottage cheese), *kefir, prostokvasha* (forms of yogurt).

The classic Russian drink, vodka, seems to have made its appearance in the mid-fifteenth century, perhaps as a result of the visit of an official Muscovite church delegation to the Council of Florence-Ferrara, where they saw how aquavit was made. The technique could easily have been taken over by Russian monks, applied to grain, and systematized in the monasteries. During the fifteenth century the three-field crop rotation system was being widely adopted in Muscovy, and it generated a considerable growth in grain production, leaving a surplus to be converted into spirits.[17] Apart from vodka, the commonest drinks were ale; mead, prepared from honey which was cultivated in forest beehives; and kvas, which was made from lightly fermented grain.

Both the state and the church took an interest in drink, partly with an eye to the potential revenue and partly out of concern about public disorder.

In the very earliest chronicles Prince Vladimir is quoted as saying that he could not consider adopting Islam as a religion because "drink is the joy of Rus, and we cannot do without it."[18] While moderate consumption of alcohol did take place, for example in monasteries, much brewing was done for public or family festivals, where there was the danger of excess. A mid-fifteenth-century statute, aimed at the peasants on a court estate, ordained that "if any man in a village or hamlet happens to have a feast or fraternity [celebration], they are not to go uninvited to drink . . . but if anyone is invited to a feast or fraternity, when he has drunk he is not to spend the night there."[19]

By the sixteenth century the increase in the number of taverns worried the church, which warned that they promoted licentious and immoral behavior, sometimes associated with pagan celebrations. "For if, in the world's custom, men and women indulge in intoxicating drink, then certain sacrilegious persons will come, playing psalteries, viols, drones and drums, and other devilish games and playing pranks before married women, leaping and singing ribald songs . . . and each man gives a drink and kisses another's wife and then embraces will be accepted and insidious speeches woven and devilish mating."[20] These were not the only results of public drinking. By the nineteenth century, when serious sociological study of the problem started, it was clear that excessive consumption of alcohol led to crime and hooliganism, and that it caused dependency which could easily undermine a peasant household economy and lead to the breakup of the family.[21]

Although the state shared the church's concern, it never mounted a concerted campaign to limit the sale of alcohol or to reduce drunkenness. The reason is not hard to find: over the centuries far too high a proportion of its revenues derived from the proceeds of selling liquor. As Alexander I remarked in the early nineteenth century, "No other major source of revenue enters the treasury so regularly, punctually, and easily as the revenue from the liquor farm; indeed its regular receipt on a fixed date each month greatly eases the task of finding cash for other expenditures." At times during the eighteenth century it seems to have constituted nearly half of the treasury's indirect tax revenue, while for most of the nineteenth century it hovered at around one-third or just under.[22]

It was levied in different ways at different times. For several centuries the most convenient procedure was to farm out *kabaki,* or taverns, to concessionaires (sometimes *tselovalniki,* sworn state officials who also served the courts and police and collected the salt tax) who would pass on a stipulated share of their income to the treasury. At a time of primitive communications, there was probably little alternative, but of course this system was wide open to abuse, since there were scant means of checking it: the unscrupulous could, and did, make huge profits by concealing the true extent of their turnover or by offering adulterated or inferior liquor at high prices. As official monitoring became more intrusive, the liquor farmers would respond by bribery, to an extent that by the 1850s the governor of Samara Province reported that "all police officials and most government officials of any consequence" were receiving a "regular salary . . . from the liquor farmers."[23]

At other times the government experimented with an excise levied directly on the distillers of liquor, and at others still with a direct monopoly, but found that all these methods were open to abuse and did little to alleviate public drunkenness. In any case, throughout the eighteenth and much of the nineteenth centuries the landowners were the main producers of strong alcohol, made a handsome profit from it by using serf labor, and had an overwhelming interest in not losing the income derived from it. Indeed, it might reasonably be argued that the liquor trade was lubricating an otherwise undermonetarized economy.[24]

The problem of public drunkenness arose not only because of the government's fiscal policies, but also from popular custom. From the earliest times East Slavs would drink heavily at festival time. Perhaps this fitted the life rhythm which the climate and seasons imposed on them: long periods of extremely hard work followed by long periods of leisure. Perhaps their orgiastic drinking helped them to escape from a drab and monotonous existence, though this is probably to impose twentieth-century preconceptions on a very different world. Most likely it had to do with the overwhelming importance of local community life. Long bouts of drinking spirits helped to bond together adult males, or at least nearly all Russian men are convinced that this is the case, whatever their women and children may think about it.

Perhaps, then, it was a malign combination of popular custom, fiscal need, and producers' interests which generated the centuries-old momentum of Russian drunkenness. The same combination almost certainly explains another peculiarity of Russian drinking, the dominance of kvas and vodka, that is to say of very weak and very strong drink, rather than the moderate drinking represented by beer and wine, which is popular in most European countries. Kvas can be easily and quickly produced in most households from any grain or from bread, has an alcohol content of less than 2 percent, and therefore served as an everyday drink for ordinary people. Vodka by contrast requires elaborate distilling equipment and entailed investment beyond the means of most households. It was comparatively speaking a luxury and could intoxicate very rapidly, especially if downed a whole glassful at a time, as Russians in company like to do (they may take it as an insult if a drinking partner refuses to). The dichotomy kvas/vodka thus preserved the very sharp division between the everyday and the festival which was an integral part of Russian peasant life.

An antidote to the heavy drinking of alcohol was provided by tea, which began to enter Russia in quantity, mostly from China, in the late eighteenth century. For a time it was a luxury beverage and served as a means by which wealthy merchant and noble families could mark out their status. From the mid-nineteenth century it was grown on plantations along the Black Sea coast in Georgia and thus became cheaper and more widely available in Russia. It is said that the pioneer planter was a Scotsman captured in the Crimean War who settled in Georgia but could not bear the thought of life without regular cups of tea. The samovar (which, though we think of it as quintessentially Russian, probably derived from the English or Dutch tea urn) then became a symbol of affluent domesticity. By the late nineteenth century, however, it was spreading among ordinary folk in both the town and the countryside. Churchmen and social reformers began to hope that it could provide a moderate stimulus and refreshment such as would rival the attractions of vodka.[25]

Another crucial element in the Russian diet, as elsewhere, was salt, partly as a seasoning but mainly for its capacity to preserve perishable produce over protracted journeys or through the long months when little could be grown in the fields. Since it is plentiful in some parts of Russia and a relatively simple mineral to extract, its treatment became the most important non-agricultural activity until the eighteenth century. It can be extracted from seawater or from brines either lying on the surface or pumped from the subsoil, then channeled into crystallization pans and left to evaporate in the sun. The industry was known from the earliest recorded times along the White Sea coast, where for example the Solovki Monastery came to play a major role in its production and trade; along the Sukhona, Vychegda, and Northern Dvina Rivers; and along much of the length of the Kama and Volga.

The conquest of the lower Volga and the Astrakhan region in the sixteenth century seems to have displaced much of the earlier trade, for there whole lakes, of very high salinity, were available. As Olearius reported: "In the lagoons or salt sloughs there are salt veins through which the salt rises. On the surface, the heat of the sun causes the formation of flakes of salt as clear as crystal and as thick as one's finger . . . The Russians do a thriving business with it, transporting it up the shores of the Volga, piling it up in great quantities, and shipping it all over Russia."[26] The grand princes imposed a levy on the salt trade. It varied from time to time and place to place, and in general was not heavy. When Tsar Aleksei tried to raise it significantly for military purposes in the mid-seventeenth century, he provoked mass urban riots.

MENTALITIES — THE KEY CONCEPTS: *MIR* AND *PRAVDA*

Living in geopolitically vulnerable and agriculturally marginal territory has formed the Russian character in ways which are only now, on the threshold of the twenty-first century, beginning to change fundamentally.

Survival itself was always at issue. At the height of sowing, haymaking, and harvesting, farmers had to work extremely hard for brief periods: this was known as *strada*, or suffering. On the other hand, for six or seven months of the year agricultural labor was impossible because of heavy frost or deep snow. To make ends meet, it was essential for a peasant to have skills other than those of agriculture: making furniture, clothes, or implements, for example, for household use or for selling on the local market. The optimum personality type was versatile, not narrowly specialized, capable of bursts of energy, but not necessarily disciplined to regular labor. As the nineteenth-century historian Vasilii Kliuchevskii remarked, "Not one people in Europe is capable of such extreme exertion for a short period as the Great Russian; but probably nowhere else in Europe can one find such incapacity for steady, moderate, measured work."[27] This versatility and capacity for extraordinarily hard work in emergency probably explains why Russians make good soldiers, provided they are properly led.

It must be added that any amount of work, whether intense or prolonged, might easily fail to bring its reward. Such was the marginality of the land that a thunderstorm or heavy rains at a crucial period might deprive the cultivator of the fruits of months of frugality and labor. Peasants did what they could to anticipate and mitigate the effects of such unforeseen mishaps by studying the "signal system of nature": changes in the sky, the sun, or the moon, in the way trees swayed or streams flowed. Perhaps that is why pagan beliefs in the spirits of the woods, fields, and rivers persisted so long among them. But however carefully they might divine natural signs, they were helpless in the face of sudden misfortune. As a result, Russians are disinclined to plan ahead or to invest steady, calculated effort in any enterprise. Instead they tend to look to good fortune to help them, while always fearing that "evil spirits" may strike at any time.

During the *strada* any setback—illness, injury, fire, labor duty for the landlord—could endanger a household's entire annual production. This hazard augmented the importance of the community. Households had a better chance of survival if they could call on help in an emergency, and they would expect to offer it in the event of a neighbor's misfortune. The custom of *pomochi* (emergency mutual aid) was not altruism but merely common sense for vulnerable communities. Neighbors would usually rally round to help rebuild a burnt-out hut or to bring in the harvest of a household crippled by illness. If possible, the beneficiaries of *pomochi* would offer vodka to their helpers, so that the work could be rounded off with a bout of celebration: drinking, singing, and dancing. But if they were too poor to offer hospitality, it was accepted that help should be given anyway.[28]

Community solidarity was needed not only at times of emergency. The narrowness of the margins of survival made it unusually important that members of rural settlements should reach a consensus on such matters as use of timber and common lands, gleaning rights, access to water, and the upkeep of roads and bridges. Conflict was not merely damaging: it might threaten the community's existence. The ideal of the rural community was *mir*, which means "peace" but in time came to be adopted as the name of the community itself. In England the "king's peace" was imposed from above, through sheriffs and royal courts. In medieval Rus, the prince was too far away and communications too poor; the community had to devise its own means of preserving harmony. Our sources do not tell us how this was done, though it seems likely that regular meetings of heads of households were the normal practice, to thrash out problems and disagreements, and if possible to reach a consensus which did not override individual interests too flagrantly. "Joint responsibility" *(krugovaia poruka)* was a well-developed custom long before it became an administrative device, to facilitate tax collecting and recruitment, in the seventeenth century.[29]

It was all the more important because, in practice, conflict, latent or open, was rife within rural communities, between indigent and affluent, young and old, men and women. Peasants were suspicious of both the rich and the poor, for they undermined community principles, the poor by draining resources from their neighbors, the rich because they did not need their neighbors. As a popular saying had it, "Wealth is a sin before God, and poverty is a sin before one's fellow villagers."[30] Egalitarianism and mutual harmony were not often achieved, but they remained ideals for all that.

"Joint responsibility" affected the peasant's attitude to all social institutions: law, authority, tradition, property. It was especially marked in relation to the land. Peasants regarded the land as belonging to God but not to any human being. It was a resource available to all who cultivated it and to their dependents, as and when they needed it. In some regions, from the seventeenth century, as state obligations became more onerous and in some regions land was beginning to be scarce, the mir would give tangible form to this view by periodically redistributing strips of land among its own members, awarding more to larger households and less to smaller ones. The tax burden would then be reapportioned correspondingly. Even where redistribution was not practiced, however, belief in the land as a common resource persisted. When the money economy became generally accepted, in the second half of the nineteenth century, this belief did not stop peasants from buying and selling land, but they continued, perhaps contradictorily, to take it for granted that a basic minimum would always be available to them, and that in times of emergency, such as war, revolution, or famine, all land could be claimed by the community.[31]

In post-Soviet Russia, feelings about the land remain divided. While the president and the government endeavor to create a full-scale market in land, the Duma and much of public opinion continue to regard individual freehold property in land as immoral.

Since the village was a tightly knit and interdependent community, Russians have always been acutely conscious of the distinction between "insiders" and "outsiders," an attitude which they readily transfer to the international plane. The contrast between *my* (we) and *oni* (they) is very marked, and the judgment *on—ne nash* (he's not one of us) correspondingly damning. The phrase *u nas* (in our village, at our workplace, in our country) is very evocative and frequently used; Russians are always surprised that English has no precise equivalent.

In a certain sense the village assembly was democratic, in that all households participated in its decisionmaking. All the same, it was not democratic in any sense we would now recognize. Heads of households were the oldest males in extended families. Younger men and women were excluded, or at least played only a subordinate and indirect role in village politics. For them especially, membership in the community entailed continuous restraint and self-control, the avoidance of behavior which might weaken family life, undermine the economic viability of the household, or even merely arouse malicious gossip. Both the Orthodox Church and peasant custom laid down very strict norms in fasting and in sexual behavior, as if to underpin a self-denial necessary both because of poverty and because of the overriding need to maintain community values.[32]

These values were summed up in the single word *pravda*. It meant "truth," but also much more, in fact everything the community regarded as "right": justice, morality, God's law, behaving according to conscience. The criterion for any decision taken by the village assembly was that it must accord with pravda. Pravda was the collective wisdom of the community, accumulated over the generations. The whole of life was regarded as a struggle between pravda and *nepravda* or *krivda* (crookedness). Pravda was order and beauty, where the home was clean and tidy, family life was harmonious, the fields were well cultivated and the crops grew regularly. *Nepravda* was a world of disorder and ugliness, where families were riven by conflict, the home was dirty and untidy, the fields were neglected and famine reigned. The orderly world was created by God and was under the protection of the saints, the disorderly one was the province of the "unclean spirit" *(nechistaia sila),* the devil. Outside the community, officials were judged according to whether their behavior exemplified pravda or not. The grand prince or tsar was assumed to embody it through his status as God's anointed: if he manifestly did not, then he must be a "false tsar," and the true one had to be found.[33]

Given the rigid and demanding norms of community life, it is not surprising that, at least subconsciously, peasants yearned to escape them, to break away and begin a new life of *volia* (freedom). Many young men did so, either by simply establishing a new household or, more radically, by fleeing to the frontier and becoming a brigand or perhaps joining the Cossacks (the term "cossack" derives from a Turkish word meaning "free man," as distinct from serf). Hence migration rates were very high, as we shall see. Volia is not freedom as that is understood in modern democratic societies, for which another word exists: *svoboda.* Rather, volia is the absence of any constraint, the right to gallop off into the open steppe, the "wild field" *(dikoe pole),* and there to make one's living without humble drudgery, by hunting or fishing, or if necessary by brigandage and plunder. Volia does not recognize any restriction imposed by the equivalent freedom of others: it is nomadic freedom rather than civic freedom. The scholar Dmitrii Likhachev has called it *"Svoboda* plus open spaces." It helps to explain the otherwise unbelievably rapid penetration of Siberia, a territory which, in the words of the writer Valentin Rasputin, "originated in runaway serfs and Cossacks."[34]

Members of a village community not only needed each other; they also needed if possible a protector, someone from the elite who could direct a minimum of material wealth in their direction, provide for them in case of disaster, and help to mitigate or divert the disfavor of the mighty. One reason, then, why serfdom became so widespread in Russia was that it could be useful to the serfs as well as the serf-owners. Not that all serf-owners fulfilled their role properly. Some of them merely practiced repression and exploitation. However, they too had an interest in the survival of their serfs. Some kept granaries to supplement the peasant diet in case of famine, or provided employment to tide villagers over a period of idleness and poverty. In all cases, however, whether the patron was good or bad, the elected village elder *(starosta)* was the key intermediary who communicated to him the village's needs, brought back his commands, and saw that they were carried out.[35]

MIGRATION AND COLONIZATION

The difficulties of agriculture in the heartland of Rus, the openness of the frontiers, and the relentless demands of tax collectors and recruiting sergeants spurred a substantial minority of more enterprising peasants from the sixteenth century onward to abandon their unrewarding holdings and to seek their fortune in the south and east. Over the centuries this intermittent but never altogether ceasing flow of population was a powerful motor of imperial expansion and shifted the center of Russia dramatically southward and eastward. In fact Kliuchevskii called migration and colonization "the fundamental feature of Russian history."[36]

According to the household tax census of 1678, some 70 percent of the peasant population lived in the pre-sixteenth-century territories of Muscovy, whereas just over two centuries later, in 1897, only just over 40 percent did so, while nearly 60 percent lived in territories assimilated since the mid-sixteenth century: the Central Black Earth zone, the mid- and lower Volga basin, the southern Urals, and Siberia. In making this move, households or individuals were not only leaving behind familiar communities and undertaking long, hazardous journeys: they were also moving from forest to steppe, where the soil was more fertile but the dangers much greater, and from universal settled agriculture to interaction with nomads. They were entering a region where the reach of the Russian state, wanted or unwanted, was less assured.

On arrival, new agricultural techniques had to be learned and adopted. The soil was better, but also much heavier: the *sokha,* or wooden plough, which had sufficed to break up the light soils of the north, could not cope with the black earth, and had to give way to the *plug,* or metal plough. This in turn required oxen to pull it, which meant more systematic stockraising. Timber was much scarcer, as were fishing grounds, so that the cultivation of cereals became dominant. Those used to waterlogged soils now found that drought was the more serious threat. In the long run, though, the rewards for the adaptable and successful were considerable, since wheat and maize, marginal or impossible farther north, flourished here, as well as sunflowers, sugar beet, and tobacco, all of which were much more marketable than the rye and oats of northern soils.[37]

From the sixteenth century on, many of the settlers in these parts were drawn by the state into frontier defense service on one of the "lines" *(za-seki)*—loose chains of fortified towns, fortresses, and blockhouses joined by felled trees, ramparts, and trenches, running from southwest to northeast. Over the next three centuries they were established ever farther to the south and east. Fugitive peasants, impoverished service nobles, brigands, Cossacks, and even Tatars desirous of land and income would take themselves thither and enroll for service, no questions asked. The terms of service restricted their freedom of movement: they had to man the guard posts, patrol the frontiers, and be ready to join the cavalry detachments deployed to repel invaders; but in return they were guaranteed sufficient land to live on, some protection, and supplementation of their income in time of famine. Some were allowed to own a few serfs, but no larger serf estates were established till the frontier had moved much farther on to the southeast by the early eighteenth century. Those who did not live close to a fortress would gather in relatively large villages, with all the homes clustered along the main street, both in order to ensure that everyone was near a source of water and to simplify common defense. The huts were built not of wood but of baked clay or bricks.[38]

In regions of settled non-Russian population, much mutual trading and intermarriage took place. The cultural level of the incoming Russians or Ukrainians was not much higher than that of the indigenous peoples: they did not bring with them a consciously superior culture, religion, or way of life. Rather, a syncretic culture emerged, elements of animism or shamanism combining with elements of Christianity, and Russians sometimes adopted the diet, clothing, and even the language of the natives.[39] Since the steppe had always to some extent brought peoples together as well as keeping them apart, the Russian incursion did not bring with it as many unfamiliar bacteria to spread disease and decimate local populations, as happened in both North and South America in the sixteenth to eighteenth centuries.

All the same, the process was not always painless. The Russian state preferred sedentary to nomadic subjects, since they were more peaceful and easier to tax, and it did what it could to fix nomads on agricultural land, as well as awarding grazing grounds to incoming agriculturalists. This policy naturally aroused implacable hostility in places. The Bashkirs proved especially resistant to Russian incursion and repeatedly rebelled between the late sixteenth and late eighteenth centuries.[40] The north Caucasian mountain peoples, notably the Chechens, fought tenaciously for several decades to withstand Russian domination before they were finally overcome in the 1860s. Forced to yield their pastures to settlers and their horses to the army, surrounded by fortification lines and Cossack settlements, the Kalmyks abandoned any hope of survival in the lower Volga steppe and in 1770 tried to migrate en masse to their ancestral homelands in central Asia. Only a third of them or fewer succeeded in reaching their goal. The rest, at least 100,000, succumbed on the long desert journey to hunger, disease, heat or cold, and the raids of rival Kazakh nomads.[41]

There is a paradox at the heart of this settlement of Russians in the borderlands. Peasants who hated the state and were fleeing its depredations nevertheless in effect became its agents. The colonizers whom Kliuchevskii placed at the center of his history of Russia were at one and the same time escaping from the imperial state and also seeking its sponsorship. The motives of those who left their homes resembled those of Englishmen who went to the American colonies, but because they had to build their new life in geographically contiguous and dangerous territories, the state was able to reclaim them, and they themselves welcomed its protecting hand. The whole process facilitated the huge population growth which made the Russians much the most numerous people in Europe by the eighteenth century, and also made it possible for them to achieve this growth without radically improving their agriculture. As David Moon has pointed out, "by settling and ploughing up ever greater areas of forest and steppe . . . most Russian peasants were able to persist with their traditional, labour-intensive and land-extensive, agricultural methods."[42]

RUSSIA'S FRONTIER SITUATION

The same openness which made possible almost unlimited colonization also made Russia a ready receptacle for the most diverse cultural influences, infiltrating from all parts of Eurasia. For most of her early centuries Russia was more an Asiatic country than a European one, receptive to the animism and shamanism of Mongolia; to Islam from Persia, Turkey, and the heirs of Mongolia; and to an eastern form of Christianity which emerged on the boundaries of Europe and Asia.

The polarity between East and West has afflicted Russia's political and cultural life at least since the sixteenth century. Most of Russia's demotic sociopolitical institutions took shape before then and were derived in large part from Asiatic practice, notably the communications system, tribute and taxation, the census, military conscription, and the village community with its ethos of joint responsibility and mutual surveillance. From the sixteenth century onward, however, Russia's elite culture was reoriented in the opposite direction, toward western Europe, where the most attractive commercial opportunities lay, but from where the most serious military threats also came. Russians themselves have been acutely aware of the East–West polarity, but have tended in the nineteenth and twentieth centuries to oversimplify it, seeing in Western influence impulses of self-reliance, dynamism, and development, while identifying the East with superstition, fatalism, and stagnation.[43]

More recently culturologists and social scientists have pointed to the "binary nature" of Russian culture, to its tendency to seek extreme solutions to problems and to lurch from one set of cultural patterns to their diametrical opposite. Three obvious examples, which we shall examine more closely later, are the abrupt replacement of an eclectic paganism with Orthodox Christianity toward the end of the tenth century, the reforms of Peter I in the early eighteenth century, and the revolution of 1917. The attempted post-Soviet transformation may come to be judged as yet another. In each case the new was presented as the complete supplanting of the old, the dismissal of absolute evil and the introduction of absolute good. As Iurii Lotman and Boris Uspenskii have commented, "Dualism and the absence of a neutral axiological zone led to the new being regarded not as a continuation but as an eschatological replacement of everything . . . The natural result of this was that the new emerged not from the structurally 'unexploited' reserve, but as a result of the transformation of the old, as it were, of its being turned inside out. In this way repeated changes could in fact lead to the *regeneration* of archaic forms."[44]

In a society marked by such extreme discontinuities, the elites, animated by one kind of mentality, would try to introduce reforms, conceived as being for the benefit of everyone, but would come up against the mistrust and conservatism of the masses, intensified by the fact that, in such a harsh climatic and geographic milieu, novelty and experimentation could genuinely be hazardous, even disastrous. The result has been a chronic, unresolved conflict between elites and masses, between the state and local communities. In these circumstances, change is distorted by violence, the closing of minds. and the tendency to reproduce old patterns and therefore old conflicts.[45]

Such a society tends to generate both utopias and anti-utopias. In a sense the first utopia was the Orthodox liturgy, taken over in the tenth century ready and complete in such a form that, as the chronicles report, those Rus envoys who first heard it "knew not whether we were in heaven or on earth." The liturgy projects an ideal of beauty, order, and truth, but one contemplated from the outside. The worshippers at a Russian Orthodox service are not participants in the liturgy but rather observers, sometimes inattentive ones. During the celebration they may come and go, walk around the church, light candles, venerate the icons, and even—though they are not supposed to—chat discreetly with their neighbors. What is going on is a theatrical performance, a mystery rather than a communal rite, as is indicated by the fact that the preparation for the principal event, the eucharist, takes place behind closed doors.

The word "icon" means an image, and in Orthodox usage an image of a holy personage or event. But it is more than an image in the normal sense in which we use that word, for an icon is not simply a representation of a phenomenon: it attempts to go further, to bring the viewer into contact with the spiritual world underlying what he sees. In the term used by semioticians, it is not merely a sign but a symbol, or, in the words of Iosif Volotskii, an early sixteenth-century divine: "By painting images of the saints on icons, we do not venerate an object, but, starting from this visible object, our mind and spirit ascend towards the love of God, object of our desire."[46]

Among a largely illiterate population, visual messages were at least as important as they are in our own day of television and display advertising, and sacred images of all kinds were an integral part of the divine liturgy, of the experience of being in a church or holy place. More than that, an icon would commonly be found in an ordinary house, and even in a peasant's hut. It would occupy a corner of the best room in the house (known as the "red" or "beautiful" corner), where honored guests were received and where major events in the life of the family were celebrated. Many people had portable icons, which they carried around with them, to be able to pray anywhere, as occasion presented itself, or as a kind of talisman, to protect them against mishap. So an icon was much more than an image, more part of a way of life, and in that role its spiritual message was paramount.

Actually, the church itself was an icon, in the sense that it conveyed visually certain sacred truths, as it still does today. Approaching the typical Orthodox "cross-in-square" building, the worshipper enters through the vestibule, or narthex, to the west, a liminal area where the profane and secular intermingle. Passing beyond it, he sees before him the lightest area of the building, under the main dome, and, grouped around it on the columns, the icons (in the more normal sense), each probably lit up by candles placed there by believers wishing to say a prayer or commemorate some person or event. To each side are aisles, somewhat less well lit, with more icons.

In front of the viewer is the iconostasis, row upon row of icons depicting patriarchs and prophets, apostles and saints, biblical tales, church festivals, and in the center the figure of Christ blessing the congregation, with the Virgin Mary to one side and St. John the Baptist to the other. Above, in the dome itself, will be the figure of Christ Pantokrator, Lord of Everything, looking down on his flock. In the center of the iconostasis, the two doors are closed, for behind them is the most sacred section of the church, the sanctuary, where the communion cup and wafer are prepared. Those doors, known as the "royal" or "holy" doors, are opened only at the most solemn moment of the service, when the eucharist is about to be celebrated. As the early twentieth-century theologian Pavel Florenskii stated: "The iconostasis is the boundary between the visible and the invisible world . . . a boundary which impinges on the consciousness by means of a massed rank of saints, a cloud of witnesses surrounding God's throne, the sphere of heavenly glory proclaiming a mystery."[47]

The layout of the church also communicates the fact that the word is less important in Orthodoxy than in Western churches, especially Protestant ones. There are no pews for the congregation to sit and listen, and the pulpit, if there is one, is situated in a relatively inconspicuous location. The services are long, and laypeople are not necessarily expected to stay for the entire duration. The music is provided entirely by the cantor, who intones the words of the scriptures, and by the choir, which sings them. The congregation does not join in, and there is no organ, for the Orthodox believe that only the human voice can offer dignified worship to God. The layout of the church, the closed doors, the intoning and incense—everything suggests that the worshippers are witnesses of a reflection of heaven rather than participants in a communal event, and that they are intended to admire, enjoy, and receive spiritual comfort rather than to understand rationally or to contribute.

As for the icons themselves: although we Westerners have become more accustomed to them in recent decades, they are still disconcerting if we regard them as representational. The figures are elongated and their gestures emblematic rather than natural. Their relationship to the visual background is not quite clear—whether for example they are standing on the ground—and that background itself has its features carefully selected and slightly exaggerated. The light is clear, monotone, radiant, and comes from no obvious source. The perspective is unsettling: its implied lines seem to converge on a point in front of the picture rather than behind it, as is usual in postmedieval Western art. All of these effects suggest that the human figure is being used both to draw the viewer in (the reverse perspective) and to suggest truths which are above or beyond the human.

As we have seen, Russian popular culture reflected the duality of pravda and nepravda. The latter, in the form of unclean spirits, could turn up unexpectedly at any time or place. They were especially potent in forests and swamps, during the dark time of the year, and during pregnancy and child-birth, places and circumstances in which human beings were more than usually vulnerable. They even had a bridgehead inside the household, in the bathhouse, usually a little log hut set at a short distance from the main dwelling. The *bannik,* or bath sprite, could be extremely dangerous if offended, causing a fire which might spread to the main building. For fear of him, people would avoid bathing alone or at night, and would leave soap, fir branches, or a little water for him on leaving, saying a formal "thank you."[48]

Folksongs and folktales expressed the same duality. Very often the tragedy or the humor which was their salt turned on the contrast between a world of order and culture, and another world characterized by poverty, hunger, nakedness, drunkenness, and disorderly behavior. In the latter, the world of darkness *(kromeshnyi mir),* the church was replaced by the tavern, clothes by rags or canvas makeshifts, proper speech by coarseness and obscenity, moral behavior by drunken brawling. Semiotic systems were jumbled up or inverted. Scenes, gestures, and discourses from the antiworld were used to reveal the truth about what we normally take to be the ordered world. This was the function of the *shuty* and *skomorokhi,* the jesters and strolling players, against whom the church constantly inveighed, but who remained beloved of the common people. The laughter they evoked alleviated the threat from the *nechistaia sila,* mocked the pretensions of the elites, and showed up the reality behind their assumed attitudes. As we shall see, even tsars (Ivan IV, Peter I) sometimes had recourse to their inversion of the world's normal values.[49]

A paradoxical version of this tension between two worlds was presented by the *iurodivye,* usually referred to in English as "fools in Christ." Found only in Byzantium and Rus, and in the latter mostly from the fifteenth to seventeenth centuries, they were maverick "holy men" who would go around naked or in rags, sometimes with their faces blackened, with chains round their waists or deliberately drawing attention to sores on their bodies: in short, they flouted all normal conventions regarding attractiveness and even decency of the person. Some of them transgressed morality, by blaspheming, throwing stones at people, or playing spiteful practical jokes. Vasilii, the Moscow *iurodivyi* after whom the Cathedral on Red Square was named, once blinded some girls (though he later restored their sight). This was asceticism of a strange and striking kind: renouncing beauty, comfort, convention, sometimes even morality or reason.

Their distinctive mode of self-abnegation gained attention and aroused a certain sympathy among the poor and oppressed. They would call out and abuse passersby or would chant prophecies. They would use their distance from normal hierarchy and hypocrisy to denounce the vices of the rich and powerful in a manner not open to those who observed social convention. In short, they employed the devices of the world of darkness to throw light on the world of morality and convention. This was a paradoxical and hazardous procedure, and many of them were reviled for it, especially by the church. On the other hand, their asceticism and devotion to truth led a few of them to be venerated and even canonized as saints.[50]

It may be that the *iurodivyi* was himself a product of the openness of Rus (like Byzantium) to religious influences from the East. In some respects he recalls the shaman, who was also an ascetic vagrant, fond of iron objects, and given to soothsaying and the committing of apparently immoral or sacrilegious acts.[51] Even if this is the case, though, he assumed a distinctive place in Russian culture as a mediator between the ordered world and the world of darkness.

He was almost the only person who was able to do so. As we shall see, the bipolar world found its reflection in many aspects of Russian politics and culture, in the behavior of tsars, in the plans of reformers, in the dreams of revolutionaries, in the creations of art and literature. There were few indeed who were able to move comfortably between one pole and the other. The stark oppositions of pravda and nepravda, of "us" and "them," of state and local community have colored, even determined, much of Russia's turbulent history.[52]

I

Pre-Imperial Rus and the Beginnings of Empire

I

KIEVAN RUS, THE MONGOLS, AND THE RISE OF MUSCOVY

SLAVS AND VIKINGS

The Slavs entered the written records of European history quite suddenly, during the reign of the East Roman emperor Justinian, when they appeared across the Danube from the direction of the Carpathians. In 626, together with the Avars, a Mongol people, they unsuccessfully besieged Byzantium itself. Over the next two centuries they settled in the Balkans. Associated Slav tribes also penetrated into central Europe, as far as the Elbe basin and northern Bavaria, where they came up against the Franks. A loosely marked German-Slavic frontier ran for several centuries along the Elbe and Saale Rivers and through the forests of Bohemia. Yet other Slavs filtered into the lakes and forests south and east of the Baltic Sea, along the upper Dnieper, the Neman, Western Dvina, and Volkhov Rivers, where they mingled with Baltic and Finnic-speaking tribes.

It seems probable that the Slavs' original homeland was in the area between the Bug, the Pripet, and the Dnieper Rivers, and that migrations of peoples across the Asian steppes caused their dispersion from this center into regions protected either by mountains or by forests. Their economy was based on arable tillage and stockraising, and proved adaptable to more northerly soils and climate. Archaeological remains indicate that they had adopted relatively advanced Roman techniques of ploughing, manuring, and the rotation of crops. Their agriculture gradually became more productive, probably through the use of metal-tipped ploughs and the introduction of winter rye, which was especially suited to damp northern climates. In time it left enough surplus for artisans and merchants to establish a livelihood.

At this stage the Khazar kaganate, a multiethnic tribal confederacy ruled by a Turkic seminomadic aristocracy, dominated the Pontic and Kuban steppes from the Dnieper to the Caspian, and the relative security it afforded against attacks from the south and east doubtless facilitated the settlement of Slav agriculturalists. Where the Slav tribes settled on the steppe itself, they constructed their settlements in the form of small stone fortresses, and they paid tribute to the Khazars to protect them. The territory of Khazaria included the future Kiev, while in the south the kaganate vied with the Abbasid caliphate for control of the Caucasus and with Byzantium for the Crimea. At times the Khazars allied themselves with Byzantium, forming a forward defense line for it against the nomads. Beyond Khazaria, in the middle Volga basin, another Turkic people, the Bulgars, had their own kaganate.[1]

It was in this condition that the "Rus" found the Slavs as they came down from the north. In the past there was lively historical debate about the identity of the Rus, but today there does not seem much doubt that they were Scandinavian Vikings, or "Varangians," as the Slavs called them, merchant-warriors seeking to dominate the trade routes which traversed territory settled by Slavic, Baltic, and Finno-Ugrian peoples. The word "Viking" originally meant "pirate." These Vikings came from kingdoms whose population was growing fast and whose agricultural land was severely restricted both by climate and by mountainous terrain. During the eighth to tenth centuries they spread out all over northern Europe, and parts of southern Europe too, in search of land, trade, booty, slaves, or just military glory. They differed from previous and some later invaders in that they were not nomads but settled peoples, with already a relatively high level of material culture.[2]

Initially the trade which attracted them was focused on the River Volga and its many tributaries, especially the Kama. The point where the latter flowed into the Volga marked the intersection-point of a caravan route extending westward into Europe and eastward into central Asia. Here the Bulgars had established a major commercial network, buying up furs, wax, and honey from peoples who lived farther north and transporting them southward, to the Khazar kaganate, to which they also paid tribute. The Rus would bring their furs to the Bulgar market and exchange them for silver.[3]

From the late eighth century another trade route also interested the Rus people increasingly: it ran from the Gulf of Finland and Lake Ladoga down the Narva or the Volkhov and Lovat Rivers, along a short stretch of the

Western Dvina, and then by portage to the Dnieper, which flowed all the way down to the Black Sea. This route contained one serious obstacle, however: in the lower reaches of the Dnieper, rapids—a series of granite ridges, some stretching right across the river—were a hazard to navigation. The deep, fast-flowing water of spring drove boats helplessly onto them, while in the shallow water of other seasons they were impassable, and cargoes had to be offloaded for transportation by land over a stretch of up to seventy kilometers. Guaranteeing this section of the route required a well-organized kaganate able to raise a strong army.

Once that hurdle was surmounted, however, the Dnieper route gave the Rus access to Byzantium, the richest market of all. They brought to it slaves, hides, furs, honey, and wax and returned northward with corn, wine, silk, and luxury goods. According to the *Chronicle of Past Times (Povest vremennykh let)*, the Slav tribes living along this route eventually welcomed their incursion. Having initially refused them tribute, the Slavs had "set out to govern themselves." It had transpired, however, that

there was no law among them, but tribe rose against tribe. Discord thus ensued among them, and they began to war against one another. They said to themselves, "Let us seek a prince who may rule over us and judge us according to the law." Accordingly they went overseas to the Varangian Russes. [And they] said to the people of Rus, "Our whole land is great and rich, but there is no order in it. Come to rule and reign over us."[4]

This chronicle was written some two centuries later, with the intention of glorifying the dynasty of Riurik, eldest of the three brothers who were said to have responded to this appeal and settled among the Slav tribes. So the story may be a flattering invention. On the other hand, it is not unknown for relatively primitive peoples to accept a ruler from a higher culture, to end feuding among themselves, to bring trade, and also to organize external defense. It is a function the descendants of the Rus frequently exercised for other peoples in later centuries.

This is certainly the service the incoming Vikings performed. They set up fortified trading settlements along the route "from the Varangians to the Greeks," that is, from Scandinavia to Byzantium. The first was just upstream from Lake Ladoga, a key junction where the southern route to the Dnieper diverges from the southeastern one to the Volga and Caspian. Other fortified towns were subsequently built along the River Volkhov, notably where it flows into Lake Ilmen, near present-day Novgorod. When steppe politics

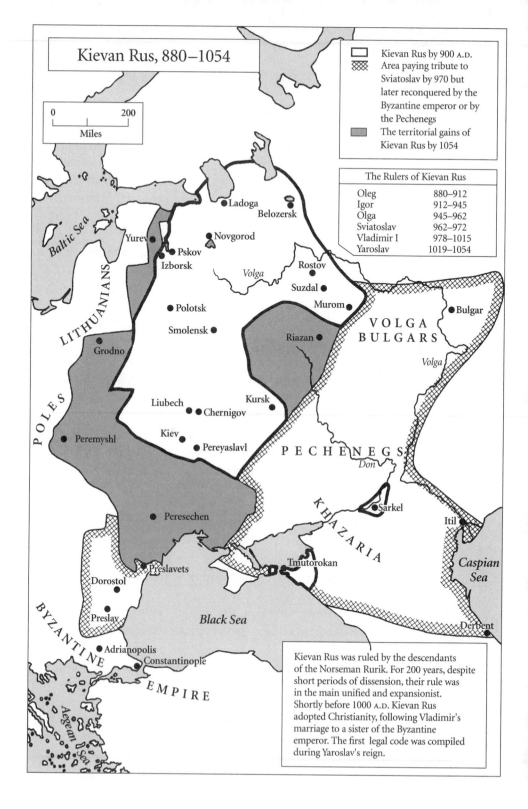

Kievan Rus, 880–1054

0 — 200
Miles

Kievan Rus by 900 A.D.

Area paying tribute to Sviatoslav by 970 but later reconquered by the Byzantine emperor or by the Pechenegs

The territorial gains of Kievan Rus by 1054

The Rulers of Kievan Rus

Oleg	880–912
Igor	912–945
Olga	945–962
Sviatoslav	962–972
Vladimir I	978–1015
Yaroslav	1019–1054

Baltic Sea

LITHUANIANS

POLES

BYZANTINE

EMPIRE

Aegean Sea

Ladoga
Belozersk
Yurev
Novgorod
Pskov
Izborsk
Rostov
Volga
Suzdal
Polotsk
Murom
Bulgar
Smolensk
Riazan
Grodno

VOLGA
BULGARS

Volga

Liubech
Kursk
Chernigov
Kiev
Peremyshl
Pereyaslavl

PECHENEGS
Don

Peresechen

Sarkel
Itil

KHAZARIA

Caspian
Sea

Preslavets
Tmutorokan
Dorostol
Preslav
Black Sea
Derbent
Adrianopolis
Constantinople

Kievan Rus was ruled by the descendants of the Norseman Rurik. For 200 years, despite short periods of dissension, their rule was in the main unified and expansionist. Shortly before 1000 A.D. Kievan Rus adopted Christianity, following Vladimir's marriage to a sister of the Byzantine emperor. The first legal code was compiled during Yaroslav's reign.

made it possible, the Vikings established a stronghold much farther south, on the middle Dnieper, where a crossing point coincided with wooded hills rising nearly 100 meters above the river. It was as close to the Black Sea as was compatible with some degree of natural protection against steppe raiders. On this location the Rus built their principal southern city, Kiev—ostensibly named after a ferryman who was its founder. It lies near where major tributaries join the Dnieper, and in the middle of a fertile agricultural region.

The Rus kaganate of the mid-ninth century was a loose federation of elite warriors living on trade and booty and drawing tribute from the Slav, Baltic, and Finnish agricultural peoples of the forest and forest-steppe land. According to the Arab traveler Ibn Rusta,

> [The Rus people] have no cultivated lands. They eat only what they carry off from the land of the Saqlaba [the woodland Slavs, Balts, and Finns]. When a child is born to any man among them, he takes a drawn sword and places it between his hands and says, "I shall bequeath to thee no wealth and thou wilt have naught except what thou dost gain for thyself by this sword of thine." They have no landed property nor villages nor cultivated land; their only occupation is trading in grey squirrel and other furs.[5]

By the mid-ninth century the Rus kaganate, with its Slav followers and its commercial contacts, was already a formidable force. In 861 it mounted a raid against Byzantium itself; it was unsuccessful, but roused the imperial state to the realization that it faced a new and dangerous foe. In 907 the kaganate concluded commercial agreements with Byzantium which gave it permanent trading rights within the imperial city. In return for exemption from customs dues, the Rus were to limit the number of their representatives allowed to enter the city, and they were to leave their weapons outside—stipulations which suggest Byzantine nervousness at the prospect of dealing with an unfamiliar and warlike people.

Rus showed its effectiveness in other ways too. Prince Sviatoslav (962–972) sacked Itil, the capital of the Khazar kaganate, ending its domination of the Pontic steppes, and secured for a time the lower reaches of the Don and the shore of the Sea of Azov, considerably enhancing the Rus trading capacity by diversifying its routes. But decisively weakening the Khazars opened the way to the incursions of the nomadic Pechenegs, who soon deprived him of his conquests.[6] It was many centuries before the descendants of Rus returned to the Sea of Azov.

By the mid-tenth century, then, the Varangians had achieved some remarkable successes and had attracted support from many of the East Slav tribes, with which they were already intermarrying; as a result the distinction between Vikings and Slavs quite quickly blurred and then disappeared altogether, leaving a predominantly East Slav language and culture. Together the "Viking-Slavs" formed a kind of tribal superalliance, with its center in Kiev, designed to repel the threat from the Pechenegs, and to enable them to conduct raids in the manner of predatory merchant princes against vulnerable targets, including Byzantium itself.

This alliance was partly a voluntary one, dictated by obvious geopolitical needs, and partly imposed by the superior wealth and coercive power of the Kievan prince. To become permanent, it needed to move beyond the stage of resting on a deal between tribes or between local warlords and to become a sovereign state, at least as far as that was practicable in medieval Europe. The history of Kievan Rus is the story of the attempt to achieve such statehood, an attempt which seemed at times to be successful, but which ended— as did the earlier Carolingian empire in western Europe—in fragmentation and breakdown. In judging its failure, however, one should note the remarkable territorial extent of Kievan Rus at its height, much larger than any comparable European realm except the Carolingian, which was even more short-lived. It was, moreover, the first wholly non-nomadic polity to establish itself durably on the steppes of Inner Eurasia.

At the base of society was the local community, which, with the growth of settled agriculture and statehood, was making the transition from kinship to a neighborhood basis. This transition was in full swing during the ninth and tenth centuries, during which time the names of tribes gradually disappeared from the chronicles, indicating that kinship was ceasing to be the normal mode of political organization. With settled agriculture, and even more with the development of handicrafts and trade, differentiation into richer and poorer was taking place. Also into weaker and stronger: the prince and his *druzhina* (retainers) were detached from the rest of the community and formed a privileged and well-armed superior stratum. However, they were not, as Soviet historians used to maintain, a feudal ruling class, since they did not possess extensive landed estates, but rather small domains and wealthy townhouses. What they levied from the rest of the community was accordingly not dues based on ownership of land, but rather tribute extorted by superior military power. The prince invested his leading warriors (or boyars) with *kormlenie*, the right to levy tribute from a community, passing a proportion of it on to him while keeping the rest as legitimate income to provide for their own needs. The boyars performed their function by dealing not with individual households, but with communities as a whole, on the basis of "joint responsibility." They exercised criminal jurisdiction on the same basis: each community had to investigate serious crimes and either find and hand over the criminal or else pay a special collective fine.[7]

For this reason, and for military purposes, it was vital that the local community have an assembly. In the kinship communities this was known as the *verv* (a word which implies a bond), though gradually the term *mir* (which, as we have seen, means peace or harmony) took hold. In towns, which began as military, administrative, and religious centers for tribes and gradually attracted commerce and manufacture, the term *veche* came into use (connected with the word meaning "to know"). All these assemblies grew out of tribal gatherings and had nothing in common with parliaments. They were not representative assemblies: they offered a place to all free adult male members of the community, usually those who owned land or ran a business, however small. Slaves and women were not represented, and probably not immigrants either.

The lower orders were slaves, not vassals, and those who paid tribute were free peasants or artisans. The system resembled that of the ancient Greek city-states more than it did medieval west European feudalism: it was financed mainly by trade and only secondarily by agriculture. Towns and surrounding countryside formed one political unit, and membership of an assembly implied the right and duty to take up arms in defense of the community.

The state of the sources makes it difficult to say very much about these local assemblies: their conduct of business was traditional and oral, and has left few traces. The chronicles, however, quite frequently contain phrases indicating that the prince "took counsel with his people," in a context which suggests that not just his personal advisers or council of elders were involved. This would be natural, since the prince might at any moment have to appeal to the free population of a town or district for military support against enemies. He could not afford to ignore their interests and opinions. Indeed the history of princely feuds shows that not infrequently the sentiment of an urban assembly might decisively swing events in favor of one claimant or another.

In its most fully developed form, the veche, the assembly could be convened by the prince or by its members through the simple device of ringing the church bells. The city of Novgorod, whose assembly had a particularly proud tradition, reserved a special bell for the purpose. Citizens would meet on the market square or in front of the church, or possibly in a field just outside the walls. There was often no definite procedure, even no chairman, and so the meetings tended to be dominated by the strongest faction in town or by the richest, the most experienced, or the "best families." Sometimes opinions would change very quickly or diverge wildly, and then an attempt would be made to reach a consensus. If this could not be done, however, then conflict might break out, including actual fighting between divergent parties. On the other hand, we have a complete record of a meeting in Kiev in the mid-twelfth century at which immaculate order was preserved and the procedure was conducted by the prince, metropolitan, and *tysiatskii* (commander of the urban militia).[8]

The most important tasks of a veche were to decide on matters of war or peace and, when necessary, to appoint a new prince. Not that all princes began their rule by being thus selected, but if they were not then they might have to impose themselves by force. The very task of selection was likely to provoke divisions, especially if it ran counter to treaties or agreements between the princes themselves.[9]

The fighting of wars was a delicate matter for agreement between prince and veche. A prince accompanied by only his druzhina was a feeble contestant: he needed the support of the much more numerous and sometimes better-armed urban militia *(opolchenie)*. This was especially true of defensive warfare against nomadic invaders. Recent research suggests that all free men had the right and duty to wear armor and helmets and to bear arms, which included sword, spear, ax, mace, and arrows, and this of course made them potentially dangerous to a prince as well as helpful to him. The urban militia included cavalry as well as infantry, though by the twelfth century the right to fight on horseback was probably becoming the monopoly of a specialized professional group in the *druzhina*. The basic unit of the militia was the "hundred" *(sotnia)*, headed by a *sotskii*, or "centurion." Large towns also had "thousands," commanded by a *tysiatskii*, who was, by virtue of his function, a highly authoritative figure within the community: he might either be elected or be appointed by the prince.[10]

Just as the Greek city-states had great difficulty in concluding alliances for common action and tended gradually to lose influence to their own former colonies, enriched as the result of trade and successful warfare, so also the principal cities of Rus tended in time to fragment and to lose their peripheries: their former *prigorody*—satellite or subordinate towns—would acquire their own independent authority, which they would legitimate by inviting a prince to take up residence. The "spare" scions of the ruling Riurikovich dynasty were usually only too happy to oblige.

CONVERSION OF THE SLAVS

It was easier for the superalliance to stabilize itself if its leader could claim a supernatural sanction. The death of Sviatoslav in 972 was followed by feuding among his sons. Vladimir, a younger son, overthrew his half brother Iaropolk in order to seize Kiev and become prince. In order to give legitimacy to this act of *force majeure* he embarked on a campaign of religious persuasion, attempting to unify his peoples, with their diverse faiths. He raised huge idols of their various gods—Norse, Slav, Finn, and even Iranian—on a hilltop overlooking Kiev.

Having accomplished this, however, he suddenly abandoned the eclectic pagan faith and embraced Christianity. This must have been a difficult decision for the leader of a warrior host. His father, Sviatoslav, when pressed to convert, is said to have replied, "But my druzhina will laugh at me!"[11] All the same, Christianity had two palpable advantages for a prince who aspired not just to make war, but also to rule peacefully an extensive territory settled by many different peoples: it condemned the practice of blood feuds, and it offered a written script for the promulgation of law and order, backed by a supernatural sanction for monarchical power.

It also held out the prospect of closer relations with Byzantium. The Byzantines had been dealing with the Slavs as the Roman Empire had done centuries earlier with the Germanic tribes, by a mixture of military precaution, trade, diplomacy, and evangelization. The aim was to induce them to become peaceful neighbors and perhaps eventually to incorporate them into the empire, once they were converted, acculturated, and hence potential citizens. The decisive stage in this process was reached during the ninth century.

Two especially effective missionaries, the brothers Cyril and Methodius, were sent out from Byzantium in the 860s to convert the pagans, beginning with the kingdom of Moravia, north of the Danube. They introduced into their missionary work a vital new element which was to influence decisively the development of Christianity in eastern Europe: they learned the Slavonic language spoken in Moravia and devised an alphabet for it (Glagolitic) to form the basis for the translation of the liturgy and the gospels. The German clerics working in the region insisted that only Latin was a suitable vehicle for the scriptures, and their view eventually prevailed in Moravia. But Cyril went on to the new Balkan state of Bulgaria, where Khan Boris and his son Simeon introduced Byzantine Christianity with a new alphabet modeled on the Greek. This was known as Cyrillic, and its use was intended to reflect the closeness of the Slavonic churches to Greek Christian culture. A new Bulgarian patriarchate was established in 924.

Byzantine Christianity was not the only option open to Rus. Through its trade and diplomacy it was exposed to Islam among the Persians and Arabs and to Judaism in Khazaria, while in the West its agents encountered Catholic Christianity: Vladimir's grandmother, Olga, had invited a mission from the Holy Roman Emperor Otto I. The chronicle records that Vladimir sent emissaries to inquire into the teaching and rituals of Islam, Judaism, Catholicism, and Orthodoxy. They reported that the Catholic ritual was without beauty and that Islam did not permit the consumption of alcohol—which would have made impossible the primary bonding ceremonial of the druzhina. Judaism they passed over in silence, but the Orthodox divine service they described as being so beautiful that "we knew not whether we were in heaven or on earth."[12]

Even if one does not take the chronicle literally, it is evident that Vladimir made a conscious choice of faith from the options which geopolitics laid before him, and that he was influenced at least to some extent by the sensuous qualities of the Orthodox liturgy as something which would impress his subjects. No doubt the most important consideration, though, was that he wished to maintain close relations with Byzantium: he already had trading links with it, and as an earthly empire it seemed much more venerable and imposing than the seminomadic kaganates or the upstart and fragmented kingdoms of western Europe.

Having taken his decision, he acted forthrightly, even harshly. He demonstratively smashed the pagan idols: Perun was dragged by horses down the hill, beaten continuously by twelve men with rods, and dumped in the Dnieper. He commanded besides that the citizens of Kiev should betake themselves to the riverbank to be baptized by immersion: "Whoever does not turn up at the river tomorrow, be he rich, poor, lowly, or slave, he shall be my enemy!"[13] To what extent they performed this ceremony willingly is open to question: when priests in Novgorod tried to imitate the humiliation of Perun, there was a popular riot. Iurii Lotman and Boris Uspenskii see in this crude and peremptory conversion the first symptom of a damaging tendency in Russian society to seek change through extreme and polarized action rather than through gradual evolution.[14] Though the princely command may have affected the external behavior of his subjects, it seems clear that pagan rituals continued to be observed for many generations to come. Peasants in particular retained a great affection for their pagan gods and often incorporated them into Christianity when they adopted it, creating a "dual faith" of a type common enough all over medieval Europe.

Vladimir himself took the title of grand prince and renounced his numerous wives and concubines in order to marry Princess Anna, sister of the Byzantine emperor, Basil. Basil agreed to this arrangement, as his empire was going through a major crisis, and he was desperate for support in his struggle against rebels in Anatolia. Vladimir duly despatched reinforcements which enabled him to defend the imperial capital successfully.

Greek craftsmen were sent from Byzantium to build churches in Rus. Bulgarian clergymen brought their holy books in the Cyrillic script and the Slavonic language. At the same time, Greek churchmen arrived as bishops to head the new church, though gradually native clergy replaced them except at the very highest levels.

By the end of the tenth century, then, what we now call Orthodox Christianity had spread from Byzantium to the Balkans, Rus, and part of central Europe. It had certain distinctive features which made it already very different from Western or Latin Christianity. First of all, the language of liturgy and scriptures was close to the vernacular: this had the effect of making preaching and conversion easier, but at the cost of cutting Orthodox churches off from both Latin and even Greek culture, and therefore from general European religious and intellectual developments. As Simon Franklin and Jonathan Shepard have commented, "Church Slavonic provided both a bridge and a barrier: a bridge to the faith, and therefore a barrier . . . to direct participation in the cultures of the other learned languages of Europe."[15] This tendency to isolation was reinforced by the establishment, not of a single universal church, but of a series of national churches, each headed by a local patriarch or even by the monarch. Moreover, the Eastern churches did not undergo the Gregorian reforms of the tenth and eleventh centuries, and therefore retained a married parish clergy much more intimately tied to worldly interests than the Catholic clergy.

The growing differences between Eastern and Western churches came to a head in the eleventh century. In the 1040s the Byzantine patriarch closed all the Latin churches in the capital city, accusing them of heretical practices. Pope Leo IX responded by sending legates to Constantinople, demanding that this step be reversed and that the Byzantine church acknowledge his claim to supremacy within Christendom. The patriarch refused to recognize the legates' status and denounced the claim. The legates replied by excommunicating him in a bull which they placed on the altar of St. Sophia cathedral itself. A Greek church council was convened, which in its turn excommunicated the legates and condemned the heresies of the Latin church. That schism has never been healed, and the rift between the Orthodox and Catholic churches remains a basic feature of Christianity even today.

The new Christianity which gained ground in Rus from the late tenth century was received as a complete whole, assimilated in an integral package, without any sense of history, evolution, or inner conflict, beautiful and to be revered, but not open to discussion or amendment. Rus had not experienced centuries of theological and ecclesiastical controversy, nor had she observed successive ecumenical councils gradually chiseling out the contours of the credo. Her rulers and perhaps her people accepted the new faith wholesale, as a harmonious, intellectually and spiritually satisfying answer to their needs. For them, moreover, it was a faith which manifested itself at least as much in its liturgy as in its dogma. Orthodoxy is reticent in making dogmatic statements about God, regarding Him as beyond the reach of rational understanding and accessible to the human heart only through the symbolism of the liturgy. So East Slav Christianity is marked by a sensuous, hieratic, and monolithic quality which has remained with it over the centuries. The singing and intoning of the liturgy, the frescoes, mosaics, and icons communicated the essence of the faith. They, rather than theology or a formulated personal belief, became the central feature of the Christianity of Rus.

Note too that Christianity was assimilated as the ideology of a universal empire, and thus as the ally of absolute (or at least potentially absolute) worldly power. For centuries it was embodied in a missionary church headed by foreigners and requiring princely support in the midst of a still largely pagan population. Christianity was an intensely political religion, whose function was to guarantee much-sought-after peace and secular stability. It was also strongly historical in outlook, binding a young state into a long tradition of patriarchs, prophets, and apostles, whose culmination was to be the second coming of Christ and the last judgment. Although in everyday politics the princes of Rus might sometimes adopt an assertive and even truculent tone toward Byzantium, culturally and spiritually the elites, both clerical and secular, took a deeply reverent attitude toward the second Rome.

During the Kievan period the relationship between church and prince remained relatively unproblematic. Each backed the other almost automatically, from mutual need. The *Nomocanon* (or *Kormchaia Kniga*), the Byzantine canon law code, stated that the emperor was supreme head of the church, should protect both its physical inviolability and its dogmatic purity, and should ensure the upholding of the canon law. These provisions were carried over to Kiev, with the assumption that there the prince would fulfill the role of the emperor. For its part the church would exhort its congregations to obey their earthly ruler.

The unity of the ruling dynasty was so important to the church that it propagated the legend of Boris and Gleb, Vladimir's sons, who declined to assert their dynastic rights by means of violence. When Boris heard that his brother Sviatopolk was intending to murder him to seize his birthright, he decided not to resist evil, and spent a night in prayer: "Lord Jesus Christ, who didst appear on earth in human form and freely offered Thyself to be nailed to the cross, accepting thy passion for the sake of our sins—give me now also strength to accept mine." Gleb later died in a similar spirit. They were subsequently canonized, the first East Slav saints, and titled "protectors of the land of Rus," in order to establish the principle that the unity of the realm justified the ultimate self-sacrifice. The ideal of meek acceptance of suffering for the sake of the community as a whole and the "land of Rus" became a lasting component of Russian piety.[16]

41

In the same spirit, Feodosii, abbot of the Monastery of the Caves, outside Kiev, bolstered dynastic legitimacy in 1076–1078 by refusing to recognize Sviatoslav's accession to the throne, since it infringed the superior right of his elder brother, Iziaslav. Not only did he dare to take a stand on the tacitly agreed seniority principle, but he persuaded Kiev's townsmen of the justice of the case: in due course they expelled the usurper and invited Iziaslav to take the throne.[17]

The church also played a major role in social life. Certain categories of the population, including refugees, redeemed slaves and the destitute in general, were denoted "church people" and were governed entirely by ecclesiastical law, which also regulated certain aspects of the life of the whole population, in matters to do with marriage, family, and inheritance.

From the very beginning monasticism was at the heart of East Slavic Christianity. It originated at a time when Byzantine monasticism was still renewing itself and expanding after the final defeat of the iconoclast heresy. The key to this renewal was the largest and most enduring of all Byzantine ecclesiastical institutions, the self-governing monastic republic of Mount Athos, set up in the tenth century on a mountainous peninsula which projects from Thrace into the Aegean Sea. In time Mount Athos became the spiritual powerhouse of the Eastern Christian ecumene (as it still is today), passing on and developing the tradition of icon-painting, and also the contemplative and ascetic techniques of the "hesychasts," or "quiet ones," as they were cultivated in late Byzantium.

Most early monasteries in Rus were founded by princes and other notables to ensure their own renown and perpetuate their memory. An exception was the Monastery of the Caves, founded in 1051 in sandy, wooded hills on the bank of the Dnieper outside Kiev by a monk, Antonii, who found other monasteries too restless for the solitary, contemplative way of life he craved. When his new foundation became popular and he attracted disciples, he allowed them to stay and drew up a regulation for their common life. Thereafter the Monastery of the Caves became a favored home for Orthodox monks who wished a cenobitic community life, but with plenty of scope for private prayer and contemplation. The first abbot, Feodosii, was a graduate of Mount Athos.[18]

THE ATTEMPT TO CONSOLIDATE THE KIEVAN STATE

To consolidate the superalliance, Vladimir distributed his sons to various cities within it: Vysheslav to Novgorod, Iziaslav to Polotsk, Sviatopolk to Turov, and Iaroslav to Rostov. Each son had a druzhina at his command, and each was given the right of kormlenie, which enabled him to raise tribute from the local population and demand maintenance for his officials in return for mobilizing troops from among them to defend the vulnerable steppe frontiers against nomadic raids. Otherwise local communities continued to observe their own laws and customs and to conduct their own economic life.

Relations with the Pechenegs, who dominated the southern steppes at this time, were complex. Kievan Rus needed their compliance to continue commerce with Byzantium, and also benefited from trading with them: their livestock was useful to Rus as haulage and as a source of food and clothing. On the other hand, like all nomads, the Pechenegs would periodically raid the territory of Rus to acquire grain, luxury goods, and slaves. They became especially dangerous after the collapse of Khazaria in the second half of the tenth century removed a threat from their rear. Vladimir constructed and manned a series of forts on and around the lower Dnieper to keep them at bay.

By the time of his death in 1015, then, Vladimir had done a great deal to unite a previously fragmented realm, convert it to a single faith, provide it with a single (if rudimentary) administrative and fiscal system, attach it to a powerful ally, and defend it from its most dangerous enemies. He gave the Riurikovich dynasty a real claim to exercise authority over the peoples of Rus as a whole.

Vladimir's work of conquest, administrative consolidation and the inculcation of Christianity was continued by his son Iaroslav, who was grand prince of Kiev from 1019 to 1054, though he was not able to rule uncontested till 1036. He built new stone fortifications for his city, with a Golden Gate as the magnificent entrance. Inside them he constructed a number of palaces and churches, entrusting Byzantine architects and master masons with the work. The most imposing was the Cathedral of St. Sophia, erected in conscious emulation of the mother church in Constantinople and in a similar architectural style.

To bolster the loyalty of his followers, Iaroslav began the work of giving the Kievan Rus state a historical dimension. Monks of the Monastery of the Caves were commissioned to compose chronicles recording the principal moments in the evolution of the East Slavs and linking them to a vision of world history as ordained by God. This was a task of theology, state-building, and community-building all at the same time.

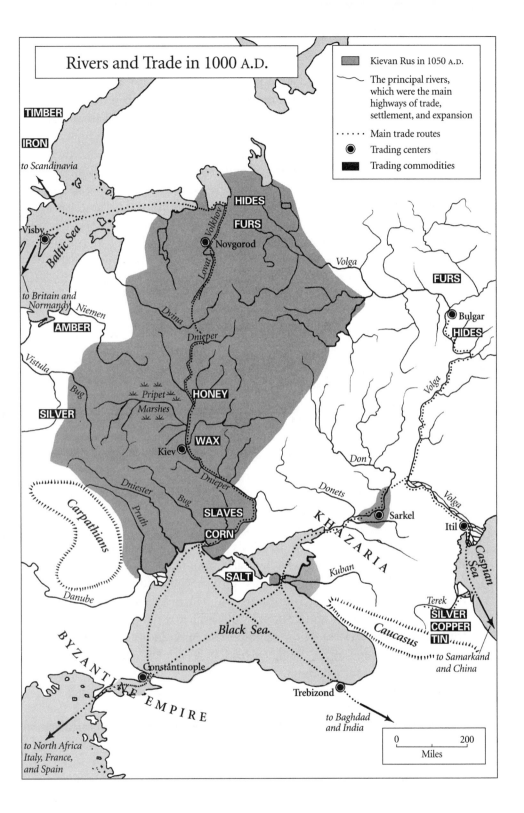

Rivers and Trade in 1000 A.D.

Kievan Rus in 1050 A.D.

The principal rivers, which were the main highways of trade, settlement, and expansion

Main trade routes

Trading centers

Trading commodities

TIMBER

IRON

to Scandinavia

Visby

Baltic Sea

to Britain and Normandy

Niemen

AMBER

Vistula

Bug

SILVER

HIDES

FURS

Novgorod

Volkhov

Lovat

Dvina

Dnieper

Pripet Marshes

HONEY

WAX

Kiev

Dnieper

Dniester

Bug

Pruth

Carpathians

Danube

SLAVES

CORN

SALT

Kuban

Black Sea

Constantinople

BYZANTINE EMPIRE

to North Africa Italy, France, and Spain

Volga

FURS

Bulgar

HIDES

Volga

Don

Donets

KHAZARIA

Sarkel

Volga

Itil

Caspian Sea

Terek

SILVER
COPPER
TIN

Caucasus

to Samarkand and China

Trebizond

to Baghdad and India

0   200
Miles

The oldest version of the first chronicle, *Povest vremennykh let* (*Chronicle of Past Times*, often known as the *Primary Chronicle*), was probably compiled in the years 1037–1039, and was extended by the monk Nikon in the 1060s and 1070s. Developed from Byzantine models in technique and subject matter, it served as the basic text for all subsequent Russian chronicle writing. It reflected the need felt by both princes and prelates to give Rus a distinctive identity within the Eastern Christian ecumene. Hence its subtitle, "A narration of past years, of where the land of Rus came from, who began to rule in Kiev, and how the land of Rus came into being." It traced the story right back to the sons of Noah and attributed the origins of Rus to the apostle Andrew, said to have traveled not just to the Crimea (which he probably did) but up the Dnieper, where he prophesied on the site of the future Kiev: "On these hills the grace of God will shine forth, there will be a great city, and God will erect there many churches."[19]

A similar message was conveyed by Ilarion, the first Slav churchman to be appointed metropolitan of Kiev.[20] In his sermon "On Law and Grace," delivered in the later 1040s, he presented the emergence of Rus as the fulfillment of divine providence, presaging ultimate victory over Judaism and Islam. Abraham's children by his maid Hagar are depicted as the people of bondage, the law. and the Old Testament, while his children by his wife Sarah are seen as the offspring of freedom, grace, and the New Testament. Vladimir, Ilarion preached, had come "in the likeness of Constantine the Great" to found a new church, "transporting the Cross from the New Jerusalem, the city of Constantine, and establishing it throughout all the land," and to build a great city, "shining in splendor as though in a crown"; his work had been continued by his son Iaroslav.[21]

The other great monument of Iaroslav's reign was the law code known as *Russkaia Pravda*, which was based on local custom rather than on Byzantine precedent and, in revised and amended form, maintained its authority in the daughter realms of Kiev right through to the late fifteenth century.[22] As we have seen, the word *pravda* means "that which is right," in all senses: truth, justice, and fairness. The most important innovation of the code was to restrict the operation of the blood feud as an acknowledged means of settling conflicts. Murder, insult, injury, or the violation of property were henceforth normally to be punished by the levying of a fine, and much of the text of *Russkaia Pravda* is taken up with the precise calibration of the penalties to be exacted for particular kinds of offenses inflicted on particular categories of people. At this stage justice was expected to be enforced within the community, using its own procedures, but in later revisions the position of the grand prince and of his investigators, judges, and courts was gradually strengthened and blood vengeance outlawed altogether. The grand prince became unequivocally the supreme judge.[23]

Iaroslav also attempted to codify the principles under which princely rule should be passed on within the Riurikovich dynasty. The deaths of both his father and his grandfather had been followed by internecine warfare among the sons, and Iaroslav was determined to try to forestall any such development after his own death. His testament admonished his sons: "If ye dwell in amity with one another, God will dwell among you, and will subject your enemies to you, and ye will live in peace. But if ye dwell in enmity and dissension, quarreling with one another, then ye will perish yourselves and bring to ruin the land of your ancestors, which they won at the price of great effort."[24] Although the full text of his will has not survived, he appears to have drawn up a hierarchy of the principal cities of his realm and distributed them among his sons, stipulating that at the death of one of them, a younger male member of the dynasty should inherit his throne, the others each moving up by one step on the ladder.

That, at least, is the usual interpretation. But the available texts are fraught with ambiguities, so that it is not quite clear what Iaroslav intended, except that he regarded Kiev not as a simple unitary realm, but as a federation ruled over jointly by members of the dynasty according to some notion of seniority. Any such pattern would have been impossible to maintain if the main wealth of each prince had been in land, since it would have been impracticable for them to keep switching from one domain to another. Where mentalities remained tribal rather than patrimonial, and the main revenues came from commerce and tribute, it is possible to imagine that it might work as conceived.

In fact, however, it never did. Soon after Iaroslav's death, his composite realm was once again torn apart by feuding brothers and cousins, though there were periodic attempts to reunite and to compose conflicts and differences. It was also faced with a new threat, in the form of the Kipchaks (also known as Cumans or Polovtsy), nomads who appeared from the steppe in the 1050s, and soon proved better able than their predecessors to penetrate the defenses erected by Vladimir and Iaroslav. In addition to conducting pillaging raids, they would storm and capture whole towns, enslaving the inhabitants for sale in the markets of the Black Sea. They also disrupted Kiev's trade links with Byzantium, in order to extort their own tribute from it. As with the Pechenegs, Kiev's relations with them were complex, involving cooperation and commerce as well as hostility. In 1094 Grand Prince Sviatoslav married the daughter of the Kipchak khan. Apart from the normal imperative to try to reach agreement with powerful neighbors, it was also the case that disunity among the princes impeded any attempt to pursue a coordinated policy of resistance.

In the end, however, the princes of the dynasty managed briefly to reunite to deal with the Kipchaks. Meeting at Liubech in 1097, those from the southern territories agreed on a formula for composing their differences and acting together. In 1103 Sviatopolk of Kiev and Vladimir of Pereiaslavl led a joint military expedition into the steppe which achieved the first major victory over the Kipchaks. It was followed up by successful defensive campaigns and a further offensive one in 1111. In that way the princes gradually broke the power of the Kipchak tribal federation for a generation or more, during which time it was Rus which conducted raids, seizing booty and slaves from its adversaries.

This cooperative success led to a final flowering of Kiev as a political center. In 1113, on the death of Sviatoslav, the citizens of Kiev ignored the dynastic inheritance arrangements and invited Vladimir to come from Pereiaslavl to be their prince. His success against the Kipchaks secured him a natural authority among the rival princes. He received from the Byzantine emperor a fur-lined crown which, as the "Monomakh crown" *(shapka Monomakha)*, became the permanent emblem of the Rus grand princes and later of the Russian emperors.

The city was in upheaval at the time because of the growing problem of debt, which generated intense embitterment, since debtors were enslaved. In itself, however, mushrooming internal debt resulted from the economic polarization which resulted from growth and was a mark of the enrichment of the city, with artisans producing glassware, pottery, ceramics, enamelware, jewels, and icons, which were beginning to command an international market. Vladimir reacted to the debt problem rather as Solon had done in ancient Athens, by canceling long-standing debts, lowering interest rates, limiting lords' authority over indentured laborers, and regulating the circumstances in which debtors might be enslaved. Kiev was going through the same kind of social crisis as the early Athenian polis, generated by the transition from an aristocratic social order based on kinship to a more open social order based on commerce. Not only did economic polarization threaten social order and stability, but the enslavement of citizens undermined the city's military potential, since slaves could not bear arms. By reducing the incidence of debt Vladimir restored social peace and military capacity to Kiev at least for a time.[25]

Vladimir Monomakh was the most learned of Kievan princes. He was a patron of the monasteries where the chronicles were written and manuscripts collected and treasured. His *Testament (Pouchenie)* was an attempt to impart a moral vision to monarchy in Rus. He glorified the world God had created and enjoined his successors to live in it in peace, while protecting the poor and unfortunate. "When robbed, avenge not; when hated, respond with love; when slandered, be silent. Overcome sin, free the oppressed, render justice to the orphan, protect the widow . . . Our Lord has promised us victory over our enemies through three means of conquering: repentance, tears, and almsgiving."[26] This was not practical statecraft, but it projected the image of a humble and peaceful Christianity which was to prove a powerful ideal in a fractured and violent world.

47

After the 1130s the Kievan confederation lost such unity as it had achieved and gradually fragmented into separate, even warring principalities. This was a natural tendency in medieval Europe, where the sinews of sovereign state-hood were simply not strong enough to operate over great distances or to contain the pressures generated by ambitious subordinate princes and their families. For this reason Charlemagne's empire fell, as at various times did other kingdoms and self-proclaimed empires such as those of Burgundy, Poland, Bohemia, Serbia, and Bulgaria. Rus was no exception.

In Rus, however, the breakup took place in a somewhat different form and for slightly different reasons. Its major centers derived their riches not only from successful warfare but also, as we have seen, from commerce and manufacture. The new towns founded during the tenth and eleventh centu-ries developed their own sources of wealth and their own hinterlands. Recent research suggests that this wealth was greater than supposed by earlier gener-ations of historians.[27] The towns thus became economically less dependent on Kiev, and politically more self-reliant too. Kiev remained the wealthiest single city and the symbolic center of Rus, but its relative importance de-clined as some of its "daughter" cities began to flex their own muscles. As in ancient Greece, "daughter" colonies were multiplying and claiming their share of the common inheritance.

Changing patterns of trade aggravated this fragmentation. By the twelfth century, Byzantium was in obvious economic decline, and the trade route "from the Varangians to the Greeks" became less important. The launching of the crusades at the end of the eleventh century and the crusaders' subse-quent conquest of territories in the Levant meant that much trade between Europe and Asia shifted away from the overland route through Rus and flowed instead through the Mediterranean and the Middle East. The territo-ries of Rus were becoming a commercial backwater. As a result they derived a greater proportion of their income from internal economic activity, in other words agriculture and small-scale manufacture.

The changes which took place in the twelfth century ended any hope of creating a unitary state or even a stable confederation. The princely superalliance disintegrated, and individual princes increasingly regarded their territories not as dominions held in trust for the dynasty as a whole, but as patrimonies *(votchiny),* to be passed on from father to sons (with provision for unsupported female heirs). Landownership began to supplant commerce and command of trade routes as the principal lever of power, and rent to replace tribute as the main source of income. The boyars' right to collect that tribute was turning into something more like feudal domination, with the right to extract feudal dues. At the same time, local mir communities were turning into purely peasant institutions as members of other social classes drifted away to secure their income and property rights. Even before the Mongols arrived, Rus was becoming a feudal society, in which princes and boyars were landlords levying dues from peasant communities whose members were bound by joint responsibility. Only in the far north, where there was little cultivable land and therefore no landlords, did mir communities retain their full traditional powers.[28]

Before its final collapse, Kievan civilization produced a strange literary masterpiece which survives as testimony to its dual pagan-Christian roots. This is the *Lay of Prince Igor (Slovo o polku igoreve),* which was apparently written toward the end of the twelfth century by someone close to the princes, perhaps a court minstrel. It recounts a failed campaign conducted against the Polovtsy by Prince Igor of Novgorod-Severskii, which ended with his captivity. The author praises the courage and daring of Igor but laments that he did not receive better support from his fellow princes, and suggests that without such support he may have acted rashly. Compared with the chronicles on the same subject, the *Lay* contains strikingly little Christian imagery. On the contrary, pre-Christian gods are evoked, and Igor's troops are likened to birds and other animals. The action takes place against the background of the movement of heavenly bodies, and at a decisive moment there is an eclipse. The general conception, in fact, is pagan or pantheist, while the highest ideal is presented as "the land of Rus."[29]

THE MONGOLS AS MASTERS OF EURASIA

That was the condition of Rus when in the mid-thirteenth century a new and more terrible enemy appeared from the steppes. These were the heirs of Chingiz Khan, greatest of the chiefs of the Uralo-Altaic tribes whose homelands lay between Lake Baikal and the Great Wall of China. They were typical denizens of the Eurasian steppe heartlands, dependent on cattle for their livelihood, roaming the open plains in search of convenient and nutritive pastures for their animals, raiding sedentary societies adjacent to their lands, but also trading with them. The basic units of social organization were tribal, but their menfolk, especially the younger ones, were specialists in war and campaigned in sworn brotherhoods *(anda)* which formed around the banner of a leader, a *khan,* remarkable for his fighting ability or his charismatic qualities. There was an aristocracy of those who possessed more animals or other wares, but membership in this aristocracy was not the main criterion in selecting military commanders: fighting and leadership qualities were decisive, since a nomadic society is utterly dependent on its capacity to make war successfully.

In the late twelfth century something happened which is decidedly unusual in a nomadic society: a stable system of rule was established above the tribal level—a tribal superalliance. Significantly, its creator, Temuchin, who was elected Chingiz (Universal) Khan in 1206, was an outsider among the tribes of his time, though his father had made an earlier attempt to unite the Uralo-Altaic tribes under his own Mongol clan, and had been murdered for his pains by envious rivals. Temuchin attracted warriors to his side by his personal charisma and his success in combat, first of all against the tribe of his father's murderers, then in other campaigns.

The growth of his empire can be partly explained by the momentum of his early successes. If he had not continued his conquests, his commanders would probably have reverted to intertribal feuding. But as the victories accumulated, Chingiz Khan evidently came to believe that he had a special providential role to play in world history, charged by the Supreme Being (Heaven, the Eternal Sky) with the mission of bringing warring realms under his leadership and thus inaugurating an era of universal peace and prosperity. Where a tribal leader could have derived such grandiose ideas is not clear: from imperial China, perhaps, where Temuchin spent some time as a young man, or as a spiritualized reflection of the geopolitical reality that steppe empires are formed in the heartland of the continent and, in order to survive, have to extend right over it.

To carry out his mission, Chingiz Khan expected devoted service from all his followers, regardless of rank. According to the Mongol Statute of Bound Service, all young men were required to undergo regular training in the skills of war and to make themselves available for military service up to the age of sixty. From the age of five or six a boy would begin to mount regularly on horseback and to develop the strength and endurance which would enable him to ride all day with little pause or nourishment. This early discipline was supplemented by periodic bouts of hunting: animals from a huge area would be corralled by relays of hunters gradually converging on the spot where the khan was waiting; then the commanders, followed by the other ranks, would be let loose to shoot down the animals with their bows and arrows.

50

The requirements of the Mongol service state applied to its civilian population and to all its conquered peoples. They had inferior status, in that they did not participate in the decisionmaking assemblies, but they were expected to furnish tribute and military recruits. Penalties for evading these dues were extremely harsh. Subject peoples could expect "peace" and "harmony" only if they obeyed implicitly the Mongol authority. These stipulations were laid out in the Great Yasa, the Mongol legal code, attributed to Chingiz Khan but compiled only after his death.

The Mongols practiced thoroughgoing religious toleration. In their view all faiths reflected something of the divine reality and contributed to the ideal of universal peace. Temples and priests, of whatever denomination, were granted a *tarkhan,* or charter of immunity, which exempted them from tribute payment and other dues binding on the rest of the population.

The election of Chingiz Khan took place in a *kurultai,* a gathering of the clan leaders. He executed some of his closest male relatives, to eliminate rivals. He introduced reforms which gave the Mongols some of the features of a sedentary state: he tightened the organization of the armed forces into tens (each usually based on an extended family), hundreds, and thousands, each of which had its own function, its own leader, and its own assigned pasture lands, and he added a new, larger unit of ten thousand, the *tiumen.* He surrounded himself with a special guard of elite troops who were exempted from the tribal system, as were the leaders of the *tiumeni.* In this way he emancipated himself finally from tribal jealousies. Toward the end of his life he wrote to a Taoist monk: "I look upon the nation as a newborn child and I care for my soldiers as if they were my brothers."[30] He was creating a new form of community, a transformation of the hitherto loose and semidemocratic association of the tribes, and it unleashed remarkable energies among the steppe peoples.

Perhaps even more important for the leader of an illiterate people—who apparently remained illiterate himself—he grasped the importance of written records for exercising authority over extensive territories and large numbers of peoples. He adapted an Uigur script to the Mongol language, and he ordered trusted associates to learn it and to record important decisions for implementation. He borrowed from China the idea of a census of the population and of their cattle holdings for the allocation of recruitment and taxation. He perfected the system of communications and postal relays. Rule over a great empire, however fleeting, would not have been possible without these innovations.[31]

In 1211–1215 his united cavalry swooped down on northern China, conquering it and its capital, Beijing. He also took over some of the latest weapons from China's technologically highly developed arsenal, and the wealth of China was tapped to benefit the Mongol ruling elite. With these supplements to the traditional steppe nomad way of life he embarked on an even more ambitious campaign to exploit his commanding strategic postion at the heartland of Eurasia. As a result the Mongols created the largest territorial empire in the history of humankind—though in its full form it was relatively short-lived.[32]

The Mongols owed their military successes to a number of factors. The superior size of their armies may have been one of them, though one suspects that Russian chroniclers exaggerated it: after all, before reaching Rus, they had had to travel thousands of miles across open steppe in all weathers. But there is no doubt about their careful preparations, their painstaking previous reconnaissance of their future opponents (in stark contrast to the insouciant ignorance displayed by the princes of Rus),[33] their dispatch of envoys to sow dissension among them, and their exploitation of the psychological effect of sudden and ruthless assault. Their horses were both speedy and robust, while their cavalrymen were experienced and accurate in handling strong, long-distance bows and arrows. While in China, moreover, they had absorbed many lessons on the techniques and strategy of siege warfare, decisive in the relatively urbanized context of Rus. Their handling of large numbers of troops in complex offensive operations over extensive territory was unparalleled until the Napoleonic wars. Their mobilization of populations and resources was also uniquely effective, and the twentieth-century military historian Liddell Hart has called them the first people in world history to wage "total war."[34]

In 1219–20 the Mongol armies moved on the Khorezmian empire of central Asia and Persia. Then they passed round the southern coast of the Caspian Sea and traversed the Caucasus and Crimea. In this way they came to confront the Kipchaks on the Pontic steppes. The Kipchaks called for the help of the princes of Rus, warning "Our land they have taken, your land they will come and take tomorrow." In this situation only the staunchest alliance of all available forces could conceivably have fended off the enemy. In the event it proved impossible to create such an alliance: the princes of Rus were not even able to cooperate with one another, let alone with the Kipchaks, whom they were accustomed to regard as their bitter foes. Nor perhaps could they have appreciated just how dangerous the new invaders were.

51

At any rate, when Prince Mstislav of Galich summoned a council of princes in Kiev, only two of his colleagues joined him, also both called Mstislav, from Kiev and Chernigov. On learning of their proposed resistance, the Mongols sent an embassy to the princes of Rus, declaring: "We hear that you are sending an army against us, responding to the Polovtsy. But we have not attacked your lands or your towns, nor have we marched against you. We have come, sent by God, to make war not on you, but on our serfs and stableboys, the heathen Polovtsy. Make peace with us." The Russian princes rejected this overture as a typical device of steppe warfarers, aimed at splitting their opponents: it had, indeed, earlier been used to separate the Kipchaks from the Ossetians. Peace was rejected and the envoys killed.[35]

All the same Rus was effectively split. Even the three Mstislavs could not cooperate. Two of them joined with the Kipchaks, and in the ensuing battle on the River Kalka (1223), near the Sea of Azov, they were defeated. What might have been accomplished with greater or more united forces is suggested by the fact that the Mongols, exhausted by their long trek across the steppe, could not thereafter manage an attack on Volga Bulgaria and returned to Mongolia.

Chingiz Khan died shortly thereafter, but in 1228 a kurultai elected his son Ögödei as his successor. In 1235 another kurultai decided to renew the campaign in the west against Volga Bulgaria and Rus. The far western lands, including Rus, were designated as an *ulus* (an autonomous territory) for Batu, the grandson of Chingiz Khan.

The princes of Rus did not make good use of the breathing space they were granted before this decision was put into effect. By the late 1230s they were engaged in vicious and prolonged fighting over the control of Kiev. This meant that their forces were exhausted and they themselves at loggerheads when in the winter of 1237 Batu's *tiumeni* crossed the middle Volga and appeared at the borders of the principality of Riazan, having already attacked and more or less destroyed Volga Bulgaria. From Riazan they demanded a tribute of one-tenth of all their armed men and armaments. The prince of Riazan, Iurii Igorevich, refused and summoned his fellow princes for help. No help came, however. Riazan's army was massacred and its principal city laid waste. A joint force dispatched belatedly by the grand prince of Vladimir was defeated at Kolomna, farther northwest, at the confluence of the Oka and Moscow Rivers.

The experience of Riazan was repeated in many other cities. Over the next three years they were stormed, their inhabitants ruthlessly put to death, and their buildings destroyed. In Vladimir many of the inhabitants took refuge in the Cathedral of the Assumption, where they were burned alive or hacked to death by the assailants if they tried to escape. Suzdal suffered a similar fate: "They plundered the Church of the Holy Virgin and burned down the prince's court and burned down the Monastery of St. Dmitrii, and the others they plundered. The old monks and nuns and priests and the blind, lame, hunchbacked, and sick they killed, and the young monks and nuns and priests and priests' wives and deacons and their wives, and their daughters and sons—all were led away into captivity."[36] A few towns, such as Kozelsk and Smolensk, resisted for some time before being overcome. The Mongols never attempted to take Novgorod, which, as the richest town in Rus, might have been a specially coveted prize. They were not superhuman, and it is possible, though not certain, that a more coordinated and organized resistance could have repulsed them, or at least prevented them from establishing such uncontested dominance. At one stage they had to pull back for eighteen months to replenish and regroup.

Batu conducted one final campaign farther west, in Moldavia, Hungary, and Transylvania, and won a great battle against the Poles, Bohemians, and Teutonic Knights at Liegnitz, near Breslau (1241). Then, however, the weakness of Mongol political structures revealed itself: when the great khan Ögödei died back in Mongolia, Batu decided he should return to the Mongol capital, Karakorum, as the only way of thwarting the dynastic ambitions of Ögödei's son, Güyük. As a result, Batu was unable to consolidate his control over the newly conquered regions and withdrew to the lower Volga to set up the city of Sarai-Batu, capital of his branch of the Mongol Empire, the Kipchak khanate, or the Golden Horde, as it has become known to historians.

MONGOL RULE

What was the effect of the Mongol conquest? There can be little doubt of the overwhelming psychological impact it had on the people of Rus. The chronicles bear ample witness to that, even if their descriptions are at times rhetorical rather than precise. Recent scholarship has suggested, however, that the actual physical destruction may have been less than the chroniclers' verbal fireworks would have us believe. After all, not *all* the cities of Rus were sacked, and there is evidence that even those which were did not have all their buildings destroyed and that they recovered relatively quickly. Economic activity resumed, trade with the West (most of it from Novgorod and Pskov) was not seriously disrupted, and some trading routes to the East were facilitated, for example by the subjugation of Volga Bulgaria. Indeed, the Golden Horde offered relative stability and a maintained network of caravan routes across the heartland of Eurasia and thereby opened up promising new trading opportunities, plugging Rus into the affluent economies of Asia, especially China, which was far wealthier than any European society of the time, even Byzantium. The Kievan state had earlier developed trading relations with the Pechenegs and Kipchaks; there was absolutely no reason why they should not do so with the much better organized Mongols.[37]

In the political sense, though, Rus was humiliated and subjected to superior authority. It became part of the Golden Horde, and its princes were required to take themselves to Sarai to kowtow—bowing with their foreheads to the ground—before Batu or, later, his son Sartak in order to express their allegiance and to have their patent *(iarlyk)*, the authorization of their rule, confirmed. Occasionally they were commanded to undertake the even longer journey to the great khan in Karakorum. They had to allow their populations to be registered in a census, and then to be taxed and recruited into auxiliary militia units according to the census data. A *darughachi* (viceroy or governor) was placed at the side of each prince to supervise his conduct of affairs and to countersign all official documents.[38]

On the other hand, the Mongols did not occupy and settle Rus as they did some other parts of their empire. It had too little to offer them in terms of either commerce or grazing lands. Instead they left the existing principalities intact and ruled them from a distance, sending their permanent agents, the *darughachi*, to extract from Rus the resources they needed.

The possibility of accommodation with the Mongols was shown by Novgorod, whose distant geographical location amid dense forests probably enabled it to maintain some kind of independence from them, even though the city was under pressure from the West, where the Swedes and Teutonic Knights were attempting to gain a foothold on the River Neva and Lake Ladoga. Its prince, Aleksandr, decided that the Mongols were the more dangerous foe and used every opportunity to gain their benevolent neutrality while he turned against his western adversaries.

By the early 1260s, then, a pattern had emerged. The Tatars exercised indirect authority, but nevertheless made unmistakable their intention to insist on their ultimate sovereignty by demanding the periodic symbolic submission of the Russian princes, and by drawing regular tribute from the conquered peoples, as well as recruits for their armies and sometimes also for forced labor, when roads, bridges, or postal stations had to be built. Their *iam* (postal relay) system, with roads linking stations roughly a day's ride apart, ensured communications by courier throughout the empire and rendered their control relatively tight. Local populations were obliged to feed horses and to service envoys as required.

For about three-quarters of a century this empire performed the unique feat of dominating the whole of Inner Asia and the neighboring sedentary states (some of them for much longer). No Eurasian empire before or since has held sway over so much territory. The later Russian Empire came closest, as we shall see, but never subjugated Persia or China. While it lasted, the Mongol Empire almost created a united Eurasia, with trade from Venice going to Beijing, and Chinese goods becoming widely available on the Black Sea. One European by-product of this abrupt universalism was the Black Death. It derived from a bacillus long familiar in Yunnan and Burma: in the face of it Europeans were like New World natives on the arrival of the Spanish *conquistadores,* overwhelmed by a hitherto unknown disease.[39]

For the princes of Rus Mongol overlordship was by no means intolerable. The Mongols put a limit to their mutual feuding, as the Varangians had done earlier for the East Slav tribes, and provided them with powerful backing for their authority in case of social rebellion. The position of prince vis-à-vis veche was powerfully enhanced.

For the people, however, Mongol domination was much harsher. In 1262 violent risings against taxation and recruitment took place in a number of the northeastern cities, the resistance being led by the veche. Townspeople objected particularly to the practice of taking away for slavery or conscription householders who could not or would not pay their dues.[40] These and other urban revolts of the late thirteenth and fourteenth centuries were probably motivated not only by plunder of homes and trade and by ethnic or religious humiliation, but also by the fact that the Mongol overlords deprived the veches of what had hitherto been their main functions, election of princes, decisions on war and peace, the allocation of taxation, and recruitment to the militia. Every one of these functions was now handled by the Mongols themselves or by the princes acting as their agents. The Mongols and the princes, in short, often now had a common interest; at the very least, princes were reluctant to intervene to protect restive townsfolk. Many rebellions coincided with the taking of the census, which symbolized the hated subjection and prepared administratively for conscription and the levying of tribute.[41]

From the mid-fourteenth century the Golden Horde relaxed its grip to the extent of allowing the princes of Rus to take over for themselves the roles of *darughachi* and *basqaq* (tribute collector), that is, to keep order and to supervise population registration, taxation, and recruitment, while still betaking themselves periodically to Sarai to perform their symbolic acts of subjection. This change was the first sign that central direction from the Mongols was slackening, and, like other subordinate rulers in China and

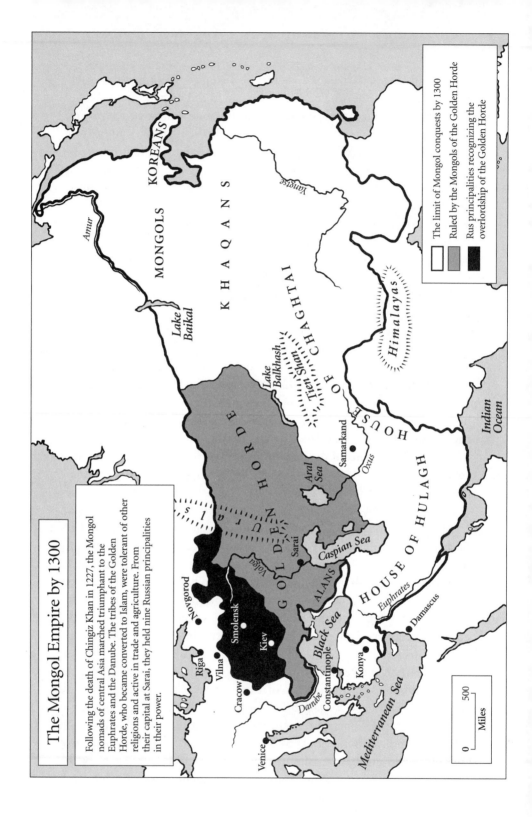

The Mongol Empire by 1300

Following the death of Chingiz Khan in 1227, the Mongol nomads of central Asia marched triumphant to the Euphrates and the Danube. The tribes of the Golden Horde, who became converted to Islam, were tolerant of other religions and active in trade and agriculture. From their capital at Sarai, they held nine Russian principalities in their power.

The limit of Mongol conquests by 1300

Ruled by the Mongols of the Golden Horde

Rus principalities recognizing the overlordship of the Golden Horde

KOREANS

MONGOLS

KHAQANS

Amur

Yangtse

Lake Baikal

HOUSE OF CHAGHTAI

Lake Balkhash

Tien Shan

Himalayas

Indian Ocean

GOLDEN HORDE

Aral Sea

Samarkand

Oxus

S i b e r i a

Sarai

Caspian Sea

HOUSE OF HULAGH

Volga

ALANS

Euphrates

Damascus

Novgorod

Smolensk

Kiev

Black Sea

Konya

Riga

Vilna

Constantinople

Cracow

Danube

Mediterranean Sea

Venice

0   500
Miles

Persia, the Rus princes were able to seize the opportunity to strengthen their own power base, though still unequivocally under overall Mongol control.[42]

It was not only the princes who benefited, but also the Orthodox Church, which, perhaps paradoxically, flourished under Mongol suzerainty to a greater degree than at any other time in its history. It became a uniquely privileged institution, receiving a *tarkhan* exempting it from the tribute which bore so heavily on other sections of the community. Clergymen were not registered and were not liable for forced labor or military service. The church was thus able to develop its lands unmolested and in a favorable competitive position.

The church received not only material benefits. With the fragmentation and humiliation of the political authority of the veches and the princes, it stood out as the one institution able to speak for the "land of Rus" as a whole. Orthodoxy became the embodiment not only of religious but also of national identity and even of lost political unity. Unlike Islam, which had expanded explosively several centuries earlier in the Middle East, the Mongols' religion had little to offer subjugated peoples other than the legitimation of their subjugation. In the long run, even the Mongols themselves accepted the religion of their most numerous conquered peoples and converted to Islam, while their Christian subjects were confirmed and strengthened in their Christian faith.[43]

While trade and princely power laid out the main arteries of the northeastern realms, we may regard the monasteries as providing the humbler cells which contained their lifeblood. In his *Course of Russian History,* Vasilii Kliuchevskii showed how the spiritual and economic achievement of the monasteries laid the foundation for Muscovy's geographical settlement patterns, its economic wealth, and its spiritual culture.[44] If Russia was a colonizing country, as he maintained, then it colonized not least through its monks.

There was of course a paradox at the heart of this "monastic colonization": in the long run the most successful foundations were bound to violate their own basic principles, rather as, say, the Cistercians did in medieval western Europe. By amassing landed property and other earthly riches—and by enserfing the peasants living on their territories—monasteries which had started as schools of asceticism, poverty, and retreat from the world became centers of prosperity, luxury, and involvement in the world. Later, when the lands of Rus emerged from the Mongol overlordship, this inner conflict was starkly revealed.

The philologist and historian Nikolai Trubetskoi has claimed that "The Tatar overlordship was for Rus above all a religious epoch. The retreat into monasticism and the creation of new monastic refuges became a mass phenomenon."[45] The German historian Günther Stökl has built on this insight, suggesting that there were two types of spirituality at work in the medieval Rus church. One was the relatively active and open piety of the Kievan elites, closely related to the authority of the princes. The other was the more withdrawn, ascetic devoutness evident during the Mongol suzerainty, cut off from the secular power and identifying with the people rather than with the state.[46]

The Mongol domination enabled some principalities to strengthen themselves at the expense of the others. Their success depended partly on geographical features, and partly on the personal characteristics of their leaders. The three leading principalities proved to be Galicia-Volynia, eventually under Lithuanian and Polish rule; Novgorod; and Rostov-Vladimir-Suzdal. In all three cases they drew some advantage from being either relatively distant from the steppe whence came the constant threat of nomadic raids, or situated in remote and wooded country which it was more difficult for raiders to attack.

Galicia, Volynia, and Lithuania

Galicia and Volynia lay on relatively fertile soil close to the borders of Poland and Hungary, on the Dniester and southern Bug and not far from the lower course of the Danube. Galicia also dominated the upper waters of the Vistula, which gave it natural contacts with Poland and the Baltic. The two principalities were thus well placed for trade with new European kingdoms to replace the lost Byzantine and Middle Eastern contacts. Galicia was united by the descendants of Iaroslav the Wise, while Volynia became the patrimony of the senior branch of the descendants of Vladimir Monomakh. The two were united in 1199 by Prince Roman Mstislavich of Volynia, who temporarily ruled Kiev as well. His son Daniil was faced with challenges from the boyars of Volynia, who at one stage invited the Hungarian king to rule over them, but he was able with the help of Volynian townspeople to reunite the two territories in 1234.[47]

Thereafter the Mongol invasion compelled them to seek allies, whom they found farther north, in the pagan principality of Lithuania. During the thirteenth century the Lithuanian prince Mindaugas had managed to unite the various Baltic and East Slav tribes of the Neman and Western Dvina basins. His successors, notably Gediminas (1316–1341), expanded southeastward into territories weakened by the Mongol assault, including Volynia, Polotsk, and Turov-Pinsk (the latter two making up much of present-day Belorussia). Galicia, on the other hand, broke away and became part of Poland.

Until the late fourteenth century the Lithuanian princes professed a warlike religion which featured oaths of fealty sealed by blood sacrifice. Gediminas centralized and systematized the cult, building a temple in Vilnius, where he also established his court. All the same, he and his successors not only permitted but actually encouraged the development of Christianity, partly in order to attract immigrants, partly to solicit the support of other Christian powers. Lithuania was right on the border between Catholic and Orthodox Europe, and both denominations were allowed to build their churches in the principal towns. Orthodoxy, however, had far more adherents among the population.

59

Although we know little about Gediminas' system of rule, it seems likely that he left a good deal of power with the warrior elite of the former tribes, the *bojarai,* consulting them and the leading members of his own family before embarking on campaigns. As a new and still vigorous pagan power, Lithuania was able to use military techniques learned from its Christian neighbors, while exploiting the divisions between them to expand its domains. She profited as Moscow later did from the debility and fragmentation aggravated by the Mongol incursion. She made good use of her location athwart the trade routes from northern Europe to both Byzantium and the Golden Horde, and herself exported the products of the forest, such as wax, honey, and furs. At the same time Lithuania's marshy and wooded territory afforded some protection against both nomadic horsemen and the heavy cavalry of the Teutonic Knights, so that it was possible for the Lithuanian grand princes to create and maintain their own forces of mobile light cavalry backed by a partisan-style light infantry. They were able to attract immigrants, interested in trade, manufacture, or warfare, from more vulnerable principalities.

Under the joint rulership of Algirdas (1341–1377) and Kestutis (1341–1382), Lithuania—at this stage generally in alliance with Tver—further annexed Briansk, Chernigov, Novgorod-Severskii, Podolia, Pereiaslav, and Kiev. Smolensk also fell to Lithuanian troops in 1403. These were the heartlands of the old Rus, and their acquisition enabled Lithuania to take over the law, culture, and traditions of the Kievan principality and to claim a special status as "gatherer of the lands of Rus." Those claims were enhanced in 1362 by victory over an army of the Golden Horde at the Battle of Blue Waters, at the easternmost bend of the River Dnieper. At this stage Lithuanian troops were able to advance unmolested into the southern steppe lands as far as the shore of the Black Sea.

However, Lithuania, though large, was geopolitically highly vulnerable, caught between Orthodoxy and Catholicism, between Poland, the Teutonic

Knights, and the Golden Horde. Her still basically tribal structure threatened her with decline and disintegration no less abrupt than her ascent. Jogaila and Vytautas (sons respectively of Algirdas and Kestutis) fell out with each other, and Vytautas looked for support to the Teutonic Knights. Jogaila responded by turning to Poland, which, as it happened, was itself in the midst of a succession crisis, the male line having died out. Jogaila's approach enabled the crisis to be solved: he married Queen Jadwiga and became himself king of Poland, taking the new name of Władysław Jagiello (1386–1434). He pledged himself and his nobles to accept the Catholic faith and the permanent dynastic union of Lithuania with Poland. Jogaila destroyed pagan idols and promoted mass conversions of both pagans and Orthodox to Catholicism. Catholic boyars were granted privileges, including the sole right to become governors of provinces. This was the Union of Krewo (1385–86), which originated as a dynastic arrangement between the two crowns but two centuries later became a full amalgamation of the two states.

In this way the western territories of Kievan Rus came under the Polish crown and the Roman Catholic Church and developed their own distinct languages and cultures, for some centuries known as Rusin or Ruthenian, and today as Ukrainian and Belorussian. The Polish-Lithuanian state saw itself as an *antemurale* power, the bastion of western Catholic civilization against Islam, Orthodoxy, and the crude, militant colonialism of the Teutonic Knights. Jogaila/Władysław explicitly aimed to recover all the lands of Rus which had been, in his words, "under the perpetual rule of the Polish crown." For this purpose he adopted Ruthenian as the language of his chancellery, to reflect both the ethnic origin of his principal servitors and his ultimate ambitions.

By the early fifteenth century, Lithuania-Poland was much the largest territorial state in Europe. Its land extended as far as the Ugra and Oka Rivers, just west of Moscow, and southward down the Dnieper to a small and precarious foothold on the Black Sea between its estuary and that of the Dniester. Expansion farther eastward was blocked by the Golden Horde at the Battle of the Vorskla River (1399). In 1410 a joint Polish-Lithuanian army defeated the Teutonic Knights at the Battle of Tannenberg, conquering the whole of Samogitia and occupying the approaches to the Hanseatic city of Riga. For a brief period it could be said that Lithuania stretched from the Baltic to the Black Sea, though it is not clear how stable its control was over the outlying southern regions, for the Lithuanian mode of warfare was not really suited to the open steppe.

Many Orthodox Lithuanian *bojarai* made the transition to Catholicism relatively painlessly, for with their new faith came the steadily growing rights of the Polish nobility, the *szlachta*. The *bojarai* and *szlachta* were amalgamated into one estate by the agreement of Horodlo (1413), which exempted them from most taxes and from the obligation of military service. Members of the combined estate had the sole right to elect state officials, including the king himself, to occupy official posts, and to treat state land as a personal or family possession. Polish-Lithuanian nobles became so powerful not least because they were the dominant force in the economy. They exploited the ever more profitable Baltic grain trade to nibble away at the lands and traditional rights of the peasants till they had reduced them to serfs obliged to perform labor duties on their estates. They closed cathedral chapters to all but *szlachta* candidates, thus eliminating an important channel of social mobility for poor but educated townsfolk. They commanded the army and monopolized both the court and the royal administration. They and they alone were the deputies in the Sejm (Diet) and their provincial equivalents, the Sejmiki.

61

In effect, members of the Polish-Lithuanian *szlachta* were the citizens of an aristocratic republic, and their increasing power and wealth were gained at the expense of the combined monarchy. This was exactly the opposite path from that being taken in Muscovy in the fifteenth century, where, as we shall see, monarchical power was steadily narrowing the prerogatives of princely families and their servitors.

At this time Jews were streaming into Poland-Lithuania in large numbers, squeezed out by endemic anti-Semitism in western Europe and seeking security in the religious toleration of their adopted homeland. They proved very convenient to the *szlachta,* who offered them patronage and employment in low-status but essential jobs, as stewards, shopkeepers, tavernkeepers, moneylenders, and tax collectors. The Jews successfully sought the protection of the crown and managed to preserve certain rights for themselves, such as self-assessment for taxation and self-government through their own *kahal,* or commune. Jews thus occupied a well-buttressed intermediate segment in Polish-Lithuanian society. Until the mid-seventeenth century they were able to lead their own way of life and practice their own form of worship more securely there than almost anywhere else in Europe.[48]

Lord Novgorod the Great

Lord Novgorod the Great (as the city-state liked to call itself) was from the earliest times a major trading center, thanks to its position close to the Baltic Sea, astride the river route "from the Varangians to the Greeks" and close to the Valdai Hills, where the Volga rises and begins its course to the Caspian

Sea. The greatest source of its wealth, however, was the immense forests which lay to its east and north, around Lakes Ladoga and Onega and all the way to the White Sea, extending as far as the northern reaches of the Pechora River and the Arctic slopes of the Urals. Novgorod was able to exercise only a loose control over the Baltic and Finno-Ugrian peoples who populated these expanses, but collected tribute from them to use in trading. Up to the eleventh century, that trade, primarily in fur, but also in honey, mead, and waxes, went down the Volga to Bulgaria, down the Dnieper to Kiev and Byzantium, and westward to markets in the Baltic and Scandinavia.

Two centuries later, the Volga trade had been blocked by the rising principality of Rostov, while the southern route was becoming unprofitable as a result of the decline of Byzantium. Only the western trade route remained, and the citizens of Novgorod exploited it with vigor. The Swedes had their "Gothic court" at the heart of the city, while the "German court" displayed the wares offered by the Hanseatic League. As late medieval Germany grew more wealthy, it offered a lively and growing market for furs and also for Novgorod's developing specialties, gold- and silverwork. The Hansa had its own compound in the city, known as Peterhof, which offered stables, inns, warehouses, stalls, and even a jail. The Hansa's mutually binding commercial laws and sophisticated credit arrangements provided an excellent means of developing Novgorod's trade, which went through the Hansa ports of Riga and Reval (today Tallinn). Twice a year merchant convoys would sail from Reval to the island of Kotlin (today Kronstadt), where wares would be transferred to Novgorodian riverboats for passage up the Neva to Lake Ladoga and the River Volkhov. Such convoys enjoyed customs privileges and the special protection of the Novgorod authorities, while in Peterhof Germans lived under their own laws and protected by their own officials (hence the jail).[49]

Until 1136 Novgorod was under the ultimate sovereignty of the grand prince of Kiev as his second city, and its own local prince was recognized as being the first in line for the succession to Kiev itself. Grand Prince Iaroslav, in gratitude for the support given to him by the chief citizens and boyars of Novgorod in winning the Kiev throne, accorded them special privileges, including a kind of extraterritorial sovereignty in one half of the city, while the prince ruled the other half. In an act of insubordination in 1136 they used this power to put in place their own elected mayor (*posadnik*) and military commander (*tysiatskii*), who was to command the militia levied from the city's *sotni*, or "hundred," areas. They also asserted their right to invite and reject potential princes, concluding with each of them a treaty governing their mutual relations, in particular the prince's military obligations and the revenue to which he was entitled. The Council of Lords (*sovet gospod)*, formally elected by the veche, became the executive power in the city. It was presided over by the archbishop (a status established in 1165), a custom which symbolized the close relationship between boyars and church. The stone cathedral of St. Sophia was erected in the boyar half in the mid-eleventh century, in emulation of the St. Sophia's in Kiev, and indicated that the city's status derived from commercial wealth rather than princely power. The city now referred to itself as "Lord Novgorod the Great," or alternatively "the patrimony of St. Sophia."

63

Thereafter Novgorod, unlike other principalities, did not fall under the domination of any particular branch of the ruling dynasty, but played the field, inviting nominees from different, often competing, branches. This feature, together with its wealth, made it an especially coveted prize in the rivalry between the princes. The city had, moreover, a strong sense of public relations: at an early stage, in addition to St. Sophia's Cathedral, it boasted a stone kremlin (not merely a wooden one, like most other towns). Its citizens enjoyed a comparatively high level of literacy, as the recent discovery of birch-bark documents testifies. Like New York in the United States or Cologne in the Rhineland, Novgorod commanded enormous wealth without commensurate political power, and thus tended to become the supreme prize in other people's contests.

With the Mongol invasion of 1238–1240 great changes took place, as they did elsewhere in Rus, but in a different direction. Novgorod's northwestern location and the diplomatic skill of its prince, Aleksandr, ensured that the city was never conquered, and that it occupied a relatively privileged position in the domains of the Golden Horde. No Mongol troops were stationed on its territory, and no tax collector came from the Horde. Instead Aleksandr agreed to pay a substantial tribute in return for a special charter guaranteeing the city's right to self-rule.

If the Mongol threat was relatively distant, however, other sources of danger were much closer. The Swedes had established themselves in Finland and were pressing ever farther eastward into the forests and lakes between the Gulf of Bothnia and the White Sea, where trapping and fishing promised immense fortunes. The farther north and the colder the climate, the finer and denser the fur. In 1240 the Swedes sailed up the Neva, to try to crush their Novgorod rivals in the region, but were repulsed, a victory to which Aleksandr owed his title of Nevskii.[50]

As if the Swedes were not enough, during the thirteenth century much of the Baltic was being overrun by the Teutonic Knights, a militant order of crusaders which had originated in the Holy Land and, with the approval of the pope, had turned its attention northeast, to the pagan peoples of the

The Republic of Novgorod obtained self-government from Kievan Russia in 997, and complete independence in 1136. The Republic styled itself "Lord Novgorod the Great" and was governed by a grand prince and an assembly of citizens. Novgorod was for over three hundred years a flourishing trading and cultural center, and successfully fought off attacks by the Teutonic Knights, the Swedes, the Lithuanians, and the Mongols. In 1478 it was finally crushed into complete submission by Ivan the Terrible and annexed to Moscow. The town itself was largely destroyed by fire in 1695.

The Republic of Novgorod, 1136–1478

Ponoy

White Sea

Pogost-na-more

Spasskoi

Ilomanets

Pudozhskoi

Lake Onega

Onega

FINNS

Lake Ladoga 1284
1295
1313

Olonets

Vyborg

Baltic Sea

SWEDES

1240, 1348
Gulf of Finland

Kopore
Oreshek
Ladoga

Vologda

Reval
1223

Yama

Volkhov

Nebolchi

Dorpat

NOVGOROD

1242
1253

Pskov

Staraya Rusa

Izborsk
1269
1298
1323

Porkhov

Torzhok
1238
Tver
Volga

Riga

Opochka

Velikie Luki

TEUTONIC KNIGHTS

LITHUANIANS

Dvina

1213

1245
1253

Polotsk

Volokolamsk
1238

Moscow

MONGOLS

Territory of the Republic of Novgorod, 1136–1478

Province of Pskov, gaining its independence from Novgorod in 1348

Principal military attacks on the Republic by the Swedes, the Teutonic Knights, the Lithuanians, and the Mongols; with dates

0   100
Miles

1396

Baltic coast. Just as their predecessors had been diverted to Constantinople, so the Knights turned against Orthodox Christianity in Rus. In 1241 they occupied the fortress of Izborsk and the major trading city of Pskov. Aleksandr decided that the Mongols were the more serious danger, and therefore should be appeased. First, however, it was necessary to turn back the Teutonic Knights, which he did in a battle on Lake Peipus in 1242. Thanks to the film director Sergei Eizenshtein, this encounter has gone down as one of the great battles of world history. Recent research reveals, however, that the armies on both sides were of relatively modest size, and that the Novgorod force outnumbered the Knights threefold. These facts, however, scarcely detract from the importance of the battle, which established the Narva River and Lake Peipus as a permanent dividing line between Orthodoxy and Western forms of Christianity.[51]

Aleksandr Nevskii's policy had numerous and powerful opponents in Novgorod itself, especially among the artisans and merchants who were strong in the veche. They were anxious to reach a peace agreement with the Teutonic Knights so as to continue trading in the Baltic. At one stage his younger brother, Andrei, succeeded in gaining the support both of the veche and of the khan, and he ruled for five years. But Aleksandr's diplomacy paid off in the end. He managed to regain the confidence of the khan and deposed his brother with the help of Kipchak troops. He later called them in twice more to put down pro-Western risings.

An even more serious crisis arose in 1257, when the Mongols tried to supervise the census and tribute-gathering directly. When their officials arrived and "began to ask for tithe and *tamga* [customs dues]," the citizens of Novgorod sent them packing. The Mongols returned the following year with troops, who paraded through the streets escorting Aleksandr. Opposition to the census then collapsed.[52] Having thus enhanced his standing with the Mongols, Aleksandr claimed and received from them the title of grand prince of Vladimir, senior among the princes of Rus, which he held till his death in 1263. This was the only time when a Novgorod prince held a title which adequately reflected the city's economic importance.

Rostov-Vladimir-Suzdal

In the long run, neither Novgorod nor Lithuania-Poland proved able to provide a focus for the emergence of a post-medieval East Slav state claiming Rus as its heritage. In the case of Novgorod this failure was due to political disunity, in the case of Lithuania to religious divisions and the growing orientation toward Western, Latinate culture.

In the twelfth century the petty principalities of the north and east, in the triangle formed by the upper Volga and the River Oka, looked even less promising. Slavs had arrived there relatively late: only in the eighth and ninth centuries did the tribe of the Viatichi make its appearance, driving out or subjugating the indigenous Finno-Ugrian tribes. The Viatichi remained pagan long after other Slav tribes had converted to Christianity. The Soviet ethnographer Lev Gumilev has argued that the intermingling of the Slav and Finno-Ugrian peoples created a new ethnic stock, the Great Russians, distinct from the East Slavs of Kievan Rus, who lived farther south and west. According to this interpretation, subsequent interaction with Tatar and Turkic peoples further accentuated the distinct Eurasian features of the Great Russian people.[53]

The great advantage of the Volga-Oka region was that it was distant from the steppes and its heavy forest cover made it uncongenial to nomads. Furthermore, it boasted enormous supplies of timber, fish, and furs, and these were what first attracted colonizers from the southwest. Furs generated increasingly abundant revenues as European courts and markets became more affluent during the later Middle Ages. The cities of Rostov, Suzdal, and Vladimir-on-the-Kliazma became considerable commercial centers. In the thirteenth century Novgorod controlled their trade almost entirely, and the subsequent struggle for it was a key to dominance within Rus as a whole.

Vladimir Monomakh sent his son Iurii Vladimirovich to rule in Rostov. Iurii married a princess from the Kipchaks and became known as Iurii Dolgorukii—Iurii of the Long Arms. He acquired that name through his ruthless and ambitious policy of territorial aggrandizement, actively developing the principality of Rostov, building churches and palaces in Suzdal and Vladimir, making land grants to peasants and monasteries who relocated to his territory. He campaigned against the Bulgars and Novgorod in order to gain control of the riches to be acquired by exploiting the northern forests.

Iurii's sons, Andrei and Vsevolod, had even greater ambitions. Andrei moved his capital to Vladimir and established his own residence just outside it, in the village of Bogoliubovo (hence his commonly accepted surname, Bogoliubskii). He intervened in the princely rivalries in 1169 to expel the current ruler of Kiev, sack his city, and install his own brother, Gleb Iurevich, on its throne. Then he took the much-cherished Byzantine Mother of God icon from a Kievan church, set it in gold, silver, and precious stones, and bestowed it on his own newly built Church of the Intercession in Bogoliubovo. It later became a much-loved national emblem. Vladimir also acquired magnificent "Golden Gates" on the model of Kiev, and a Cathedral of the Dormition, named after the one in the Monastery of the Caves. Andrei tried to carve out for his city a metropolitanate separate from Kiev, but was over-ruled by the patriarch of Constantinople. In short, Andrei consciously raised the prestige of Vladimir, in the context for the moment of Kiev's symbolic seniority, but aiming perhaps in the long run to supplant it in that respect too and to emulate Byzantium itself. In these respects his brother, Vsevolod III (1175–1212), known revealingly as "Big Nest," continued his policies.[54]

67

PRINCES AND LOCAL COMMUNITIES

As we have seen, the changes which took place in the twelfth century ended any hope of creating a unitary state or even a stable confederation. In all parts of Rus, the princely superalliance fell apart. Princes increasingly re-garded their territories as patrimonies (votchiny) rather than as dominions held in trust for the dynasty as a whole. Landownership rather than com-merce and command of trade routes was becoming the principal lever of power, and rent was replacing tribute as the main source of revenue.

In the countryside these changes resulted in the princes' subjugation of the local assemblies, now known variously as the mir or *volost*, which governed a large village or a complex of small ones. Each was headed by an elected elder, a *starosta* or *sotskii* (hundred-man). Correspondence between princes or monasteries and these elders shows that it was the responsibility of the mir to regulate the use of common facilities, such as pastures, woods, and water-courses, and to allocate and collect tribute and dues. The mir decided the magnitude of each household's allocation by reference to the amount of land it held and the common facilities to which it had access. The mir had to investigate crimes and if possible to catch criminals. The prince's court had the job of judging serious crimes, but even then "good people" from the mir had to participate in the court proceedings if the verdict was to be bind-ing on all.

The mir (or several *miry,* depending on size) was also an ecclesiastical unit, in effect the parish. Its members built the church, chose the priest, and allotted land to him for the use of his household and for ecclesiastical busi-ness. Sometimes the church building would be used for mir assemblies and the treasury would be kept there. Often the *sotskii* was also the church-warden.[55]

As the center of gravity of the Rus economy moved from trade toward agriculture, the princes acquired more land, whether by force, custom, or economic domination, and began to regard it as their private patrimony. Therewith the boyars' right to collect tribute, kormlenie, was becoming more like the right to extract feudal dues, while local *miry* were tending to turn into peasant communes. In this way, already in the Kievan period, and more intensively under the Mongols, Rus was becoming in some respects a feudal society.[56]

At the same time, essential aspects of feudalism, as it was known in western Europe, were missing. There was little sense of a permanent and mutually binding personal loyalty between lords and vassals. Indeed vassalage was absent: inferiors were not bound by any oath to serve their superiors, and the superiors were not bound by any law or moral obligation to protect their inferiors and provide for them in times of dearth. In Rus the superior acted like an occupier, demanding an income but not obliged to offer anything in return. Peasants and townsfolk obeyed while they had no choice, but if oppression became intolerable or if other opportunities beckoned, they moved on in search of a more congenial master. Their right to do so was secured by custom. By the same token, a lord could at any time quit the service of one prince and seek out another. This was freedom of a kind, but not one resting on law or stable institutions.[57]

The designation commonly applied by historians to each of the Rus principalities during this time of fragmentation is *udel*. An udel was a princely holding, that portion of a father's property—and sovereignty—inherited by a son as a result of the division of the property among the various heirs, which included the widow and any daughters otherwise unprovided for. In English the term is often translated as "appanage," but this is fundamentally wrong, since an appanage was a territory provided for the upkeep of the younger sons of monarchs within a system of primogeniture, and it reverted to the crown when no longer needed for that purpose. An udel, however, was a permanent holding within a system of partible inheritance. Once a son inherited it, he could bequeath it to his own sons, again with a portion for each heir. There was therefore a natural tendency with each passing generation for udel principalities to become smaller and more numerous, a process which could not continue indefinitely without their falling below a size at which defense or even sensible economic exploitation was possible.[58]

This system posed a painful dilemma for the princes: they each needed a male heir, to ensure the smooth passage of authority and property, but preferably not more than one, or their properties would be diminished and civil strife might ensue. They tried to overcome the dilemma by making elaborate wills providing for each of their sometimes numerous heirs, but in practice these were usually not enforceable once a prince had died.

Each udel centered on a town of greater or lesser importance, and typically had its focus in a river valley, along which the lines of trade and settlement would flow. The larger principalities, those with significant towns, became known as grand principalities and conducted relations directly with the khan of the Golden Horde. The grand prince of Vladimir had nominal precedence over all of them, but in practice the khan would vary according to circumstances the award of the principal *iarlyk*, the patent which entitled the holder to act as his agent for tax collection, recruitment, and the enforcement of authority.

69

Each prince was nominally sovereign in his own territory, which he usually divided into two categories: his domain, cultivated by his slaves and managed by his courtiers *(dvornye liudi, dvoriane)*; and other lands, held by his boyars, the members of his *druzhina*, and cultivated by free ("black") peasants or monasteries paying him tribute, part of which was to be passed on to the grand prince and ultimately to the khan. Those latter lands were administered by the prince's *namestniki* (lieutenants) or *volosteli* (governors of a volost), who were chosen from among his most trusted servitors. They raised the revenues from the territory—tribute, taxes, excise dues, court fees, and fines—while enjoying the right to keep back a substantial, and in practice unverifiable, proportion for themselves, customarily one half. As we have seen, this system of revenue-farming was known as kormlenie. The taxable population also had certain labor obligations to perform: cartage, the upkeep of roads and bridges, providing horses, board, and lodging for the prince's officials when traveling on duty. These obligations and the dues in money and kind were provided by each community as a whole, and the portion to be paid by each household was determined in the mir assemblies. The mir was gradually changing its nature and functions, becoming a mainly peasant institution, and one sharing out dues and labor obligations rather than tribute, hence more closely tied to the work process. The extent of all these obligations was largely governed by custom, which meant that the prince endeavored to avoid sudden changes in them, for fear of provoking discontent.[59]

Kormlenie was more than a fiscal device. It was also a form of what anthropologists call "generalized exchange," a means by which local communities could get a measure of their superior by making gifts and gauging his reaction. In the same way they could draw him into a network of mutual obligation and thereby blunt the power of the prince.[60]

The princes were bound to one another by treaty, which usually stipulated the contribution they must make to a joint military effort. The grand prince of Vladimir, or later of Moscow, would command the leading detachment, while his appointed *voevody* would lead secondary detachments which the junior princes and boyars would assemble and bring to the muster. Soldiers were also raised from the communities of town and village, commanded by a "thousander" *(tysiatskii)* appointed by the prince. After a campaign they would disperse again to their home territories. In practice it was difficult to persuade a prince to participate in a military campaign unless he had a direct and obvious interest in it.

Each prince of any consequence had a loosely organized "council" of his principal boyars and courtiers, whom he would consult either individually or together, according to the nature of the business he wished to discuss. He would do this because he was anxious to retain their services and needed their advice, information, and support.

For the same reason, the prince would award his boyars land, as he would to his most trusted courtiers. With the decline of trade, land was now the most cherished good. But the resultant complex calibration of dues and jurisdictions could easily lead to conflict. Most princes regarded with distaste their servitors' right to quit their service, but there was little they could do to prevent it, as their powers of enforcement were simply too limited. To lose a boyar was especially damaging, since in offering his services to another prince he was also transferring to him his land with all its revenues. The result was that many princes' holdings were a complex and intermingled patchwork, which constantly undermined claims of territorial sovereignty. Authority was personal rather than territorial, so in a sense this intermingling did not matter. All the same, most princes found the arrangement highly inconvenient, and some would stipulate in treaties concluded with each other that they would neither attract nor accept servitors from each other's territories. In the early stages of its growth, Moscow had an interest in maintaining the right of free movement, which mainly worked to its benefit, and usually did so in its treaties, but in practice denied the right to leave to its own servitors, or denounced them as traitors and tried to recall them.

It made most sense to attract servitors from the borders of a neighboring territory, so that minimal intermingling would result from their departure, and in the fifteenth century Muscovy put a lot of effort into attracting boyars and princes from the borders of Lithuania.[61]

THE RISE OF MOSCOW

At the start of the fourteenth century, no one could have foretold that of all the principalities of Rus, Moscow would eventually play the leading role. Originally a fortified frontier post of the principality of Suzdal, it was first mentioned by the chronicles in that capacity in 1147. It seems to have become a separate principality around the time of Aleksandr Nevskii's death in 1263, having been set aside for his two-year-old son, Daniil. It became a serious contender among the principalities in 1301–1304, when it pushed out from the immediate surroundings of Moscow by annexing Mozhaisk in the west, Pereiaslavl in the north, and Kolomna in the southeast. These acquisitions gave it control over nearly all of the Moscow River, with its tributaries, up to its confluence with the Oka, as well as the upper basin of the Kliazma and a substantial slice of relatively fertile territory north of it, providing access to Vladimir itself. Along its southern frontier the Oka offered a degree of natural protection against nomadic raids. This was a territory that could be defended as a base for economic life.

The principality of Tver, likewise a relative newcomer, was also expanding at about the same time, and for some decades was a real rival to Moscow. Its natural defenses were somewhat less favorable, but it was farther from the steppe and its geographical situation was much more favorable for trade, on the banks of the Volga and relatively close to Novgorod. A long-term alliance between Tver, Novgorod, and Lithuania, which at one stage seemed probable, would have placed the center of gravity of Rus farther west and closer to the Baltic Sea.

By the early part of the fourteenth century, Tver and Moscow were the only principalities with a strong enough economic and military base to lay claim to the *iarlyk*. The princes of Moscow came from a junior line of the dynasty, the Danilovichi (through Aleksandr Nevskii's younger son), and, under the succession principle inherited from Kiev, had no legitimate right to seniority. They were thus doubly dependent on the favor of the Golden Horde. When a rising took place in their rival's main city in 1327, Ivan I of Moscow was sent with a huge Tatar army to restore order in Tver. As a result he was rewarded with the *iarlyk*. Ivan (1325–1341) turned out to be an ideal agent, who regularly paid the khan's tribute punctually and in full. As a result the Horde ceased sending its own tribute collectors to Rus, and Moscow took over the responsibilities of the tribute-gatherer. This assumption of fiscal power proved to be a turning point, for thereafter the *iarlyk* remained almost uninterruptedly with Moscow, at first perhaps because the khan wanted a counterweight to the potential alliance of Tver, Novgorod, and Lithuania, later because it was strong enough to be the only principality capable of ensuring regular tribute payment.

In addition to the authority conferred by the *iarlyk*, Moscow managed by a combination of good fortune and good judgment to prevent the fragmentation of its udel. Ivan I left a testament for his three sons, Semen, Andrei, and Ivan, assigning a more or less equal division of territory among them, but recognizing Semen's seniority within the family. He took his sons to Sarai and persuaded the khan to ratify the testament, as if consciously assuming the role of founder of a dynasty worthy to exercise the *iarlyk* in perpetuity. After his death, his sons confirmed the arrangements but took an additional step: to avoid conflict, they acknowledged Semen as the senior political authority and fixed the territory assigned to each brother as a patrimony, thus breaking definitively with the Kievan tradition that both land and sovereignty were the affair of the dynasty as a whole. Similar arrangements were confirmed in the testaments of later grand princes. Patrimonies were now owned by individuals and implied responsibility for a family rather than for the dynasty as a whole. Thus the will of Prince Dmitrii Donskoi (1389), grandson of Ivan I, stated unambiguously: "I bless my son, Prince Vasilii, with my patrimony, the grand principality."[62]

THE ORTHODOX CHURCH

While the principalities of Rus were sundered, the church was in a much more favorable position than any secular prince to act as a focus for the loyalties of the East Slavs. The leading prelate, the metropolitan, first of Kiev, then of Vladimir, was the only public figure in whose title was inscribed a claim to authority over all the land of Rus: *vseia Rusi.* The church was independent of the princes: its diocesan boundaries did not coincide with the shifting princely territories, and its bishops were usually appointed by clergy and laity. As we have seen, it received special immunities from the Golden Horde. Its prelates were of high social standing, often coming from princely or boyar families, and not infrequently they acted as intermediaries between princes, or between them and the khan—for which purpose a special diocese was established at Sarai.

It was, then, crucial where the metropolitan of all Rus chose to locate his see. In 1299 Metropolitan Maksim transferred it from Kiev to Vladimir, because of the instability of life in the south, exposed to the hazards of steppe warfare. Vladimir, however, soon began to decline in the face of the rivalry between the principalities of Tver and Moscow. In 1322 Metropolitan Petr made a choice in favor of Moscow, which had supported his candidacy. A mere year after his death in 1326 he was canonized in a ceremony designed to make Moscow the lasting center of the Orthodox Church in Rus. His tomb became a shrine for all Orthodox believers and greatly enhanced the standing of the city.[63]

It was normal for princes, boyars, merchants, and other wealthy people to endow monasteries with money, goods, or land to compensate them for the obligation to say prayers for their souls. By the fifteenth century the accumulation of these gifts made the church an extremely powerful landowner and gave it a strong stake in commerce and industry. Given the close connection between property and authority, these commitments, together with the extensive jurisdiction of ecclesiastical courts, meant that the church formed a kind of state within a state, intermingled territorially and jurisdictionally with the princes' realms. It had to maintain an army of servitors of its own: clerks, treasurers, judges, bailiffs, stewards. The metropolitan of Moscow even had his own armed regiment and *voevoda*, which, as a vassal of the grand prince of Moscow, he had to provide if it was needed for battle.[64] In a sense the church was the greatest political power in the land of Rus. Even though much of its wealth was used for the relief of orphans, widows, invalids, and other social victims, this combination of wealth and authority could not but arouse the envy of the princes. Some of the bitterest political controversies of late medieval Rus were to be concerned with ecclesiastical landholding.

There was also the question of the church's political commitment: although its metropolitanate was in Moscow, should its loyalty lie primarily with the grand principality of Moscow or with the wider Orthodox ecumene, whose head was the Byzantine patriarch? In particular, what should be its attitude toward the Orthodox believers in Lithuanian lands, coming under increasing Polish Catholic dominance?

Metropolitan Aleksii, who became regent in 1359, when Dmitrii (later known as Donskoi) began his reign at the age of nine, was anxious to promote the interests of both Moscow and the church. Perhaps because of Byzantium's evident political weakness, he considered that Moscow's continued strength was crucial to the future of Orthodoxy as a whole, and he did his utmost to ensure that the Moscow see would be entitled to the loyalty of all East Slavs, including those who lived under Lithuanian rule. At first he had the support of the Byzantine patriarch in this policy, but when the latter faced the threat of a Lithuanian conversion to Catholicism, he agreed to the creation of a separate metropolitanate in Galicia.

Aleksii's successor, Kiprian, was an entirely different figure. Whereas Aleksii was a robustly political cleric, staunchly attached to the grand principality of Moscow as an instrument of ecclesiastical policy, Kiprian has to be seen against the background of the changes taking place in the Byzantine patriarchate during the fourteenth century. Never having fully recovered from the Latin domination of the thirteenth century, Byzantium now saw most of its territories overrun by the Ottoman Turks, until it became little more than a tiny besieged enclave in the midst of Muslim dominions. As its worldly realm declined, the patriarchate came proportionately to outweigh the Byzantine imperial court in prestige and diplomatic importance. As if to reflect the growing significance of spiritual matters, the patriarchate was taken over in the mid-fourteenth century by a party known as the "hesychasts." They proposed that individual human beings could attain to a more direct personal knowledge of God through prolonged ascetic discipline combined with repeated prayer. In particular they recommended that through concentration on a simple prayer, addressed to Jesus and repeated in time with the rhythm of breathing, the believer could reach a higher sphere of knowledge and make direct contact with the "energies" of God.

Hesychasm represented a reaction against both the traditional hierarchical and ritualistic Byzantine church and the new Hellenist humanism which was gaining ground among intellectuals. One might say that among its aims was that of transforming an obviously ailing worldly empire into a spiritual ecumene through the preaching of religious practices which could be adopted everywhere, even in territories where the church itself was oppressed by the secular power. Not that its proponents undervalued the church: on the contrary, they were endeavoring to save it, to rediscover its essential values at a time of crisis, and to ensure that it had the wherewithal for survival. The center of the movement was Mount Athos, the "monastic republic" in northern Greece which acted as disseminator of the texts and the learning of Byzantium to the Slavic Orthodox communities, a function which became even more crucial after the Ottoman conquest of the Balkans.[65]

Metropolitan Kiprian had spent several years as a monk at Athos. A Bulgarian by birth, he was initially sent by the patriarch as a diplomat to compose the differences between Lithuania and Moscow. When he became metropolitan in 1378, his appointment was contested in Moscow, where Grand Prince Dmitrii installed an alternative candidate, supported by the Golden Horde. Nevertheless, Kiprian set out to reunite the two sees of Moscow and Lithuania without subordinating himself to the political ambitions of any single ruler. Some scholars believe that he exercised a decisive influence in persuading Grand Prince Jogaila of Lithuania not to come to the aid of Mamai's Tatar army at the Battle of Kulikovo. At any rate he was eventually accepted by Dmitrii.[66]

Against the divisive secular ambitions of the princes of Rus, Kiprian emphasized their spiritual unity under symbolic Byzantine leadership. He insisted on having the emperor remembered in the liturgy, and when Vasilii I of Moscow objected to this practice in 1393, Kiprian presented to him an epistle from the patriarch exhorting him: "For Christians it is not possible to have a church and not to have an emperor, for the empire and the church have a great unity and a commonality, and it is impossible to separate them."[67]

The ideal of maintaining a strong spiritual sphere, separate from and not wholly dominated by the coarse, overbearing princes of this world also animated the monastic movement which played such a major role in the colonization of the immense forest territories of northern and eastern Rus from the thirteenth to fifteenth centuries. As the towns declined in relative importance and saw their rights of self-rule curtailed, monasteries were more often founded outside them, without powerful or wealthy patrons and therefore dependent on their own resources.

The reasons for this development were spiritual as well as economic. Most of the early monasteries had been cenobitic in their lifestyle—that is, they emphasized the communal life: manual work, meals, and liturgical devotions were all performed together, at set times and in set ways. But now a new type of monastic regimen was spreading, coming from Byzantium through Mount Athos: this was the solitary, ascetic life, conducted by each monk in his own way, through his own self-discipline. The moving force now tended to be individuals, animated by the spirit of asceticism, contemplation, and prayer.

The dense forests of northeastern Rus offered an ideal setting for the lifestyle they yearned to adopt. The remoteness, the cold and dark, the dangers from wild animals, constituted an environment in which the novice had to provide for himself, to learn new skills, and to master his own emotions.[68]

The *vitae* of the saints of Rus offer us many examples of a biography which becomes the "type" of the Russian holy man. Born in a well-to-do family, he shows early signs of unusual piety, reading the scriptures and zealously attending services, practices not always welcome to parents who would like to see their son take over the family business. Entering a monastery against their advice, he willingly performs the dirtiest and most unpleasant tasks, but also becomes discontented with the lax discipline and excessive worldliness of his fellows. Sometimes even before taking his vows, he leaves the brotherhood and sets up a little hermitage in the forest, living in a self-erected log hut or even in the hollow of a tree, and feeding on berries and roots, or on bread left for him by occasional visitors. Cold in winter and tormented by mosquitoes in summer, he spends his time in prayer and psalm-singing. The aim of the isolation and asceticism was to achieve spiritual concentration, sometimes employing the contemplative techniques derived from Byzantium.

Typically, the lone forest-dweller does not manage to maintain his isolation for long: brothers from his former monastery come to join him, or pilgrims happen to pass by. Other huts and shelters appear, and the lonely monk becomes the focus of a *skit*, where several brothers live a basically solitary life but gather occasionally for joint celebration of divine service. Sometimes the final outcome of the original hermit's lonely initiative may be a whole new cenobitic foundation. Not infrequently peasants are then attracted to the area, both for spiritual comfort and for economic opportunity: virgin forest is cleared for agricultural work, with the prospect, at least in early years, of an abundant yield. The result may at length be a large, bustling, and wealthy community—a resounding success story, except that its outcome contradicts the ideals of those who initiated it. Not infrequently, in the midst of this hive of activity, another young novice becomes discontented, yearns for solitude, and takes off toward the northeast, starting the whole cycle over again.[69]

Such was the biography of Sergii of Radonezh (born 1314), who together with his brother left his parents' home, moved some distance into the forest, and built there a log cabin and a chapel dedicated to the Holy Trinity. His brother eventually became discouraged and left, but Sergii stayed on alone, occasionally visited by monks or priests who would take divine service together with him. Gradually he gained a reputation for holiness and spiritual insight. Other monks came to join him, forming a *skit* and then a larger community, of which they asked him to become the abbot. At first Sergii refused, loath to give up the contemplative life for one of administration, but on the insistence of the local bishop he eventually took it on. His monastery lay in the patrimony of a cousin of Prince Dmitrii, who was sufficiently impressed by his reputation to seek out his advice. He began, initially with reluctance, to play a role in political life, advising the princes of Rus on their duties in relation to the church, to the Byzantine patriarchate, to Lithuania, and to the Golden Horde. His foundation to the northeast of Moscow, the Monastery of the Holy Trinity (to which his own name was later added), became a major center for the training of monks and future ecclesiastical hierarchs. Eventually, in the late sixteenth century, it became the site of the Moscow patriarchate, Sergiev Posad.[70]

Sergii's choice of the Holy Trinity as the dedication of his monastery was not fortuitous. The Trinity assumed a special significance in hesychasm, which taught that, by praying silently to Christ, one could overcome the limitations of the flesh and attain to a vision, not of God himself, but of the divine "energies" which emanated from God and manifested themselves in the form of the "light of Tabor" (as Gregory Palamas, the originator of the doctrine, called it). This communion with the light was considered to be the work of the Holy Spirit, and was held not only to bring peace to the individual soul but to help in the overcoming of earthly passions and feuds. Father, Son, and Holy Spirit thus each played a crucial role. In his life of Sergii, his hagiographer Epifanii Premudryi emphasizes this aspect of his spiritual insight.[71]

77

These colonizers also kept alive the spirit of Cyril and Methodius. Stefan of Perm (1340–1396), son of a clergyman in Ustiug on the Northern Dvina, the "land of midnight" (as his biographer Epifanii Premudryi describes it), became a monk in Rostov, where he learned Greek and assembled a collection of Greek books. He was moved to take his learning to the pagan Zyrian people living in the neighborhood, and for that purpose invented a Zyrian alphabet and synthesized Zyrian words, so that he could translate the scriptures and liturgy for them. Epifanii explicitly places him in an honorable list of disseminators of the Orthodox faith going right back to Paul and the apostle Peter.[72]

The hesychast spirit—the search for peace, inner concentration, and personal devotion—also inspired icon-painting during the late fourteenth and fifteenth centuries, which most experts would identify as the crowning period of Russian religious art. The icon as a genre derives from Byzantine Christianity. But at quite an early stage Russian images began to develop their own distinctive features: less imposing and statuesque, their human figures seem both more humble and more intimate. As well as taking their motifs from Byzantine tradition, the icon painters of Rus drew on material from life around them, as if to insist that this world is potentially transfigurable. The discipline of the icon painter was supposed to develop and sustain his spiritual insight. As the twentieth-century theologian Pavel Florenskii has said, "Icon painters occupy a more exalted position than most lay people. They are supposed to be meek and unassuming, to observe spiritual and bodily purity, to devote themselves to prayer and fasting, and frequently to consult their spiritual fathers."[73] In other words they were to adopt the ascetic practices of the hesychasts, for it was held that only thus could they attain the insight necessary to communicate in their work the mystery of the divine becoming human.[74]

The new tendency was exemplified in the work of a group of artists around the Moscow court and the Trinity Monastery in Sergiev Posad, led by Feofan the Greek, who, as his name suggests, came from Byzantium. He painted frescoes from the 1370s to the 1400s in Novgorod, Nizhnii Novgorod, and Kolomna and in the Archangel and Annunciation Cathedrals of the Moscow

Kremlin. His pupil, Andrei Rublev, worked with him on the Annunciation Cathedral, and then continued his work in Zvenigorod, in Vladimir, and in the main cathedral of the Trinity Monastery. His most important work, the Trinity, was an expression of the hesychast ideal which animated Sergii: the calm light-blue coloring, the meek and trusting gestures of the three angelic figures, speak of the attainment of peace and intimacy through deep spiritual knowledge.[75]

Compared with their predecessors, both Feofan and Rublev were less monumental, freer and more dynamic in their presentation of human personality. Their human figures and the draped garments enfolding them display strong feelings through gesture and implied movement, while the buildings and natural scenes surrounding them are depicted with somewhat greater naturalism (though without the detailed mimesis and use of perspective beginning to enter western European art at the time). The work of Rublev, in particular, is wrought in glowing colors and suffused with a gently melancholy lyricism which is far from pessimistic in its effect.[76] (A century and a half later, a church council of 1551 recommended Rublev as a model for all icon painters.)

THE BREAKDOWN OF THE GOLDEN HORDE

Under Dmitrii I (1359–1389), Moscow consolidated its authority over the principalities of Rostov, Suzdal, and Nizhnii Novgorod and extended its territories far toward the northeast, into Starodub (east of Suzdal), Kostroma, Galich, Uglich, and Beloozero, whether by some kind of financial transaction or by invasion has never been clear.[77] These acquisitions greatly increased Moscow's access to the wealth of the forests and lakes of the north while curtailing the territory which had been the key to Novgorod's affluence.

This expansion coincided with a period when the Golden Horde, having been a stable overlord for more than a century, began to fall apart. Until the late fourteenth century it remained indisputably the leading power in Eurasia. It dominated the great trading route down the Volga, from the Baltic to the Middle East, Persia, and India; it protected the caravan trade passing across the steppes from central Asia and China to the Black Sea and the ports of the Mediterranean. The incomes it derived from these lucrative sources, together with the tributes from its subordinate lands, ensured that it was not only a powerful but also a wealthy state. On the other hand, this wealth generated an increasingly sophisticated urban civilization which was difficult to reconcile with continuing nomadic rule. The far-flung, highly diverse territories of the Horde, each developing in its own way, were becoming more difficult to administer adequately from horseback.

Eventually the accumulating pressures brought about an explosion. The assassination of Khan Berdi-bek in 1359 inaugurated a series of coups, in which short-lived rulers succeeded one another on the throne of Sarai, while one of the more enterprising generals, Mamai, set up his own independent horde in the steppes west of the Volga and proceeded to claim the lands of Rus as part of his *ulus*. Faced with two demanding, unstable, and mutually jealous claimants for acknowledgment and tribute, the princes of Rus fell prey to confusion and apprehension. Yet they also had the opportunity to exploit the divisions among their masters, if only they could unite to take advantage of them.

Meanwhile, farther east a Mongol warlord, Timur (Tamerlane), had seized control of the Chagatai *ulus* and was using it as a base to establish a great central Asian empire, with its capital at Samarkand. One of his generals, Tokhtamysh, broke away to move westward with his own army, seize power at Sarai, and reunite most of the fragments of the Golden Horde. Only Mamai eluded his grasp.

Before facing Tokhtamysh, Mamai decided to deal with the restive Russians in his rear. In 1378 he sent an army toward Moscow, but Dmitrii repulsed it in an engagement on the River Vozha. Taken aback by this unexpected defeat, Mamai made more thorough diplomatic preparations for a second attempt. He allied himself with the merchants of Genoa, to whom he promised trading rights on the rivers of Rus, with Jogaila of Lithuania, and with the prince of Riazan, and then led a much larger army northwestward to demand obedience. Hitherto Moscow had avoided any major military conflict with the Golden Horde and its remnants. Now, however, Dmitrii gathered troops from a number of principalities and received the blessing of Sergii of Radonezh to oppose Mamai with military force, on the grounds that he was a usurper, and hence not Moscow's legitimate overlord.

The two armies met on 8 September 1380 at Kulikovo Field, near the upper Don River. Since in the event Riazan remained neutral and Lithuanian troops did not arrive, Dmitrii took the initiative and crossed the Don to a position where rivers protected both his flanks. There he was able to withstand the Tatar onslaught and to throw Mamai back. This was an unambiguous victory for Muscovy. It was far from being a decisive one, however, for it was won against a mere rebellious fragment of the Golden Horde. Soon afterward Tokhtamysh defeated and overthrew Mamai and then mounted his own punitive expedition to reestablish suzerainty over Rus, in the course of which he sacked the city of Moscow (1382). The princes of Rus resumed paying tribute and seeking patents of rule from the khan of the Golden Horde.[78]

All the same, Kulikovo Field was a symbolic turning point, for it demonstrated that when most of the princes of Rus worked together, they were capable of standing up even to large Tatar armies. By the end of the fifteenth century, then, Moscow was not only the religious center of East Slav Orthodoxy and the acknowledged protector of the church, but also the tried and tested leader of a potential national movement against Tatar domination.

In 1395 Timur himself moved westward to try to destroy his former protégé, now bitter rival, Tokhtamysh, who had concluded alliances with Moscow, Poland, and Lithuania to consolidate his position. Timur pursued a policy of laying waste the lands of opponents. When he approached Moscow, Vasilii I led an army against him, while Metropolitan Kiprian brought the miracle-working icon *Our Lady of Vladimir* to the city. Suddenly Timur changed course and withdrew, an unexpected development which many attributed to the influence of the icon. Actually, Timur had already achieved his main aim of defeating Tokhtamysh and had no further reason thereafter to concern himself with Moscow.

As often happens with steppe armies, however, Timur experienced a serious setback in his hour of victory. One of his own lieutenants, Edigei, rebelled against him and won dominance of the steppe lands west of the Volga for some twenty years. In 1408 Edigei besieged Moscow and plundered several towns around it. Nizhnii Novgorod and Vladimir were ransacked by associated Tatar warlords. But these random campaigns themselves testified to the fragmentation and progressive enfeeblement of the Golden Horde.

By this time the achievements of the Danilovichi were being undermined by dynastic disunity after the death of Vasilii I in 1425. As it happened, for several generations, at the death of each Muscovite grand prince there had been only one eligible candidate, whether by collateral or by vertical succession. As we have seen, Dmitrii Donskoi had attempted to convert this de facto system of succession into a legally binding one. Vasilii I had both a son, whom he named as his heir, Vasilii II, and several brothers, one of whom, Iurii Dmitrievich, refused to recognize the new system and therefore Vasilii II's claim to the princely throne. He in turn had two sons, Vasilii Kosoi and Dmitrii Shemiaka, both of whom took their father's side and continued his struggle after his death on their own behalf. For that reason dynastic civil war flared up intermittently for some thirty years, in spite of the efforts of the Trinity-Sergii Monastery to mediate. Vasilii II's ultimate victory more or less established the system of vertical succession for good.

THE SPLIT IN THE ORTHODOX CHURCH

There were some in Byzantium who saw the task of preserving an Orthodox ecumene as insufficient on its own. They also wanted to reunite the two Christian churches of Constantinople and Rome. As the plight of Byzantium became more critical, their concern naturally intensified, in the hope, apart from anything else, of receiving military help from the Catholic states. During the 1430s negotiations took place to prepare the convening of an ecumenical council in the full sense, to include both Orthodox and Catholic representatives. One of the leading Greek participants in those negotiations, Isidor, was consecrated metropolitan of all Rus in 1436 by Patriarch Joseph, even though another candidate, Iona, had already been elected by bishops in Moscow and was awaiting the patriarchal blessing. Vasilii II received Isidor with some reluctance—so at least he later maintained—but allowed him to take up his office.

Not long afterward Isidor departed for the Council of Ferrara (later moved to Florence, 1438–39), where the great issue of reunion of the Orthodox and Catholic churches was to be decided. Owing to the political weakness of Byzantium, the advantages in negotiation were all on the side of the Roman delegates, and in the end the Orthodox, including Isidor, felt themselves compelled to sign a statement accepting the Roman position without modification, not only on the *filioque,* the credal issue which had divided the two parties in the eleventh century, but also on purgatory, the eucharist, and papal primacy, which were further serious issues of contention.

Capitulation to Rome brought little in the way of military aid to Byzantium. Pope Eugene IV preached a crusade calling on the faithful to come to its rescue, but the army he managed to muster was defeated at Varna by Sultan Murad in 1444. Meanwhile, the Greek envoys found on returning home that their capitulation to the Catholics was bitterly resented, and several of them recanted. Isidor attempted to brazen it out on his return to Moscow, entering the city in solemn procession "carrying before him a Latin crucifix and a silver crozier," but he probably guessed what kind of reception awaited him. He was arrested and confined in the Chudov Monastery, from where he subsequently escaped, possibly with the connivance of Vasilii, and fled via Lithuania to Rome.[79]

The tribulations of the civil war within Muscovy prevented the swift election of a successor. But in 1448 Iona was officially raised to the metropolitanate of which he had been brusquely deprived eleven years earlier. The announcement of his consecration contained no mention whatever of Constantinople or the patriarchate. In effect, Moscow had declared itself an autocephalous church.

In the same year Vasilii II, wanting to forestall the kind of dynastic disorder which had disfigured his own reign, designated his eldest son, Ivan, as
his successor, without any reference to the competing khans of the Golden
Horde. He began also to apply to himself the epithet *gosudar,* or "sovereign,"
implying that he no longer acknowledged any earthly overlord.[80] To secure
the planned succession, during the final years of his reign he eliminated most
of the udel principalities of his cousins. He compelled the city of Novgorod
to pay a large indemnity for having supported his enemies. He asserted his
authority over it by requiring it henceforth to display only the grand prince's
emblems on its coinage and by prohibiting the city veche from concluding
treaties with foreign powers.

By the end of his reign in 1462, Vasilii II was undisputed head of the ruling
house, with huge wealth and dignities, and with the right and capacity to
decide how other members of the dynasty should behave. Furthermore, he
had secured the same rights for his eldest son. He had finally replaced the
steppe system of lateral succession with primogeniture (for the ruling house
only). In 1452–53 he became the first Rus prince to take a Tatar prince into
his service, with the establishment of the khanate of Kasimov.[81]

All these developments were, however, overshadowed by the long-dreaded
fall of Byzantium to the Ottoman Turks in May 1453. The great Orthodox
ecumene, of which the Russian church had been a part, now existed only in
a humbled and fragmented form. Even the Russian church itself was divided
between the metropolitan sees of Moscow and Lithuania. Since it had hitherto been the principal bearer of the national consciousness of Rus, the humiliation of the ecumene and the ecclesiastical split left all Orthodox believers in Rus facing a crisis of apocalyptic proportions. The church of Rus, and
therefore the potential Russian nation, had to work out its own destiny without further reference to the spiritual father in whose flock it had always
previously sought its security.

At the very moment, then, when Moscow was launching its career as a
sovereign state, its people lost their external spiritual anchor. Moscow was
now the only major sovereign state whose people were Orthodox believers.
Should the grand prince of Moscow replace the Byzantine emperor as their
earthly protector? And how should he assert and maintain his sovereignty
in such vulnerable and troubled lands? The religious and geopolitical dilemmas were both crucial and difficult to resolve. No wonder that over the
following decades Muscovites gave vent to feelings of both apocalyptic doom
and unprecedented exhilaration.

2

IVAN IV AND THE EXPANSION

OF MUSCOVY

In the 1460s Moscow began to recover from dynastic crisis and embarked on a course of territorial expansion which in its earlier stages had analogies elsewhere in Renaissance Europe—in the Habsburg lands and Poland, for example, or in England and France—but which in the end assumed unparalleled dimensions. Moscow was geopolitically situated in such a way that its expansion was ultimately far more extensive (all the way from the Baltic and Black Seas to the Pacific Ocean and the oases of Central Asia) and lasted much longer (right up to the late twentieth century) than that of any other European state.

However, the very circumstance which gave Moscow the opportunity for such aggrandizement—the absence of natural frontiers in northern and central Eurasia—also made it permanently vulnerable to external invasion, ensured that its population would be uniquely diverse, and left it with the most labile and unstable borders of any major power. All of these factors have remained etched into the administrative structure and cultural ethos of Russia, right up to the present day. They have conditioned Russia's greatness and its weakness.

Furthermore, Moscow embarked on this process with many basic questions about its identity as a state unresolved. Was it a Chingizid successor khanate, a member of the Mongol steppe confederation? Or was the legiti-

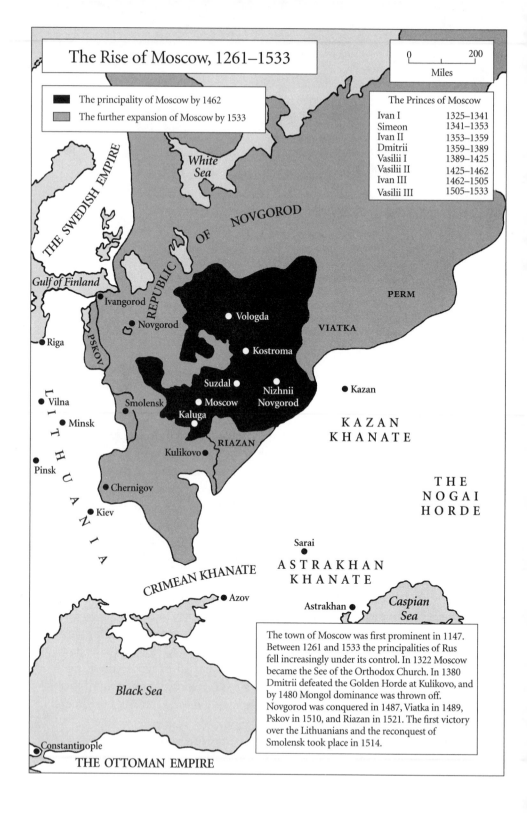

The Rise of Moscow, 1261–1533

0 ————————— 200
Miles

- ■ The principality of Moscow by 1462
- ▨ The further expansion of Moscow by 1533

The Princes of Moscow

Ivan I	1325–1341
Simeon	1341–1353
Ivan II	1353–1359
Dmitrii	1359–1389
Vasilii I	1389–1425
Vasilii II	1425–1462
Ivan III	1462–1505
Vasilii III	1505–1533

THE SWEDISH EMPIRE

White
Sea

REPUBLIC OF NOVGOROD

Gulf of Finland

Ivangorod

Novgorod

PSKOV

Riga

PERM

Vologda

VIATKA

Kostroma

Suzdal

Nizhnii
Novgorod

Kazan

L I T H U A N I A

Vilna

Smolensk

Moscow

Minsk

Kaluga

KAZAN
KHANATE

RIAZAN

Kulikovo

Pinsk

Chernigov

THE
NOGAI
HORDE

Kiev

Sarai

CRIMEAN KHANATE

ASTRAKHAN
KHANATE

Azov

Astrakhan

Caspian
Sea

Black Sea

The town of Moscow was first prominent in 1147.
Between 1261 and 1533 the principalities of Rus
fell increasingly under its control. In 1322 Moscow
became the See of the Orthodox Church. In 1380
Dmitrii defeated the Golden Horde at Kulikovo, and
by 1480 Mongol dominance was thrown off.
Novgorod was conquered in 1487, Viatka in 1489,
Pskov in 1510, and Riazan in 1521. The first victory
over the Lithuanians and the reconquest of
Smolensk took place in 1514.

Constantinople

THE OTTOMAN EMPIRE

macy of its ruler derived from the Byzantine tradition, only recently brought to an abrupt end by the Ottomans? If so, what was its relationship to that tradition? Was its principal significance in Orthodox belief or in imperial authority?

Throughout the late fifteenth and the sixteenth centuries Moscow continued to be faced with fundamental strategic dilemmas generated by its geopolitical situation. Constant danger threatened from two directions across long-open frontiers: in the west from Lithuania-Poland, and in the south and east from what remained of the Golden Horde, now a semiagricultural realm on the steppes of the lower Volga, and from the successor khanates of Crimea, Siberia, Kazan, and Astrakhan. Nor did conquering more territories necessarily ease the problem: on the contrary, they made Moscow a direct rival of Sweden, Denmark, the Ottoman Empire, and the Teutonic Knights. The more extensive Moscow's territories became, the greater her resources, yet also the more straggling and vulnerable her borders and the more numerous her potential enemies.

With the end of the fifteenth-century dynastic civil war, Moscow came into its own as promoter of the unity of Orthodox and East Slav peoples, though in circumstances tinged with foreboding aroused by the fall of Byzantium. The church was eager for the grand prince to use the titles *samoderzhets* (autocrat) and *tsar* (*basileus*, emperor) to signal his assumption of both the religious and imperial heritage of Byzantium, but the grand princes were hesitant about following this advice. They first claimed the title *tsar* (at that stage in the sense of khan) in documents guaranteeing safe passage across Rus territory—perhaps because they genuinely had replaced the Kipchak Khan in this capacity. Thereafter they broadened their use of the term cautiously, and interspersed it with the title *gosudar vseia Rusi* (sovereign of all Rus), which implied parallelism with the metropolitan's title and rejection of Lithuania's claim to the heritage of Kiev. They also began using the emblem of the double-headed eagle, in its Byzantine form, on the princely seal. It was not till 1547, however, at the coronation of Ivan IV, that the term *tsar* definitively came into usage as the correct ceremonial designation of the grand prince of Moscow. Even then it was not clear whether it signified khan or *basileus*.[1]

Ivan III (1462–1505) was an able, cunning, flexible, and ruthless politician who subordinated everything to his ultimate goal of expanding control over the territories of Rus. To this end he was prepared to sacrifice even the most intimate family ties, as is demonstrated by his divorce of his first, childless wife and his treatment of his daughter, whom he married to a Lithuanian and eventually abandoned to imprisonment and death in her adopted country. In these respects, Vasilii III (1505–1533), though chosen by his father as heir only after long hesitation, proved to be a worthy successor. From the 1460s to the 1520s, through dynastic marriage, inheritance, pressure, or outright conquest, under the rule of Ivan and Vasilii Moscow brought under its authority the princely territories of Iaroslavl, Rostov, Tver, and Riazan.

The greatest prize, however, was Novgorod. Its anomalous position as economic giant and political weakling had depended on the patronage of the Golden Horde, whose relative decline during the fourteenth and early fifteenth centuries precipitated a concomitant decline in Novgorod's status. Half a century or so after the death of Aleksandr Nevskii, in the early fourteenth century, the townspeople abolished the title of prince of Novgorod altogether and instead began to recognize the formal suzerainty of an external ruler, usually that of Tver or Moscow. Without an immediate overlord, the feuding of boyar clans again weakened the city's military strength. As Moscow began its rise and Lithuania also became a power to reckon with, the citizens of Novgorod were divided over where their allegiance should lie. On the one hand, Moscow was Orthodox like Novgorod, whereas Lithuania was pagan and then Catholic. On the other hand, Lithuania offered the prospect of closer relations with traditional European trading partners as well as closer contact with the European culture of the late Middle Ages and Renaissance.

By the late fifteenth century, Muscovy was much more powerful, and within Novgorod the struggle between its supporters and those of Lithuania had become more embittered. After a stormy session in 1471 the veche decided to resist Moscow's pretensions and invite the Lithuanian prince Casimir IV to become sovereign. Ivan III of Moscow responded by sending a punitive force which defeated a much larger but probably also more inexperienced Novgorod militia army and reinstated Muscovite rule.

Ivan proceeded cautiously after his victory: he was dealing with much the largest of the states of Rus, and also the one least like Moscow in its sociopolitical structure. Knowing that not only the boyars but also ordinary townsfolk had real influence on decisionmaking, he took care to cultivate them by proclaiming Moscow's religious and national mission. For a time he preserved Novgorod's self-rule, at least in name, seeking an alliance with its citizens rather than their subordination. But in the face of continuing evidence that the pro-Lithuanian party, centered around the Boretskii family, was still active, and that the veche had not abandoned all thought of alliance with Lithuania, Ivan decided in 1478 to annex Novgorod altogether. He sent another army, which occupied the city, demonstratively dismantled the veche bell, and carted it off to Moscow. Ivan expropriated and exiled a large number of the wealthiest boyars, and in 1494 he closed the German Court and expelled its merchants.[2]

Even as its self-government was being destroyed, Novgorod was going through a period of intellectual and spiritual flowering, one of whose results was a series of heretical movements influenced by late medieval religious ferment farther west. They combined with economic and political crisis to generate instability for a further century. A once wealthy and proudly independent city had been reduced, if not yet to penury, at least to modesty in economics and a faction-ridden subordination in politics. One option for the development of Rus, as a federation of self-governing oligarchies, had been closed off.[3]

From the dispossessed of Novgorod Ivan III confiscated some three million acres of populated agricultural land, including that of the wealthiest boyars, whom he exiled, and distributed it to his servitors in return for their military and civil service. To be able to create such a land fund was vital in a realm whose area was expanding so fast, and which needed the sinews of communication and command. The land transfers laid the foundations of the *pomestie*, or service estate, system, which enabled the grand princes of Moscow to incorporate and administer new territories, attract and endow incoming servitors, and also to finance and staff their huge and expanding army.

In 1509–10 Vasilii III humbled Pskov in the same way, abolishing its traditional citizens' assembly—again the veche bell was carted away—and exiling many of its leading citizens. He awarded their lands to his own servitors and brought in Moscow merchants to dominate the city's trade.

Lithuania itself was much too strong to be dealt with in any such peremptory fashion, but Ivan provoked a series of frontier incidents, and in a series of campaigns Muscovite armies steadily gnawed away at her eastern territories, eventually reconquering Smolensk in 1514. At the same time nobles on Lithuania's eastern borders were lured by the lucrative service conditions which Muscovy could now offer: several senior boyar families came over.

At the same time Moscow succeeded in beating off a major challenge from the south. In the 1460s one of the rival steppe warlords, Akhmat Khan, gathered several lower Volga clans which constituted the remnants of the Golden Horde. Though not recognized as Kipchak khan by any of the other successor states, he nevertheless tried to compel Moscow to pay him tribute. In 1480, he concluded an alliance with Lithuania and put out feelers for help from two of Ivan III's brothers, Andrei and Boris, hoping to revive dynastic conflict within Moscow. He then assembled a considerable army, which he moved up to the Ugra River, a tributary of the Oka. Ivan concluded a counteralliance with the Crimean khan, challenging Akhmat with the same kind of rear threat that he himself faced from Lithuania. Then he used his growing administrative resources and his dominant position within Rus to assemble a no less formidable army to confront that of Akhmat. After an unsuccessful attempt to cross the river, the discipline of the Tatar army faltered, and its men began to plunder the surrounding districts. Ivan merely stood firm and waited till Akhmat had concluded that he was not going to receive the expected help either from the Lithuanians or from Andrei and Boris. Then he withdrew his forces across the steppe.

Although the Tatars remained a serious menace for another three centuries, always able to mount slave-gathering raids and at times to lay waste whole towns, never again did they threaten the sovereignty of the Russian state. Historians usually count this nonexistent battle of 1480 as the moment when the Mongol overlordship finally ceased. None of the successor states was strong enough to exact tribute. In 1502 the Golden Horde was taken over by Mengli Girei, khan of the Crimea, during an exceptionally harsh winter, and its remaining nomadic resources were moved south and west into his territory.[4]

GOVERNMENT AND SOCIETY IN MUSCOVY

To administer the huge and expanding realm of Muscovy, to raise, supply, and equip the armies required to police and when necessary defend the long, open frontiers, the grand princes needed to mobilize resources and therefore establish administrative structures beyond the dreams of their more modest and primitive ancestors. The very size of the territory assured abundant resources of soil, minerals, and people. The difficulty was to get them to where they were needed when they were needed. For this purpose a civil and military bureaucracy was essential, operating according to regular norms and leaving detailed written records. No longer could a monarch know personally all his servitors; he had to set up institutions which would function when he did not himself command, even when he was perhaps far away on some official duty. As in medieval European kingdoms, at first the grand prince's household simply expanded in size and functions to take on these new commitments. The posts of *dvoretskii* (majordomo), *koniushii* (equerry), and *kaznachei* (treasurer) lost their domestic nature and became major official appointments, responsible for a range of state functions. A staff of *diaki*, state secretaries, was created to handle their correspondence and keep their records straight. To conduct business dispassionately, it was important that these men were not members of boyar clans, and that they were educated enough to cope with bookkeeping and correspondence.[5]

In the late fifteenth century the first steps were taken to knit together the farther reaches of the sprawling realm by creating a system of communications. Ivan III undoubtedly had in mind the example of the Mongol postal system, and used the same word, *iam*, for it. A *iam* was an inn and postal station, provided with food, bedding, horses, and either coaches or sledges, according to the season. *Iamy* were set up at intervals along important routes, such as the one from Moscow to Pskov and Novgorod, the one to Smolensk via Mozhaisk and Viazma, and the one to Murom and the Oka-Volga waterway which enabled travelers to proceed onwards to Nizhnii Novgorod or Kazan. The grand prince and his principal servitors could provide any traveler—an official courier, a foreign envoy, or simply a person of status—with a *podorozhnaia*, or "route pass," requiring the holder of each *iam* to provide board, lodging, and transport as specified.

The Habsburg envoy Sigismund von Herberstein reported that the system enabled him to reach Moscow from Novgorod, some 500 kilometers, in seventy-two hours, and reckoned that this was much faster than he would have been able to travel anywhere else in Europe. His account of the facilities offered to official travelers is intriguing, reflecting both the high priority communications were given and the care expended on their maintenance:

> Anyone was permitted to ride horses at top speed, and if any horses by chance fell, or could not last, it was permissible to seize another from any nearby house, or from anyone whom one by chance met on the way, excepting only the courier of the ruler, and to take the horse with impunity. The *iamshchik* is accustomed to look for horses exhausted and left en route, to restore another horse to him from whom it was taken, and to pay the price according to the length of the trip.[6]

Ivan III and Vasilii III began converting the Muscovite army from an ad-hoc medley of druzhinas and local levies, led by boyars and udel princes, into a more or less integrated force, whose units could be swiftly mobilized and dispatched to where they were needed. The grand princes had always distrusted the followers of their lesser brethren, the udel princes, and increasingly allotted them secondary tasks on the frontiers, while giving the most important assignments to troops commanded by their own subordinate boyars and courtiers. With the absorption of other Rus territories, the leading nobles who lived there were usually stationed first in their own homeland, and then, when their loyalty was confirmed, transferred freely from one part of the growing realm to another. Army command positions were bestowed on members of junior boyar lineages *(deti boiarskie)* and on courtiers *(dvoriane)* awarded *pomestia* in return for military service. Among the old Muscovite clans whose scions made themselves responsible for Moscow's fate were the Obolenskie, Saburovy, Koshkiny, Khovriny, Cheliadniny, and Morozovy. To them were gradually added the Kholmskie from Tver, the Iaroslavkie (whose name reflects their origin), and, from Lithuania, the Belskie, Vorotynskie, Belevskie, Mezetskie, and Novosilskie. One family, the Patrikeevy, became so powerful and wealthy that in 1499 Ivan III forced its senior member, Prince Ivan Iurievich, to become a monk and imprisoned all his sons. Unable to reproduce itself, the line died out. Such drastic action was, however, rare and probably reflects a consensus of envy among other boyar families as well as Ivan III's own displeasure.[7]

The overall effect of these policies was to create a composite service nobility which was not strongly rooted in any particular locality, as can be seen from the fact that few noble families were named after a locality and that they had no equivalent of *de* or *von* in their surnames. These servitors were more pliable than the feudal nobles whom west European monarchs were painfully integrating into their retinues at about the same time. They resembled rather the commanders of a steppe army. The pomestie was analogous to the *iqta,* which had enabled Muslim cavalry armies to conquer and assimilate huge territories in the sixth and seventh centuries, and to the *timar,* used by the Ottomans during their imperial expansion: a landed estate taken from recently acquired territory and awarded to a cavalryman to maintain him in return for obedient service.[8]

Since the Muscovite grand prince was now claiming to be lord *(gosudar)* of his realm in both senses—ownership and authority—patrimonial estates *(votchiny)* came under the same regime: they now also entailed a requirement to perform service and could be confiscated if that service was withheld. Long-standing and loyal boyar families would now receive new pomestie estates to ensure that their landholdings did not diminish too greatly as a result of partible inheritance. The only real difference between the two forms of landholding was that a pomestie could not be sold, pledged, or given away.[9]

One of the principal tasks of the new *diaki* and their scribes was to compile land registers *(pistsovye knigi),* first for the Novgorod lands, and then for other territories as they were annexed, in order to make possible the equitable distribution of military obligations.[10] Townsmen and "black" peasants (those not dwelling on the estates of boyars, servicemen, or monasteries) were taxed directly by the grand prince's officials and were required to provide a certain number of infantrymen and auxiliary troops, fully clothed and equipped. As firearms developed, arquebusiers, then musketeers and artillerymen were also drawn from the urban populations. The first cannon foundry was set up in Moscow in 1475, but for many decades artillery was used sparingly, and only from fixed positions, usually in fortifications, since there was no equipment for moving heavy guns around.[11]

The Muscovite political system represented in reality (though not in its symbolism) a compromise between the grand prince and his principal noble servitors. It is worth stressing this, since both contemporaries and historians have given the impression that by the sixteenth century the grand prince/ tsar was an absolute autocrat, able to have his lightest whim obeyed throughout his realm. Herberstein wrote, for example, in the early sixteenth century: "in the sway which he holds over his people, he surpasses the monarchs of the whole world."[12] This interpretation was reasserted with elegance and force in the 1970s by Richard Pipes, who used the term "patrimonial monarchy" to describe the tsar's authority. Pipes construed it as a uniquely oppressive form of absolute monarchy, in which there is no distinction between sovereignty and ownership, so that the monarch's subjects are literally his slaves.[13]

It is true that the Russian term for the state, *gosudarstvo*, means literally "lordship," and so does not distinguish ownership from political authority. All the same, Pipes's understanding seems to me to rest on a misinterpretation of the term *votchina*, which Pipes translates as *dominium*, in the Roman sense of "absolute ownership excluding all other appropriation and involving the right to use, abuse and destroy at will."[14] Actually the holder of a votchina had no such rights, especially not those of abusing or destroying. He was bound by a whole range of obligations to use the land to the benefit of his family, and the peasants who lived on it had certain customary expectations too. In general the concept of ownership was much more diffuse in fifteenth- and sixteenth-century Muscovy than it became in later centuries, and was compatible with multiple intersecting rights.[15]

The testaments of the grand princes show that they saw their patrimonies as having been entrusted to them by God and as entailing serious responsibilities. In making their wills, they would invoke the blessing of the current metropolitan, to show that they acknowledged the church as a joint stakeholder in the destiny of the realm. Thus Vasilii II opened his testament in 1461 or 1462: "In the name of the holy and life-giving Trinity, the Father, the Son, and the Holy Spirit, and with the blessing of our father Feodosii, Metropolitan of all Rus: lo I, the much-sinning, poor slave of God, Vasilii, while living and of sound mind, write this testament." Then followed a list of his territories as they were to be divided between his sons and his widow, emphasizing the obligations they had toward each other and noting where subordinate princes also had the right to rule without interference. Similarly, Ivan III in his testament of 1504 specifically noted that his boyars and princes had their own patrimonies and purchased lands, with which his son Vasilii should not interfere.[16]

The term *votchina*, in short, was a complex concept and cannot simply be equated with freehold ownership. It was part of a religious, moral, and customary order, one which lacked the explicit legal and institutional underpinning that characterized, say, French feudalism at its higher levels, but still one which had its own accepted restraints.

So the term "patrimonial monarchy" is best interpreted not as an extreme form of absolutism, but rather as a system designed to enable local elites to mobilize resources by any means they deemed expedient. It was a kind of "statization of personal power."[17] The symbols of absolute sovereignty were deployed to back up the personal power, even personal whim, of local landowners and urban elites. These symbols enabled ordinary people to conceptualize the state, or at least sovereign authority, in the form necessary to make the grand prince's power effective at all. After all, because of its size and vulnerability, Muscovy had to accomplish the massive mobilization of the population at a much earlier stage in its institutional history than any other European state. Since it did not have the bureaucratic sinews for these tasks, it had to project and make credible its authority in any way it could. The statization of personal power was the only way to achieve it at the time. If you like, this was "statization before the state," analogous to the way in which, as Ernest Gellner tells us, nationalism preceded the nation.[18]

In the long run, however, this premature form of "state-building" impeded the later fashioning of more mature and stable structures. It obstructed the development of law and the establishment of durable institutions, as well as the appearance of any distinction between the public and private spheres. The center was strong, and local communities were strong, but there was little other than the personal caprice of powerful placemen to mediate the relations between them.[19]

Above all, the Muscovite grand prince relied implicitly on the cooperation of the great boyar clans, heirs to a dignity not much less imposing than his own. (The term *boyar* originally meant "great man," "rich man," or "warrior.")[20] They were the indispensable stakeholders in the Muscovite enterprise: without their unswerving support and loyalty there was little the prince could achieve, and nothing of lasting significance. He had to accommodate their susceptibilities, for all sorts of reasons, but not least because a generation or two earlier their forefathers had been free warriors, able to attach themselves with their retainers to whichever sovereign lord they wished— and then to leave him for another should his terms of service prove insufficiently rewarding. The erosion of this "right of withdrawal" had been gradual and hesitant, for no grand prince had any wish to provoke an armed revolt.

Conversely, however, the boyar clans also needed the grand prince, for the custom of dividing their land among all heirs ineluctably reduced and fragmented their estates if they were not periodically awarded more. Besides, without a stable and strong ruler, feuding among boyar clans always threatened to get out of control and in the end to divide the realm. The chronicles were written partly in order to remind everyone that such had been the lamentable fate of Kievan Rus. As a result, by the late fifteenth century grand prince and boyars had a common interest in projecting the myth of absolute monarchical authority. This is the key to understanding the Muscovite political system.

Boyars had the right of access to the court, and the senior ones among them gave the grand prince counsel in regular meetings, which may be loosely referred to as the Boyar Duma (though the term was not invented till the nineteenth century). Any official decree was expressed in the formula "the boyars advised and the grand prince resolved," a form of words which reflected the expectation that the monarch's power, though absolute, was exercised in a collegial manner, by consultation with senior colleagues.

Advancement to the status of boyar came only to young men who belonged to an existing boyar family and who were next in line according to the family's succession system. Thereafter promotion to regular membership of the Boyar Duma was awarded only to boyars who had given years, or even decades, of meritorious service, usually in both military and civilian capacities. Until the late fifteenth century there were only some fifteen members of the Duma. Thereafter it grew quite rapidly, to reflect the expansion and diversification of administrative needs and military tasks. The symbolic importance of membership in it was considerable, for the boyars had no institutions of their own: they were not awarded titles, they had no escutcheons or heraldic devices, and they did not attach the names of any of their landed estates to their family name.

Because pedigree and the prince's service were the decisive criteria in gaining entry to his council, boyars took care that genealogy and official positions were meticulously noted in court records, in the *rodoslovnye* and *razriadnye knigi* (genealogical and official service books). A system of *mestnichestvo*, or precedence, evolved to ensure that official posts were awarded in accordance with the seniority of each clan. It was analogous to the ranking of the khan's warriors, which determined their share in the booty of successful warfare. The rigid provisions of *mestnichestvo* show how great the real power of the boyar clans was, and it sometimes obstructed the appointment of the right man to the right job—for which reason it was less rigidly applied to military personnel—but it was necessary to ensure that conflict among the boyar clans was minimized and the fragile unity of the state preserved. Like the village community, the grand prince's court needed its own mir.[21]

To replace the uprooted udel princes, Ivan III and his successors sent their own nominees from the Moscow court to exercise authority in the provinces. Known as *namestniki* (vice-regents), they were responsible for collecting taxes, preserving public order, acting as appeal judges, and keeping communications in good repair. In accomplishing these tasks they were expected to cooperate with the local community. The prince would issue charters, outlining the duties of his *namestniki* and stating what functions he expected volosti to fulfill—one of which would always be to provide the local vice-regent with kormlenie.[22] Towns had no separate status and were subject to the same authorities and the same tribute system as the villages. Kormlenie was a crucial aspect of the statization of personal power: it enabled princes to watch over local communities without paying their officials, while it also enabled communities to make their own arrangements with local power-holders, partially reprivatizing the relationship.[23]

The role of the mir or volost in local government remained crucial. Individual households owned the arable land which they cultivated, but the mir regulated access to fishing rights and to common facilities, such as woods, meadows, pastures, watercourses, and beehives. It was thus able to distribute the tax burden among its own members, taking into account the amount of access each household had to communal facilities. The mir was also expected to carry out policing and to catch dangerous criminals, as well as to provide basic justice for its inhabitants, according to local customary law. The *namestnik* or *volostel* did not have enough staff to carry out these functions, especially in view of the vast distances involved, so that the *starosta*, the elected volost elder, often had in practice to act as his lowest-level agent. Communities were bound by joint responsibility, and it was gradually extended to matters of state service, including taxation and recruitment, so that if one household fell behind on its payments, the remaining ones had to make up the difference. Similarly, if a soldier from the village proved unsuitable or deserted, the community had to find someone else to serve in his place.[24]

Ivan III endeavored to amalgamate the customs and laws of the recently assimilated principalities in a single code, the *Sudebnik* of 1497. It was concerned mainly with the procedures of law courts, evidently in the expectation that once they were coordinated and brought under the Muscovite crown, the law itself could automatically be applied in the same manner everywhere.[25]

In practice, then, internal administration was a matter of delicate compromise among the prince, his officials, and local communities. Each needed the other two because of the hazards of life in exposed and bleak territories, and each had expectations of the other based on a shared Christian culture molded largely during the Mongol overlordship and articulated into something approaching an ideology during the late fifteenth and early sixteenth centuries. The grand prince's court became the arena where the rewards and penalties of this compromise were allocated, and at the same time a focus for networks of personal patronage stretching out into the localities.

95

If the linchpin of this compromise was the grand prince/tsar, its substance was in the boyar families, both those native to Moscow and those who had come over from some other principality, and in the links which they forged to their social inferiors. One remarkable feature about Muscovy, underestimated in most Western historiography, was that those links turned out to be very tenacious indeed, strong enough to build a successful expanding realm in the late fifteenth and early sixteenth centuries, to survive the crises of the late sixteenth and early seventeenth centuries culminating in the Time of Troubles, and then to build and consolidate the largest territorial empire on earth—one which lasted for several centuries, far longer than its British counterpart, right down to very recent times.

Sustaining this system was a distinctive political culture which probably emerged during and after the mid-fifteenth century dynastic crisis.[26] The civil war within the Danilovich clan had threatened to plunge Moscow back into fragmentation and then submission to whatever superior local power should arise in its place. This frightening experience taught the lesser princes and the boyars that unrestricted feuding among themselves was mortally dangerous, and that they needed to agree on certain fundamentals. Paramount among these was the authority of the grand prince, as a guarantee against the ever-present danger of disintegration.

The boyars had no institutions of their own. They thought above all in terms of *rod,* kinship and pedigree. Each of them aimed to advance the interests of his own kin at court, but within the consensus that the tsar must be obeyed; besides, there was a much better chance of successful and profitable warfare if they stuck together. As Edward Keenan has pointed out, "It was these clans, closely organized extended families of tradition-bound cavalrymen, that provided the crucial nucleus of the military forces of the Muscovite princes, it was these clans that effected, and benefited from, the mobilization of the available resources of the Russian village, and it was these clans, or rather superclans, that controlled, and were the principal players in, the game of politics at the Moscow court."[27]

The boyars, through their stewards and servitors, were administrators and judges, patrons and exploiters of the peasant communities over much of the realm (other communities, of course, were on monastic lands, or were "black" communities in the forests and along the rivers and lakes of the north). No princely supervision could effectively restrain their exploitation of the peasants, but their own interest limited it, for they needed the survival and if possible prosperity of the villages in their charge.

What sustained the boyars in carrying out their various functions was a strong sense of honor. One of the main functions of law in Muscovy was to protect them against dishonor, whether in word or deed, through an elaborate range of penalties. The system of partible inheritance gave each male member of any family a tangible interest in the protection of the whole family's wealth and honor. But at the same time, it was important not to divide the clan's landholdings too much, and so, where there were many sons, only certain among them were recognized as the senior partners and received the most generous shares. Families would try to ensure that one in particular would be endowed with enough wealth to be able to hold his own at court, where it was vital to have someone to speak for the whole clan.[28]

Women played a crucial part in the maintenance of the *rod*. Since the head of the household was often away at war or on official duty, women had to run the household and often to oversee the estate management as well. Marriage and childbirth were essential to the survival of the *rod*, as also was the transmission of codes of honor and morality from one generation to the next. For this reason families tried to ensure that any female family member not directly provided for by a husband or father could inherit land and property for her subsistence. Traditionally, too, a woman brought her own property with her into marriage and kept it distinct from male holdings so that in the event of the husband's death it could be used to ensure her continued well-being. One scholar has concluded that "By the end of the fifteenth century, the majority of married women and widows from well-to-do social ranks had the right to own and dispose of both movable and immovable property almost on a par with men."[29]

With the growth of the centralized state during the fifteenth and sixteenth centuries the freedom and in some respects the rights of high-born women were curtailed. Pomestie land was awarded to a particular serviceman. In theory at least a woman could not hold it or dispose of it, though in practice families tried to ensure that she could at least draw the usufruct of it if she needed to. As for votchina land, the clear distinction between the husband's and wife's portions became blurred in the obligation to provide military servitors from it. This blurring usually worked to the disadvantage of the woman.[30]

Increasingly during the sixteenth century a noble-born woman would sleep and eat separately and would be confined to an enclosed and protected part of the house known as the *terem,* to ensure that she would not receive unwanted male visitors. As one observer put it, "She sits behind three-times-nine locks, behind three-times-nine keys, where the wind never blew, the sun never shone, and young heroes never saw her."[31]

Her rigid seclusion may have derived from Byzantine practice.[32] In any event, it was motivated by the desire to preserve the woman's honor, which was protected by law even more fiercely than a man's, in order to ensure that no illegitimate births disrupted property-owning arrangements, now crucial to the functioning of the state.[33] At the same time, seclusion also testified to the increased influence of the church on the everyday life of elite families and especially on the regulation of marriages. The church's teachings on sexual ethics were severe, and any hint of impropriety could fatally stain a woman's reputation.

The importance of hierarchy and stability in Muscovite family life was highlighted in a popular handbook on religion, morals, family life, and household management known as *Domostroi,* probably written during the 1550s. It is uncertain who wrote it, or even whether it was composed by a single person. Traditionally it has been supposed that Silvestr, the priestly adviser of Ivan IV, was the author, and he may indeed have compiled the religious chapters. But it seems most improbable that he composed the sections offering practical advice on the conduct of trade and husbandry. A much more likely author, from internal evidence, would be a wealthy merchant involved in international commerce, who might have encountered the handbooks on etiquette and household management which circulated quite widely among the elites of Renaissance Europe.

Domostroi reflected the desire of the Muscovite elites to inculcate God's law as interpreted by the church, and to regulate everyday life more closely, replacing custom by law and local tradition by uniform prescription.[34] It is the work of a person of means, accustomed to being waited on by servants, to having a good cut of meat at his table, and to wearing superior fur cloaks in winter. It views society as a hierarchy, in which the higher placed have the right to expect obedience from those below them, but are obliged also to care for their welfare and the salvation of their souls. Men and women have their strictly demarcated separate realms, both in practical affairs and in spiritual life. "Husbands should instruct their wives lovingly and with due consideration. A wife should ask her husband every day about matters of piety, so that she will know how to save her soul, please her husband and structure her house well . . . Whatever her husband orders she must accept with love; she must fulfill his every command. Above all, she must fear God and keep her chastity as decreed above."[35]

We do not know how widely *Domostroi* was read and digested. Its audience must have been fairly restricted, since few Muscovites could read, even in the upper reaches of society. Presumably it reached primarily merchants, officials, priests, literate boyars, and courtiers.

Perhaps surprisingly, its outlook was replicated in very different circumstances in the peasant culture. The village community had to operate in extremely adverse conditions, in remote often infertile terrain, through long, dark, cold winters brought to an end only by the hazards of the spring floods, and amidst gloomy forests which offered food and shelter but also harbored unknown dangers—wolves, brigands, even enemy soldiers. As we have seen, in this setting the natural tendency was to imagine malign forces at work everywhere, to the extent of concluding that this world was in the grip of the devil. Such an outlook generated a tendency to exercise very strict self-control, to rein in the passions, and at all costs to minimize risk, to pursue safe, thoroughly tested forms of husbandry in agriculture, fishery, and cottage industry. Their yield was modest but secure, whereas innovation, though it might bring great rewards, might also cause disaster. Over the centuries this conservatism and risk-averse behavior gave local communities a tendency to resist change and reform, even or perhaps especially when innovation was brought from outside by well-meaning reformers.

Peasants, like most Muscovites, operated with a view of morality which emphasized human beings' weakness and vulnerability, their proneness to passion and sin—drunkenness, sloth, greed, lust—any of which might disrupt productivity or family arrangements and with them the precarious household economy, and thus threaten the survival of the whole community. Villages tended to improvise their own arrangements to share risk, by mutual action to discourage deviant behavior, and to punish it and minimize its effects when it took place. In this setting decisionmaking had to be collegial and consensual, with all households involved, free and frank in the discussion of alternatives, but endeavoring to avoid open splits, and authoritarian in the enforcement of any decision once reached. The system adapted naturally to the practice of joint responsibility in the allocation of tax and recruitment burdens.

There has been a tendency to portray fifteenth- and sixteenth-century Muscovy as a backward and poverty-stricken society. It is true that its expansion took place well away from the main arteries of international trade. That is one reason why that expansion was not much contested, and then only in areas such as the Baltic, close to major commercial routes. However, Rus did supply certain products in high demand on the world market. In order to meet this demand, especially for sable fur, which was highly prized in the courts of Renaissance Europe, Moscow had expanded during the late fifteenth and early sixteenth centuries into the areas of the Viatka, Vychegda and Kama Rivers, in rivalry initially with Novgorod and thereafter with the khanate of Kazan. The grand prince exacted tribute from the local peoples, the Zyriane, the Permiaki, the Voguly (Mansi), and the Iugra (Khanty), in the form of furs, and also licensed a limited number of traders to engage in the very lucrative trade.[36]

In addition, there was always plenty of local trading, in fish and meat, in salt, in alcohol, in honey and wax from beehives, and in the products of the forest, including implements made of wood. So there were two kinds of merchants: the large, specialized, wealthy ones licensed to conduct international trade or to operate an official monopoly, and the small, nonspecialized ones, most of whom were also peasants and/or artisans, dealing in whatever they produced, perhaps during the long winter months, or in whatever they were able to catch in forest or river or buy at a favorable price.[37]

MOSCOW THE THIRD ROME

It was a fateful confluence of events which destined that Moscow should emancipate itself from the Tatar yoke very soon after Byzantium fell to the Ottoman Turks. The disaster which had befallen the Eastern Christian ecumene plunged Orthodox believers into gloom and foreboding. The grand principality of Moscow, which had always accepted the role of junior partner in religious matters, was suddenly thrust into a position of responsibility for the whole of "right-thinking" Christendom, at the very time that it was also seeking a new basis for its own statehood, no longer under the shadow of the Golden Horde. Furthermore, as it happened, the more eschatologically minded were expecting the end of the world in the year 7000, that is, 1492 (the Orthodox calendar claimed to count the years from the creation of the world).

The result was a feverish reappraisal of the mission of the Orthodox Church in Rus, and in particular of its relations with the secular authority.

The church held immense tracts of land, populated by millions of peasants and townsmen. It was also the supreme spiritual authority, mediator with God, and spokesman for the peoples of Rus as a whole, in a way which no prince had hitherto been able to emulate. Now, however, one prince, that of Moscow, was beginning to raise rival claims, just at the moment when the church's supreme spiritual pastor, the Byzantine patriarch, had been decisively weakened, first by the split within the Orthodox Church over the Council of Florence, then by the fall of Constantinople to Islamic rule.

The Muscovite church could claim to have kept to the strait and narrow path where its senior pastor had gone astray. The decision of the Byzantine Church at the Council of Florence to reunite with Rome and to accept Rome's doctrinal authority now looked like an act of apostasy punished by God. That is how it had been treated when Isidor returned from the council to Moscow, and that is why Moscow had disavowed the ecclesiastical authority of the patriarch in electing Iona to be metropolitan in 1448. Spiritually, the break with Byzantium came slightly before events precipitated a physical break. In both senses the Orthodox Church in Muscovy had suddenly become more dependent on the grand prince of Moscow. It now had to explore the consequences of this unaccustomed dependency.

These developments, taken together, both required and enabled the grand prince to seek a new basis for his legitimacy, whereby the church would play an important but no longer necessarily a dominant role. The Muscovite Danilovich princes had always hesitated to trace their lineage right back to pre-Mongol Kievan Rus, for they had been members of a junior line and were therefore not entitled to supreme authority, according to the old dynastic principles. Now, however, in chronicles and in court ritual, they began to emphasize the descent of the ruling dynasty from St. Vladimir, and through Vladimir Monomakh they evoked the sovereign emblems of Byzantium itself. The first such claim was advanced in the *vita* of Dmitrii Donskoi, apparently written in the Trinity-Sergius Monastery in 1454 or 1455, that is, immediately after the fall of Byzantium. It described Dmitrii as "the most fertile branch and the most beautiful flower from the God-planted orchard of Tsar Vladimir, the New Constantine who baptized the land of Rus, and he was a kinsman of Boris and Gleb, the miracle workers."[38]

The Muscovite grand princes hesitated, however, actually to claim that a *translatio imperii*—a transfer of imperial authority—had taken place, since that would imply an obligation to attempt to reconquer Constantinople from the infidels, as legates from the old imperial city periodically reminded them.

Moscow, then, had confused views about its own origins: one might say that it was creating for itself two "virtual pasts."[39] Apart from Byzantium, it could and did evoke the heritage of the Golden Horde, and even of the Chingizid line, to which it had no dynastic claim. Legitimate rule over a wide variety of steppe peoples implied a very different view of religion, not exclusively Orthodox, but eclectic and tolerant.

One thing was clear, though: whether one took a Byzantine or a Chingizid view of Moscow's legitimacy, its newfound grandeur required the regular raising of large armies, and to provide for his military servitors the grand prince needed a plentiful supply of cultivated land. The most obvious source from which he could obtain it was the church. (There was of course plenty of uncultivated land in Moscow's now extensive territories, but *pomeshchiki*—holders of a pomestie—needed land which could be exploited without delay to grow produce.)

In that way, Moscow's new role faced the church with a double danger: that it might lose both much of its landed wealth and also, if the Muscovite prince chose to make it only one among several religions, the power to define the faith of the people of Rus.

The threat these developments presented to the church was first fully appreciated in Novgorod, the territory whose humiliation had been most abrupt and whose church had previously enjoyed both the greatest independence and the most extensive landholdings. It was also the city with closest links to the Baltic and the markets of Europe, and therefore most open to the new religious teachings of the late Middle Ages and the Reformation. Already in the late thirteenth and fourteenth centuries, in reaction to the political and religious challenge presented by the Mongols, groups of believers in Novgorod and Pskov urged the importance of a thorough knowledge of the scriptures and of a spiritually pure way of life, especially among the clergy. They exhorted believers to perform confession and communion among themselves, before the cross, if the clergy were unworthy to take the sacraments. These zealots were later condemned as *strigolniki,* or "shaven ones."[40]

During the 1470s a new sect appeared, known as the Judaizers, some of whom were priests and some laymen: the name was fastened on them by their adversaries and does not necessarily imply that they confessed the Jewish faith. None of their own documents have survived, so that one must reconstruct their beliefs on the basis of the accusations made against them. It seems that they were antitrinitarians, and perhaps considered Christ to have been human rather than divine; that they objected to the worship of icons; and that, like the *strigolniki,* they considered the Orthodox Church hierarchy to be corrupt and therefore unworthy to administer the sacraments. They denied the value of monasticism, and, if one reads between the lines of the accusations against them, they were seeking "wisdom" and a form of life which made possible the "love of one's neighbor." The lists of books found in their homes show them to have been highly cultured: apart from the scriptures, they included classical Greek literature, Arabic and Hebrew works, and texts on philosophy, law, rhetoric, history, astronomy, and mathematics. Altogether they sound rather like the humanists of the early Reformation in western and central Europe, such as the Brethren of the Common Life in the Netherlands.[41]

The movement evidently had considerable support among the townspeople and the "white" (parish) clergy, and Ivan III favored it, perhaps because it encouraged a law-abiding piety and could provide him with well-educated, cosmopolitan people to staff his offices in church and state. In addition, its opposition to ecclesiastical wealth offered him arguments for expropriating church lands. In 1480, after a visit to Novgorod, he took two priests of "Judaizing" persuasion back to serve in the Kremlin cathedrals. At the same time, one of his leading diplomats, Fedor Kuritsyn, was the principal figure in a circle of Moscow humanist reformers.

Opposition to the "Judaizers" naturally came from the prelates. Archbishop Gennadii (1484–1504) of Novgorod was determined to oppose the new tendency and to vindicate the church's right to identify and deal with heresy. He began by trying to ensure that the church could deploy its own ideological armory properly against the heretics. He founded a circle of writers and translators, who produced an up-to-date Slavonic translation of the Bible, and he sent an agent, Dmitrii Gerasimov, previously an ambassador in the Muscovite service, to the West to acquire the latest ecclesiastical learning. He also commissioned a long report from an envoy of the Holy Roman Empire, Jörg von Thurn, on the way in which the Catholic Church dealt with heresy. Gennadii was especially impressed by what he learned of the Spanish Inquisition, and he took the initiative in convening a church council to discuss the current heresy and to establish a permanent state-supported inquisition. The council was held in 1490, but Ivan III opposed the full implementation of Gennadii's program: no inquisition was set up, and the worst he was allowed to do to the heretics was to seat them backward on horses, with their clothes turned back-to-front and an inscription on their caps reading "Behold the Army of Satan!" The heresy was not fully condemned till 1504.[42]

One of the texts which Gerasimov brought back from his travels was the *Legend of the White Cowl*, allegedly from the Vatican archives, but he may well have composed it himself, having in mind the interests of his patron. It purported to be a popular legend, according to which a white cowl, of the kind worn by senior Orthodox prelates, representing the true faith and the "radiant resurrection," had passed from Rome, which had abandoned Orthodoxy by adopting Apollinarianism, to Byzantium, which in turn had spurned the true faith at the Council of Florence.

> The ancient city of Rome has broken away from the glory and faith of Christ because of its pride and ambition. In the new Rome, which has been the city of Constantinople, the Christian faith will also perish through the violence of the sons of Hagar [Muslims]. In the third Rome, which will be the land of Rus, the Grace of the Holy Spirit will shine forth. Know then . . . that all Christians will finally unite into one Russian realm because of its Orthodoxy. For in ancient times, by the will of Constantine, Emperor of the Earth, the imperial crown was given from the imperial city to the Rus Tsar. But the White Cowl, by the will of the King of Heaven, Jesus Christ, will be given to the Archbishop of Novgorod the Great. And this White Cowl is more honorable than the crown of the Tsar, for it is an imperial crown of the archangelic spiritual order.[43]

What was being asserted here was less a "transfer of empire" than a transfer of spiritual authority within the Orthodox ecumene. The same idea was used by other clerics to bolster the authority of the church, but in a specifically apocalyptic context. The most famous example of its kind is the epistle by Filofei, abbot of the Eleazarov Monastery in Pskov (like Novgorod recently annexed to Moscow), to Misiur Munekhin, Muscovite state secretary in Pskov. The date of the epistle is not clear, but in it Filofei warned against the grand prince's intention of confiscating land from the church in Pskov. He also admonished the prince to root out abuses among the clergy and to exercise charity in his dealings with the poor. His glorification of the role of Moscow thus carried a powerful sting in the tail. "If thou rulest thine empire rightly, thou wilt be the son of light and a citizen of the heavenly Jerusalem . . . And now, I say unto thee: take care and take heed . . . All the empires of Christendom are united . . . in thine, for two Romes have fallen, the third stands, and there will be no fourth."[44]

The warning was clear: Moscow now bore responsibility for the fate of the true Christian faith, handed on from the churches of Rome and Byzantium. If the grand prince of Moscow failed to be worthy of this awesome mission, then there would be no further chance—"there will be no fourth"—and the end of the world was inevitable. In this vision of providence, Moscow took over authority within the Byzantine ecumene, but could exercise that authority properly only if it allowed itself to be guided by the church.

The theory of "Moscow the Third Rome" thus originated with senior clergymen in Novgorod and Pskov, who were trying to defend the landholdings and prerogatives of the church. Their method was to extol the state, but to do so in a form which suggested that the state's greatness depended on the church. As one scholar has put it, the theory "magnified the power of the ruler" but also "stressed his obligations," in a manner not necessarily congenial to him.[45]

Crucial therefore both to the theory of the state and to church-state relations was the question of ecclesiastical landholding, which also became a hotly contested issue in the late fifteenth and early sixteenth centuries. The traditional view among scholars is that on this question there existed two parties among senior clergymen, the "possessors" (*stiazhateli*, or "acquisitive ones") and the "nonpossessors" *(nestiazhateli),* and that the two clashed at a church council in 1503, when Ivan III backed the nonpossessors and tried to launch a program of massive secularization of church (mainly monastic) land. The leader of the possessors was supposedly Iosif Volotskii, abbot of the large monastery at Volokolamsk and protégé of Gennadii, and of the nonpossessors Nil Sorskii, a prominent figure in the movement of "trans-Volga elders," who came from hermitages in the north of the country. However, according to recent scholarship, the sources do not offer unimpeachable evidence that church landownership was an issue at the council or that two well-defined parties clashed over it; moreover, neither Iosif nor Nil expressed an unambiguous view about monastic landholding in his writings.[46]

Whether or not the council of 1503 passed a resolution on church landownership, it is quite clear that by the end of the fifteenth century the Muscovite grand princes were trying to get a grip on the process by which patrimonial land and the peasants living on it were accumulating in the hands of the monasteries, both through inheritance from pious benefactors and through straightforward purchase. If they could not restrict it, they at least wanted to register it. Furthermore, Ivan III had expropriated monastery land in Novgorod after its annexation, and it was obvious that his successors could try at any time to continue the process elsewhere, a development which the church wanted to restrain.

As for the disputes within the church, they may not have focused specifically on monastic landowning, but they were vehement and they bore on fundamental aspects both of the religious life and of church-state relations. Iosif had started from a quasi-papal view of church-state relations, close to that of Gennadii. He even wrote that the church was the guardian of moral standards for the world as a whole, and had a right to condemn an earthly ruler who was dominated by sin and passion, "for such a Tsar is not God's servant, but a devil and a torturer." Later, however, he played down the church's role as moral judge of the ruler, for he came to believe that the future of the Russian church lay in a close alliance with the grand principality of Moscow, under which the state would underwrite the church's authority to proceed against heresy and would support its ownership of land and its authority over peasants and townsfolk living on that land. Iosif believed monasticism should be cenobitic, and he devoted a lot of attention to elaborating the rules under which monks should live. He held that monasteries needed landed property and other wealth if they were to fulfill their functions properly—including care for the poor and sick—but that their wealth should be collective, while individual monks should be bound by their oaths of poverty and should not own property. To exercise its functions the church and its monasteries needed to be wealthy, but the monks themselves should be poor. In the face of the heretics' challenge, Iosif reasserted that the clergy should be pure in spirit and that monasteries should justify their wealth by charitable activity and by looking after the physical and spiritual well-being of their peasants.[47]

Nil Sorskii and the Trans-Volga Elders held to an older view of the church: that it was part of the Orthodox ecumene whose head was the patriarch of Constantinople and that it should avoid too close an association with any earthly ruler, reserving for itself the right to stand back and judge whether princes were acting in accordance with God's law. Although Nil did not object in principle to the cenobitic mode of life, his ideal was the *skit*, the hermitage where two or three brothers lived together and tended to their own needs without hiring labor. This was the ancient Syrian tradition, and it was the one which was most widely practiced on Mount Athos, where Nil had spent time in his youth. His writings are imbued with the spirit of late Byzantine hesychasm, which he had found in full flower there: he emphasized not the rules of the common life, but the need for each individual believer to find his own path through asceticism, contemplation, and regular silent prayer.[48]

Perhaps the most remarkable exponent of the latter viewpoint was Maksim the Greek, a learned monk who was invited to Muscovy in 1518 by Vasilii III to translate religious texts into Slavonic (a continuation of the work begun by Gennadii's circle). A Greek by origin, born around 1470, he had studied in the Florence of Lorenzo de Medici, and became a Dominican monk for a while. However, having consorted with Renaissance humanist thinkers and studied the Greek and Latin classics, he renounced the whole milieu and returned to the faith of his fathers in the Vatopedi Monastery on Mount Athos. Here he had at his disposal a fine library which contained the writings of the church fathers. From his years on Mount Athos he brought the conviction that monks must live an ascetic and contemplative life, maintaining themselves by their own work. He wrote that on Athos the monks "live without villages, only by their own industry and unceasing labor and by the sweat of their faces do they acquire for themselves all their daily needs. There is no excess silver lying in their treasuries, nor among the [monastery] people, as is the custom here."[49]

On Athos and after his transfer to Moscow, he wrote a large number of treatises which show him to have been strongly influenced by hesychasm. A convinced proponent of Orthodox ecumenism, he taught that the ruler should be anointed by the bishops and guided by the divine law as expounded by them, and that the metropolitan of all Rus should be chosen only with the approval of the patriarch of Constantinople.

These attitudes were increasingly unwelcome to Vasilii III, who wanted to assert the independence of the secular power and the right of the Moscow church to run its own affairs. In 1525 Maksim was arrested and tried for heresy. He spent the remaining thirty years of his life in confinement, though he continued to be revered as a source of wisdom, and he was consulted by Ivan IV.[50] His arrest seems to mark the moment when the state finally distanced itself from the heretics and concluded a compromise with the followers of Iosif. Pulling back from any concerted confiscation of monastic lands, Vasilii III agreed to accept and enforce the church's view of heresy, in return for which the church renounced its hesychast heritage and its post-Byzantine ecumenical ambitions and agreed to become in effect a Muscovite state church, protected by the grand prince/tsar.

This settlement was embodied in the collections of texts and emblems assembled in the early years of the reign of Ivan IV by Metropolitan Makarii, a disciple of Gennadii and Iosif, who himself came originally from Novgorod. He put together two compilations of readings, in some ways like the texts assembled by Chinese emperors to demonstrate that they possessed the "mandate of heaven." They were the *Great Reading Menaea (Velikie Chetii-Minei)* and the *Book of Degrees of the Imperial Genealogy (Stepennaia Kniga Tsarskogo Rodosloviia).* Taken together they demonstrated both the secular and the spiritual pedigree of the Muscovite prince. The first included lives of the saints, resolutions of church councils, sermons, epistles (including the one by Filofei of Pskov), and excerpts from historical documents, edited and presented so that they could conveniently be read from the pulpit on each day of the ecclesiastical calendar. They were selected and arranged to show that from the creation onward God had intended to found a truly Christian empire on earth, and that Rus was now destined to fulfill this purpose.

Moscow thus became symbolically both the "Third Rome" and the "Second Jerusalem," inheritor of both the Roman Empire and the Christian Church. Believers heard daily in church how the princes of Rus were descended from the Roman emperor Augustus through his brother Prus, and how Vladimir Monomakh had received regalia from the Byzantine emperor Constantine in explicit recognition of his status as tsar. Makarii also began the collation and editing of chronicles from the various lands of Rus to create the *Illustrated Digest (Litsevoi svod)* as a consistent and continuous narrative tracing Moscow's heritage back through Kievan Rus to the Roman Empire and to the ancient Jews.[51]

"Moscow the Third Rome," then, was not originally a political theory, but rather a moral and religious one, and it should be understood as part of a complex of symbols and narratives which emphasized the sacred and exclusive heritage of Rus. It had a paradoxical and double-edged potential, since it could be interpreted in an optimistic or a pessimistic way, and it could be used as a loyal or oppositional statement in relation to the secular power. In practice Moscow's secular officials seldom evoked it, because of its ambivalence and also because it tended to strengthen the standing of the church, already strong enough in their eyes. Disseminated from the pulpit, however, it had considerable popular appeal and inculcated among ordinary Orthodox believers the conviction that their country had a special and exclusive mission to fulfill in the world. For an embattled people on vulnerable terrain that was both a comforting and potentially an intoxicating vision.[52]

IVAN IV: PERSONALITY AND IDEOLOGY

In 1533, then, when Ivan IV came to the throne, Muscovy was assuming ever more grandiose geopolitical and religious goals. The conquest and assimilation of the great Novgorod republic had been completed, and Muscovy was advancing claims to be considered paramount not only among the successors of Kievan Rus, but among all Christian powers. Yet she was also extremely vulnerable, and could not become a great power in any sense, in either Europe or Asia, without achieving greater security. In the Baltic area the Teutonic Knights were still a considerable force, while Denmark and Sweden were rising and ambitious powers, and to the west Lithuania was a formidable rival, territorially of comparable size but with more fertile soil, while her claims to be considered the heir of Kiev were no less convincing than those of Muscovy. Moreover, Lithuania was supported by the Catholic kingdom of Poland: taken together the two lands formed the largest territorial realm in Europe.

In some ways even more dangerous were the successor states of the Golden Horde, the Crimean khanate, the Nogai Horde, and the khanates of Siberia, Kazan, and Astrakhan, now Islamic societies, increasingly sedentary in their mode of life, but retaining something of the formidable mounted striking power of their nomadic predecessors. They were backed, moreover, by the strongest state in the Middle East, the Ottoman Empire, at the zenith of its renown and influence after its subjection of the Balkans and the final conquest of Byzantium. The defense of the open southern steppe frontier against the roaming Crimean Tatar horsemen was to remain a constant and debilitating drain on the resources of the still thinly populated and relatively infertile Muscovite realm.

The circumstances in which Ivan acceded to the throne in 1533 demonstrated the extent to which Muscovy, in spite of these external dangers, was still capable of tearing itself apart internally. His father died when he was only three years old, leaving the widow and son in the care of her family, the Glinskie. Regencies are always a hazardous period for a monarchy, and this was no exception. The Glinskie, Belskie, and Shuiskie, currently the most powerful boyar clans, fought each other viciously for predominant influence over the young prince and over the wealth and patronage of the court. It was a terrifying milieu for Ivan to grow up in, especially after the death of his mother in 1538. Yet he himself was never directly threatened, nor was violence inflicted on him: awe in the face of the *gosudar vseia Rusi* remained the one fixed point in the turbulent world of boyar feuding. Ivan could see and understand that his courtiers were acting on his authority yet leaving him no real power. He acquired from his childhood a permanently smoldering resentment of all boyar clans, which from time to time would burst into flame.

At his coronation in the Uspenskii Cathedral in the Kremlin, in January 1547, the young Ivan received the title of tsar, the first Muscovite ruler to be thus formally styled at the outset of his reign. Metropolitan Makarii made the sign of the cross over him and placed on his head the crown of Monomakh *(shapka Monomakha)* as a symbol of the dual derivation of his authority from both the church and the Byzantine Empire. Ivan was claiming not only sovereignty, independence from other powers, but the actual superiority of his realm, as the universal Christian monarchy, to all others on earth. He persuaded the patriarch of Constantinople, doyen of Orthodox churchmen, to send him a document ratifying this status, but declined to

invite him to place the crown on his head. He wanted the publicly acknowledged status which the patriarch could give him, but no direct subordination
to the Greek church, which bore the taint of defeat and subjection to the
infidel.[53]

On the other hand Ivan did want to be connected with the heritage of the   109
Byzantine Empire: hence the Byzantine regalia and the *shapka Monomakha*.
Subsequently, in the Gold Room of the Kremlin palace and in the Archangel
Cathedral frescoes and icons were painted placing Ivan in a long line of
princes which went right back to Old Testament Israel and included Roman
and Byzantine emperors. The baptism of Rus under Vladimir was depicted,
as was the presentation of the Byzantine regalia to Vladimir Monomakh.
Each prince was portrayed bareheaded and with a halo to suggest that he
enjoyed saintly status in the Byzantine mode.[54]

In concordance with these frescoes, Ivan held an awesome concept of his
own mission: no less than to conduct humanity through the snares and hazards of the present unstable era to ultimate salvation or damnation. That
was the implication of the sacred status of the land of Rus, in which he had
learned to believe from his tutors and from Makarii. However, the implications he drew from his vision of monarchy differed somewhat from Makarii's
teachings, and this discrepancy was to widen in the course of Ivan's reign.
Makarii, like the young Iosif Volotskii, believed that the monarch should
above all be pious and offer an exemplar of the virtuous, God-fearing life.
"He keeps himself pure before the Lord in all matters . . . he is never absent
from the required church services . . . Leaving aside all royal entertainments,
the hunt and all other amusements, he must strive to do the will of Christ
in everything, to preserve the state given to him, establishing it in justice
and preserving it from the heterodox barbarians and Latins." It followed
that he was bound by God's law. "If the Tsar, who wears the purple vestments
and royal crown, places his hope in the loftiness of his birth and begins to
be proud of his office, so that he becomes filled with anger towards our
office, and does not submit himself to the holy precepts of the sainted fathers;
if he dares to behave in such a manner, he will be condemned as one who
fights against the word of God."[55]

Nor was this merely Makarii's personal opinion. The church remained a
dominant spiritual and physical presence in Muscovite Rus, thanks both to
its huge landholdings and to the unifying national role it had assumed under
Mongol suzerainty. Public ceremonial reflected its salience. Each Epiphany,
for example, the tsar stood bareheaded on the frozen Moscow River, among
his boyars, while the metropolitan blessed the waters and sprinkled them
on those assembled. Even more remarkable, in the Palm Sunday procession

through the center of Moscow, the tsar would lead a donkey on which the metropolitan was seated, in reenactment of Christ's entry into Jerusalem. The Epiphany ceremony was adapted from a Byzantine model, the Palm Sunday procession from a Catholic one: in both cases, the tsar's pious humility before the representative of Christ was more emphasized than in the original.[56]

Ivan, by contrast, especially as he grew older and more confident of his powers, took the view that his responsibility for ultimate things entitled him to absolute and untrammeled power, gave him the right to dispose unrestrainedly of human life and property, even to be free of the moral law if he should consider it necessary. "Is it fitting for the Tsar to offer the other cheek when he is struck on one?" he asked Prince Andrei Kurbskii. "It is the most perfect commandment, but how can the Tsar govern his realm if he allows himself to be dishonored?" It followed that his moral worth as a man was completely separate from the standards demanded of him as a monarch. "Though I am a sinner as a man, as Tsar I am righteous."[57]

In taking this view he was influenced by the teachings of a minor Lithuanian nobleman, Ivan Peresvetov, who had seen service with the Ottoman sultan. Having enlisted with Muscovy, Peresvetov suffered at the hands of the greedy and factious boyars, who, in his own account, left him destitute. Recalling his Ottoman experience, he presented Ivan with two treatises, *The Legend of the Fall of Tsargrad* and *The Legend of Sultan Mehmet*, which together recounted the Ottoman conquest of Byzantium in 1453 and reflected on the factors which had humbled a once great empire.

Peresvetov took a totally different view of the causes of Byzantium's fall from that of Makarii or the propagators of the White Cowl legend. Byzantium's fatal weakness, he asserted, was not the apostasy of its church, but the avarice, feuding, and disloyalty of its aristocrats, which had made it impossible for the emperor to present a united front against Ottoman aggression. For Ivan the parallel with the behavior of the Muscovite boyars was obvious. Peresvetov contrasted the feebleness of the last Byzantine emperors with the firm and wise leadership of Mehmet II, who disdained the claims of pedigree, selected his advisers and servitors according to merit, and ruled dispassionately, firmly, and, when necessary, with exemplary harshness. Peresvetov believed that a good ruler must inspire fear or "awe." "Without awe one cannot establish justice [*pravda*] in the realm. Justice means that the tsar must not spare even his favorite, if he finds him guilty . . . A tsardom without awe is like a horse without reins."[58]

Peresvetov was not an uncritical admirer of Ottoman practices: he did not, for example, envisage that military leaders should all become the tsar's personal slaves. His overall approach reflected the influence of the European Renaissance, perhaps especially that of Machiavelli. It is not clear whether he had actually read him, but Machiavelli's influence was all-pervasive in European political thinking at the time, and someone with Peresvetov's concerns would certainly have been aware of him. One assumption permeates the thinking of both: that a ruler who is indulgent toward human weakness promotes greater evil, in the form of anarchy and civil war, than one who is harsh, even cruel, in suppressing ambition, avarice, and the spirit of rebellion among his subjects. The state, in other words, is an autonomous sphere and has its own morality, its *raison d'état,* which is not necessarily that of the church.[59]

Peresvetov was not a religious thinker. He was concerned mainly with mobilizing the resources of people and territories efficiently. The army, he believed, should be recruited, trained, and financed by the monarch, so that its individual formations should not become pawns in boyar feuds. Its officers should be promoted on the basis of merit rather than pedigree, or *mestnichestvo.* He did not put forward specific proposals as to how those officers should be provided for, but a system of service estates would conform to the logic of his argument.[60]

IVAN'S ATTEMPTED REFORMS

Ivan began his reign in the most inauspicious circumstances. Fires broke out in Moscow, and much of the center of the largely wooden city was burned down. Rumor among the market stalls and alleyways had it that the Glinskie had started the fire deliberately. Ivan's uncle, Iurii Glinskii, was dragged out of the Dormition Cathedral in the Kremlin and lynched. Ivan IV had to face the mob in person and refuse categorically to deliver up any more members of the family before the angry crowd would disperse. Thereafter the remaining Glinskie fled to Lithuania.

Ivan reacted to these events in a manner which indicates his seriousness, his piety, and his desire to make contact with the common people. If he was to implement the concept of monarchy suggested to him by Peresvetov, he had to try to build a state which would be free both from the prelates' tiresome moralizing and from the magnates' destructive squabbles. That meant reaching out beyond bishops and boyars and forging links with local elites, with the *zemlia* as opposed to the *gosudarstvo.*

The concept *zemlia* was a crucial one in Muscovite politics: it referred to the local communities and their leaders, as distinct from the court and the central officials. Hitherto, as we have seen, taxation, justice, and local administration had been handled by princes, boyars, and other officials as part of their votchiny, in other words as part of their estate management, making no distinction between public and private affairs. This was kormlenie, and it formed the centerpiece in the relations between local communities and the prince.

In conformity with his ambitious vision of the Muscovite state's mission, Ivan wanted both to mobilize better the resources of local communities and to draw them into closer relations with the state. With these two goals in mind, he tried to end or at least curtail kormlenie by abolishing the post of *namestnik* and handing over taxation, justice, and local administration to local assemblies, known as *zemstva,* and courts, known as *guby.* In doing so, he was giving official status to existing local assemblies of town and village, the *miry,* and to their elected elders, or *starosty.* These arrangements were set out in the new *Law Code (Sudebnik)* of 1550.[61]

The reform proved difficult to implement in practice, for reasons which were to be replicated many times in the following centuries. Members of the mir assemblies were bound by joint responsibility for taxation and other duties, which meant that they had to compensate any shortfalls and derelictions of duty out of their own pockets. Elders were in an invidious position in enforcing these requirements, and served reluctantly. Furthermore, no intermediate institutions were set up between these tiny local assemblies and the central government, nor was provision made for horizontal links among them. Given the immense distances and poor communications, neither commands from above nor feedback from below reached their destinations more than fitfully. In the end, especially once war became protracted, it was simpler to fall back on well-tried methods. In any case, the old "fed" officials did not simply disappear, and to retain their loyalty it was easiest to allow their personal power to continue.[62]

In 1549 Ivan convened a so-called Council of Reconciliation in order to attempt a new start, both moral and institutional, after the initial disorders of his reign. He prefaced it with a thirty-eight-mile penitential procession in bare feet to the Monastery of St. Sergius. Having thus made his own peace with God, he reproached the boyars for their disloyal and avaricious behavior while also confessing his own sins and pleading for general repentance. This was an attempt, in the style of Makarii, to put his reign on a pious and God-fearing footing. On a few later occasions, he also consulted with representatives of local elites about policies he was considering, for example, in 1566, over whether to continue the war in Livonia and how to pay for it. Some historians have given these assemblies the name of *zemskii sobor,* or "gathering of the lands," but they had no such name at the time, nor were they in any sense a regular institution. They do, however, indicate that Ivan felt the need to distinguish state concerns from court intrigues, to extricate the "sovereign's affairs" (gosudarevo delo) from the jealous eyes of the boyars, and to communicate directly with the zemlia.[63]

For the same purpose, Ivan supplemented the advice of his boyar counselors with that of a few personally selected confidants of lower social status, whom some historians refer to as his "Chosen Council," though there seems to be no contemporary warrant for this term. He also endeavored to coordinate the central administration more satisfactorily by consolidating and enlarging the permanent offices of state. The pomestnyi prikaz supervised the distribution and maintenance of service estates, the razriadnyi prikaz oversaw the appointment of officers to military posts, the posolskii prikaz conducted foreign affairs, and so on. Some prikazy looked after particular territories, as survivals from the domain administrations of the old udel principalities. The head of the three prikazy mentioned above, together with the administrator of the kazna, or treasury, gained the right to attend meetings of the Boyar Duma, and were therefore normally themselves boyars. As the Russian historian R. G. Skrynnikov has pointed out, "Only with the formation of the prikaz system did the Boyar Duma finally constitute itself as the highest organ of state power."[64]

In a realm with overarching religious claims, it was obviously important to make sure that the church was well run, and in accordance with the sovereign's aims. Furthermore, Ivan wanted to curb the church's wealth and if possible take over some of it himself. In 1551 he convened a church council and submitted to it a long series of questions, one hundred in all—hence the council's generally accepted name of Stoglav, or "a hundred headings." In the Byzantine spirit, he himself participated in the debates. Many of the council's provisions aimed at improving standards of literacy and morality among priests and monks. The council resisted any widespread secularization of church lands, but agreed to return lands which had been transferred to the church during the tsar's minority, and to accept land in future only with his authorization. Monastic tax exemptions were reviewed.

The proponents of closer unity among the various churches of the Orthodox ecumene raised the question of whether the Slavonic scriptures and the liturgical practices of the Russian church needed to be modified to bring them more into line with Greek models. The council, however, explicitly upheld existing practices, such as making the sign of the cross with two fingers raised instead of three, as was generally done elsewhere by Orthodox believers.[65]

In practical terms, no less important to Ivan's mission was the army, which had to be large, well equipped, and mobile enough to deal with emergencies on several frontiers. This meant first of all ensuring that the boyars who were its senior commanders were both obliged to perform military service and well supported while they discharged that service.

Ivan set up a force of 1,000 elite cavalrymen by endowing chosen members of boyar and princely families, and sometimes more humble servitors too, with estates of up to 200 cheti (approximately 100 desiatinas, or 270 acres) within seventy versts of Moscow. To receive such a military command and the estate which went with it was a great honor: beneficiaries who already held estates elsewhere did not lose them, and they were inscribed in a special roll (the "book of the thousand"). On the other hand, their conditions of service were onerous: they were required to live permanently on their new estates, from where they could be sent at short notice to any of a variety of military or civilian tasks—becoming a regimental commander, taking charge of a garrison on the frontier, becoming vice-regent of a province, or heading a delegation to a foreign potentate.[66]

It was to ensure that enough land was available for his new "thousanders" that Ivan had raised at the Stoglav Council the question of secularizing church lands. Further, to establish his prior right even to boyar holdings, in 1551 and 1562 Ivan reduced the scope of *votchinniki* to dispose of their votchiny as they saw fit. They were forbidden to sell or bequeath them without official permission, while their right to pass them down the female line was curtailed. Estates without a direct heir passed to the treasury.

Having confirmed these guidelines, in 1556 Ivan issued a decree *(Ulozhenie o sluzhbe)* laying down the military duties of all who held landed estates, whether votchiny or pomestia: roughly speaking, each holder of 150 desiatinas (about 400 acres) of "good, cultivable land" had to provide one fully equipped soldier with a horse for the tsar's service as and when required. This decree was a milestone in Russian law, for it established the principle that all land was held at the tsar's pleasure and on condition of performing state service as required. Enforcement of the principle was patchy, and tended to decline the longer an estate had been in the hands of the same family, but the principle itself conferred on the tsar considerable reserve powers.[67]

The nucleus of the army remained the mounted "junior boyars" (landed servitors or the younger sons of boyar families), with their helmets, armor, swords, bows and arrows. They were archaic by the standards of the time, but sufficient to discourage roaming bands of steppe horsemen. To face the armies of European powers, Ivan had to supplement them with a new force of musketeers *(streltsy)*, recruited from the *posad* (urban) communities. Like service nobles, they were provided with a source of income, in the shape of workshops and allotment lands, so that they could feed themselves and practice a trade as well as train regularly with their firearms. By the early 1560s there were about 7,000 musketeers available for the field army, while another 3,000 were detailed off to protect Ivan's country residence at Vorobievo, just outside Moscow. By the early seventeenth century they had evolved the tactic of advancing in line, increasing frontal firepower, which other European armies were also adopting at that time. Similar arrangements were made to guarantee a supply of trained bombardiers to man the growing artillery arm. A special chancery, the *pushechnyi prikaz*, was set up to supervise the production of artillery and ensure that it was regularly tested.[68]

THE COSSACKS

Ivan IV was the first Russian ruler to try to solve the nagging problem of the southern frontiers by drawing the Cossacks into a permanent alliance. The Cossacks were the hunters and brigands, horsemen and stockraisers who roamed the "wild country" *(dikoe pole)* left by the breakup of the Golden Horde. This was indeterminate steppe territory surrounded by established states: Muscovy, Poland, the Ottoman Empire, the Crimean khanate, the Nogai Horde, and the north Caucasian tribal kingdoms. Cossacks had no state formation of their own, but lived in loose military fraternities, cultivating the skills of horsemanship crucial to survival on the plains. The name by which they were known is Turkic and means "free man." In its essentials they adopted the lifestyle of the nomads.

The first concentrations of Cossacks were in the lower reaches of two great rivers, the Don and the Dnieper. In the early stages many of them were Tatars, survivors perhaps of the Golden Horde or other nomadic hosts, but many too were Slavs, hunters, fishermen, and traders who had strayed from the borders of Poland or Muscovy, peasants or even landowners fleeing from justice or injustice in their homeland. In time the Slavic element became dominant and most Cossacks adopted the Orthodox faith.[69]

Cossacks lived at first in settlements of tents made of hides, reminiscent of the nomadic *iurty*, though as their way of life stabilized they began to build wooden or clay houses *(kuren)* grouped in a *stanitsa*, a village or fortified camp. They would use islands or even churches as strongholds to which they could retire with their flocks if attacked. They practiced a mixture of primitive democracy and ruthless authoritarianism, characteristic of communities that live in a highly vulnerable environment and whose members are dependent on each other to survive in it. They were intensely proud of their status as "free men" and were prepared to defend their *volia* (liberty) to the utmost. At the same time, in preparing and conducting military campaigns, they obeyed their leaders implicitly, and indiscipline was harshly punished, sometimes even with the death penalty.

With the passage of time their institutions became more elaborate, but the basic unit remained what it had long been in the steppe: the *krug*, or circle, which was a gathering of all the members of a band or army unit. It elected their leader (*hetman* on the Dnieper; *ataman* on the Don) and took decisions on the most important affairs, whenever possible by consensus rather than by voting. The Army Circle in Cherkassk was the nearest thing the Don Cossacks possessed to a supreme sovereign body: it would conduct negotiations with foreign envoys, conclude alliances, and declare war or negotiate peace. It would also elect the army ataman, who was military leader and head of the administration.

Until the late seventeenth century or so, the Cossacks despised agriculture as unworthy of free men, and in any case futile in such a vulnerable environment. They were thus compelled, like all nomads, either to seize agricultural produce or to trade in order to purchase it. They would sell fish, meat, hides, or honey, but they would also attack and plunder merchant ships, especially on the Caspian, and sometimes even attempt raids on shore settlements to capture goods, produce, or slaves. These expeditions were mounted by expert Cossack oarsmen on quite small but extremely maneuverable boats, which could make use of darkness, calm, or a favorable wind to surprise and overwhelm their victims. Against organized naval forces, however, or even a well-defended merchant ship, they could do little and were liable to be overwhelmed themselves.[70]

The Cossacks' way of life was, then, inherently a vulnerable and economically incomplete one. They depended on the outside world for economic exchange (or plunder), and increasingly they turned to it also for protection, in spite of their tradition of *volia*. Thus the Dnieper Cossacks had an arrangement with the Polish king, whereby they served him as frontier troops in return for pay, partly in money and partly in kind.

Ivan IV concluded a similar agreement with the Don Cossacks, to draw them into his campaigns against Kazan and Astrakhan. It became more permanent in 1570, when Ivan granted them a charter, under which they would serve him as frontier defense troops, to warn of and repel nomadic raiders, while he confirmed their right to the territories around the lower Don. In the early seventeenth century the Russian government augmented its side of the bargain by promising a regular allowance, consisting of grain, firearms, and ammunition—all items which Cossacks could otherwise obtain only by exchange or plunder. This was the beginning of a long process by which the

Cossacks were gradually integrated into the Russian imperial army and administrative system, while losing most of their own self-governing institutions.[71]

THE CONQUEST OF KAZAN

In 1552 the army reforms and the alliance with the Cossacks enabled Ivan to achieve the greatest triumph of his reign. For at least half a century, his predecessors had been trying to find a way to cope with the khanate of Kazan, the strongest of the successors of the Golden Horde, which blocked the lucrative trade route to the Middle East down the Volga and across the Caspian Sea. At times Muscovite princes had intervened in its internal conflicts to place their own candidates on the khan's throne, but at other times they had had to watch helplessly while opponents of Muscovite influence were installed there.[72]

In the end Ivan decided to cut short the maneuvering. In justification he cited a number of mutually conflicting arguments. Kazan, he claimed, had in the past acknowledged the suzerainty of Moscow as the heir to the authority of the Golden Horde, and in rejecting that authority now the khans were violating their own oaths. Inconsistently, he also cited his own standing as the champion of Christianity against the infidel, and as the tsar of Rus, responsible for reassembling the patrimony of the Riurik dynasty and the "lands of Rus," which he asserted Kazan had been "since antiquity."[73]

He took advantage of a Cheremis rebellion against the khanate to construct a fortress at Sviazhsk, on the western bank of the Volga, and in October 1552 used it as a base for his final successful assault on the city, in which his artillery and the newly established *streltsy* played a key role.

This was a historic turning point, which fundamentally and permanently altered the balance of power on the Eurasian steppes. The loose alliance of successors of the Golden Horde was broken, and the Nogai Horde, the khans of Siberia and Astrakhan, the princes of Piatigorsk and Kabarda all acknowledged themselves vassals of the tsar. Furthermore, although Rus had earlier absorbed non-Russian peoples in the course of territorial expansion, the conquest of Kazan marked the first defeat and annexation of a non-Russian sovereign state. Establishing a stronghold on the mid-Volga enabled Moscow to open up stable trade relations with the Middle East via the Caspian Sea and the Caucasus and also to embark on further expansion across the Urals into Siberia.

To consolidate his grip on Kazan, Ivan deported most of the Muslim population from the city and brought in Russian merchants and artisans to take

Muscovy, 1533–1598

☐ Moscow in 1533

← Unsuccessful military expedition against
the Mongols of the Crimea, 1556–1559

☐ Muscovite conquests by 1598

◉ Cities founded 1584–1594, with dates

SWEDISH EMPIRE

*Arctic
Sea*

Baltic Sea

Kexholm

INGRIA

Pskov

Dvina

Arkhangel
1584

Urals

Ob

Surgut
1594

Obskii Gorodok
1585

SIBERIA

Tobolsk
1587

Tiumen
1586

LITHUANIA

Polotsk

Moscow

Smolensk

Volga

Kazan

Chernigov

Kiev

Volga

Voronezh
1586

Samara
1586

Saratov
1590

THE
NOGAI
HORDE

CRIMEAN

Tsaritsyn
1589

Bakhchisaray

KHANATE

Astrakhan

Black Sea

Terek

Caucasus

Caspian Sea

OTTOMAN EMPIRE

| 0 | 400 |

Miles

Ivan IV became the grand duke of
Moscow in 1533. In 1547 he was
crowned "Tsar of All the Russias."
He conquered the Mongol khanate
of Kazan in 1552, the khanate of
Astrakhan in 1556, and the Mongols
east of the Urals in 1584. In 1583 the
Swedes conquered Ingria, and Russia
lost all access to the Baltic Sea; but
this was regained under Tsar Fedor,
1584–1598.

their place. Over the following years he had to deal with repeated rebellions by disaffected Tatars, which he suppressed ruthlessly. To mark his triumph, Ivan had a great Orthodox cathedral constructed in the center of Kazan. At the heart of Moscow, in Red Square outside the Kremlin, he built the Cathedral of the Holy Veil (later known as St. Basil's), with eight chapels, each celebrating a Muscovite victory, grouped around an octagonal nave. The onion domes surmounting each chapel imparted to the whole structure an unforgettable swirling exuberance, which even today gives Red Square its characteristic ambience.

Ivan also commissioned a new style of icon painting, which is epitomized in the icon known as the *Church Militant*. It portrays a victorious Christian army, led by the warrior-saints of old Rus and presided over by the Mother of God, marching toward Moscow, while in the background infidel Kazan is in flames. The use of icons to convey political messages was an innovation which ran counter to the purely spiritual content of past icon painting, as handed down by Rublev and others. Ivan Viskovatyi, one of Ivan's most prominent chancery officials, objected to such images—for example, one depicting Christ clothed in armor on the cross—as heretical. A church council of 1554 rejected his arguments, however.[74] Thenceforth it was considered legitimate to deploy religious imagery in the interests of the state.

In the following years, in spite of their oaths of allegiance, the surviving Tatar khanates attempted to reverse the Muscovite victory. In 1555 the Crimean Horde invaded the territory of Muscovy and nearly defeated a Russian army under Ivan Sheremetev, who was severely wounded. Khan Derbysh-Ali of Astrakhan, supported by Turkish janissaries and artillery, simultaneously drove Russian troops out of the Volga-Don portage area. Cossacks of the lower Volga responded by falling on the khan's headquarters and destroying it, so that Derbysh-Ali not only was unable to exploit his victory, but was forced to flee his realm. The khanate of Astrakhan was incorporated into Muscovy. Ivan wanted to follow up this success by invading the Crimea in order to root out a permanent source of danger. He began to build a fleet on the Don and Dnieper Rivers, manned by *streltsy*, but eventually had to abandon the plan, as his forces were insufficient to accomplish it.[75]

THE BALTIC WARS

At this point Ivan turned his attention to the Baltic. He believed that a realm of the size and importance of Muscovy needed both to be able to trade with the powers of Europe and to build strategic strongpoints against them in case of conflict. For these purposes Ivan aspired to control a significant portion of the coastline of the Baltic Sea, together with one or more port city. By the mid-1550s Muscovy's only European trading partner was England, and that as a result of a chance landfall in 1553, when Richard Chancellor, seeking a sea route to China along the northern coasts of Europe, had sheltered from storms in the White Sea. The following year, Queen Elizabeth chartered a Russia Company to take advantage of the trading opportunities thus created, and English merchants were granted trading privileges and tax exemptions inside Muscovy. England needed great quantities of timber, rope, and tar for her navy, and hoped to find a new route to Asia along the Volga. For their part the Russians purchased English metal products and chemicals for making munitions.[76] The drawback was that this commerce, however advantageous, had to be conducted either over the long and hazardous route through the Arctic Sea or through ports controlled by others on the Baltic.

By the 1550s the Teutonic Knights were in terminal decline. Their original crusading urge had long spent its force, and in any case there were no pagans left to convert. The Knights' last surviving branch, the Livonian Order, ruled Livonia as a more or less normal feudal authority, but it was rent both by religious strife resulting from the Reformation and by political conflict with the growing number of townsfolk on its territory. It looked like a good moment for Moscow to assert its interest in the Baltic.[77]

In 1558, accordingly, Moscow demanded that Russia's Baltic trade, which passed mainly through Riga and Reval, no longer be conducted by Livonian merchants, but henceforth be taken over by Russians. Not receiving a favorable reply, Ivan sent a Russian army under A. D. Basmanov, which captured the key trading port of Narva and set about building a new fortress city, Ivangorod, on its opposite bank. This was an auspicious start to the Baltic campaign, and it was followed by further successes during the next few years, including the capture of Polotsk and Derpt. Ivan proceeded in Livonia and Lithuania as he had in Kazan, by expropriating local landowners in order to award their estates to Russian immigrants.

He was unable to bring his plans to fruition, however, for his aggression provoked a reaction from the other Baltic powers, anxious not to be left out of the carve-up of Livonia. Denmark and Sweden entered the war, Denmark taking the large island of Ösel, while Sweden conquered Reval and north Estland. Gustav Kettler, head of the Livonian Order, placed his state under the protection of Lithuania. Worse still, the Russian action provoked the final union of Poland and Lithuania, agreed at Lublin in 1569. Ivan's warmaking had stirred up a hornets' nest, and his armies became steadily less successful. The old vulnerability in the south had by no means been eliminated, so that Moscow had to keep looking to its rear and diverting armies to protect it. In the end Moscow lost Polotsk, Narva, Ivangorod, and Derpt, captured during the war, and also strategically vital territory in Karelia and at the eastern end of the Gulf of Finland which it had annexed from Novgorod long before war was joined.

Meanwhile, in 1571 a Crimean Tatar army under Devlet-Girei slipped through Muscovy's depleted southern defenses and sacked Moscow itself. The Tatars plundered the monasteries and merchant suburbs and then set fire to the city. According to an eyewitness, as smoke filled the streets crowded with terrified refugees, alarm bells sounded in all the churches and monasteries, then crashed to the ground and fell silent one by one as the fire reached them.[78]

These perceived failures meant that the tendency of landowners to come over to the service of Muscovy from Lithuania now began to reverse. Since the rights of votchina owners were being curtailed, and the monarchy was trampling ever more unceremomiously on the presumed privileges of the highborn, some of them decided to exercise their ancestral prerogative of seeking service where they chose. They noted that their counterparts in Poland-Lithuania, the szlachta, had more secure rights, including that of electing the monarch.

The most egregious example of this tendency was Ivan's personal friend, Prince Andrei Kurbskii, military leader and member of the Boyar Duma, who in April 1564 went over to Lithuania, from where he wrote a series of epistles denouncing Ivan's tyranny as contrary to God's law. Ivan replied, using biblical arguments to show that all earthly power comes from God, and that rulers have special responsibilities which exempt them from a narrow interpretation of God's law. He considered Kurbskii's transfer of allegiance to be not the exercise of an honored feudal right, but rather treason to his realm and its universal claims.[79] Military reverses and growing evidence of boyar defections steeled his determination to become the absolute ruler he believed God intended him to be.

His mounting secular ambition encountered resistance from the church as well as the boyars. Filipp, metropolitan of Moscow, accused him publicly of "spilling the innocent blood of faithful people and Christians . . . Tatars and heathens and the whole world can say that all peoples have justice and laws, but only in Rus do they have none." Ivan did not react immediately, but later had Filipp arrested and strangled in a monastery prison.[80] Thereafter no senior prelate dared to rebuke him openly.

But there were religious movements whose challenge to both church and state was even more radical. One of Ivan's chosen "thousand," Matvei Bashkin, perhaps influenced by antitrinitarian views from Novgorod, preached that Christ was not God, but a man, and that the church was not a temple but a "gathering of the faithful." To fulfill this vision, he released his own slaves and called for equality, mutual love, and the abolition of social hierarchy. In 1553 he was arrested and imprisoned in the Volokolamsk Monastery, stronghold of the Josephites.[81]

Even more extreme was Feodosii Kosoi, a former slave who escaped to a monastery on the White Sea, where he gathered a circle of like-minded colleagues and preached a return to the gospels and the Acts of the Apostles, the tenets of which he thought should be made available to all believers, through a rejection of the church with all its saints, icons, and rituals, nowhere mentioned in the scriptures. True Christianity, he asserted, lay not in pagan temples or idolatry, which he believed ecclesiastical Christianity amounted to, but in a life of contemplation, silent prayer, and hard work in a property-sharing community.[82]

In these teachings one can detect echoes of contemporary Protestantism, as well as of hesychasm and of "nonpossession." Almost certainly there were more heresies abroad which have not come down to us. But even the evidence we have shows that there was a current of opinion which rejected not only the concept of a propertyowning church allied with the state, but any kind of hierarchical, ritualistic church, in favor of a stripped-down spiritual and communal Christianity. That was to remain a tangible undercurrent in Russian thought thereafter.

The circulation of such ideas and the authorities' nervous reaction to them obstructed the development of printing. The first printing press, the *pechatnyi dvor,* was opened in Moscow in 1564 by the former deacon of a Moscow church, Ivan Fedorov. Fedorov had the sponsorship of Metropolitan Makarii, but after the latter's death came under attack from influential churchmen who suspected him of not doing what Makarii had intended, propagating the true faith, but instead of disseminating heresy. Fedorov closed his press and fled to Lithuania, where he eventually reopened it in Lvov.[83]

THE *OPRICHNINA* AND IVAN'S LATER YEARS

In December 1564 Ivan suddenly withdrew his court from Moscow and, taking with him the contents of the state treasury and several revered icons, withdrew to the settlement of Aleksandrovskaia Sloboda, a minor princely residence to the northeast. From there he sent the boyars and church leaders an epistle, declaring his intention of abdicating and accusing them of treason and of embezzling state funds on a massive scale. When he tried to punish the guilty, he complained, the Boyar Duma and church intervened to obstruct him. If they did not wish him to abdicate, they should give him the right to set up his own separate realm (*oprichnina*: the word used in law to denote the widow's portion of an inheritance), in order to guarantee him an income and to give him the freedom to proceed as he saw fit against peculators, traitors, and heretics.

Ivan's histrionic behavior dramatized Muscovy's need for the symbolism of firm and undivided authority. The boyars hastened to send envoys begging him to resume the throne and promising to let him proceed as he saw fit. Returning to Moscow, Ivan divided his realm into two: the oprichnina, where he would have unlimited jurisdiction; and the *zemshchina* (the territory of the *zemlia*), where the Boyar Duma would rule according to custom. He absorbed into the former most of the surviving udel domains, as well as some service estates in the region of Moscow and extensive territories in the north which had originally belonged to Novgorod.

Ivan used the revenues from these lands to provide for a new combined army and police force, which was to act as his bodyguard, defend the frontiers, and root out corruption, treason, and heresy. Its members were given special powers of investigation and arrest, with curtailed judicial procedure or none at all. The oprichnina had its own court in Moscow and functioned, among other things, as a kind of monastery. It followed an ascetic regimen, which however was in practice interrupted periodically by orgies of sensuality and sadism. Ivan referred to his *oprichniki* as "brothers." Dressed in long black cloaks, almost like monks, they rode on black horses, each carrying a dog's head and a long broom: "This means that first of all they bite like dogs, and then they sweep away everything superfluous out of the land." Those accepted into this elite were supposed to be carefully checked for their probity: for this purpose Ivan placed a letterbox within his court, "box 200," as it was known, for the receipt of denunciations.[84]

One of the oprichnina's first acts was to expropriate many leading boyars and holders of udel domains and to exile them to the region of Kazan. They were not allowed to take movable belongings with them and were escorted by royal troops, but when they arrived new estates were provided for them. In effect, Ivan was treating Kazan as later tsars would treat Siberia: as a distant part of the empire to be assimilated and developed by semioutlaws whose presence too near the center of power was undesirable. However, a few years later Ivan pardoned most of them and let them return to their former estates. He had discovered that he could not govern in utter contravention of the traditions and interests of the ruling class and therefore invited them back, leaving only the most dangerous in banishment. In practice, many of them were unable to resume their former lives on estates now neglected or plundered, and some sold their land to monasteries, which was the precise opposite of what Ivan wished to achieve.[85]

Thereafter the rational element in the creation of the oprichnina lapsed. Ivan's "brotherhood" degenerated into a licensed army of rapacious and cruel brigands, far more damaging to the interests of the state than the boyars and udel princes they had been meant to tame. The most grotesque of their exploits was the destruction of Novgorod in 1570. Ivan betook himself there because of suspicion that the city elders were once more in treasonous contact with Lithuania. His *oprichniki* blockaded the urban precincts, plundered the monasteries, killed most of the monks, and then arraigned leading citizens on charges of treason in kangaroo-court hearings. In the end some 2,000 to 3,000 people were put to death, much of the once wealthy city was destroyed, and its trade was undermined for decades to come. Famine and plague broke out at the same time, so that it is impossible to determine how many deaths were due solely or mainly to oprichnina violence.[86]

Ivan had every intention of carrying out a similar devastation of Pskov, but Nikola, a local "fool in Christ" *(iurodivyi),* warned him that he should cease tormenting people and leave for Moscow; "otherwise your horse will not bear you back." When Ivan removed the bells from the Trinity Cathedral, his horse suddenly fell from under him. Horrified, he broke off the Pskov inquisition and hastened back to Moscow.[87] He may have aspired to be a Renaissance prince, exempted from any normal morality, but all the same he could not remain indifferent either to superstition or to an appeal from the old morality of Rus, staged in such dramatic form.

"Fools in Christ" had existed earlier in Rus and also in Byzantium, but they became more frequent and popular figures during the reign of Ivan IV, and he himself felt a certain respect for them which he evinced for few others. His Cathedral of the Holy Veil in Moscow soon became popularly known as St. Basil's, named after one of them. "Fools in Christ" could be seen as representing an extreme, even grotesque, form of the spiritual and moral ideals of hesychasm, in reaction against the official church militant of Iosif Volotskii and also against Ivan's extreme espousal of *raison d'état.* Exemplifying the words of Paul in 1 Corinthians, "The wisdom of this world is foolishness with God," they practiced radical asceticism, renouncing all pride and even self-respect, defying the world, its hierarchy, and its norms by going about naked and unwashed. But they did this in the name of a special mission, which was to speak truth to the world, and especially to the powerful, as could not be done by those involved in it.[88] The extreme authoritarianism of the Muscovite state was beginning to generate its own counterculture.

Not long after the reverse at Pskov and the sacking of Moscow, Ivan dissolved the oprichnina and thereafter forbade even the mention of its name. Evidently it had become clear to him that it was not fulfilling its function of purifying the land and fortifying his authority. On the contrary, it was sowing destruction and division, making authoritative rule more difficult. Historians have differed profoundly about how it is to be interpreted. Models in Ivan's mind may have included the Spanish Inquisition, the orders of military knights in the Baltic, or even the Jesuits. Alternatively, one could regard it as a kind of artificially created steppe khanate or the de facto revival of an udel principality, where Ivan could rule as in his own domain, unbound by the restraints operating on the sovereign monarch of a Christian realm.[89]

The notion of the oprichnina as a steppe khanate is lent credence by a "happening" which Ivan staged in 1575, when he briefly installed on his throne Simeon Bekbulatovich, a Tatar prince in his service, calling him "grand prince of all Rus" (but not tsar), allowing him to rule over the *zemshchina,* and asking his permission to proceed against traitors in his own udel.[90] Bekbulatovich was the grandson of Akhmat, the last khan to claim leadership of the Golden Horde, so Ivan's act could be seen as a kind of theatrical semiotics, a demonstrative retreat from trying to create the complicated institutions needed by a rising European power, a grotesque restoration of Chingizid legitimacy and of the relative simplicity of the steppe khanates. It was easier to enforce *raison d'état* on an udel domain or a khanate than to gain the consent of the church and the Boyar Duma.

Ivan was a bitterly divided personality, and not only because of his psychological makeup. He was trying to find a new basis for sovereignty, adequate both to the enormously increased size and diversity of his realm and to the grandiose historical mission it claimed to be fulfilling. He wanted to rule according to God's law, but he also felt that princes should have a special dispensation and was determined to possess absolute power, in order to create huge armies without having to humor boyar sensibilities about rank and precedence. His intense piety and dedication to the task he felt God had entrusted to him alternated with periods of grotesque sensuality, sadism, and debauchery in which at times he took a fierce pride, as if to assert that tsars, because of the burdens they bore, could be forgiven for sinning on a grander scale than other men. Underlying this inner turmoil was a threefold outer split between the Third Rome, the steppe khanate, and the aspiring European power, between the pious, God-fearing Byzantine ruler, the

125

horse-borne nomadic warlord, and the rational, ruthless Renaissance prince. All the political and religious traditions of Eurasia seemed to meet and conflict in Ivan's outsize and anguished personality.

When he became tired of the inner conflict, or when he was terrified that his enemies would overthrow him, he sought refuge in the idea of a personal union with Poland, such as had once saved the Lithuanian principality, or even of fleeing to England. He several times pestered Queen Elizabeth with letters sounding her out on the conditions under which he might, if necessary, seek asylum in her realm.[91]

Overall, Ivan's reign revealed in dramatic and even lurid form the paradoxes of the attempt to create a universal empire on the vulnerable and thankless soil of the northeast European plain. In the military sense, Muscovy was becoming a major power. In the economic sense, too, it promised much, because of the abundant resources of its population and territories. But as yet its technology was too primitive to mobilize those resources readily, while the fissile, parochial and patrimonial nature of Russia's inherited social structure still made it difficult to present a united front where it was needed. Given these obstacles, Ivan achieved a great deal, but what he achieved was far outweighed by the human cost, both to himself and to his hapless people.

By the end of his reign, much of central Muscovy was deserted, as peasants fled exorbitant taxes and labor duties to seek either easier conditions on monastic lands or to try their fortune on the open frontier. Many individual boyars were ruined, but as an elite they survived, and their clannish conflicts would continue to weaken the sinews of the state throughout the seventeenth century. Meanwhile the newer service nobility on their *pomestia* had achieved a higher and more durable status, but still had a raw and impecunious air. The clergy were demoralized by heresy hunting, while the townsfolk found themselves ever more heavily taxed, as well as fixed to their abode by "joint responsibility."

Above all, Ivan had not followed through what he had started, the task of creating institutions which would link strong local communities with the central administration and thus mobilize durable public support for the state which had to organize the defense of the whole population. Instead, he had inaugurated a tradition that in order to unite and mobilize, Russian rulers had to be harsh and overbearing, even to violate God's law, to the extent of risking disunity and demoralization, and of undermining the ideals which the monarchy itself professed. In the absence of intermediate institutions and settled laws, the authority of the state in the localities amounted to no more than the private caprice of the notables the monarch had coopted or

appointed there. What he set in motion was not state-building, but the statization of personal dominance. Thus was launched the peculiarly Russian
style of governance: a huge, diverse and vulnerable empire resting on personalized powerbroking.

As if this were not enough, Ivan, who of all people should have realized
the dangers of a disputed royal succession, struck and fatally wounded his
son, Tsarevich Ivan, who had been popular with the *zemshchina,* in a fit of
rage, when the latter tried to protect his pregnant wife from his father's
violence. Ivan himself died in the spring of 1584, in an agony of contrition
over his misdeeds and having taken the vows of a monk. Of his two surviving
sons, one, Dmitrii, was the offspring of his seventh marriage and hence was
not recognized as legitimate by the church, while the other, Fedor, was men-
tally retarded and in poor health.

Under Ivan IV Muscovy had made its first attempt to play a fully Eurasian
geopolitical role. It had been quite unable, however, to create the institutions
needed to sustain such a role. For that reason, at the turn of the sixteenth
and seventeenth centuries, it underwent a crisis which nearly destroyed it.
But it proved, all the same, to have the strength to survive and to make a
second attempt on its Eurasian destiny later.

1. St. Sophia's Cathedral, Novgorod

2. Andrei Rublev's icon of the Holy Trinity

3. Sixteenth-century Novgorod icon of St. George and the dragon

4. Late sixteenth-century German print of Ivan IV

5. A street in seventeenth-century Moscow, from Adam Olearius, *Description of a Journey to Muscovy*, 1663

6. Engraving after the portrait of Peter I by Karl Moor, 1717

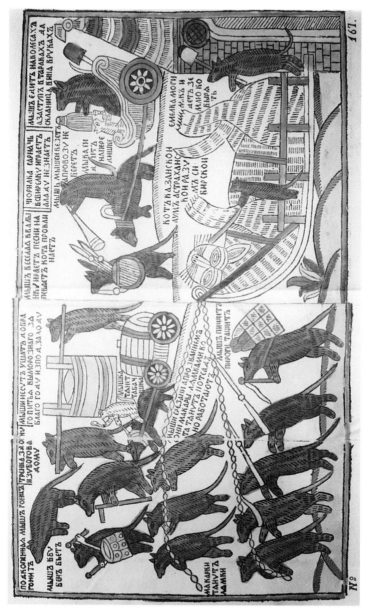

7. Popular print: *The Mice Bury the Cat*

8. Admiralty Wharf: the construction of the Russian navy

9. Nevskii Prospekt, St. Petersburg, in winter

10. Merchants of Nizhnii Novgorod at tea, ca. 1850

11. Old believers from Semonovskii uezd, Nizhnii Novgorod guberniia, late nineteenth
century

12. A peasant ploughing his field, late nineteenth century

13. Peasant officials with land commandant, late nineteenth century

14. Monument to General M. D. Skobelev, Moscow, ca. 1890

15. A Tatar encampment, ca. 1900

16. A village Sunday-school class, addressed by a Baptist preacher

II

The Troubled Building
of Empire

3

THE TURBULENT

SEVENTEENTH CENTURY

THE CREATION OF THE MOSCOW PATRIARCHATE

In spite of ill health, Fedor Ivanovich ruled for fourteen years (1584–1598) while Boris Godunov, brother of his wife, acted as regent. The final symbolic self-elevation of Muscovy took place in the 1580s, when a separate Moscow patriarchate was created. It is significant that this happened at a time when a relatively weak and childless ruler was on the throne and the end of the Riurikovich dynasty seemed likely. Ivan IV had been unwilling to contemplate the possibility of a patriarch at his side, for he feared he would be a rival, a kind of co-sovereign. This was one aspect of the Byzantine imperial tradition which was not welcome in Moscow. But a weak ruler whose line might die out was in a much less strong position to resist the aspirations of the Muscovite church hierarchy.

The patriarch of Constantinople had already confirmed the imperial title of Ivan IV and had addressed him as "Tsar and Sovereign of Orthodox Christians of the whole Universe . . . among Tsars like the apostolic [*ravnoapostol-nyi*] and ever-glorious Constantine." The eastern patriarchs were, however, much more willing to acknowledge Moscow's right to an empire than to a patriarchate, for if a Moscow patriarchate existed, it would outshine their much more venerable ones by virtue of the power, wealth, and independence of the realm to which it would be attached. They ignored Moscow's first request in 1584.

In the end, Moscow resorted to a mixture of cajolery, bribery, and diplomatic pressure to get its way. The Orthodox Church under the Ottomans had lost most of its worldly wealth. When Patriarch Ieremei of Constantinople visited Moscow in 1588, looking for financial help, Muscovite churchmen took the opportunity to persuade him in return to sanction the creation of a Moscow patriarchate. There were two views in Moscow about how this might be done. The proponents of a new Orthodox ecumene hoped that Ieremei might be persuaded to transfer the seat of the ecumenical see itself from Constantinople to Moscow, which would then become formally as well as in practice the leader of world Orthodoxy. The party which one might describe as "Muscovite nationalists," on the other hand, distrusted the Greeks as no longer wholly right-thinking in religious matters, and were therefore determined to have a separate Moscow patriarchate, to which a Russian should be elected. Some of them even schemed to have the ecumenical see and its Greek patriarch transferred to Vladimir, to become subject to Muscovite sovereignty.

Ieremei reacted favorably to the proponents of the ecumenical line but found himself blocked by the Muscovite nationalists. He was not prepared to contemplate being shunted off to Vladimir. However, he did issue a charter recognizing Moscow's right to a patriarchal see, in terms which implied full acceptance of its status as the Third Rome. The Muscovites used this charter to put their case to the Orthodox Church synod in Constantinople, which with reluctance approved the creation of the new patriarchate. The synod, however, insisted that Moscow be the fifth, or lowest-ranking, of all the Orthodox patriarchates, a resolution which could not be shaken by all the generosity and persuasive powers of Muscovy.

In spite of this setback, the significance of the new foundation was enormous. The proclamation announcing the establishment of the Moscow patriarchate was the only document ever issued by a tsar which expressly subscribed to the concept of "Moscow the Third Rome."[1] Moscow was the first patriarchate created in the Orthodox ecumene for over a thousand years, and its appearance symbolically sealed a momentous shift of power which had already taken place within Orthodoxy. It did so, however, in a form which laid bare the full extent of the suspicions and jealousies which poisoned the relations between the Greeks and the Russians—and not only because the texts and liturgical forms used on both sides diverged significantly. The Russians regarded the Greeks as effete and decadent, and their religious practices as having been corrupted by prolonged contact both with the Catholic Church and with infidels. The Greeks, for their part, saw the

Russians as uncouth upstarts, holding more power and earthly wealth than was good for them.[2]

THE END OF THE DYNASTY: A NEW CHALLENGE

When Fedor Ivanovich died in 1598 he left no heir. The ending of the Riurikovich dynasty placed the Muscovite state and the peoples of Rus in a wholly new situation. Up till that time, if we may take the chronicles as a guide, the collective consciousness of Rus had focused on three concepts: the "land of Rus," the princes of Rus, and Orthodox Christianity. It is intriguing that a potential fourth concept, "the people of Rus," was absent, perhaps because of the ethnic diversity of the Rus territories.[3]

Of these concepts, Orthodoxy was the cardinal one, and it illuminated the other two. The grand princes and tsars claimed that their authority derived from God, and embodied this claim symbolically in the coronation ceremony. In the epic poem *Zadonshchina,* which recounts the victory of Moscow over the Golden Horde at Kulikovo, Grand Prince Dmitrii Donskoi is depicted as appealing to "princes, boyars, and all men of courage" to join him and fight for "the land of Rus and the Christian faith," as if the two were inseparable from each other and also from his own title.[4] Even Prince Andrei Kurbskii, when he attacked the tyranny of Ivan IV, did not cast doubt on the God-given monarchy or the special status of the "holy land of Rus": he merely insisted that Ivan had "defiled" both by his debauched and bloodthirsty behavior.[5]

Now, with the end of the dynasty, a vital element in this trinity was removed. Had Moscow developed a strong enough corporate identity to survive without it? That question, more than any other, underlay the turmoil into which Rus was plunged during the ensuing decades. The boyars, the church, the service nobles, townsfolk, Cossacks, and peasants faced a decision about who was to rule over them and, perhaps even more important, how that person was to be chosen and on what moral basis he was to exercise his authority. All grievances and concerns—enserfment, the growing burden of taxes and state service, ethnic assimilation, the defense of the frontier—were subsumed in these two vital questions, posed directly for the first time by the end of the dynasty.

When Fedor Ivanovich came to the throne in 1584, a zemskii sobor had been convened, not to elect him, since he succeeded by inheritance, but to witness and endorse the coronation ceremony which conferred legitimacy on him. On his death in 1598 the patriarch, who in the absence of an obvious successor was the principal authority figure in the country, convened another sobor, this time with a more tangible function, to elect an heir. It chose Boris Godunov, who as regent had in effect been running affairs for most of his predecessor's reign. He was the obvious choice, and there is little reason to doubt that most service people and Moscow townsfolk—crucial in proclaiming a new tsar—favored him. Boris himself twice refused the crown, insisting that his right to it must be unambiguously demonstrated.[6]

The procedure was unprecedented, and hence left room for doubts about the legitimacy of Boris' succession. There were other grounds for such doubts: Dmitrii, Ivan's son by his last wife, had been removed from court and exiled in 1591 to Uglich, where he had died in unexplained circumstances. Suspicion persisted that Boris had ordered his murder in order to eliminate a potential successor to Fedor.

Boris was an able ruler and, in the human qualities needed by a leader, certainly far superior to both his predecessors, but he could never lift from his shoulders the shadow of contested legitimacy. This was unfortunate, since he had little choice but to carry out policies which strengthened the powers of the administration and increased the burdens being borne by all classes of the population. The devastation inflicted by the recent Baltic wars and the need to provide continuous defense, especially on the southern frontiers, made these impositions necessary to the survival of the Muscovite state.

Peasants, threatened by heavy taxes, military service, or labor dues—or a combination of these ills—often found it difficult to cultivate the soil efficiently, fell into debt, and bound themselves to landowners or monasteries who could discharge that debt.[7] They became slaves or were reduced to compulsory labor dues *(barshchina)* on the lord's domain in order to be awarded plots of their own. Alternatively they simply fled, looking for more secure or remunerative service elsewhere, or making for the open frontier, where they could become Cossacks. Many villages in central Russia became almost depopulated, while the landowners, whether boyars or service nobles, who relied on their produce were left without means to defray the burdens of state service. In 1587–88, and again in 1601–1603, famine broke out, huge numbers of beggars swarmed into Moscow, and a naked *iurodivyi* walked the streets denouncing Godunov's government.[8]

Boris, both as regent and then as tsar in his own right, tried desperately to restore both the economy as a whole and the taxes which derived from it for the upkeep of state administration and army. In 1584–1588 the regime was so desperate for revenue that it abolished many of the tax exemptions on monasteries and landlords and instituted a land census, in order to determine the labor and tax obligations which were due under the law. Finally, Boris made the regime for military service personnel on the southern frontiers much more demanding.

It was as a result of these two measures that the progressive enserfment of many peasants took place, together with the fixing of the urban and service population. Hitherto the peasants had still to some extent been free agents: they had been entitled to leave their landowner and seek service elsewhere, provided that they first paid off their debts and that they made their move in the week preceding or following St. George's Day (26 November), when the harvest and all other normal autumn work had been accomplished. Their departure could mean serious difficulties for the holders of service estates, whose land was worthless to them unless they had a labor force to cultivate it. They petitioned the tsar, and from 1580 or 1581 the government began "temporarily" to suspend the St. George's Day entitlement in some regions. The extension of these provisions meant that by the mid-1590s all peasants whose holdings were registered in a land cadastre were officially bound to the land.[9]

During the later years of Boris' reign, however, the chaos gripping the country aggravated the tendency for peasants, and sometimes landowners as well, to ignore all official prohibitions and simply to abscond whenever they saw fit. Townsfolk sometimes did so too, as their obligations were also growing and their freedoms being curtailed. The wide open plains and impenetrable forests made it relatively easy for a bold and hardy traveler to vanish. The treasury began to be deluged with petitions from landowners and urban assemblies asking for the search and return of fugitives, without which taxes could not be paid nor services discharged. As the census was completed in the various localities it became more difficult for their inhabitants simply to disappear, and the task of reclaiming them became a little easier.

Because of the sheer quantity of search petitions, Godunov passed an ukaz in 1597 imposing a deadline of five years on such searches, so that the military and the courts should not become overburdened. In 1607 that period of grace was lengthened to fifteen years. Later in the seventeenth century it would be abolished altogether. In this way the combined pressure of debt, the fiscal needs of the state, and the economic needs of the landowners gradually reduced the peasants from a relatively free state to one of serfdom, which did not differ greatly from slavery.[10]

The power of the state was secured, then, not through institutions of the kind Ivan IV had tried to create, which offered feedback or reflected the aspirations and abilities of local communities, but through the legitimization

135

of personal despotism. Private whim became the transmission belt of political power, rather than state authority mediated through law and institutions. The very term "state" *(gosudarstvo)* retained about it something of the sense of "domain."[11]

To be accepted as legitimate, burdens of this kind would have needed to be imposed by a ruler of unimpeachable authority. Boris was not that. Moreover, he reacted to evil gossip and rumors of conspiracy by setting up a special office to receive and investigate denunciations and by arresting, exiling, and imprisoning his potential opponents. His most obvious boyar rival, Fedor Nikitich, head of the Romanov family, was compelled to take monastic vows under the name of Filaret. Fedor's son, Mikhail, and other members of the family were exiled, and some of them died in circumstances which aroused suspicions of murder.

THE TIME OF TROUBLES

The tsar was "God's anointed," and the state had not become separated from his person. For that reason, and in the absence of intermediate institutions and corporate bodies, the only way opposition could organize and justify itself was by asserting that the person on the throne was a "false tsar" and then rallying round an alternative "real tsar."[12] Boris was especially vulnerable to such a procedure.

Sure enough, in 1603 a young man appeared in Poland, claiming to be Tsarevich Dmitrii, not after all murdered. In reality he was probably Grigorii Otrepev, once a junior boyar, subsequently a monk, and he may have been provoked and aided by the Romanovs to launch his anti-Godunov enterprise. But once he chose Poland as a base, he became the instrument of quite different forces. The Polish church had just created the Uniate Church and wanted to spread it throughout the lands of Rus. The Poles were also anxious to assemble an all-European coalition, to include Moscow, against the Turks and Tatars who permanently menaced their southern frontiers. A Catholic-sponsored tsar on the throne of Muscovy would serve both purposes admirably, and perhaps a union of the two crowns, as earlier with Lithuania, could be engineered.

With the support of Polish magnates and Jesuits, then, and ultimately of the Polish crown, the pseudo-Dmitrii crossed the border into Muscovy, where he attracted a large and diverse following: anti-Godunov boyar clans, hard-pressed service people from the southern frontier, Cossacks reasserting their *volia*, peasants bridling at their new obligations, and the uprooted and hungry generally. Some of them viewed him as a Christlike figure, miraculously resurrected. In effect, Dmitrii provoked an insurrection of southern Muscovy, of those living in and on the edge of the "wild field," those who bore the brunt of the economic crisis and the defense burdens against the more secure and older-established heartlands and the north. Initially he failed to make any headway against government troops sent to repel him, but the sudden and unexpected death of Boris in April 1605 opened the capital city to him.

"Tsar Dmitrii" was proclaimed by the townsfolk, crowned in the Uspenskii Cathedral, and seemed to be well on the way to achieving the aims of his sponsors. However, pious Muscovites soon noted that, though Orthodox himself, he had Jesuit advisers, that he did not observe the strict regimen of Orthodox fasts, and that he had not insisted that Marina, the bride he had brought from Poland, convert to Orthodoxy before their marriage. Besides, there was no way that he could reconcile the disparate and even mutually contradictory demands of his followers. In May 1606 he outraged Orthodox susceptibilities by holding his wedding, with sumptuous feasting and celebration, on Friday, an Orthodox fast day. Boyars who had failed to profit by his succession stirred up discontent, and the townsfolk launched a pogrom of the Polish guests. "Dmitrii" was killed and Marina arrested.

Vasilii Ivanovich Shuiskii, head of one the great boyar clans, was now proclaimed tsar without any kind of sobor. He claimed legitimacy as member of a senior line of the Riurikovich dynasty. But he was no better able than his predecessor to unite the population. Some boyars opposed him from clan rivalry. More serious, most of the Cossacks refused to accept from him the exercise of authority to which they might have submitted from a "true tsar." Their opposition injected a powerful note of social protest into the upheavals. Resistance to Shuiskii was especially fierce, as ever, in the south and east. A runaway slave, Ivan Bolotnikov, raised an army and issued a proclamation, which has not survived, but which evidently called on the poor and oppressed to murder boyars and merchants and to seize their property. Cossacks, escaped slaves and serfs, and discontented service gentry flocked to his banner, and he was able to advance northward far enough to threaten Moscow itself. However, many service nobles, alarmed by the peasants' demands for freedom, deserted Bolotnikov, and Shuiskii managed to rally an army strong enough to defeat him. Shuiskii then installed a police regime, more severe than Godunov's, which restored many fugitives to their masters. He began the registration of serfs, and punished landowners who harbored runaways.

"Pretenderism" had by now become a chronic disease, and another Dmitrii duly appeared, having, as it were, eluded his murderers twice. With genial contempt, he was widely known as the "brigand" *(vor)*. Like his predecessor, he elicited support from Polish nobles, and managed to establish an armed camp at Tushino, just outside Moscow (on the site of what was later the first Moscow airport). There he was joined by many followers of the previous pseudo-Dmitrii, including even Marina, his widow, who claimed to recognize him. He established his own alternative court and set about besieging the capital city. Shuiskii, desperate for the relief of Moscow, appealed for help from the towns of the north and east. He also enlarged the arena of conflict by concluding an agreement with Sweden, ceding territory on the Gulf of Finland in return for military assistance. For the Swedes this was a golden opportunity: they were endeavoring to extend their Karelian territories eastward and southward, and in the long run to take over the heritage of Novgorod to enrich their own poorly endowed homeland. The Poles, on the other hand, were worried that Shuiskii's move placed their own imperial plans in jeopardy, and in May 1609 the Polish Sejm voted funds for King Zygmunt III to intervene to forestall the Swedish advance. While the Swedes helped Shuiskii to advance on Tushino, Polish troops occupied Smolensk.

Shuiskii's campaign broke off when he himself was overthrown by an urban uprising in July 1610. At this point his boyar opponents had just struck a deal with the Poles under which Zygmunt's son Władysław would become tsar in personal union with Poland. At the time this seemed the best way of preserving boyar rule and keeping the lower orders down. The conditions the boyars presented are of great interest as indicating the way in which an aristocracy with a corporate identity might have developed in Russia. They were prepared to see Władysław crowned provided that he undertake to uphold the Orthodox Church (in a later version he was required to convert to Orthodoxy himself) and to guarantee the rights of members of the individual estates to enjoy a fair trial and not to be demoted from their rank without due cause being demonstrated. Supreme power would be shared with a combined Boyar Duma and zemskii sobor *(duma boiar i vseia zemli)*, with whose agreement taxes and the salaries of service people would be set and the award of patrimonial and service estates decided. Such a document could have laid the basis for a constitutional monarchy in personal union with Poland.[13]

To put this agreement into effect, Polish troops were admitted to Moscow, and a large delegation, including Filaret (who had been appointed patriarch by the second "Dmitrii" and then deposed by Shuiskii in favor of his own candidate, Germogen), proceeded to Smolensk to meet Zygmunt and negotiate the details of the accession of his son. To their dismay, Zygmunt passed over Władysław's ambitions, announcing that he intended to rule himself and to combine the Muscovite and Polish thrones. The delegates sent for the advice of Patriarch Germogen, who warned them to accept no arrangement which did not require the new tsar to convert to Orthodoxy. He followed up his warning by issuing a public announcement that no one should take an oath of loyalty to a Roman Catholic ruler. The negotiations broke down, and the leaders of the Muscovite delegation were imprisoned by the Poles, among them Germogen, who died in his cell in January 1612.

Subsequent events suggest that Germogen's appeal was a cardinal turning point. Orthodoxy had the capacity to unite the various strata of Muscovite society in a way that no other force could. The message of Metropolitan Makarii about Rus's special mission as an Orthodox power, repeated in every church pulpit over the decades, had borne its fruit. The boyars, hitherto undisputed trustees of the realm at times of crisis or disputed succession, had lost the key to that power: their attempt to overcome their own differences by bringing in a Polish king made them look weak, divided, and treacherous.

So someone else had to generate the degree of national unity and purpose necessary to calm social upheaval and expel the foreigners. In 1610–11 it looked like an impossible task. All the same, it was accomplished. The decisive actors were the church and the mir communities of the north and east, the regions of Muscovy's newly acquired wealth and those least affected by the troubles. Before his death Germogen had begun to send letters to elders of the city assemblies calling on them to raise a "militia of the land" (zemskaia rat) to prevent the infidels from finally taking over in Moscow. After his death, Avraamii Palitsyn, cellarer of the Holy Trinity Monastery, took over and continued his efforts.

The first attempt to raise a "militia of the land" broke down on the irreconcilable conflict of interests between Cossacks and fugitives on the one hand, who wanted the full restoration of volia, and on the other the merchants, clergy, service nobility, and boyars, who reckoned that Rus could not survive without some kind of service state. The Riazan landowner Prokopii Liapunov, who tried to head the militia, was murdered by Cossack leaders impatient with his demands.

However, a second attempt was made. In September 1611 the elders of Nizhnii Novgorod, led by a merchant, Kuzma Minin, proclaimed the establishment of a militia (opolchenie) and opened correspondence with other cities, appealing for subscriptions for it. "Let us be together of one accord . . . Orthodox Christians in love and unity, and let us not tolerate the recent disorders, but fight untiringly to the death to purge the state of Muscovy from our enemies, the Poles and Lithuania."[14] The scion of an old princely family was appointed to lead the militia: Prince Dmitrii Pozharskii.

It is significant that the movement for national revival was inaugurated in Nizhnii Novgorod. Called after the original leading trade center of old Rus, it was the entrepôt where the riches of the northern forests, lakes, and rivers reached the Volga and the commercial arteries of the country. It was a major focus of Rus's wealth and her communications system, one whose self-government had not been destroyed by the depredations of the service state and which had kept out of the bitter social conflict of the preceding years.

The Nizhnii Novgorod program rejected the idea of rule by the "brigand or any of his followers" or by non-Orthodox Christians. On this basis it proved possible to assemble a military council representative of the elites of Rus. Pozharskii gathered his militia at Iaroslavl, a large town on the Volga much closer to Moscow, where even some of the Cossacks joined him, at the urging of Palitsyn. From there he was able to storm the capital city and expel the Polish garrison in October 1612. Meanwhile the military council had sent out invitations to all towns and districts to send their "best, most sensible and trustworthy people," each equipped with a mandate, to a "council of the land" (sovet vseia zemli), which would elect a new tsar.

At that council in February 1613 Mikhail Romanov, son of Filaret, was elected tsar. This solemn event has often been represented as the final stage in the rallying of Russian national forces and as marking the end of the Time of Troubles. In fact, it was a close-run thing, and it left Russian society still riven by conflict, while substantial tracts of territory remained in the hands of foreign powers. Many of the boyars were in favor of inviting a member of a foreign royal family to assume the Russian throne, on the assumption that an outsider would be able to mediate between boyar clans better than a native appointee, who would inevitably be a member of one of them. Once the Poles had been driven out of Moscow, the obvious candidate was Karl Philipp, younger brother of Gustav Adolphus of Sweden. One invitation addressed to him specifically appealed to him "so that, having him as sovereign, the Russian state might as before be in peace and tranquillity, and that bloodshed might cease." One is reminded of the East Slav tribes calling in the Varangians centuries before with the same motive in mind. Some of Karl's supporters wished to stipulate that he convert to Orthodoxy before mounting the throne. Others did not even insist on that condition: the mood in Russia was markedly less anti-Protestant than it was anti-Catholic.

At the beginning of 1613 opinion in the sobor favored Karl Philipp, but then Cossacks and townsfolk demonstrated in Moscow against the idea of a foreign candidate. They accused the boyars of wanting to elect someone unfamiliar with Russia so that they could run the country in their own interests and draw the lion's share of the revenues. The demonstrators' candidate was Mikhail Romanov. Since he was a member of the family from whom Ivan IV had taken his first wife, and nephew of the last Riurikovich tsar, his election would represent something as close to a return to pre-Trouble traditions as could be devised, and its proponents played up this advantage by broadcasting the myth that Tsar Fedor Ivanovich had on his deathbed bequeathed the throne to Fedor Nikitich Romanov, Mikhail's father (Metropolitan Filaret, currently in Polish captivity).[15]

Avraamii Palitsyn also spoke in favor of Mikhail. According to him, "many of the gentry and lesser boyars, merchants from many towns, atamans, and Cossacks all came openly and declared to him their opinions, bringing their written depositions concerning the election of the tsar, asking him to convey them to the ruling boyars and commanders." Avraamii did this. According to the official account, "they listened, and thanked God for such a glorious beginning." The next day Mikhail was duly elected, in spite of concerns about his youth (he was barely seventeen) and inexperience, and also about the danger of having a close relative of the tsar in Polish captivity.[16]

Never at any stage was there a suggestion of presenting the new tsar with any conditions or restrictions on his authority. Most participants in the council evidently felt that the overriding necessity was to have an authoritative ruler at all, someone whose sway would be generally acknowledged. Becoming tsar at this juncture was a hazardous and in many respects thankless undertaking, and Mikhail, currently in residence at the family estate at Kostroma, could only with difficulty be persuaded to assume the responsibility at all. He had to be assured that his candidacy had received widespread support and that the provisional government would be able to clear the roads and villages of marauding bands, so that he could be secure on his journey to Moscow to his coronation.[17]

No sooner had Mikhail accepted the poisoned chalice and undergone the coronation ceremony than he had to send to all the towns not occupied by foreign troops asking them to contribute supplies and a supplementary tax levy to begin the task of putting the army into proper shape, suppressing maverick Cossack bands, capturing brigands, restoring law and order, and reviving the economy of the devastated country. He also asked the Stroganov family for a special contribution from their lucrative enterprises in the Urals, which was granted. Once again the wealth of the recently conquered and barely assimilated eastern lands came to the rescue of the jeopardized heartland. Without its newly acquired territories it is clear that Russia could not have survived the Time of Troubles. The northern forests, the Volga lands, and Siberia had saved it from being partitioned among Sweden, Poland, and the Ottoman Empire. Russia as Eurasian empire was becoming a reality, and its European and Asian portions were mutually dependent.[18]

EXPANSION EASTWARD

Assimilation of the peoples of the former Kazan and Astrakhan khanates gave Muscovite Rus its first experience of colonial administration. Russian merchants, clergymen, Cossacks, and peasants were all encouraged to settle in the newly acquired regions, to establish a strong Russian ethnic presence there, to take advantage of the new economic opportunities created by the conquest of the entire Volga basin, and to build and man fortresses on the new frontier.

Once they had suppressed early revolts aimed at restoring the khanates, the Muscovite authorities adopted a tolerant policy toward the main local ethnic groups, the Mari, Chuvash, Cheremis, Mordvins, and Udmurts. They were given the status of "*iasak* people"—people subject to tribute—which meant that they could not become serfs or slaves. Officials were instructed "not to embitter" them, and to show "benevolence and friendliness" in collecting the tribute. An early campaign of conversion to Orthodoxy was swiftly abandoned, since it seemed likely to stir resentment and thus undermine peace and order. At the same time, the local peoples were forbidden to bear weapons, and had to give hostages for good behavior.

An effort was made to persuade the Tatar *murzy* (nobles) to convert to Orthodoxy, but it was not pressed beyond the point of provoking hostility, and even those Tatars—the majority—who remained Muslims were admitted to the Russian imperial nobility. This concession had the strange and presumably unintended effect that in some places Muslim landowners were able legally to enserf Russian Christian peasants. There could be no clearer sign that, as early as the late sixteenth century, the Russian Empire was beginning to take precedence over the embryonic Russian nation.[19]

By the mid-seventeenth century, social stratification in the Volga region was onion-shaped, with Russians predominating in the relatively small uppermost and lowest tiers, and the indigenous people occupying the much larger middle ones. The lowest stratum consisted of private serfs, mostly failed settlers, lower in status than the *iasak* people. Religious and ethnic assimilation mostly tended upward, which meant that some Russians were drawn toward Islam or animism. On the other hand, it became progressively more difficult for non-Russians to move into the highest tier without converting to Orthodoxy.[20]

But by this time the frontier had moved on. After the conquest of the Volga khanates, the way lay open across the central and southern stretches of the Urals to the rich forests, lakes, and river country which Novgorod and Moscow had already begun to exploit from the north. In 1558 a certain Grigorii Stroganov, member of a wealthy former peasant family which had founded a successful saltworks at Solvychegodsk, received a charter from Ivan IV allowing him to colonize "empty lands" along the Kama River, with exemption from taxes and customs for twenty years, in return for providing for the defense of the frontier against Nogai and Tatar horsemen. Here in the following decades the Stroganovs established a commercial family empire, still focusing on the extraction of salt but extending to fishing, hunting, mining, and agricultural operations. They defended their acquisitions with fortified towns, manned by musketeers, as was stipulated in their charter.[21]

Kuchum, the khan of Siberia, however, whose capital, Isker, lay on the far side of the Urals, regarded this territory as his own, and launched persistent raids, using troops recruited from among the native Mansi and Khanty people. The Stroganovs brought in Cossacks to assist in defense. Among them was a certain Ermak Timofeevich from the Don, who was on the run, having participated in a raid on the Nogai which had subsequently been disavowed by the tsar. Encouraged by the Stroganovs, Ermak in 1582 led an expedition across the Urals, which not only proved successful in harrying the Siberian Tatar troops, but actually captured Isker in the face of a much larger army (though probably one without firearms).[22]

The tsar was quick to recognize the potential significance of Ermak's victory and sent supplies, reinforcements, and a military governor (voevoda) to consolidate it. They arrived only after the Cossacks had already pulled back, constantly harried by Tatar troops and having lost Ermak in an ambush in August 1584. However, the newcomers built a fortress at Tiumen, on the Tura River, in 1586, and the following year another at Tobolsk, on the westernmost bend of the Irtysh. Local Tatar princes and their vassals were drawn into the tsar's service. Together with the Cossacks, they inflicted the final defeat on Kuchum in 1598 and subjugated his khanate.

The way now lay open into the flatlands of Siberia. By 1620 Russian troops were beginning to colonize an area stretching up to the Enisei valley, in 1627 they built a fortress at Krasnoiarsk, in 1632 another at Iakutsk, on the River Lena, in 1643 they discovered Lake Baikal, and by 1648 an advance party had reached the Pacific coast at the bay of Okhotsk.

The Expansion of Muscovy, 1550–1700

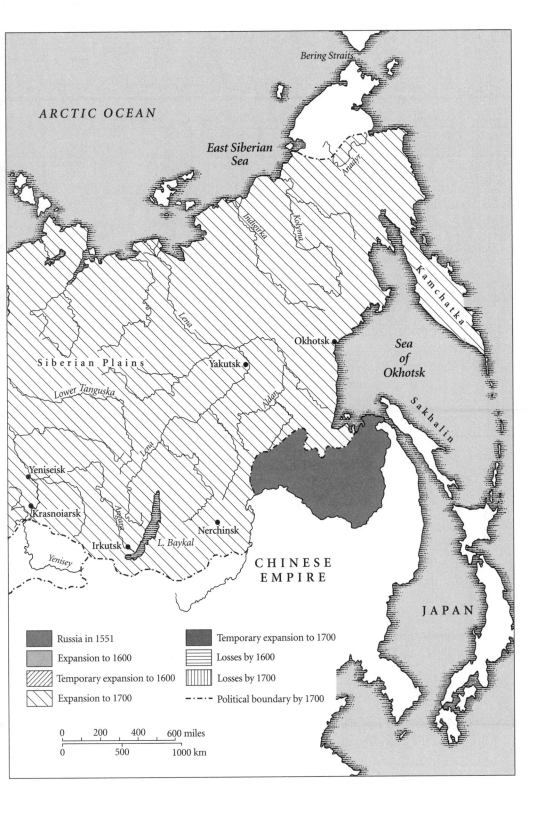

ARCTIC OCEAN

East Siberian
Sea

Bering Straits

Anadyr

Indigirka

Kolyma

Kamchatka

Okhotsk

Sea
of
Okhotsk

Lena

Siberian Plains

Yakutsk

Lower Tunguska

Aldan

Sakhalin

Lena

Yeniseisk

Angara

Krasnoiarsk

Nerchinsk

Irkutsk

L. Baykal

CHINESE
EMPIRE

JAPAN

Yenisey

Russia in 1551

Expansion to 1600

Temporary expansion to 1600

Expansion to 1700

Temporary expansion to 1700

Losses by 1600

Losses by 1700

Political boundary by 1700

| 0 | 200 | 400 | 600 miles |

| 0 | 500 | | 1000 km |

Of course, by no stretch of the imagination could this thrust into the wilds be called territorial occupation. The bands of adventurers who accomplished the initial explorations were Cossacks and freebooters, prepared to risk their lives for the huge profits which could be made, either out of booty seized from the natives or from the fur trade. The courts of Renaissance Europe were hungry for the more exotic types of fur—marten, sable, ermine—which had long ago been exterminated farther west. Bringing back a few samples of the right kind of pelt could set up a merchant for life. The state's fur revenue tripled between 1589 and 1605, and had grown eightfold by the 1680s, at which stage it constituted a tenth of total revenues. The prized animals were soon severely depleted by hunting, which helps to explain the rapidity with which the eastward movement took place. In one sense, the colonization of Siberia was a kind of "fur fever," analogous to the California gold rush of the mid-nineteenth century.[23]

The native tribes were in no position to prevent this exploitation of their territories, since they had no firearms and no tradition of acting in common. Tribes were often divided one from another by ancient and bitter feuds. Some of them in any case welcomed the newcomers, who appeared to pay them generously for furs whose value they counted at very little. Others, however, fought hard within their limited means, especially the Samoieds, in the Arctic regions of western Siberia, and the Buriats, Tungus, and Iakuts farther east. Resistance and rebellion were always crushed ruthlessly, using whatever forces were to hand. Thereafter the settlers, and later the voevody and their officials, would coopt the tribal leaders as their agents in collecting *iasak*. A few hostages would be taken from each tribe until the required number of pelts was handed over.

Russian officials recognized the exposed situation of the settlers and did what they could to avoid alienating or provoking the natives. For the most part, their beliefs, traditions, and legal systems were left untouched, though the *iasak* levies inevitably put some strain on these. According to standing instructions from the Siberian Chancellery (set up in 1637), the levies, as in the Volga, were to be taken "with kindness and not with cruelty"—but in practice that meant only if kindness sufficed: if necessary, punitive expeditions would be dispatched to chase up the required contributions.[24]

"Settlement," then, meant the construction of a wooden stockaded fort (*ostrog*), a church, an administrative office for tax and recruitment officials, and a few dwelling places. Much of the Russian "settler" population was in fact on the move, looking for better opportunities elsewhere or fleeing justice back home. Some peasants came to settle in southwestern Siberia, where the soil was relatively fertile and the climate not quite so harsh as farther east and north. On the other hand, the sheer size and remoteness of the region made it a paradise for fugitives and vagabonds—those escaping from serfdom, or uncaptured brigands, whose depredations on both natives and settlers gave Siberian life something of a "wild east" quality.[25] Brigands who had been captured also tended to finish up there, since from an early stage Russian officials used the region as a place of exile for convicted criminals and prisoners of war, many of whom were drafted into the Cossacks, and were then expected to keep order against their own kind!

147

The acquisition of such a huge territory transformed the nature of the emerging Russian state. By the mid-seventeenth century—within a few decades of the Time of Troubles—the realm still widely known as Muscovy had become the largest empire on earth, with a greater diversity of peoples, religions, climates, and economies than any rival. It was tempting to interpret this achievement as a fulfillment of the promise of its status as "holy Rus." On the other hand, none of the newly assimilated peoples were Christian: Russia had become a Eurasian empire populated not only by Orthodox believers, but by numerous animists, Buddhists, and Muslims. It had annexed territories containing untold wealth in human and natural resources, but little of that wealth could be exploited, because of the immense distances and the rigors of the climate. Instead the Russian authorities used Siberia as a kind of dumping ground for the delinquent and the unwanted. It became a huge appendage which never knew cardinal features of Russian life, such as the service gentry and serfdom. At the same time, defending it was an extremely onerous responsibility, since the endless migration eastwards had left an enormously long southern frontier, running undefended for thousands of miles over steppe and desert. It was the most dramatic instance of Russia's tendency, determined by her geopolitical situation, to expand to fill out the territory available—freed on this occasion by the collapse of all the successors to the Mongol Empire—until she fetched up against either insurmountable natural frontiers or another power strong enough both to put up effective resistance and to offer a stable political border.

The Pacific Ocean afforded a natural frontier (though even then, only for a century or so, till Russian explorers pushed further, across the straits into Alaska). The political border was provided by China, undoubtedly a great power, even if in the 1650s one not yet fully recovered from its own "time of troubles" following the collapse of the Ming dynasty. Its tribulations allowed a Cossack force under Erofei Khabarov to establish itself in the Amur River basin, which lay beyond what might be seen as the natural frontier between northeastern Eurasia and China, the Iablonoi and Stanovoi mountain ranges. Here was a kind of Pacific Riviera, warmer and more fertile than anywhere in Siberia, a potential granary to feed the population of its frozen wastes, and it also offered a convenient commercial route to the Pacific. Khabarov defeated the local tribes and established a tribute-collecting system. When aggrieved tribal leaders turned to China he was able to fend off early attacks by improvised Chinese frontier forces. By the time the new Manchu dynasty had completed its conquest of China and had had time to react to the news that "man-devouring demons" were at large on the Amur, the Russians were quite well ensconced there and colonists were beginning to arrive in large numbers.

At first the Russians were unresponsive to diplomacy. They rejected a Chinese offer of guaranteed trade in return for withdrawal from the Amur basin. However, once the Manchus had mobilized a large army, enough to besiege and storm the Russian fortress of Albazin in 1685, this intransigence had to be reconsidered. The territory was simply too far away from European Russia to be defended against a determined adversary of any size. Besides, the Russians had done little to endear themselves to the indigenous tribes. The Treaty of Nerchinsk (1689) represented just the kind of deal the Russians had begun by rejecting: they were required to evacuate the entire Amur basin in return for trading privileges along a regular caravan route which entered China at Kiakhta, on the Selenga River. It was stipulated that leaders of official caravans should perform the kowtow before the Chinese emperor.[26] This was to be the basis of Russo-Chinese relations for two centuries.

WHY MUSCOVY SURVIVED

For the first two decades of the seventeenth century, the Muscovite state was threatened with outright destruction. That it survived at all was owing to three main factors: (1) the strength and solidarity of local mir communities of town and country; (2) the wealth originating in the northeast and from across the Urals, which financed the popular militias; and (3) the popular standing of the Orthodox Church, which enabled it to act as a focus for the loyalty of different social classes with mutually conflicting interests.

The eventual military victory of the militias and the successful convening of a zemskii sobor showed that the tendency to social disintegration in Muscovy could be overcome and that there was a potential state-bearing people of Rus. In the most representative of all its assemblies that people chose to restore autocratic monarchy—that is, a monarchy derived from God and constrained by God's law alone, not by any earthly laws, agreements, or institutions.

The degree of devastation suffered by the country during the Time of Troubles can scarcely be exaggerated, especially since it compounded an economic decline which had set in during the second half of Ivan IV's reign. Both the destruction wrought by war and the mutual distrust generated by anarchy and banditry brought even small-scale economic exchange to an end over large areas of central and southern Russia. The towns were especially hard hit, and some took a century or more to recover. Only in the north and east, where the depredations of strife were less severe, did something like normal economic life continue. As a result, these regions, and the new wealth of Siberia, were to be the main sources of state revenue for much of the seventeenth century.[27]

149

Once survival was assured and the sinews of the administration had begun to recover, the unsettled questions of the sixteenth century reasserted themselves. What was Muscovite Russia's mission? There were three possible visions of its identity: (1) as the center of an East Christian ecumene, replacing Byzantium as the guarantor of Orthodoxy; (2) as a Russian nation-state, that is, a national home for all East Slavs; and (3) as a north Eurasian multiethnic empire and European great power.

For most of the seventeenth century, these three visions haunted statesmen and prelates, not as distinct and separate programs, but rather intertwined in enticing and hopeful patterns. The trouble is, they were not wholly compatible, as gradually became clear.

URBAN LIFE

Most trade and industry was limited in scope, conducted for a local village and small-town market by peasants during the long season of the year when agriculture and fishing were difficult or impossible. Itinerant merchants conducted more distant commerce at trade fairs held periodically in the larger towns. The greatest of these fairs was held every July and August from 1624 at Nizhnii Novgorod, whose location gave it ready access by river to markets extending from the Baltic to the Middle East.[28]

A few large towns were also opening trading centers, *gostinye dvory*, or "guest courts," where merchants offered their wares under arcades, in rows of stalls, each row specializing in some particular class of product. The actual "guests" *(gosti)* were not confined to the arcades: they were large-scale merchants who possessed a license to carry on foreign trade, to run the mint, and to administer the main customs houses. They also possessed the crucial privilege of distilling liquor, as well as being freed from billeting duty, from certain taxes, and from the obligation to surrender horses or carriages to the postal service. They had the right to have their affairs and their litigation dealt with by the tsar or his personal representative rather than by the Boyar Duma or the chanceries. In other words, their status equalled that of the most favored courtiers, though their fortunes, not being in land, were far less secure and seldom outlasted a generation.[29]

150

At any one time there were very few of them, seldom more than thirty in the whole empire, though the subordinate merchant "hundreds," the *gostinnaia sotnia* and the *sukonnaia sotnia,* contained far more, with more modest privileges. Most *gosti* lived in Moscow, and, apart from their own trade, they were required to administer the imperial monopolies, which included most of the more lucrative branches of commerce, such as furs, salt, dyes, potash, leather, and of course vodka. Since trading in these commodities involved receiving excise payments and delivering them to the treasury, these merchants often contracted to collect other forms of tax as well—in other words became imperial tax-farmers.[30]

Most international trade was conducted through foreign merchants, who had much readier access to credit and shipping than Russian ones. The Russian merchants resented foreign domination of their most lucrative commerce, and from time to time petitioned the tsar to curtail it, on the grounds that foreign competitors did not have to bear equivalent burdens. The tsar usually ignored these requests, as foreign merchants were much better than domestic ones at raising loans and at acquiring arms or luxury goods when needed. The *gosti* dealt with them at the ports. Vasilii Shorin, for example, dealt with Dutch and English traders at Arkhangelsk and with oriental ones at Astrakhan. He would sell them furs, hides, hemp, and tallow in return for their wares, usually luxury items like velvet, satin, silk, paper, spices, and dyes, for which he could find a ready and lucrative market at court and in the larger towns. He also operated an internal trading business in more mundane but essential items such as fish, salt, and grain. For all these purposes he ran a fleet of rivergoing merchant vessels.[31]

Not even this highest category of traders had their own autonomous corporation. Such organizations as they and their inferiors possessed, the *sotni,* or "hundreds," were set up and maintained by the state as agencies for royal monopolies and certain types of official service, such as tax-farming and moneylending. The risks they ran were considerable: robbery, fire, and shipwreck were endemic, and there was no insurance industry. Contracts and loans were quite often not honored and were almost impossible to enforce, unless one had a powerful patron. For many reasons, therefore, merchant families took care to keep their links with the court and the great boyar families in good repair. As far as trade and industry were concerned, patronage and protection did the duty of credit and contract.[32]

Nor were there any institutions which represented the whole urban population. The lower urban orders were known as *posad* people: a *posad* had originally been a suburb or quarter of a city, but gradually came to denote those people, other than officially registered merchants, who owned commercial or industrial property within the city walls. They had their own assembly and their own functions, for the discharge of which they were jointly responsible: these included building and maintaining roads and bridges, collecting taxes and excise payments, and acting as constables, watchmen, and firefighters. These duties were onerous and unpaid. It was a constant grievance of the *posad* people that they faced competition from landowners or merchants who did not shoulder comparable burdens.[33]

At the lowest level of urban society were the slaves. There were slaves already in the city-states of Kievan Rus, but their number increased markedly during the sixteenth and seventeenth centuries. At their maximum number, in the early seventeenth century, slaves probably constituted some 10 percent of the population. At the same time, the nature of slavery changed: indenture (limited service contract slavery) became more common, though in practice this tended to become full slavery when slaves could not buy themselves out or pay off their debts.

Unusually, in Muscovy slaves belonged to the same East Slav ethnos as their owners. Such a situation is historically anomalous: slaves are not normally conationals of those who possess them. Perhaps as a result, Muscovite slaves had somewhat greater rights of property and judicial process than slaves elsewhere. They could sue and be sued, for example, and they always enjoyed the same right as free people to participate in the rituals of the Orthodox Church.

One could become a slave through being captured in war, through indebtedness, or through selling oneself. Relatively speaking, the last was very common in Muscovy. People sold themselves because they were hungry or had no other means of social support. The constant wars and the open nature of the terrain weakened extended families, and for those who fell upon hardship the easiest way out was often to attach oneself as a slave to the wealthy or powerful. Slavery also meant an escape from taxation, from military service, and from other official obligations. There was a large increase in the number of slaves during the difficult later decades of the sixteenth century, and especially during the famine years 1568–1570 and 1601–1603. Slavery, in short, was a form of welfare provision in a society where kinship ties were relatively weak and the state made no provision.

During the seventeenth century, the government began trying to restrict slavery among the peoples it colonized as a result of imperial expansion. In the 1649 *Ulozhenie* (Law Code), for example, there are several articles protecting Tatars and others from enslavement, presumably in order to ensure their continuing status as *iasak* people, payers of tribute.

Slavery declined further during the later seventeenth century. As the state became stronger, it was anxious to be able to tax and recruit a greater proportion of the population, and therefore ceased to provide legal defense of slavery. In 1700, for example, absconded slaves serving in the army were simply allowed to remain there. At the same time, "wandering" *(guliashchie)* people, without social classification, were required to register in the taxable estates, which usually meant becoming a peasant-serf. When the government moved from taxing by sown area to taxing by household, peasants responded by living in larger households, which tended to absorb slaves, or at least to make it unnecessary for the indigent to depart and sell themselves. Finally, as happened in the late Roman Empire, the status of peasant degraded into serfdom and become almost undistinguishable from slavery; in 1723 the two estates were amalgamated. Confusion persisted long thereafter, as can be seen from the fact that serfs were often sold as chattels, without land, in spite of official efforts to restrict the practice.

At the same time the government was opening the first almshouses and requiring monasteries to make better provision for the indigent, especially old soldiers without means of subsistence. Landowners were being enjoined to set up granaries for famine relief. In other words, the welfare functions of slavery were being taken over by others.[34]

RECOVERY FROM THE TIME OF TROUBLES

After the Time of Troubles the mood among most people—except those, like brigands and some Cossacks, with a direct interest in disorder—was naturally to yearn for peace and prosperity. As the zemskii sobor of 1613 showed, they were profoundly conservative in outlook and sought stability in a restoration of *starina*, the "old days" (even though they had not found those "old days" so attractive at the time). They recreated—or rather created—a monarchy with unlimited authority of a kind Ivan IV had aspired to but had never been able to achieve. The boyars and churchmen who had obstructed Ivan now supported untrammeled autocracy to protect them against social rebellion and foreign invasion.

Mikhail Romanov (1613–1645) chose to exercise his powers in close partnership with both the "land" and the church. He owed his power to both: he saw advantages in regularizing the relationship, and in practice he probably had no alternative, given the extent of the problems facing the country and the resources needed to overcome them. Besides, the patriarch, Filaret, was his own father. Mikhail gave him the title "Great Sovereign and Patriarch" and left him complete authority over the territories and functions subject to the church. Filaret used these powers and the enhanced standing of the church to make himself the senior partner in what, while he was alive, was a ruling duumvirate (1619–1633). The basic policy of the two was to continue the cooperation of church and "land" which had generated national unity, to ensure that taxes and dues were equitably allocated and that service nobles were held to their obligations.[35] As we shall see, the need for a practical and fair allocation of the service burdens in time generated a bureaucracy capable of carrying out the requisite censuses and cadasters.

The first essential was to get rid of the importunate foreigners and restore the integrity of the state. This could not be achieved without cost. The Treaty of Stolbovo (1617), which ended the war with Sweden, brought Novgorod back into Muscovite territory, together with Swedish recognition of the tsar's title, but it also ceded Ingermanland and eastern Karelia and left Sweden dominating the Baltic Sea, including its eastern extremity, for another century.

The Poles proved even less accommodating. They were unwilling to acknowledge Mikhail's title, and in 1617–18 they launched another military offensive, which brought them to the walls of Moscow itself. However, they lacked the stamina for a long siege, and in the end both sides agreed to an armistice and an exchange of prisoners—which, among other things, set Filaret free to play his role in government. Moscow ceded Chernigov, Smolensk, and some other western territories.

This precarious peace confirmed what was already obvious: that the country's most urgent task was to put its army in a condition to face its major foes. The cavalry levies which were adequate to cope with steppe nomads could not face up to a modern infantry regiment, equipped with the latest firearms and trained to move in close formation. The *streltsy*, who were supposed to be the Muscovite equivalent, were part-time soldiers, more accustomed to internal security duties and to standing guard at court than to the heavy fire and rapid maneuvering of modern warfare.

The limitations of the army manifested themselves when Moscow tried to take advantage of Polish involvement in the Thirty Years' War to regain Smolensk in 1632–1634. To prepare for the campaign, Moscow signed on foreign mercenary infantry—at great expense, for they were in high demand elsewhere in Europe—and purchased huge quantities of iron and lead for casting cannon and making bullets. Dutch specialists were invited to build a modern arsenal in Tula. Anxious for quick success, so that the mercenaries could be released, the Muscovite commander, Boyar M. B. Shein, committed all his troops to the siege of Smolensk, but was unable to take it because he could not move his heavy artillery into the required positions. In the face of setbacks, his mercenaries began to desert en masse: they lacked the commitment and tenacity of the Polish defenders.[36]

Moscow needed, then, its own standing infantry forces, trained in the latest military tactics, to generate its own esprit de corps and to sustain protracted operations. From the 1640s musketbearing infantrymen were recruited inside Russia as well as from abroad, and were trained according to a handbook imported from the Netherlands: usually commanded by foreigners, these "new model" regiments took the brunt of the fighting against European armies.

Their recruitment was on a new basis. Whereas previously landowners had been expected to provide soldiers for campaigning in proportion to the amount of land they held, henceforth soldiers were recruited on the basis of the number of households. The quantity was easier to compute, and the system accommodated itself readily to "joint responsibility." One recruit per twenty households was a typical expectation. As a result many more soldiers were being recruited from among the common people than previously, and they served for much longer. By the 1680s the army was probably about 200,000 strong, or roughly double its size a century earlier. The population had certainly not doubled in the meantime, so the military participation rate among adult males had increased sharply, perhaps to as high as 4–5 percent. Desertion became much commoner, and if a culprit could not be found, his community had to supply a substitute. Deserters often figured in civil disorders.[37]

To finance this military expansion, taxation was screwed up to the maximum. Salt was perhaps the most easily taxable item, since it was highly visible at its point of production and was traded everywhere. In 1646 Tsar Aleksei imposed a uniform and high rate of salt tax to replace a variety of commercial dues. The new levy turned out to be a disaster. Not only did it provoke "salt riots" in Moscow in 1648, but it disrupted the salt trade, as Olearius reported. "A year later . . . it was necessary to calculate how many thousands had been lost on salt fish—used in Russia more than meat—that spoiled because it was not properly preserved, owing to the high price of salt. Besides, much less salt was sold than before, and remained in the packing houses, it turned into brine and dribbled away."[38]

On top of existing dues, "musketeers' money" *(streletskie dengi)* was levied, in cash or kind, throughout the century. Additional special levies were imposed seven times in the early years of Mikhail and eight times between 1654 and 1680, falling especially heavily on townspeople. Most of this income was spent on the army: in 1679–80, for example, some 700,000 rubles, or 62 percent of the total budget estimates. And this is to ignore compulsory labor duties imposed on the population—again, especially in the towns—such as cartage and the upkeep of roads and bridges.[39]

Russia was becoming a "fiscal-military state" to an even greater extent than any other in Europe. Its whole social structure was determined by the need to recruit soldiers, to levy taxes, and to impose state service of various kinds.[40] In addition, it was now trying to enforce an official morality restricting gambling, heavy drinking, performances of *skomorokhi,* and illicit liquor brewing and salt refining. It aimed to track down vagrants and escaped slaves or serfs, fix their location, and register them. To carry out all these roles, it needed an increasingly elaborate and differentiated bureaucracy. The system of *prikazy,* or chanceries, evolved haphazardly, as we have seen, initially from the exchequer of the tsar's domain lands. Some of them were responsible for administering particular territories, such as the *Kazanskii prikaz* or the *Sibirskii prikaz.* Some had specific functions, some of which we have already observed, such as the Petitions Chancery, the Treasury Chancery, and the Ambassadors' Chancery. The *pomestnyi prikaz* oversaw the grant of service estates and the fulfillment of obligations springing from them: it began to employ surveyors to establish boundaries and to arbitrate the disputes arising from them. The *razriadnyi prikaz* drew up and monitored military service rosters. The *razboinyi prikaz* supervised the investigation and prosecution of serious crimes, such as murder and robbery. And there were many others. One of the most important was set up in 1654: the *prikaz tainykh del* (Secret Chancery) reported directly to the tsar and supervised other chanceries for him.[41]

The proliferation of bureaus employed a growing stratum of clerks and other official personnel. By the mid-seventeenth century some 1,600 people were employed in the central and local offices of the chanceries; by 1700 their number had risen to 4,600. Their operations entailed an increasingly impersonal and rule-bound method of transacting official business, one which always risked affronting the susceptibilities of a people who were used to seeing monarchical power as personal and exercised according to traditional or divinely ordained moral norms.[42]

In the localities the voevoda had representatives of the more important chanceries attached to him and was supposed to oversee their interaction with the institutions of the "land," especially the *guba*, the mir, and the volost. In practice the voevoda and his assistants dominated this relationship, since he had far more resources at his command than the tiny mir and volost assemblies.

All this did not mean that the state ran everything. It could not, nor did it try to. On the contrary, it had to work with local communities to keep order and to mobilize the country's resources as efficiently as possible. The communities had to decide the precise distribution of the various burdens, and their elected officials had to put those decisions into effect, in the process acting both as representatives of the community and as low-level officials of the government. Among these dual-function officials were the collectors of excise and liquor tax, the elders in charge of administration *(zemskii starosta)* and of criminal justice *(gubnoi starosta)*, the latter being responsible for policing as well. Each had his own assistants and scribes.

There was always difficulty in filling these offices, for their exercise was burdensome and the holders were not only unpaid but bore the risk of being made financially responsible for mistakes committed. Where offices remained vacant, the local voevoda would send his own officials to fill the gap. The northern regions were more self-reliant, since they were so remote and had few or no landowners from the service class. Here local communities were freer of the voevoda and more genuinely self-governing.

There was occasional provision for mutual consultation between the government and local communities in the form of gatherings of representatives of the "land," the institution to which historians have given the name zemskii sobor. It was not an embryonic parliament, since it had no agreed status, nor were its delegates normally elected: the assemblies of mir and volost were too small and remote to be able to send elected delegates regularly to a national body, and there were no intermediate popular institutions. Usually the delegates of the zemskii sobor were selected by the tsar from among local servitors who happened to be on hand in Moscow at any one time.

On the other hand, while they existed these gatherings did give the tsar a forum in which he could listen to the grievances of at least some of his people and also elicit their reaction to his own plans and those of his advisers. This was especially important at a time of emergency or the danger of war. While the zemskie sobory lasted, they did at least provide a rudimentary form of social feedback and constitute a check on the abuse of power by appointed officials. They offered an arena where traditional and God-given limits on monarchical power could be evoked. When they were no longer summoned, the "land" gradually lost its stake in affairs of state, and the civic basis for potential Russian nationhood remained undeveloped.[43]

So the proposals and grievances of mir and volost were handled, if at all, in the form of the collective *chelobitnaia,* or "loyal petition." (Its name implied that it was delivered with a kowtow, one of the few Russian customs which derived directly from Asian practice, probably via the Mongols.) These might be complaints about corrupt or overbearing officials or about high taxes, or they might be requests to mediate in a dispute between two local clans. They would be delivered by a special envoy directly to the tsar, or they might be presented at a zemskii sobor. The regime took these petitions seriously, always answering them and satisfying most of them—perhaps because petitioners took care to make sure they had a good chance of success before submitting them, but also because they represented the government's almost only source of information on popular moods, not distorted by powerful intermediate personalities.

When the population suspected its petitions were not reaching the tsar, the consequences could be violent. In 1648 the townsfolk got together with the service gentry, who had gathered for their annual muster to report for duty on the southern defense perimeter. Both presented their petitions together, the townsfolk complaining of excessive taxes and unfair competition from foreigners and other nontaxpayers, the gentry asking for an unlimited right to chase and reclaim fugitive serfs. Both complained of the greed and corruption of Aleksei's leading adviser, the boyar Boris Morozov and other courtiers.

Returning from his annual pilgrimage to the Trinity-Sergius Monastery, Aleksei refused to receive the petition in person or to speak with the petitioners. They felt insulted and complained that both Aleksei and his father "were wont personally to take our bloody-teared petitions from us." The townspeople ran amok, plundering the mansions of Morozov and his associates, and stormed the Kremlin, demanding the delivery of the boyars they suspected of being guilty of embezzlement and of blocking their requests. Because the *streltsy* refused to shoot on the crowd, Aleksei Mikhailovich had to accede to their demands and deliver individual advisers to them for death by lynching.

The year 1648 was a major turning point. It marked the moment when the Muscovite state ceased to base its cohesion on a putative personal relationship between the tsar and all his people. Aleksei was so alarmed at the popular violence in the capital that he declined ever to receive a petition personally again. Instead he created a special office, the *chelobitnyi prikaz,* to take in petitions and give them preliminary consideration. He satisfied both townsfolk and service gentry in drafting the *Ulozhenie* the following year. However, the tsar, alarmed by signs of incipient solidarity between two quite distinct social groups, never called another full zemskii sobor. Instead he relied on the procedures and personnel of his chanceries, and on his voevody, to keep him informed of local affairs and in particular of impending trouble.[44]

158

All the same, the last zemskii sobor was a very important one. It drew up the first code of laws to be issued for a century and a half, and thereby did something to limit the personalization of public affairs. Previously politics had been seen as a matter of great individuals who were either wholly good or wholly bad: petitions focused on morals and on replacing individuals. The tsar was expected to concern himself personally with individual cases and to give judgment in the name of God. The *Ulozhenie* established law as the rhetorical framework within which decisions would be taken. The growth of bureaucracy also meant that the tsar would legitimately expect his officials to handle the great bulk of casework. From the mid-seventeenth century, gentry petitions showed that they had registered this change. They increasingly used the language of law and institutions; they now expected the state to chase their fugitive serfs, not to have to do it themselves. None of this meant that the rule of law was secured, but the adoption of a *legal* discourse changed the way in which personal power was perceived.[45]

The peasants did not accept their aggravated bondage passively. As in the sixteenth century, those anxious to avoid the heavy burdens imposed on them were liable to abscond, to seek a monastery or a richer landlord who could offer them better patronage: in spite of the penalties, many landowners were short of working hands and would take them in. Or they could make for the southern and eastern borders, where they enrolled among the Cossacks or garrison defense troops. Desperate for manpower in these regions, the authorities were not assiduous about identifying and returning them. In fact, in some years, voevody along the southern fortified perimeter were actually *forbidden* to return fugitive peasants without permission from Moscow. As one historian has commented, "Frontier life provided southerners with an opportunity to move on, to renegotiate their relations with the government by putting themselves temporarily out of its reach."[46]

As a result of such defections, the poorer *dvoriane* and *deti boiarskie* found their landholdings becoming worthless for want of a labor force to cultivate them. In 1637 a representative sample of them, participating in a zemskii sobor, petitioned the tsar in the accustomed extravagantly servile language to repeal the five-year limit on reclaiming fugitives. "Order, lord, our fugitives and slaves to be returned to us . . . so that our pomestia and votchiny will not be laid waste and the remaining peasants and slaves will not leave us, your slaves, and so that we, your slaves, serving in your never-ending royal service from vacant lands and paying your royal taxes, will not perish completely."[47]

As we have seen, eventually their plea was satisfied. At the zemskii sobor of 1649 the *Ulozhenie* finally abolished the time limit for recovering fugitives. All peasants, both seigneurial and "black," were fixed to the place where they had been registered in the census of 1646–47.[48] This provision was of cardinal importance, for it ended once and for all the peasants' long tradition of free movement. It did so, however, not by embedding them in institutions, but by fixing them to the land and to the person of the landowner. They became payers of taxes and performers of officially imposed tasks, but the manner in which they discharged these obligations depended almost entirely on the lord and his steward.

Serfdom was not an institution defined by law, even in the sense in which law was understood in an absolute monarchy. The *Ulozhenie* nowhere mentioned the word "serf": it merely laid down what penalties should be imposed on peasants who fled and on those who harbored them. Nowhere did it stipulate who might become a serf and in what circumstances, what services serfs might be expected to perform, or how they might be treated.[49] Not until the late eighteenth century did the state attempt to intervene in the landlord-serf relationship, in order to restrict abuses. Until then serfdom was simply another aspect of the state underwriting personal power.

Townsfolk requested a similar binding of their own kind, the *posad* people, so that they would not have to discharge dues and provide recruits for those who had absconded. They also requested a monopoly on trade and manufacture within their city walls. They received what they wanted on both counts, and thus, in the words of one historian, "at their own request became a closed caste."[50]

Serfdom had a profound and lasting formative influence on all Russian social and political institutions. It perpetuated and strengthened a collectivist outlook on social problems; "joint responsibility" was confirmed not just as an administrative device but as the manner in which Russians of both town and country tackled the difficulties of survival in a harsh environment. It probably made possible the conquest, consolidation, and defense of a huge and diverse empire; on the other hand it also impeded the development of private property and of personal and political freedoms. It confirmed the dominance of persons, rather than of institutions and laws, throughout society, at the very time when authorities were just beginning to introduce from above an impersonal and bureaucratic mode of administrative procedure.[51]

POLAND, LITHUANIA, AND THE COSSACKS

West Russian civilization as it had developed in the Grand Duchy of Lithuania was evolving in a very different manner. Here it was not the monarchy which was dominant, but the landed nobility, and it imposed serfdom in its own way. During the sixteenth century Poland, provider of grain to the Baltic and much of western Europe, was at the height of its power and prosperity. In 1569, by the Treaty of Lublin, the personal union with Lithuania was turned into a permanent state amalgamation. The monarchy and the grand duchy were to keep their separate laws and administrations but were to be ruled by a common monarch and Diet. With the dying out of the Jagiellonian dynasty, the monarch was henceforth to be elected by members of the nobility *(szlachta)*, gathered in the Diet: they were also to retain supervisory powers over taxation, war and peace, and foreign treaties. The nobles won for themselves powers not unlike those of Athenian citizens and, as if to celebrate the fact, called their state a commonwealth *(Rzeczpospolita)*. The towns also enjoyed self-governing status under royal charter, and were ruled by elected municipal councils under Magdeburg law. These arrangements ensured that corporate life and the sense of law became stronger in western Russia than in Muscovy.

The Ruthenian nobles of Ukraine were part of the *szlachta* and were able to profit from their status, owing to their fortunate geographical situation on the fertile black-earth soil of the steppe and steppe-forest regions.[52] The sixteenth century saw a sharp upswing in the demand for grain in the cities of northern and western Europe, and they were admirably placed to supply it. They used their growing dominance of the political system to impose fresh dues on their peasants. In this way they turned them into serfs, but of a different kind from those of either medieval western Europe or contemporary Muscovy. Whereas in Muscovy serfdom was imposed to meet the military needs of the autocratic state, in Poland-Lithuania it was created to facilitate the commercial farming of the landowners.

The Thirty Years' War, however, brought a sharp setback to the rising tide of Polish prosperity, a circumstance which, if anything, intensified the demands which the landlords and their Jewish stewards made upon the serfs. The result was to generate harsh social polarization and lively resentment of Jews and landlords among the ordinary Ukrainian peasants.

To defend the vulnerable granaries of the steppe, the Polish king built a line of frontier fortresses and concluded agreements with some of the Zaporozhian Cossacks who lived on and around the lower Dnieper, under which he provided supplies in return for their manning the strongpoints. Those whom he enrolled in the frontier defense force were known as the "registered Cossacks." They did not, however, include the headquarters of the Zaporozhians, which was the "Sech," a fortified island south of the Dnieper rapids, where representatives of the various "hosts" (armies) would meet periodically to elect a new hetman. Most Cossacks wavered between the "registered" agents of the Polish king and the fiercely independent denizens of the Sech.

Sixteenth-century Poland was a country beset by religious turmoil. Catholic humanism flourished early in the century but was displaced by Protestantism, which, in both Lutheran and Calvinist forms, gained an eager following in the cities and among the nobles. Because of the monarchy's policy of toleration, many radical sects, including the Anabaptists, Mennonites, and Czech Brethren, found a home there. The Jews, who had been settled in Poland some centuries, had a well-established tradition of freedom of worship in their synagogues.

By the latter part of the century, the Jesuits were trying to stem these trends by opening a large number of schools and colleges, devoted to propagating the Tridentine Catholic faith. Although their religion was militant and intolerant, the Jesuits did not spurn the achievements of Catholic humanism, and their curricula included the study of the classical heritage and such subjects as mathematics, rhetoric, and philology. Their aim was to create a universal Christian civilization, which would synthesize ancient classical and modern Catholic traditions. They aspired to overcome the split between Catholicism and Orthodoxy which had occurred at the Council of Florence. We have already seen how they used the turmoil within Muscovy to advance those aims in the early seventeenth century.

The Orthodox Church suffered gravely from the Polish counter-reformation. Lithuanian and Ruthenian nobles were attracted by the western Latinate culture of Poland, and by the enhanced status of nobles within the commonwealth: conversion to Catholicism seemed a natural way to take full advantage of these benefits. Orthodox congregations were increasingly reduced to the poorer and lower-status strata of society. Besides, the Orthodox did not have at their command anything approaching the degree of learning and culture which the Jesuits possessed, so that there was little they could offer the wealthy or educated.

For that reason, some Orthodox bishops supported the idea of a reunion with the Catholic Church, recognizing the supremacy of the pope, provided they were allowed to preserve their liturgy and self-government, both of which were in danger from poverty, neglect, and a low level of culture. Some even hoped that, with the help of the Jesuits, they would find it easier to provide a systematic pastoral and theological training for ignorant Orthodox parish priests. The result was the Union of Brest (1596), which established a Greek Catholic Church, self-governing under the ultimate authority of the pope, with a married clergy and an Orthodox liturgy and scriptures.[53]

During the seventeenth century, however, the Orthodox Church itself began to revive. An Orthodox hierarchy, separate from the Uniate Church, was reestablished. Orthodox brotherhoods set up schools in Kiev and Lvov under the direct patronage of the patriarch of Constantinople, with a curriculum modeled on that of the Jesuits. They looked for support from the Cossacks, whom the Orthodox metropolitan of Kiev, Iov Boretskii, called "descendants of glorious Rus," whose "ancestors, together with Vladimir, were baptized and accepted Christianity from the church at Constantinople." "No one," he added hopefully, "in the whole world does so much for the benefit of persecuted and oppressed Christians . . . as the Zaporozhian Host."[54] The Cossacks were impressed: Hetman Sagaidachnyi symbolically enrolled the entire Zaporozhian Host in the Kiev brotherhood.

Outstanding among the proponents of a revived Orthodoxy was Petr Mogila, abbot of the Caves Monastery, who in 1632 was elected metropolitan of Kiev. He set up in his monastery a theological college on the Jesuit model, and provided it with a catechism and an Orthodox Confession, a formulation of the faith equivalent to the Augsburg Confession drawn up for Protestants a century earlier. In this way he hoped to prepare clergy properly for parish work in the Ruthenian lands. The college's syllabus laid great emphasis on Latin as the highway to both ancient and modern learning, and included philosophy, logic, physics, Greek, Slavonic, rhetoric, grammar, poetry, arithmetic, music, and singing. Theology was taught according to the system of Thomas Aquinas. This was a full-scale humanist education, according to the standards of the epoch.

To give his alumni consistent materials for their subsequent pastoral work, Mogila convened scholars to work on the liturgical texts, to compare them with the Greek originals, and to eliminate mistakes and inconsistencies which disrupted the conduct of services and the teaching of the scriptures. His aim was to restore the "ancient piety," but in fact he was a kind of belated Erasmus, bringing modern learning and thinking to bear on Orthodox spirituality and in effect therefore introducing new elements into it. He insisted, for example, on the efficacy of sermons for inculcating a full understanding of the faith among the laity: the kind of reflective and personal reinterpretation of belief which sermons promote had scarcely figured in Orthodox practice up to that time. For that reason, and because of his emphasis on Latin, he had many opponents among the Orthodox, especially the Cossacks. All the same, as we shall see, his work evoked a lively response in Moscow.[55]

By the 1640s the Cossacks of the Dnieper were becoming extremely discontented, the unregistered because they were spurned and unrewarded, and the registered, who often had landed estates, because the Polish king did not confer on them full noble status. The Zaporozhian Host was infuriated when in 1638 the king attempted to replace their elected hetman with a Polish nobleman appointed by himself. Their discontent reached boiling point when in 1646 King Władysław reneged on a deal he had made with them, to grant them a charter of nobility in return for their joining him in a campaign against the Ottoman Empire.

There was thus ample background discontent when a minor squabble over property arose between Bogdan Khmelnitskii, a registered Cossack with an estate near Chigirin, and a Polish nobleman named Daniel Czaplinski. Khmelnitskii took his case right up through the courts to the king himself but did not receive satisfaction. Feeling that his grievance reflected general social injustice, Khmelnitskii fled to the Sech and persuaded the Zaporozhian Host that the time had come to rebel. Concluding an alliance with the Crimean Tatars, who brought them four thousand well-equipped cavalrymen, the Cossacks marched northwest, defeating a Polish advance detachment and attracting new Cossacks wherever they appeared. Encouraged by their success, Ruthenian peasants took the opportunity to loot Catholic churches and Polish landed estates, murdering the priests, the lords, and their Jewish stewards. For the Jews especially, this was a disaster of major proportions: tens of thousands of them died in the disorders, in the towns and villages and on the estates.

Probably Khmelnitskii had not anticipated the extent or the radical nature of the rebellion he had stirred up. Certainly he had no wish to liberate the serfs: indeed, he ordered his forces to suppress them. Many peasants and unregistered Cossacks fled eastward from his reprisals into the southern reaches of Muscovy, where their settlements (slobody) were given tax-exempt status. This is why Ukraine east of the Dnieper (left-bank Ukraine) was often subsequently known as slobodskaia Ukraina.

Whatever his motives, Khmelnitskii did not exploit the full momentum of his rebellion, which might have allowed him to advance on Warsaw itself.

He concluded a couple of unsatisfactory agreements with the king, but then suffered reverses at the hands of the Polish army and decided that the Cossacks on their own would never achieve their desired status within Poland. Accordingly, he appealed to the tsar of Muscovy to come to his aid and to take Ukraine under his protection.

164

In doing so he was opening up a vista of new possibilities for Moscow. Patriarch Paisios of Jerusalem, currently in Kiev, was working to free the Orthodox Church from infidel domination by creating an alliance between Muscovy, the Cossacks, and the principalities of Moldavia and Wallachia. Patriarch Nikon of Moscow supported these aims as part of his own program of recreating the ecumenical Orthodox Church, with Moscow as its center. Tsar Aleksei was at first hesitant, reluctant to encourage rebels against legitimate monarchy, and remembering the difficulties the Muscovite army had encountered twenty years earlier in dealing with Poland. Eventually, however, he allowed himself to be persuaded that the opportunities outweighed the risks.

The resulting treaty of Pereiaslavl (1654) laid bare the appreciable differences between Russian and Ukrainian concepts of law, corporate status, and obligation. Khmelnitskii expected the tsar's envoy, Vasilii Buturlin, to join him in taking an oath to abide by the terms they had agreed. Buturlin, however, declined, on the grounds that the tsar could not bind himself by oath to a subject. Taken aback, Khmelnitskii walked out of the negotiations. So pressing was his need for military aid, however, that he subsequently returned and consented to accept Buturlin's assurances of good faith in place of an oath. The Cossacks pledged the tsar "eternal loyalty," while he promised them supplies and confirmed them in their privileges, including the right to elect their own hetman and to receive foreign envoys not hostile to him. He also confirmed the status of the Ukrainian nobility and the municipalities.[56]

With the Cossacks on their side and their own army reformed, the Muscovites' campaign against Poland went much better this time. Not only did they capture Smolensk; they also occupied the whole of left-bank Ukraine and much of Lithuania. Had he not been distracted by a rival Swedish attempt to seize Lithuania, Aleksei might have toppled the Polish king, Jan Casimir, altogether. As it was, under the Treaty of Andrusovo (1667), Moscow received Smolensk and the whole of left-bank Ukraine plus Kiev and the territory of the Zaporozhian Host. Aleksei augmented his title: he was now "Tsar of all Great and Little and White Russia."

This was the first time the Ukrainians had had their own state recognized in international law, and it took the Cossack name of Hetmanate. The circumstances in which they received it meant that they would have the greatest difficulty in ever establishing its independence. The Cossacks were one social stratum, not a whole nation, and their link to the Ukrainian peasantry was weak, not to say antagonistic. The same was true of the Russian boyars and service nobility, of course, but they had a long-established monarchy and considerable wealth to back them up. At any rate, over the next century or so the tsars gradually whittled down the privileges and exemptions of the Cossacks, while the frustrated Hetmanate periodically flirted with the idea of returning to the Polish fold. In this way the integration of the western branch of the East Slavs into Muscovy began hesitantly and in an atmosphere laden with misunderstandings.

PATRIARCH NIKON'S REFORMS AND THE SCHISM

The Time of Troubles left the church triumphant but intensely conservative. Most clergymen and many laypeople regarded the Troubles as God's judgment on Rus for having strayed from the true path, and they aspired to restore the "ancient piety" in its fullness. This, however, was becoming more difficult to accomplish. Muscovy had already absorbed substantial territories inhabited by peoples of non-Orthodox and indeed non-Christian faiths; the pursuit of its imperial mission during the seventeenth century was to bring it yet more. Nor could Russia remain hermetically sealed from European religious developments: the Protestant Reformation in its various guises, and the Catholic Counter-Reformation. The Orthodox Church had made appreciable concessions to tsardom to become the established church of a Russian nation-state, and now it found that that role accorded ill with a state which was no longer national.

The lingering effect of the Troubles mingled with these later developments to generate a mood of uncertainty and foreboding, which in places became tinged with apocalyptic expectancy. Documents show that from the late 1630s the authorities were trying to eradicate the eschatological teachings of a monk, Kapiton, who preached that the end of the world was at hand, that the Antichrist was already ruling, and that the faithful should flee from churches, with their tainted priests and sacraments, into hermitages, where they should renounce the vain riches of this world and practice strict asceticism in preparation for the second coming of Christ. For a time Kapiton established his own monastery, where he insisted that all monks perform manual labor, and any fields they could not cultivate themselves were handed over to the local peasant communities. His teachings gained a following in northeastern regions such as Vladimir, Iaroslavl, and Kostroma. As the authorities stepped up their persecution, some of his followers reacted with mass self-immolations, shutting themselves up in their wooden chapels and churches and setting fire to them.[57]

166

Others reacted to the crisis not by fleeing the church, but by trying to purify it in order the better to seek salvation within it and in order to permeate the world with Christ's teachings. In the trans-Volga region a movement arose in the 1630s among parish priests determined to raise the spiritual and educational level of the clergy, through better preparation for ordination, heightened discipline, regular fasting, confession, communion, and the frequent preaching of sermons. They wanted to make divine service more comprehensible and accessible to ordinary people, and at the same time to cleanse the faith from the taint of drunkenness, debauchery, and surviving popular pagan practices. They demanded for example a ban on public performances by *skomorokhi,* strolling players and minstrels, which frequently took place on holy days in public squares after divine service. Some of these zealots made themselves extremely unpopular in their parishes by forbidding favorite entertainments or denouncing the vices of the rich from the pulpit.

The reformers, known as Zealots of Piety *(revniteli blagochestiia)* or "lovers of God" *(bogoliubtsy),* became influential at court after the accession of Aleksei Mikhailovich in 1645. His confessor, Stefan Vonifatiev, was a sympathizer, as were two of his leading advisers, Boris Morozov and Fedor Rtishchev. Members of the movement ran the Moscow Printing Press and used it to publish works of popular religious edification, including collections of patristic writings, the Orthodox catechism of Lavrentii Zizanii (first published in Ruthenia), and a *Book of Faith,* a summary statement of Orthodox dogma by a Kiev abbot. Several of their publications were drawn from the Ruthenian Orthodox revival, and their aims had much in common with the program which Mogila was propounding in Kiev. Not all its members, however, accepted the notion of injecting foreign learning into the process. Some of the reformers, notably the redoubtable Archpriest Avvakum from Iuriev, felt that homespun truths were sufficient and suspected foreigners of *khitrost* (cunning, sophistry), which would adulterate the simple, strong native faith.[58]

A prelate associated with the Zealots, Metropolitan Nikon of Novgorod, was elected patriarch in 1652. His elevation should have marked the movement's triumph, but in fact it laid bare the tensions within it between the modernizers and the conservatives, between the cosmopolitans and the native fundamentalists. Moreover, his own ambitions took him in directions of which neither side approved. Their vision was limited to Muscovy, where they wanted to create a church which was morally pure, liturgically sound, and close to the ordinary Russian people. By contrast, Nikon aspired to rise beyond Muscovy and attempt the restoration of the entire Eastern Christian ecumene in a form which would guarantee the continued dominance of church over state. He was, if you like, a kind of Pope Gregory VII of the Orthodox Church. Whereas most Zealots advised against war with Poland, Nikon was eagerly aware of the opportunities such a war would create for his program. In this, as would ultimately become apparent, he differed even from Aleksei, for the latter was planning war in the interests of empire rather than of ecumene.

167

Nikon's contact with Greek and Ukrainian churchmen had made him acutely conscious of the many discrepancies in liturgy and scriptures between Russia and Byzantium. At first, like most Russians, he regarded the Greek versions with suspicion, as the product of a church which had capitulated to the "Latin heresy" and had lived for two centuries under infidels. In time, however, he became convinced of the exact opposite, partly under the influence of a Kievan translator and ecclesiastical scholar, Epifanii Slavinetskii, whom Rtishchev brought to Moscow.

All Nikon's beliefs were held with total conviction and expounded with a tactless arrogance which sometimes disconcerted even his closest supporters. Having become patriarch, he hastened to assemble scholars and texts in order to study, compare, and correct the printed service books, so that the practices of the Muscovite church should not be distorted by "archaic" errors and should be fully adapted for its exalted ecumenical role. As early as February 1653 he instructed congregations to make a number of changes in the ritual, including bowing to the waist instead of to the ground and making the sign of the cross with three fingers instead of the traditional two. During the next two years he added further amendments, none of them doctrinally significant, but altering, for example, the traditional Russian spelling of the word "Jesus."

Nikon was wrong in assuming that his reforms reversed recent unjustified changes and returned to ancient canonical procedures universally accepted among Orthodox. Over the centuries the various Orthodox churches had adopted divergent practices in the details of the liturgy, and some of Nikon's "restorations" were actually relatively recent innovations. Furthermore, he introduced his reforms without calling a church council to discuss them, which was uncanonical and in itself repugnant to many. In 1655, however, he belatedly corrected this error and, with the support of the tsar and of Greek prelates he had invited, forced the changes through.

What was even more important, he offended the Russians' view of their religious faith. They saw it as an indissoluble whole, in which dogma and ritual fitted seamlessly together. To them a change in the externals of the faith meant a change in the substance, and this in turn meant undermining the image of "Holy Rus" which had been daily preached to them from the pulpit. Some clergymen and laypeople were reluctant to implement Nikon's instructions, council or no council. In many cases their opposition to Nikon was motivated also by disputes over ecclesiastical appointments and benefices.[59]

Before matters came to a head, however, Nikon and Aleksei had fallen out. As we have seen, the tsars regarded the notion of Moscow the Third Rome—Moscow as the head of a renewed Orthodox ecumene—with misgivings, for it threatened to give the already powerful church the decisive voice in politics as well as in religion. Aleksei was also alienated by the increasingly high-handed and intolerant behavior of the prelate whom at first he had called his "bosom friend." In July 1658, offended by the tsar's coolness toward him, Nikon suddenly, in the middle of divine service, took off his patriarchal robes, donned the simple habit of a monk, and announced that he felt himself no longer worthy to occupy the office of patriarch. This gesture was probably intended to compel concessions from Aleksei, but it had the opposite effect: Aleksei accepted his resignation.

He had no quarrel with Nikon's reforms, though. On the contrary, they were as essential to his imperial purposes as they had been to Nikon's ecumenical ones. He spent several years trying to get them generally accepted, but found that the opposition to them mounted, and that a coherent party of Old Ritualists, or Old Believers, among whom a leading figure was Archpriest Avvakum, was emerging to resist their acceptance. In order not to provoke further conflict, Aleksei held off from deciding what to do about the patriarchate till he could settle the issue of reform. Meanwhile he placed Nikon in confinement.

Eventually Aleksei convened a church council in 1666, to deal with both issues. It was attended by the Eastern patriarchs, whose authority was needed to convince waverers. With their backing the council approved Nikon's textual amendments and liturgical innovations. Far more significant, it also pronounced an anathema on all those who refused to put them into effect, and decreed that they were to be delivered up to the state for punishment. It also reversed the Stoglav council's rejection of scriptural and liturgical amendments, denouncing it as motivated by "unreason, naivety, and ignorance," and explicitly condemned the *Legend of the White Cowl*, which, it will be recalled, recounted the transfer of ecclesiastical authority from Byzantium to Rus.[60]

The council of 1666–67 thus upset the church's existing authority structures and repudiated its traditions. Even more important, it converted the Russians' existing national myth into a heritage of the opposition—opposition not only to the church leadership but also, given Aleksei's position, to the tsar as well. The Old Believers pointed out, with irreproachable logic, that hitherto all Russians had daily performed rituals now deemed so abominable that they merited anathema. "If we are schismatics," they argued, "then the holy fathers, tsars, and patriarchs were also schismatics." Quoting from the *Book of Faith*, they charged Nikon with "destroying the ancient native piety" and "introducing the alien Roman abomination." "To make the sign of the cross with three fingers," they protested, "is a Latin tradition and the mark of the Antichrist." Avvakum, who was arrested for his opposition, wrote to Aleksei from his prison cell: "Say in good Russian 'Lord have mercy on me.' Leave all those Kyrie Eleisons to the Greeks: that's their tongue, spit on them!"[61]

Avvakum was wrong about the origin of the three-fingered sign of the cross. But he was right in feeling that the culture and language of the church were becoming Latinized. Through Polish and Ruthenian models and the influence of Mogila's academy, it was adopting a homiletic style suffused with Baroque dialectic and imagery and reflecting the confident, activist outlook of the Jesuits. Avvakum counterposed to these stylistic innovations his own Russian idiom, which in a sense was no less innovative. He wrote an autobiography which was widely circulated and cherished among Old Believers and later became accepted as one of the classics of early Russian literature. It mixed Church Slavonic expressions with a rich vocabulary drawn from contemporary colloquial discourse. Doubtless Avvakum felt that the church's apostasy justified him in raising the status of demotic language, employing it to treat of sacred matters. As he said in his autobiography, "I love my native Russian tongue, and I am not fain to decorate my speech with philosophical versifying, for God listens not to our fine words, but wants our deeds!"[62]

The council's anathema was not an idle gesture. Aleksei supported it, and soon his Secret Chancery mounted inquisitions to seek out those who clung to the old liturgy. This officious enforcement of a deeply divisive resolution ensured that a conflict which, however serious, might otherwise have remained within the church, became a touchstone of people's whole attitude to authority. Making the sign of the cross with two fingers became a powerful semiotic statement. It constituted a rallying point for all those who objected to changes going on in the whole of Russia's political, economic, and cultural life: the adoption of Western clothes and the reading of Western books; the

170

incursion of a Baroque, semi-Polonized culture; the final fixation of serfdom; the erosion of Cossack liberties; heavy taxation; the enfeeblement of communal self-government; the undermining of parish councils' freedom to choose their own priests; the general transition to a more bureaucratic and impersonal style of rule. Aleksei had won his Canossa against Nikon, but that victory was purchased at a high price.[63]

The combination of religious and secular motifs fanned the flames of apocalyptic prophecy. Propagators of doom had predicted that the end of the world would come in 1666. What had happened seemed to confirm the warnings of Kapiton and his followers, that the Third Rome had indeed fallen, the Antichrist had arrived, and Judgment Day was at hand. To keep themselves undefiled by contact with the Antichrist's agents, whole congregations, at the approach of soldiers or officials, would shut themselves inside their wooden churches and set them alight in defiant acts of self-immolation.

Opposition to ecclesiastical reform also provided the occasion for a series of rebellions which made the late seventeenth century one of the most turbulent periods in Russian history. They began in 1668 in the island monastery of Solovki, in the White Sea. Even before Nikon became patriarch, this establishment had a long history of resistance to the tightening of church discipline. A number of religious and political exiles were concentrated there and had gained influence in its internal affairs. Abbots sent by Moscow to restore order were given a hard life, and at least one of them was beaten up and imprisoned.[64]

The monks refused to accept the new prayer book, and petitioned Aleksei to be allowed "to die in the old faith, in which your Majesty's father, the true-believing lord, Tsar and Grand Prince Mikhail Fedorovich of all Rus and the other true-believing Tsars and Grand Princes, lived out their days."[65] Aleksei reacted by sending an army to enforce obedience, but with the support of the local peasant population, who kept them supplied, the monks withstood siege for eight years before finally succumbing in January 1676.

Many Old Believers fled to the south, to the Don, where they became involved in a rebellion whose origins had little to do with church reform, but everything to do with the wider issues of centralization, authoritarianism, and the overriding of local communities. Relations had long been turbulent between the Don Cossacks and the Muscovite tsardom. During the 1650s and early 1660s the Cossacks' position deteriorated, for a number of reasons. The center of gravity of Muscovite policy had shifted westward, to the territory of the Zaporozhian Cossacks and the war against Poland. The Ottomans took advantage of these preoccupations to build a large new fortress near Azov, blocking the access of the Don Cossacks to the Black Sea, hitherto one of their most fruitful sources of booty. At the same time the Muscovite government, alarmed by the growth in the number of fugitives, began to reduce the number of Cossacks it was prepared to register and pay. It cut regular disbursements to the Don and ignored repeated requests to restore them. This meant that the Cossacks must either contrive somehow to increase their income through raids for booty or else take up agriculture, which they despised.

These difficulties form the background to the insurrection led by Stepan (Stenka) Razin. Razin was one of the most successful military commanders among the Don Cossacks and had also been chosen by his men to head diplomatic missions. In 1665 his brother was executed by the army commander on the Polish front, Prince Iurii Dolgorukii, for disobeying orders.

Razin had a grievance, then. Even so, it was not so much insubordination as normal Cossack practice when during 1667–1669 he led plundering expeditions, first on the lower Volga, where he captured and took over merchant vessels, then in the Caspian Sea, where he seized some Persian ships. When they returned to the Volga, Razin's Cossacks were confronted by a Muscovite flotilla commanded by the local voevoda, Prince Ivan Prozorovskii. Razin realized he could not take on properly equipped fighting ships and accepted the government's demands that he surrender his booty, captives, and heavy guns. In return he received a full pardon from the tsar.

His submission did not last long, however. Razin became convinced that the grievances of the people of the lower Volga—the townsfolk and *streltsy* of Astrakhan, the Kalmyks and Nogai, as well as the Cossacks—were such that he could espouse them and lead a successful rebellion. Initially he convened a *krug* and raised his standard in the name of Tsar Aleksei against the boyars, whom he dubbed "traitors." In the summer of 1670 he captured Astrakhan and the major fortress city of Tsaritsyn, where he established a Cossack regime and promised to divide property equally.

From there he advanced up the Volga toward Moscow, gathering around him a large and diverse army of insurgents. In addition to Cossacks and *streltsy,* Tatars, Chuvash, Mari, and Mordvins joined him, indignant at growing taxes and mounting official pressure to convert to Orthodoxy. A large number of Russian peasants also flocked to his banner, alienated by the recent final imposition of serfdom, as well as by the increasing demands for recruits and taxes. They took the opportunity to drive out or murder their lords and to plunder their estates. Russians and non-Russians took part in the rebellion side by side, with very similar grievances and aims: this was a rising of the border people as a whole against the empire which imposed on them relentlessly increasing demands.

During the autumn and winter of 1670–71 much of the middle Volga between Saratov and Nizhnii Novgorod was consumed by the insurgency. Monasteries and gentry estates were ransacked; clothes, jewelry, and wine were pillaged; nobles and officials were seized and lynched.

At this stage Razin stated that the Tsarevich Aleksei Alekseevich, who had recently died, was in his ranks. He also claimed to have the support of Nikon, recently deprived of his patriarchate and imprisoned. In other words, his rebellion was no longer in the name of the tsar, but was now directed against him, in the name of a new tsar and a new church. That he should claim Nikon's support for the Old Belief *against* the very reforms Nikon had sponsored was not wholly illogical, since those reforms had been pushed through while Nikon was in prison. Some Old Believers did in fact join Razin's ranks.

In September 1670, assaulting Simbirsk, Razin finally came up against a properly organized army, led by Prince Iu. N. Bariatinskii, which took a heavy toll of his well-motivated but motley forces. Meanwhile the government hastily reduced tax burdens in the southern regions, paying salaries to those Cossack regiments which remained loyal. His reputation dented by defeat, Razin could not revive his fortunes by summoning up new supporters. In May 1671 he was captured, taken to Moscow in an iron cage, and hanged, drawn, and quartered on Red Square as a rebel and traitor. With the degradation and destruction of its leader, the insurgency collapsed.[66]

Razin's legend, however, lived on. He became a hero of popular legend and song for the next couple of centuries, and the notion survived that he might one day be resurrected and return to lead the ordinary people in a final emancipation from unjust and tyrannical oppressors. Old Believers, since they impugned the very legitimacy of both state and church, nourished such expectations. The symbiosis of Old Belief and Cossackdom, merging at times with the discontents of Tatars, Bashkirs, and other non-Russians, created a threat to imperial authority in the southeast for at least a century to come.

In 1682, when the death of the childless Tsar Fedor Alekseevich left a disputed succession, Old Believers joined with discontented *streltsy* to raise mutiny in Moscow itself. The insurgents demanded redress of their grievances, an improvement in their pay, and the restoration of the traditional form of worship. This rebellion became part of the dynastic conflict between the families of Aleksei's two wives. The Regent Sofiia at first supported it, since it served her interests, but later turned against the *streltsy* when it became clear how much of a threat they posed to her authority.

The most important consequence of the schism, however, was not in the rebellions it helped to provoke. It was that the Old Belief survived and, over the next two centuries, gained in strength. Its adherents moved outward to the frontier territories, and especially to the far north, where they were safer from the Secret Chancery and its successors. In those remote regions local communities could maintain a rugged independence of the authorities. Old Believers were on the whole peaceful people, desperately asserting tradition and principle against what seemed like overwhelming force.

173

The authorities saw the Old Belief as a *raskol* (schism) within the church, and therefore as separate from other sectarian movements which sprang up among peasants and the urban lower orders during the late seventeenth and eighteenth centuries. This view is probably unhelpful. Since the Old Believers denied the "Nikonian" church's priests and sacraments, they had to improvise their own arrangements, and in doing so moved far from official Orthodoxy. They broke up into numerous splinter groups, each with its own distinctive beliefs and ceremonies. Natural conservatives willy-nilly became extreme radicals and innovators, and the solutions these "schismatics" adopted sometimes looked remarkably like those of "sectarians."

At issue were the most fundamental questions of authority and community. Old Believers, like sectarians, clung to a vision of cohesive local *miry* bound by *pravda*, God's law and personal obedience to the tsar. That was what they understood Rus to mean; that was the vision which had been propounded to them regularly in the pulpit by the church of Iosif Volotskii and Metropolitan Makarii. It was confirmed by the anthems they listened to and by the icons and frescoes they gazed at during the long hours of divine service. Now all this was set aside in favor of a semi-Latinized religious culture and a new kind of authority which seemed to take no account of God's law or of personal bonds of loyalty.

So the Old Belief in all its variants was only part of a spectrum of religious movements, all of which were trying in their different ways to recapture a vision of community and authority which they felt was part of their identity. Their view was most cogently expressed by Semen Denisov, abbot of the Old Believer community at Vyg, on the shores of a river which flows into the White Sea. His treatise, *Vinograd rossiiskii* (The Russian Vineyard), was a martyrology of the early generation of Old Believers and also an evocation of the Holy Rus they had lost. According to him, Rus had been a people penetrated by the divine will, the one abiding Christian realm in a world threatened by Satan in the form of Catholicism, Protestantism, and Western rationalism. But alas, the Russians themselves had been corrupted, first by the Council of Florence, then by the impious reforms of Nikon.

All the same, if the hierarchs had succumbed to temptation, purity had survived among ordinary people. "In Rus," Denisov wrote, "there is not one single city which is not permeated with the radiance of faith, not one town which does not shine with piety, nor a village which does not abound with the true belief." True, the tsar and the church, with which the people had been accustomed to identify, were now in the grip of the apocalyptic beast. But Denisov believed that Rus would revive and return to the true faith, because of the staunch and uncorrupt faith of her people. He evoked at length the memory of the saints of Rus, who "by their piety, faith and virtue unite the Russian nation with Christ in one single flock."[67]

In reformulating the religious-national myths of Makarii for his own time, Denisov abandoned the eschatology of the first-generation Old Believers: he saw some kind of future for Rus other than an imminent Second Coming. But since the essence of Russian nationhood was now no longer to be found in tsar or church, it must reside entirely in the "land," among the people in their local communities, their "towns shining with piety," and their "villages abounding with the true belief." Unwittingly, Denisov undermined the doctrine of Christian autocracy and proposed in its place the concept of a democratic Christian nation.[68]

This idea of a people bearing within themselves their own salvation inspired the Old Belief thereafter and influenced all Russian sectarian movements. In effect the Old Belief carried encoded within itself the spurned Russian national myth, in the form of an eschatologically tinged vision of a sacred people. Old Believers were reluctant antimonarchists; they continued to believe in the divinely appointed nature of monarchy even while they reviled current monarchs as the Antichrist and refused to pray for them in their services. Denying state and church in their current form, they could look only to local communities of the faithful for hope of salvation. During the next two centuries this belief withstood official persecution and discrimination and not only survived but flourished. By the early twentieth century, some 250 years after the schism which gave it birth, the Old Belief probably numbered some ten to twelve million believers, or more than a fifth of adult Great Russians. To that several hundred thousand other sectarians must be added.[69]

The schism thus opened up a fateful split in Russian society, when large numbers of conservative and patriotic Russians became alienated from the imperial state and the Orthodox Church and took the decision to conduct their spiritual and community lives as far as possible outside the framework they offered. The eschatological idea of Russia as the "new Israel," a "prophetic land" with a "chosen people," remained as a powerful substratum in Russian culture and politics, which reemerged in very different forms two centuries later.

4

PETER THE GREAT AND

EUROPEANIZATION

By the later decades of the seventeenth century Russia was already a Eurasian empire, heir to the lands of the Golden Horde and of more besides. To maintain that status it also had to become a European great power. Given its geopolitical situation, it had no alternative. Unlike Spain, which had also conquered a huge empire at about the same time, it had no Pyrenees at its back to shield it against European armies while it evolved at its own pace. Its immediate western neighbors were all formidable powers. Sweden commanded most of the east coast of the Baltic, including the entire Gulf of Finland, while Poland's frontier ran in places beyond the Dvina and Dnieper, almost to the walls of Smolensk and Kiev. Meanwhile the Ottoman Empire ruled over the whole of the Balkans and a good deal of the Caucasus, while its client, the Crimean khanate, dominated the northern coast of the Black Sea and constantly threatened the extensive steppe lands beyond it.

To become a serious rival to these powers, during the seventeenth century Russia had reformed its army to take account of the lessons of the Thirty Years' War. It adopted European administrative models, especially those operating in Prussia and Sweden, which like Russia faced the problem of creating powerful armed forces out of limited resources. In those countries, however, the context of reform was quite different: institutions in Prussia and Sweden functioned well not least because the people staffing them were imbued with a Pietist or neo-Stoic spirit which regarded impartial and efficient administration, self-abnegation in the interests of the collective, as a religious duty. In those countries administrative reform was thus a natural accompaniment to cultural and educational reform.[1]

176

Without this indwelling religious mentality, the Russian state, in order to mobilize scarce resources, had to operate through intensified coercion. In doing so, it risked crushing or at best enfeebling the barely perceptible civil institutions—in justice, local government, religion, philanthropy, and so on—which might nourish and sustain a conscious public spirit on the Swedish or Prussian model. The result of such enfeeblement was to reinforce and invigorate the patron-client networks which took the place of institutions. Modernization reinforced archaism; increasing state control meant entrenching personal caprice. That was the paradox which Russian governments faced from the late seventeenth century onward. It was accentuated by the tendency to introduce reform in total packages, rejecting previous ways as utterly wrong.

There was no single straightforward model of European culture from which to borrow. There were two alternative models, though they had a common core. One, which came to Russia through Ukraine and Poland, derived from the post-Tridentine Catholic Church and from the Jesuits; the other, which came via the Baltic from Scandinavia, the Netherlands, and England, was Pietist and neo-Stoic. They had much in common: both were confident of man's capacity to understand nature through reason and to change it by disciplining himself, overcoming his sinful nature, and directing his energy in accordance with science. In this outlook they diverged radically from traditional Russian culture. On the other hand, the two European tendencies also differed from each other on cardinal points. The Catholic tendency required obedience to the church's authority, while the Protestant one stressed self-discipline and the development of personal piety through study of the scriptures.

Aleksei's own life experience inclined him more to the Catholic tendency, but throughout his life he evinced a lively interest in European social graces, learning, and technology. He had been brought up on classical learning, tinged with Polish religious culture in the spirit of the mid-seventeenth century, and had supplemented it by reading Western thinkers and scientists of the Renaissance and after. He discovered much more about Western culture during his Polish campaign. His English doctor, Samuel Collins, reported that since the tsar "had been in Poland and seen the manner of Princes' houses there . . . he begins to mode his Court and Edifices more stately, to furnish his Rooms with tapestry and contrive houses of pleasure abroad."

He was also inspired to a greater concern with agriculture and industry and paid close attention to developments in the numerous branches of the economy in which he held a monopoly.[2]

There had been several attempts during the seventeenth century to imitate Mogila's Kiev institution and set up an Orthodox college in Moscow. Aleksei's favorite, the boyar Fedor Rtishchev, for example, invited Kievan scholars to settle in Moscow to teach the Russians "liberal sciences" *(svobodnye nauki)*, among them a Belorussian poet and scholar, Simeon Polotskii, who became tutor to the tsarevich. No actual institution emerged for these contacts until in 1685 a "Slav-Greek-Latin Academy" was opened in the Zaikonospasskii Monastery in Moscow on the basis of a charter drawn up by Polotskii and implemented by his pupil Silvestr Medvedev. Its curriculum included both Latin and Greek and also grammar, rhetoric, poetry, physics, and theology.

The patriarch of Moscow, Ioachim, was opposed to Catholic influences, and the academy therefore sought Greek teachers in its early stages. It soon turned out, however, that Greek scholarship had declined under Ottoman rule, and that most of its best scholars had in any case been educated in Italy or France. Against the intentions of its founders, then, the academy was soon teaching largely in Latin, with a syllabus strongly marked by Jesuit influences. The first directors were dismissed for their excessive predilection for Latin, but their successors did not change the policy: it was virtually impossible to teach a modern theological or humanist syllabus in Greek.[3]

At the same time as the academy was set up, Moscow, with the consent of Constantinople, finally took over the Kievan metropolitanate. In that way, the Orthodox believers of the territories of Rus came under a single patriarchal jurisdiction for the first time for more than two centuries.[4]

We have seen that already by the mid-seventeenth century the rhetoric of politics was moving away from a personal and moral context toward an impersonal and legal one. In 1682 a further major step was taken in this direction when *mestnichestvo*, the awarding of officials' posts on the basis of kinship, was abolished, and the lineage records which had sustained it were burned. The decree ordering the abolition specifically mentioned the "general welfare" *(obshchee dobro)* as a motive for the reform. This was probably the first time the public welfare, a typically Pietist or neo-Stoic motif, was mentioned in Russian official documents. The intention was to replace kinship as the decisive factor in court politics by law and official procedure. In practice, though the abolition of precedence changed the framework and the rhetoric of factional politics, it did not end the dominance of factions. The abolition was intended to be the first act in a far-reaching reform of the army, but the death of Tsar Fedor Alekseevich in 1682 delayed further implementation.[5]

Warfare and international trade brought unprecedented numbers of foreigners to Muscovy, especially from the countries of western and central Europe. A large number came either as military advisers to train the "new formation" regiments or as officers to exercise a command in the army. Others were traders. Most of them settled in Moscow itself, as the center of wealth and influence. Especially numerous were representatives of the seafaring nations of northern Europe: England, the Netherlands, Denmark, and Sweden. They traded in the *gostinyi dvor* in Kitaigorod, the original foreigners' quarter just outside the Kremlin. The Dutch formed a distinct "hundred" with their own *sotnik*, recognized by the authorities. Some of them lived for decades in Moscow, became semi-Russified, and even converted to Orthodoxy.

A few were medical people, reflecting the fact that the medical profession was just beginning to develop beyond the tsar's personal physicians at court. An apothecary's store was opened in Moscow, which sold medicines to "people of all ranks." A special *aptekarskii prikaz* was set up to invite foreign medical specialists, to organize the training of Russian doctors and surgeons, and to provide specialist medical services for the army. In the Azov campaign of 1695 there were seven Russian and fourteen foreign surgeons accompanying the troops. This was the beginning of the first profession in Russian society.[6]

The foreigners were viewed askance by many of the natives. After the expulsion of foreign rulers and the triumphant reassertion of Orthodoxy in the early seventeenth century, many believers regarded all foreigners as heretics or infidels. As a result they were compelled to live in a special new suburb just outside the city walls known as the "German settlement" (*nemetskaia sloboda*).

Each of the two main tendencies in European culture had its supporters in Russia. During Aleksei's reign Afanasii Ordyn-Nashchokin was leader of the party which sought closer relations with the Protestant countries. He came from Pskov, of which he was voevoda in 1665–1667, and inherited his hometown's feeling of closeness to the Baltic. As head of the *posolskii prikaz* in 1667–1671, he supported the idea of an alliance with Poland against Sweden in order to gain a permanent and secure outlet to the Baltic. He also wanted to promote an alliance of European nations against the Ottoman Empire, of which Muscovy would be part. Ordyn-Nashchokin pioneered the systematization of diplomatic links with the major European countries, which Russia had scarcely begun at that time, both in order to improve relations with them and to find out more about how they operated. Official envoys and international merchants were encouraged to dispatch regular reports on countries they visited.

Ordyn-Nashchokin also favored the creation of institutions which would increase wealth through trade, both internally and with other countries. While in Pskov he tried to encourage richer merchants to form joint companies with the poorer *posad* people and to provide cheap credit for them from the local treasury. He set up a commercial court, with its judges elected by trading people, to ensure that disputes would be settled in a manner which was equitable or at least had the confidence of local merchants. Richer merchants opposed the idea, as it threatened to undermine their dominance of local trade, but the tsar upheld it. In international treaties, too, Ordyn-Nashchokin tried to ensure that there were commercial clauses which enabled the authorities in both countries to uphold the quality of merchandise and to enforce court rulings.

In his political thought Ordyn-Nashchokin can be seen as a neo-Stoic, while in his economic concepts he was a mercantilist, as he showed in the New Commercial Statutes of 1667, which he compiled and drafted: they provided for the maximization of international trade on the basis of contract law protected by sovereign states. His attempts to regularize and legalize what had previously rested on personal relations or on the whim of the rich and strong won him few friends, either among merchants or among foreign office clerks. His son Voin provided his opponents with ammunition by quitting the diplomatic service and remaining abroad, taking with him official documents. Aleksei explicitly did not accuse the father of the son's treason. All the same, in 1672 Ordyn-Nashchokin withdrew into a monastery, where he died in 1680.[7]

After Aleksei's death, under Tsar Fedor and then the regent Sophia, her principal adviser, Vasilii Golitsyn, continued Ordyn-Nashchokin's work, but his orientation was more toward Catholic Europe. The abolition of *mestnichestvo* was largely his doing: he intended to begin the reform of the army command under meritocratic principles. As head of the *posolskii prikaz* he concluded a "permanent peace" with Poland (1686) and allied Muscovy with Poland, Venice, and the Habsburg monarchy in a "Holy League" for common action against the Ottoman Empire. This was the first time Muscovy had been admitted to an alliance of European powers. Golitsyn planned to follow up this achievement by regularizing Russia's foreign relations and sending permanent diplomatic representatives to the major European powers.

Golitsyn had absorbed the seventeenth-century European fascination with science and technology, even though he never visited western Europe. His Moscow residence "was a meeting place for educated foreigners who came to Moscow," including Jesuits, who were not universally welcome. It had German maps on the walls, while "on the ceilings the planetary system was painted. Many clocks and thermometers of artistic workmanship decorated the rooms." He was stripped of his boyar title after the coup of 1689 in which Sophia was overthrown, and was sent into exile.[8]

As a military leader he was less successful, but that is partly because he was the first to tackle the formidable task of ending once and for all the threat of Tatar raids from the south and seizing the potentially fertile steppes north of the Black Sea. The problem was that the Russian army had to be moved, with all its supplies and equipment, across hundreds of miles of uncultivated, sun-baked plains before it could even begin campaigning. When Golitsyn attempted it in 1687, the Crimean khan simply burned the steppe grasses in front of his troops, so that his horses had no fodder. In 1689 he tried again, loading fodder onto his supply train and setting out earlier, in order to complete the campaign before the fiercest heat of summer. Though delayed by springtime floods, he managed to reach the fortress of Perekop, which guarded the isthmus leading to the Crimea. However, his supplies ran out, and he had to abandon the siege.[9]

The sudden death of Fedor in 1682 precipitated a resurgence of the factional infighting which Golitsyn's reforms had been designed to alleviate. Two half-brothers survived him: Ivan, of Aleksei's first marriage to Mariia Miloslavskaia; and Peter, of his second, to Natalia Naryshkina. Under normal practice, Ivan, as the older brother, would have succeeded to the throne; but he was feeble-minded and sickly, while Peter was healthy, energetic, and already a favorite of Moscow townsfolk. Patriarch Ioachim suspected the Miloslavskii clan of pro-Catholic tendencies and therefore supported Peter, who was proclaimed tsar.

However, the proclamation provoked a rebellion among the *streltsy*, which enabled Sophia Miloslavskaia to come to the rescue of her younger brother, Ivan. The *streltsy* feared that army reform would strip them of their privileges, including that of plying a trade, and they had grievances against some of their officers, who were corruptly withholding their pay. Many of them, moreover, were Old Believers. They stormed the Kremlin and murdered members of the Naryshkin family and their clients. Sophia did not support their demands, but she made use of their action to ensure that Ivan had his share of sovereign power. On 26 May 1682 both Ivan and Peter were crowned as joint tsars upon a specially constructed double throne. The accompanying manifesto pointed out that in ancient Rome it had been common practice for two emperors to rule jointly. Sophia, though not officially installed as regent, actually fulfilled that role for the next few years, and even harbored plans to have herself crowned.[10]

In 1689, however, on hearing rumors of a further *streltsy* coup, Peter fled to the Trinity Monastery and organized his own countercoup, using regiments favorable to him. Sophia was imprisoned, while some of her leading supporters were executed or exiled. Peter ruled jointly with Ivan till the latter's death in 1696.

The turbulence of the late seventeenth century marked the closing down of certain visions of Russia's future. The idea of leading an Eastern Orthodox ecumene had perished with Nikon's fall. Russia was in any case now a multifaith community and could no longer promote its own internal cohesion by propagating Orthodoxy. Nor could Russia become a nation-state any more: in anathematizing the Old Belief, official Russia and its church had repudiated the national myth.

Russia was therefore now committed to becoming and remaining a multiethnic north Eurasian empire, which in its turn entailed becoming a European great power. The service state and serfdom provided it with the means to build and sustain that empire, so that over the next two centuries Russia reached its fullest territorial extent and earned a reputation as one of the strongest European powers. That was a remarkable achievement for a state situated on infertile and landlocked territory remote from the major international trade routes. At the same time, the internal structural consequences of that achievement were to last even longer and to complicate Russia's further evolution after the mid-nineteenth century.

RUSSIA AS EUROPEAN POWER

At the end of the seventeenth century Russia was a Eurasian empire, but it was only just beginning to become a European power. In 1636 the "Grand Design" of the French statesman, Sully, had recommended the exclusion of Muscovy, along with the Ottoman Empire, from Europe. But nearly seventy years later the Abbé St. Pierre's "project for perpetual peace" (1713) recognized that peace in Europe could not be guaranteed unless Russia were part of the system.[11] Her entry into the European constellation of alliances coincided with the end of the expansion of the Ottoman Empire. By the "Eternal Peace," concluded with Poland in 1686, Russia became an associate member of the anti-Ottoman Holy League, which also included Austria and Venice. This was the first time Russia had joined a major European alliance, its first step toward being a full member of the European diplomatic system, which it needed to be if it was to maintain its Eurasian empire. Its western frontiers were open to any power strong enough to invade. All the military and diplomatic capacities of a great power were required to prevent that from happening. That was the leitmotif of Russia's foreign policy in the eighteenth and early nineteenth centuries: becoming and remaining a European great power.

The European diplomatic system which Russia was joining was in an unstable balance. The period when a single power, often with messianic pretensions, could aspire to dominate Europe was long past, terminated at the Treaty of Westphalia (1648), if not before. Instead a number of more or less equally matched powers jostled with one another to maintain a rough equilibrium, sometimes known as the "balance of power." To cope with this new situation, the diplomatic consensus was that states were selfish, that each had its own *raison d'état,* but that if they all pursued their own ends they would cancel each other out and thus collectively generate some kind of peace. In the words of a recent diplomatic historian of the eighteenth century, "The motive and rule of all action was to advance the interests of the state—meaning first of all its power, security and wealth, but also, almost equally, its monarch's honor and prestige *(considération)* and rank among other princes."[12]

This was the world which Russia had to fit into, and it was one which Peter I found congenial. He was temperamentally suited to the energetic but pragmatic pursuit of the interests of the state he headed. His country was far less well fitted for the role. First of all it needed a supply of diplomats who would absorb and assimilate the rules of the European game. European states were beginning to appoint permanent diplomatic representatives to each other's courts, nearly always aristocrats, whose job it was to cultivate each other's company and thereby soften the asperities of universal *raison d'état* while also finding out as much as possible about their host country. This new diplomatic network adopted French, the language of monarchy and aristocracy par excellence, as its common tongue. Peter I was the first Russian monarch who consciously trained young members of aristocratic families to undertake this role, and thus to plug Russia into the European network as a full member.[13]

This was not entirely an innovation. Muscovite rulers had long been aware of the value of good diplomacy and intelligence. All their experience of steppe rivalry and warfare had taught them the importance of a thorough knowledge of potential opponents and the desirability of weakening them by fomenting internal dissensions among them. They had also been acutely aware of the significance of the symbolic aspects of relations between rulers, of getting one's own prince or khan respected and feared, the extent of his realm and the abundance of his resources properly appreciated. Muscovite envoys would frequently insist that their sovereign's long list of titles and dependent territories be read out in full on state occasions.

Actually, Muscovy had set up the first foreign office of any European state, the *posolskii prikaz* of 1549, but it had been staffed largely by clerks rather than by boyars, and its responsibilities included relations with semidependent communities such as the Don Cossacks and the Kalmyk tribes. In other words, it was a relatively junior office, and it exhibited a certain ambivalence about what were Russia's internal and what her external affairs—an enduring feature of Russian statehood.[14]

183

At first Russia had conducted her foreign relations by means of special embassies, that is, delegations of senior statesmen visiting foreign monarchs for limited periods to conduct specific business. It was not till the late seventeenth century that Russia first sent a permanent embassy abroad, initially to Poland, then to Sweden, the two states with which it had closest relations.

In the early eighteenth century, however, the situation changed rapidly. By 1725 there were twelve permanent Russian diplomatic missions established in various European capitals. Moreover, Peter I made sure that they were staffed by members of the leading aristocratic families, who were left a good deal of discretion about the details of how they conducted business. For that reason he required that aspiring diplomats prepare themselves thoroughly for their function by learning French and spending time as youths in other European countries. The idea was that, unlike their bearded, long-robed predecessors, they should be European gentlemen in the full sense, part of the "aristocratic international," able to hold their own on equal terms with their foreign colleagues. To this end Russia created the most painstaking system of diplomatic training of its time, and was also among the first to build up a classified archive of diplomatic documents, so that officials could readily brief themselves and quote precise precedent or the texts of treaties whenever it was expedient.[15]

By the mid-eighteenth century Russia was fully part of the European diplomatic scene. Sir George Macartney, British ambassador to St. Petersburg, remarked in 1765 that it was "no longer to be gazed at as a distant glimmering star," but was now "a great planet that has obtruded itself into our system, whose place is yet undetermined, but whose motions most powerfully affect those of every other orb."[16]

Not surprisingly her arrival was regarded with some misgivings by other powers. One English journalist called her "the most monstrous empire, in extent, that ever spread over the face of the earth," while another, more astute, remarked on the intensive Russian preparations for all their campaigns, diplomatic or military: "They triumph by intrigue before they take the field; they bribe, cajole and overreach."[17] As if other powers never did the same! But the sentiment shows that Russia was regarded as being in some ways alien: now that the threat of the Ottoman Empire was beginning to recede, it looked as if another semi-Asiatic power was about to take her place, one in some respects more to be feared.

Appearances were partly deceptive, however: the Russian concern for symbolic display and her meticulous preparations resulted from a constant awareness of potential weakness. Hence her attachments to "balances of power," while they existed, but also her periodic attempts in the nineteenth and twentieth centuries to replace them with more permanent and universal settlements, such as the Vienna Congress system after the Napoleonic wars.

THE BALTIC SEA

Russia could not become a European power in the full sense while deprived of secure access to both the Baltic and Black Seas. At the beginning of the eighteenth century, Sweden still held the strategically vital Baltic provinces of Ingria, Karelia, Finland, Estland, and Livland (Livonia). Poland had ceded the eastern (left) bank of the lower Dnieper at the Treaty of Andrusovo (1667), but had kept a grip on much of the upper Dnieper, as well as on most of the length of the Dvina.

In March 1697 Peter set out on a grand tour through the Baltic and northern Europe. This was the last of the special embassies soon to be abandoned as a feature of Russian diplomacy, and was unusual only in that the tsar himself was a member of it, under an incognito (Bombardier Petr Mikhailov) so transparent that he became offended if his various hosts did not treat him with proper dignity. The embassy was initially designed to enlist allies for an anti-Turkish campaign, but in the course of his journey Peter came to feel that concentration on the Baltic would make better sense, for a number of reasons. Conquest of the Baltic coastline would give Russia a secure natural frontier in the northwest and would also open up unencumbered trade with the wealthy countries of northern Europe.

Perhaps even more important, as an observant traveler Peter became profoundly impressed with the scientific, technological, and economic achievements of Protestant Europe, and decided he needed to make Russia part of this world. It was not quite his first experience of it: in his youth he had violated Muscovite taboos by visiting the "German suburb" outside the capital and engaging in long (often drunken) conversations with the traders, craftsmen, and mercenary soldiers living there. He had begun to study navigation, ballistics, and fortification under the Dutchman Franz Timmerman, and took to wearing a Dutch sailor's uniform himself. His European tour was an exploration of the world from which these fascinating foreigners came. Several north European countries were beginning to assimilate the "scientific revolution" into their economic and social institutions, and Peter witnessed, even participated in, the process at first hand. He studied artillery in Königsberg, carpentry in Amsterdam, and shipbuilding in London, while his observation of the arsenal, the Royal Mint, and the Royal Society inspired him with ideas about how the state should patronize science and technology.[18] Peter also finally became convinced of the need for permanent diplomatic representation at the major courts of Europe.

Giving Russia secure access to the Baltic meant taking on the Swedish Empire, which at this stage was a formidable prospect. Sweden was in some respects a Russian Empire in miniature, expanding from an inadequate northern resource base and insecure frontiers to absorb ill-defined territory to the south and east. By the late seventeenth century Sweden had nearly achieved her aim of dominating the Baltic Sea and its coastlines, along with its international marine commerce. Its well-trained infantry army and her efficient mobilization of resources made it, Peter felt, an example for Russia to emulate. The morale of the Swedish people was also an enviable model: an activist Lutheran faith, combined with national unity and relatively easy movement between social classes, created an unusually cohesive society by the standards of the time, something which Peter admired.[19]

For all these reasons, however, Sweden proved a tougher opponent than perhaps Peter, with his youthful impulsiveness, anticipated. In 1700, having concluded an alliance with Poland and Denmark, he led a large army northward to besiege Narva, the easternmost port on the Gulf of Finland. If he expected an easy victory against the young and inexperienced Charles XII, he was disabused. Denmark quit the alliance, and a Polish army failed to take Riga, so that Russia was soon fighting on her own. Even so, her army was four times the size of the Swedish one and should have taken Narva easily, had it not been for the high quality of the Swedish troops and the inspired leadership of their boy-king, who relieved Narva and destroyed the besieging force.

Ever willing to learn, Peter drew from this serious setback the lesson that he should build a modern navy to assist in operations on the Baltic and that his army, for all its size, was not well organized or equipped to cope with the finest potential European adversaries. His awareness of these needs became the mainspring of his reforms.

Charles did not follow up his Narva victory, but turned against Poland first, leaving Peter the breathing spell he needed to accomplish his reforms. In 1703 the Russian army defeated a minor Swedish force and conquered a foothold in Ingria, at the eastern end of the Gulf of Finland. This was a major strategic acquisition, and Peter decided to celebrate it by founding a great new city, St. Petersburg, to become the capital of an empire which now saw itself as part of northern Europe.

Not only did Peter move Russia's capital city boldly into a former peripheral zone; he also gave the armed forces a whole new dimension, a navy, beginning with the construction of a Baltic fleet. An Admiralty was built on the bank of the Neva, and alongside it a wharf which was soon filled with the frames of warships, being built to take their place at the island base of Kronstadt, a few miles down the Gulf of Finland. By 1725 the Baltic fleet had 36 ships of the line, 16 frigates, 70 galleys, and more than 200 other vessels. It embodied Russia's determination to be a permanent presence in the seas of northern Europe. As the preface to the Naval Statute proclaimed, "A potentate who has only land forces has a single arm. He who also has a fleet has two arms."[20]

Eventually Charles became aware of the serious threat the Russian army still posed to the Baltic provinces, which were a vital source of grain for the Swedish Empire. In 1707, having finally defeated the Polish army, he occupied Grodno and from there crossed the Berezina to take Mogilev, where he awaited the arrival of a further army under General Löwenhaupt, with extra supplies and munitions from Livonia. Löwenhaupt however was unexpectedly intercepted by the Russians on the way. Desperate for provisions to feed his troops and hoping to find new allies among the Little Russian Cossacks, whose hetman, Mazepa, was discontented at Peter's failure to defend Ukraine properly, Charles advanced southeastward into Ukraine instead of making directly for Moscow.

Peter's response aimed to make maximum use of Russia's incomparable strategic advantage, space. He ordered that where territory could not be defended, it should be evacuated, buildings and bridges burned down, and all provisions destroyed, so that the enemy should find neither food nor shelter. It was a strategy which only Russia among European powers could afford to employ consistently, but it was also extremely demanding and costly for the ordinary Russian people, who had no choice but to see their homes and livelihoods shattered. At the same time Mazepa's headquarters was annihilated, along with his considerable store of food and ammunition, on which Charles was relying. Thus, when the Swedes besieged the town of Poltava (June 1709), their exhausted and ill-fed troops proved no match for the reformed Russian army and were decisively defeated. Charles himself, wounded, fled with difficulty to the Ottoman Empire.

The Russian army took advantage of the opportunity to turn northwest up the Dvina, capture Riga, and from there gradually occupy the whole of Sweden's southern Baltic provinces. The new Baltic fleet defeated the Swedish navy at Hangö in 1714. The Russians were poised to invade Finland and briefly threatened Sweden itself across the Gulf of Bothnia, Cossacks reaching the edge of Stockholm. Thereupon Sweden sued for peace, and Peter was able to impose his own terms on them.

The Treaty of Nystad (1721) gave Russia control of Livland, Estland, Ingria, part of Karelia around Vyborg, and all the islands from the Kurland border right round to St. Petersburg, one of which, Kotlin (renamed Kronstadt), became the headquarters of the Baltic fleet. The treaty also permitted the Swedes to purchase 50,000 rubles' worth of rye each year from their former provinces. The Russians declared themselves guarantors of the new Swedish constitution of 1720, which had ended absolutism and restored legislative power to the Riksdag. In other words, they claimed the right to interfere in Swedish internal politics, giving themselves a lever to project their power the other side of the Baltic, should they think it desirable.

Such intervention proved to be far from straightforward, however. Any indication that Russia might overrun Sweden or gain decisive influence there aroused either resistance from other European powers, alarmed that Russia might ultimately transform the Baltic into its own interior lake, or, on the contrary, prompted them to balance her there by ensuring themselves a share in the loot. In 1727, by the Union of Hanover, Denmark, Sweden, and Prussia joined with Britain and France to prevent Russia from making effective use of its dynastic link with the Duchy of Holstein. On the other hand, in 1765 Russia, Prussia, and Denmark were actively discussing the possible partition of Sweden.

Nothing came of any of these plans. During the following century, in spite of three wars (1742–43, 1788–1790, and 1808–09), Russia never succeeded in decisively influencing Swedish internal politics. Sweden's monarchy, unlike Poland's, was hereditary, not elective, and her political structure did not encourage the free play of faction and "confederation," such as gave Russia a powerful lever inside Poland. Nor was it easy for Russia to back up a political threat by moving troops in, since Finland and the Gulf of Bothnia lay in between. All the same, as long as she controlled Finland, Sweden represented an enormous danger to the new Russian capital city. This threat finally became intolerable during the Napoleonic war, and Russia made use of the lull following the Treaty of Tilsit (1807) to conquer Finland.[21]

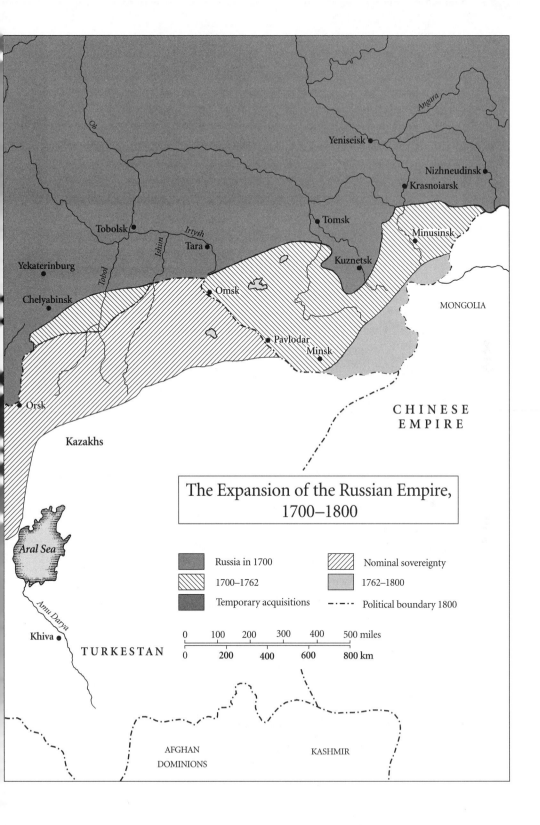

Yeniseisk

Nizhneudinsk
Krasnoiarsk

Tobolsk
Irtysh
Tara

Minusinsk

Tomsk

Ob

Angara

Yekaterinburg

Ishim

Kuznetsk

Tobol

Chelyabinsk

Omsk

MONGOLIA

Pavlodar
Minsk

Orsk

CHINESE
EMPIRE

Kazakhs

The Expansion of the Russian Empire,
1700–1800

Aral Sea

▓ Russia in 1700	▨	Nominal sovereignty
▨ 1700–1762	▨	1762–1800
▓ Temporary acquisitions	–·–	Political boundary 1800

Amu Darya

Khiva

TURKESTAN

0	100	200	300	400	500 miles
0	200	400	600	800 km	

AFGHAN
DOMINIONS

KASHMIR

Victory in the Great Northern War involved Russia ineluctably in European diplomacy and military rivalry from the 1720s. Her royal family was now marrying into the princely houses of Europe, sometimes to support diplomatic campaigns, and always in the process acquiring dynastic territorial interests. In general, Russia needed allies to counterbalance Turkey in the south and whoever seemed likely to dominate the Baltic in the north. By midcentury this approach dictated an anti-Prussian policy, for Prussia was rapidly becoming the dominant power in northern continental Europe, by means of fiscal and military policies not unlike those of Russia herself.

In the greatest war of the period, the Seven Years' War (1756–1762), Russia, fighting alongside Austria and France, invaded Prussia. This was the moment when Peter the Great's military reforms really paid off, both the efficient mobilization of a large population and the inculcation of high morale. In spite of shortcomings in the command and serious supply difficulties, its excellent artillery and hardy, speedily maneuverable infantry enabled the Russian army to defeat the Prussians at Gross Jägersdorf and Kunersdorf. Some foreigners were horrified at the readiness of Russian commanders to achieve victory at the cost of huge casualties; after the indecisive and bloody battle of Zorndorf (1758) Frederick the Great, hitherto contemptuous of Russian arms, is reputed to have exclaimed, "It is easier to kill these Russians than to defeat them."[22] The Russians were able to take over East Prussia and to mount a raid on Berlin itself. Then, however, the Empress Elizabeth died, and, in an egregious switch of strategy, the incoming tsar, Peter III, ordered the evacuation of East Prussia in order to prepare for action against Denmark, the rival of his own home state of Holstein.[23]

The outcome of the Seven Years' War showed that Russia was not only a full member of the European concert of great powers, but potentially a dominant one. It suggested that her army was at least the equal of any in Europe, but that her leaders still had difficulty in formulating and sustaining any permanent concept of the "state" and its interests independent of the family possessions and connections of the ruling dynasty.

POLAND

One of the abiding issues of Russian imperial and foreign policy has been the problem of weak states on the border. Such states have both posed a threat and offered an opportunity. They posed a threat first because their internal disorder might spread into Russia itself, and second because, if they collapsed, they might tempt another, much stronger power into occupying the vacuum thus created. The classic example of this kind was eighteenth-century Poland, the more sensitive since the border affected was on the flat north European plain, the direction from which European great powers were most likely to invade Russia.

We have seen earlier how Poland-Lithuania in the first half of the seventeenth century was able to jeopardize the very existence of a separate Russian state. However, its power and status had gradually declined during the late seventeenth and early eighteenth centuries. The monarchy, already elective by the late sixteenth century, had lost its control over the army and had become the plaything of noble factions and foreign intriguers. The bastion of the nobles was the Diet, where the "republican" constitution permitted a single member to veto a resolution—a right reputedly not exercised lightly, but nevertheless one which enfeebled the state's capacity to take controversial decisions. The constitution also allowed the right of confederation, which entitled groups of citizens to combine to uphold what they held to be the law by means of armed action.

The latter provision positively encouraged Russia to do what it had always done when preparing for conflict with one of the steppe khanates: cultivate factions inside the target realm and if possible induce them to transfer their loyalty to Russia. In a sense, this was the reverse of the use Poland had earlier made of the Uniate Church. During the eighteenth century Russia intervened several times on behalf of Orthodox believers and other non-Catholics, encouraged by Orthodox clergy inside Poland. It also involved itself decisively in each royal election in favor of candidates prepared to promote Russian interests. It deliberately obstructed Poland's revival by impeding attempts to reform the constitution, and on one occasion sent troops into the Diet to arrest deputies unfavorable to the Russian cause.

Poland, however, was not a steppe khanate; she was a European power, and it followed that other European powers had a legitimate, though far from altruistic, concern about her fate. Russia's interest was to keep Poland weak, a client state which could act as a territorial buffer. The other powers resented and resisted Russia's special status, and in the end the most acceptable solution for Poland's neighbors proved to be the partition of the country in three stages, in 1772, 1793, and 1795, among Prussia, Austria, and Russia, and the termination of its existence as a sovereign state. This was the way the eighteenth-century European "concert" dealt with one of its own declining members.[24]

The deal offered Russia both new opportunities and new hazards. With the acquisition of its share of Poland (which after 1815 included the capital city, Warsaw), Russia took over the entire area of Ruthenian culture and regained all the territories once ruled over by Kievan Rus, with the single exception of Galicia (still part of the Habsburg domains). The long-standing claim of Muscovy to act as "gatherer of the lands of Rus" was vindicated. But Russia also assumed responsibility for two peoples who proved to be the most difficult of all to assimilate into her empire, a large number of Poles and most of Europe's Jews.

THE OTTOMAN EMPIRE

The greatest prize of all for eighteenth-century Russia was the huge area of steppe country between the southern defense perimeter and the northern coast of the Black Sea. Strategically and economically, these territories were essential to Russia's consolidation as Eurasian empire and European great power. Strategically, since if Russia could not establish readily defensible frontiers, or at least frontiers guaranteed by a stable power on the other side, she was permanently vulnerable. The Crimean Tatars were less formidable than the Mongols had been, but all the same for more than two centuries their raids had proved ferocious and costly, and repelling them had been a principal determinant of Russia's military policy and even of her social structure.

Economically, the region was crucial because the steppes offered the largest expanse of fertile soil in Europe, most of it rich "black earth" *(cherno-zem)*, in a warm climate which guaranteed a long growing season, all of it virtually unexploited because of its geopolitical vulnerability. For an empire hitherto largely confined to thinner soils and a harsh climate, this prospect was exceedingly attractive.

Looking beyond that, Russia could see the prospect of being able to conduct its commerce and project its naval power through the Bosphorus and Dardanelles into the Mediterranean, enabling it to escape from its landlocked position within frozen seas and to participate in the abundant and promising Levantine commerce which had replaced the trade of earlier centuries across the Eurasian continent.

Finally, above all these worldly considerations shone the ultimate crusading call, to reverse the setbacks suffered over the centuries by Christendom against Islam, to topple the crescent and restore the cross on the Cathedral of St. Sofia in Constantinople. Russia's statesmen had abandoned the aim of reestablishing and leading the East Christian ecumene, but all the same its echoes evoked powerful cultural and religious responses, which lent an extra fervor to the efforts of soldiers and diplomats.

The Ottoman Empire was a formidable and enduring adversary. For two and a half centuries it was Russia's most constant preoccupation and its most frequent wartime enemy. Yet in a sense it was also Russia's alter ego. Like Russia, it was a multiethnic realm straddling the border between Islam and Christianity, and it included numerous subjects of both faiths. Like Russia, it was an autocracy with an ostensible religious mission which in practice observed toleration toward nonestablished faiths. It had a further, less obvious similarity with Russia: its supposedly leading people, the Turks, whose language was used for official documents, and by whose name the empire was often known, were in fact largely a subjugated peasant people whose culture and traditions were alien to the ruling elite.

In the fifteenth to seventeenth centuries the Ottoman Empire had reached the peak of its power. Its unsuccessful siege of Vienna in 1683 marked the beginning of its protracted decline. In a long series of eighteenth- and early nineteenth-century wars, Russia established its dominance, first over the northern coast of the Black Sea, then over the Caucasus mountain range and its southern outliers. These successes guaranteed Russia the right to send its merchant ships out through the Dardanelles and Bosphorus—the Straits in universal diplomatic parlance—into the Mediterranean and thence to trade with the rest of the world. They also brought Russia predominance in the vital stretch of land between Black Sea and Caspian where three Asiatic empires met, the Turkish, the Persian, and its own.

Russia, then, was more successful than the Ottoman Empire between the late seventeenth and the early twentieth centuries. Understanding the reasons for this superiority gives one a clue to the distinctive features of the Russian Empire. One certainly was that Russia's nobility, and following it her intelligentsia, became far more thoroughly Europeanized than that of Turkey. Peter the Great's radical reform of social, cultural, and educational life was matched in the Ottoman Empire by a brief spell of superficial borrowing of furniture and landscape design which has earned it the sobriquet of the "tulip period." Otherwise, the Ottoman assimilation of European culture and technology came later and more reluctantly than in Russia. As one of George I's diplomats remarked in 1721, "The Russians should be feared more than the Turks. Unlike the latter, they do not remain in their gross ignorance and withdraw once they have completed their ravages, but, on the contrary, gain more and more science and experience in matters of war and state, surpassing many nations in calculation and dissimulation."[25]

Furthermore, in spite of its huge size, Russia was the more united empire. In the Ottoman Empire, Syria, Egypt, the Balkans, and even parts of Anatolia were for long periods effectively under the rule of prominent regional families, who controlled the local economy and had their own retainers. Rather than exercise direct authority over them, the Ottoman regime had to reach agreements with them about taxation, recruitment, and law enforcement.[26] In Russia, nobles were transferred too frequently and possessed landed estates in too many regions to achieve this kind of identity with any one locality. Furthermore, non-Russian elites were more fully integrated into the empire's ruling class. Given Russia's size, it suffered remarkably little from centrifugal localism.

The Russian state was also more effective at mobilizing the resources of people and territory. The poll tax may have been extortionate, but it did bring in appreciable revenues, and the same was true of the liquor monopoly, however corrupting it may have been for the people. At times of crisis the Russians experienced inflation, but not a total breakdown of public finances, and it never suffered the humiliation of having its debt administered by an international board put together by the European banks, as the Ottomans did after 1881. Moreover, the Russian export trade to Europe, albeit mainly of raw materials and agricultural products, remained healthy throughout, while the Ottoman balance of trade wilted in the face of European competition. While Russia's overseas commerce was largely carried in foreign ships, she did not suffer the long-term crippling handicap of the "capitulations," which allowed foreign merchants to trade on privileged terms inside the Ottoman Empire.[27]

As we have seen, the geostrategic problems of the Pontic steppes had defeated Vasilii Golitsyn. Peter's first attempt to reach the Black Sea coast, in 1695, was no more successful. But in 1696 he avoided the long march over the steppes by building a flotilla of naval and supply vessels at Voronezh and then brought them down the river Don in 1696 to support an army of some 60,000 men. The army laid siege to the key Ottoman fortress of Azov, while his ships cut it off by sea. In July the fortress capitulated. This was a great success, and Peter planned to follow it up by constructing a harbor at Taganrog, thirty miles west of Azov, and cutting a Volga–Don canal to solve the problem of rerouting Volga trade toward Europe.

He tried to renew the advance after his Poltava victory, striking south through the Balkans against an Ottoman Empire newly weakened by its defeats at the hands of the Habsburgs. The Greek prelates living under Ottoman rule were urging Russia to follow up its success in Ukraine by allying itself with the *hospodars* (princes) of Moldavia and Wallachia in order to liberate the Balkan Christian peoples from "Hagarites and *basurmane*."[28] In the summer of 1711 Peter campaigned with a force of over 40,000 men, but the expected help from fellow Orthodox believers failed to materialize, and soon the Russian army found itself surrounded by a larger Ottoman force and cut off from supplies. In order to extricate himself and his men, Peter had to agree to peace terms which included surrendering Azov, and with it Russia's one precarious foothold on the Black Sea.

In 1736 General Münnich renewed Golitsyn's attempts to conquer the Crimea by main force. He got even farther than his predecessor, actually breached the ramparts of Perekop and took the fortress, but was able to do little in the peninsula and had to abandon it because he had run out of supplies, the Tatars having burned the granaries and poisoned the wells. Once again there were no gains from the war: Azov and Taganrog remained barred to Russian ships.[29]

PETER THE GREAT'S REFORMS

To hold together his sprawling empire, with so many commitments around its borders, and to mobilize its resources for its European great-power role, Peter I set out to create institutions of the kind he had seen during his youthful journeys in the countries of Protestant northern Europe. He both was and was not successful. In one sense he transformed Russia into a country fitted for her new European status; yet below the surface, he not only left the country unchanged, but even consolidated its non-European characteristics. He himself was convinced that he was bringing about fundamental change, dragging Russia "from darkness into light," to use an expression favored by his eulogists. It is true that he was able to operate with a directness most European "enlightened absolutists" could only dream of, but that is because in many respects he was working *with* the grain of Muscovite society, perpetuating and even intensifying its archaic features. Other European monarchs had to work hard to weaken existing hierarchies, to struggle against entrenched corporations, to break down long-standing privileges and immunities. Peter's task was much simpler: he was renewing the service state, not undermining it.

The humiliating defeat before Narva provoked him to completely overhaul the army, taking to their logical conclusion reforms which his father had pursued more tentatively. The pomestie-based cavalry had already ceased to be the mainstay of the army, but remained at the heart of the country's social structure, and the pomestie had in practice become heritable property, regardless of whether service requirements were fulfilled or not. Peter needed both to restructure the army and to reinstate the service principle. In place of the semifeudal levies which still supplied many of Russia's troops, he created an entirely standing army, not disbanded every winter, but permanently on a war footing, and manned by soldiers who served for life. He placed the burden of recruiting, training, and equipping the army directly on the state, and his reform of regional government amounted to little more than a device for raising troops locally and paying for their upkeep.

From 1705 he imposed the *rekrutchina* (regular call-up), under which recruits were drawn directly from the village, usually at the rate of one per twenty households, selected by the landlord (or in the case of "black" peasants by the communal assembly) and sent to an assembly point with minimal supplies and clothing, thereafter to be taken care of by the state. Recruitment was backed by "joint responsibility": that is, if a recruit failed to report for duty or deserted, then the neighboring households had to provide a replacement.[30]

By the end of Peter's reign, this system was producing a standing army of some 200,000 men, not quite the largest in Europe—the French army slightly exceeded it—but still quite enough to place Russia in the European superleague; especially since, as it turned out, the regiments thus raised were remarkably effective. Given the persistent underresourcing of the troops and the harsh discipline with which they were treated, their outstanding performance is paradoxical.

The key to the army's success was the creation of pride and esprit de corps among its soldiers. A serf called up for the army became a completely new person. He was freed from serf status. Since he was to serve for life, his departure from the village was permanent—and was marked as such, by a form of civil funeral, accompanied by wailing and lamenting. (By the late eighteenth century, the term of service was twenty-five years, but twenty-five years in the Russian army must be considered virtually a life sentence.) In his regiment he was provided with a uniform, regular pay, and the opportunity for promotion and decoration—none of which he could have hoped for in the village. The Military Statute required his officers to take care of his welfare by all possible means. The military justice system gave him the right to appeal against certain kinds of abuse, and occasionally even redress.[31] In short, in the army he was a kind of "citizen," with rights and resources he could not dream of back at home.

In practice, of course, his pay was often late, curtailed, or embezzled by his superiors. He might have to sew his tunic, mend his boots, and grow his turnips himself. In peacetime soldiers had to spend a lot of their time as amateur tailors, cobblers, and market-gardeners. To do this, they formed *artels,* just as they would have done had they been peasants seeking employment. An artel was a working collective usually comprising a platoon of twenty to thirty men: one of their number would be elected to act as "elder," receive revenue from the commanding officer, add to it any other available source of income, and use the total to supplement the deficiencies of the state supply system. The elder would organize manual labor in the workshop and the fields. In some ways a platoon or company was like a village community, and the regular meetings of the artel resembled the familiar *skhodka.* In more than one sense the Russian soldier was a "peasant in uniform."[32]

So the artel performed functions which in most armies fall to noncommissioned officers or the quartermaster's office. Created out of necessity, it nevertheless generated its own internal cohesion. Studies of combat morale suggest that improvisation in adversity and the sense of being bound by strong ties to one's comrades are crucial, especially when reinforced by competent leadership and strict but not inhuman discipline.[33]

The Russian army, partly inadvertently, promoted these assets. A good general was one who could foster them and make use of them. Perhaps the finest was General Aleksandr Suvorov, who in the late eighteenth and early nineteenth centuries was credited with not having lost a battle over a period of thirty years. He maintained uncompromising discipline, but also took great care of the material welfare of his men and did his utmost to get to know them. To the horror of his aides and subordinates, he would turn up unannounced at a regimental bivouac to share a frugal meal with ordinary soldiers and listen to their accounts of recent fighting. He insisted on regular religious ritual as a way to promote contact between officers and men, as well as to ease for all of them the terrifying unpredictability of armed combat. Unlike most officers, he allowed his troops to live off the land, knowing that their artels would not allow them to desert or become totally undisciplined. Most important of all, believing that Russian units were more cohesive than their adversaries, he conducted bolder and more demanding maneuvers than most of his contemporaries thought advisable. That is how he was able to storm and capture two Ottoman fortresses, Ochakov (1788) and Izmail (1790), previously thought impregnable.[34]

Overall, then, we may say that soldiers became in a sense "imperial citizens." They constituted the social base for an imperial Russian consciousness which was weak or absent in the villages. That is why tsars identified themselves so strongly with the army, seeking in it the microcosm of an empire whose solidarity elsewhere was shadowy and uncertain.

THE NATURE OF THE IMPERIAL STATE

Many of Peter I's reforms arose from the necessity of recruiting, supplying, and paying for the army. But they were not hastily improvised purely for that purpose. Peter had an overall conception of the way the state should function, one that he had assimilated in Protestant Europe. In his personal faith he was a neo-Stoic. He believed that as monarch he had been called by God to mobilize the resources of his realm in order to increase its power and wealth and to improve the well-being of its people. He was a child of the late seventeenth century, inspired by the recent advances in science and technology to believe that human capacities could be made effective if the latest knowledge and skills were applied to them, and that it was the task of the state to do this. The relevant branch of knowledge was known at the time as "cameralism," and Peter, though he never studied it, imbibed its principles, like his contemporaries in Sweden and Prussia.[35]

His activist view of the state was displayed in the ceremonies he devised to project himself both to the Russian public and to foreign courts. They were derived not so much from the second Rome as from the first, pagan and pre-Christian, with a cult focusing on the person of the emperor himself, and emphasizing his achievements rather than God's grace. The annual Palm Sunday procession, in which the tsar on foot led the patriarch seated on a donkey, was allowed to lapse, while those religious ceremonies which he continued were decked out with military and secular emblems. After victories in the field he would enter the capital city through Roman-style triumphal arches, past scenery depicting an imperial eagle along with Zeus, Hercules, and Mars. He took the Latin title *Russorum Imperator,* while epithets previously associated with the tsar, "pious and gentle," were dropped. After the final victory over the Swedes, the Senate awarded him the additional dignity of *otets otechestva,* equivalent to *pater patriae,* which the Roman Senate had bestowed on Emperor Augustus.[36]

All this is not to suggest that Peter abandoned Orthodox Christianity or ceased to be an Orthodox believer in some sense himself. There is no question, however, that his personal beliefs contained elements very alien to Orthodox tradition, and that he reduced the standing of the Orthodox Church, subordinating its functions to the needs of the activist state. In 1721 he abolished the patriarchate, replacing it with the "Most Holy Synod"—not really a synod at all, but a collegiate administrative board composed mainly of bishops, under the supervision of a lay overprocurator, appointed by the tsar and acting for him.[37]

The new relationship of church and state was expounded by Peter's leading church reformer, Feofan Prokopovich, one of a long line of Ukrainian churchmen who gave the Orthodox Church its shape during the seventeenth and eighteenth centuries. Although he had received a full Jesuit education, including a spell at the College of St. Athanasius in Rome, Prokopovich adhered to the extreme Erastian Protestantism preached by Thomas Hobbes and practiced by the Church of England, which had impressed Peter during his visit to London. Prokopovich's treatise, *The Spiritual Regulation* (1721), claimed that autocracy was necessary because human beings were naturally acquisitive and pugnacious and would constantly make war on one another were they not restrained by a firm sovereign authority. A patriarch was dangerous because he rivaled the sovereign and offered an alternative to him. "For the common people do not understand how the spiritual authority is distinguishable from the autocratic, but marveling at the dignity and glory of the Highest Pastor, they imagine that such an administrator is a second sovereign, a power equal to that of the Autocrat, or even greater."[38]

No doubt Peter had in mind the difficulties his father had experienced in dealing with Nikon. But his subjugation of the church had a more far-reaching implication. In Byzantium the monarch's adherence to divine law was guaranteed by the patriarch. Now in Russia, with one pillar of the Byzantine "symphony" removed, the monarch himself became the guarantor. One might read into that state of affairs the corollary that the monarch's authority was not limited by God's law, since it was itself an *expression* of God's law.[39]

Under Prokopovich's leadership, priests were required to keep a record of parishioners' attendance at communion and confession and also to read out decrees from the pulpit, administer oaths of loyalty, and keep registers of births, marriages, and deaths. In the absence of other local officials they became the lowest-level functionaries of the imperial state. They even had what one might term security-police duties. According to an ukaz of 17 May 1722, "If during confession someone discloses to the spiritual father an uncommitted but still intended crime, especially treason or rebellion against the Sovereign or the State, or an evil design against the honor or health of the Sovereign and his Family, and in declaring such evil intent shows that he does not repent of it . . . then the confessor must not only withhold absolution and remission from the sinner, but must promptly report him to the appropriate place." The "appropriate place" was the Preobrazhenskii Prikaz, successor to the Special Chancery.[40]

Under the new dispensation, relations between priests and their parishioners changed markedly. This was partly because priests were becoming better educated in the seminaries. Since their training was based on Polish and Latin models, though, it did not reflect particularly well the specifically Orthodox form of Christianity. Perhaps more serious was that the relationship between parish and priest was undermined. Priests were no longer chosen by parish meetings, but appointed by bishops, who were in a much better position to validate their qualifications. Partly as a result, the parish itself began to atrophy, leaving most of its ecclesiastical functions to the diocese, and its secular functions to the mir assembly. The program of the Zealots of Piety was being belatedly and one-sidedly carried out: parish priests were better trained, conducted services according to the reformed prayer book, and rooted out pagan practices, but at the cost of a close relationship with their parishioners.[41]

Peter's restless, activist faith naturally found monasteries uncongenial. Unlike his Anglican counterpart, Henry VIII, he did not close them down, but he did reduce their numbers and endeavored to regulate them so that they would function efficiently as agents of social security. Their role was to help the poor and sick and to offer a refuge to invalids, beggars, and army veterans. To make sure they did so, he expropriated their revenues, allocating them instead a fixed state subsidy, conditional on strict discipline and the fulfillment of approved charitable duties. Admission to monasteries was to be limited to men over thirty and women over fifty. Monks were expected to be literate, but were forbidden to write anything without permission from their superior, or even to have writing implements in their cells, since "nothing so ruins monastic tranquillity as vain and useless writing."[42]

In a sense Peter's church reform was a "Protestant reformation," as some scholars have remarked.[43] Peter subordinated the church to the state, took over its finances, and restructured it to carry out educational, charitable, and social work. The problem was that many of the prerequisites of a Protestant reformation were lacking. There was no tradition of covenant theology or natural law, both crucial elements in the political culture of Protestantism. Congregational and parish life were relatively undeveloped, and were actually weakened by his reform. Above all, there were no scriptures in the vernacular language which ordinary people could read in order to form and develop their own personal piety. Congregational and scriptural traditions of a Protestant kind were nourished, if at all in Russia, by the Old Believers, who were bitterly opposed to Peter's innovations.

Consequently, there emerged a dangerous incongruity between the view of the church held by most believers and its actual situation in the Petrine state. Most clergy and laity continued to see the tsar as God's Anointed, ruling in harmony or "symphony" with the church, but the state was pursuing a totally different agenda, with the church as an instrument for secular policies. One ecclesiastical historian has called this mismatch "the cardinal falsehood of the Synodal period," while another has claimed that Peter inaugurated a "real and profound schism . . . not so much between the government and the people (as the Slavophiles thought), but between the authorities and the church."[44]

From 1762 to 1764 Peter III and Catherine II completed the expropriation and rationalization of the church's wealth by taking charge of all its remaining landholdings and replacing the income from them with an official endowment to dioceses and monasteries, which totaled only about a quarter of the previous revenues. Only one senior clergyman, Metropolitan Arsenii of Rostov, protested against these provisions. He was tried for *lèse majesté*, defrocked, and imprisoned for life.

The effect of these reforms was, then, if anything, the opposite of a Protestant reformation. The Orthodox clergy became a segregated and relatively impoverished estate, wearing distinctive and archaic dress and holding no *chin*, or official rank. Characteristically, the clergy were, along with the serfs, the only social estate not invited to the Law Code Commission of 1767.

With Peter's new symbolism and his ecclesiastical reforms, monarchical authority in Russia assumed a whole new dimension. In the West the concept of monarchical absolutism had arisen out of the struggle with the papacy and out of the need to overcome the immunities of ancient privileged institutions. Transferred to Russia, where papacy was not an issue and there were no such institutions, absolutism took on a completely different coloring and implied a sacralization of the monarchy itself. During the eighteenth century, court ceremony and official laudatory literature implied that the monarch was the equal of Christ, or even Christ himself, and hence divine. As the Russian scholars V. M. Zhivov and B. M. Uspenskii have commented, "The sacralization of the monarch lasted the whole Synodal period [1721–1917], and throughout it was in conflict with traditional religious consciousness. That conflict could not in principle be resolved, since the sacralization of the monarchy was a constituent part of the structure of the state and in particular of the Synod."[45]

Sacralizing the monarchy is not quite the same as sacralizing the monarch. Peter deified not himself, but the state. Like neo-Stoics elsewhere, he had an exalted concept of the state, believing that it stood above individual and family ties, ethnic and religious loyalties, even above the person of the monarch. Peter was the first Russian ruler who attempted to distinguish between the authority of the state and the person and property of the monarch. The distinction was articulated in the text of the Spiritual Regulation, and recruits entering the army took an oath to "the sovereign and the state" (*gosudariu i gosudarstvu*), as if the two, though closely connected, were separate. This was Russia's first hesitant step away from the patrimonial state toward a functional or bureaucratic one.[46]

Peter also sketched out a new source of legitimacy at this stage. This was the idea of "progress," which he conceived as improving the capacity of the state to promote the "common welfare." His propagandists, in a style which recalled earlier messianic pretensions, claimed that this improvement was an abrupt and total transformation "from darkness into light," "from nothingness to being." Some of this messianic dedication to progress and welfare later passed into the tradition of the Russian intelligentsia.[47] The transition had its paradoxical aspects, though, since, as we have seen, Peter accomplished his goals by reinforcing features of old Muscovy or—in his own rhetoric—deepening the darkness.

To embody his notion of an impersonal state dedicated to progress, Peter set out to design an administrative machinery—a "regular state" he called it—which would function automatically, even in the absence of the monarch (when he was on campaign, for example), through officials appointed for their proven ability and probity rather than birth or personal connections. At its center was the Senate, which replaced the Boyar Duma as the tsar's council and coordinator of affairs. To handle routine matters he replaced the *prikazy* with "colleges," each of which had its own strictly delineated function—justice, manufacture, revenue, and so on—and its own offices in the localities. To eliminate personal and family interest from the conduct of affairs, each college was headed by an administrative board of several persons, who were supposed take decisions in common, while their subordinates were bound by precise regulations, procedures, and spheres of jurisdiction.

However, Russia was not Sweden, where the equivalent institutions were embedded in a political structure whose main social estates had corporate bodies and were represented in parliament. In Russia, where life chances were distributed through patron-client networks restrained only by the tsar, "colleges" were bound to function differently. Bodies of men, as well as individuals, can generate their own collective interests and promote them so forcefully as to frustrate the best-designed mechanism.

Peter in any case was ambivalent about the distinction between state and sovereign, and certainly did not always observe it himself. He was constantly tempted to poke into his newly created machinery personally, to see that it was working properly. To watch over the Senate and the colleges, he appointed a procurator-general, with a subordinate in each office, and also placed in each college his own personal representative, the *fiskal*, "who should see that all business is conducted zealously and equitably."[48] *Fiskaly*

were encouraged to denounce malpractice and corruption and were sometimes awarded part of the property of those whose misdeeds they uncovered.
In this way, to overcome the discrepancy between personal and state interests, he generated a routine of exhaustive paperwork and malicious denunciations which was to pervade Russian bureaucratic life and to provide ample
fuel for the infighting of patronage factions.

At bottom, Peter's reliance on *fiskaly* represented his tacit recognition that
his cameralist concept of governance, based on impersonal subordination,
division of functions, and formal regulations, harmonized ill with the networks of personal dependence which had hitherto formed the sinews of the
Russian state.[49]

Peter's personal life and court ceremonial reflected his own ambivalence
about the abrupt reorientation of Russian culture he was promoting. Alongside the regular court, he built a mock one, consisting of wooden buildings,
where he periodically held an "All-Mad, All-Jesting, All-Drunken Assembly,"
whose name suggests a parody of the church council he had abolished. Its
ritual varied, but usually a "prince-Caesar" would be elected to head the
revels. On one occasion the assembled dignitaries were required to wear
fancy dress with animals' tails, while on another a stark naked Bacchus paraded in a bishop's miter bearing the insignia of Cupid and Venus, while
the servitors were all given comic names based on the word *khui* (prick).
This was Peter's version of carnival, an occasion for riotous relaxation and
unbuttoned entertainment, mocking and subverting established institutions,
including those he headed, but ultimately reinforcing them.[50]

Senatorial rule, as it developed over the next century, certainly did not
succeed in implanting "regular" government throughout Russia. It did, however, encourage the impression that there was an impersonal set of guidelines
called the "law" which its members and subordinates ought to ascertain and
observe. By the same token it induced a certain caution about allowing personal and clannish interests to predominate automatically in all political conflicts. For that reason it generated mountains of paper on all contentious
matters, as each official provided himself with recorded evidence against the
possible intrigues of rivals or the denunciations of *fiskaly*. As a result, the
Senate and the colleges accumulated a huge backlog of unsettled cases, which
grew from reign to reign. To get anything done required the sovereign's
personal intervention, which meant defeating the object of establishing the
Senate in the first place.[51]

The same ambivalence about legality and personal authority governed Peter's attitude toward his own ruling class, the nobility. On the one hand, he
wanted to see nobles imbued with his own ideals and activated by a sense

of honor, cultivating the skills of administration and handling public affairs with probity and efficiency. On the other he distrusted them and felt the constant need to cajole, admonish, and even browbeat them into discharging their duties.

204   Peter's ambivalence was on display even in the naming of the nobility. He amalgamated the various ranks of the Muscovite aristocracy into a single new social estate, to which he gave the Polish name *shliakhetstvo*, implying that its members were citizens of a "commonwealth." In practice, however, he and his successors normally used the term *dvorianstvo*, which implied a very different status, that of courtier.[52]

He required that the nobleman's sense of honor, derived from birth and pedigree, be supplemented by training in a skill useful to the state, and by military or civilian service, entered at the lowest level. Aristocrats thus had to join the army as privates, though the blow was softened by allowing them to enroll in the prestigious new Guards regiments. The young officer or civil servant would then proceed up a promotion hierarchy minutely defined in the Table of Ranks. This Table, instituted in 1722, finally replaced *mest-nichestvo*, which had been abolished some thirty years earlier. It was intended to ensure that pedigree and family status were supplanted as criteria of promotion by merit, achievement, and seniority in the service. The table was based on the military hierarchy but applied equally to the civil service and the court, with the result that top civilian officials were commonly known as "generals." It contained fourteen parallel ranks: by working up to the eighth, a non-noble could win hereditary noble status not just for himself, but for his descendants. Merit and dedicated service, in short, were assumed to be hereditary.

The Table of Ranks proved exceptionally durable. It lasted till 1917, offering a framework not only for state service but also for social life among Russia's elites. One's rank determined one's whole way of life, including the manner in which one was addressed and one's precedence on official occasions. Anyone who arrived at a court reception in too grand a conveyance or too ostentatiously dressed had to answer to the Master of Heraldry for his impudence.

At the same time, Peter stopped granting pomestia in return for state service, replacing them with a regular salary. The two categories of landed estate, pomestia and votchiny, were amalgamated. Peter intended to convert both of them into entailed properties, normally inherited by the eldest son, so that they could provide for noble families in perpetuity. But here, significantly, he failed. Depriving younger sons and female inheritors of their shares of landed estates violated too harshly the norms of kinship in Russia, which required provision for all heirs. Soon after Peter's death his entail law was repealed.[53] The tsar's domination of public life was still limited—not by God's law, but by kinship and patronage. These, not autocracy, were still the bedrock of Russian society.

Initially at least, Peter's reforms served, not to create a new nobility, but rather to bolster the dominance of the old Muscovite boyar families. This is not altogether surprising. In their early stages, meritocratic reforms often reinforce old social hierarchies, since existing elites are usually in a better position to offer their offspring the education and personal connections which launch them on their career. At any rate, an analysis of the top four service ranks in 1730 shows that thirteen of the families represented in them were among the twenty-two families with members in the Boyar Duma a century and a half earlier. They were the Buturliny, Cherkasskie, Dolgorukie, Golitsyny, Goloviny, Kurakiny, Pleshcheevy, Romodanovskie, Saltykovy, Shcherbatovy, Sheremetevy, Veliaminovy, and Volynskie.[54]

Of course, not all of them were equally or permanently powerful. Their individual fortunes rose and fell. Under the Empress Anna, for example, the Saltykovy were in the ascendant. Under Elizabeth it was the turn of the Trubetskie and the Vorontsovy. But whatever the precise constellation of the moment, it is clear that the backbone of the military and civilian command in the mid-eighteenth century comprised families of long-standing pedigree. In broad terms, in fact, their dominance lasted from the mid-seventeenth to the mid-nineteenth centuries, during which time Russia's relative internal stability was upheld by a ruling class centered on the imperial court and extending outward through the estates of the great aristocratic families, with their clients among the gentry of the provinces. As John LeDonne has put it, "Russian society was a command structure in which the ruling class collectively owned half the population and controlled the destiny of the other half, exercising its power through the agency of interconnected patronage networks, and governed the dependent population in pursuance of selfish ends, the maintenance of the status quo and the maximization of military power."[55]

The Table of Ranks gave this ruling class a formal hierarchical framework and enforced a degree of meritocracy; Western culture increasingly gave it a sense of identity and of separateness from the dependent population. Peter introduced many of the social forms he had observed in the Netherlands and England: newspapers, coffeehouses, Western dress, with breeches and tight-fitting jackets replacing the loose kaftans of Muscovy, and clean-shaven heads in place of beards and flowing locks. Evening gatherings (known in Russia as *assamblei*) were instituted in aristocratic townhouses, with cards,

205

dancing, and a buffet supper; women of noble blood were required to come out of seclusion to attend these. A new alphabet was introduced to simplify the process of learning to read.

Peter's new capital city, St. Petersburg—named after the apostle, not the tsar, but cross-echoes were inevitable—was designed to accommodate these activities and to celebrate the changed nature of the imperial state. Laid out on a generous scale on former marshland and constructed in stone according to the latest European architectural designs, its location and its appearance symbolized Peter's determination that Russia should become a full member of the European concert of powers. The Aleksandr Nevskii Monastery commemorated the monarch who five hundred years earlier had defeated the Swedes and consolidated Rus's outlet to the Baltic. Architects were invited from Italy, Austria, and Germany to design public buildings, starting with the Cathedral of St. Peter and St. Paul (started 1712), with its Scandinavian-looking spire and bell tower. Streets were laid out in straight lines converging on a huge square on the banks of the Neva where the Winter Palace was built. Outside the new capital, Peter started work on a Versailles-style summer residence, Peterhof, with a terrace of fountains running down from the palatial main windows toward the sea.

Peter insisted that nobles who wished to present themselves at court should build themselves a residence in St. Petersburg. Foreigners were no longer confined to the outskirts, but were permitted, even encouraged, to settle within the city. Merchants dealing in international commerce were required to relocate their business from Arkhangelsk (hitherto the only port through which foreign trade had been allowed) to St. Petersburg and the Baltic.[56]

EDUCATION AND CULTURE

At the beginning of the eighteenth century a country which was joining the ranks of European powers needed a Europeanized educational system at all levels. The only mass education available in Russia, that of the Orthodox Church, was ill adapted to meet such needs, and hence Europeanization meant either inviting in large numbers of Jesuits or else radical secularization. Peter the Great preferred secularization.

His most famous innovation was the School of Mathematics and Navigation, based on the Royal Mathematical School at Christ's Hospital in London. The founding charter of 1701 stipulated that "student volunteers are to be enrolled, and others in addition by compulsion, and those without means are to be allotted a daily ration." Evidently Peter anticipated that there would not be many willing students. British teachers were brought over to direct studies in arithmetic, geometry, trigonometry, navigation, and geography. Later these utilitarian subjects were buttressed by social graces as drawing, painting, fencing, and dancing appeared on the curriculum, and by European culture too, with the addition of Latin, French, and German.

Graduates of the Mathematical School were expected to teach in "cipher schools" in the provinces, housed in monasteries and parish church outbuildings, where "children of the nobility and chancellery rank, of secretaries and clerks . . . aged from ten to fifteen are to study numbers and some part of geometry." At the end of their studies they would receive a diploma, "and without such diplomas they are not to be allowed to marry or to give pledges of betrothal." Later Slavonic grammar and spelling were added and the prohibition on marriage was eased.[57]

Peter had great difficulty in finding for his schools students who were literate enough to cope with the curriculum, and who would not dissipate their time and stipends on the "pursuit of Bacchus and Venus" rather than of learning. Yet in time, as their austere functionalism eased and elements of culture and social grace penetrated the curriculum, the schools became more accepted, especially among the nobility, who found that education and culture were an excellent way of marking themselves off from lower social classes.

The foundation in 1732 of the secondary schools known as Cadet Corps accentuated this tendency. They emphasized literature, music, and social etiquette as much as they did navigation and fortification. Some alumni distinguished themselves in cultural life: a group of students led by Aleksandr Sumarokov founded the first Russian theater at the court of Empress Elizabeth. The Cadet Corps became the nursery of a whole distinct *dvorianskii* way of life, centered on school, regiment, state service, and landed estates. The graduates spoke French and were ready to become full-fledged European diplomats, to assume command in the army, or to supervise a whole district administration. To supplement their qualifications, some young nobles were sent abroad to study, usually at German universities, from which the more serious-minded brought back German attitudes to learning and public service, at first on Pietist, later on post-Kantian idealist models.[58]

Peter was also alive to Russia's need for institutions of science and technology capable of functioning at the highest international level. He corresponded with the philosopher Gottfried Leibniz, who had ambitious schemes for spreading the benefits of learning and technology. He recommended that Peter appoint foreigners to jump-start the process in Russia and at the same time found libraries, museums, and research institutes capable of disseminating existing knowledge and of generating new ideas for improvement and economic development.

208

Peter implemented much of his program. He opened Russia's first public library and first museum (the Kunstkamera in St. Petersburg) and sponsored expeditions to remote regions to seek minerals, make maps, and report on natural resources, a crucial step in a country of such widely scattered abundance. To crown these efforts, he decreed the establishment of an Academy of Sciences on the model of the Royal Society in London, in the hope not only of discovering and developing Russia's immense latent resources, but also of making her a center of world science, to "put other civilized nations to the blush, and to carry the glory of the Russian name to the highest pitch." That part of the program had to be postponed, since, when it opened in 1726, the academy had an entirely foreign staff, mostly Germans (except the director, Lavrentii Blumentrost, who, despite his surname, was Russian). A university and a *gimnaziia* (grammar school) were attached to the academy so that Russian students might receive the kind of secondary and higher education which would qualify them for it.[59]

One young provincial who took advantage of the new opportunities was Mikhail Lomonosov (1711–1765), son of a fisherman from the far northern Arkhangelsk Province who, by joining a caravan of salt fish, made his way to Moscow to study in the Slav-Greek-Latin Academy. Significantly, he had to start his career by faking his way out of the tax-paying estate: he declared himself a nobleman in order to enroll in the academy. But this initial deception past, there was no further barrier to his talent. He transferred to the newly opened Academy of Sciences, becoming its first Russian student, and was sent to study in Germany. On his return he displayed an amazing versatility, teaching at different times chemistry, mineralogy, rhetoric, versification, and Russian language and making serious contributions to the study of each. His career marked a stage in the Russification of learning: he hated his German colleagues and, together with Ivan Shuvalov, one of the most influential members of the Empress Elizabeth's court, sponsored a campaign to have a purely Russian university opened in Moscow, along with two secondary schools, one for non-nobles. The university opened in 1755, with faculties of law, medicine, and philosophy, and lectures were delivered either in Latin or in Russian. Significantly, it had no theological faculty: ecclesiastical learning continued on an entirely separate track.[60]

Peter might be accused—and was—of putting the cart before the horse, of promoting abstruse scientific research while the overwhelming majority of the population could not even read. Perhaps even more serious, since science was inculcated by foreigners at a time when the Orthodox Church was being downgraded, it acquired the reputation of being godless. Some Russians even whispered that learning was the work of the Antichrist. A suspicion of all scholars implanted itself among many ordinary Russians: it has proved extremely tenacious.

209

However, the opposite process also took place, at least among the nobility. During the next two centuries, Russian learning in the humanities and in the social and natural sciences gradually established itself as being among the finest in the world, enjoyed prestige in polite society, and received priority in state expenditure—no small matter in a poor country.

Furthermore, the spread of learning took place in a form whose implications were egalitarian or at least meritocratic. From Peter's time onward, completing secondary or higher education entitled one to enter state service higher on the Table of Ranks than the less well educated. Besides, the spirit of science itself reinforced egalitarianism: once tried and tested in it, one became a member of the "international republic of learning," a community indifferent to the hierarchies of state and army. In this way the Russian state nurtured powerful antibodies for the future.

III

Russia as European Empire

STATE AND SOCIETY IN THE

EIGHTEENTH CENTURY

AUTHORITY, INSTITUTIONS, AND LAW

Peter I's far-reaching overhaul of government and society represented renewal not just in a symbolic but in a real sense. Yet, as we have seen, in
making his leap "from darkness into light," Peter was consolidating, even
strengthening, some of the features of Muscovite society which were, from
his point of view, most inimical to "progress." His accomplishment stands as
a prime example of Lotman's insight that in Russia the most radical changes,
despite appearances, actually reinforce the traditions of the society they are
meant to change.[1]

During the eighteenth century real power fluctuated among three groups
of institutions: (1) the visible state: Senate, Holy Synod, colleges; (2) the
monarch's advisory council (under various names); and (3) the monarch's
personal favorites. Not all who rose to the top of the system were content
with it—not least because their prominence could easily turn out to be fleeting. In 1730 members of the Supreme Privy Council (institution type 2) tried
to make the Empress Anna on her accession pledge herself to certain "conditions" which would have required her to obtain the council's consent before
marrying, appointing an heir, deciding on war or peace, raising taxes, spending revenue, and making senior official appointments or land grants. If they
had succeeded, Russia might in theory have become a limited monarchy
of the eighteenth-century English Whig type. But, as their counterpetitions

showed, most nobles felt that if monarchy was to be limited, then the nobility as a whole should be properly represented on the assemblies fulfilling that function. They regarded the "conditions" as merely a ploy by the Golitsyn and Dolgorukii families, currently dominant in the council, to perpetuate their clans' authority. They encouraged Anna to refuse them, which she did.[2]

In a similar spirit, and perhaps inspired by Montesquieu, Ivan Shuvalov, favorite of the Empress Elizabeth, proposed in 1754 that the monarch and her subjects should take an oath to observe certain "permanent and fundamental laws" which would, for example, guarantee the inviolability of landed property and the right of nobles to be tried only by their peers. Ivan's brother Peter headed an official commission which tried to embody these ideas in a code of laws. It completed much of its work, but its recommendations were not followed up.[3]

Catherine II (1762–1796) had a more direct interest in institutions and law than any of her predecessors, for her claim to the throne was weaker than theirs: she was not an offspring of any branch of the Romanov dynasty. Without the stable support of her subjects, embodied in institutions and laws, she was always vulnerable to any chance conspiracy among the Guards officers. In her early years her principal adviser, Nikita Panin, had plans to systematize Peter I's "regular state." He proposed the creation of an Imperial Council, which would not only advise the monarch but also have supreme executive responsibility and be functionally divided, operating as a kind of council of ministers within the framework of a code of laws. His proposals would in practice have confined the monarchy within a power network guaranteed by the great aristocratic families, those who had proved themselves by birth, rank, merit, and experience.

Even this advice, though to all appearance impartial, was subject to the shifting circumstances of court rivalry. When his opponents appeared to be in the ascendancy in the empress's entourage, Panin withdrew his proposals, fearing no doubt that their implementation would consolidate his adversaries' influence.[4]

Catherine had her own ideas about how government might be reformed and legal order introduced. These she had imbibed from the Enlightenment thinkers she had read in conscious preparation for imperial responsibility. She felt that it was important to have the law validated by representatives of her peoples, and so in 1767 she convened a Law Code Commission consisting of elected delegates from the various estates of society, and composed for it her own set of recommendations, articulated in a *nakaz,* or memorandum.

She had a vision of the rule of law, and it was very close to that of Peter I.

She believed that law is a means by which the state mobilizes the resources of society to augment its own strength and wealth and to provide for the welfare of the population. It was not in her eyes an impersonal force mediating between autonomous and sometimes competing social institutions, but rather an instrument through which the monarch exercises authority and puts moral precepts into effect. "In a State, that is, in a Collection of People living in Society where Laws are established, Liberty can consist only in the Ability of doing what everyone ought to desire, and in not being forced to do what should not be desired." This was the view of the German cameralists rather than of French or British Enlightenment thinkers, one which many German monarchs were busy putting into practice in their relatively smaller states, from Prussia downward.[5]

215

The Law Code Commission contained elected representatives of the nobility, townsfolk, Cossacks, *odnodvortsy* ("single householders," descendants of the militarized servitors who had manned the southern frontiers), "black" peasants, and non-Russians. Serfs and, symptomatically, the clergy were unrepresented. The deputies brought with them their own *nakazy (cahiers)*, articulating the grievances and aspirations of their constituents. When the commission first met, in July 1767, it soon became clear that each estate had its own narrowly conceived interests, put forward without any attempt to envisage new legislation in the context of the state or the population as a whole. Since their assemblies operated in a purely local context, without a broader institutional framework, they had no way of conceptualizing the overall interests and needs of the Russian state.[6]

In the end, with the outbreak of war against Turkey in 1768, Catherine prorogued the commission's plenary sessions so that deputies could disperse to report for military service. She never reconvened them, but the subcommittees continued work, and the commission's secretariat produced a ten-volume digest of existing law in 1780. Catherine used the information thus generated, but she did not want lawmaking to consist merely of adjudicating and balancing among sectoral interests, and probably felt that she and her advisers could provide the overarching concepts better than any elected assembly. Therewith a permanent dilemma of Russian statehood became manifest: that representative institutions tend merely to buttress existing privilege and hence to entrench social conflict.

In this respect, the problem she faced was different from that of almost every other eighteenth-century European monarch. Whereas they had to use both authority and law to break down the privileges and immunities of corporations and local institutions, her problem was the opposite: the excessive weakness of those bodies. Because of the way the Russian state had developed, they were too puny to act even as a transmission belt for governmental authority; as a result, patron-client relations and tribute-taking were still the main elements in the distribution of authority and wealth.

216

Reserving central lawmaking for herself, then, Catherine set about the task of strengthening intermediate social institutions—the area of Peter's greatest failure—and creating a social class to fill the gap. She grappled seriously as no predecessor had done with the problem of local government. She divided the empire, including its recent conquests and acquisitions, into fifty *gubernii* (provinces) and some 360 *uezdy* (districts). Each province was headed by a *gubernator*, or governor, who was the monarch's personal appointee, and who headed a cluster of local offices subordinated to central colleges. (There were also sometimes *general-gubernatory* in charge of two or more provinces which for some reason required special attention, for example in the border-lands.) Each district was headed by a police official *(ispravnik)* in alliance with the local gentry assembly *(dvorianskoe sobranie),* which elected officials to fill the functional posts. The district marshal of the nobility *(predvoditel dvorianstva)* presided over the assembly and represented the local interest in all governmental affairs.

Because the nobility occupied such an important place in this scheme, Catherine granted them a charter in 1785. They had already been freed in 1762 from the obligation to perform state service. Now nobles were to have their own association in each guberniia and each uezd. Those associations would not entirely control their own membership, since anyone at the appropriate service rank who held a minimum of land and serfs would be entitled to join. However, noble status could be annulled only for a deed incompatible with the honor of a nobleman, and then only after a trial conducted by other nobles. Landed nobles thus became the first estate in Russian society to possess legally guaranteed corporate rights. In effect, moreover, thanks to the charter, their land and their serfs became their private property.[7] This was part of the settlement which for the first time produced viable local government in a nonmilitary form in Russia. A ruling class, united by a Westernized culture and the ownership of serfs and defined by the first eight levels of the Table of Ranks, now staffed central and local government, the military command, and the diplomatic service. As John LeDonne has remarked, "Serfdom was inseparable from the political supremacy of the nobility, the legitimacy of the ruling house, and the destiny of Great Russia."[8]

At the same time, serfdom placed nearly half the population beyond the reach of state and law. It proved impossible in practice to enforce through the courts a consistent conception of who was entitled to enserf whom, and of how serfs should be treated.[9]

Catherine also granted a charter to the towns, though in a much weaker form, and contemplated granting one to the state peasants, which would have secured for them property rights and corporate status, defendable at law, through their village communities. A draft was completed but was never issued, for reasons unknown. Perhaps she was afraid to arouse fruitless expectations among the private serfs, whose status had actually been weakened by her reform.[10]

In the absence of fundamental laws and of effective corporations other than those of the nobility, we may regard the leading noble families and their interconnections as constituting the substance of the Russian state. Without their sustained efforts and their identification with the new Europeanized order, Russia might have fallen victim to another Time of Troubles after Peter's death, as it had done after that of another ruthless and domineering tsar, Ivan IV.[11]

At the center of the new society and "state" were the army officers, and especially those of the Guards regiments. Even the very highest families could occupy positions of command in those regiments with honor, and those of humbler origins could strive for promotion to them. As LeDonne has put it, they constituted "a political association of the ruling families in the capitals and their clients in the regiments" and "embodied the very function that defined the ruling class, the defense of the collectivity against foreign (and domestic) enemies."[12] Their corporate spirit, though never embodied in specific institutions, was crucial to the survival of the state between Peter's death in 1725 and the accession of Catherine II in 1762. Peter I tried to eliminate even biology as a restraint on the monarch's will by abolishing the existing system of succession. As a result during the eighteenth century descendants of the two families of Aleksei Mikhailovich occupied the throne in haphazard order by virtue of support from the Guards regiments—and were removed from it by the same means.

The creation of a new-style nobility proved in fact to be fruitful and self-sustaining. Initially, young aristocratic males were reluctant to go to "cipher schools" to learn mathematics, navigation, and engineering. But surprisingly quickly, they began to internalize the Petrine spirit. The turning point was probably the opening of the Cadet Corps, which, as we have seen, in spite of their title, were intended to train future civil servants as well as army officers. In addition to practical knowledge they imparted the culture, etiquette, and social graces expected of those who would have to mix with the aristocracies of Europe.[13]

Over time nobles came to see in these acquisitions the decisive criteria which distinguished them from non-nobles, in other words to regard them as a matter of pride. For the sake of their own status, they imbibed and propagated a culture which some of their fellow countrymen regarded as the creation of the Antichrist.

As youths, some nobles were sent to study in universities in France or Germany, at first in supervised groups like unruly schoolboys, later as individuals by their own personal choice. As a result, by the late eighteenth century many of the best noble families spoke French in society, and sometimes even at home, relegating Russian to communication with servants, serfs, and small children. They began to internalize west European culture and to make it part of their own spiritual life, deploring its absence in Russia, rather in the way that late nineteenth-century Indian princes, having been educated at English public schools, would on their return home yearn for the sophisticated social and intellectual intercourse they had known in their youth.

Russia, however, was no colony; it was a sovereign state and one of the strongest European great powers. The colonial-style rift in its culture, between elites and masses, was the more incongruous. Some historians as a result have regarded the Russian nobility as alien to Russia. Vasilii Kliuchevskii wrote of nobles "who tried to be at home among foreigners and succeeded only in being foreigners at home," and Marc Raeff similarly suggested that the experience of European travel and education "denationalized" them.[14]

Michel Confino has questioned these assertions, pointing out that nobles continued to serve in Russian institutions, that on completion of service they could retire to their estates and devote themselves to local affairs, and that most of them retained tender memories of their village childhoods, when they might have been cared for by serf nurses along with serf children.[15]

Confino is surely right: Russian nobles were thoroughly Russian in culture and far from unpatriotic. In fact they might be regarded as the first consciously patriotic Russians. But Kliuchevskii and Raeff have a point too: the nobles' Russianness was very different from that of the peasants, and for that matter of most merchants and clergymen. It was an imperial Russianness, centered on Cadet Corps, Guards regiment, and imperial court, and imbued with social and cultural values derived from France and Germany. Even their landed estates were islands of European culture in what they themselves often regarded as oceans of semibarbarism. The Russianness of the village was important to them, but they knew it was something different. This is the split between *rossiiskii* and *russkii,* between imperial and ethnic Russia, which became crucial during the nineteenth century. A Russian nation could not be created without amalgamating the two, but the pressures of empire tended to drive them ever further apart.

FISCAL NEEDS AND ECONOMIC CONSEQUENCES

The main fiscal device by which the governments of Peter I and his successors paid for the huge new military expenditure was the poll tax, which was introduced in its full form in 1724. It was levied on all males registered among the taxable *(tiaglye)* estates, that is, the peasants (including serfs) and townsfolk. There is controversy over whether by itself it led to an immediate major increase in the tax burden, but three things are quite certain. First of all, since it was levied at the same rate for everyone, regardless of the amount of land or property held, it was highly inequitable, and bore very hard on those least able to pay it. Second, since communities were bound by "joint responsibility" to make up shortfalls, it gave them an additional incentive to ensure that no one fell below the poverty line. In other words, the poll tax generated or reinforced a fiscally motivated egalitarianism. Third, although that very fact made the tax easy to calculate, it also required a regular census of the population to make it effective. Such censuses proved difficult and expensive to carry out, and they had the effect of perpetuating the fixation of the taxable population, rural and urban, to the places where they lived and worked. In 1724 internal passports were introduced, and Peter launched an official campaign to have all "paupers, vagabonds, and footloose people" returned to the communities where they were to be taxed.[16]

The military and accompanying fiscal reforms afford good examples of the way in which Peter I proceeded by consolidating old institutions rather than by creating new ones. He used the relatively simple and uncluttered structure of traditional Russian society to achieve his aims where rival European monarchs had to contend with entrenched privileged corporations. But this absence of intermediate institutions also had its damaging consequences. There were, for instance, no local officials who could be trusted to carry out the census other than landowners, who would be sure to underreport their own serfs. For that reason, the censuses were conducted by army officers also responsible for quartering their troops, giving the whole process an air reminiscent of the levying of tribute by an occupying force.[17]

The development of manufacture had similar paradoxical consequences. Peter was a mercantilist by conviction, that is, he favored encouraging private economic enterprise protected by the state through such means as guaranteed contracts and protectionist tariffs. Needing new textile mills to turn out military uniforms, and ordnance factories and metalworks to produce weapons and ammunition, he invited entrepreneurs to build factories and, when they could not find enough hired labor, "assigned" working hands to them from nearby peasant communities. This system of state-protected and state-nourished "private" enterprise, manned by industrial serfs, worked well during the eighteenth century. It enabled Russia to supply its large army and to become the leading iron exporter of Europe. But it also consolidated a manufacturing system based on patronage and on primitive levels of technology and skill which in the long run proved difficult to adapt to the Industrial Revolution.[18]

The most durable effect of the fiscal and industrial reforms, then, was to fix Russia's economic development in a rigid and rather stagnant mode for a century and a half, at the very time when the acquisition of new and fertile lands in the south and the west offered the opportunity to raise productivity, both agricultural and industrial, to new levels. The center of the problem was the relationship between the landlord and the serf. During the eighteenth century many nobles received from the tsar gifts, sometimes very generous, of land and "black" peasants, who thereby became serfs. The resources put at their disposal should have enabled them to become significant entrepreneurs and to begin mobilizing Russia's abundant natural resources. However, their official duties and their dependence on a backward peasant economy hindered them from taking advantage of that opportunity.

Landlords were above all state servants: they were mostly ignorant of agriculture and were in any case absent for long periods commanding a regiment or governing a distant province. It was the peasants who provided the know-how, the tools, the animals and seeds. For the running of their estates, therefore, the landowners depended on their stewards and on the relationship the latter were able to strike up with the peasant communities. Some ran their affairs by having their own nominees elected to the crucial position of village elder, but many communal assemblies had their own favored candidates, and a steward would usually advise against overruling them, since he needed to work with someone who enjoyed the villagers' confidence.[19]

In that way most landlord estates came to be run as gigantic peasant holdings, farmed in strips according to risk-averse methods which had ensured the village community's survival in the past but which firmly discouraged innovation. Those holdings now had moreover to bear burdens altogether greater than in the past. Nobles coveted the articles of display and conspicuous consumption which they observed at their wealthier neighbors' or while abroad as diplomats and army officers. They adorned their estates with Westernized commodities: fine furniture, paintings, designer gardens, and interior decoration. They dressed in French-style clothes and imported French wines. All these acquisitions entailed an outlay far beyond the reach of any peasant holding, no matter how large. A few landlords managed to improve their husbandry and turn out produce or raw materials needed on the market. But most lacked the knowledge of agriculture or of accountancy which might have enabled them to identify which aspects of their estates could make a profit. It was simpler instead to put extra pressure on the peasants by raising their dues, to mortgage part of the estate, or to exploit connections at court to request official loans.[20] The whole system in effect perpetuated the kormlenie which was supposed to have been abolished two centuries earlier.[21]

Official loans were usually forthcoming: the authorities did not want to see their principal servitors bankrupt. In 1754 a Nobles' Bank was set up for the express purpose of offering them credit at favorable terms. The result was an accumulating mountain of debt: by 1842 half of all serfs were mortgaged to credit institutions as security for loans, and by 1859 two-thirds.[22]

Arguably it was not the serfs who suffered most from this arrangement, but the townsfolk. They did not enjoy the special favor of the tsar and had to bear the burden of taxation and official duties unprotected. The town, its institutions and inhabitants, continued to fulfill the same function as the village: it provided recruits, taxes, and other services to the state. The *posad* people had their own assembly, like villagers, and its members were similarly bound by "joint responsibility," fixed at their dwelling places, and forbidden to leave unless their elected elder gave permission. Fugitives could be hunted down and reclaimed, and the community had a strong interest in doing so, since otherwise it had to discharge the unpaid dues of the absconded.[23]

In recompense for these obligations, the state did not grant the townsfolk any kind of monopoly in trade and manufacture—though merchants did have the right to own serfs between 1721 and 1762. Peasants, landlords' employees, and others were able to trade on urban streets, often at lower prices than the townsfolk, because they did not bear the latters' burdens.

Catherine II modified the situation by granting a charter to the cities in 1785, but it was much less generous than the one awarded to the nobility. It treated merchants (defined as those with capital of more than 500 rubles) as an elite, with their own special duties and privileges. They were freed from the poll tax and from corporal punishment and were given the right to substitute payment for military service. Citizens were divided into six categories, each in theory an independent corporation, entitled to conduct its own affairs and to elect representatives to a municipal council, which oversaw the town's affairs as a whole, under an elected mayor. This was an elaborate structure, and it had the disadvantage that under "joint responsibility" the merchants' exemption from poll tax increased the burden upon other townsfolk. Besides, towns remained part of the structure of the service state: they had no special liberties and could not, for example, take in and provide freedom for serfs. As a result, urban corporations remained largely a fiction.[24]

Because of the restrictions imposed on burghers, the countryside, for all its economic deficiencies, was in some ways a more secure place for ordinary people to live. A serf was at least sure of a plot of land and a minimal income, and agriculture or cottage (kustar) industry was a safer source of revenue than urban commerce or manufacture. The proportion of the population living in the towns declined from 11 percent in the 1740s to 7 percent in the 1860s—in striking contrast to demographic trends elsewhere in Europe.[25]

In the countryside, by contrast, population growth was very high during the late eighteenth and early nineteenth centuries. All the partners in serfdom had an interest in promoting it. The landlord welcomed more working hands and commonly quoted the number of his serfs as an indicator of his status. The village commune needed as many workers as possible to share the burden of paying dues, while households valued early marriage and abundant children because they created claims for new allotments of land.[26]

Population growth generated both new needs and new opportunities. Fortunately, it coincided with the opening up of the new lands in the south, which meant that cheaper grain became available, transported up the Dnieper and Volga to most parts of European Russia. These new resources freed peasants, especially in the less fertile north, from the constant pressure of wringing produce out of ungrateful soil, and enabled them to take up other ways of making money, not always agricultural. The seigneurs were usually happy to see their protégés earn an income and transferred them from barshchina (labor dues) to obrok (dues in money or kind), at least for part of the year, giving them permission to leave the village when necessary.

Peasants working away from home would form an artel, an association of working men who would hire themselves out together to an employer. They usually owned their tools in common and would often lodge together. They would elect a starosta, or elder, who would negotiate with employers, receive the wages, divide them out among the members, and generally keep an eye on work discipline. In some respects the artel resembled the village assembly, and it embodied the conviction that work practices, as well as relations with the outside world, were best handled communally, by consensus.[27]

As a result, by the late eighteenth century there were whole rural areas where kustar industry, rather than agriculture, provided the main source of income. North and east of Moscow there were villages which specialized in linen and silk weaving, and later cotton, for the rapidly growing Moscow clothes market. In Vladimir and Kostroma gubernii was another textile re-

222

gion, centered on the Sheremetev estate at Ivanovo, which during the nine-teenth century became a sizable industrial city. In Nizhnii Novgorod guber-niia tanning and metalworking developed, again on Sheremetev estates, one of which, Pavlovo, became known as "the Russian Sheffield" on account of its specialization in locks, knives, scissors, and surgical instruments. Another example of a highly specialized village was Mstera, Count Panin's estate in Vladimir guberniia, where peasants produced cheap icons, prints, and litho-graphs, which were transported by peddlers all over Russia.

Icons and prints weighed relatively little, but for most products *kustar* industry enjoyed a significant advantage over large-scale manufacture. Given poor communications, it was difficult to transport goods over a long dis-tance: the small-scale flexibility of *kustar* work, for a regional or local market, was therefore more appropriate. Far from providing ruinous competition, the early stages of heavy industrial development actually *encouraged* it by providing basic tools and by training peasants in their use.

The early industrial entrepreneurs were sometimes peasants, nearly always privately owned serfs rather than state peasants. Landlords were crucial, not just in giving permission but in smoothing the road to productive activity, by providing initial capital, making raw materials available, backing up labor discipline, and securing trading privileges, favorable transport tariffs, and the like. They could also intervene to ensure that at the death of a serf entre-preneur, his capital was not dispersed among the members of his commune. Some of the major industrialists of late nineteenth-century Russia were only one or two generations removed from a serf patriarch who had built a mill or a tannery, employed working hands, and accumulated enough wealth to buy from his lord both his own freedom and the property which his labor had created.[28]

Russia's native tradition of early industrialization was thus rural and small-scale, though supplemented by a few large, state-supported enter-prises. It proved enough to sustain her armed forces, state apparatus, and great-power status right up to the first half of the nineteenth century. At that point it reached its natural limits and thereafter constituted a brake on further development. Crucially too, the economic structure placed enormous emphasis on protection, whether of the state or the landlord. Patron-client relations, rather than property and contract, were the surety on which invest-ment was based.

The way in which the state extracted wealth from the economy intensified the archaizing effects of this economic structure. It was not only the poll tax which tended to level and communalize the population. By the middle of the eighteenth century the demands of the Seven Years' War made it clear that additional sources of revenue would have to be found. The easiest way to do this was to increase indirect taxes, especially that on alcoholic liquor: it was far simpler to coax money out of thirsty drinkers than to send punitive expeditions to coerce reluctant poll-tax payers. Russian popular custom demanded bouts of heavy drinking at times of celebration; not to consume large quantities of alcohol on such occasions was to acquire a bad reputation.

The state liquor monopoly was farmed out and was a source of enrichment to its agents—officials, landowners, and publicans (the latter often Jews in the western provinces)—right up to the 1860s, when it was replaced by an excise levy. By 1759 the liquor revenue constituted about a fifth of the state budget, and this rose to 40 percent by the 1850s. The tax-farmers *(otkupshchiki)* had no scruples about boosting their income by illegal methods: adulterated, shortweight, or inferior products masquerading as expensive ones. Provincial officials often considered bribes for overlooking these infringements as a normal part of their income. As one commentator put it, "the police officials themselves are farmed out to the tax farmers."[29]

From 1769, initially in order to finance the Turkish war of 1768–1774, the state regularly issued paper money *(assignaty)*, unbacked by gold or silver. Naturally enough, as a result, the paper ruble declined in value, and by 1817 was worth only 25 kopecks. During the 1820s and 1840s the treasury attempted to restore financial probity by treating *assignaty* as state debt, buying them back and destroying them, but never had enough bullion to complete the exercise. The high cost of the Crimean War and of crushing the Polish rebellion (1863–64) then unleashed a further round of financial instability.

It would be an exaggeration, but not a grotesque one, to say that the empire was kept financially afloat on paper money and on the drunkenness of the common people. War had to be avoided whenever possible, because it threatened financial ruin. To maintain its empire, the Russian state was overreaching itself, overstraining what the resources of land and people could sustain at current levels of technology. Its demands, moreover, were cramping enterprise, obstructing the development of an internal market and of investment such as might have improved that technology. Now of course tax-farming was far from unknown in other empires: both ancient Rome and seventeenth- and eighteenth-century France relied heavily on it. But in both cases, and in Russia too, it obstructed the equitable collection of revenues, hampered economic growth, and reduced the state's ability to mobilize real wealth.

For the peasants these arrangements were burdensome and unjust but not altogether intolerable. Neither the state nor the landowners had any interest in exploiting them to the extent of ruining them. Furthermore, being bound to the land at least meant that they were *guaranteed* land and, in a normal year, subsistence, unlike peasants in some contemporary European countries who were being crowded off their traditional lands by enclosures and other devices of the market economy. Landlords even had in theory a duty to provide grain for their serfs at times of famine. Steven Hoch's study of Petrovskoe, the Gagarin estate in Tambov Province, shows that in a normal year peasants enjoyed a reasonable level of consumption, not inferior to that enjoyed by peasants in most of Europe. In bad years, on well-run estates, the steward would make grain available to the peasants from the lord's granary—though admittedly in some years, such as 1833–34, not in sufficient quantities to avert a subsistence crisis. The author concludes that the serfs were supported by "a paternalistic but limited welfare system."[30]

Paternalistic it certainly was: the lords or their stewards were, in effect, tax collectors, recruiting sergeants, policemen, and appeal judges for their serfs—a relationship which was total and open to abuse, but which guaranteed both sides minimal conditions for life.

In practice, and increasingly so during the eighteenth and early nineteenth centuries, these functions were exercised by the mir itself, especially tax collection and recruiting. In that way the mir's elected officials became ever more an appendage of the state structure, with increasingly formalized and written procedures, even while the mir retained its function as a corporate organization of peasant households.[31]

Provided that they diligently applied traditional agricultural practices, paid their dues, and obeyed the lord and his steward, peasants could lead a tolerable existence. The demands placed upon them encouraged a cautious and egalitarian approach to life. "Joint responsibility" was at the center of it. It was useful to the lord because it simplified the problem of collecting taxes and raising recruits, it helped the peasants by ensuring minimal subsistence for each household in all but the most exceptional crises, and it greatly simplified the state's administrative tasks.

"Joint responsibility" colored the peasant outlook on all aspects of life: economics, work patterns, culture, law, property, and authority. Its principles were embodied in the village assembly, the *skhod,* which consisted of all heads of households, customarily the oldest males. Very seldom was the head of household a woman. The *skhod* was responsible for apportioning the burden of taxes and dues, regulating land tenure, and managing common land (pastures, woods, and so on), determining the crop rotation, maintaining communal facilities (roads, bridges, stores, and also the church building), and supervising law and order. For the day-to-day discharge of these duties the *skhod* would elect from among its own members an elder (*starosta* or *burmistr*), who also assumed the unenviable multiple role of representing the village to the outside world, working with the landlord's steward, and acting as the lowest-level (unpaid) official of the state.[32]

The *starosta* would chair meetings of the village assembly, which might be held in a peasant hut, the church porch, or even in the open air. There was no formal procedure, so that those who spoke loudest or who were most adept at catching the elder's eye could influence decisions disproportionately, as could the "best people," the older and wealthier members of the community. This was direct democracy of a kind, but in practice usually functioned as a tradition-bound oligarchy, with its direct ties to the landlord or, in the case of "black" peasants, the nearest officials of the state.[33]

In many parts of Russia the assembly would maintain material equality by periodically redistributing the community's main resource, usually its arable land, though in the far north it might be timber or fishing rights. This procedure ensured that each household had enough for subsistence and the discharge of its share of the commune's dues. It was linked to the strip system of land tenure, which guaranteed each household a share in land of different types around the village, near and distant, dry and marshy, fertile and less fertile. Since all households went through cycles of growth and decline caused by births, marriages, deaths, and illness, these redistributions would be periodically repeated, whether as partial adjustments or as wholesale rearrangements. The commonest criterion for allotting land was the amount of labor power at the disposal of each household, though in some places a consumption norm was applied, that is, the number of mouths to be fed. In either case, the amount of land held by a household determined the share it had to pay of the dues borne by the whole village.[34]

These arrangements generated a mentality which emphasized risk minimization, egalitarianism, and dependence on patronage. On the whole, they discouraged the entrepreneurial spirit. A peasant who enriched himself was likely to travel and have good connections in the outside world, and hence to be in a far better position to abscond or otherwise to evade his communal obligations, leaving others to make up the shortfall. Resentment of successful individuals was not wholly irrational: it was rooted in the social structure.

All the same, entrepreneurialism was not absent. As we have seen above, many peasants were engaged in producing for the market, and a few were extremely successful. Some used their wealth to become moneylenders, shopkeepers, or operators of the state liquor monopoly, in which positions they could enrich themselves further. These were the *kulaki* (fists) or *miroedy* (commune-eaters) of village demonology.

The communal way of life tended also to be stifling for young men, especially if they came from large families. The apportionment of tax by household encouraged large, multigenerational households, dominated by the *bolshak,* or patriarch. Younger adult males usually had to wait for his death before they could inherit land, and even then if there were many brothers each would receive only a small portion. Often they would try to set up on their own earlier, but doing so would almost invariably provoke bitter family disputes. The long-term tendency to the fragmentation of holdings guaranteed impoverishment and conflict, unless other sources of income could be found.[35]

Communal arrangements of the mir type had been common in Europe in the Middle Ages but were in decline by the fifteenth or sixteenth centuries, along with other aspects of the feudal system, including serfdom. What is striking about the Russian case is that the absolute monarchy, supposedly a modernizing force, perpetuated and even strengthened them. Modernization entailed intensifying some of the most archaic aspects of Russian society, including serfdom, joint responsibility, the introverted village community, and the dependence of the peasants on patronage.

At the very time when the nobles were adopting a cosmopolitan European culture and taking over many "modern" attitudes as that word is usually understood, the peasants on their estates were being forced back into a more primitive way of life. Nobles lived in a world defined for them by a cosmopolitan culture, the habit of command, bureaucratic or military service, the hierarchical Table of Ranks, and competition for posts or honors. The peasants, on the contrary, inhabited an egalitarian universe whose culture was parochial, whose decisionmaking was consensual, and whose paramount priority was survival in adverse conditions. The mentalities generated by these very different life situations were so different as often to be mutually incomprehensible.

Many nobles were uneasily aware of this gulf. A few of them came to think the peasants' outlook was superior. Prince Petr Kropotkin, one of the founders of Russian anarchism, reflected in later life: "Brought up in a landowning family, I, like all young people of my time, entered life with the sincere conviction that one must command, give orders, rebuke, punish, and so on. But as soon as I had to undertake responsible business and so to enter into relationships with people . . . I realized the difference between behaving on the basis of discipline and on the basis of mutual understanding . . . between an official approach to business and a social or mir approach."[36]

It seems clear that the peasants themselves found their situation frustrating, even if they normally acquiesced in it. The ways of the imperial state and of the nobles who were its immediate representatives became ever more alien to them. Their fundamental grievance was not serfdom itself, but land tenure. Though they were prepared to give service to the state and to provide recruits for its armies, they regarded the land as theirs or as God's, a communal resource to be available to all those who cultivated it and had need of it. When a young nobleman, I. D. Iakushkin, decided to free his serfs around 1820, the peasants rejected his plan because he intended to keep the land as his own property, paying them a wage to cultivate it. "In that case, *batiushka*, let's leave things as they are: we are yours, but the land is ours."[37] They still wanted his patronage and were prepared to acknowledge subjection to him, but they insisted on their right to the land.

Did this attitude actually imply that the peasants had a coherent social ideal to counterpose to the practices of the imperial state? The "joint responsibility" and participatory self-government of the mir did offer a potential alternative ideology, but one which the peasants themselves were poorly placed to articulate. It was not badly summarized, though, in a pamphlet of 1830, apparently written by a peasant: "Freedom, the tsar, and one Christian law for all." Many peasants simply used the time-honored word *pravda* to capture it. In this context it implied that the land was for everyone who needed it and was prepared to work it, and that if need be the tsar would guarantee the fairness of the arrangements.[38]

In general, however, peasants needed outsiders to articulate their social ideal persuasively, and for that matter to organize unrest which transcended village boundaries. In the seventeenth and eighteenth centuries those outside leaders were Cossacks, whose ideal of *volia*—the democratic, participatory frontier community, with its elected leader—overlapped with that of the peasant. The Old Belief and the various sectarian movements, which often espoused some kind of egalitarianism and were opposed to the imperial state, also offered motifs which could easily intersect with peasant aspirations, in their opposition to a state which was becoming impersonal and bureaucratic, and whose officials wore strange clothes.

In 1705 *streltsy* and Old Believers in Astrakhan refused to accept the new rules outlawing beards and enforcing "German" dress. In letters to the Cossacks the rebels claimed that the "real" tsar had been imprisoned or killed and replaced by an impostor who "instead of God-respecting carol-singing uses masquerades and games" (probably a reference to the All-Drunken Assembly). "We stood up in Astrakhan for the Christian faith and against shaving and German dress and tobacco and because we and our wives and children were not admitted into God's church in old Russian dress."[39]

In 1707–08 there was serious trouble among the Don Cossacks, led by their ataman, Kondratii Bulavin. Resentments at Western dress and restrictions on

Cossack liberties were compounded by an official attempt to round up fugitives whom the Cossacks had welcomed into their communities. Bulavin claimed that "our pious tsar" was being subverted by "wicked men and princes and boyars and profitmakers and Germans" who were "leading everyone into the Hellenistic pagan faith and diverting them away from the true Christian faith with their signs and cunning tricks." Like Stepan Razin, Bulavin drew support from a variety of social, ethnic, and religious groups, some of whom were Muslims and cannot have been the least interested in the "true Christian faith," but all of whom had grievances against the imperial regime. Also like Razin, he was eventually betrayed by disaffected followers in his own ranks.[40]

The explosive mixture of Cossackdom and Old Belief was epitomized in the person and movement of Emelian Pugachev, leader of the greatest of all Russia's popular rebellions (1773–1775). Like its predecessors, the rebellion broke out in the southeastern borderlands, where Old Believers and other fugitives from imperial authority rubbed shoulders with non-Russian steppe tribesmen and where Cossacks defended the tsar's fortresses and stockades while continuing to dream of the brigands' license which had been their birthright. Pugachev was himself a Don Cossack, but his movement began among the Yaik (or Ural) Cossacks. Their integration into the imperial army was causing concern and resentment among the rank and file, who feared losing their *volia* and their participatory institutions. Pugachev converted to the Old Belief and assumed the title of Emperor Peter III, who he claimed had not been murdered after all but had meekly accepted his dethronement and then, after visiting Constantinople and Jerusalem, had wandered sadly among his people, learning of their sufferings and grievances.

In his manifesto of July 1774 Pugachev set forth the ideal which he knew would have the greatest resonance among the common people.

By God's grace, We, Peter III, Emperor and Autocrat of all the Russias . . . with royal and fatherly charity grant by this our personal ukaz to all who were previously peasants and subjects of the *pomeshchiki* to be true and loyal servants of our throne, and we reward them with the ancient cross and prayer, with bearded heads, with liberty and freedom and to be for ever Cossacks, demanding neither recruit enlistment, poll tax, nor other money dues, and we award them the ownership of the land, of forests, hay meadows, and fishing grounds, and with salt lakes, without purchase and without dues in money or in kind, and we free peasants and all the people from the taxes and burdens which were previously imposed by the wicked nobles and mercenary urban judges.

He also accused the landlords of having violated "the ancient tradition of the Christian law" and introducing "an alien law taken from German traditions."[41]

Many elements in his narrative derived from an idealized version of the old Muscovite national legend: beards, Christian law, the evocation of Constantinople and Jerusalem, the offer to restore a simple, just, and personalized service state, the rejection of secularism and "German" ways among the nobility. He synthesized them with Cossack elements—freedom, service without enlistment—and with elements he knew would appeal to peasants: the ownership of land without payment, freedom from taxes.

It is significant that his manifesto appealed both to Russians and non-Russians, though he also made specific offers directed at particular groups of followers: to the Bashkirs and Kalmyks the return of their tribal grazing lands, to the serfs of the Urals factories release from bonded manual labor.

The diversity of his appeal meant that Pugachev's campaign could recover from setbacks by moving into a new area and raising fresh followers. When he failed to capture the fortress town of Orenburg in the spring of 1774 and lost Kazan in the summer, he moved along the mid- and lower Volga basin, took the authorities by surprise, and attracted a large number of fresh adherents. The final stages of his campaign sparked a general peasant rising. Villagers would gather at the sound of the tocsin, seize whatever weapons they could lay their hands on—scythes, pitchforks, perhaps a musket or two—and march on the local manor house or the state *kabak* (tavern). Nobles and their families, stewards, publicans, tax officials, and sometimes clergymen would flee at the approach of trouble, knowing they could be murdered by the rebels.

Pugachev's weaknesses are as instructive as his strengths. In spite of the fear he aroused and the destruction he wrought, he succeeded in capturing only two major cities (Kazan and Saratov), and then briefly. His army, at times quite numerous—at least 10,000 during the siege of Orenburg—was effective against small garrisons and Cossack units but could not match up to the regular army. Here the wisdom of the policy of recruiting peasants for life manifested itself in full measure. Soldiers in the regular army were immune to Pugachev's appeals: they did not identify with the peasants' or Cossacks' complaints, and they were constrained by a harsh and all-embracing discipline.[42]

The rebellion gathered a whole medley of grievances, many of them local, but above all it represented the resurgence of a Muscovite way of regarding authority and community: simple, moral, and personalized, based on God-given pravda. It protested against an increasingly centralized, rational, secular, and impersonal state.[43]

EXPANSION IN THE SOUTH

The turning point in Russia's duel with the Ottoman Empire did not come till the second half of the eighteenth century, in reaction to a Crimean Tatar raid of 1769—which proved to be the last. By this time the Russian army was larger and had considerably improved its supply administration. Under the effective leadership of Generals Petr Rumiantsev and Aleksandr Suvorov, it was in a position to attempt a three-pronged maneuver, moving simultaneously into the Balkans, toward the Crimea, and through the Caucasus. The Russians also deployed their Baltic fleet, bringing it round through the Atlantic and Mediterranean to confront the Ottoman navy, most of which it destroyed at Chesme Bay (1770). The Crimean campaign was less successful but ended with Russia securing the vital fortresses of Kerch and Enikale, on the eastern tip of the peninsula, and proclaiming the independence of the Crimea. Here, as so often, the Russians saw the "independence" of an opponent's client state as the first stage toward its incorporation into the Russian Empire.

The Treaty of Kuchuk Kainardji (1774), which concluded the war, has been called "in a very real sense the first partition of the Ottoman Empire" and "the turning point in the relations between Europe and the Middle East."[44] Russia received the right to send merchant ships through the Straits and to keep warships on the Black Sea, and built its first port there, Kherson, on the estuary of the Dnieper. Within ten years Russia had incorporated the Crimea (1783), the first time the Ottoman Empire had lost Muslim subjects to a Christian state. In the Caucasus Kabarda became part of the Russian Empire.

No less important than territorial matters were the rights the treaty accorded to the tsar in religious affairs. The Porte undertook "to protect constantly the Christian religion and its churches," and the wording of the relevant clause implied that the Russian envoy in Constantinople would have the right to make representations on behalf of Christians if this undertaking was not observed. Here the ghost of the East Christian ecumene reasserted itself as an instrument of great-power diplomacy. Given that the Russians had persistently raised the question of Orthodox believers' freedom of wor-

Western Russia under Catherine the Great

The provinces of Russia in 1750

Territory annexed by Russia in 1762–1796, giving Russia an outlet on the Black Sea and a common frontier with Prussia and Austria

FINLAND

Helsingfors

Arkhangel

ARKHANGEL

ST. PETERSBURG

ESTONIA

LIVONIA

NOVGOROD

Novgorod

Pskov

Vologda

Viatka

Perm

KURLAND

Niemen

Vilna

Tver

MOSCOW

KAZAN

Kazan

Ufa

PRUSSIA

LITHUANIA

Minsk

SMOLENSK

Moscow

NIZHNII
NOVGOROD

UFA

Warsaw

WHITE RUSSIA

Pinsk

Orel

Stravropol

Samara

PODLESIA

AUSTRIA

Lutsk

KIEV

BELGOROD

VORONEZH

Kiev

Dnieper

Belgorod

ASTRAKHAN

Dniester

PODOLIA

Jassy

ZAPOROZHE

Odessa

Taganrog

Astrakhan

KUBAN

Kutchuk-
Kainardji

CRIMEA

Sebastopol

KABARDA

Tarki

Caspian
Sea

Black Sea

Constantinople

THE

OTTOMAN

EMPIRE

Kars

PERSIA

0	100	200	300 miles
0	250		500 km

ship to destabilize Catholic Poland, the suspicion naturally arose that they intended to do the same to the Turks, especially since the ambassador sent to Constantinople in 1775 was Nikolai Repnin, who had been envoy in Poland.[45]

Under Catherine II's favorite, Count Grigorii Potemkin, Russia rounded off the work of Kuchuk Kainardji by annexing the Crimea, together with the Kuban steppe and the adjacent Taman peninsula. This success enabled Potemkin to build a line of forts right across the north of the Caucasus range, from Taman to the mouth of the Terek, and thus to block raids by the mountain tribes into the steppe. Russia was also at last able to undertake the construction of a Black Sea fleet.

The fears which Kuchuk Kainardji and its sequel aroused in Europe were articulated by Lord Elgin in a letter of 1788 to Prime Minister William Pitt: "Who could say where the court of St. Petersburg would stop if, after forming a solid footing not only in the Crimea, but in other parts of the Black Sea, and striking there at the vitals of the Ottoman Porte, she should seize some unlucky moment when the rest of Europe was unable to assist that country and erect her standard in Constantinople?"[46]

His concerns were justified. Potemkin, as governor of New Russia—the region newly conquered from the Ottomans—harbored just such ambitions. He wanted to use the Terek fortifications and the Black Sea fleet as a power base from which to encourage Caucasian tribal leaders to rebel against the Turks. He expected Balkan Orthodox subjects to be similarly inspired by Russian success and to join the anti-Ottoman campaign. His ultimate aim was the recreation of the Byzantine Empire on the ruins of the Ottoman, with the replacement of the crescent by the cross on the Cathedral of St. Sophia in Constantinople. In preparation for this great event, Catherine had her grandson named Konstantin.[47]

If achieved, this "Eastern Project" would have combined Russia's great-power aspirations with her Orthodox ecumenical ones. The fear that just such a superimposition of political and religious power might prove possible continued to haunt European statesmen throughout the nineteenth century. They never quite became accustomed to Russia's characteristics as a power: her huge size, her labile borders, her latent messianic pretensions, and the nature of her sociopolitical system baffled and repelled them. They were accordingly always liable to band together to obstruct any arrangement which seemed likely to accord Russia too much power in the Balkans and around the Straits.

In reality, partly because of this resistance, Russia's further advance along the Black Sea coast and into the Balkans proved to be surprisingly slow. As a result of war in 1787–1792 she gained the territory between the Bug and

Dniester and was able to found the great port city of Odessa. In 1806–1812 she incorporated Bessarabia—roughly the eastern half of Moldavia—between the Dniester and Prut, where the indigenous inhabitants were Romanians. Finally, in 1828–29 she gained the Danube delta and obtained a protectorate over the Danubian principalities of Moldavia and Wallachia, which remained nominally under Ottoman suzerainty. Under the supervision of the Russian viceroy, Count P. D. Kiselev, the principalities received an aristocratic form of constitutional government.[48] This was another instance of Russia's exercising a shadowy semisovereignty in a territory which she might one day hope to annex.

Slow progress reflected fundamental dilemmas which the Russians continued to face throughout the nineteenth century. Although they wanted the Ottoman Empire to be weak, they did not wish it to collapse altogether, possibly allowing a stronger European power, and one hostile to Russia, to control the Straits. As Foreign Minister Nesselrode wrote in 1830, "If we have allowed the Turkish government to continue to exist in Europe, it is because that government, under the preponderant influence of our superiority, suits us better than any of those which could be set up on its ruins."[49] Russia was therefore torn between attempts to destroy the Ottoman Empire and attempts to prop it up for as long as possible. In 1833, for example, against the apparent tendency of her policy, she sent troops to save the sultan and his capital from the invasion of his rebellious vassal, Mehmet Ali of Egypt.

As far as the Straits themselves were concerned, in the abstract Russia's interest would have been to have the right to send its own warships through them, but to block them to the incursion of anyone else's. This could be achieved, however, only if Russia was on friendly terms with Turkey, and even then only in the teeth of hostility from other European powers.

Russia would have liked to pursue its traditionally successful policy of attracting local elites to its side and then using them to subvert its opponent. In the Balkans this device appeared especially promising, since the relevant elites were Orthodox Christian and might be expected to welcome Russian influence on those grounds alone. But the secular and religious elites of Serbia, Bulgaria, Greece, and the Danube principalities, as Peter I had found in 1711, never entirely overcame the suspicion that Russia was merely using them as pawns in a great power struggle. Nor was it consistent for an autocratic tsar to support rebels against legitimate monarchy.

Add to these dilemmas the geopolitical fact that the Balkans contain many mountains and rivers, natural obstacles to a south-moving army, in LeDonne's words "so many skerries and shoals against which the force of Russian expansion would have to spend itself," and it becomes understandable that Russia's progress there was slow and frustrating, and still incomplete by the end of the eighteenth century.[50]

THE CAUCASUS

Once Russia had established itself fully on the north coast of the Black Sea and was committed to developing the wealth of the region, it was drawn ineluctably into the neighboring strategic cauldron of the Caucasus mountain range and beyond into the Transcaucasus area, between the Black and Caspian Seas. General Rostislav Fadeev explained why this should be so in the 1850s, but his thoughts applied just as cogently sixty years earlier.

> Domination on the Black and Caspian Seas, or in extremity the neutrality of those seas, is a vital interest for the whole southern half of Russia, from the Oka to the Crimea, the area where the principal strength of the empire, material and personal, is more and more concentrated . . . If Russia's horizons ended on the snowy summits of the Caucasus range, then the whole western half of the Asian continent would be outside our sphere of influence and, given the present impotence of Turkey and Persia, would not long wait for another master.[51]

The potential "other master" Fadeev hinted at was Britain, but Turkey, if not Persia, was still quite powerful enough to project her influence into and beyond the Caucasus, using ethnic and religious ties to cause trouble for Russia's wealthiest regions. During wars with the Ottoman Empire, the Caucasus always became an additional front, and even during peace the north Caucasian hill tribesmen constantly threatened the productive agricultural settlements on the Kuban plains not far to the north.

To contain these threats, Russia exploited every opportunity to pursue a forward policy and project her power over the Caucasus range and closer to the Turkish and Persian borders. Here the mountains were somewhat lower, but still formidable, and the crucial arteries were the basins of the Rion and Kura/Araxes Rivers. This was the ancient land of Colchis, home of the mythical Golden Fleece. Here in the Middle Ages Queen Tamara (1184–1212) had ruled over the kingdom of Georgia, whose people had been Christians since the fourth century. Subsequently, under Mongol pressure, the kingdom had broken up into smaller principalities, but they had survived as battered and besieged buffer states between the Muslim empires of Persia and Turkey. From west to east they were Guria, Mingrelia, Imeretia, Kartli (which included the largest city, Tiflis), and Kakhetia. Here lived a population largely of peasants and landed nobles, speaking a variety of dialects, though the literate still cherished the medieval Georgian culture and its language.[52]

Even more embattled were the Armenians. Their homeland was in the eastern half of Anatolia, where their kingdom was subjugated by Pompey in the first century B.C.E. and became part of the Roman Empire. At the beginning of the fourth century they became Christians of the monophysite persuasion, in which, like the Copt and Syrian churches, they have remained to the present day. From the ninth to the eleventh centuries, under the Bagratid dynasty, they enjoyed a wide measure of self-rule under the ultimate suzerainty of the Abbasid caliphate. Later they fell under the Ottoman Empire, in which they formed a separate *millet,* or ethnoreligious community. In the early seventeenth century their principal city of Erevan was conquered by the rising Safavid empire of Persia, and from then on they were divided between the Ottoman and Persian Empires. Because of the insecurity of their homeland, many Armenians became traders and professional people, living in cities all around the Black Sea and throughout the Middle East, where their social position resembled that of the Jews in central and eastern Europe.

Armenians were also divided from one another by region and by social class. The remote hilly country in which the rural population lived impeded communication, especially as Muslims established their dominance under Ottoman or Persian patronage, and as a result Armenians spoke a multiplicity of dialects, many of them mutually incomprehensible. They had two literary languages, a western one based in Constantinople and an eastern one based in Erevan, as well as a written ecclesiastical language, *grabar.* Many Armenian peasants were very poor, especially those in eastern Anatolia, hundreds of miles from the Armenian merchants and professional people scattered in Smyrna, Constantinople, Rostov-on-Don, and the Crimea.

In the early eighteenth century, Russia had begun to expand into the eastern Transcaucasus. At that stage the condition of Persia offered special opportunities. A loose confederation of tribes only intermittently dominated by the shah, it was undergoing a period of weakness and disunity. Peter I set up consulates there for the purposes of trade, but when Russian merchants were molested at Shirvan by Dagestani tribesmen, he attacked along the Caspian coast and took the towns of Derbent and Baku. He hoped thereby, with the help of the Georgian kingdom and of Armenians living in the region, to establish Russia on the western and southern coasts of the Caspian. He and his successors lacked the means, however, to pursue these aims or even to hold on to their recent gains, and it was not till the end of the eighteenth century that Russia's campaign against Persia resumed.[53]

What provoked the renewal of Russia's attempt to dominate the western shores of the Caspian was the Persian invasion of eastern Georgia and conquest of Tiflis in 1795. Despite early setbacks the Russian army conquered Derbent and Baku, and by the Treaty of Gulistan (1813) annexed several khanates in the Kura basin and along the Caspian coast, containing about half the Azeri population of Persia. By the Treaty of Turkmanchai (1828) Nakhichevan and Erivan were added, so that Russia's southern frontier ran along the Araxes River and included the eastern half of historical Armenian territory. Probably not more than 20 percent of its population was Armenian at the time of annexation, but thereafter thousands of Armenians immigrated from Persia and the Ottoman Empire, seeking what they hoped would be greater security in a Christian realm. Persia was thus crowded out of the Transcaucasus and much of the Caspian shoreline.[54]

The Georgians, too, though living in their own kingdoms, welcomed the prospect of Christian protection against their Muslim neighbors. In 1783 King Heraclius II of Kartli and Kakhetia offered Russia an ideal opportunity by seeking a guarantee against Persian aggression. In return for assurances of military protection, he made the Bagratid royal succession and the conduct of foreign policy subject to Russian approval. These assurances could be made effective only if Russia had the means to mount military operations over the Caucasus, and for that purpose it built a new fortress on the Terek, Vladikavkaz (Lord of the Caucasus), and a military highway from there over the Caucasus range to Tiflis, the capital of Georgia.

In spite of their promises the Russians could not prevent the Persians from devastating Tiflis in 1795, taking some 30,000 captives back home. But the defense and maintenance of the Georgian Military Highway, as a key to the domination of the Caucasus, became one of the main aims of Russian foreign and military policy. It was an exceedingly demanding one, for the highway led through harsh and precipitous terrain inhabited by some of the most warlike people in the world. Living in steep and isolated valleys, divided from one another by high mountain walls, these were tiny peoples, each speaking a separate language and each jealously defending its own independence. They were tribes or even clans, not nations, and the extended family was the dominant force in each. So to use national terms is an oversimplification, but with that reservation one can speak of the numerous Dagestani peoples in the east, closest to the Caspian Sea, and, moving west from there, of the Chechens, the Ingush, the Ossetians (long-standing allies of the Georgians and partly Christianized), the Kabardinians (core of a major kingdom in the sixteenth century), the Balkars, the Karachais, the Circassians, and the Abkhazians. They were transhumant nomads, pasturing their cattle and sheep on the alpine meadows in the summer, and descending to the plains bordering the mountains in the winter. Like other nomadic peoples, they also conducted raids into settled territories, to obtain slaves and booty.

Among them the most consistently effective warriors were the Chechens, who in peacetime had no internal hierarchy, no princes or barons, but rather a multitude of clans, some of them feuding with others. At time of war, however, the clans would drop their squabbles, join forces, and elect military leaders, whom they would obey for the duration of the war. Most of the other peoples had native aristocracies and more or less stable feudal systems. In religion they were mainly animist, and Islam was only just beginning to establish itself during the eighteenth century.

The building of the Terek forts and the Russian encroachments on the Caucasus made inroads into the tribes' traditional way of life and actually provoked the spread of Islam as an ideology of resistance. A good focus for the emergence of a democratic Islamic resistance proved to be Sufi brotherhoods. Sufism was originally a contemplative movement, but the intense relationship which existed between mentor (*murshid* or *sheikh*) and initiate could be used in time of danger to fire collective militant action. Hierarchy and obedience to the tribal *beg* were replaced by egalitarianism, self-sacrifice, and devotion to the Prophet. The brotherhoods repudiated the chieftains and their compromises with imperial envoys: here the traditional Russian policy of co-opting indigenous elites backfired and actually provoked widespread and effective resistance.[55]

The first Muslim insurrectionist leader was Sheikh Mansur, who in 1785 declared a *ghazawat* (holy war) against the importunate unbelievers. He preached that the north Caucasian clans should abandon their petty feuds and unite in the name of Islam to repel the invaders from the north. He assembled an army of some 20,000 from various peoples and besieged the Russian fortress of Kizliar, but failed to take it. However, his army certainly obstructed Russian strategic aims, and it was six years before he could be captured. If the Turks had supported him, they might have prevented Russian penetration of the Caucasus, but the Ottoman authorities distrusted the Sufism of the Naqshbandi order which inspired Mansur.[56]

Faced with this kind of impediment to their mastery of the Caucasus, the Russian authorities were uncertain how to react. They described their dilemma as that of "the samovar or the sword." Some felt that the only way to proceed in such unfavorable terrain was to continue the traditional policy of forging alliances with individual princes and military leaders, lavishing gifts and favors on them and gradually drawing them into permanent subjection. Others, discerning that this policy fueled the very popular opposition it was meant to preempt, maintained that only military action could overcome the resistance. Since it was impossible to storm hundreds of mountain valleys at once, such action would have to be patient, protracted, and determined.[57]

With hesitations and interruptions, that was the policy which was pursued. Its most determined proponent was General Ermolov, governor of the Caucasus (1816–1827), who proceeded by destroying swathes of forest and burning down whole villages, in order to deprive the indigenous peoples of the environment which sustained their way of life and thus induce them to submit. "I desire," he proclaimed, "that the terror of my name should guard our frontiers more potently than chains of fortresses." His punitive expeditions naturally encouraged Russian soldiers to rape and pillage on their own behalf. When rebuked by the emperor for such excesses, Ermolov replied that "condescension in the eyes of Asiatics is a sign of weakness, and out of pure humanity I am inexorably severe. One execution saves hundreds of Russians from destruction and thousands of Muslims from treason."[58]

The "executions," of course, were not confined to those who were guilty, even in the eyes of the Russians, and Ermolov's policy certainly fanned the flames of resistance. The greatest of all the north Caucasian Muslim leaders, Imam Shamil, took over a movement which was already well established when he raised his banner in 1834. Though a Dagestani by origin, he based himself among the Chechens, the most intractable of the mountaineers. Overriding inherited hierarchies, he proclaimed the rule of Islamic law and enforced it ruthlessly. He also used the Sufi brotherhoods and their disciples as the kernel of informal armed bands which would descend at any moment on a Russian outpost or convoy, exploiting surprise and mobility to inflict maximum damage, then melt back into the uplands and forests. Although he was several times close to defeat and capture, he exhibited an almost miraculous capacity to recover, relocate, raise new armies, and harass the Russians from yet another quarter.

So brusque was his treatment of traditional clan chieftains that not all Chechens, let alone the other peoples, wholeheartedly supported his leadership. When the Ottoman Empire failed to support him during the Crimean War, his reputation began to fade, and more and more villages surrendered to the Russians. In 1859 the Russians were able to storm his stronghold, Mount Gunib, held by the relatively small forces remaining loyal to him, and to take him prisoner. The viceroy of the Caucasus, Prince A. I. Bariatinskii, received him with full military honors, and he was later given an honorable confinement in an official residence before being allowed to undertake a pilgrimage to Mecca. Such was the attitude of a traditional multiethnic empire toward a respected opponent.

Thereafter the way was open for the Russian army, free of other commitments, finally to impose its will, which it did by a systematic campaign of tree-felling, crop-burning, road-building, and destruction of villages. This campaign was especially ruthless at the western end of the Caucasus, among the Circassians, who were a numerous people and relatively close to the Ottoman Empire. No outside help came to them, however, and by 1864 all armed resistance had been overcome. The Russian authorities then resettled many Circassians on the plains, but at least 300,000 of them, more than half their population, and by some estimates a million Caucasians altogether, preferred exile instead and set sail for Turkey.[59]

Overall, then, methods which had served the Russian authorities well enough over the centuries on the steppes provoked ferocious resistance in the mountains and impelled them to undertake policies which were genocidal. Their victory entailed one of the first mass deportations of modern history and left an enduring legacy of hatred and a desire for vengeance which has made the Caucasus a permanent festering sore in the Russian body politic.[60]

THE "REGULAR" STATE UNREALIZED

In the second half of the eighteenth century and the first half of the nineteenth century the sinews of the Russian state were still mainly ones of personal dependence. Local communities were for most purposes self-governing and distributed taxes and military obligations among their own members. To obtain service from the mass of the people, the government relied principally on its rural agents, the landed nobles, and, where they did not exist, on the police and military. Revenues came to the state either through the landlord's steward, the police, the military, or the excise farmer who ran the state tavern. In each case there was little effective check on how much the receivers actually collected: only the desire not to ruin the source of their income restrained their acquisitiveness. Within those limits landowners and state officials could dispose more or less as they liked of the products and labor power of townsmen and peasants under their authority. The relationship between subjects and officials was still not very different from that which had pertained in the tribute-gathering nomadic empires and khanates of old.

Given the extent of its burdens as a great power, Russia probably had no choice but to use the means most readily available of mobilizing the population and its resources. But by the mid-nineteenth century those means had become insufficient, even counterproductive, and constituted a threat to continuing great-power status.[61]

Already for at least half a century statesmen had been warning that this critical point was not far away, that the time would soon come when it would be necessary to bring the majority of the population more effectively under the control of state institutions, mediated by the rule of law and financed by a more equitable tax system tapping the true sources of the country's wealth. Patronage would be replaced by state authority and tribute by an ordered fiscal system, while conflicts arising in both would be settled by courts of law. Beyond these institutional issues, Russia's rulers yearned for a more conscious support from the population, generated not by habit or coercion but by willing identification with the state—in short, for patriotism and civic consciousness. By the end of the eighteenth century these qualities were widespread among the nobility and the upper ranks of officialdom, who observed them also among the citizens—normally the elites—of the European countries where they derived their higher education or spent time as diplomats.

The French Revolution and the Napoleonic wars confronted Russia more acutely than ever with their desirability. Napoleonic France looked like a country where modern representative institutions, the rule of law, and universal military service had engendered an unprecedented level of patriotism and effectiveness on the battlefield.[62] Some of its institutions functioned well too in other parts of Europe for more than a decade, including Poland, so that they could not be dismissed as unexportable products of the French genius. They looked like the wave of the future, and Russia as a great European power could not afford to be left far behind.

Such were the considerations which were to animate Alexander I for much of his reign. They were sharpened by the experience of his predecessor, Paul.

FREEMASONRY

By the second half of the eighteenth century, as we have seen, nobles were beginning to respond well to the state's educational initiatives. The results were not always what official educationalists might have expected, though. Some young nobles internalized the ethic of service at least as fully as Peter can have anticipated, but with results he would certainly not have approved.

With the Orthodox Church eased out of the secondary and higher education systems (except for the training of their own clergy), nobles began to look elsewhere for their spiritual life. Some of them discovered freemasonry. Its attraction was that it offered a framework of community and ritual for the servitors of the secular, mobilizing state. It also offered a network of personal connections useful to a young man in advancing his career, and provided him with some protection even when he was in other European countries. It was thus well suited to a secularizing state resting on personal patronage.

One of the first lodges in Russia was opened in St. Petersburg in the 1750s, and included graduates of the Cadet Corps. Its grandmaster was Ivan Elagin, director of the court theater. By the 1760s, it has been estimated, perhaps a third of the higher civil and military officials (above grade eight) were masons. When they joined a lodge they took an oath obliging them to be "an unshakable witness to the majesty and great wisdom of my Maker Most High, a loyal subject of my gracious Sovereign, a straightforward and worthy son of my dear Fatherland, a peaceful and good citizen," and to "endeavor to help the poor, comfort the unhappy, and defend the oppressed."[63] Peter I would have approved of every word of this oath, but he had tried to impose these ideals through his *fiskaly*. To have them taken up by active, patriotic, self-aware citizens was to unleash forces which all the *fiskaly* in the empire could not control.

One of the most active freemasons was Nikolai Novikov, a member of Elagin's lodge, whom Catherine II selected as a young man to be secretary of a subcommittee of her Law Code Commission, the one concerned with the formation of a "third estate" or "middle class." He was an apt choice, for he was a pioneer of what might be seen as Russia's distinct middle-class, or perhaps more accurately professional, ethos, based not on wealth or commerce but on culture, learning, and service to the community. He founded several satirical journals which directed their ridicule at a corrupt bureaucracy and an idle society, at those who, though noblemen, fell short of the ideal of "noble man." Through his masonic connections Novikov was able to take over the lease of Moscow University's printing press and launch a wide-ranging publishing program. He issued not only religious tracts and masonic devotional works but also textbooks and grammars, translations from foreign thinkers, and some of the first documentary publications on Russian history. He devoted the income from their sale to charitable activities, such as famine relief and the provision of elementary education, in which children were to be "trained in piety and prepared for further study for the sake of themselves and their Fatherland." These were probably the first Russian charitable associations independent of either church or state.[64]

Catherine II initially approved of freemasonry, since it seemed to supplement, free of charge, the government's own efforts in the fields of education, justice, and the relief of poverty. It was only gradually, and especially after the French Revolution, that she became doubtful about confidential cliques with aims which could be construed as subversive or heretical.

Specifically, Catherine suspected Novikov of involvement in a plot, backed by Prussia through the masons, to overthrow her in favor of her son, Paul. The fact that philanthropy and enlightenment could be promoted only through a clandestine society proved to be his undoing. He was arrested in 1792, accused of heresy and treason, and sentenced to fifteen years in the Shlisselburg fortress.[65]

A similar fate befell Aleksandr Radishchev, another nobleman who internalized official values too thoroughly for his own good (though, as far as is known, he never became a mason). As a young man, he was personally chosen by Catherine to study in Germany, where among other things he was instructed to learn "natural law" and "moral philosophy." This he certainly did, though not quite in the way Catherine had intended. He was impressed by "natural law" as a universal ideal to which monarchs themselves should be subject, and he was strongly influenced by the German Pietist form of Enlightenment thinking, which emphasized the duty of the good citizen to actively promote improvement and the general welfare. From his later work in the Senate, where he had to investigate alleged abuses of authority, he came to believe that although monarchical power was justified, it needed to be tempered by the rule of law and the separation of powers. He expounded his vision of civil patriotism and civil society in an article of 1789, "What Is a Son of the Fatherland?"—a title which ironically echoed Peter I's claim to be "Father of the Fatherland." He concluded that the good citizen should have the virtues of an aristocracy—honor, ambition, nobility of soul—complemented by the civic merits of upright behavior and love of one's fellow men.[66]

That the Russian aristocracy did not display these virtues he showed at length in his didactic travelogue *A Journey from St. Petersburg to Moscow*, in which he fleshed out his indictment of Russian society. At each stage in his journey the narrator comes into contact with some evil: corruption, drunkenness, prostitution, superstition, the recruitment system. Serfdom is shown to be both an immoral institution and an impediment to the economy. At the end of the text an "Ode to Freedom," supposedly from another hand, attacks monarchy unrestrained by the rule of law as the fount of these evils and warns of the danger of tyrannicide and of peasant revolution.

Somehow this work slipped past the censor, was published anonymously, and became an overnight celebrity among educated Russians. Catherine was thoroughly alarmed and ordered that its author be sought out. Radishchev was arrested, stripped of his noble title, charged with sedition, and sentenced to death. Catherine commuted his sentence to ten years' exile in Siberia. Radishchev's work did much to launch the peculiarly Russian nineteenth-century literary tradition: realist, conscience-stricken, critical of existing society.[67]

244

6

THE REIGNS OF PAUL,

ALEXANDER I, AND NICHOLAS I

By the end of the eighteenth century the new state traditions and the culture associated with them had taken root, but only in one social class, the nobility. To bridge the gap thus opened between the nobility and other social strata, a monarch could proceed in one of two alternative ways: he could confirm and strengthen nobles' freedoms, in the hope that they would gradually broaden out into the rule of law for everyone; or, on the contrary, he could restrain nobles' privileges and use his autocratic power to promote equality and justice.

The former approach was likely to be more effective, but would intensify existing inequalities and injustices, while the latter would be far more difficult to implement: it would entail abolishing serfdom and would curtail the only genuine freedoms currently available to any social class. Moreover, it meant bypassing the patronage networks maintained by the great noble families. All the same, it was what Paul set out to do. He abolished the noble associations, together with their right to elect local officials, whom he appointed instead. He subjected landed estates to taxation, like any peasant plot, and abolished the gentry's emancipation from state service along with their exemption from corporal punishment. To see that nobles served like any other social estate and hatched no plots against himself, he used his intelligence service (now called the *tainaia ekspeditsiia*) to spy and report on them. The right of serfs to petition the monarch about mistreatment was restored, and Paul was the first sovereign to place legal limits on serfs' obligations by prohibiting the exaction of forced labor on Sundays.

At the same time he tried to isolate Russia from the contagion of the French Revolution by forbidding the import of books and journals and prohibiting travel abroad—which was the normal way for a wealthy young aristocrat to round off his education. If such policies had been pursued for long, they would have undermined Russia's distinctive aristocratic culture and degraded its capacity to participate successfully in European diplomatic life.

Paul was inconsistent in promoting greater social equality, since he awarded his favorites land populated by peasants no less bountifully than his mother had done. There is not much doubt, too, that his character was unbalanced: he was given to furious outbursts of rage. But his madness, if that is what it was, reflected the objective situation of the Russian autocracy, its huge claims matched by only limited resources.

At any rate, the nobles and especially the Guards officers resented the humiliations he imposed on them. In 1801 a group of them, led by the governor-general of St. Petersburg, Count Petr Palen, deposed and murdered him. Undermining privilege, disdaining patronage networks, and promoting equality was shown to be a disastrous policy for a monarch to pursue.[1]

THE REIGN OF ALEXANDER I (1801–1825)

Paul's successor, Alexander, also set out to challenge the omnipotence of patronage, but in a completely different way: not through despotism but by means of the rule of law. His reign was a turning point no less decisive than that of Peter the Great. It marked the moment when the "regular" state was beginning to acquire substance, when senior officials expected its framework to be filled out by the practice of "equity" or the "rule of law." Senatorial government had proved cumbersome and ineffective in many respects, but it had generated the expectation of legality and correct procedure, and the sense that the widespread sway of patronage and personal whim was somehow illegitimate. The very accumulation of unsettled cases in the Senate's files demonstrated that Russians of all social estates were taking it seriously as supreme arbiter in the power hierarchy.[2]

The circumstances of Alexander's reign offered him a supreme challenge, the French invasion of 1812, but also a supreme opportunity, a mood of patriotic unity such as Russians had not experienced for two centuries. It was a time when government, society, and the masses might have been drawn into a closer association resting on "regular" institutions and the rule of law. That was what many educated Russians both wished and expected to happen, and when it did not they were disappointed and embittered. The question "Who is to blame?" *(kto vinovat?)* began to seem crucial.

At the outset of the reign the auspices were favorable. Alexander was welcomed by elite society, partly because he was not Paul, but partly because he was a charming and courteous person and was known to be an admirer of his grandmother and a pupil of the Enlightenment. The tutor whom she had chosen for him, Frédéric-César La Harpe, was a Swiss "republican," that is to say someone who believed in citizenship and the rule of law. Alexander was impressed by his teachings, but combined his devotion to them with a kind of premature world-weariness which indicated tensions within his personality. He alternated the harsh exercise of authority with a yielding disposition, a readiness to relinquish real power to representative and responsible institutions. He told his tutor that he hoped to create a constitution and a representative assembly which would supersede his own authority and enable him to "retire to some spot where I will live contentedly and happily, observing and taking pleasure in the well-being of my country." It was sentiments of this kind which moved the philosopher Nikolai Berdiaev to call Alexander "a Russian *intelligent* on the throne."[3]

Alexander was one of the most sensitive and educated men of his generation, but he was no melting aesthete. He combined delicacy and responsiveness of character with a readiness to act firmly, even ruthlessly, when he felt it to be necessary. The internal tension induced by trying to blend these contradictory qualities inclined him to be secretive and to show different aspects of his personality to different individuals.

When it came to fulfilling the expectations aroused by his accession, the same difficulties arose as under Catherine and Paul. As we have seen, one could proceed either by extending and consolidating the privileges of the one social class which already possessed a measure of political independence, the nobility—broadly speaking the Whig approach—or one could act like a Jacobin and try to spread civil rights more broadly among the population as a whole. There was also a dilemma about how reform might be decided upon, formulated, and carried out. If it meant curbing the privileges of the nobles, then they could hardly be expected to implement it. In that case it was important that autocracy, the ruler's freedom of action, remain unimpaired. But then what would remain of the rule of law or representative institutions?

Alexander never solved this fundamental dilemma. He was divided on the issue, and he learned to disguise his views when talking to people. In his youth he had been subject to the influence not only of La Harpe, but also of his father's court at Gatchina, with its imposing military ceremonial. There he got to know Aleksandr Arakcheev, a minor landowner and artillery officer who had been Paul's chief adviser and impressed Alexander too by his blunt, even brutal honesty. In short, the circumstances of his life made the exercise of absolute authority seem natural, especially since it might be needed even to carry out the reform plans he never entirely dropped.

In the early years of his reign, Alexander took seriously the "Whig" view, presented by the so-called senatorial party, that the Senate should be elected by the *dvorianstvo* and should act as a repository and guarantor of the laws, but he eventually rejected it.[4] He gave much more attention to a private coterie of friends, highly educated young aristocrats, which he called the "Confidential Committee" *(neglasnyi komitet),* or sometimes in jest the "Committee of Public Safety." One of them, Pavel Stroganov, had actually attended meetings of the Club des Jacobins in Paris. The circle met frequently and probably discussed, among other things, the abolition of serfdom. But it remained true to its title, confidential, and its deliberations were not recorded, still less published. It eventually dispersed, having achieved very little.

Alexander was tenacious, though. He never altogether abandoned the hope of consolidating "regular" government and of extending its authority deeper into Russian society. His views about how this might best be done changed radically, however, in the course of his life. At times he tried to approach the problem from the side, as it were, by trying out reforms in the most westernized regions of the empire, such as Poland and Finland, and emancipating the serfs in the Baltic provinces. At other times he redesigned his reform on a military or on a religious model. He could see that institutional changes were not enough, and his protean, many-sided personality was capable of hoping that any or all of these models might provide the key to the transformation he desired.

In the institutional sense, his greatest innovations were the ministries, introduced in 1802, and the State Council in 1810. The latter was conceived as the lynchpin of a scheme put to him by his most radical adviser, Mikhail Speranskii, under which government would be "regularized" according to the most advanced theories of the day, with separate administrative, judiciary, and legislative branches at the center and in the localities, the legislature to be elected by the propertyowners of town and countryside. If realized in full, this scheme would have ensured that part of the authority of the state was filtered through publicly elected institutions entitled to comment publicly on legislation and on the conduct of the government.

As it turned out, only the ministries and the State Council functioned in the way Speranskii intended. The State Council consisted of elder statesmen appointed by the emperor, whose job it was to advise him on legislative matters and to provide draft laws which he could accept, reject, or amend. It thus assumed the legislative functions of the Senate. Ministers took over the functional executive responsibilities of the colleges, with the vital difference that they were headed by individuals rather than by committees. Alexander had concluded that the colleges were capable of handling only routine business, and that very slowly. Restoring executive power to individuals made it possible to discharge business much more efficiently, and Alexander tried at first to restrain personal caprice by requiring ministers to consult regularly with one another and with him before taking major decisions. Gradually, however, this habit waned, so that ministries had a tendency to lapse back into being centers of personal patronage, as the old *prikazy* had been, galvanized by their close association with the imperial court. All the same, the very existence of ministries aroused the anticipation that impartial and functionally delineated exercise of authority could now be expected, in other words a bureaucratic rather than a patronal regime. A start was made to the professionalization of the civil service: from 1809 a university degree or a written entrance examination was required for admission to the higher grades on the Table of Ranks.[5]

In time a few ministries managed to convert their fiefs into functional offices with real administrative capacity, especially after permanent ministerial agents were introduced in gubernii and uezdy and the governors-general were abolished in 1837. The Ministry of the Interior became the most powerful department, taking the police under its authority.[6]

THE CHALLENGE OF NAPOLEON BONAPARTE

Alexander's greatest challenge, but also his greatest opportunity, was presented by Napoleon Bonaparte. The French invasion of 1812 was the most dangerous military threat any Russian ruler had faced since the Time of Troubles. Even before then, however, Napoleon radically disrupted the European concert of powers which Russia had joined and to which it had molded itself. He did so by taking to extremes the concert's own guiding principle, jostling and expansive state egoism, to create a French empire encompassing most of Europe. Meeting this challenge stretched the *ancien régime* monarchs to the utmost: they wavered uncertainly, Russia included, between confronting Napoleon and allying themselves with him.[7]

249

Napoleon was a disruptive influence in a subtler sense, too. His principles of government were rooted in Enlightenment thinking, and his reconstruction of France represented in exaggerated form what Alexander would have liked to achieve: a meritocracy resting on convinced patriotism and successfully mobilizing the nation's resources. The postrevolutionary French nation-state was in itself both an enticing and an unsettling model for Russia.

Alexander reacted, as ever, ambivalently. In 1806, at his instigation, the Orthodox Church anathematized Napoleon as the Antichrist, but then had to withdraw the anathema in 1807, when the Tilsit agreement inaugurated a period of alliance—albeit uneasy—between Russia and France. Accounts of the meetings of the two emperors at Tilsit, and the following year in Erfurt, testify that they had long conversations in private and suggest that they found much in common with each other, though it is not known what they discussed.[8]

Whatever their affinity, however, it fell victim to the incompatibility of their ambitions. There were many reasons why Russia did not fit into Napoleon's Continental System, notably the damage it inflicted on Russia's trade with Britain and most of Europe, but the most important one was Poland. Napoleon had recreated Poland as a semi-independent state in the form of the Duchy of Warsaw and had armed it for war against Austria. Here the nation-state model was a direct threat to Russia. The fear that Poland was a dagger menacing Russia rather than a buffer state protecting her in the last resort convinced Alexander that war against France was necessary.[9]

In 1808–09 he prepared for the forthcoming war by invading the Swedish dependency of Finland, occupying the Aland Islands, and moving the frontier several hundred miles back from his capital city. Facing the prospect of guerrilla warfare within the newly conquered territories, Alexander promised to uphold all existing liberties of the Finnish estates and people, and summoned an elected Diet, which he addressed personally. Finland thus became a grand duchy ruled by the tsar, but otherwise separate from the political arrangements of the Russian Empire.[10]

The war which ensued when the Grande Armée invaded Russia in 1812 was of a kind which Napoleon had not experienced before. Russia was able to exploit its strategic advantage, immense territorial depth, as Peter I had done against Charles XII, in fact even more radically, but only at incalculable cost—a cost so great that the generals did not admit to themselves or to their emperor that they were paying it until the French were in Moscow itself. In confronting other European powers, Napoleon's hitherto successful strategy had been to seek battle with their main army, when his own tactical skill, together with the numbers, superior maneuverability, and higher morale of his troops almost invariably brought him victory. It did so even against the Russians, when their generals at last stood their ground at Borodino in September 1812, but only at a very heavy cost in casualties, debilitating for an army so deep in enemy territory.

251

Besides, even victory did not guarantee the success of the invasion. Kutuzov abandoned Moscow, as the defeat at Borodino compelled him to do, but he did not surrender or even send envoys to Napoleon to discuss a settlement. Occupying Moscow brought Napoleon no ultimate triumph nor even much satisfaction, since the city burst into flames soon after he entered it. As the smoke swirled round the Kremlin, Napoleon, assuming the Russians had deliberately started the fire (which is far from certain), exclaimed: "This is a war of extermination, a terrible strategy which has no precedents in the history of civilization . . . To burn down their own cities! A demon has got into them! What ferocious determination! What a people!"[11]

Probably he was overestimating the consistency of the strategy being employed against him. One reason both Alexander and his generals hesitated to withdraw in front of the Grande Armée was that they feared the effect Napoleon might have on the serfs, whom at one stage he had promised to emancipate. Landowners remembered Pugachev and feared their serfs might once more seek *volia*.[12] To forestall internal disorders, Alexander ordered that half a battalion be stationed in each guberniia. There were reports from Smolensk that some serfs had declared themselves French citizens and that an "Old Believer sect" had enrolled 1,500 serfs by promising them freedom when Napoleon arrived.[13] In fact Napoleon had no intention of emancipating the serfs: they were too convenient to him in their present status. Once that became clear, the disorders died away.

Thereafter peasants contributed fully to the war effort by defending their homes and crops or, on the contrary, when strategy demanded it, destroying them and retreating into the woods. Once Napoleon had decided that to face the winter in a devastated Moscow made no sense and had begun to withdraw, those peasants became a major factor in the campaign. They joined the Cossack and light cavalry units harassing the French army in its painful retreat along the way it had come. Their knowledge of the countryside was invaluable to irregular Russian detachments. Sometimes they formed their own guerrilla units, but the authorities were nervous about such private military enterprise unless under the command of a regular officer. A certain Captain Naryshkin handed out spare weapons to a peasant partisan group, so that they could attack French soldiers looking for forage, and was disconcerted to receive orders to desist. He later testified, "Astonished by an order which fitted so poorly the noble behavior of the peasants, I replied that I could not disarm those whom I had armed and who were destroying the enemies of the fatherland, nor could I treat as rebels those who were sacrificing their lives to defend their independence, their wives and homes."[14]

The government did set up a popular militia *(opolchenie)* to reinforce the army, recruiting it from the regions most affected by the invasion. But it was very cautious about who was mobilized. State peasants were not wanted: only private serfs were called on, since in their case the landlords took the decision about who should fight. Nor were genuine volunteers encouraged: when one serf turned up of his own accord at a recruiting center, he was treated as a fugitive and sent to the police "to be proceeded with according to the law."[15]

Overall, peasants played a vital part in the defeat of Napoleon, and in doing so displayed great courage and fighting spirit. But their patriotism, though genuine, was of a kind unwelcome to their superiors: it was the assertion of the pravda of their local communities, the aspiration to be free Orthodox believers under church and tsar. The war, like the Time of Troubles, awakened in them aspirations Russians did not usually express: they believed that if they fought for their country, then the good father tsar would award them *volia.* This explains why the most serious peasant disorders took place toward the end of the war, when the chance to fight was receding and with it the opportunity to win freedom. After a disorder of December 1812, in Penza guberniia, the peasants responsible confessed that they had intended to kill all the officers, go to the front themselves, and defeat the French, then beg the tsar's forgiveness and request *volia* in return for their valor.[16]

The Russian campaign of 1812 was, then, a genuine people's war, of a kind Napoleon had not had to fight elsewhere, except in Spain. But it did not imply that the Russian people enthusiastically supported the existing order. They had been animated by fears and hopes which one might describe as both apocalyptic and millennial: fears of the destruction of their homeland, hopes of casting off bondage and becoming free citizens under the tsar.

THE HOLY ALLIANCE AND THE BIBLE SOCIETY

Alexander's victory over Napoleon encouraged him to see his reforming aspirations in a new light. For one thing, he was the savior not just of Russia, but of Europe too. It was Alexander who insisted among his fellow monarchs that Napoleon had to be totally defeated, his model of Europe rejected, and a new international order created in its place. Russian troops took a full part in the Battle of Leipzig (1813) and paraded victoriously down the Champs Elysées in Paris in 1814, champions of what was now seen as the leading continental power.

Alexander thus dominated the Congress of Vienna in 1815, and his vision was embodied in the Holy Alliance. It was intended to keep the peace in Europe and to defeat the twin threats of atheism and revolution by means of concerted action among the powers. As Alexander wrote to his ambassador in London, Count Lieven, the alliance was "to apply more efficaciously to the civil and political relations between states the principles of peace, concord, and love which are the fruit of religion and Christian morality."[17]

To propagate his concept inside Russia, he ordered copies of the alliance's founding document to be widely circulated and displayed. It is important to note that the religion which inspired him was not really Orthodox Christianity. He intended to inculcate a kind of "inner" or "universal" Christianity, nondenominational in form, which would peacefully reconcile the peoples of Europe. He reorganized the Holy Synod, so that it absorbed all Christian churches, and amalgamated it with the Ministry of Education under his close friend Prince Aleksandr Golitsyn. The resultant hybrid Ministry of Spiritual Affairs and Popular Enlightenment has been aptly dubbed the "ministry of religious-utopian propaganda."[18]

The difference between Alexander's Christianity and that hitherto practiced by the Orthodox Church is shown by his insistence that the scriptures should now be made available to all the peoples of the empire in their native languages. He wanted the common people to acquire an altogether more conscious, informed, and personal Christian belief than was fostered in most Orthodox parishes or than could be imbibed from a Bible in an antiquated tongue. He sponsored the creation of an Imperial Russian Bible Society (as a branch of the British and Foreign Bible Society) to undertake the work of translation, publication, and distribution. Its steering committee contained representatives of different churches, including a Lutheran pastor and a Roman Catholic bishop. It set up new printing presses and began issuing New Testaments and complete Bibles in languages of the empire such as German, Finnish, Estonian, Latvian, Lithuanian, Polish, Armenian, Georgian, Kalmyk, and Tatar. For the purpose it used retail outlets, such as apothecaries' shops, which had never previously been used for selling books.[19]

Significantly, the language which caused real difficulty was Russian itself. Of course, the Bible already existed in the Church Slavonic of Archbishop Gennadii, but Alexander explicitly wished "to give Russians the means of reading the word of God in their native Russian tongue, which is more com-

prehensible to them than the Slavonic language." Many Orthodox churchmen felt that the modern vernacular lacked the venerable dignity to convey
the full meaning of the scriptures. Some were also alarmed by Golitsyn's
"superministry," with its eclectic and evangelical Christianity. Their suspicions seemed to be confirmed when the Bible Society began to issue editions
of Pietist and freemasonic thinkers whose exalted and mystical style appealed
to Alexander.

In 1824 the Bible Society was denounced in a vituperative pamphlet by
Archimandrite Fotii of the Iuriev Monastery, near Novgorod. He warned of
certain "Illuminists"—that is, freemasons—who were plotting to destroy
"all empires, churches, religions, civil laws, and order" and to replace them
with a universal rationalist faith. The Bible Society was their agent in Russia,
distributing pernicious books and "degrading the word of God" by peddling
it "in the apothecaries' shops, along with tinctures and ampoules." Fotii appealed to Alexander: "God defeated the visible Napoleon, invader of Russia.
Let him now in Your Person defeat the invisible Napoleon."[20]

Fotii's was the voice of a church demoralized by more than a century of
subjection to the secular state, lacking confidence in its own capacity to re-
buff the intellectual and spiritual challenge posed by other forms of Christianity. His memorandum was on one level a reformulation of the apocalyptic fears which had animated Old Believers; in another it was the first
example of a persistent modern Russian genre: the denunciation of a cosmopolitan and godless international conspiracy aiming to undermine the simple
faith of true-believing folk and thus to destroy the country.

By this stage Alexander had become susceptible to Fotii's insinuations.
He was worried by the secret societies in Germany, Italy, and Spain which
threatened his Holy Alliance, and he was aware that there were clandestine
groups with masonic origins in Russia too. He decided to restore the Holy
Synod and to dismiss Golitsyn as head of the Bible Society. Golitsyn's successor, the conservative Metropolitan Serafim of Novgorod, stopped distributing New Testaments in Russian and ordered stored copies to be burned.[21]

The only senior churchman who continued to insist on the importance of
translating the Bible was Metropolitan Filaret of Moscow. Against Serafim's
contention that a vernacular Russian Bible would merely "provoke idle
minds to controversy" he countered: "Everything which is necessary to salvation is expounded in the holy scriptures with a clarity such that any reader
moved by the sincere wish to be enlightened can understand it."[22]

Nevertheless, even Filaret's attempt to publish an up-to-date catechism
was seriously delayed because he had included in it the Ten Commandments
and the Lord's Prayer in modern Russian. Not until 1859 did the Holy Synod

reward his patience and at last give permission for the translation to go ahead. The New Testament appeared in 1862 and the whole Bible in 1876. It proved immensely popular: reprints were needed immediately, and in St. Petersburg the Society for the Dissemination of the Holy Scriptures distributed 1.4 million copies of the New Testament from 1863 through 1865.[23]

255

The halting of the Russian Bible delayed for half a century the time when literate Russians had access to the scriptures in a form they could easily read and study. Peter the Great's "Protestant" reformation remained superficial: without widespread Bible-reading the state domination of the church threatened to hollow out its spiritual life, leaving the way open to the sects.

EDUCATION AND LEARNING

Both Catherine II and Alexander I broadened the educational system, starting the task of filling up the lower levels, which Peter had ignored. In 1786 Catherine issued a National Statute of Education, which provided for a two-tier network of schools, primary at the uezd level, secondary in the guberniia, which were to be coeducational, free of charge (that is, financed by state and local community), and open to all classes of the population except serfs. The new educational program made no use of the existing network of church schools: the statute propounded a secular Enlightenment ideology strongly influenced by Prussian and Austrian models. Pupils were issued with a handbook outlining the "Duties of Man and Citizen," whose religious outlook was deist rather than Orthodox. Among the aims of education were "a clear and intelligent understanding of the Creator and His divine law, firm belief in the state, and true love for the fatherland and one's fellow citizens."[24]

In practice, not much of Catherine's planned network materialized, in her reign or for some decades afterward. Nevertheless, the aim had been declared, and the principle laid down that education was nondenominational, indeed largely secular, and was not the preserve of the privileged or of males, but that it should be open to all, free of charge, with a ladder leading from the lowest to the highest level. Perhaps because these principles were necessary to draw enough qualified personnel into state service, they passed into the lifeblood of Russia's pedagogues and educational officials and survived all later attempts to narrow them. The system remained democratic, cosmopolitan, and secular in spirit.[25]

Alexander I opened new universities in St. Petersburg, Kharkov, and Kazan. With universities of non-Russian origin also functioning in Vilna and Dorpat, the empire now had six higher educational institutions, each of which was supposed to supervise and appoint teachers to the secondary schools in their region. They were all self-governing, appointed their own rectors and professors, determined their own curricula, disciplined their own students, set their own examinations, and awarded their own diplomas. The ideal of freedom of research underlay the organization of seminars and the promotion of younger scholars. Only in Vilna and Dorpat were there theological faculties, Catholic and Lutheran respectively, so that the "Orthodox" universities remained purely secular in their teaching, though they were supposed to inculcate "sound religious and moral principles." At times they were accused of spreading libertinism and atheism, and Alexander I made an attempt to impose the principles of the Bible Society and Russian patriotism, especially in St. Petersburg; but they proved too alien to established practices and were soon abandoned.[26]

In the late eighteenth century, private scholarly activity also took wing, partly through institutions which developed with the encouragement of the imperial state. This activity was extremely important in a country which had grown rather haphazardly to immense size and diversity, with little systematic knowledge of its own human and natural resources. The Free Economic Society, founded in 1765, sponsored the study of Russia's agriculture and agrarian arrangements, and later of its economic conditions in general, and encouraged serious proposals for their improvement. The Moscow Society for the Study of Russian History and Antiquity (1803) and the Imperial Archaeographic Commission (1837) began assembling archive materials from all over the country, ensuring their preservation, and publishing edited collections of them. One of the main results was the multivolume *Complete Collection of Russian Chronicles,* whose appearance began in 1846 and has continued throughout the nineteenth and twentieth centuries. Sergei Soloviev, author of the most complete history of pre-nineteenth-century Russia (published 1851–79), based his work on these compilations.

Similarly, the Russian Geographical Society (1845) sent expeditions out to study and record the country's geology, botany, zoology, climate, and ethnography. Thus for example a survey of the northern Urals in 1851–1853 produced two learned reports and a detailed map of the region. The philologist Vladimir Dal used materials collected by such expeditions in his collection of *Proverbs of the Russian People* (1862) and his *Interpretive Dictionary of the Russian Language* (1864–1868), which recorded and explained a wide variety of regional and dialect usages.[27]

Without information of this kind, it was impossible to know what human and natural resources Russia had at her disposal, or in what conditions her numerous and varied peoples lived. The societies which gathered and published the data were themselves significant innovations, since they offered the first Russian examples of civil assocations independent of—though in some cases partly supported by—the state. They also began the process of making Russians more aware both of their own identity and of the numerous non-Russian peoples in their midst.[28]

257

POLAND AND THE JEWS

Even after the partitions of 1772–1795, Poles could not be absorbed as if they were Mordvins. They had a well-tested concept of citizenship and nation-hood, which ran counter to the whole theory and practice of political author-ity in Russia. As in England, Polish political rights rested on a broadening of feudal aristocratic privilege to embrace a wider population. This broaden-ing had begun belatedly in the last years of the commonwealth and was clearly articulated in the constitution of 3 May 1791. Both in its traditional aristocratic and in its new democratic forms, the Polish ideal was incompati-ble with Russian autocracy. On the other hand, the continuing split between the *szlachta* and the rest of society made it impossible for Poles to mount a concerted challenge to Russian rule. Unable either to throw off Russian domination or to submit peacefully to it, Poland became a permanent source of problems within the empire.

Tsar Alexander I was sensitive to the problem and appointed his close friend, a leading Polish aristocrat, Prince Adam Czartoryski, as his foreign minister. For a time he encouraged Czartoryski's proposal for a "Europe of nations," in which Poland would be united and independent under a Russian protectorate.[29] And after the defeat of Napoleon, he granted the "Congress Kingdom of Poland" a constitution which, under personal union with the Russian crown, guaranteed its inhabitants their own citizenship, their own government and elected legislature (the Sejm), and even their own army. Polish was the official language and the Catholic Church had established status in the Congress Kingdom. Similar arrangements were being made for Finland at the time, and many educated Russians hoped they would be pro-totypes for a future all-Russian constitution.

In reality the Polish constitution proved short-lived. Many Poles never reconciled themselves to Russian domination, even in this relatively mild form. In 1830 a patriotic society tried to assassinate the viceroy, Grand Duke Konstantin. They failed, but seized control of central Warsaw and an-nounced that Russian rule was over. Their coup compelled all elite Poles to decide for or against participation in insurrection. Even Czartoryski reluctantly made up his mind to sponsor it, and agreed to head an independent Polish government.

The splits within Polish society, however, in the end made their new-won independence untenable. It was imperative to satisfy the peasants' land hunger speedily if they were to support the insurrection led by their superiors, but the *szlachta* temporized, even in this emergency, reluctant to sacrifice wealth and social standing until it was too late. The Polish army fought gallantly, many of its officers recalling the glorious days of the resistance against Napoleon, but without the backing of a majority of the Polish population it could not indefinitely resist the Russians.[30]

Defeat was devastating for Polish nationhood. The Diet and the Polish army were abolished, the University of Warsaw was closed, and Polish affairs were handed over to Russian ministries in St. Petersburg. The Uniate Church was subordinated to the Holy Synod as if it were part of Russian Orthodoxy. Officers who had served in the rebel army were cashiered, their lands were expropriated, and they were exiled to Siberia. Some managed to forestall their fate by emigrating, mostly to France. At the Hotel Lambert in Paris, Czartoryski became a kind of "king over the water," and the Polish emigration, with its brilliant poets, musicians, and elder statesmen, aroused the sympathy of a European public already disposed to regard Russia with apprehension and revulsion.[31]

In a very different way, the Jews proved just as difficult to assimilate. With their ancient religion and culture, and a level of literacy and communal cohesion far higher than that of Russians, they usually excelled at any trade, manufacture, or profession they undertook. On the other hand the great majority of Jews were very poor, as a result of long-standing insecurity and discrimination in Poland. From the outset the government regarded them with misgivings as likely to outperform Russians and drive them from business. When Moscow merchants petitioned in 1791 to be shielded from Jewish competition, the government issued a decree forbidding Jews to settle in the capital cities, and then created the Pale of Settlement, to which they were to be confined, in Ukraine, New Russia (the steppe territory to the north of the Black Sea), and the former territories of Poland.

All the same, the imperial regime did try, as with all nationalities, to find some way of integrating Jews. The Jewish Statute of 1804 confirmed their right of self-government in the local commune, or *kahal*, though insisting it be separated from the religious establishment, the rabbinate. Jews were allowed to attend Russian schools or to found their own, to open commercial and manufacturing establishments, and to buy or lease land in the Pale. On the other hand, they were barred from the liquor trade, which had been a major source of income for them in Poland, and from military service, instead of which they had to pay a special tax.[32]

The Jews' own poverty, and the suspicion with which they were regarded by much of the population, made it difficult for them to take up many of the opportunities offered, for example by buying land or commercial property. Quite apart from that they suffered from the imperial government's endemic tendency to proclaim well-designed reforms which it was subsequently unable to deliver. It proved quite alien to Jewish tradition to separate the secular functions of the *kahal* from the religious ones of the rabbinate, and so in 1844 the *kahal* was abolished, though in practice it continued to exist, as Russian substitutes were ineffective.

Under Nicholas I "assimilation" was viewed not as a long-term aim but as a short-term bureaucratic ploy, to be manipulated in carrot-and-stick fashion. Conversion to Orthodoxy was demanded before officials would grant Jews rights to which they were theoretically entitled. In 1827 the exemption from military service was abolished, and Jews from unconverted families would be taken off at the age of twelve for military training, after which they would serve in the army for the full term of twenty-five years.[33]

Up to the mid-nineteenth century, Jews suffered from poverty, from popular prejudice, and from the imperial regime's inability to match aspirations with practical measures. There was as yet, however, no ethnic or racial doctrine specifically directed against them. That was a product of a later era, when the Russian Empire was trying to find its place in a Europe of nation-states.

THE DECEMBRISTS

A generation later than Nikolai Novikov and Aleksandr Radishchev the kind of thinking they exemplified had become much more widespread, especially among the younger members of aristocratic salons and at Moscow University. Their outlook was consolidated and enriched by the war of 1812, in which many of them were involved as army officers. The experience of defending the fatherland inspired in them a certain solidarity with other classes of the population through "relationships formed at the bivouac and on the battlefield in the sharing of equal labors and perils," as Sergei Trubetskoi put it. It sharply intensified their sense of what it meant to be Russian.[34] As Ivan Iakushkin, an ensign in the Semenovskii Guards observed, "The 1812 war awoke the Russian people to life."[35] It seemed both immoral and perhaps dangerous after this awakening to subject them once more to the deprivations and indignities of serfdom.

259

260

Those officers who had taken part in the campaigns of 1813–1815 had also observed something of political life in other countries, and were attracted by what they saw of popular patriotic movements, representative institutions, and the rule of law, all benefits which Russia lacked. The experience of war and of western Europe both intensified patriotism and suggested a new and broader context in which it could develop, in the shape of a nation of citizens liberated from bondage and able to contribute through elected representatives to the making of the laws by which they were governed.

Those who wished to promote such a vision had some reason for believing the emperor was on their side, for, as we have seen, he had discussed constitutional schemes with his young "Jacobins" and with Speranskii, and he had granted a constitution to Poland and Finland. After 1815, however, the perception took hold that he was under the thumb of Arakcheev and was more interested in religious or military utopias than in the rule of law for Russians. As Aleksandr Muraviev commented acidly, "Poland received a constitution, while Russia as a reward for 1812 received—military settlements!"[36]

To many, then, the formation of secret societies seemed to offer a better prospect of effective action than relying on the emperor, and they had models before them in the shape of the freemasons and the anti-French patriotic societies of the countries occupied by Napoleon, such as the Carbonari and the Tugendbund. The first Russian secret society, the Union of Salvation, began with a restrictive and nonimperial concept of the nation: its initial aim was "resistance to the Germans in the Russian state service." However, it soon broadened its agenda and turned to promoting the "welfare of Russia" by advancing the idea of regulating serfdom, or possibly abolishing it and transforming the autocracy into a constitutional monarchy. This was the first time a political movement had been created in Russia with such an ambitious aim, and how it was to be accomplished was never really settled. Eighteenth-century Russian history suggested that a coup by Guards officers, of whom there were a number in the Union, offered the likeliest prospect of success. But at what stage should it be attempted? Few were in favor of violent action, so the best prospect seemed to be to wait for the next monarchical succession and refuse to take an oath of allegiance to the incoming emperor till he should swear to grant a constitution.[37] Since that might mean waiting for decades, such a plan almost amounted to inaction.

To give the movement's ideas wider currency, the Union of Salvation turned itself into the Union of Welfare, with a public arm devoted, like the masons, to philanthropy, education, justice, and morality. These were laid out in a Green Book, which bound every member to seek public office if possible, but in any case to promote the aims of the Union through personal example, practical activity, and the denunciation of official abuses. Members were required to be male, Christian, nonserf, and Russian. By the latter was meant "those who were born in Russia and speak Russian," a definition which might include Tatars, Germans, and Jews, among others. Foreigners were also acceptable if they had "rendered outstanding services to our fatherland and are ardently devoted to it."[38] In this way the Union's concept of nationhood included elements which were linguistic, religious, political, and even moral.

The exclusion of serfs was characteristic. In spite of the demotic sympathies awakened by the Napoleonic war, the Union was unambiguously elitist, as its concept of citizenship implied. The Green Book did not recommend freeing the serfs, merely treating them humanely on the grounds that "subordinates are also people."[39]

The members of the Union later became known as Decembrists, because of the attempted coup in 1825 which grew out of their activity. But most of them, even those in its secret wing, had no definite political strategy in mind. For the most part, if they took its ideals seriously, they did so by trying to live out its precepts in everyday life. As Iurii Lotman has shown, they were trying to overcome the duality which existed between the Enlightenment culture in which they had been educated and the reality of life at court and on their estates, where most relationships were unadornedly hierarchical. They did not so much reject social etiquette as try to behave as if they really felt the sentiments normally expressed only for convention's sake. Many of them rejected the prevailing patriarchal notions of family life, seeing marriage not mainly as a means of perpetuating the *rod* (kin), but rather as a partnership of two equal adults joined by mutual affection and committed to the humane upbringing of children. In reaction against hierarchy and frivolity, they practiced an intense cult of sincerity and friendship among equals. The poet Aleksandr Pushkin grew up in this environment, and although he was never a Decembrist himself, his early poetry celebrated precisely those ideals. They were part of the atmosphere in which young nobles lived; the main significance of the movement was that its members tried to practice them consistently even in a discouraging environment. In essence, they were behaving as if "civil society" already existed.[40]

There were, however, a few very determined political activists. One of them was Pavel Pestel, son of the governor-general of Siberia. Unlike most of his colleagues, he was a republican by conviction and was prepared to envisage violent action, including regicide if necessary, to introduce the new order. He wrote a handbook setting out his ideas on the structure of the future Russian state, and gave it the title *Russkaia pravda,* consciously using the word which best conveyed ordinary people's understanding of the moral code under which they should be ruled and also recalling the eleventh-century law code of Iaroslav.

Like Peter I, Pestel believed that government existed to promote the welfare of its subjects and that, provided it did so, it was entitled to expect their allegiance. The present regime, however, did not, and therefore Russia needed "a complete transformation of the order of government, and . . . the issuance of a complete new Code or collection of laws that will preserve everything useful and destroy all that is harmful."[41]

Pestel envisaged Russia not as a multiethnic empire but as a nation-state of Great Russians. Georgians, Tatars, Letts, even Germans would abandon their separate languages and traditions and become Russians. He conceded that the Poles and Jews might prove unassimilable. In that case, it would be prudent to grant the Poles independence, but the Jews he recommended expelling from the country, so that they could "establish a separate Jewish state" in "Asiatic Turkey."[42]

The capital of the new nation should be Nizhnii Novgorod, renamed Vladimir, in honor of the first Christian prince of Rus. Serfdom was to be abolished, and former serfs were to receive a certain minimum of land, expropriated from the landowners, plus the right to purchase more if they had the means. All citizens were to enjoy the same rights and to be represented in the legislative assembly, which Pestel called the *veche,* in memory of the popular assemblies of pre-Mongol Rus.[43]

Overall, Pestel's ideal was the post-1789 French unitary nation-state, which had swept away all the compromises and anomalies of the *ancien régime.* He simply assumed the straightforward identity of the civic and the ethnic. Pestel was prepared to engineer this identity by authoritarian means where it did not exist, and in this respect he anticipated the later policies of Mikhail Katkov and Viacheslav Pleve.[44]

Pestel's concepts and strategy found few supporters in the Union of Welfare, which underwent a fictitious dissolution in 1821 partly to get rid of him. He refused to accept the decision and continued the Union's work in Tulchin, Chernigov guberniia, where he was posted. In this way, a split came about in the movement: the two wings have generally been known as the Northern and Southern Societies, because of their geographical locations in St. Petersburg and Tulchin. They did not fully trust each other, but to some extent cooperated.

The Northern Society was less radical both in its strategy and in its political concepts, which can be compared with those of the more democratic-minded English Whigs. According to Nikita Muraviev, the author of its constitution, serfdom was to be abolished, but former serfs would not be guaranteed anything more than a house and garden plot. Land above that minimum they would have to buy or rent from existing owners. The rule of law was guaranteed, and citizens were to be represented in the legislative assembly (called the Supreme Duma), but election to public office would depend on property qualifications.[45]

The Northern Society was run by a triumvirate from ancient aristocratic families, Nikita Muraviev, Evgenii Obolenskii, and Sergei Trubetskoi, who were cautious and vacillating in their strategy. Pestel tried in vain to convince them of the need for determined action, if necessary regicide, and the installing of a dictatorial provisional government. However, the dominance of Guards and aristocratic families in the Northern Society was being diluted by the influx of new members from lower ranks. Among them the key figure was Kondratii Ryleev, son of a bankrupt landowner and himself a romantic poet who was nourished on the civic virtues of the Roman republic and sang of their supposed revival among Slavic heroes of antiquity. He was the central figure in a coterie of ardent civic rebels, inspired not only by the classical city-states but also by contemporary revolutionary movements in Greece and Spain.[46]

In 1822 Alexander abolished all secret societies, including masonic lodges, but did not hunt down those involved. As he ruefully remarked to the governor-general of St. Petersburg, "You know that I have shared and encouraged these illusions and errors. It is not for me to be harsh."[47] It is true that Muraviev's constitutional proposals were very similar to those of Speranskii, whom Alexander had long sponsored.

The sudden death of Alexander, on 19 November 1825, faced the secret societies with a sudden and grave dilemma. They had no fully matured plan of action, but if they were going to act at all this was the ideal moment, especially since there was some confusion over the succession: Konstantin, the next in line, had orally renounced the throne but never confirmed his intention in writing. The conspirators had little support among the common people or even among rank-and-file soldiers, for whom their ideas had no resonance. In the end on 14 December, when Konstantin's renunciation was confirmed and his younger brother Nicholas was preparing to take the oath, the Northern Society drew up such battalions as they could muster on Senate Square and declared for Konstantin. The officers deliberately deceived their men into thinking that Konstantin would abolish serfdom and improve soldiers' terms of service.

The leaders lacked all conviction or sense of direction. Trubetskoi, appointed provisional "dictator," simply disappeared and was later found to have taken refuge in the Austrian embassy. General Miloradovich, governor-general of St. Petersburg, whom Nicholas had sent to parley with the rebel troops, was shot and killed, and eventually Nicholas reluctantly gave orders to disperse the insurgent units with artillery. When the cannons opened fire, the soldiers fled the square. The Southern Society mobilized some troops which at one stage were on the point of attacking Kiev, but were swiftly dealt with by a cavalry detachment.

The fiasco of December 1825 was a critical moment in Russia's evolution. The Decembrists were nobles and army officers who tried to act as if the service state wanted genuine service and as if civil society really existed. Actually it did, among their tiny elite, but that was precisely what cut them off from the mass of people. Vacillating between the empire which had raised them up and the people they wished to serve (however paternalistically), they could devise no sensible political course. When plunged into action in spite of themselves, they had no confidence in themselves and could not summon sufficient seriousness of purpose or popular support to achieve anything.

In high society there was probably considerable support for the aims of the Decembrists—but not at the cost of rebellion. That was the outlook of, for example, Pushkin. But by precipitate, poorly planned action, the Decembrists made themselves mortal enemies of the regime with whose ideals they had much in common. From then on, civil society and the rule of law became ideals which tsars tended to regard as hostile. There was already a split between educated society and the people; to it another was now added, between society and the regime.

THE REIGN OF NICHOLAS I (1825–1855)

Nicholas I was horrified by the way in which his brother's reign had ended. He followed the interrogation of the participants in the Decembrists' conspiracy with fascinated attention. He was especially dismayed by the way in which sedition had broken out among the landed nobility, on which the state relied to rule most of the empire. The secretary of the investigating commission, A. D. Borovkov, drew up a summary of the Decembrists' views on the condition of the empire, and Nicholas kept it by him as a kind of agenda for action. He did not agree with them, but he realized that their concerns were important indicators of what needed to be done.

Borovkov concluded his report with the following recommendation:

It is necessary to grant clear positive laws, to implant justice by introducing speedy legal procedures, to raise the moral education of the clergy, to strengthen the nobility, which has fallen into decay, ruined by loans in credit institutions, to revive trade and industry by unshakable charters, to improve the position of the cultivators of the soil, to stop the humiliating sale of human beings . . . in a word to correct countless failings and abuses.[48]

This was a formidable program. It amounted to completing the creation of a "regular" state and using it to generate civil society and a productive economy. Nicholas decided at the outset that the imperial bureaucracy could not do the job. In any case he did not trust the top bureaucrats: they were landed nobles, whose unreliability had been proved in December 1825. He resolved accordingly to reanimate the personal element in the monarchy, not by abolishing the ministries but by creating alongside them his own personal chancellery, the first department of which would be a kind of civil service inspectorate.

The Third Department constituted a political police, whose officials were explicitly authorized to act in accordance with conscience rather than formal legal procedure, whenever they judged it necessary to uncover sedition, correct injustice, or protect the weak. Nicholas declared that "men with evil intentions, striving to seize their neighbors' property, will become afraid to carry out their ruinous schemes when they come to believe that the innocent victims of their greed have a short, direct path to the protection of the imperial majesty."[49] The Third Department, in short, was to be an instrument of vigilant and ubiquitous monarchical benevolence, reviving the moral and personal approach to government which Peter (in theory not in practice) had tried to eradicate in favor of the pragmatic and the institutional.

The Second Department had a totally different aim, which might seem to run counter to a personalized notion of government. It was to draw up and publish the first complete collection of the laws to be issued since the *Ulozhenie* of 1649, together with a digest in which the present state of the law would be summed up. This was a huge undertaking, since tens of thousands of laws, edicts, decrees, and other enactments had been promulgated since then, many of them mutually contradictory. However, under the direction of Mikhail Speranskii, the Second Department accomplished its task: both a complete collection and a digest were published by 1833.

Nicholas also founded an Imperial School of Jurisprudence, on the same principles as the Cadet Corps: that is, as a secondary school giving selected candidates a specialized legal training alongside a general education. Its graduates soon formed the backbone of the universities' law faculties and of the judiciary in the higher courts. Taken together, the law code and the Imperial School of Jurisprudence fostered the attitude that law was not merely a malleable instrument to be manipulated by the powerful, but an objective state of affairs, ascertainable by the courts, and enforceable even to protect the weak and patronless. By the end of Nicholas' reign, a reserve of senior officials existed who were properly trained in law, qualified to guide and enforce the decisions of the courts. The framework of a "regular" state was in place for the first time, and its creation helped to prepare the way for the reforms of Alexander II. For all his reversion to personalized authority, then, Nicholas I was in his own way a constructive statesman.[50]

Reforms carried out by the minister of state domains, Count P. D. Kiselev, hinted at what might be achieved within a "regular" framework but also the restraints operating on reform in Russian society. He endeavored to do for the nonenserfed (state) peasants what Catherine's aborted charter might have achieved for them: define and secure their legal rights and obligations, including those of self-government, and encourage their economic productivity. Plans were drawn up to ensure that each household had enough land for subsistence and the discharge of official obligations; in a few cases land was actually reclaimed from the gentry for this purpose. Officials encouraged and advised on improved sanitation and medical care.

The motives behind Kiselev's reform were similar to those which underlay the military settlements (discussed below). If it had been successful it might have been extended to private serfs, as a preliminary to their emancipation. But it suffered from corrupt and insensitive administration coupled with peasant suspicion and occasional resistance. In 1840–1843 it was decreed that potatoes should be grown to create a reserve public food supply in case of famine. The Ministry of State Domains sent round circulars instructing state peasants to plant potatoes on a certain proportion of their land. Handbooks were issued on their cultivation, storage, and cooking, and priests were required to explain their benefits. Many peasants, however, averse as ever to risk, objected to the unfamiliar crop, and some forcibly prevented the planting of them. Here and there, encouraged by Old Believers, who regarded the new plant as "the devil's apple," they refused to comply, and rioted when efforts were made to compel them. In the end after widespread disorders the scheme was dropped.[51]

As for the private serfs, Nicholas did very little to improve their condition, though he was aware that the unlimited personal power of nobles over half the population weakened the state's authority and undermined the rule of law. But he also knew that he had no institutional structures with which to replace personal enserfment, and that an attempt to tamper with it might well raise hopes which could not be satisfied and would therefore generate unrest. He declared to the State Council in 1842: "Serfdom, in its present form, is an evil obvious to all; but to touch it now would of course be an even more ruinous evil."[52]

Nicholas was the first Russian ruler since Ivan IV to sponsor the formulation of an explicit and positive state ideology, intended both to distinguish Russia from the countries of western Europe and to define the symbols which were intended to appeal to the population. But his attempt was much less convincing than Ivan's because of the contradictory situation in which he found himself, as leader of a multinational empire which claimed Rus as its heritage but was busy inculcating an external, Western culture. His minister of education, Count S. S. Uvarov, sent a circular to officials in 1833, instructing them that "the education of the people be conducted . . . in the joint spirit of Orthodoxy, Autocracy, and Nationality (narodnost)."[53] The first two watchwords were an assertion of the distinctive identity of Russia, while the third was an obeisance to the latest developments in European culture, a pale reflection of post–French revolutionary nationalism.

The problem about this triad was that one of its pillars, the Orthodox Church, was too impoverished and too beholden to the state to play an independent role; in any case, it could not be expected to appeal to nearly half of the empire's population, which was non-Orthodox. Another, nationality, was even more problematic. Did it imply that the Russian people— like the church—had a role in legitimizing the monarchy? Surely not. And if the Russian people were the bearers of empire, then why were so many leading officials Germans?

These problems of interpretation left only the third pillar: autocracy. That at least made sense to most of Nicholas' subjects, of whatever faith or ethnic origin. The tsar was the supreme patron, anointed by God, severe in dealing with abuse, but unfailingly just and benevolent toward his loyal subjects: that was the image, and it was widely, even enthusiastically, accepted. Right up to 1905 autocracy was in practice the one truly distinctive feature of the Russian state, the one adhesive which might credibly be said to have held the variegated and ramshackle structure together. That is why monarchs and senior officials clung to it obsessively.

The pillar of autocracy was the army. It was the cardinal legitimizing institution of the monarchy: as long as it won regular victories on the battlefields of Europe and Asia, the tsar's right to rule would not be seriously in doubt. Besides, the appearance and moral outlook of the army were emblematic of the disciplined and devoted service which the tsar looked for in all his subjects. Nicholas I said of it: "Here there is order, there is strict unconditional legality . . . no one commands before he himself has learned to obey; no one steps in front of anyone else without lawful reason; everything is subordinated to one goal, everything has its purpose."[54]

Nicholas, following his predecessor, even hoped to use the army as a model for social reform. In the military settlements first set up just before the Napoleonic war, soldiers lived in buildings arranged in symmetrical rows and equipped with the most modern hygienic devices (including "English latrines"). Like peasants, they had their families with them, and they received land, livestock, and tools. While one regiment was on maneuvers, two others cultivated the soil. In this way, both emperors hoped, the army might become self-financing and also act as a showpiece for modern agricultural methods.

It was not to be. The soldiers hated their way of life, "regimented" in both senses of the word. There were several serious rebellions, at least one of them provoked by the fumigation of buildings during a cholera epidemic, which the men interpreted as the *cause* of the disease. For all the dreams of monarchs, peasantry and soldiery could not simply be amalgamated. Eventually the settlements had to be closed down.[55]

In other ways too the preoccupation with military virtues had its downside for the monarchy. From Paul onward, all the Romanov tsars were brought up to identify first and foremost with the army on the barrack square, and most of them never shook off the comforting obsession with military parades. Close-formation march and punctilious drill looked good to one's own subjects and to visiting foreign potentates, but they were a mere prerequisite to battlefield efficiency and, when overdone, an obstacle to it. From the time of Paul onward, some officers took the view that disciplined and devoted military service to Russia could best be offered in a different kind of army, commanded by professionals rather than aristocrats and manned by citizens rather than serfs. Such thinking, which flowed with impeccable logic from giving paramount priority to the army, was strengthened by the bonding experience of fighting together as comrades during the 1812 war; it formed part of the impetus behind the Decembrist rebellion and underpinned an alternative military mentality which came into its own after the Crimean War.[56]

LITERATURE, "THICK JOURNALS," AND THE RUSSIA QUESTION

In the long run one of the most fateful developments which proceeded from Peter the Great's promotion of culture, education, and social life was the creation of an institutionalized Russian literature. In the eighteenth century, apart from the initiatives of Novikov and Radishchev, there was little sign of this happening. Writers were usually dependent for their living on a patron, and they wrote accordingly, in genres such as the ode, the elegy, or the epic narrative poem.

By the early nineteenth century the form of patronage was beginning to change. Peter had brought women more or less forcibly into social life, but a century later they had carved out their own territory, in the form of salons: regular gatherings in the sitting rooms of polite society, where conversation was not only elegant, but also well informed and witty. They were modeled on the Parisian example, and like the French original nearly all Russia's salons were run by women. Here a social life—even public opinion—began to take shape independently of the imperial court.

Some salons came to include a literary component. Hostesses would cultivate well-known writers, who augmented the prestige of their company, while the writers themselves gained by making the acquaintance of the wealthy and influential. They might read preliminary drafts of their writings and receive from those assembled an informed reaction. The presence of a warmhearted, hospitable, and tactful hostess was crucial in softening the sensitivities which could be generated on such an occasion. In this way, a literary public began to form—or at least a public which enjoyed literary entertainment, had the leisure to partake of it, and the education and taste to make discriminating judgments about it.[57]

For the development of a national literature, it was essential that there be a generally accepted language in which the works could be written. Church Slavonic was too archaic and too closely associated with a specifically ecclesiastical culture for the post-Enlightenment world. The secular language of the chancelleries was not suitable, either, for Peter's reforms in technology, war, and public administration had created great linguistic confusion. Words and expressions imported wholesale from Swedish, Dutch, and German enriched vocabulary, grammar, and syntax but also dislocated them without any systematization of the innovations. Polite society increasingly used French, the language of diplomacy and ideally suited to witty and refined conversation.

However, Russian was never wholly discarded as a medium for social intercourse. It remained the official language of a great power, with the capacity for further development. Furthermore, after Napoleon's invasion of 1812, French was no longer universally used in high society, especially not in Moscow. In 1783 a Russian Academy had been founded, on the model of the Académie Française, and it promoted the recovery of Russian by standardizing the linguistic innovations and issuing an authoritative dictionary and grammar (1789–1802).[58]

The historian and novelist Nikolai Karamzin complimented the Academy on its "systematic formulation" of the language,[59] and he was the first major writer to demonstrate that modern Russian could be an adequate vehicle for literature. Its diction, based on the simple and elegant syntax of French, was close to that of polite society, which made it suitable for the discussion of literature and for the new genres coming into fashion, such as epigrams, album inscriptions, and light verse. Karamzin wrote romantic stories, exemplifying the new "sentimental" approach to human relations. They involved ordinary contemporary people, appealed to the intimate feelings of his readers, and were especially appropriate to salon discussion. Later he adapted this style to the writing of history. His multivolume *History of the Russian State* (1804–1826) superseded the dry fragmentation of the chronicles and wove an accessible and engaging narrative thread for the nonspecialist reader. It provided raw material for polite conversation, public debate, and academic controversy for decades to come, especially since Karamzin's adulation of the autocracy as the decisive formative influence in Russia's history was not unanimously accepted. It was the first stage in the creation of Russia as an "imagined community" for an educated nineteenth-century audience.[60]

Some educated Russians still contended that the "Frenchified" usages being imported into Russian lacked the dignity and the links with the past which enriched Church Slavonic and the Muscovite chancellery language. But literary professionalization, taking place gradually in the salons, pushed inexorably toward the adoption of a language which brought educated Russians closer to the major European cultures and which opened up new scope for self-expression and systematic discourse. This was to be the language of Pushkin, Gogol, Tolstoi, and Dostoevskii, as well as of Russian science and learning. These benefits were purchased, of course, at the cost of widening the cultural rift which already existed between the mass of Russians and the educated elites—and also between the secular elite and the church, which preserved its own linguistic forms for many decades to come. Russian intellectuals henceforth belonged to a secular and international "republic of letters" far removed from the culture of the church and ordinary people in their own country.

The major literary figure of the first decades of the nineteenth century was Aleksandr Pushkin (1799–1837). He employed the new Europeanized usage but was able to draw on folk culture as well, for example in his verse novel *Evgenii Onegin*, which paints a very broad picture of Russian society, contrasting the gentry's urbane way of life with that of the ordinary people. Perhaps Pushkin's greatest strength was his capacity to think himself into the mentality of individuals of different social and cultural origins, and to show in his ironic but affectionate verse how their behavior and attitudes are formed by their milieu and upbringing. This was a talent of peculiar importance in Russia, where a culture imported from abroad had by now thoroughly rooted itself among the elite and was beginning to penetrate other social classes as well. The main characters in *Evgenii Onegin* understand and misunderstand one another through the cultural filters of Byron, German idealism, and English romantic novels.

We may think of Pushkin as the bard of the Russian Empire at its apogee. He was educated in the exclusive Imperial Lyceum, nursery of Russia's highest elite, and always looked back to it as his "homeland." The ties he formed there enabled him to associate on easy terms with the best aristocratic families. He was close to the Decembrists but was never considered reliable enough to be drawn into their ranks, nor would he have approved of rebellion or regicide. Recognized in his early twenties as Russia's leading poet, he was courted by Nicholas I and submitted to the tsar's personal censorship—an arrangement which proved frustrating and humiliating in practice, since it was handled through the insensitive Third Department chief, General Aleksandr Benkendorf.

In his later years Pushkin was haunted by the question of why the Decembrists had failed. Was Russia really fundamentally different from other European countries, whose culture it had assimilated? He never abandoned poetry, but he began to write more prose, including both a novel and a chronicle of the Pugachev revolt. He also did what he could to advance the cause of literature as an independent calling, in both the professional and the political senses. The journal which he founded, *Sovremennik* (The Contemporary), became for decades the leading "thick journal," a forum for literature, scholarship, and thought and a meeting place for like-minded intellectuals. In campaigning for authors to be properly paid, and hence professionally self-reliant, he had to fight off those among them who wished to guarantee their incomes by service to powerful patrons. A particular *bête noire* was Faddei Bulgarin, former Polish patriot and officer in Napoleon's army, who, to live down his past, reported to the Third Department on his fellow writers and published works aimed at immediate commercial success. Literature was still halfway between patronage and the marketplace.[61]

272

All the same, in the post-Decembrist period, when mutual distrust between the regime and educated society became entrenched, printed literature began to assume a special importance—as it had in England in the era of Milton, during an analogous period of intense religious and political conflict, or in France in the era of Voltaire, during the long guerrilla war between the Enlightenment and the *ancien régime*. The authorities were by now suspicious of all forms of intellectual endeavor, including the creative arts. But in these circumstances, literature had certain inbuilt advantages over other forms of intellectual or creative production. Since, unlike music or painting, it dealt in words, it could deal directly with social or political issues. Yet the ambiguity and semantic richness of artistic literature made it relatively difficult to police. It posed the censor far more tricky problems than other varieties of verbal production. It was hard for him, without appearing naive or malicious—and he was a member of polite society too—to fix a single unambiguous meaning on a text and declare it unacceptable.

For that reason much of Russia's spiritual, religious, political, and intellectual life for the next half-century was conducted in the form of artistic literature, and in the reviews and criticism which surrounded it. Literature and its institutions replaced wholly or in part the church, the academy, universities, schools, public libraries, voluntary associations, and much of civil society, creating a functional overload which was uniquely stimulating to writers but also tempted them to exaggerate their potential role and to overwhelm literature itself.

In this process the central role was played by journals, which during the mid-nineteenth century gradually took over from salons the task of acting as intermediaries between writers, critics, and readers. They brought together like-minded people with literary interests, who read and debated each other's works and discussed matters of mutual concern in all spheres of intellectual life. The journals reflected this breadth of interest. Starting out as almanacs, anthologies, or occasional collective volumes, they gradually assumed a regular institutional form, absorbing every kind of intellectual and scholarly concern—unlike for example English literary journals, which usually specialized in literature alone. Not for nothing did they become known as "thick journals": a monthly number could easily run to 600 or 700 pages, embracing history, the arts, the social and natural sciences, political and social commentary, and book reviews on every conceivable subject. Professors not only wrote popular articles on their specialties but even excerpted forthcoming scholarly works, complete with footnotes. By the later nineteenth century, a good monthly journal was the equivalent of a gradually unfolding encyclopedia, offering its subscribers a complete extracurricular program of self-education.[62]

Much of the spiritual energy for the journals came from small, informal circles of intellectuals meeting frequently to discuss each other's works and ideas in general. After the Decembrist rebellion society salons were sometimes under observation by Nicholas I's Third Department, so that full freedom of argument required greater seclusion. A smaller room in an aristocratic townhouse might be the venue, but student garrets provided the perfect milieu, the more appropriate since the participants in the debates were usually young men in or on the fringes of higher education. In these circles, or *kruzhki*, the cardinal values were friendship and complete honesty; their members shared not only their thoughts but also their private experiences and feelings.

In this heady atmosphere, "nobility" was defined by character, not by membership of a superior social estate. The *kruzhki* were miniature republics, which rose above distinctions of wealth and birth so that their members could cultivate friendship and truth on equal terms. P. V Annenkov, a young intellectual who recorded the life of the 1830s *kruzhki* in his memoirs, went so far as to suggest a parallel with the *obshchina*, or village commune.[63]

Unlike the village commune, however, the members of the *kruzhki* could choose their associates and could also break with them at any time. Ardent attachment to one's colleagues was usually fortified by contempt for those outside the magic circle and by hearty detestation of rivals. As Aleksander Herzen said of the circle of his friend Nikolai Ogarev, "they were bound by a common religion, a common language, and even more—by a common hatred."[64]

This was the exalted but fractious atmosphere in which literary journals took shape. An early example of the type was *Moskovskii telegraf* (The Moscow Telegraph), under the editorship of Nikolai Polevoi (1825–1834). Its title reflected its ambition of acting as a kind of rapid communications system for a fragmented public. Like the editors of the eighteenth-century *Encyclopédie* in France, Polevoi saw his mission as being the dissemination of information and opinion in order to form and sustain an educated public capable of generating social and economic progress, no matter how obscurantist the regime might be. An admirer of west European technical achievements, economic development, and constitutional government, he hoped to publicize them among Russian readers by blending the edifying with the popular, and he steered round the censorship by resorting to allegory or indirect allusion if direct statement seemed too risky. In the end Nicholas I's officials decided all the same that Polevoi's "Jacobin tendencies" were too obvious, and in 1834 *Moskovskii Telegraf* was closed.[65]

274

The thinker who put into perspective the role of literature in Russian life was Vissarion Belinskii, son of a provincial army doctor, and hence a man of lower social standing than most of his colleagues. During the 1840s, in *Otechestvennye zapiski* (Notes of the Fatherland) and *Sovremennik,* the monthly originally launched by Pushkin, he put across his vision of literature not just as entertainment or even education, but as a vital spiritual force which could engender a sense of community, even create a Russian nation. A Hegelian in outlook, Belinskii believed that literature was the vehicle through which the Universal Spirit would come to self-awareness and self-expression in Russia, the means whereby the Russian people would make their own distinctive contribution to world culture and the development of mankind.

Literature, he declared, would heal the rift within Russian culture, reintegrating the common people by giving a detailed and authentic account of their life and assimilating their spoken language, not for ethnographic reasons but for moral and cultural ones, to express the Russian national essence. It followed that the mainstream of Russian literature would be realism, or what Belinskii called the "natural school." By describing the life of the common people vividly and sympathetically but also critically, the writer would arouse the concern and compassion of the reader and stimulate improvement and progress. He identified Pushkin's long narrative poem, *Evgenii Onegin,* and the first part of Gogol's novel, *Dead Souls,* as exemplars of the new tendency.[66]

By the 1840s one question overshadowed all others in the polemics conducted on the pages of the "thick journals," and it provided a fundamental marker by which membership in this or that camp could be determined. It was quite simply "What is Russia?"

Although others had raised it earlier, it was posed in acute form in 1836 by a retired Guards officer, Petr Chaadaev. In a letter to a minor journal, written, significantly, in French, he asserted that Russia was a cultural nonentity. Suspended uneasily between the civilizations of Europe and Asia, it had not borrowed anything culturally fruitful from either. "Alone in the world, we have given nothing to the world, learned nothing from the world, and bestowed not a single idea upon the fund of human ideas. We have not contributed in any way to the progress of the human spirit, and whatever has come to us from that progress we have disfigured."[67]

To a generation still recovering from the Decembrist fiasco and trying to understand what made Russia's evolution different from that of other European powers, this bald pronouncement mounted a timely challenge. Chaadaev had touched on a raw nerve. He effectively, if one-sidedly, conveyed the still precarious and shallow nature of Russia's imperial culture as it had developed since Peter I, its lack of organic development and ethnic substance. It was difficult to accept what Chaadaev said, but impossible to ignore too. Even Chaadaev, in his later writings, retreated from the full stringency of his indictment and suggested that Russia's lack of experience was evidence of youthful freshness and potential.[68] One way and another, his challenge posed the most important question Russian intellectuals had to face for decades to come.

Some, who became known as "Slavophiles," reacted by declaring that Chaadaev was mistaken, that Russia did have its own distinctive culture and its own valuable contribution to make to mankind's progress. On this view, Chaadaev had been blinded to them by the superficial and seductive civilization of "the West." At this point "the West" became hypostatized in Russian cultural discourse as a single homogeneous complex of concepts and institutions in opposition to which "Russia" had to be defined. Both the "Slavophiles" and the "Westerners" were at one in this fundamental mindset.

The Slavophiles had their natural home in Moscow, in the old capital city, away from the bustle, the Europeanized architecture, and the cosmopolitan energy of St. Petersburg. The leading Slavophile thinkers came from landowning families, and their milieu was still the salon rather than the kruzhok. Ivan Kireevskii, after studying the Greek church fathers, rebutted Chaadaev by asserting that Russia had its own rich cultural heritage, derived from Byzantium and transmitted by the Orthodox Church. Russia had actually preserved the integrity of the Christian faith, which the West had lost, thanks to the popes' greed for secular power and to the countervailing but equally sterile individualism and rationalism of the Protestants. What gave Russian institutions, especially the village community, their peculiar value, was sobornost, conciliarity or congregationalism, the capacity to take decisions in common, by consensus, and for the greater good of the collective rather than of the individual.

Aleksei Khomiakov, the major theorist of sobornost, defined it as "unity in multiplicity," the principle by which the individual finds his strength and his true purpose in common reflection and action with others. Only thus could the individual fulfil himself as a person, "not in the impotence of spiritual solitude, but in the might of his sincere spiritual union with his brothers, with his Savior."[69] In "the West," by contrast, human beings were spiritually impoverished, caught in the toils of a heartless laissez-faire economy, and consumed by individualism, rationalism, and atheism. Renewal for European civilization could come only from Russia, where the people, ignorant and poverty-stricken though they often were, nevertheless were still illuminated by the full light of Christianity. Their innate sobornost was best exemplified by the village commune, which Konstantin Aksakov called "a moral choir [in which] one voice is not lost but is heard in the harmony of all voices."[70]

Conservatives though they were, the Slavophiles did not accept the autocracy in its current form. They considered that Peter the Great, inspired himself by Western principles, had undermined the inherited unity of monarch and people by interposing between them a Germanized bureaucracy. In the words of Aksakov, "There arose a rift between the tsar and his people, and the ancient union of land [*zemlia*] and state was destroyed. In its place the state imposed its yoke on the land . . . The Russian monarch became a despot, and the people who had been his free subjects became slaves and prisoners in their own land."[71] This despotism had given rise to serfdom and censorship and had subjected the church to the bureaucracy instead of to a properly elected *pomestnyi sobor* (church council).

To rectify this state of affairs the Slavophiles proposed that the tsar should reconvene the zemskii sobor as a regular institution representing the estates of Russian society. They rejected Western parliamentarism and did not consider that the tsar should be bound by constitutional guarantees, but they believed that he did need the regular contact with his loyal subjects which a zemskii sobor would provide. They also wanted to restore sobornost to the church by reinstating the pomestnyi sobor as its supreme governing body, and at the lowest level by reinstating the parish council as an autonomous body empowered to choose its own pastor, run its own finances, and look after the material affairs of the congregation.[72]

The Slavophiles opened new avenues in the search for a Russian national identity. Their historiography was misleading: for example, many of the abuses they identified, such as serfdom, long predated Peter the Great. But they were the first thinkers to warn that there were dangers in the gulf which had opened between the imperial elite and the ordinary Russian people, and to propose ways of overcoming it.

The "Westerners" were a much less homogeneous camp than the Slavophiles. It would be difficult to single out common elements in their thinking, except for the generally held assumption that Russia was fundamentally like other European countries, only delayed in its evolution by geographical and historical circumstances. Like the Slavophiles, many Westerners operated within a Hegelian framework and looked forward to Russia's becoming the most advanced European civilization in the next stage of history, borrowing from Europe but at the same time transforming its own youthfulness and inexperience into a blessing which would enable it to offer leadership. As Leah Greenfeld has pointed out, both Slavophiles and Westerners were "steeped in *ressentiment*," resentment of a dominant and apparently superior neighboring civilization, and both prophesied a great future for Russia. No doubt that is why Aleksandr Herzen, an ambivalent member of the Western camp, referred to the Slavophiles jokingly as "nos amis les ennemis."[73]

The crucial difference between Slavophiles and Westerners was over the question whether, in borrowing from European culture, Russia was denying its own nature, as the Slavophiles believed, or on the contrary taking vital steps for its own renewal and development. Belinskii scoffed at those who considered that a man dressed in a frockcoat could not be a Russian and that "the Russian spirit is present only where there is a homespun coat, bast shoes, raw vodka, and pickled cabbage."[74] Russia, he pointed out, belonged to Europe "by its geographical position, because it is a Christian power, because its civic culture is European, and because its history is already indissolubly linked with Europe." Nor, as an undoubted power of independent standing, need it fear being swamped by European innovations: it could absorb and assimilate them without damaging its own distinctive essence, just as "the food ingested by a human being is transformed into his flesh and blood and maintains in him strength, health, and life." It had been the achievement of Peter the Great to accomplish precisely that.[75]

Konstantin Kavelin, who taught the history of Russian law at Moscow University, attempted to refute the historical analysis of the Slavophiles in a long paper published in *Sovremennik* in 1847. Titled "A Brief Survey of the Juridical Way of Ancient Rus," it asserted that the kinship *(rodovoi)* principle as the basis for legal consciousness had long ago been replaced by the individual principle, thanks both to Christianity and to reforms carried out by the state, especially by Peter the Great. The strong state was responsible for progress, civilization, and, paradoxically, individual liberty in Russia.[76]

This paper aroused intense interest and controversy and brought forth a Slavophile rebuttal from the Moscow landowner Iurii Samarin. Eventually the discussion merged with the controversies of the late 1850s regarding the emancipation of the serfs, in which Kavelin spoke out for gradual social change impelled by a benevolent reformist monarchy, designed to protect private economic enterprise and the position of the landed gentry as the guarantee of culture and civilization.

By that time Kavelin's moderate position had been rejected by many.

Among them was Aleksandr Herzen. Illegitimate son of a Moscow noble-man, ardent habitué of the Westernizing *kruzhki,* enthusiastic proponent of (successively) German idealism and French socialism, Herzen was outspoken in discussion in his criticism of autocracy, serfdom, and police arbitrariness. In his youth he believed, in Hegelian spirit, that socialism of the kind preached by the French thinker Saint-Simon would bring the Absolute Spirit to fulfillment in western Europe in a reign of freedom and justice. These beliefs twice led to his arrest and exile, where, as a minor official, he had ample opportunity to observe the abuse of personal power prevalent in Nich-olas I's Russia.

278

Inheriting his father's fortune in 1847, he was able to travel to western Europe, where he arrived just in time to see the revolutions of 1848 in France and Italy. What he witnessed disabused him of his admiration for Western liberty. Even before the outbreak of revolution, he was shocked by Frenchmen's attachment to their private property: the high stone walls of Provence topped with broken glass "affronted the Slavic soul," as he wrote in a letter. The spectacle of the republican General Cavaignac crushing a workers' rising in Paris in June 1848 finally convinced him that bourgeois "freedom" was mercenary, egoistic, and repressive—more or less as the Slavophiles contended.

Here was a "Westernizer" confronted with the actual West, and as a result seeing new virtues in his homeland. Perhaps "young" Russia, unencumbered by the weight of deadening social institutions, might lead humanity toward the great future. Perhaps too, the peasant commune, which he had once pilloried the Slavophiles for extolling, might have a positive role to play, especially since, in a primitive and unconscious manner, it embodied the virtues of socialism. "The commune saved the Russian people from Mongo-lian barbarism and from imperial civilization, from the gentry with its Euro-pean veneer, and from the German bureaucracy. Communal organization, though severely shaken, withstood the interference of the state. It has sur-vived, fortunately, until the development of socialism in Europe." Later in life he urged that the commune and the workers' artel should be set free from "lifeless Asiatic crystallizations" by contact with European socialism, so that they could develop their potential.[77]

Toward the end of his life, Herzen combined Westernism and Slavo-philism in a new hybrid. He was the founder of the distinctively Russian style of socialism, which rejected parliaments, constitutions, and the rule of law in favor of the free cooperation of equals exemplified in the commune and artel. What Russian peasants and workers needed to make it work, he preached, were "land and freedom," a slogan which became the watchword of the first generation of Russian socialists. Ambivalent about revolution, since he recognized that it could easily destroy the culture which did exist in Russia, he hoped at times, like Kavelin, that the monarch would launch fruitful reform, and on that basis publicly lauded Alexander II's 1857 manifesto foreshadowing the emancipation of the serfs. This gesture forfeited the support of a more radical newer generation of thinkers, who did not believe autocracy could achieve anything creative.

Increasingly isolated toward the end of his life, Herzen nevertheless launched yet another great and lasting Russian institution, the émigré press. The Free Russian Press, set up in London in 1852, issued a series of memoranda and periodicals in a format designed to make it easy to smuggle them into Russia. As the first uncensored Russian publishing house, it placed before readers both ideas and facts inaccessible to them at home. It is said that his newspaper *Kolokol* (The Bell) became essential reading for high officials within Russia itself, if they wanted to find out what their subordinates were concealing from them.

Altogether, the *kruzhki* of the 1830s–1850s, together with their journals and other associated publications—including eventually those of emigration—played a major role in the evolution of Russian politics and culture. Their crucial feature was that they exemplified a style of social interaction which did not depend on hierarchy and patronage, but on cooperation and the exchange of ideas among equals. They thus implicitly challenged the fundamental operating principle of the empire. Out of the *kruzhki* came Russia's greatest writers and its principal revolutionary thinkers of the following generation, but also its leading liberals and also some of its most important government officials.

THE CRIMEAN WAR

The approach to the Crimean War exemplifies the difficulties Russia faced in dealing with the Ottoman Empire and the European powers. The Treaty of Adrianople (1829) acknowledged Russia's control over the entire mouth of the Danube, over the eastern Black Sea coast all the way from the Sea of Azov to Poti, and over Georgia and eastern Armenia. Even more important than the territorial gains were the provisions of the treaty which guaranteed Russian merchant ships passage through the Straits; any infraction of this right, howsoever caused, was to be considered a "hostile act" and gave Russia the right to "immediate reprisals against the Ottoman Empire."[78] The Treaty of Unkiar Skelessi (1833), following Russian intervention against the Egyptian rebel Mehmet Ali, further provided that in time of war Turkey would close the Dardanelles (the westernmost straits) to foreign warships: this was long-established Ottoman practice and created no new obligations. However the Russian text of the treaty implied that the Bosphorus (on which Constantinople stood) would remain open to Russian warships, allowing them to penetrate to the heart of the empire.[79]

In the words of John LeDonne, this was "an attempt to transform the Turkish core area into a Russian protectorate" and "to project Russian naval power from the Black Sea . . . into the Mediterranean."[80] Combined with the provisions of Kuchuk-Kainardji concerning the Russian right to protect Christians in the Ottoman Empire, it offered evidence for the notion that Russia was trying to convert Turkey into a client state.

Not being ready to go to war against other European powers, Russia was prepared to try to alleviate suspicions of this kind, and in 1841 signed the Straits Convention, which removed the ambiguity and made it clear that Russian warships, like all others, were barred from the Bosphorus as well as the Dardanelles. Furthermore, in 1844 Nicholas I went to London to endeavor to reach an agreement with Britain to consult and work together if the Ottoman Empire seemed on the point of collapse or was under attack from another power. He thought he had achieved this, but in fact he had managed also to sow in the minds of British statesmen the impression that that collapse was exactly what he was trying to bring about. This naturally heightened their suspicions of Russia's intentions.[81]

These altercations help to clarify why relatively trivial incidents should have occasioned such suspicion of Russia as to lead to the Crimean War (1853–1856). The establishment of a Latin patriarchate of Jerusalem in 1847 and the French renewal of claims embodied in a treaty of 1740 to protect Christian sites in the Holy Land struck at the heart of Russia's ill-defined but jealously guarded prerogatives inside the Ottoman Empire. Attempts to set up a joint Catholic-Orthodox guardianship of the holy places failed, and in 1853 Nicholas I sent Prince A. S. Menshikov to Constantinople to demand that Russia's right to protect Christians in the Ottoman Empire be reaffirmed. Both the demand and the arrogant personality of the envoy who made it ensured its rejection. Menshikov's understanding of the Treaty of Kuchuk-Kainardji implied that some 40 percent of the empire's population was entitled to invoke Russian protection in some unspecified form. That such a demand should be made convinced the other European powers that Russia was determined to destroy Turkey and take over Constantinople, especially since Russia backed it up by a military occupation of the Danube principalities till it was satisfied. British and French fleets were sent to the

Dardanelles, while Austria, on whom Nicholas I had been relying for support, assumed a posture of disapproving neutrality.

In this way Russia found itself in the situation its diplomats had traditionally tried to avoid at all costs, fighting not only the Ottoman Empire but two European great powers as well. In a desperate bid to appease them, Russia withdrew its troops from the Danubian principalities, but even this concession could not avert war. Britain and France decided to concentrate on preventing Russia from projecting its power into the Mediterranean, and therefore landed their troops on the Crimean peninsula in order to destroy the Black Sea fleet at its base in Sevastopol. In this they were eventually successful, though only after two years of heavy fighting.

Russia was forced to sue for a peace which proved to be extremely onerous. By the Treaty of Paris (1856), Russia had to see its claim to protect Christian subjects of the Ottoman Empire handed over to the European powers; likewise its protectorate over the principalities. Worst of all, it was required to cease maintaining a fleet in the Black Sea and to remove all naval installations along its coast. This was a signally humiliating condition for a great power to have to observe on its own shores, especially when those shores were strategically so vital. It was a mark of the fear which other powers entertained of Russia's potentiality that they should impose it, and of Russia's sense of weakness that she should accept it. At a stroke Russia ceased to be a leading guarantor of the status quo and became a revisionist power, dedicated to regaining sovereign power over its own coastline.

The whole Crimean crisis showed that the vague and portentous diplomacy, the appeal to religious sentiment, and the attempt to gain allies on a potential enemy's territory, all of which had served Russia well in dealing with its Eurasian steppe adversaries, generated alarming and destructive crises when applied in Europe, and actually undermined the peace and stability which Russia had been at pains to preserve. Before it was over, too, the faltering conduct of the war provoked public discussion which soon raised fundamental questions about the empire's future.

IV

Imperial Crisis

7

ALEXANDER II'S UNCERTAIN

REFORMS

THE POST-CRIMEAN CRISIS

For one hundred and fifty years Russia had been a successful empire and a European great power on the basis of personalized forms of authority backed up where necessary by police and military. The Crimean War served notice that that period was over.

The European situation in the second half of the nineteenth century was much more testing for Russia than the first half had been. For a century and a half the morale of her army had been high, and she had been able more or less to keep up with the military technology of her rivals, in artillery at times excelling them. The Crimean War demonstrated that this was no longer the case. The hardiness and team spirit of Russian soldiers remained as strong as ever under good leadership, as was shown by their tenacious defense of Sevastopol under Prince Aleksandr Menshikov. But their small arms were outclassed by the new rifles at the disposal of the British and French troops, which could fire both farther and more accurately. Furthermore, the Russian army had not received the supplies it needed to maintain its fighting capacity in a long campaign.

In short, it had become quite clear that Russia's industry and communications were wholly inadequate for the conduct of a major European war, even when it was fought on her own territory against an enemy coming from more than a thousand miles away. With no railway running south of Moscow, all her supplies and armaments had to be hauled along rutted, bumpy roads which became ribbons of mud in spring and autumn. The sheer size of the empire and the number of its vulnerable points told against her: many men and ships had to be kept away from the main theater of war, in the Baltic region for fear of an Anglo-French-Swedish landing there, or in the Caucasus to provide for an Ottoman attack assisted by rebellious local tribes.

Besides, war proved far more damaging to Russia's political stability than to its adversaries'. As in 1812, many peasants saw war as an opportunity to gain their freedom, and volunteered for the militia in far greater numbers than could be absorbed. Even when the war ended, peasants still insisted on heading for the Crimea, where, they staunchly asserted, "the Tsar sits in a golden chamber and gives freedom to those who come, but those who do not or are too late will remain as before, serfs to the lords."[1]

The loss of the war and the ensuing peace settlement of the Treaty of Paris (1856) were even more damaging than they seemed on the surface. It was bad enough that Russia lost territory on the Danube and the right to station warships on the Black Sea, the major artery of its most flourishing international trade. Worst of all, however, was the damage the defeat inflicted on Russia's great-power status within Europe and on the reputation of tsarist authority within the country. The Romanov dynasty had identified itself so completely with military power that the loss of a war in the region where it had the greatest hope of expansion made autocracy for the first time seem ineffective. It is no accident that within a few years political movements appeared which rejected monarchy outright and aimed to overthrow it.

Over the next half-century events in Europe continued to threaten Russia's international standing. In the early nineteenth century it had been the leading continental member of the Holy Alliance, which had offered a tolerably stable framework for resolving conflicts. In the second half-century it was a humiliated and struggling power in a far more anarchical European constellation. The unification of Germany in 1871 created a major new rival on a strategically vulnerable frontier, and also signaled that power in Europe was moving into the hands of industrialized nation-states. Russia, of course, was neither industrialized nor a nation-state. The same was true of the Ottoman and Habsburg empires, but although their gradual enfeeblement opened up opportunities for Russia, it created dangers as well. The rebellions of Balkan peoples against their imperial masters posed an acute dilemma: they offered the chance for intervention and for the acquisition of influence and even territory, but on the other hand Russia was reluctant to risk going to war with a major power; nor did it wish to be seen supporting rebels against legitimate monarchs, even when the rebels were Orthodox and the monarchs Catholic or Muslim.

Throughout this period, Russia, for all its large population and immense territories, was operating from a position of weakness of which its statesmen were all too aware. A great power must be ready if necessary to go to war. But for Russia war meant heavy expenditure which overburdened the state's finances, generated inflation, and undermined the economic development necessary to manufacture the instruments of war. Worse, war could easily mean internal disorder. Two of the likeliest theaters of combat, Poland and the Transcaucasus, were the homelands of rebellious peoples only recently subdued. In Poland Russian artillery was not issued with shells lest they should fall into the hands of insurgents; if war threatened, mobilization had to be delayed while those shells were retrieved from specially locked storage depots.[2]

Even without such extreme precautions, the Russian army had to be dispersed around the empire on internal security duties, instead of being concentrated where strategic threats were most likely. In 1873 N. N. Obruchev, the General Staff's principal theoretical adviser, warned that "the armed forces of Russia in their present condition are insufficient to guarantee her security."[3] Aleksandr Gorchakov, foreign minister for a quarter of a century (1856–1882), remarked in 1876 that "we are a great and powerless country." He added, "One can always dress up finely, but one needs to know that one is dressing up."[4] "Dressing up" remained a major element in Russian diplomacy: speaking the language of a great power which was ready to back up words with force, even when statesmen secretly lacked the confidence that force could be made effective.

THE DECISION TO REFORM

After the Crimean War even the most resolutely conservative statesmen had to agree that the system needed radical change, starting with its lynchpin, serfdom. Such a consensus had been building for a long time. As we have seen, Nicholas I himself had condemned serfdom in 1842. His reservation then, that "to touch it now would of course be an even more ruinous evil,"[5] no longer held good: after the Crimean fiasco, it seemed more dangerous to Russia's standing in the world *not* to touch serfdom.

Alexander II was himself a cautious and conservative person by temperament, in no way a natural radical, but on his accession he found himself in a milieu in which all his advisers were dissatisfied with the existing state of affairs and were busying themselves with reform proposals, some of them far-reaching. Many of them had cut their intellectual teeth and learned new ways of thinking in the semiclandestine *kruzhki* of the previous reign, and they were unanimous that the war had revealed fundamental weaknesses. The Slavophile Iurii Samarin declared, "We were defeated not by the external forces of the Western alliance, but by our own internal weakness . . . Stagnation of thought, depression of productive forces, the rift between government and people, disunity between the social classes, and the enslavement of one of them to another . . . prevent the government from deploying all the means available to it and . . . mobilizing the strength of the nation."[6]

Slavophiles and Westerners concurred that serfdom was the key to the problem. As the westerner Boris Chicherin put it, "Someone bound hand and foot cannot compete with someone free to use all his limbs. Serfdom is a shackle which we drag around with us, and which holds us back just when other people are racing ahead unimpeded." He quoted as an example the tsar's revocation of the decree forming a volunteer militia for fear of arousing vain hopes among the serfs of being freed.[7] Konstantin Kavelin, former member of the Granovskii circle, was dismissed from his post as tutor to the tsarevich for publishing a memorandum stating that serfdom made it impossible to reform the educational system, the legal system, the passport regulations, conscription, taxation, police, or censorship.[8]

Reformers had before them the model of the west European nation-state, which they had learned to admire in the course of studies, travel, or diplomatic service there. History seemed to be moving in the direction of nation-states, and most Russian statesmen assumed that Russia too would have to do so, however cautiously. What seemed to distinguish the new-style European great powers was on the one hand the rule of law, the market economy, and strong civic institutions, and on the other hand a newfound identification of the population, especially in the towns, with the nation and its rulers. Russian reformers set out to emulate these features by adopting a dual strategy, both civic and ethnic. The civic strategy entailed strengthening the institutions of civil society and through them loyalty to the state, while the ethnic strategy meant inculcating in the whole imperial population, including non-Russians, a sense of belonging to Russia.

The civic and ethnic strategies were not pursued together, since they were in partial contradiction with one another. Rather, each was adopted fitfully when the other did not seem to be working well. In general, during the 1860s and 1870s the emphasis was on civic measures, in the 1880s and 1890s on ethnic ones, or Russification. Overall the reforms, if fully accomplished, would have meant transition away from a society based on ascriptive hierarchy, kinship, patronage, tribute, and state service toward one based on meritocracy, personal rights, the rule of law, and the taxation of wealth.

Reformers faced an immediate practical obstacle. If the Crimean War made it politically possible to put their ideas into practice, it also deprived them of the means to do the job properly. As always, war had brought turmoil to Russia's finances, generating inflation, a mounting state debt, and a negative balance of payments, threatening the convertibility of the ruble and the solvency of official credit institutions—all this at a time when statesmen knew they would have to invest far more in industry and communications. The ominous fiscal climate meant that radical reform had to be carried out in a cramped and pennypinching manner which threatened to thwart its very purpose.[9]

EMANCIPATION OF THE SERFS

Freeing the serfs was the key to the whole process, since serfdom was the cement which had held the system together for two centuries. It was both complicated and hazardous to dismantle it, especially since landowners and peasants had incompatible views about what a just emancipation settlement would entail. The government convened provincial sessions of the nobility to advise on the practical details of the reform, but did not consult the serfs.

The nobles did not oppose emancipation as such. Many of them could see the reasons for it, and in any case they accepted that once the tsar had decided to go ahead with it, opposition would be both futile and illegitimate. They did however try to save what they could for themselves from the ruins of serfdom. In the southern provinces they did this by bargaining to retain as much arable land as possible and by making the peasants pay heavily for the allotments transferred to them. In the north, where land itself was less valuable, landowners concentrated on trying to obtain some monetary compensation for the loss of personal service.

The government went some way to satisfy these aspirations. It insisted that former serfs must own land, that they could not be left destitute to seek paid employment or to roam the countryside as vagabonds. On the other hand it also reserved substantial landholdings for the holders of pomestia (*pomeshchiki*): one does not ruin one's ruling class at the stroke of a pen.

The result, perhaps inevitably, was a complex of measures which satisfied nobody and left behind damaging anomalies and grievances. In principle the freeing of roughly half the peasants from personal bondage should have opened the way for all peasants to become full citizens of the empire, with the right to own property, go to law, enter the market on their own account, and participate in political life. In practice the emancipation edict of 19 February 1861 stopped well short of accomplishing that. For reasons of fiscal prudence and internal security, plans to provide peasants with credit, to reform the passport and tax systems so that they enjoyed greater mobility and suffered a lighter debt burden, were postponed—as it turned out, for decades.[10]

In the event, then, though no longer bound to the landowners, peasants were fixed to the volost and the "rural association" (essentially the village commune) on whose territory they lived. As a member of it, each household received an allotment of land, of a minimum size laid down for each uezd, and made annual redemption payments to cover the purchase price. The landowners received compensation for the land they considered they had lost and in all circumstances had the right to insist on retaining at least a third of their previous holding.

From the peasants' point of view, the results of the state's relatively solicitous attitude to the landed nobility were frustrating. They had cherished expectations that they would receive the land which they felt was theirs by God-given right. Now they were dealt a double blow: some of "their" land was being taken away from them, and for the rest they were told they would have to pay. Not only were they being robbed for the benefit of someone who was no longer to be their protector, but God's land was being made an object of monetary exchange.[11]

Peasants reacted with incredulity and resentment, which was dramatically expressed in the village of Bezdna in Kazan Province. An Old Believer by the name of Anton Petrov announced that the tsar had actually granted the peasants all the land; to discover his real intention, though, it was necessary to read the emancipation charter attentively and to decode the figures in the appendixes. Peasants flocked from many nearby villages to hear him expound this doctrine, and they took a resolution not to disperse till "the tsar's will" had been put into effect. When troops were sent to deal with them, the peasants stood firm and shouted "*volia*" in defiance of threats to shoot. In the end several of them were killed.[12]

It is not clear whether they literally believed what Petrov told them. But one thing is certain: the peasants were utterly convinced that their demands represented pravda, and they were prepared to stand for it even against bullets. In their eyes the terms of the emancipation were not merely burdensome but violated God's law.

From the government's point of view the most serious problem with emancipation was that it undermined the crucial link between lord and peasant which had sustained the framework of state service. Supplanting personal whim with the rule of law seemed essential, but how was it to be done? Here Slavophile ideas came into their own. It was decided to replace the lord's authority with that of the village commune and the volost (an amalgam of several villages), which were given new powers as the basic unit of local government. The commune, with its elected elder and officials, would be responsible for law and order within its area, would hold ultimate title to the land, and would allocate the tax burden and the redemption payments for the land allotments. Peasants, in short, were to become self-governing, though bound as before by joint responsibility and still liable to the poll tax and to corporal punishment. For them it was an incongruous mixture of empowerment and renewed dependence.

The commune and volost were purely peasant institutions: nonpeasant rural inhabitants were not subject to it and had no influence over its decisions. The peasants therefore remained a segregated class. Perhaps even more serious, there was no link between the volost and the rest of the administrative network, other than the police constable appointed by officials of the Interior Ministry. This meant that tax collection, recruitment, public hygiene, and other measures necessary to modern governance came to the peasants as police directives, imposed from outside and alien to their world. It might be claimed, in fact, that the emancipation, far from integrating the peasants into society, deepened their isolation from it. When, during the next two generations, economic and social change integrated the peasants anyway, there were no readily available channels for their aspirations and grievances to be fed into the political system.

Emancipation inevitably raised the question of reforming all the empire's political institutions. Some senior statesmen, aware that Russia's elites remained fragmented and discontented with the regime, felt they should have some kind of institutional representation. Petr Valuev, minister of the interior, suggested in memoranda of 1861 and 1862 that the first steps should be taken toward representative government by creating a cabinet or council of ministers and by giving the nobility and the regions of the empire some kind of voice in the State Council, on the lines of the Austrian Reichsrat.[13]

Some nobles raised similar proposals. During the drafting of the emancipation provisions, they had organized themselves for the first time to participate in the legislative process. Frustrated by the result, several provincial committees decided to exceed their instructions and make further recommendations, on matters about which the tsar had not consulted them. Here even conservatives, piqued at being snubbed, turned out to have a tolerably generous view of what civil society might entail. They were prepared to renounce some of their privileges in order to create a more open and equitable society. They called for such things as freedom of speech, equal rights for all social classes, equitable taxation, elected local government, and some kind of representative assembly in St. Petersburg. The Tver gentry complained of a "strange misunderstanding hindering the realization of Your [Imperial Majesty's] good intentions" and concluded that "the summoning of elected representatives from all the Russian land offers the only means for achieving a satisfactory solution to the problems posed, but not solved, by the statutes of 19 February."[14]

The tsar rejected their representations out of hand, not, he told Valuev, because it would limit his powers, but because he believed that any kind of constitution might provoke the disintegration of such a huge and diverse empire.[15] Furthermore, to demonstrate unambiguously that he was not prepared to have intermediate institutions encroach on his prerogatives, Alexander dissolved the Moscow provincial gentry assembly and forbade its members to petition him.[16] This was the old Russian paradox: that a reforming autocrat needs autocracy more than ever.

Whatever the emperor's wishes, however, the gentry's brief experience of political self-organization, though fruitless in the immediate sense, rendered them more effective both in implementing the terms of the emancipation in the decades which followed and in acting as the backbone of the new local government assemblies.[17]

In the economic sense, however, the emancipation of the serfs marked the beginning of a period of decline for the landed nobility. Over the period 1862–1905 their landholdings fell from 87 million to 50 million desiatinas, and the losses accelerated thereafter. The latifundia, which had been especially dependent on serf labor, dwindled with particular rapidity. Many landowners sold up altogether and took up professional careers in the cities. The decline was uneven, however: a substantial minority of landowners, often those with medium and small holdings, managed to modernize their agricultural methods and/or to diversify into food processing, industry, or commerce. They did not abandon the inherited sense of being the backbone of the Russian state structure. When they organized themselves to defend their own interests after 1905, they still called themselves nobles rather than landowners: that is, they saw themselves as an honored and responsible status group rather than an economic interest, a *soslovie* (social estate) rather than a class.[18]

LOCAL GOVERNMENT

There were to be no elected representatives at the center, but Alexander did allow representative government to be created at the intermediate adminis- trative level, the uezd and the guberniia. Here assemblies, known as zemstvos (derived from *zemlia*) were to be elected by landowners, urban dwellers, and peasants under a voting system based partly on *soslovie*, partly on property qualification. Municipal councils were set up in 1870 on similar principles, but with stiffer property qualifications which ensured that a tiny group of wealthy patricians dominated them. The hybrid voting system reflected the regime's ambivalence about whether Russia was now a civil society or still a hierarchical one based on state service. Significantly, the zemstvos and municipal councils were introduced only in provinces where Russians con- stituted both the elites and a majority of the population. There were to be no zemstvos in Poland, the Baltic, or the Caucasus, and hence no experi- ments with self-government for non-Russians. Alexander was still haunted by the prospect of the empire breaking up.

Peasants, though represented, were outnumbered in nearly all zemstvo assemblies, which tended as a result to reflect the outlook of the landed nobility. The new system certainly strengthened the political experience and skills of the latter, and also for the first time brought professional employees to the small towns and villages in appreciable numbers. Teachers made up about half their number: the remainder were lawyers, doctors, *feldshera* (medical orderlies), veterinary surgeons, statisticians, bookkeepers, and clerks. They were often known as the "third element," because they comple- mented the activity of the state officials and the zemstvo delegates. Through their involvement in local government work these professionals gained a lively sense of self-esteem. They revived and renewed the imperial Russian ethic of service in a more democratic form, dedicated now to the people rather than to the state.[19]

Many members of the "third element" became ambivalent about the state, even hostile to it, in the course of their work. On the one hand, the state was their best source of assistance and revenue; on the other, it often seemed to obstruct their endeavors. When doctors or schoolteachers tried to convene congresses at an all-Russian level to discuss common problems, the police would deny them permission to meet, or would close their meetings on the ground that the discussions were becoming political. The efforts of profes- sional people to overcome such obstruction and exercise their imputed right to organize themselves provided much of the impetus toward further politi- cal reform in the early twentieth century.[20]

This active and growing social stratum formed the core of what the Russians called *obshchestvennost*. The term is difficult to translate, but might be rendered as "educated society," as "politically aware society," or even as "public opinion." Its existence implied a civil society, which in fact had not yet matured, and so its relations with the ruling regime were tense. Its own members believed themselves to constitute a kind of "alternative establishment," more truly representative of the Russian nation and more genuinely able to serve it than the regime was. When famine broke out in the Volga basin in 1891, along with a cholera and typhus epidemic, professional people, especially those employed in local government, raised funds and labored heroically to relieve the sufferings of the peasants. Subsequently they argued that they had proved more effective than the government in dealing with the crisis, although research suggests that they depended greatly on finance and facilities provided by the regime and its local officials.[21]

LAW COURTS

The judicial reform of 1864 brought to an end the old system of closed and separate justice for the different estates and gave the judiciary complete independence from the administration. It institutionalized the principle that the law was an impersonal force which dealt impartially with individuals, and hence it implicitly challenged collective responsibility, ascriptive hierarchy, and arbitrary personal authority. Civil and criminal courts were opened up to the public and were given the right to try all social estates, with the partial but telling exception of the peasants, most of whose cases went before segregated volost courts. Serious criminal cases were to be heard before a jury and a judge appointed with life tenure, and the accused was entitled to a qualified defense lawyer, if necessary at public expense. Lesser cases were to come before justices of the peace elected by the local uezd zemstvo. The investigation of suspected criminal offenses was taken out of the hands of the police and assigned to a new official, the investigating magistrate.

This was perhaps the most radical of all Alexander II's reforms, and the one which fitted least well into the inherited political structure. Judges could henceforth not be dismissed, even when their decisions displeased the authorities, as Alexander discovered to his dismay when he tried to expel a member of the Senate (in effect now the empire's supreme court) in 1867; to his credit, he decided reluctantly to obey his own law.[22] A whole new profession was created, that of *advokat*, or defense lawyer, with a Bar Council to supervise training and oversee professional probity. Among its future members were Kerenskii and Lenin, along with many of Russia's leading politicians of the first two decades of the twentieth century. The *advokaty* were the only profession in Russian society with a direct interest in both the rule of law and freedom of speech, and courtrooms were the only forum in which both were consistently upheld. Perhaps for that reason, the government took fright at the institutionalization of the profession and in 1874 forbade the formation of further branches of the Bar Council, when only three existed (in St. Petersburg, Moscow, and Kharkov). In 1889 Jews were debarred from membership. In practice, moreover, the government did not prevent unqualified attorneys from pleading before courts, so that the professional standing of the *advokat* was undermined from within.[23]

The professionalization of lawyers accompanied and almost certainly assisted an evolution taking place in attitudes toward property, the family, and gender. Hitherto family relations had generally been seen in the context of the *rod,* or kin group, with strong authority vested in the eldest male, in men over women, and in parents over children. Descent and inheritance went through the male line, and illegitimate children enjoyed no rights. Members of the *rod* had a right to a share in both movable and immovable property for their sustenance. As a result of these traditions women traditionally enjoyed somewhat more secure property rights than in many European countries: they could reclaim their dowries, and in case of need had a right to a share of the kin's land and other property to support themselves, though it reverted to the male line after their death. On the other hand, a husband's permission was required before a wife could take a job, start a course of education, or enter into financial transactions. The church had jurisdiction over family affairs: divorce was difficult to obtain, and marital separation was not recognized at law.

Already in the early nineteenth century, among the educated strata, a newer view was gaining ground, that marriage was a bond of affection between two equal partners, and that children on reaching adulthood were the legal equals of their parents. It seemed to follow from this perception that, where marriage had broken down, procedures for ending it and redistributing property and the care of children should be simple and based on principles of equity rather than on patriarchal moral judgments. Lawyers, imbued with Western legal concepts, increasingly took the view that property should be owned by individuals recognizing their responsibilities rather than by extended families. They naturally also believed that secular law courts were better placed to accomplish this than ecclesiastical courts.

There was a gradual evolution in the legal disposition of these matters, not so much because of legislation—which was slow and uncertain—but because of the decisions of courts, where the Westernized training of judges and lawyers produced its effects. The Civil Cassation Court in the Senate, to which many family and property cases came for review, tended more and more to come down on the side of acknowledging women's property rights, and recognized marital separation at least thirty years before it received statutory sanction.[24] In this way by the late nineteenth century the law courts were gradually fostering the view that legal and property rights were vested in individuals rather than in patrimonial extended families.

EDUCATION

Legislation of 1864 made it much easier to open primary and secondary schools, provided the founders observed moral and religious principles, opened their doors to entrants of any social estate, and submitted to regular inspection by an uezd school council. The removal of social discrimination was a return to a long-established principle in Russian educational practice, temporarily suspended under Nicholas I, and it was combined with the restoration of "ladders" up the educational hierarchy, so that success at one level would ensure the possibility of transfer to the succeeding one.

Higher education reform raised the most fundamental questions about the tsarist system and faced it with some of its most testing challenges. On the one hand the regime needed experts trained and qualified to the highest standards, and for that purpose authorized freedom of enquiry and communication of knowledge as that was practiced at the best European universities. At the same time, fulfilling those requirements fostered an independent and critical spirit among students and graduates which was the absolute antithesis of the values cherished in a patrimonial and hierarchical society.

This duality underlay the formation of what became known as the "intelligentsia," which one may trace back as far as the 1830s: these were people with at least secondary education, of a Westernized kind, trained for service in the imperial system but often repelled by that system, troubled by the cultural and economic distance between elites and masses, and anxious to do something to bridge that gap. They were, if you like, the more radical and determined wing of *obshchestvennost*, ready to take concrete action in support of their principles.

In spite of the regime's doubts, the higher education system was thoroughly reformed in the 1860s. Its doors were opened for the first time to former serfs, and restrictions on the sons of clergymen were considerably eased. Universities regained the right to govern themselves, to choose their

own professors, to establish their own research programs and teaching sylla-
buses, and to admit, assess, and discipline students. Students, however, were
not permitted to form their own associations. Women were allowed to attend courses but not to take degrees.[25]

From 1865 to 1899 the number of university students grew roughly fourfold
(from just over 4,000 to just over 16,000), and their profile become socially
more varied, with much larger numbers of sons of peasants, *meshchane*
(lower-rank townsfolk), and, until 1879, clergy. Clergy sons were admitted
in the early 1860s in an attempt to improve the educational level of the
church, but it was soon found that many of them used their university qualifications to escape the church altogether, and so restrictions on their admission were reimposed.[26]

The inbuilt tension within higher education played itself out in the lives
of students. For all except those who came from wealthy and established
noble families, entering college meant a sharp rise both in social status and
personal expectations. It often also entailed transplantation from family life
and a rural or small-town environment to the anonymity of the big city.
The transition could be extremely unsettling, especially for women, who
faced a far harsher choice than men over whether to submit to family pressures and become wives and mothers or to try for a career and financial
independence.

Given the Russian tendency to see all aspirations in a universal context,
this change in environment, along with abrupt arrival at adulthood, generated in many a veritable worship of *nauka* (learning or science). The future
historian Pavel Miliukov recalled that he entered Moscow University in 1878
"as if it were a temple."[27] Its sacred portals aroused in freshmen hopes of
acquiring not only a general education, but also a total world view and a
moral philosophy which would enable them to act for the good of society
as a whole. Educated Russians began to believe that science would bring
them deliverance.

Often a reaction set in on closer acquaintance with crowded lecture halls,
monotonous lectures, unsatisfactory libraries, and lack of contact with professors. However, many students found substitutes in their own self-help
organizations: study circles, mutual aid funds, shared libraries, and so on.
Such associations were forbidden, strictly speaking, but in practice survived
discreetly, and provided their members with practical experience of cooperation and a sense of personal dignity which deepened their repugnance for
subordination and hierarchy. As we shall see, such experience inspired the
"going to the people" movement of the 1870s, as well as the student strikes
and clashes with authority in the period 1899–1906.[28]

CENSORSHIP AND THE MEDIA

In the late 1850s and early 1860s the authorities wanted to encourage freer discussion of social problems—the term *glasnost* (openness) was introduced then as a political watchword—and they eased the operation of the hitherto very rigid censorship, although the new provisions were not encoded till 1865. Daily newspapers were no longer submitted to prior censorship, which was also ended for books and periodicals of more than 160 pages, and for all academic works. But the Ministry of the Interior retained the power to withdraw from circulation any publication deemed to have a "dangerous orientation" and to prosecute the publishers. Periodicals could be fined, suspended, or, on repeated offenses, closed down.

By retaining these powers, the government thought it was giving itself a guarantee against subversive or damaging media influences. In practice that guarantee proved less effective than anticipated. All the advantages were on the side of the media. As Petr Valuev noted in an internal memorandum of 1866, the press "appeals to passions by using alternately truths, half-truths, and downright lies." The government often could not reply for fear of breaching state security, while if it remained silent—and still more if it fined or closed a newspaper—the public assumed it was in the wrong.[29]

On the other hand only wealthy or well-connected media outlets were in a position to benefit fully by the new opportunities. In other words, the new regulations raised the stakes in the publishing business. They undoubtedly aided the circulation of information and ideas. On the other hand, they made life much more hazardous for editors and publishers, who could no longer shelter behind the censor. They now had to take the crucial decisions themselves. The situation favored bold editors with strong financial backing: they could excite the curiosity of the reading public by probing at the ill-defined frontiers of the permissible. Russia's literate readership was growing fast, so that it was well worth risking fines in order to sell a good story and thereby hook new readers.

Popular journals could be and were closed down if they were deemed to "justify acts forbidden by law," to "incite one section of the population against another," or to "insult an official person or establishment." *Sovremennik*, originally Pushkin's offspring, suffered this fate in 1866. Its editor, the popular poet Nikolai Nekrasov, however, took many of its contributors to a new journal, *Otechestvennye zapiski*, which for two decades thereafter offered regular helpings of critical and radical thinking veiled in "Aesopian" language. In 1884 it too was closed as "an organ of the press which not only opens its pages to the spread of dangerous ideas, but even has as its closest collaborators people who belong to secret societies."[30]

The best way to play the hazards of the new game was to articulate views which were mildly nonconformist, but to which the authorities could not openly object without appearing ridiculous or contradicting their own principles. Espousing a nondynastic kind of Russian nationalism was a favorite device, especially during wars or international diplomatic tension. During the Balkan crisis of 1875–1878, for example, many newspapers took up the defense of "our brother Slavs and Orthodox believers," even when official policy was to seek a settlement acceptable to the Ottoman Empire. General Mikhail Skobelev on his white horse pandered to this mood, as did General Mikhail Cherniaev when he resigned from the Russian army to go off and lead the Serbian volunteers. The diplomatic humiliation of Russia at the Congress of Berlin (1878) aroused vehement denunciations of official cowardice, led by the redoubtable Mikhail Katkov in his daily *Moskovskie vedomosti* (Moscow News).[31]

Nor was this necessarily a journalistic ploy: editors like Katkov and A. S. Suvorin, of the daily *Novoe vremia* (New Time) believed that to remain a great power Russia needed to forge a strong demotic national consciousness, like that which had become evident in postunification Germany. Both of them held that shared devotion to the tsar could create and sustain this kind of political nationalism even among the very diverse tribes and nationalities which made up the Russian Empire. They also took pride in Russia's "civilizing mission" in the Caucasus and central Asia, which they believed was not properly appreciated in the West.

Another effective press strategy, notably in the cheaper "one kopeck" newspapers and in *Russkoe slovo* (Russian Word), owned by I. D. Sytin, a supporter of Lev Tolstoi, was to highlight social problems, reporting vividly and in detail on crime, alcoholism, prostitution, and disease and on the sufferings of the peasants, workers, and immigrants to the city, in fact on any victims of oppression and exploitation. These papers specifically aimed to encourage ordinary Russians to feel a sense of dignity and moral worth, as well as compassion for those around them. Again, the authorities might not welcome such reporting, but they felt they could scarcely prohibit it, provided it was tolerably accurate.

In questions of imperial, ethnic, and social policy, then, by the end of the century, with journals and newspapers as a forum, a certain "public opinion" was beginning to take shape, not wholly dependent either on the government or on the radicals for information and ideas. It conceived of Russia as having its own distinctive and valuable identity, consisting in the capacity to rule peacefully over a great variety of peoples and in the tendency, whether inspired by Orthodoxy or by a veiled socialism, to seek collectivist and cooperative solutions to social problems rather than individualist ones.[32]

MILITARY REFORM

The most hotly contested of Alexander's reforms was that of the army, whose main feature, the introduction of adult male conscription, was consequently delayed till 1874. Dmitrii Miliutin, the war minister, aimed to create an army which was better equipped, more professionally led, and manned by conscious citizens of Russia. As his supporter, Minister of the Interior Petr Valuev, remarked, "Military service is a kind of national elementary education."[33] Their model was the Napoleonic army and, more recently, the Prussian one, which had brought unity to Germany. In both those countries, of course, the new-style army had been created only after revolution or massive national humiliation, and Russia proved no different. Even after the Crimean War, it was difficult to persuade the hereditary nobility that they should lose their virtual monopoly over the officer corps, or the grand dukes that top command positions were no longer their automatic right. As we have seen, the imperial court was bound up more closely with the army than with any other institution, and its grip was the more tenacious.

All the same, in the end, Miliutin succeeded in establishing the principle that all adult males should have the obligation to perform military service, with education, not social origin, determining the length and nature of the service. Recruits without primary education were to do a full six years, which were to include literacy classes: all soldiers were required to be able to read. After completion of service, soldiers would be released to civilian occupations, with the obligation to do a period of training each year and to report to their regiments if some crisis compelled mobilization of the reserve. The Cadet Corps were abolished, and other military schools were set up with the specific purpose of training officer cadets from non-noble backgrounds as well as offering them a general secondary education.[34]

However, the nobles fought for and retained their own elite military colleges, and under Alexander III (1881–1894) the Cadet Corps were restored. At the same time, regular literacy classes for ordinary soldiers were dropped. Right through till 1917 the high command remained the preserve of court patronage, while lower down well-trained but plebeian officers struggled to preserve their status and a degree of professionalism in the face of condescension and sometimes contempt from their superiors.[35]

THE ORTHODOX CHURCH

By the late eighteenth century the Orthodox clergy had become virtually a closed caste, even though there were no formal restrictions on entry to or withdrawal from it. Very few nobles entered the clergy, since doing so meant a sharp loss of social status, and in any case they had the wrong type of education. Ordinary peasants and townsfolk *(meshchane)* did not usually have the means for years of study in a seminary. As a result, most priests were the sons of priests, and most priests' daughters became the wives of priests. To be the son of a clergyman and not to become a clergyman oneself meant being demoted into the lower "tax-paying" orders and possibly having to serve as a private in the army. To avoid this fate, priests were desperately anxious to find parishes for their sons and sons-in-law, a task which became progressively more difficult as their numbers grew, without any increase in the number of parishes or in diocesan finances. Add to this that no pension was provided for retired clergymen. An aging priest in Vladimir guberniia wrote to his bishop with unusual candor in 1791: "To take care of me and my impoverished family and wife, order a student at the Suzdal seminary to marry my daughter and then appoint this son-in-law to my position."[36] Most of his colleagues were trying, perhaps more discreetly, to achieve something similar.

Under this kind of pressure the church as an organization was turning into an employment agency and social security office for its numerous semi-indigent families and their dependents. This subsidiary but nevertheless vital function thwarted several attempts, in the 1820s, 1840s, and 1860s, to reform the church's structure by cutting down the number of parishes, and the number of clergy whom parishioners had to support, in order to improve the funding for those remaining. Clergy resisted redundancy or even transfer, which could be a disaster for them and their families, and bishops usually refrained from compulsion.[37]

In the spiritual sense the Orthodox Church reflected the uncertainty of the Russian people about their status in their "own" empire. The church did not really embody the messianic Russian national myth, since, as we have seen, that was more effectively done by the Old Believers, who in addition enjoyed a higher level of literacy and a more cohesive parish life.[38] In the cities, Lutherans, Catholics, and Baptists were all more successful at recruiting immigrants newly arrived from the countryside. So too were the socialist parties.

In the field of charitable and social work the church's record was variable. Its numerous monasteries played a considerable but uneven role in providing for the needs of the poor, the sick, the old, and special categories like army veterans. However, the confiscation of monastery lands in 1762–1764 considerably diminished their capacity to respond to this kind of need. At the same time the parishes, as we have seen, were becoming more constricted in the kinds of activity they could promote. Some Orthodox theorists in any case taught that charity should not be organized, but should come straight from the heart, as a loving impulse from the giver to the receiver. This sounds like an evasion of the issue, but it was not altogether so: there is plenty of evidence of spontaneous charity, offered compassionately by people of all social ranks to beggars, cripples, old people, and convicts.[39]

Even making allowance for these factors, however, the absence of organized church involvement in charitable work during the nineteenth and twentieth centuries is striking. Where it existed, it usually resulted from the energy and enterprise of individual parish priests, such as Aleksandr Gumilevskii in 1856–1866 in the Peski suburb of St. Petersburg, or Father Ioann Sergiev from 1855 for nearly half a century in Kronstadt, the island naval base just outside the capital, who raised funds to set up a hostel for beggars, a workhouse for the unemployed, and a trade school for indigent children. Father Ioann became a nationally known figure as John of Kronstadt, whose spiritual reflections were translated into several languages, and he was later canonized by the Orthodox Church; but Gumilevskii attracted official suspicion as a political subversive and was transferred to a parish well out of the capital city.[40]

The church, then, was poverty-stricken, embattled, and overshadowed by the secular state. Yet at this apparent low point of its fortunes a remarkable spiritual revival was germinating which goes back to the semiburied tradition of hesychasm. Since hesychasm had been the preserve of the "nonpossessors" in earlier centuries, it is perhaps not surprising that it recovered its vigor at the very time when the church had been deprived of its property by the state.

The source of the revival was Mount Athos, where in 1782 St. Nicodemus the Hagiorite collated and published a selection of patristic texts on contemplation and prayer under the title *Philokalia* (Lover of the Good). This was translated into Russian by a Ukrainian monk, Paisii Velichkovskii, and published in St. Petersburg in 1793. Paisii founded a monastery in Moldavia, Niamets, where the hesychast disciplines were consciously fostered: it served as a refuge for monks whose houses had been closed or who were dissatisfied by the secular spirit of the current monastic regime in Russia itself.[41]

Gavriil, metropolitan of St. Petersburg from 1783, founded hermitages (*skity*) inside Russia where contemplation and prayer could be pursued in the hesychast manner, and invited monks from Moldavia to run them. One of the most active was at Sarov, in Nizhnii Novgorod province, where in the first decades of the nineteenth century *starets* Serafim both practiced the hesychast discipline and invited visitors who sought spiritual guidance. His mission marked the moment when hesychasm turned outward, from the cultivation of personal spirituality, to work in the world, the offer of comfort and counseling to ordinary people. Serafim was criticized by his colleagues for diluting his discipline in this way, but he replied: "Learn to be peaceful and thousands of souls around you will find salvation."[42]

Metropolitan Filaret, after the rejection of his proposal to translate the Bible, was suspended from the Holy Synod. Thereupon he set up his own *skit* not far from the Trinity Monastery, without official approval. He called it the Gethsemane Hermitage, and lived there for more than a decade, not returning to St. Petersburg till after Nicholas I's death.[43]

The leading center of the contemplative "holy men" was Optyna Pustyn, a hermitage near the town of Kozelsk, in Kaluga guberniia, revived from almost complete neglect by Metropolitan Platon of Moscow in the early nineteenth century. There three successive *startsy*, Leonid, Makarii, and Amvrosii, maintained the hesychast tradition for nearly a century (1828–1911), continuing and broadening the social commitment displayed by Serafim. Nor was it only the masses whom they attracted: intellectuals and men of letters also made the pilgrimage to Optyna Pustyn. Ivan Kireevskii, the Slavophile thinker, went there frequently, not only to consult on his translation of the church fathers, but also to seek the personal advice of the *startsy*. At the time of his religious crisis, Gogol visited it at least twice, and the religious thinkers Vladimir Soloviev and Konstantin Leontiev sought the spiritual counsel of the elders of Optyna. Lev Tolstoi went several times, even though he rejected the Orthodox Church as an unworthy exemplar of Christianity: he was on his way there again when he died in November 1910.[44]

Dostoevskii spent three days at Optyna Pustyn in 1878 after the death of his infant son. According to his wife, he returned "much reassured and at peace with himself . . . He saw the famous *starets* Father Amvrosii three times, once among a crowd of people and twice alone, and felt the most deep and penetrating influence from conversation with him."[45] He described Amvrosii in the figure of Father Zosima in his novel *The Brothers Karamazov:*

> All sorts of people, the simplest and the most aristocratic, would flock to see the *startsy* of our monastery, to fall at their feet and confess to them their doubts, their sins and sufferings, and to ask for advice and instruction . . . The *starets* would come out to the crowd of simple

pilgrims awaiting him at the gates of the hermitage . . . They would fall before him, weep, cry out, kiss his feet, kiss the ground on which he stood; women would hold out their children to him and bring before him those possessed by hysteria. The elder would talk to them, say a short prayer, bless them, and let them go.[46]

In his novel Dostoevskii suggests that Zosima had difficulties with his monastic superiors and some of his colleagues, because he did not observe the strict rule of the house and because of the unruly folk he attracted into its grounds. The hesychast movement, and especially its diversion into social work and popular witness, never had the wholehearted support of the Holy Synod, even though individual bishops advanced and assisted it. It remained in some respects an exotic outgrowth of the church, though one of enormous potential for Russia's distinctive cultural and religious life, not least because it attracted people of all social classes.

THE POLISH REBELLION

Right at the outset Alexander II's civic reforms faced a challenge in the most sensitive region of the empire. By restoring a degree of Polish autonomy, promoting the expansion of primary education, planning the reopening of Warsaw University, and encouraging public discussion of the emancipation of the serfs, Alexander stimulated the Polish elites to feel themselves once again leaders of a potential nation. While some Poles, led by Marquis Alexander Wielopolski, believed it was in Poland's best interests to work with the Russian government to take reform further and regain Polish civic nationhood, others wanted to use the opportunity to move swiftly to full independence and the reclamation of the eastern territories in Lithuania and Belorussia which Poland had lost in the eighteenth-century partitions.

A year of patriotic street demonstrations culminated in the summer of 1862 with attempts on the life of Wielopolski and of the viceroy, Grand Duke Konstantin. Wielopolski tried to deprive the radicals of their manpower by conscripting young Polish men into the Russian army. Instead, the potential recruits headed for the woods and formed partisan bands. Insurrection broke out in January 1863 and lasted more than a year. Unlike in 1831, there were no large-scale engagements between armies. This was guerrilla warfare, and much therefore depended on the attitude of the peasants. They proved to be ambivalent. Some of them supported the rebels, helping them with supplies and information. But a large number held back, feeling no strong identification with the Polish national cause. Some of them suspected that they might actually be emancipated on more favorable terms by the Russian government than by their own landlords.[47]

Probably for this reason, in the end the Russian army managed to regain control of the countryside, and the leaders of the rebellion were captured and executed. However, the fact that the rebellion had broken out at all cast doubt on the policy of promoting local institutions, expanding education, easing censorship—in short, some of the cardinal points of the government's current reform program.

305

The question of how to conduct the repression generated a significant division of opinion among Alexander's advisers. Some, like Interior Minister Valuev and Foreign Minister Gorchakov, were anxious to continue the traditional imperial policy of ruling through a co-opted client aristocracy. This implied allowing the Polish gentry to dominate the region as before, prosecuting only the obvious ringleaders from among them. Others, led by War Minister Miliutin, took the view that the Polish gentry as a whole had conclusively proved their disloyalty to Russia and that they should be ruthlessly expropriated and shorn of power, Russian officials being brought in to take over their estates and to Russify Poland. This represented a new approach, dedicated to bypassing aristocracies and converting the whole empire into something more like a nation-state, directly responsible for the welfare of the whole people. The implications of such a change of policy for the empire as a whole were far-reaching. As one of its opponents, Aleksandr Koshelev, remarked, "It is impossible to act in one part of the empire in the spirit of radical democracy and elsewhere to hold on to other, healthier principles."[48]

All the same, by and large the second policy was adopted. Hundreds of Polish noblemen were exiled to Siberia and their estates awarded to incoming Russians. The government also took the opportunity to emancipate Polish—and also Belorussian and Ukrainian—serfs on far more generous terms than those offered to Russian ones. Polish peasants gained freehold rights to the lands they were allotted, and compensation was paid to the landlords through a tax levied on all owners of land, not on the peasants alone. The Polish rural district council, the *gmina,* included all social strata, and was not a segregated peasant institution as in Russia. In the long run, of course, these measures laid the basis for a cross-class Polish civic consciousness which remained absent in Russia itself.[49]

However, the immediate effects of the suppression of the rebellion were extremely damaging to Polish nationhood. The remnants of its separate status were abolished: the former Congress Kingdom became known in official parlance as the "Vistula region" of Russia. Polish officials were often replaced by Russian ones, and Russian was imposed as the language of public business as well as of education. The Catholic church was forbidden to maintain correspondence with the Vatican, and bishops who disobeyed were dismissed, while in Lithuania and Belorussia mass conversions from the Uniate to the Orthodox Church were enforced.[50]

RUSSIAN SOCIALISM

Members of the intelligentsia, as we have seen, were looking for a scientifically-based doctrine which would enable them to be of service to the people. The one which proved most compelling was socialism. It came from western Europe in a variety of forms, but they all underwent a transformation on reaching Russia: they took on a pronounced messianic streak which ultimately derived from the long-suppressed national myth of "Holy Rus" as the bearer of true Christianity. Russian socialism was also strongly marked by the tradition of "joint responsibility" which had been consolidated and extended by the post-Petrine state. It elevated to an ideal the egalitarian, self-contained, and participatory peasant land commune and workers' artel.

The first thinker to articulate a distinctively Russian vision of socialist revolution was Mikhail Bakunin, who came from a family of wealthy landowners in Tver guberniia. Characteristically, he had little contact with the peasants on the family estate: he came to socialism by way of German philosophy. He was particularly inspired by Hegel, who assigned a cosmic significance to ideological and political struggles, seeing them as the means by which humanity—and with it the Absolute Spirit, or God—comes to full self-knowledge and is reconciled with itself. Bakunin believed that revolution was imminent in Russia, and that it marked the moment when the dialectic reaches its culmination and the contradictions hitherto inherent in human existence are finally resolved in one great purgative conflict. As he put it, "The urge to destroy is a creative urge!"[51]

He believed the Russian people would be the bearers of this theophany because in Russia the alienation of the masses from the state was at its greatest. There was a strong element of Russian, or Slav, nationalism in his outlook. He held that the Slavs in their local communities still exhibited a primeval human solidarity which the rationalizing, Germanized state bureaucracies of the modern era were destroying. "The Slavs," he asserted, "are predominantly peaceable and agricultural . . . Living in their separate and independent communes, governed according to patriarchal custom by elders, but on an elective basis, and all making equal use of the commune's land, they . . . put into practice the idea of human brother-hood."[52]

Bakunin was not a penetrating or even coherent thinker: he had little to say about how the uprising he envisaged might be carried out or even what its practical political aims might be. But he is crucially important because he identified the Russian peasant commune as the bearer of a millennial upheaval which would sweep away impersonal rational bureaucracy throughout Europe and restore primitive human solidarity. "Russian democracy," he proclaimed, "with its tongues of fire, will swallow up the state power and light up all Europe in a bloody glow!"[53] This proved to be a contagious and attractive vision, not only in Russia but especially there.

If Bakunin was the fiery prophet of revolutionary socialism, Aleksandr Herzen was its hesitant sage. His experiences in France and Italy in 1848 had left him hoping that in a socialist society nourished by the traditions of the village commune liberty could be defended without the need for high stone walls, policemen, and bewigged judges. The first step had to be to emancipate the peasants from serfdom and to offer them land. "Land and freedom" became the slogan of the first generation of Russian socialists. Herzen was uncertain about how this should be done, especially since he knew that a peasant rising à la Bakounine would destroy much that he cherished. At one stage, in the late 1850s, he hoped the tsar might introduce socialism as an extension of the emancipation of the serfs. When the terms of the 1861 edict were announced, it became obvious that this was an illusion, and Herzen, for all the influence of Kolokol, was elbowed aside by younger, more energetic, and less ambivalent thinkers.[54]

Nikolai Chernyshevskii crystallized Herzen's ideas in a novel, What Is to Be Done?, which remarkably was passed by the censor and appeared in the journal Sovremennik in 1862. It portrays an artel of seamstresses, young women who had broken away from patriarchal families dominated by husband or father in order to pool their resources and make clothes for sale. In the background, somewhat veiled (because of the censorship) but unmistakable, is a conspiratorial circle of young men, political activists preparing for a coming revolution. Rakhmetov, their leader, trains himself by an ascetic regime of theoretical study, body-building, moderate food, and abstention from sex. One might say that in him the Petrine ideal—the selfless official working tirelessly for improvement—combined with that of the Orthodox monastery and the socialist phalanstère. The image, though a fictional one, exercised a powerful appeal on readers and influenced two generations of revolutionaries, including Lenin.[55]

Chernyshevskii's novel highlighted one notable feature of Russian social-

307

ism: the major place accorded in it to the "woman question" and the unusually active role played by women within the movement. As we have seen, during the earlier part of the century, concepts of family life and gender roles had been changing under the influence of the Enlightenment and the Romantic movement, and it had come to be widely accepted in aristocratic and professional circles that a woman should be as well educated as a man in order to be an equal companion to her partner and a fruitful influence for her children.

These expectations were probably more at odds with inherited traditions in Russia than in most of Europe. But the more secure property rights which Russian women enjoyed gave them a certain basis for independent action. One may hypothesize, then, that they were both more frustrated and potentially more autonomous than in many other countries.

The 1860s reforms deepened this paradox: they undermined the inherited wealth of many noble families, making it harder for them to provide for their younger women, while they also opened up, albeit hesitantly, new female educational opportunities. Many young women from the elites now both needed to set up on their own and had somewhat better facilities for doing so. The generation conflict, serious enough between fathers and sons, became explosive when it took place between fathers and daughters. Many middle-aged men were outraged that their daughters were not content to seek security in a traditional marriage or to accept a life of dependence and service within their own family, but wanted to go into the big, bad city, sit unchaperoned in lecture halls or even anatomy theaters, then open their own bank accounts and set up their own businesses. So the question of self-realization was especially acute for women, and it became an important part of the socialists' ideal of self-emancipation within a more mutually supportive society.[56]

The first revolutionary organizations date from the 1860s, their appearance provoked by the disappointment of the 1861 emancipation edict and nurtured by the distinctive atmosphere of Russia's higher education institutions. Students' experience of mutual aid, and their reading of Chernyshevskii, inspired them to found conspiratorial groups with ill-defined aims, which included making contact with workers, spreading revolutionary propaganda, and murdering government officials.

One member of such a groupuscule, D. V. Karakozov, attempted to assassinate Alexander II in 1866. He left behind him a manifesto which throws light on the motives and feelings of revolutionaries of the period. "Brothers, I have long been tormented by the thought and given no rest by my doubts why my beloved simple Russian people has to suffer so much! . . . I have looked for the reason for all this in books, and I have found it. The man really responsible is the Tsar . . . Think carefully about it, brothers, and you will see that the Tsar is the first of the nobles. He never holds out his hand to the people because he is himself the people's worst enemy."[57] The idolization of the people, the naive faith in books, the crude division of the world into good and evil: all this was characteristic of intellectuals isolated from the masses, without practical experience, and tempted by millenarian hopes derived from Russia's "shadow" tradition.

A much more repellent figure emerged from the same background: Sergei Nechaev. He preached that the revolutionary was someone who had "broken every tie with the civil order . . . and with the ethics of this world,"[58] and he put his concept into practice. He set up a secret society, persuading its other members that it was but one cell of a vast network, whose sole representative among them was himself. He visited Switzerland, where, on the strength of his fabrications, he persuaded Bakunin to part with a good deal of money he had been saving for revolutionary purposes. Back in Russia, he alleged to his followers that one of their number was a police spy and that they must murder him. They did so, and after a police investigation Nechaev was brought to trial in 1872—a trial which the authorities decided to hold openly, in the expectation that the evidence presented would awaken public repugnance toward the revolutionaries. In fact, as it turned out, the newspaper reports inspired many young people with admiration for Nechaev's courage, for his single-mindedness, and even for his break with conventional morality.[59]

Others, however, rejected his example with abhorrence, as one which would pervert the fine aims of the movement. During the 1870s there was a wave of peaceful attempts to bring the revolutionary movement out of its claustrophobic isolation, to make contact with the masses, and to convince them of the necessity of common action to end the existing system. The thinker who inspired this wave was Petr Lavrov, a retired military engineer who had been involved in one of the student circles and was exiled to Vologda guberniia. His *Historical Letters* (1869) was widely read and became a kind of Bible of the intelligentsia. He preached that intellectuals, since they owed their education and culture to the sweat and toil of the masses, had a duty to repay the debt by going out to them and sharing the fruits of their learning. He believed revolution would ultimately have to be the work of the people themselves, but he rejected Bakunin's idea that blind destruction would prove fruitful. Instead, he argued, the level of culture and consciousness of the peasants must first be raised, so that they could bring their own socialist potential to full fruition and not dissipate it in indiscriminate violence.

During the mid-1870s thousands of young people, mostly students, tried to put his message into practice. Some of the early attempts to contact the people were aimed at Old Believers and sectarians, on the strength of their record of alienation from regime and church. By this time, however, the Old Believers had long ago lost their oppositional fervor, and in any case regarded the atheism of most of the radicals with alarm and repugnance.[60]

Urban workers proved much more responsive. In 1869 Mark Natanson set up a circle at the St. Petersburg Military-Medical Academy, and after his arrest in 1871 it was continued by Nikolai Chaikovskii. Its members rejected the "Jesuitism and Machiavellism" of Nechaev. Chaikovskii used to call the circle "an Order of Knights" and insisted: "We must be clean and clear as a mirror. We must know one another so well that, should there arise difficult times of persecution and struggle, we are in a position to know a priori how each of us will behave."[61]

The circle began by collecting socialist books, at first for their own use, then for distribution among workers. They included Marx's *Das Kapital*, Lavrov's *Historical Letters*, Louis Blanc's *History of the French Revolution*, and works by Herzen and Chernyshevskii. Distribution was supplemented by the formation of clandestine study and discussion groups which proved popular.[62]

By 1873 members of the circle felt it was time to go out to the heartland of the *narod* (the people), the villages. This was a much more drastic step than urban agitation, for it meant abandoning one's studies and any hope of a career, and probably breaking with family and friends. All the same, several thousand young people took that decision. In the words of one participant, "these revolutionary young folk, full of belief in the people and in their own strength, gripped by a kind of ecstasy, set out on the long journey into the unknown . . . All their boats were burned. There was no return."[63]

As the language of this account implies, the mood among participants resembled that of Victorian missionaries departing for "darkest Africa." They were going to try to reknit the torn ethnic fabric of Russia by living among the peasants, learning about their way of life, but also bringing them the fruits of socialist theorizing from all over Europe. They indicated their longing for ethnic unity first of all by the clothes they wore. The young men dressed in red shirts, baggy trousers and overalls, and kept their hair long, while the women trimmed their hair short and wore plain white blouses, black skirts, and heavy boots. They were not only imitating workers but also deliberately blurring gender distinctions in defiance of social convention. Some of them learned a trade which could make them useful in the countryside: cobblery, joinery, stove-setting. Others took jobs for which their studies had prepared them, as schoolteachers or medical orderlies, or became volost clerks.[64]

How did the peasants respond to them? Traditionally, historians have asserted that they regarded them and their propaganda with incomprehension and suspicion, and often turned them over to the authorities. More recent research suggests that this was not always the case. There were undoubted difficulties in establishing communication with villagers, who revered the tsar and held religious beliefs which most students considered grossly superstitious. Osip Aptekman found on settling in a village in Pskov guberniia that "My outlook on the world is completely different from theirs. We have two categories of ideas, two mentalities, not only opposite to but contradicting each other."[65]

All the same there were techniques for establishing human contact. Aptekman, when he became a medical orderly, discovered that he could win the peasants' confidence by asking them attentively about their lives while he treated them. Vera Figner, an orderly in a Samara rural zemstvo hospital, also found that they responded well when she questioned them sympathetically and in detail and gave them proper instructions on how to take their medicines. When she and her sister Evgeniia opened a school offering tuition free of charge, they found that not only children but also adults came to them to learn basic literacy and arithmetic, which was useful to them in their everyday affairs. "Every moment we felt that we were needed, that we were not superfluous. That awareness of being useful was the force which attracted our young people to the villages; only there was it possible to have a pure heart and a peaceful conscience."[66]

Peasants did in fact share some of the radicals' ideas, for example about egalitarianism in landholding and the desirability of village communities being left to govern themselves; but they saw them in a completely different context, in which local pravda was guaranteed by a distant but benevolent father-tsar. Two activists in Kiev guberniia discovered that the peasants were hoping for all the land finally to be given to them as a reward for the universal military service recently introduced by Miliutin. The two of them circulated a forged manifesto, supposedly from the tsar, which appealed to the peasants to seize the land from the pomeshchiki who were thwarting his intention to give it to them. The peasants responded by setting up a *druzhina* (militia) before the police got wind of the conspiracy and broke it up.[67]

This episode suggests that the peasants were prepared to take political action if they thought they had the tsar's approval. Most radicals, however, felt that attracting peasant support by means of deliberate deceit violated the moral principles on which their movement rested.

312

Village authorities—elders, clerks, policemen, sometimes the priest—could not but become aware of the strangers in their midst, for the young people were conspicuous by their speech, by their behavior, sometimes by their clothing. They were completely vulnerable, for their movement was peaceful and largely unorganized. They could not resist arrest, nor had they local bases to escape to. Several hundred were picked up and imprisoned. At that point everything suddenly changed for them: from an active life of commitment, they were abruptly plunged into passivity and solitary confinement. Furthermore, many of them discovered that their comrades were not shining knights, but were yielding to the pressures of the investigation and beginning to provide information to the authorities. Some committed suicide; others went insane. Eventually two great trials were held in 1877–78, one of 50, the other of 193 defendants. The trials were open and offered those defendants who had kept their heads the chance to make their case in public, personally or through their *advokaty.*

The whole experience of "going to the people" *(khozhdenie v narod),* as it became known, suggested that peaceful socialist propaganda was of limited use under the current regime, and that tight conspiratorial organization was essential. In 1876 Mark Natanson and others set up what might be called the first political party in Russia, in the sense that it had a central committee and branches in many of the provinces. Called Land and Freedom (Zemlia i Volia) after Herzen, in December 1876 it organized a demonstration of more than 200 people, including workers, outside the Kazan Cathedral in St. Petersburg.

From the outset Land and Freedom was troubled by a split which soon grew into a permanent division, between those who favored continuing peaceful propaganda and those who argued that only the violent overthrow of the regime could make real change possible.

Those who recommended violence were encouraged by the affair of Vera Zasulich, who in January 1878 shot and wounded the governor-general of St. Petersburg, General Trepov, in his reception room. Her case was brought to open criminal trial, before a St. Petersburg jury appointed in the normal way. To the authorities' horror, even though no one denied that an attempted murder had been committed, the jury acquitted her, accepting the plea of her *advokat* that she "had no personal interest in her crime," that she was "fighting for an idea." The public in the courtroom applauded the verdict.[68] Evidently the jury—propertyowners of St. Petersburg and peasant officials from nearby villages—were susceptible to the argument that the regime itself was immoral. Even Dostoevskii, who was thoroughly monarchist in political views, confessed to a friend that were he to hear of a terrorist outrage being prepared, he would not report it to the police, for fear of public exposure and ridicule.[69]

In 1879, in accordance with this mood, a secret congress of Zemlia i Volia resolved on a policy of systematic terror with the aim of disorganizing and overthrowing the government and replacing it with a regime which would convene a constituent assembly and prepare the way for popular rule. A few members dissented, notably Georgii Plekhanov, a former student of the Mining Institute, who tried, not very successfully, to set up a rival organization. The majority reconstituted themselves as Narodnaia Volia, which can be translated as either the People's Freedom or the People's Will. On 26 August 1879 the Executive Committee of Narodnaia Volia condemned Alexander II himself to death for "crimes against the people," and from then on devoted itself to putting that verdict into effect.

313

PAN-SLAVISM AND THE TURKISH WAR OF 1877–78

Continued tension between regime and educated society stimulated the appearance of the first independent public movement with an agenda which concerned both foreign policy and, even more deeply, the nature of Russia as a state and a community. Especially strong among the wealthy and educated members of Moscow society, the Pan-Slavs were inspired by the example of Germany to hope that Russia could both renew its national identity and strengthen its standing in Europe by sponsoring nation-building among the Slav and Orthodox peoples of central and southeastern Europe.

The reason for the appeal of Pan-Slavism was partly geopolitical: after the reverses which had followed the Crimean War, it seemed desirable for Russia to seek compensation within Europe. Cultivating relations with Slav and Orthodox peoples looked like a practical means to contain and perhaps roll back the power of the Habsburg monarchy and the Ottoman Empire.

Pan-Slavism also appealed to the suppressed messianism in the Russian cultural and religious tradition. In this sense, it had something in common with populist socialism. The poet Fedor Tiutchev wrote as early as 1849 of "the city of the Constantines" as one of the "secret capitals of Russia's realm," and he evoked an unfading empire stretching "from Nile to Neva and from Elbe to China . . . As the Spirit foresaw and Daniel prophesied."[70]

The messianic mood was articulated by Nikolai Danilevskii, who declared in his *Russia and Europe* (1869) that the Romano-Germanic domination of Europe was coming to an end and would be replaced by a Slav-Orthodox domination. In Danilevskii's view, the new Slavic civilization, with its capital at Constantinople, would synthesize the highest achievements of its prede-cessors in religion (Israel), culture (Greece), political order (Rome), and so-cioeconomic progress (modern Europe), and would supplement them with the Slavic genius for community and social justice. The Slav peoples would be held together by "deep-rooted popular confidence in the tsar." Echoes of "Moscow the Third Rome" were unmistakable in his writing, transmuted into contemporary geopolitical prophecy.[71]

The most popular exponent of such ideas was Dostoevskii, who in his novels and his journalism projected the concept of Russians as a people marked out by God both for special suffering and for fulfillment of a special mission. He believed that their humble and passive spirit enabled ordinary Russians to understand and sympathize with the cultures of other nations; hence in a Russian state other nations could come to flowering, on condition that they acknowledged the legitimacy of Russia's political authority. Applied to the Balkans, this doctrine implied that Russia would assume leadership of the Slav and Orthodox peoples in a crusade to destroy the Ottoman Em-pire and reinstall the cross on the Cathedral of Hagia Sophia in Constantin-ople. Dostoevskii believed that such a campaign would be the first step to-ward the inauguration of "eternal peace" in Europe in the Slav spirit.[72]

Some Pan-Slavs hoped that Russia's incorporation of the other Slavic and Orthodox peoples would be accompanied by the creation of a federal assem-bly, a zemskii sobor representing the various peoples and enabling them to communicate their aspirations to the tsar. In this way empire would go hand in hand with democratization.[73]

There were problems with this vision, though. Not all Slav peoples were content to accept the role assigned to them by self-appointed Russian proph-ets. Most Polish intellectuals, being Catholics, were not willing to recognize themselves as part of the Orthodox cultural domain, and still less to accept continuing Russian rule, of which they already had more than enough expe-rience. Even the Orthodox Slavs of the Balkans, though happy to accept Russian help in their struggles against the Ottomans, did not wish to see their nationhood subsumed in a Russian-dominated empire.

Even more serious, the Pan-Slav program could be effected only if Russia went to war at least against the Ottoman Empire, and probably against Aus-tria too. With the formation of the German Empire in 1871, Pan-Slavism moved from the realm of cultural vision to that of Realpolitik. It became a means of containing the growth of German influence in eastern Europe. General Rostislav Fadeev believed that a major showdown between Germans and Slavs was imminent: Russia, he argued, must either use its Slavic ties to establish itself on the Danube at the expense of Austria or else renounce any thought of influence in Europe and retreat behind the Dnieper to become a purely Asiatic power. "Slavdom or Asia," he used to repeat ad nauseam to Russian diplomats.[74]

Fadeev was dismissed from the army for propagating his ideas. The truth was that Russian diplomats were most unwilling to risk a major European war, for whatever purpose. Their aim was to restore a stable balance of power, already sufficiently disturbed by the emergence of a united Germany. Besides, the tsar was reluctant to be seen encouraging rebellion against legitimate monarchical authority.

The Serb and Bulgarian revolts of 1875–76 against Ottoman rule raised these dilemmas in sharp and unavoidable form. Army officers, society ladies, and merchants formed Slavic Benevolent Committees which collected money to send volunteers to Serbia. The authorities did not publicly support them, but tacitly permitted officers and men from the Russian army to take leave and join the Serbian army. One of them was a friend of Fadeev, General Mikhail Cherniaev, hero of Russia's recent triumphs in central Asia.

When, in spite of these efforts, the Serbs were defeated, the Russian government could no longer temporize. Russia either had to come to the Serbs' aid or see its influence in the Balkans sharply diminished. Eventually Alexander II decided to declare war on Turkey, but on the grounds that it was failing to implement reforms demanded by the European powers, and only after concluding an agreement with Austria that excluded the formation of "a large amalgamated Slav state."[75] In the end, then, Russia went to war to enforce European agreements rather than out of solidarity with the Balkan Slavs.

The war proved to be a complicated one. Turkey, long known as the "sick man of Europe," was by no means a pushover. For one thing, she was able to foment risings in the Caucasus, among the Muslim peoples of Dagestan and Chechnia, only recently pacified. Ottoman troops landed on the Black Sea coast, and, to rouse the local population to rebellion, they brought with them Abkhazians who had been driven out a decade or so earlier. The Russians were able to crush these rebellions, but at the cost of keeping more than 60,000 men in the Caucasus, under the command of General M. T. Loris-Melikov. Later these troops attacked successfully south and west into Anatolia, captured the town of Kars, and cut off the port town of Batum.

In the Balkan theater Russian troops crossed the Danube, forced the Shipka Pass across the Balkan mountains, the most serious barrier to their southward progress, and held it against ferocious Turkish counterattacks. But their further advance fetched up against the fortress of Plevna, which they tried three times to storm, in vain. Eventually they took it only after a long siege. Thereafter things went better, and after a great battle at Plovdiv the Russians entered Adrianople in January 1878 and seemed poised to take Constantinople itself. But European alarm at the prospect of Russia's expanding toward the Mediterranean was reviving. The British sent a fleet to enter the Sea of Marmora, next to Constantinople. So the Russians pulled back and instead concluded a treaty with Turkey at San Stefano: it acknowledged Russia's right to "guarantee" reform in the Ottoman Empire. It also ceded to Russia the port of Batum and the Anatolian town of Erzurum and created a large Bulgarian state which had access to the Aegean Sea and included virtually all of Macedonia. It was expected to become a dependency of Russia.

Again the European powers reacted in common alarm at the prospect of Turkey's fragmenting and Russia's replacing her in the Balkans. Bismarck called a congress in Berlin which eventually agreed to confirm the Russian annexations in the south Caucasus and also to leave her a foothold on the Danube in southern Bessarabia (lost in the Crimean War), but only at the cost of dismantling Bulgaria: its southern half, renamed Eastern Rumelia, was to remain part of the Ottoman Empire, as was Macedonia.

The Pan-Slavs were furious. They believed that what Russia had won at great cost on the battlefield had been surrendered by her diplomats. At a Slavic Benevolent Society banquet in June 1878 Ivan Aksakov denounced the Congress of Berlin as "an open conspiracy against the Russian people, [conducted] with the participation of the representatives of Russia herself!"[76]

Pan-Slavism, then, attempted to bring empire and people closer through an aggressive, nationally oriented foreign policy analogous to that of Prussia within Germany. It had considerable support in educated society and in the press, but found little resonance among ordinary Russians: insofar as it did, it was connected in their minds with revolt against legitimate monarchy.[77] Overall, then, it was poorly suited to a multiethnic empire, not all of whose peoples were Slav or Orthodox, and which was vulnerable to ethnic conflict, international war, and popular rebellion.

For a couple of decades, Russia solved the problem of containing Germany by means of a truncated replacement of the Holy Alliance. In 1873 Russia, Germany, and Austria signed the Three Emperors' League, but it was plagued by constant friction between Russia and Austria. When it lapsed in the late 1880s, Russia had no option but to fall back on a naked balance of power by concluding a defensive alliance with France. This was a step taken reluctantly: France was a republic (against which the Holy Alliance had originally been directed) and had till recently been politically unstable. The tsar hated standing bareheaded in respectful silence while the republican battle hymn, the *Marseillaise,* was being played. But in spite of all that the alliance was concluded in 1891 and was followed up by joint military planning between the two partners.[78]

On 1 March 1881 Narodnaia Volia achieved its greatest success: as Alexander II was returning along a St. Petersburg embankment from a military parade, he was blown up by a bomb. Yet this very triumph revealed the movement's fundamental failure. It was quite unable to take power or to convene a Constituent Assembly. It could not even influence the policies of the new tsar, Alexander III, except in a negative manner. On the contrary, most of the members of the Executive Committee were discovered and arrested as a result of police investigation and infiltration.

Already a year or so earlier Alexander II had responded to the rising wave of terrorism by bringing in an emergency government charged both with suppressing terror more efficiently and with taking measures to attract the support of the general public. He put at the head of it General M. T. Loris-Melikov, the Armenian who had distinguished himself during the Turkish war of 1877–78. Loris-Melikov soon concluded that "police and punitive methods are insufficient" and stressed the importance of "indicating the government's attentive and positive response to the needs of the people, of the social estates, and of public institutions" and of measures to "strengthen society's trust in the government and induce social forces to support the administration more actively than they do now in the struggle against false doctrines."[79]

To achieve this he took up again some of the reformist ideas which had remained unfulfilled in the 1860s, though they had been circulating in confidential official memoranda ever since. He proposed to give peasants securer civil rights, enhance their legal status, and make it easier for them to acquire their allotment land as property. He wanted to augment the powers of zemstvos and municipalities and to strengthen their tax base. Boldest of all was his proposal that elected representatives of zemstvos and larger towns (together with delegates from Siberia and non-Russian areas to be appointed by the tsar) should sit in a preliminary committee of the State Council, to examine draft laws before they were submitted to the full session of the State Council and then to the emperor for decision. This was a timid first step toward the participation of elected representatives in legislation, and it was given preliminary approval by Alexander II on 1 March 1881—a few hours before his assassination.[80]

When his successor, Alexander III, convened his ministers to decide whether or not to proceed with this proposal, the procurator of the Holy Synod, K. P. Pobedonostsev, denounced it vehemently. In his eyes it was the formation of a "talking-shop," the first step on the slippery slope to a Western-style constitution, in short *finis Rossiae.* "Russia has been strong thanks to autocracy, thanks to the limitless mutual trust and the close tie between the people and the tsar . . . We suffer quite enough from talking-shops, which, under the influence of worthless journals, simply stoke up popular passions."[81]

When considering this plea, one must remember that for two years government officials had with good reason feared attempts on their lives by revolver or bomb. However, when Pobedonostsev rejected Loris-Melikov's suggestions for institutionalizing public participation in government, he did not offer any alternative. Loris-Melikov resigned, taking with him most of his colleagues.

The Pan-Slavs came up with an alternative. In 1882 N. P. Ignatiev, former ambassador in Constantinople and now minister of the interior, put forward a scheme for the revival of the zemskii sobor, to convene at the coronation of the tsar in Moscow at Easter 1883. It was to communicate to him the aspirations of "the land" and to make proposals for reform, particularly of peasant institutions. Pobedonostsev, however, regarded the proposal in the same light as the earlier one of Loris-Melikov: the first stage to a constitution and "revolution, the downfall of the government and the downfall of Russia." Alexander III turned the idea down, and Ignatiev resigned.[82] The obsession with autocracy as Russia's distinctive glory won the day.

Instead of drawing civil society into timid partnership, the government made provision for emergency rule to be introduced in any part of the empire where public order was deemed to be endangered. Emergency rule meant that the minister of the interior, provincial governors, or police chiefs could summarily restrict civil liberties, dismiss officials (including judges), countermand the decisions of zemstvos and municipalities, close newspapers or educational institutions, search property, and arrest individuals without court procedure. In ten provinces, mostly in Ukraine but including St. Petersburg and Moscow, an emergency regime was introduced forthwith. The "temporary" legislation authorizing it remained in effect till 1917. Certain areas of Russia, in other words, could at any time have judicial guarantees suspended and be placed under police rule.[83]

During the 1880s and 1890s further measures were taken to restrain the undesirable effects of the 1860s reforms. Senior officials continued to be alarmed by the lack of supervision over peasant institutions. Dmitrii Tolstoi, as minister of the interior, argued that the scattered nature of the peasant population, their low economic and cultural level, and their isolation from law courts and government offices required that village communes be placed under the supervision of government-appointed officials, "not hampered by excessive formalism." In 1889 "land commandants" *(zemskie nachalniki)* were introduced, each with a territory of several volosti to oversee. Appointed whenever possible from among the local gentry by the minister of the interior, they were empowered to countermand the decisions and personnel appointments of village assemblies and courts. This was a partial revival of the personal authority of the pre-1861 serfowner, especially since in practice the control of the government over the land commandants was feeble. One of them later noted in his memoirs: "In his bailiwick the land commandant is . . . all-powerful and virtually unrestrained."[84]

Ever since the 1860s, as we have seen, officials had been worried about the unreliable political sentiments of some local government assemblies. In 1890–1892 the qualifications for participation in zemstvo and municipal elections were tightened to favor landowners and the upper bourgeoisie, while provincial governors were given a wider range of powers to veto and amend the decisions of local government assemblies. An attempt by Tolstoi to subordinate the zemstvos and municipalities completely to the Ministry of the Interior was rejected, but the "self-government" enshrined in their original conception was circumscribed.[85]

By the end of the century, then, Russia's internal politics hovered uneasily between two incompatible systems. Alexander II's reforms had severely shaken the traditional personalized power structure but had not managed consistently to replace it with institutions of civil society or the rule of law. To plug the resulting authority gap, the regime had nothing else at hand but the police, backed up by emergency powers. Having set out to demolish an old building and erect a new one, the regime had then changed its mind and started repairing the ruins: the resultant hybrid architecture threatened the equilibrium of the entire edifice. The regime was in an insoluble dilemma, caught between perception of the need for civic institutions and inability to introduce them without undermining its own stability.

8

THE RISE OF NATIONALISM

The 1860s–1880s saw the last major expansion of Russian territory, into Central Asia. Whereas earlier the military authorities had built defensive lines in the steppe to keep the nomads out, now they aimed finally to incorporate all the territory grazed by those nomads, and then beyond them to establish new frontiers with stable and predictable powers.

It was many centuries since the region had been under a single ruler. Mainly steppe in the north and desert in the south, it had a few valuable oasis areas, notably Khiva near the mouth of the Amu Darya River, the Zeravshan valley between Samarkand and Bukhara, and the very fertile Fergana valley, watered by the rivers of the Pamir Mountains, where an intensively irrigated agriculture was practiced. Cities like Merv, Bukhara, and Samarkand had once been great centers of international trade between Europe, the Middle East, Iran, India, and China, along the so-called silk roads; but over the centuries they had fallen into relative decay with the growth of oceanic transport and the decline in transcontinental trade. The whole region had long been within the Persian sphere of dominance, and the ancient settled people was Iranian in language and culture (called Tajik by the Turks). Over the centuries, and especially after the Mongol invasion of the thirteenth century, the Tajiks had absorbed a large number of former Turkic nomads. Around and among this mixed settled population were nomadic peoples of two kinds: those who remained on the steppe all year round, moving their flocks from one grazing area to another; and mountain nomads who took their flocks up to alpine meadows in the summer and brought them down to the lowlands in the winter.

In the twelfth and thirteenth centuries the Mongols had imposed a nomadic overlordship over the region, first under the immediate successors of Chingiz Khan, later under Timur (Tamerlane), who came from Samarkand. In the sixteenth century an Uzbek tribal confederation, also claiming descent from Chingiz Khan, ruled over much of the territory, but thereafter its control faded and fragmented, leaving a number of khanates and emirates (kingdoms and military governorships) exercising a fluctuating hegemony over tribal leaders.

The linguistic and cultural heritage of the region was mixed, with Turkish as the language of administration and military command, while Persian was adopted for trade, culture, and religion. Uzbeks operated as the ruling class over most of the region, and tended to become gradually more sedentary, adopting Persian as the language of commerce and civilized discourse. Sedentary Uzbeks and Tajiks of the oases, both being bilingual, gradually became more or less indistinguishable, and were known to the Russians as Sarts (a Sanskrit word meaning "merchant"). In the Kipchak steppe to the north lived the Kazakhs and, nearer to the Aral Sea, the Karakalpaks. In the Tien Shan Mountains farther to the east were the Kirgiz, while in the southwestern desert area and along the eastern Caspian coastline lived the Turkmens (Turcomans), western Turkic peoples belonging to the same linguistic family as the Azerbaijanis.[1]

Islam had established itself among the oasis peoples well before the Mongol invasion and, in its orthodox Sunni form, experienced a flowering both before and after it. Central Asia was for centuries a major center of Islamic learning: its scholars traveled widely throughout the Muslim world and made signal contributions to philosophy, jurisprudence, and science. Ibn Sina (Avicenna), the great Aristotelian scholar of the eleventh century, came from Bukhara. With the fragmentation of the sixteenth century, however, and the rerouting of world trade, the prosperity which supported this culture declined. Besides, as Shiism became dominant in Iran and the Russians gradually occupied the Volga region and the steppes, central Asian Islam became more isolated and provincial. Even the duty of pilgrimage to Mecca became difficult to perform.[2]

The nomadic peoples were much slower to adopt Islam. Most of them were shamanists, who worshipped the sky god Tengri and revered holy places connected with ancestors or with natural phenomena such as groves, springs, and rocks. Islam came with Sufi missionaries, who traveled from one community to another, adapting themselves to the nomadic lifestyle in order to spread the faith and gain the sympathy of tribal leaders. The Sufi sheikhs (elders) played a major role in the consolidation of the power of the khans, by bestowing on them the aura of divine election and by mobilizing popular support for them through the Sufi networks. In return Sufi orders received valuable land and buildings, so that their *waqf*, or charitable trusts, were able to dispense both patronage and social welfare on a considerable scale. In the remoter areas, it was probably not till the eighteenth century that Islam took a real hold. Many tribes and settlements had their own *ishan*, that is, a locally revered religious leader who articulated the community's legends and customs (often with survivals from shamanism), conducted rituals and prayers, and offered counseling and comfort.[3]

Russia began to have an interest in central Asia as early as the late sixteenth century, when a caravan trade route was established between Tobolsk and Bukhara. In 1730–1734 the Lesser and Middle Hordes, two of the major Kazakh tribal confederations, acknowledged Russian overlordship. The Russian governor-general in Orenburg did not at this stage interfere with the internal life of the Kazakhs, but used his authority simply to impose peace along the ill-defined frontier.

Only in the early nineteenth century, when the khan of Kokand began to harbor his own ambitions to unite central Asia and sent nomadic troops to disrupt the caravan trade, did the Russians intervene further, sending armed detachments into the steppe to establish fortresses there and to attract individual tribal leaders to the Russian side. In this way towns such as Kokchetav and Akmolinsk were founded. By the 1850s Russia had a loose line of strong-points stretching all the way from the southern Urals to Alma Ata.

There was another reason for Russia to take a closer interest in the region at this time: it was becoming a huge and ill-defined power vacuum between the two fastest-growing empires in Asia, those of Britain and Russia. In both countries those responsible for imperial administration worried that their dominion over numerous unruly foreign peoples was a kind of confidence trick, and that if the appearance of overwhelming might was punctured, for example by the incursion of a serious rival, then the collapse of empire might be sudden and cumulative. That is why the British annexed Sind and Punjab in the 1840s and began sending commercial, diplomatic, and military missions into Afghanistan. The prime minister argued in the House of Commons that "Whatever may be the principle which may regulate the conduct of civilized nations when coming into contact with each other, when civilization and barbarism come into contact there is some uncontrollable principle

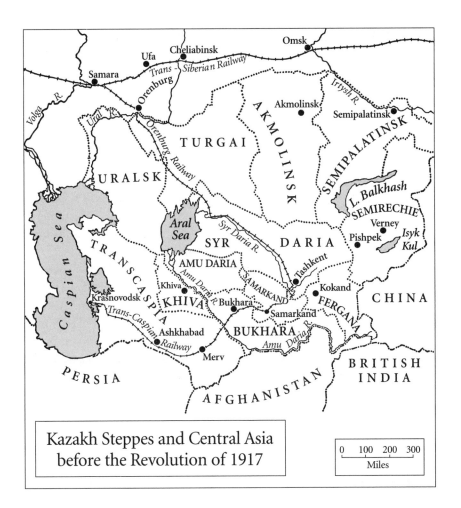

Kazakh Steppes and Central Asia before the Revolution of 1917

0   100   200   300
Miles

of a very different description, which demands a different course of conduct."[4]

What he meant was that in Asia no gentlemen's agreements were possible: when a crisis took place, one must respond with a demonstration of power and the establishment of firm authority. Russian foreign minister Gorchakov put the same doctrine slightly differently:

The situation of Russia in central Asia is similar to that of all civilized states which come into contact with half-savage nomadic tribes without a firm social organization. In such cases, the interests of border security and trade relations always require that the more civilized state have a certain authority over its neighbors, whose wild and unruly customs render them very troublesome. It begins first by curbing raids and pillaging. To put an end to these, it is often compelled to reduce the neighboring tribes to some degree of close subordination.[5]

As for the kind of power to be deployed, Prince Bariatinskii, the new viceroy of the Caucasus, warned: "England displays its power in gold. Russia, which is poor in gold, has to compete with force of arms."[6]

It was difficult, however, to do this in a planned or systematic manner, and the distance between central Asia and St. Petersburg meant that the emperor's instructions took two to three months to reach his subjects there. The initiative in reacting to crises lay with the local proconsuls and generals, who were well able to expand "missions" and "expeditions" into full-scale invasion forces if they thought it expedient. Both General Mikhail Cherniaev, the local military commander, and N. A. Kryzhanovskii, his civilian superior as governor-general of Orenburg, were ambitious men with competing agendas. In 1864–65 Cherniaev reacted to local unrest by conquering the major trading cities of Chimkent and Tashkent. Kryzhanovskii, probably jealous, rebuked him for exceeding his powers but justified his policy: "It seems to me that it is time to stop pandering to the languages and customs of our weak neighbors [the khans of Khiva and Kokand and the emir of Bukhara]. We can compel them to conform somewhat to our customs and impose our own language on them. In Central Asia we alone must be the masters so that with time through us civilisation can penetrate there and improve the lives of those unfortunate offspring of the human race."[7] War Minister Dmitrii Miliutin responded wearily: "Major General Cherniaev merely communicates to me accomplished facts compelling me either to confirm measures wholly incompatible with our general aims or to revoke those measures, which would injure the prestige of our authority."[8] Cherniaev was eventually dismissed, but not before he had changed the course of Russian policy—or at least enormously speeded its implementation—and secured a public relations triumph among newspaper readers back in the homeland.

Cherniaev's successors did not alter the fundamentals of his policy. The khan of Kokand accepted Russian peace terms which included an indemnity and security for Russian merchants trading in his territory. The khanate of Khiva and the emirate of Bukhara became Russian protectorates, though nominally self-governing. In 1876, after a rebellion, the khanate of Kokand was abolished altogether. During the following years the remaining Turkmen tribes were subjugated, though not before they had inflicted a major defeat on the Russian army at Gok Tepe (1879). It was avenged by General Skobelev, fresh from his triumphs in the Balkans: he massacred the entire male population of the fortress town of Dengil Tepe in 1881. As in the Caucasus, Russia launched its rule by means of conspicuous violence to show who was master. Skobelev explained: "I hold it a principle that in Asia the duration of peace is in direct proportion to the slaughter you inflict upon the enemy. Strike hard and keep on striking till resistance fails; then form ranks, cease slaughter and be kind and humane to the prostrate enemy." An American visitor to the region seemed to offer confirmation of this policy. He remarked that "what was strange for Mussulmans, [they] spoke in the highest terms of the Russian Emperor. The conduct of general Tchernaief made a most favorable impression upon [them] and from that time on there was not the slightest trouble of any kind on the part of the native population."[9]

It was not the Russian intention for the moment to make the central Asians full subjects of the empire. They were classified as *inorodtsy,* or aliens, and central Asia became a colony in a more or less normal sense: that is, it was geographically cut off from the metropolis (by desert and steppe), it had a lower socioeconomic and cultural level, and it provided raw materials, mainly cotton, for metropolitan industries. All the same, the assimilation of huge new Asiatic territories and several million Muslims strengthened the Russian feeling of being an Asiatic as well as a European power.[10]

A governor-generalship of Turkestan was created to oversee the newly conquered territories; its first holder, General K. P. Kaufman, had previous experience in the military administration of Poland. Russian rule did not at first much affect the religion, customs, and legal systems of the indigenous peoples or their subjection to khans and beks, but tighter integration into the Russian economic system brought considerable changes. In the oases this meant more intensive cultivation of cotton, with the necessary irrigation, establishment of textile mills, and laying of railways, usually staffed by Russian immigrants.

In the steppes the changes were even more far-reaching. Land was expropriated from the traditional elites, the khans and beks, to redistribute among ordinary tribal members. This policy also made it easier to award land to peasants being resettled from overcrowded and poverty-stricken regions of European Russia. But of course those lands were traditional nomadic pastures, and the appearance of Russian farms on long-established migration routes affronted the local population. The Russian government tried in response to encourage the nomads to raise grain and hay and to improve the quality of their cattle, sheep, and horses. This involved restraining traditional feuds between tribes, favoring the more docile and/or economically more efficient at the expense of others. At the same time the Russian authorities encouraged the spread of official mosque-based Islam, as more likely to promote law, order, and economic enterprise, at the expense of the more home-spun doctrines of the ishans.[11]

For all these reasons grievances built up among the local peoples, both nomadic and sedentary. There were intermittent outbreaks of unrest, usually led by a Sufi sheikh or an ishan. This was not necessarily a sign of religious fanaticism: rather, with the secular authorities humbled by the Russians, religious specialists seemed the natural leaders of the community. Many of those involved were either urban unemployed or displaced nomads. The most serious incident took place in 1898, when a mob of about two thousand, led by an ishan, broke into a barracks in Andizhan in the Fergana valley and murdered twenty-two Russian soldiers.[12]

Russian domination could not but have a gradual impact on the internal evolution of Islam. As in other colonized societies, this evolution tended toward two poles: some Muslims admired the colonizers and wanted to re-form the indigenous faith in order to absorb some of their qualities, while others rejected the colonizers as infidels and reasserted the fundamentals of their own beliefs.

The first tendency, known as Jadidism (New Method), originated in the 1880s in the Volga basin, where Russian rule over Muslims had lasted longest. It was originally a movement in favor of Europeanizing Muslim education by encouraging universal literacy and by assimilating secular teachings, in particular science, technology, and the Russian language. It broadened out, especially in the writings of a thinker such as the Crimean Tatar Ismail Bey Gaspirali, to embrace social and political reform: democracy, equal rights for women, and the encouragement of a written national language for the peoples of Turkestan. Gaspirali hoped by these means to unite the Muslim and Turkic peoples of the empire. Others went further and called for the creation of a Pan-Turk union which would have dismembered both the Russian and Ottoman empires. Jadidism never gained mass support, but it was influential in the education system and among young people from elite families. Like the Young Turk movement in the Ottoman Empire, it stimulated the search for new doctrines of social solidarity, whether in the form of Turkestani nationalism, Pan-Islamism, or Pan-Turkism.[13]

When the 1905 revolution lifted the taboo on political organization, Gaspirali's ideas helped to inspire the creation of an All-Russian Muslim League, demanding the abolition of discrimination against Muslims and supporting the constitutional aspirations of the Russian liberals. Despite its name, the focus of its program was the creation of a Turkestani nation within the Russian Empire, composed of the various Turco-Tatar peoples and tribes, enjoying the rights promised by the liberals.[14]

With the opening of the State Duma in 1906, there was a brief prospect that such ideas might come to fruition. The Muslim Union had thirty-one deputies in the Second Duma. Under the new electoral law of 1907, however, central Asian Muslim representation in the Duma was abolished altogether, and thereafter the authorities supported the khan of Khiva and the emir of Bukhara in closing Jadid schools and suppressing their newspapers. The dramatist Abdalrauf Fitrat bitterly attacked Muslim leaders for supplanting the dynamic religion of the prophets with a diseased faith, hostile to progress and obsequious toward the secular authorities. Disappointed in Russia, some Muslim leaders began to look to the Ottoman Empire to sponsor their movement, on the principle that "Our blood is Turkish. Our language is Turkish. Our faith is the Holy Koran of Islam, and therefore we are one nation." Some emigrated to Turkey to continue their political and publicist work in a more congenial environment.[15]

In 1916 the sporadic unrest in the Ferghana valley coalesced with the resentment of the steppe nomads to generate a large-scale anti-Russian insurrection. The immediate precipitant was the ending of Muslim exemption from military service. As lists of potential recruits were drawn up, crowds attacked draft board centers, police stations, and other administrative buildings in the main towns. The army had to be brought in to restore order, with great bloodshed, and in the aftermath hundreds of thousands of Muslims fled across the border into China. It has been estimated that some 17 percent of the population of Turkestan was lost, either through death or through emigration, and in some districts a much higher proportion.[16] Russia's domination of central Asia seemed to be turning out almost as damaging as her conquest of the Caucasus.

THE FAR EAST

Although it had possessed territory in the Far East ever since the seventeenth century, poor communications had hindered Russia from populating it properly or even attempting the serious exploitation of its resources. All that connected the Pacific coast with the heartland of Russia was a *trakt*, a grass-and-dirt track running through the taiga and across the frozen plains. Passable in winter and summer, it became muddy, swampy, and in places flooded at other times of year. As late as 1890, the writer Anton Chekhov took nearly three months to reach Sakhalin by traveling the length of it.

In the 1850s Russia had taken advantage of China's weakness during the Taiping Rebellion to reoccupy the "Pacific Riviera," the basin of the Amur

River and the territory between the Ussuri and the ocean. The initiative had been taken by an insubordinate young naval officer, Gennadii Nevelskoi, who without authorization circumnavigated the hitherto poorly charted Sakhalin, proved that it was an island, and then planted the imperial flag on the mainland shore opposite, artfully naming the spot Nikolaevskii Post (Nicholas' Outpost). His ploy succeeded: the emperor deplored his disobedience but declared that wherever the Russian flag had been raised it must not be lowered.

The main agent of Russian expansion in the region was Nikolai Muraviev, who was appointed governor-general of Eastern Siberia in 1847. A convinced supporter of reform under Alexander II, he also believed that Russia could retain its great power status only by projecting its power determinedly into eastern Asia, taking advantage of Chinese weakness and forestalling other European powers, which, in his view, had no mission in Asia comparable to Russia's. Encountering caution in St. Petersburg, he provided himself with his own army by setting up the Transbaikal Cossack Host, recruiting peasants, convicts, and descendants of the Don and Zaporozhe Cossacks. During the Crimean War he used the presence of an Anglo-French naval squadron off Sakhalin to reinforce Russian garrisons along the coast. Then, in two treaties, Aigun (1858) and Beijing (1860), which China negotiated from extreme weakness, he secured the entire Amur basin as well as the territory between the Ussuri and the ocean. At the extreme southern end of it, in 1860, the town of Vladivostok (Ruler of the East) was founded, looking out toward Korea and Japan, as the base of Russia's Pacific fleet. Russia had, with a vengeance, opened a "window to Asia."[17]

The question was how to follow up this success. Vladivostok and the whole Maritime Territory were desperately exposed, garrisoned by relatively few troops and cut off by several months' travel from effective reinforcement. Not until the completion of the Trans-Siberian Railway in 1903 was this picture substantially altered. That huge undertaking was always conceived as a means of projecting Russian power into eastern Asia. Sergei Vitte, its leading protagonist, was concerned mainly about the economic benefits it would bring. But even he, as minister of finance fully aware of the costs of war, was anxious that Russia should be equipped to project the military might of a genuine Eurasian power. Whereas in Europe Russia was a backward country, an importer of capital, and the object of others' imperialist designs, in Asia she could become a full imperial power in her own right. In 1893 he told the tsar: "On the Mongol-Tibetan-Chinese border major changes are imminent, which may harm Russia if European politics prevail there, but which could bring Russia countless blessings if we forestall western

Europe in east Asian affairs . . . From the shore of the Pacific and from the heights of the Himalayas Russia will dominate not only the affairs of Asia, but those of Europe as well."[18]

Whether or not Vitte himself took such flights of fancy wholly seriously, the Foreign Ministry, cautious as ever, was unmoved by them. The trouble was that the only person coordinating foreign, economic, and military policy was the emperor himself, and Nicholas II proved susceptible to forceful individuals with grandiose schemes.

Besides, Russia had an extremely dangerous rival in the region. Nobody yet realized the full potential of Japan as an Asian great power, but it had been building up its army and navy ever since the Meiji restoration of 1868, and there were powerful voices in the military and at court urging that Japan should make up for the lack of minerals at home by emulating the European powers and seizing for itself an empire in Asia. In 1894 Japan attacked China in Korea and Manchuria and was prevented from permanently annexing the Liaotung peninsula (the southern extremity of Manchuria) only through concerted action by Russia, Germany, and France. Russia took the opportunity to conclude a defensive treaty with China which permitted it to build a railway line across Manchuria, branching off from the Trans-Siberian. This was a considerable prize, for it promised to open up Manchuria's abundant mineral wealth to Russia. A Russo-Chinese Bank was set up to finance construction of the line, and proved very attractive to French investors. Russia also exploited the Kiaochow crisis of 1897 to demand a lease on Port Arthur, at the tip of the Liaotung peninsula, from which the Japanese had just withdrawn: it offered an ice-free base for the Pacific fleet, and a neighboring trading port, to which a branch was planned from the Manchurian railway.

These developments greatly reinforced Russia's presence in Manchuria, and it took advantage of the Boxer rising (1899–1900) to strengthen it further: after the suppression of the rebellion Russia simply refrained from withdrawing its troops. At this stage, though, acute divisions opened up inside the government. Vitte, with the support of Foreign Minister Lamsdorf, urged that Russia should pull out of Manchuria, as the continued maintenance of an army there was a heavy expense and a provocation to other powers, especially Japan, which should not be offered unless Russia was ready to go to war. General A. K. Kuropatkin, the war minister, on the other hand, argued that Russia could perfectly well remain in northern Manchuria, creating there a protectorate, possibly under nominal Chinese suzerainty.

At court there were some who wanted to pursue an even more forward policy. In 1898 a Russian timber company had been set up on the Yalu River, inside Korea, by a retired Guards officer with connections at court, Captain

Russia at Its Greatest Extent

North Sea

Barents Sea

NORWAY

SWEDEN

Stockholm

Novaia Zemlia

Kara Sea

Berlin

Baltic Sea

Riga

L. Ladoga   *L. Onega*   Arkhangel

Vienna   Warsaw

Vistula

W. Dvina

N. Dvina

Ob

Budapest

Volga

Smolensk

Yaroslavl

Ural Mountains

Moscow

Oka

Kiev

Dniester

Dnieper

Voronezh

Kazan

Kama

Tobolsk

Sibir

Bucharest

Ob

Saratov

Volga

Ufa

Tobol

Odessa

Don

Tsaritsyn

Tara

Constantinople

Azov

Black Sea

Astrakhan

KAZAKHSTAN

Irtysh

OTTOMAN EMPIRE

Aral Sea

Caspian Sea

TURKESTAN

Tehran

PERSIA

INDIA

AFGHANISTAN

Kabul

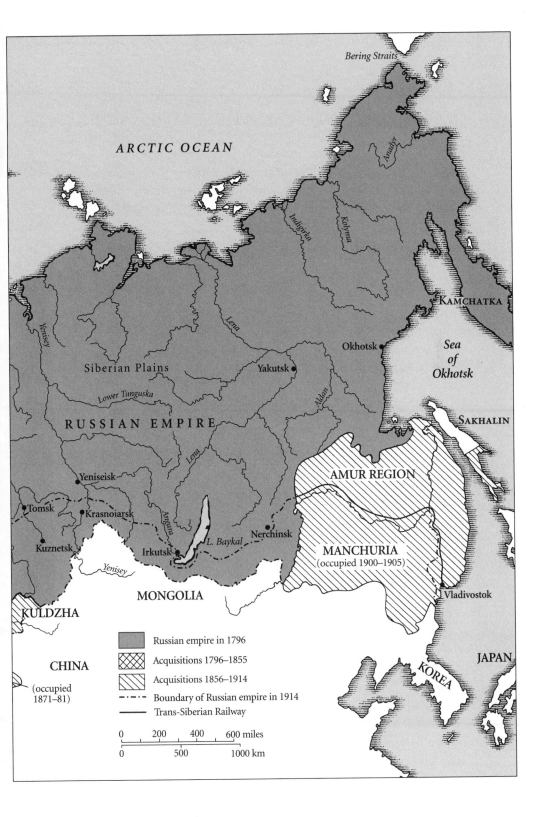

ARCTIC OCEAN

Bering Straits

Anadyr

Indigirka

Kolyma

KAMCHATKA

Yenisey

Lena

Okhotsk

Sea
of
Okhotsk

Siberian Plains

Yakutsk

SAKHALIN

Lower Tunguska

Aldan

RUSSIAN EMPIRE

Lena

AMUR REGION

Yeniseisk

Angura

L. Baykal

Nerchinsk

Tomsk

Krasnoiarsk

MANCHURIA
(occupied 1900–1905)

Kuznetsk

Irkutsk

Yenisey

MONGOLIA

Vladivostok

KULDZHA

CHINA

(occupied
1871–81)

	Russian empire in 1796
	Acquisitions 1796–1855
	Acquisitions 1856–1914
–·–·–	Boundary of Russian empire in 1914
——	Trans-Siberian Railway

JAPAN

KOREA

0   200   400   600 miles

0   500   1000 km

A. M. Bezobrazov. The emperor himself was among the shareholders, and Nicholas followed up the initiative by establishing a viceroyalty of the Far East under Admiral E. I. Alekseev, commander of the Pacific fleet. This new creation, on the model of the Caucasus, removed the region from the jurisdiction of the ministries and marked Nicholas' determination not only to pursue an expansionist policy there, but to conduct it personally. At this stage (August 1903) Vitte was dismissed, and his restraining influence was lost. Court patronage had triumphed over diplomacy and ministerial politics.

Alarmed, the Japanese sent a note in an attempt to stabilize relations between the two countries on the basis that Russia's special interest in Manchuria should be acknowledged, in return for equivalent acceptance of Japan's in Korea: neither side should maintain troops in either territory except in emergency to contain civil disorder. To these proposals Russia never sent an unambiguous reply. None of the ministries or the viceroyalty could deal with it alone, and coordination from the emperor was lacking: he was away from St. Petersburg for much of the summer and autumn of 1903. Such notes as were sent implied that Russia wanted a free hand in Manchuria but saw no need to recognize an equivalent Japanese right in Korea.[19]

The Japanese eventually reacted by abruptly withdrawing their diplomats from St. Petersburg and torpedoing Russian ships in Port Arthur. Although the immediate Japanese responsibility for the war is undeniable, the whole buildup to it showed Russian diplomacy in a very poor but not untypical light. Alarmed by a power vacuum opening up on its distant borders, Russia as always overestimated the importance of territorial acquisition (how on earth could she need *more* territory when she could not exploit what she already had?), failed to define her capabilities and objectives clearly, and was dilatory and confused in responding to Japanese diplomacy. Policy was being made not by a government, but by court cliques and individual ministers competing for the tsar's ear.

Moreover, the Russians, like everyone else, had grossly underestimated the capacities of Japan, which proved able to mobilize forces at land and sea effectively. Russia relied on the single-track Trans-Siberian Railway to move troops and equipment, and could reinforce the Pacific fleet only by sending ships halfway round the world. Never had the paradoxes of Russia's immense landlocked bulk been more strikingly demonstrated.

The Russo-Japanese war of 1904–05 was on a grand scale, dwarfing most nineteenth-century European engagements. Armies of 100,000–150,000 fought on fronts fifty to sixty miles long. This fact alone made Russia's poor communications a crippling handicap. In December 1904 the Japanese captured Port Arthur after besieging it for nearly six months, and in the following months defeated a large Russian army at Mukden, in Manchuria. The Russian Pacific fleet, which the Japanese navy had contained inside Port Arthur, was lost, and the Baltic fleet, which had sailed for more than six months in an attempt to relieve it, was defeated and largely destroyed at the Battle of Tsushima in May 1905.

Thereupon the Russians accepted the offer of President Roosevelt of the United States to mediate. The Japanese, their resources severely strained even by victory, were glad to bring the war to an end. As it transpired, then, Russia's losses were not as serious as might have been expected: she was allowed to keep the Maritime Territory and the Chinese Eastern Railway as well as a dominant position in northern Manchuria.

RUSSIFICATION

By 1881 it could be argued that Alexander II's civic strategy had led straight to the assassin's bullet. Actually, the search for an alternative had been going on ever since the Polish rebellion of 1863–64. The principal proponent of the ethnic strategy was the brilliant newspaper editor Mikhail Katkov, who propounded it in his daily *Moskovskie vedomosti* (Moscow Bulletin). Katkov began his career as an admirer of the British political model and supported Alexander's reforms for making progress toward it. The Polish rebellion persuaded him, however, that strengthening the local gentry was not necessarily advisable in a multinational empire: far from upholding law and order, they might lead the forces of sedition and separatism. "Freedom," he warned, "does not mean freedom to arm the enemy." He became convinced that Poland and Russia could not both be sovereign states: "It must be one thing or the other," he exclaimed, "either Poland or Russia . . . In the ethnographic sense there is no antagonism beween Russians and Poles . . . But Poland as a political term is Russia's natural and irreconcilable enemy."[20] This was a clear call for the abandonment of a civic strategy and the adoption of an ethnic one to bring about better integration of the empire.

The Polish model was merely the starting point for what became his overall ideal for Russia in an era when the nation-state was becoming the most successful political form in Europe.

There is in Russia one dominant nationality, one dominant language, developed by centuries of historical life. However, there are also in Russia a multitude of tribes, each speaking in its own language and having its own customs; there are whole countries, with their separate characters and traditions. But all these diverse tribes and regions, lying on the borders of the Great Russian world, constitute its living parts and feel their oneness with it, in the union of state and supreme power in the person of the tsar.[21]

Welding a cohesive political organism out of disparate ethnic material by projecting the supreme personal authority of the tsar: that was Katkov's recipe. It was to become the leitmotif of many twentieth-century authoritarian nationalist movements. Within a Russian Empire still ruled largely through traditional elites, however, it was difficult to apply consistently. Alexander II held back, restrained by existing hierarchies and by accustomed concepts of responsible imperial government. His successors, however, Alexander III and Nicholas II, felt less inhibited. They tried to draw the non-Russian regions and peoples more securely into the framework of the empire, first by administrative integration, then by inculcating in each of them as far as possible the language, religion, and culture of Russia, leaving their own traditions as subsidiary, colorful ethnographic remnants rather than active social forces. This policy was a natural accompaniment to Vitte's economic program, which aimed to develop transport and to assimilate outlying regions into a single imperial economy.

In the historical literature, Katkov is usually represented as a reactionary. In fact, however, what he proposed was radical innovation, a sharp break with Russian imperial practice, which had been to hold a balance among the different ethnic elites and to rule through them, using their wealth, reputation, and patronage to control the various peoples. Katkov was recommending instead that the imperial regime bypass the elites and take over patronage of the people directly, as had been done in the emancipation of Polish serfs and the subsequent administrative arrangements in the former Congress Kingdom. This policy, he felt, would give the empire much greater homogeneity and cohesion, and in the long term would promote a political Russian (rossiiskii) loyalty throughout it. In a sense his model continued to be Britain, with its imperial monarchy and its compound national identity binding English, Scots, Welsh, and some Irish in a shared civic consciousness without destroying their ethnic distinctiveness.

The problem of course was that even after Alexander's reforms, civic institutions were severely stunted in Russia, so that Katkov's approach would work only if the non-Russians remained underdeveloped and highly malleable. It promised reasonably well in the eastern regions of the empire but, if consistently applied, could only generate determined resistance among the more culturally advanced nationalities of western Russia, such as the Poles, the Finns, the Germans, or the Jews.

Ukraine

The most draconian application of the new principles came in Ukraine. For good reason: it had always been a region disputed between Poland and Russia, and the Polish rebellion had merely revived that ancient quarrel. It was decisive to the ethnic composition of the empire. Ukrainians formed numerically the second-largest nationality: 22.4 million according to the census of 1897, or nearly 18 percent of the population. If they were assimilated to Russian nationality, then Russians formed a secure majority, 62 percent, of the population of their own empire. On the other hand, if Ukrainians elevated their own "dialect" to a separate literary language, that of a nation distinct from Russia, then the Russians at 44 percent were a minority.[22]

By this time, too, a distinctively Ukrainian intelligentsia was beginning to take shape, not among the larger landowners of "Little Russia," who were by now thoroughly integrated into the imperial *dvorianstvo*, but among the sons of priests, townsmen, and poorer members of the old Cossack nobility of the hetmanate. As in Russia, they gathered in *kruzhki*, centered at the universities of Kharkov and Kiev.

The creation of a literary language was especially crucial for Ukrainian intellectuals. There was no Ukrainian scriptural or chancellery usage: Church Slavonic and Russian served that purpose. There remained only the myriad peasant dialects. Many educated Ukrainians themselves doubted whether it was possible or useful to develop their own literary language when Russians already had one. Perhaps the most talented Ukrainian writer of the 1830s, Nikolai Gogol, deliberately left his homeland, went to St. Petersburg, and published in Russian, because he believed that was the right way to make a contribution to serious literature.

Unexpectedly, however, a pastiche pointed the way forward. In 1798 Ivan Kotliarevskii, a minor Cossack noble, published a burlesque on Virgil's *Aeneid*, in which Greek heroes and the gods of Olympus spoke the vernacular of Ukrainian farmworkers. His satire had an unanticipated effect: it was taken seriously, because it demonstrated that by drawing on Ukrainian rural dialects one could create the makings of a literary language.

Kotliarevskii's example inspired the first major Ukrainian poet, Taras Shevchenko. His first collection, *Kobzar* (The Bard), drew on themes from Ukrainian history and folklore and synthesized urban and rural linguistic usages with Church Slavonic to articulate the full range of ideas and feelings.

Somewhat akin to Robert Burns in his concerns and outlook, Shevchenko railed against the Russian autocratic state in the name of "this land of ours which is not ours."[23] His nationalist verses remained unpublished till 1905, but circulated in manuscript and reassured literate Ukrainians that they were at least a potential nation.

This was a real question, since most of the elites of "Little Russia" were non-Ukrainian: Russian and Polish landowners; Jewish, German, and Russian townsfolk. Some of the national deficit was made good from across the border in Galicia, part of the Habsburg monarchy, where Ukrainian culture (there known as Ruthenian) was officially encouraged as a counterweight to Polish. With the help of smuggled Galician material, by the 1860s Russian Ukrainians were investigating and publishing their own folklore, collecting antiquities, and beginning to write their own history as a people distinct from the "Muscovites." *Hromady,* Ukrainian cultural societies, were being formed in the towns and launching educational programs for the newly emancipated peasants.[24]

These cumulative developments moved Minister of the Interior P. A. Valuev to warn the tsar in 1876 that "permitting the creation of a special literature for the common people in the Ukrainian dialect would signify collaborating in the alienation of Ukraine from the rest of Russia . . . To permit the separation of thirteen million Little Russians would be the utmost political irresponsibility, especially in view of the unifying movement which is proceeding alongside us among the German tribe." As a result of his warning, the tsar issued a decree prohibiting the publication of books, other than *belles lettres* and folklore, in Ukrainian, as well as the use of Ukrainian in the theatre and the import of Ukrainian books from abroad.[25]

This measure inevitably transferred the center of gravity across the border to Habsburg Galicia, a region with very different traditions. If the roots of Ukrainian distinctiveness within Russia originated in the Cossack tradition of *volia,* then in Galicia the Ruthenians had their own Greek Catholic, or Uniate, Church. They had, moreover, imbibed the strong estate consciousness present in all ranks of Habsburg society and the relatively more robust legal traditions prevalent there. All the same, the Habsburg Ruthenians remained a highly disadvantaged ethnos, economically backward and without national leaders outside the clergy.[26]

Altogether, by the early twentieth century the prospects for the emergence of a separate Ukrainian nation looked very dim. They had no elites outside the small towns, their cities were in the hands of other national groups, and their written culture was weakly developed and poorly disseminated. Only the revolutionary developments of the twentieth century, combined with the collapse of the empires in which they lived, could provide the conditions for national independence.

Bessarabia was really an extension of Ukraine toward the southwest, between the Dniester and Prut Rivers. Lost in the Crimean War and recovered at the Congress of Berlin, it had been part of Romania in the meantime. It had a mixed urban population, and its peasantry spoke a variety of Romanian dialects. It was the only European territory of the Russian Empire directly threatened by irredentism, and so the Russian government energetically promoted the settlement of Russian officials, merchants, and landowners. At the turn of the century, this raw, brash, immigrant ruling class provided a natural soil for anti-Semitic and extreme right-wing political views.

Finland and the Baltic

Finland was a highly sensitive region, since its borders were so close to the imperial capital and to the headquarters of the Baltic fleet. Ever since its incorporation in 1809 Finland had enjoyed a special status within the empire, as an autonomous grand duchy whose ruler was the tsar. It took over from Sweden the distinctive four-estate Diet, which included peasants. Though inactive at first, the Diet met regularly from 1863, and Finland had its own laws, education system, currency, and even army. The congregations of its Lutheran Church enjoyed freedom of worship and the right to run schools. Under imperial protection and with the huge Russian market available, the Finnish economy developed well during the nineteenth century, industry as well as raw materials. For this reason and also because they possessed far more developed civil rights than any other people of the empire, Finns were impeccably loyal to Russia, quite unlike the flamboyant and recalcitrant Poles.[27]

The Finnish ruling class, a nobility whose elaborate gradations are still recorded in the flamboyant Gothic Rittersaal in Helsinki, was mainly Swedish-speaking, as was the commercial and industrial bourgeoisie. On the other hand, the clergy and increasingly professional people as well spoke Finnish and began consciously to develop Finnish culture, propagating it through the primary and secondary schools which educated most of the population. Elias Lönnrot, a doctor who traveled widely among the Finns, Karelians, and Lapps, noted down their ballads and folksongs. He believed that his material represented the fragments of a lost folk epic, and he fashioned out of it a continuous narrative poem, the *Kalevala* (1835), which provided a model for the Finnish literary language. This was a good example of the way in which intellectuals can, if not invent a national tradition, at least synthesize one.[28]

The relative harmony between Finland and Russia came to an abrupt end in 1898, when Nicholas II appointed General Nikolai Bobrikov as governor-general of Finland, with a program for integrating the country fully into the empire. He intended to abolish the separate status of the Finnish army and conscript Finns as Russian soldiers, to increase the tuition of Russian in secondary schools, and to make Russian the official language of the administration. The Finnish Diet was explicitly subordinated to the State Council in St. Petersburg rather than to the emperor himself.

The Finns responded with a level of civic activism worthy of their previous autonomous status. They boycotted all Russian institutions and drew up a Great Address signed by no less than one-fifth of the population, conveyed to St. Petersburg by a Great Deputation of 500 (whom, however, the tsar declined to receive). Conscripts refused to report for duty and were shielded and concealed by their compatriots. Nor did the resistance remain passive: in July 1904 Bobrikov was assassinated.[29]

Altogether, Finland presents an absolutely clear example of a peaceful people, loyal to the empire, transformed by Russification into a disaffected and potentially rebellious one. Their mode of activity was unusual, however: their consciousness of having distinct political institutions, their high level of literacy, and the tradition of peasant independence combined to make largely peaceful civil resistance possible.

The strength of the authorities' Russifying drive is attested by the fact that they attempted to apply it even in the Baltic provinces, where the dominant elite were the German landowners, unswervingly loyal to the tsar. The Baltic barons represented a strange anomaly, unlike anything else in the empire, a medieval ruling estate which had preserved more or less all its privileges intact well into the nineteenth century. True, they no longer possessed serf rights over their Estonian and Latvian peasants, emancipated in 1816–1819, but they still had considerable economic power over them, since the former serfs had received their freedom without any allocation of land. The barons' *Ritterschaften,* or noble corporations, dominated the *Landtage,* the local government assemblies of the Baltic provinces, and Germans also controlled the municipalities, the guilds, and the Lutheran Church, where the landed gentry enjoyed patronage over the livings.

When he came to the throne, Alexander III took the symbolically important decision not to confirm the privileges of the *Ritterschaften,* as all his predecessors had done since Peter the Great. He did not abolish them as local government institutions, but gradually whittled down their authority by introducing Russian-style law courts and insisting on the Russian language for administrative and judicial proceedings. "Ministerial schools" were opened, controlled from St. Petersburg and teaching only in Russian: many Estonians and Latvians received in them an education which fitted them for employment elsewhere in the empire. In 1893 Dorpat University, a German institution, was closed and reopened its doors as Iuriev University, a Russian one. Meanwhile bulky Orthodox cathedrals with bulging golden domes were constructed in the center of Reval and Riga, alien monsters looming over the medieval Hanseatic architecture.[30]

These measures did not fundamentally weaken the grip of the German landowners on the region but did undermine their political standing and offered the Latvians and Estonians a chance to advance their own civic status. They were well prepared. Already from the late sixteenth century the German Lutheran pastors had felt the obligation to bring the word of God to their flock in their own language. The Bible had long been available in both Estonian and Latvian, and by the nineteenth century primary education was widespread. Germans also sponsored the study of folklore and the systematization of the Estonian and Latvian languages. Johann Herder, the first major preacher of organic nationalism in Europe, derived his ideas from a study of Latvian folksongs carried out while he was a pastor in Riga.

From the 1860s the local peasants had been allowed to acquire freehold property in land, and they were also beginning to enter the urban professions, as well as replenishing the working class of the booming port cities of Riga and Reval (Tallinn). By the end of the century the Estonians and Latvians had a wide range of singing clubs, teachers' associations, agrarian cooperatives, and other cultural and economic organizations. They were, apart from the Germans themselves, the most highly literate peoples in the empire.[31]

The result was an explosive mixture: archaic political institutions trying to contain rapid economic development and the pressure of disadvantaged peoples seeking a share in political life. In 1905–1907 the Baltic region was one of the most violent in the empire. Riga went through a second Bloody Sunday in January 1905, when troops fired on workers demonstrating about the first one: twenty-two were killed and some sixty wounded. Peasants went on strike, withheld their rents, and boycotted law courts run by Germans or Russians. When attempts were made to coerce them, they attacked and burned down many of the manor houses, especially in Livonia, where the barons raised vigilante squads to defend their property. Casualties on both sides were high, and the bloodshed increased when the government sent in punitive expeditions to restore order.[32]

The mutual slaughter impelled the Russian government and the German barons to an accommodation. Russifying moves were dropped, and in the Duma the Germans supported the Octobrists as adherents of a reformed monarchical empire. Some Baltic landowners, however, lacking confidence in these arrangements, began to seek a rapprochement with Germans from the cities and from other regions, abandoning their elite separatism and cultivating ties with the German Reich, as if foreseeing a time when their membership of the German nation would be more important to them than their status in the Russian Empire.[33]

The Caucasus

Russian administration in the Caucasus converted a patchwork of principalities and local fiefdoms into more or less homogeneous provinces of the empire, bringing feuding to an end and ironing out anomalies and inconsistencies, often in the face of ferocious resistance. As Georgian nobles and Armenian traders were drawn into the imperial education system, they absorbed European concepts, among them the idea of the nation-state, and began to conceive of themselves as potential national elites, with a duty to bring the national language and culture to their own dialect-speaking peasants. Often this national awareness took the form of intensified hostility to the Muslim peoples around and among them.

The imperial economic system on the whole enriched them, especially the Armenians, by furnishing a large market for the specialist products of the Caucasus—wine, brandy, olives, citrus fruits. Georgian nobles fared less well, especially after the emancipation of the serfs in the 1860s. Many of them responded as Russian landowners did, selling what remained of their holdings and seeking employment in the cities. There they found to their distaste that most urban trades and professions were dominated by Armenians. Some of them became members of clandestine nationalist and socialist organizations. In Georgia nationalism and socialism tended to go together, anti-Armenian sentiment expressing itself as anticapitalism.[34]

Modern Armenian national consciousness took shape largely in opposition not to Russia, which was regarded as a protector, but to the Ottoman Empire, where in the 1890s they were the victims of pogroms carried out by Turks and Kurds. The Armenian revolutionary party, the Dashnaks, began as the organizer of self-defense militias on Ottoman territory, but when the Russian government in 1896–1903 took over Armenian church properties, including its parish schools, Dashnak weapons turned against Russian officials too. All Armenians were suspicious of the Azeri Turks, whom they regarded as cousins of their oppressors in the Ottoman Empire.[35]

The Azeris themselves were mostly stockraisers and tenders of citrus and olive groves in the hills. Related to the Turks of Anatolia by language, they had lived for centuries in the Persian Empire and had adopted the Shiite form of Islam. They had a small urban intelligentsia which had evolved its own written language. With the development of the oil industry, many Azeris came down from the hills to seek employment as unskilled workers along the shore of the Caspian. Their national awareness was sharply intensified by the events of 1905–06: Armenians in Baku and Tiflis were a conspicuous and relatively successful middle class, easy targets for resentful Azeris, who formed the underclass in those cities. Now anti-Armenian pogroms took place inside the Russian Empire as well as the Ottoman, and again the Armenians, led by the Dashnaks, formed their own self-defense militias. At this point official Russian policy changed sharply. Realizing that the Armenians were potentially their staunchest allies in the Caucasus region, the government restored their church and schools to them and began to cooperate with the Dashnaks in restoring order.[36]

THE JEWS

The Russian government's treatment of the Jews in this period is usually numbered among its "Russifying" policies. However, the term is a misnomer, since what the regime was actually doing was gradually abandoning any hope of assimilating Jews into the Russian nation, instead rejecting them as aliens. From the 1880s, along with nomads and central Asian Muslims, they were classified as *inorodtsy*.[37]

The experience of 1878–1882 had shown that both Pan-Slavism and populism were inadequate as strategies for bringing Russian state and Russian people closer together. At the same time, anti-Jewish pogroms had taken place in parts of the Pale of Settlement after Alexander II's assassination, and they inspired Ivan Aksakov, one of the leading Pan-Slavs, with the notion that there was a possible alternative ideology, namely popular anti-Semitism, to mobilize the spontaneous dislike which peasants and workers felt for Jewish publicans, shopkeepers, and moneylenders. "The Jews within the Pale of Settlement," he preached, "constitute a 'state within a state.' . . . a state whose center lies outside Russia, abroad, whose highest authority is the 'Universal Jewish Alliance' in Paris." This alliance, he warned, was striving to achieve "anti-Christian world domination, Jewish world domination."[38]

Aksakov was elaborating a conspiracy theory which for decades had been floating around in popular gossip, and even in one or two works of ethnography and theology, but which had not before been taken up and promoted by a major political figure. It was a projection onto Jews of the embitterment many Russian intellectuals experienced at not being able to bring Russian nationhood to full flowering: they felt they were being internally undermined by some mysterious alien and international force. In a sense they were right, but the real culprit was the Russian state, which had imported an alien culture and outlawed the original Russian national myth.

Anti-Semitism was a kind of frustrated Slavophilism, born of the agonized realization that Russians had failed to fulfill their own nationhood. In the interests of empire, the Russians had suppressed their own messianic myth, while the Jews, by contrast, continued to believe they were a chosen people. Whereas Slavophiles dreamed in vain of a peasant commune based on truly Christian principles, the Jews appeared still to have cohesive communities ruled over by their religious leaders, and to have succeeded where the Russians had failed: in making a messianic religion the focus of their national identity.[39]

Anti-Semitism was not a coherent and concerted government policy. Some ministers were opposed to it, notably Vitte, who as finance minister positively welcomed Jewish energy and entrepreneurialism, with its links to international finance. All the same, from the 1880s onward the regime curtailed the already restricted rights of Jews, mainly out of fear that in the freer postemancipation economic milieu they would outperform Russian farms and businesses and drive them into bankruptcy. Jews were forbidden to acquire property in rural areas, even within the Pale of Settlement, while outside it the police were instructed to enforce residence regulations which had been widely flouted for decades: at Passover 1891 Jews were expelled en masse from Moscow. They were barred from the *advokatura* and the military-medical profession, their admittance to secondary and higher education was restricted, and they were denied the vote in zemstvo and municipal elections.[40]

The anti-Semitic campaign against Vitte reached its apogee in a document forged inside the Police Department of the Ministry of the Interior, the head of which, Viacheslav Pleve, was bitterly opposed to him. The so-called "Protocols of the Elders of Zion" purported to be the verbatim record of a meeting of international Jewish leaders, planning the final stages of their conquest of the world. Its text suggested that liberalism and the slogans of the French Revolution had been exploited by Jews to undermine legitimate monarchy throughout Europe, that industry and finance had been manipulated by them to destroy the landed aristocracy, that schools, universities, and the media had been targeted to subvert public morality. Now the only remaining obstacle was the Russian autocracy: once that too was overthrown, the Jews would establish their own world government, defended by a ruthless and efficient police state.[41]

This was a modernized version of the ancient Russian ghoul, the Antichrist from foreign lands. It came too late to have much effect on Vitte's career, but it muddied constitutional politics after 1905, and in later decades it played a devastating role in the fate of Jews all over Europe. Ironically, its nightmare vision anticipated the Soviet Communist state—and that of Nazi Germany—far more closely than it described imperial Russia.

It had little effect on the wave of pogroms which swept the Pale of Settlement during 1903–1906. These outbreaks of destructive frenzy were products of rapid economic growth and population movement, and then of radical political change, all of which reawakened old popular resentments against a people who seemed to have done well out of disrupting a traditional way of life. The pogroms have to be seen in the context of all kinds of violent disorder taking place during those years: peasant unrest, strikes and demonstrations, urban insurrection, and ethnic feuding. Traditions of *samosud* (popular justice) reasserted themselves: ordinary people took the law into their own hands and took vengeance in a crude and undiscriminating way against those whom they perceived as guilty for their misfortunes. The results were extremely destructive: between October 1905 and January 1906 more than 3,000 Jews were killed, 800 of them in the one city of Odessa, where the population's interethnic mix was particularly marked and communal hatreds were especially virulent.

Local officials and policemen often had insufficient resources at their command to deal with large-scale disorder and, especially after the October Manifesto, were uncertain where authority lay and who would back them up. Even if they were not anti-Semitic themselves, they knew that people in high places were, notably Nicholas II himself, who explained the pogroms in his own way in a letter to his mother: "The people became enraged by the insolence and audacity of the revolutionaries and socialists; and because nine-tenths of them are Yids, the people's whole wrath has turned against them. That is how the pogroms happened."[42] In this spirit Nicholas welcomed the formation of the Union of the Russian People, which created armed squads (known as "black hundreds") to defend "tsar, faith, and fatherland" against "the enemy within." It was responsible for attacks not only on Jews, but also on students and on those whom it identified as socialists. These included two Kadet politicians from the Duma, whom they assassinated; they also made an attempt on the life of Vitte. Despite these outrages, Nicholas accepted the insignia of the Union and ordered that it be publicly subsidized.[43]

Whatever Nicholas' personal beliefs, it was never government policy to encourage anti-Jewish pogroms or even to condone them: like other revolutionary outbreaks, they were a threat to law and order, as well as to the fragile interethnic accommodation on which the empire rested. But, as always, individual ministries went their own way. The police headquarters in St. Petersburg, which answered to the Ministry of the Interior, printed pamphlets which did seem to owe something to the "Protocols": "Do you know, brethren, who is the chief author of all our misfortunes? Do you know that the Jews of the whole world . . . have entered into an alliance and decided to destroy Russia completely? Whenever those betrayers of Christ come near you, tear them to pieces, kill them."[44] The minister of the interior, P. N. Durnovo, may not have personally authorized such propaganda, but he did not disavow it or forbid its circulation either.

The government cannot, then, be altogether absolved from the accusation of having used anti-Semitism as a kind of poor man's patriotism, to mobilize ordinary Russians at a time of bewilderment and disorder in support of a regime from which they normally felt somewhat alienated.

HIGH CULTURE AND RUSSIAN NATIONAL IDENTITY

Through all the changes of the nineteenth century, as we have seen, neither the imperial state nor the Russian Orthodox Church had succeeded in projecting an image of Russianness or generating a narrative of Russia's history and traditions which was capable of appealing to Russians across a broad social spectrum. For that reason writers, musicians, painters, and people active in the performing arts were intensely concerned with national identity.

In music Rus had two traditions of its own, folksong and dance, and the *znamennyi* liturgical chants.[45] The chants derived from Byzantium, where choral singing had been practiced without instrumental accompaniment, but, like Russian icon painting, it had evolved in a distinctive way inside Rus, absorbing the influence of folksong. Russian folksong was heterophonic, as opposed to harmonic or polyphonic: that is, each singer sang his own melodic line independently of the others, but listening to them and staying in the same key as they. Of the emotional coloring of the songs one scholar has written: "They are not melodies that bask in the sunshine, like those of Italy, but root-melodies that make their way out of the soil with difficulty."[46] This tendency to earthiness and melancholy has ensured that bass voices have always been highly valued and specially trained in Russia, for both liturgical and secular music.

By the nineteenth century, however, the link with the medieval liturgical tradition was tenuous. Following Peter the Great's reforms Russian church musicians had studied post-Tridentine Western examples of polyphonic and harmonic music and adapted their techniques for the imperial chapel, from where they were widely taken up by choirs. The old style gradually faded away, and even the notation in which it was written down became difficult to decipher. Almost the only surviving record was a four-volume collection of chants, compiled and published by the Holy Synod in 1772.

Meanwhile, on landed estates a new style of musicmaking was emerging, also based on Western models: orchestras and choirs staffed by serf musicians, specially trained to perform in the Italian or Austrian manner. In St. Petersburg, opera and ballet were developed with imperial support, performers and composers being imported to begin with; later, Russians were sent to study with leading musicians abroad.

The first composer to weld these disparate traditions into some sort of unity was Mikhail Glinka (1801–1857), who studied in Italy with Donizetti and Bellini. His *Life for the Tsar,* performed in St. Petersburg in 1836, is usually regarded as the first proper Russian opera. It adopted an Italian-style format, but using melodies derived from Russian folk material, and with a Russian theme: it told how a simple peasant, at the risk of his life, deliberately led a Polish army astray in 1613 so that they would not find the newly elected young Tsar Mikhail. Glinka's orchestral piece *Kamarinskaia* was a prototype of the Russian technique of developing melody by simple repetition, with ever new ornaments and ingenious orchestrations.

From the 1850s to the 1870s all Russian composers were either self-taught or picked up their knowledge haphazardly during periods of study abroad. Nikolai Rimskii-Korsakov (1844–1908), who became a professor of music in 1871, later confessed that at the time of his appointment he had never written a bar of counterpoint and did not know the name of the diminished seventh chord.[47] Perhaps partly for that reason, Russian musicians tended to profess disdain for "academic German" practices in harmony and counterpoint.

More important, they set about a proper study of Russian folk music. Milyi Balakirev (1836–1910) traveled up and down the Volga collecting and transcribing folksongs, which he published as a compilation in 1866 (it included the famous *Volga Boatmen*), while in the Caucasus he picked up motifs which he used in his piano study *Islamei*. Balakirev became the acknowledged leader of a school of composers concerned to create a distinctively Russian style of music. The influential critic Vladimir Stasov dubbed them approvingly the "mighty handful" *(moguchaia kuchka)*, and the epithet stuck. Among them Modest Musorgskii (1839–1881) was the most remarkable talent and in the long run the most influential. He insisted that Russian music should reflect the Russian way of life (he lived for a short time in an artel of the Chernyshevskii type) and that its melodies should derive from folksong, liturgy, or the rhythms of Russian colloquial speech. His orchestration was so sparse and his harmonies sometimes so strange that his followers felt bound to revise them for performance.

Revision, or at least editing, was unavoidable in his case because he died so young and left his two most important works unfinished. These were the operas *Boris Godunov* and *Khovanshchina*. Both took themes from turning points in Russian history, both depicted the collision of Russian and Western culture, and both dramatized the question of trust, or lack of it, between elites and ordinary people. *Boris Godunov* (based on Pushkin's text rather than on historical documents) shows its tsar-hero challenged by a shifty, smooth-tongued pretender bringing with him Polish troops, Jesuits, and the whole panoply of Counter-Reformation culture. Yet Boris, though a thoroughly Russian figure, is deeply flawed, weighed down with guilt over the murder of the infant Dmitrii, and therefore, it is implied, a sick man unable to lead national resistance. From time to time the Moscow crowd gathers in front of the Kremlin to watch and comment on events which they cannot influence.[48] Power in Rus is shown as necessary, but distant from the people and immoral.

Khovanshchina, yet more unfinished than its predecessor, offers an even more brutal clash between old Russian ways and Western innovations. We are shown the intrigues of the late seventeenth-century court at the time of Peter the Great's accession, and also the Old Believer disaffection of those years. The opera ends with an Old Believer community immolating itself inside a wooden church while offstage Peter's army approaches. Musically this tragic collision is symbolized by the stark juxtaposition of *znamennyi* chant with a Western military march. Commentators on and revisers of the score have been divided about whether Musorgskii supported the Old Believers or Peter: probably the truth is that he was appalled by the brutal and unmediated conflict between the two.

A letter he wrote to the critic Vladimir Stasov in June 1872 (during the celebration of the bicentenary of Peter the Great's birth) throws light on Musorgskii's powerful though inchoate feelings at this time:

> The power of the black earth will make itself manifest when you plough it to the very bottom. It is possible to plough the black earth with tools wrought of alien materials. And at the end of the seventeenth century they ploughed Mother Russia with just such tools, so that she did not immediately realize what they were ploughing her with, and, like the black earth, she *opened up* and began to *breathe*. And she, our beloved, received the various state bureaucrats, who never gave her, the long-suffering one, time to collect herself and think *"Where are you pushing me?"* . . . The times are out of joint: the state bureaucrats are not letting the black earth *breathe* . . . The people groan, and so as not to groan they drink like the devil.[49]

347

In 1862 Anton Rubinstein opened a conservatory in St. Petersburg, followed in 1866 by another in Moscow, and from then on it became possible for Russians to undertake a full academic and practical study of music before embarking on performance or composition. One of the first to undergo the full curriculum there was Petr Chaikovskii (1840–1893), who was at times regarded with suspicion by the "handful." He did more than anyone else to integrate Russian and European musical traditions, in his symphonies and concertos, which used Russian motifs in a framework of sonata form, and in his ballets, which soon became immensely popular throughout Europe and North America.[50]

Chaikovskii opened the way for later composers, who were able not only to synthesize Russian and Western styles but also to innovate on the basis of that synthesis, so that by the 1910s Russia, far from straggling behind, was in the avant-garde, experimenting with techniques and forms from which European composers learned. The most radical was Igor Stravinskii (1882–1971), who took the exploration of Russian folk tradition even further back than the "handful," to pre-Christian paganism. In *Petrushka* he drew on the music of the modern urban fairground as the setting for a ballet based on puppet theater,[51] while in the *Rite of Spring* he portrayed in ballet form archaic fertility rites and human sacrifice: its nonprogressive harmonies, its repetitive and sometimes brutal rhythms, implied a static or cyclical existence. Here the contrast between elite and popular culture came out more starkly than anywhere else among the folk music revivalists of Europe. *Rite of Spring* sounded alien both to European and to cultivated Russian ears, but was imbued with a primeval energy, exhilarating or horrifying according to one's point of view. Its first Paris performance provoked catcalls and walkouts but also signaled that a new kind of modernism had arrived in European music.[52]

The ballet company which presented Stravinskii's music on that famous occasion, Sergei Diagilev's Ballets Russes, had also drawn inspiration from developments in the Russian visual arts. In 1863 fourteen students at the Imperial Academy of Art rejected the classical subject set for the annual Gold Medal examination and walked out. They established their independence from imperial patronage by setting up an artel in the style of Chernyshevskii. They announced that they intended instead to depict the lives of ordinary Russians, especially the poverty-stricken and oppressed, and to exhibit in provincial galleries in a series of road shows, for which reason they called themselves the Wanderers (Peredvizhniki). Their work was taken up by an industrialist, Pavel Tretiakov, who founded a picture gallery in Moscow, with cheap entrance tickets, so that ordinary people could afford to enjoy paintings.[53]

Another example of industrial sponsorship aimed at developing a distinctive Russian art took shape in 1870, when the railway magnate Savva Mamontov bought Abramtsevo, the estate of the Slavophile writer Sergei Aksakov, near the Trinity and Sergius Monastery, and turned it into a center for artists to revive the techniques of Russian demotic craftsmanship in utensils, ceramics, furniture, embroidery, and icons. He set up a workshop to train local peasants in the skills and also invited well-known artists to come and study peasant motifs and incorporate them into their work. Out of this cross-fertilization came a new school of Russian applied art: domestic artifacts, interior design, theatrical scenery, and so on. Mamontov sponsored Diagilev's journal, The World of Art (Mir iskusstva), which incorporated these developments into the mainstream of Russian art, and later into the costumes and stage sets of the Ballets Russes.[54]

In art as in music, there was a tendency to move even further away from accepted motifs and techniques toward the primitive and basic. Thus Vasilii Kandinskii, who began by depicting Cossacks, churches, peasant huts, and popular festivals in a highly colored imaginative style, gradually withdrew the representational element from his canvases, leaving only colors and shapes. Natalia Goncharova and Mikhail Larionov painted scenes from the lives of peasants, workers, and soldiers, but then concentrated more and more on line and form until their pictures became abstract configurations. The ultimate limit was reached when Kasimir Malevich placed a large painting of a black square in the "red" or "holy" corner of a Petrograd exhibition in 1915.

The withdrawal of painting from representation or meaning could not have been more complete.

Animated by the apocalyptic mood in society and by the huge gap between educated and popular culture, Russian artists of all kinds were asking searching questions about the techniques of their own art form and the meaning of art in general. They generated the most radical experiments of the early twentieth century seen anywhere in Europe, as well as fundamental speculation about art and its relation to life which was to place Russia in the vanguard of aesthetic theory for much of the twentieth century.

With the abolition of the imperial theater monopoly in 1882, Mamontov also helped to finance a theater dedicated to performing Russian and foreign drama and selling tickets at a price ordinary people could afford. With the help of the actor-director Konstantin Stanislavskii, he opened the Moscow Arts Theater, which played host to a troupe run on artel principles, without the "stars" who normally monopolized reviewers' attention. Suppressing applause during the acts and music in the intervals, the players attempted to draw the spectators into the illusion of real life. Their most successful plays, including those of Anton Chekhov (1860–1904) and Maksim Gorkii (1868–1936), contained a strong element of social criticism, depicting the lives of ordinary Russians of different social classes, including the very lowest.[55]

What animated Moscow entrepreneurs like Tretiakov and Mamontov was the sense that they were rescuing and reviving a genuine Russian culture, centered on their own city and distinct from the academic, cosmopolitan culture of St. Petersburg. That is why they encouraged art which depicted the life of ordinary people or which drew on folk and religious themes (some of them were Old Believers). They took the view that their wealth should be used for public service and distributed for the benefit of ordinary people, in both the material and the spiritual sense. They hoped thereby, among other things, to gain greater social acceptance and political influence in a society still dominated by the landed gentry.[56]

Undoubtedly, however, the art form which most fully and successfully explained the aspirations of Russians to themselves was literature, and especially, because of the realist tendencies of the time, prose fiction. Pushkin had launched the trend in his later works, when he moved away from verse toward stories and chronicles.

Already in the 1830s and 1840s Nikolai Gogol decided that it was his mission to save Russia by his writings. His various works portrayed the imperial state, with its uniforms and ranks, as a Moloch which destroyed people's lives. The empire lived on "dead souls": the novel of that name plays on the administrative fiction that all serfs counted in the last census are still alive till the next one, and on the official terminology—which the Old Believers found offensive—designating a taxpaying adult a "soul." The spectacle of the mountebank Chichikov buying up these "dead souls" becomes a symbol for the unreality and inhumanity of official Russia.

Gogol hoped in the second part of the novel to redeem the nightmare empire in the spirit of Orthodoxy, but in the event he was unable to complete the text and finished by burning the manuscript. So his greatest work ends with the enigmatic image of Russia as a troika, racing headlong over the snow, in an unknown direction, while other peoples draw back in amazement and horror. A contemporary wrote of Gogol that he "broke under the weight of his own calling, which in his eyes had taken on enormous dimensions."[57]

Lev Tolstoi (1828–1910) managed to fulfill his religious aspirations outside literature, by founding a sectarian movement which became quite popular in the final decades of the imperial regime. But he also articulated an image of Russia in his literary work. His novel *War and Peace* portrays the victory of the Russians over Napoleon not as a triumph of the generals, but rather of ordinary people, "determined not by the quantity of pieces of cloth called banners picked up on the battlefield," but by "a moral victory, of the kind which convinces the opponent that they are helpless in the face of the moral superiority of their enemy."[58] Not the calculations of the generals, but the mutual solidarity of the men in their units proves to be the decisive factor in determining the outcome of battle. Tolstoi shows Kutuzov as a wise commander because he accepts the limitations of his role, unlike Napoleon, who sees a battlefield as a chessboard and believes that his orders determine what happens on it.

Pierre Bezukhov, Tolstoi's alter ego in the novel, seeks various ways to save both Russia and himself, going through a phase of freemasonry and dreaming of assassinating Napoleon, but in the end accepts the homespun teaching of a simple peasant who recommends resigned acceptance of God's will. Tolstoi's own religion rejected the entire imperial heritage, army, government, and Orthodox Church, in favor of the renunciation of violence and a community based on the ethic of peaceful mutual cooperation. The works in which he expounded his viewpoint were condemned by the church, and he was excommunicated. Significantly, this did nothing to restrain his growing popularity among people of all social classes; rather the reverse. The denial of a church burial after his death in 1910 provoked a lively public protest and sparked off student disorders in universities throughout the empire.

More than any other writer, though, it was Fedor Dostoevskii (1821–1881) who articulated a version of Russian national identity which was widely acceptable to a growing reading public. In his novel *The Brothers Karamazov* he portrayed a *starets*, or holy man, Father Zosima, brought up in the ascetic and contemplative tradition of Mount Athos, who early in life had broken away from imperial Russia, in the shape of the army, and entered a monastery. Toward the end of his life he is seen counseling and giving comfort to pilgrims of all social classes who come to consult him at crisis points in their lives. Dostoevskii's intention was that Alesha, the young "hero" of the novel, would go through an analogous temptation, that of atheist socialism, before eventually following in the path of Zosima and helping to fulfill his prophecy that "The salvation of Rus will come from its people . . . The people will confront the atheist and defeat him, and a united Orthodox Russia will arise."[59]

Although Dostoevskii did not live to bring this conception to completion, he did in his novels accomplish what one might call a "literary construction" of Russia. He believed that the Russians were a "God-bearing people," marked out for exceptional suffering but also, by virtue of that suffering, endowed with extraordinary sympathy for other peoples and hence entrusted with an exclusive mission to bear witness before them of the truths of Orthodox Christianity.

This was the messianic idea of "holy Rus" reformulated for an age of atheism, nationalism, and material progress. Russia, in Dostoevskii's presentation, did not accept these talismans of an apparently triumphant West: she was not atheist, her material prosperity was low, and her nationalism was tempered by generosity and understanding toward other nations. Those were precisely the qualities which would enable Russia to redeem humanity. Dostoevskii came closer than anyone else to combining two incompatible Russian myths. He believed that Russia was great *because* its people was humble and suffering: multiethnic empire and village commune coalesced in one vision.

By the 1890s writers were becoming impatient with the techniques of realism and even with prose itself. Associating the realist outlook with determinism, materialism, and secularism, they began to claim for art some of the functions of religion, laying claim to territory which the stagnant, unreformed Orthodox Church seemed to be abandoning. The inspiration for the generation of Symbolists was the philosopher, theologian, and poet Vladimir Soloviev (1853–1900), who urged them to seek a "real" world beyond appearances, where human beings could be truly free, live the life of the spirit, and share with God in the work of creation. The idea of "Godmanhood" (*bogochelovechestvo*), man aspiring to and participating in the divine, fascinated many in this generation. Others found more congenial the image of the Superman created by Nietzsche, or of the new, more harmonious human being promised by revolutionary socialists.

In his later works Soloviev articulated an apocalyptic mood in the face of accelerating urbanization, industrialization, and the emergence of mass culture. As in the early sixteenth century, apocalyptic visions could stimulate hope as well as foreboding, the anticipation of a great revolutionary change which would transform the life of humanity, and especially the oppressed and poverty-stricken. Poets like Aleksandr Blok, probably the most considerable figure among the Symbolists, veered back and forth between optimism and despair, between desire to serve the people and fear of being crushed by them. In a public lecture of 1908 he evoked the image of Gogol's troika, Russia rushing headlong into an unknown future, and warned: "Even as we cast ourselves at the feet of the people, we are casting ourselves under the hooves of the furious troika, to certain death."[60]

17. Barricades in the Arbat, Moscow, December 1905

18. A steam train crossing a bridge on the Trans-Siberian Railway, 1911

19. Nicholas II blessing troops in the First World War

20. Army deserters making for home, 1917

21. Lenin and his colleagues in Red Square, October 1918

22. Bagmen at a railway station, ca. 1919

23. Caucasian Muslim women listening to a Communist propagandist, ca. 1920

24. An aristocratic mansion converted into a workers' rest home, 1923

25. Tractor agitators in Samara Province, mid-1920s

26. Queues outside Lenin's Mausoleum, 1928

27. Kirov, Stalin, Kuibyshev, Ordjonikidze, Kalinin, and
Voroshilov at the Sixteenth Party Congress, 1930

28. Workers on the building site of a blast furnace at Magnitogorsk, ca. 1930

29. Construction of the opera house, Novosibirsk, late 1930s

30. Architectural model of Moscow University, early 1950s

31. Hungarian uprising, 1956: the decapitated bust of Stalin

32. Khrushchev and U.S. Vice-President Nixon in frank debate, Moscow, 1959

V

Revolution and Utopia

9

SOCIAL CHANGE AND REVOLUTION

By the 1850s the needs of empire had skewed the Russian economy to the point where the failure to exploit human and natural resources was undermining military might and therefore great-power status. The most pressing needs were to mobilize resources better, to raise the prosperity of the population, to generate funds for industrial investment, and to place the state's finances on a firmer foundation by taxing genuine wealth rather than the social classes least able to avoid payment. This was the message which Ivan Pososhkov, Petr Shuvalov, and Mikhail Speranskii had preached over the past century and a half, but in vain.

Most economic advisers in the 1860s considered that the only way to break through from stagnation to higher levels of prosperity was by building railways. These would both improve communications in wartime (a cardinal aim of Dmitrii Miliutin) and make it easier to tap the unparalleled resources hitherto inaccessible in remote regions of the empire. M. Kh. Reitern, who became finance minister in 1862, reported to the tsar that "without railways and mechanical industry Russia cannot be considered safe even within its own borders." But how was one to raise the money to build them? There were scant internal sources of capital, since "for many years the government and the upper classes have been living beyond their means." Investment would have to be attracted from abroad. That meant stabilizing the ruble and ceasing to depend on *assignats,* which in turn entailed balancing the state budget by cutting expenditure and raising tax revenue. Inevitably these goals had to be attained mostly at the expense of the peasants.[1]

At a time when landowners were being massively compensated for land "lost" during the emancipation, balancing the budget was more than usually tricky, and the difficulty explains the stingy treatment of the peasants in 1861. On the other hand, the establishment of a single official budget, published annually and audited, raised public confidence in the state finances. The abolition of the liquor tax farm and its replacement by an excise tax eliminated the last major source of personal tribute and finally laid down a clear demarcation line between private profit and public taxation. The creation of a State Bank in 1860 helped to improve Russian credit ratings, as did the disciplines it imposed on joint-stock banks set up subsequently. The state did not, however, facilitate the promotion of corporate enterprise in general by issuing a model charter for a limited company. Right up to 1917 each joint-stock company had individually to seek permission from the tsar before it could begin trading—a process which could take years and involve substantial bribes to key officials.[2]

All the same, a railway boom did take place. Track mileage increased sevenfold during the 1860s and doubled again in the following decade. Railways came to the Black Sea coast and the Caucasus region. Most daring of all was the Trans-Siberian Railway, an undertaking embarked upon with considerable misgivings, in view of the colossal investment needed. For all its shortcomings, by the time it was completed in 1903 it had begun the process of opening up the largest single underexploited geographical area in the world. It also promoted communications with Manchuria, Korea, and China, which other European powers were starting to penetrate by seaborne routes, while its offshoot into the Transcaspian strengthened control of central Asia and boosted trade with Persia and the Ottoman Empire. All these developments linked Russia's grain-growing regions and mineral deposits with her cities and ports, and they also opened the prospect of lively trade with Asiatic countries where Russia could still assume the role of the more advanced power, selling manufactures as well as raw materials and agricultural products.[3]

In spite of much incompetence and corruption among their owners and managers, the new railways were the decisive impetus for an impressive expansion of industrial output in the late 1880s and 1890s, and again in 1907–1914. They made it possible to transport heavy goods of all kinds more easily, and they also provided a market for mines and manufactures, whether in rails, locomotives, signaling equipment, or rolling stock. From 1883 to 1913 total industrial output rose by an annual average of 4.5 or 5 percent, a rate comparable with that of the United States, Germany, and Japan at their peak periods of sustained growth.[4]

This industrialization was more abrupt than in most European countries, since Russia, as a latecomer, was in a position to launch its new enterprises using the latest technology. This usually meant building very large factories, mills, and mines to achieve economies of scale. The Putilov Works in St. Petersburg, which produced ships, locomotives, and heavy machine tools, was one of the largest factories in Europe, and the capital city had many other up-to-date industrial giants, in shipbuilding, railways, machine tools, metallurgy, and chemical and electrical products. Other areas of the empire had their own specialties: textiles in Poland and around Moscow; coal, iron, and steel in Ukraine; oil in the Caucasus; ports and consumer industry in the Baltic.

The speed of Russia's industrialization meant that it lacked the intermediate "proto-industrial" and consumer-oriented forms common in western and central Europe. Instead cottage industry and heavy industry existed side by side, with very little between them. Peasants either made domestic articles for a local market at home, or they went into the city to work in a factory. In the latter eventuality, they were seldom able to take wives and children with them, and so families became divided for long periods. Men lived on their own, renting a bunk in the corner of a room or among fellow male workers in crowded barracks and dormitories. They had to adapt abruptly to urban life, with its dangers and temptations, as well as to industrial discipline.[5]

The industrial upsurge required substantial foreign investment, which had to be attracted by projecting an image of financial stability. Finance Ministers I. Ia. Vyshnegradskii (1887–1892) and S. Iu. Vitte (1892–1903) balanced the budget by ruthless levying of taxes, including the new liquor excise, which in effect replaced the poll tax, and by imposing a high tariff on imports of industrial products—the latter measure also being intended to protect Russia's infant industries. In this way it proved possible to stabilize the ruble sufficiently to place it on the gold standard in 1897, a development which much increased the confidence of foreign investors.[6]

All the same, the policies provoked lively opposition. Landowners complained that they were finding it more expensive to buy agricultural machinery and also more difficult to sell grain abroad, as trading partners retaliated by raising their own tariffs. Populist intellectuals and some officials charged that the policies were "un-Russian," since they produced goods for which the country had no need, while promoting Western individualism and mercenary values which undermined traditional Russian collectivism. Vitte's more unscrupulous opponents insinuated that he was the agent of an international Jewish conspiracy aiming to destroy Russia from inside.[7]

The effects of official policy and of economic growth on the peasantry have been the subject of much controversy among scholars in the last couple of decades. The traditional interpretation is that the peasants were emancipated on terms which hindered their own efforts to better themselves economically: they were awarded too little land, burdened with debt, and fixed to the village commune, so that their paying powers and their mobility were severely restricted. They were forced to sell their grain on unfavorable terms, were unable to raise capital, and fell into a deepening spiral of indebtedness and poverty.[8]

More recently, drawing on statistics from a variety of sources, some scholars have pointed out that peasants were able to buy land and to pay indirect taxes in a way which suggests that at least some of them were doing well, either by improving their agricultural productivity or by diversifying into nonagricultural activities. Village communes did not hold them back, but encouraged these activities in order to benefit from the extra revenue they brought in. Important to the newer interpretation is the notion that the development of heavy industry, at least in the early stages, did not drive cottage industry out of business, but on the contrary aided it by providing it with cheaper sources of tools and materials.[9]

In adjudicating between these interpretations, a regional perspective is essential. In the central agricultural provinces south and southeast of Moscow and from there toward the Volga basin a combination of factors made it very difficult to improve agricultural productivity or to derive wealth from other occupations: a dense rural population, the absence of large urban markets or seaports, and a preponderance of very small allotments trapped most households in a vicious circle of underproduction, noninvestment, and overtaxation which demoralized many and stimulated the most energetic to leave and find employment elsewhere. It was here and along the Volga that the famine of 1891, with its attendant epidemics, was most severe.[10]

By contrast, rural areas near large towns, ports, or western borders were more likely to offer scope for the enterprising and able. This was true of much of the central industrial area, as well as the Baltic, parts of the western provinces and Poland, the steppes of the Don and Kuban, and "new Russia," on the northern shore of the Black Sea. Altogether, the growth of industrial towns, plus gradual and often patchy but cumulative agricultural improvements in these regions, fostered a more prosperous, mobile, and confident population, many of whom were migrating to the cities. One paradoxical result of the uneven geographical distribution of these opportunities was that many of the fast-developing cities and regions were largely non-Russian in population; most of the poverty-stricken regions, however, were Russian.[11]

REVIVAL OF THE REVOLUTIONARY MOVEMENT 359

The assassination of Alexander II in 1881 failed in its political aims. It also led to the destruction of the Central Committee of Narodnaia Volia, most of whose members were arrested in the police investigations which followed. Many provincial organizations survived, but their capacity for concerted action was fatally undermined. Not until the late 1890s did the surviving members begin to reconstitute an empirewide organization, which they christened the Socialist Revolutionary Party.

By this time their cells had become the object of concerted police attention. Among the measures taken by the regime in the aftermath of the assassination was a thorough overhaul of the security police. The old Third Department was wound up and replaced by a new and much larger Department of Police, among whose tasks was the protection of senior officials and the thorough investigation of terrorist organizations. It had its own security bureaus (okhrannye otdeleniia), first in Moscow, St. Petersburg, and Paris (to keep watch over émigrés), then in some twenty other major cities. Sergei Zubatov, head of the Moscow okhrana, sponsored the promotion of a new generation of specially trained security officers, their operations backed up by systematic records. In short, the security police were becoming professionalized. Lenin accorded them the ultimate accolade when he recommended that the revolutionary party should be run by a "few professionals, as highly trained and experienced as our security police."[12]

By now the revolutionary parties had perfected their conspiratorial techniques, and to gain the information they required about them the police had little alternative but to deploy secret agents within their ranks. To sustain their credibility, those agents had to take their share in the tracking, the bombmaking, and the secret communications which were part and parcel of the terrorist's life. In that way the agent provocateur emerged, the double agent working for both the police and the revolutionaries. Opposition parties cut off from the public and a secret police accountable to nobody held out intoxicating opportunities to individuals attracted by the exercise of power for its own sake. They were extremely difficult for either side to detect and could orchestrate alternating betrayals and terrorist acts at their own convenience. Here the fiskal and the revolutionary, both descendants of Peter the Great, amalgamated in one sinister figure.[13]

The Socialist Revolutionaries, anxious this time not to be hijacked by the practitioners of assassination, created a separate "fighting detachment" *(boevoi otriad)* to concentrate on terrorism, so that other party members could devote themselves to propaganda and other peaceful activities. Ironically, however, the isolation of the terrorists meant their final emancipation from normal moral and political considerations. The fighting detachment fell into the hands of a police agent, Evno Azef, under whose command it conducted a concerted campaign against officials of the very regime which had hired him. From 1902 to 1906 its victims included the governor-general of Moscow, a number of ministers—including two ministers of the interior, Dmitrii Sipiagin and Viacheslav Pleve, Azef's own employers—and some 4,000 central and local officials, killed or wounded. Rarely, if ever, has any regime sustained such an onslaught of terror. When Azef's duplicity was finally revealed, in 1908, the disclosure discredited the police and permanently undermined the moral standing of the Socialist Revolutionary Party.[14] It contributed in no small measure to the public's disillusionment with politics of all kinds in the final years of tsarism.

A cardinal tenet of the revolutionary movement up to the early 1890s had been that Marx's teaching on historical evolution did not apply to Russia, whose communal institutions would enable it to build a socialist society without going through the stage of "bourgeois capitalism" and without creating an alienated and poverty-stricken proletariat, such as had been seen in Britain, the United States, and, more recently, Germany.

The first revolutionary figure to question this doctrine was Georgii Plekhanov, the man who had rejected terrorism in 1879. In a series of studies written on emigration in the 1880s he argued that Russia had already entered the era of bourgois capitalism and was creating a modern industrial system, including a proletariat of the kind Marx had described. As for the commune, it was only the remnant of a dying economic system, already being destroyed by the pressures of capitalism. Only when capitalism had exhausted its potential and the proletariat had expanded and matured would revolution become possible: to try to bring it about before then was to act in a premature and irresponsible manner.

Plekhanov believed that only his version of Marxism had the right to be called "scientific socialism," and he disdainfully wrote off the revolutionaries of the period up to 1881 as *narodniki*, "people worshippers." Though translated more respectfully as "populists," the word is still commonly used for all non-Marxist Russian revolutionaries. His assertions launched a lively debate in the 1890s between the "populists," who held that Russia had its own distinctive path of social evolution, and the "Marxists," who believed that it would follow the same road as other European countries, though with some delay caused by its relative backwardness.[15]

Plekhanov's view appealed to those who liked to regard themselves as "scientific" and to those who wished to see themselves as part of an international scene, to escape from the claustrophobia of insisting on Russia's distinctiveness. But there was a serious drawback to his doctrine: if Russia was to wait till it had a numerous and "mature" proletariat, then revolution would have to be delayed for decades, at least. In the meantime the revolutionaries would be obliged to *welcome* the growth of capitalism and of bourgeois liberalism as progressive developments. Most revolutionaries were not so patient or understanding. Dealing with the dilemmas posed by this ambivalent and dauntingly long-term perspective was one of the main preoccupations of Russian Marxists.

There were others too. Russia was a very different society from Germany, where the first major Social Democratic (that is, Marxist) party had arisen. At the second congress of the Russian Social Democratic Workers' Party, which took place in Brussels and London in 1903,[16] there was a split over the question of party organization. Iulii Martov, backed by Plekhanov, suggested as a qualification for party membership "regular personal assistance under the direction of one of the party's organisations," while his opponent, Vladimir Lenin, proposed a tighter formulation: "personal participation in one of the party's organizations." With goodwill this relatively subtle distinction could have been finessed. But the truth was that Martov and Lenin had fundamentally differing notions of the party's nature. Martov envisaged a mass working-class party, whereas Lenin had in mind a conspiratorial organization of activists, dedicated fulltime to party work. Lenin lost the vote, but because the members of the Jewish Bund, who were opposed to him, walked out over an unrelated issue, he was able to leave the congress claiming the majority.[17] From then on his faction was known as the "Bolsheviks," or "men of the majority," while his opponents contented themselves with the faintly disparaging label "Mensheviks," "men of the minority."

In fact only Lenin's conception had any chance of realization in contemporary Russia. The Mensheviks laid great store by the creation of a "bourgeois" parliamentary state, in which the rule of law would enable the working-class party to act as a legal opposition and to prepare itself for the ultimate assumption of power. That was a plausible reading of what was happening in Germany in the first decade of the twentieth century. But Russia was different. Even during 1905–06, when it looked briefly as if Martov might be right, conditions were so turbulent that few stable working-class organizations could be created.

361

Lenin, by contrast, regarded the rule of law in Russia as a sham, and he became increasingly impatient at the protracted timetable implied by the Mensheviks' policies. Although he did not clarify his view fully until 1917, it was already apparent earlier that he aimed to telescope the whole process, curtailing the "bourgeois" period of history and proceeding as fast as possible to socialism. The man who helped him to clarify his views on this issue was Lev Trotskii, who for that reason became Lenin's closest ally during and immediately after 1917.

Lenin believed this conflation of two revolutions could be achieved because, after 1905–1907, he became convinced that in Russia the peasants, thanks to their frustration over land, were not bastions of property and order but potential revolutionaries. In this respect Lenin resembled those whom Plekhanov had written off as populists. If one regards populism and Marxism as two separate traditions, then Bolshevism was a synthesis of the two. Like the Marxists, Bolshevism was internationalist in its outlook and put its faith in the working class as bearers of revolution, but like the populists it accepted the notion of leadership by a small group of intellectuals. It also (after 1905) took the peasantry seriously as a revolutionary class, and, by mobilizing the peasantry, it aspired to overstep the "bourgeois" phase of economic development and proceed straight to socialism.[18] Actually, it would make more sense to regard Bolshevism as the form of socialism best suited to politics in Russia, where it was impossible to form a mass working-class party, where the peasants were alienated and discontented, and where civil society was very weak.

One could regard populism as Russian ethnic socialism, while Marxism was imperial or Europeanized socialism. As we shall see, in attempting to synthesize the two visions in 1917, Bolshevism created an unstable amalgam of internationalism and Russian nationalism, colored with millennial expectations.

SOCIAL CHANGE AND URBAN PROBLEMS

Taken together the political reforms and the economic changes profoundly affected social relationships within Russia. A whole society was moving away from a structure based on kinship, ascriptive estates *(sosloviia)*, state service, and a traditional rural culture, where the church played an important role, toward a model based on the nuclear family, mobile social classes, economic functionalism, and an urbanized commercial culture, where the church's role was peripheral.

As in all European countries a separation was taking place between family and work: the home was ceasing to be the site of economic production and becoming more a haven for rest and personal life, and thus for privacy—a concept the Russian language had not yet adopted. Entertainment became less communal and more commercial: even the traditional *narodnye gulia-niia*, folk gatherings, or mass promenades were transplanted from village common land to parks and squares and set around with commercial booths and puppet shows.

Urban inhabitants who could afford a modest outlay would go to theaters, music halls *(estrada)*, circuses, and, by the early twentieth century, the cinema. Newspapers, as we have seen, were beginning to gain a mass market, and popular novels were selling on bookstalls. The shows townsfolk saw, the songs they heard, and the stories they thrilled to sometimes involved adventurous and successful Russian soldiers in the wilder outreaches of empire; but more usually they included material which neither the regime nor the nonconformist intelligentsia approved. Where the action did not involve crime or sexual conquest, it often portrayed a world of luxury and affluence seen as desirable in its own terms: spectators and readers would use them as a guide to their own aspirations in food, clothing, furniture, and interior decoration.[19]

In the larger cities the traditional Russian booths and stalls were being replaced as the site of everyday retail trade by permanent specialist shops, though few of them were as diverse and opulent as the Eliseev delicatessen store on Nevskii Prospekt in St. Petersburg or the Muir and Merrilies furniture store on the Petrovka in Moscow. Crowds would gather before the window displays, often people who had not the means to purchase any of the goods on show but who were nevertheless eager to discuss their various merits. Department stores were schools of taste and fashion, assisted by newspaper advertisements and the first women's magazines. Clothes ceased to be a sign of one's inherited social status and became more an index to aspirations shared by a new mass audience of consumers. Women longed for the *sak*, a loose-fitting coat which draped from the shoulders, while men aspired to a straw hat and fancy shoes—in both cases acquisitions which symbolized one's break with boorish rural culture and accession to an urbane lifestyle.[20]

The breakdown of customary social bonds manifested itself in more sinister forms too. Many of the men who came in from the countryside to work in factories left their wives and children at home to cultivate the family plot of land. Living alone in the corner of a room or in a barracks with a lot of other men, they were subject to temptations against which they had few defenses. The tavern beckoned, with its culture of everyday drinking in cheerful company, perhaps accompanied by gambling. On street corners prostitutes offered feminine solace but also venereal disease. Alcoholism, hooliganism, contagious illness, and crime proliferated in a way which deeply worried both the authorities and the oppositional intelligentsia.

As a result of such social dislocation, the towns experienced acute and mounting political tension. The great majority of new immigrants, streaming in during the 1880s and 1890s to work as domestic servants or in factories, transport depots, and shops, found no institutions through which they could express their aspirations and grievances or even achieve a sense of common identity. Trade unions were prohibited and friendly societies nonexistent. The municipalities were dominated by a wealthy oligarchy and gave no voice to the poor.

Nor did the church meet their needs much better. It is often supposed that urbanization entails a loss of religious faith. In fact it would be truer to say that it generates a religious crisis: as studies of other European countries have shown, it is a crucial moment in the evolution of religious identity. In some ways recent immigrants need religion more than before, to help them cope with the problems of adjusting to a new way of life, often without family, colleagues, or traditional moral guidelines. Besides, new forms of religious activity become possible: prayer or Bible-reading groups, charitable associations, newspapers, and journals. If the church is not ready to support and mold such activities, then the newly urbanized may drift away into sectarianism or atheism. The record of St. Petersburg in the early twentieth century suggests that this was true of Russia.[21]

At any rate, the early twentieth century seems to have witnessed a sharp upsurge of unruly public behavior, not only in the towns but also in the villages, which, as we have seen, were increasingly affected by urban modes of behavior. This trend was reported in the press under the heading of "hooliganism." It ranged from the desire to shock and offend—whistling, jostling, shouting obscenities—to attacks on life and property, such as muggings and stabbings.[22]

Actually, the statistics on "hooliganism" are not unambiguous and may reflect no more than an increasing awareness in polite society of a boorishness which had always been present. It is certain, though, that such behavior now caused more offense than before. Russia's new and still insecure urban middle classes felt more threatened by it than their counterparts in older, established civilizations.[23]

In the field of industrial relations this behavior was especially conspicuous, since channels for the orderly expression of grievances did not exist. Most workers usually accepted their downtrodden and disfranchised situation passively, but from time to time their apathy was punctuated by outbreaks of primitive lawlessness and casual violence, directed against foremen, officials, or police or against the property of their employers.[24]

Since workers had no legitimate mode of self-organization, differences among them of age, training, skill, function, and ethnic or religious affiliation had far less significance than might have been expected in a multinational empire. Old and young, skilled and unskilled, latheworkers and cleaners, Russians, Ukrainians, and Latvians—all had common grievances and, for the purpose of expressing them, were thrown together in indiscriminate solidarity. This meant that, when trouble broke out, it could spread very fast, flooding across the bulkheads which normally divide status groups within large industrial units.[25]

The authorities were not unaware of the dangers of this situation, and of the way in which the socialists might exploit them. The country's most skilled and determined antirevolutionary, Sergei Zubatov, determined to do something about it. In 1901 he set up a police-dominated trade union, in order to divert workers' discontent away from the Social Democrats, indeed away from politics altogether into purely economic channels. It proved impossible, however, to separate economics from politics: members of his union became involved in the Odessa general strike of July 1903. Zubatov's rivals accused him of fomenting disorder, and his union was closed down.

His work was continued, though, by a priest from the St. Petersburg industrial suburbs, Father Grigorii Gapon. Gapon was not quite a maverick, since his organization, the Assembly of Russian Factory and Mill Workers, had support from his diocese; but he was certainly highly unusual among secular clergymen in the degree of his determination to do something to solve the workers' question. His frame of reference was patriotic: he wanted to "build a nest among the factory and mill workers where Rus, a truly Russian spirit, would prevail." He aimed to promote this spirit by encouraging self-help, temperance, and the peaceful acculturation of the workers. To this end he set up tearooms, clubs, and mutual aid funds, as well as arranging lectures on economic and other topical themes.[26]

His movement had about it something of the revivalist crusade, and it attracted large numbers of workers, who probably responded to its patriotic and religious message, and who certainly wanted a legitimate channel for their grievances and aspirations. Gapon was sensitive to this pressure and decided that his movement needed a political as well as an economic and moral dimension. He took advice from the Union of Liberation (discussed below) and also from a group of disaffected Social Democrats, and with their help drew up a petition including political demands which combined elements of liberal and socialist thinking. Citing "capitalist exploitation" and "bureaucratic lawlessness" as the two main evils workers faced, the petition called for an eight-hour day, the right to strike, and "normal" wages, and also took a stand on political issues, demanding a constituent assembly, civil liberties, and a law-abiding government answerable to the people's representatives. Reflecting the close ties most workers still had with the village, the petition also took up the most burning peasant concerns, such as the abolition of redemption payments and the transfer of land to those who worked it.[27]

The fall of Port Arthur to the Japanese in December 1904 and the outbreak of a strike at the huge Putilov engineering works in St. Petersburg coalesced to create a mood of expectation in which Gapon decided the workers must register their petition publicly. The occasion was to be a peaceful march through the capital city, followed by the presentation of the petition along with a loyal address to the tsar. Workshop meetings took up the idea enthusiastically. Observers spoke of "a kind of religious, mystical ecstasy." On Vasiliev Island the branch president asked: "And what, comrades, if the Ruler will not receive us and does not want to read our petition . . . The response was a mighty roar: 'Then we have no Tsar!'"[28]

Alarmed by the mass mood, the government tried at the last moment to ban the procession, but merely succeeded in sowing confusion. On Sunday, 9 January 1905, the workers turned out in their Sunday best and paraded with icons and portraits of the tsar. They proceeded from the various industrial suburbs to the center of St. Petersburg, where they hoped to present their petition. There, instead of the tsar, they found nervous soldiers awaiting them. Drawn up without proper instructions, the troops panicked at the sight of such huge and determined crowds and opened fire, and in the resulting melee some 200 people were killed.

It is difficult to overstate the importance of this massacre, which was soon christened "Bloody Sunday." It simultaneously closed off two possible developments: a revived urban Orthodoxy providing for the needs of the lower orders, and a renewed patriotic and popular monarchy. Gapon's protest had been a mixture of the archaic loyal *chelobitnaia* and the twentieth-century mass labor demonstration. Old social bonds had been disrupted; now the basis for new ones was eliminated.

THE REVOLUTION OF 1905–1907

The result was a cataclysmic eruption of social disorder, in which all social strata, all regions, and all nationalities of the empire were involved, one way or another, an outburst of manifold grievances and conflicts, many of which had smoldered for decades, gradually accumulating the destructive power they suddenly unleashed now.

The workers, naturally enough, were the first to react to Bloody Sunday. Abandoning any hope of support from church or tsar, they turned for advice and organizational support to the opposition, especially to the socialists. The Social Democrats and Socialist Revolutionaries were slow to respond: their leaders were still in emigration, cut off from their potential constituents and preoccupied by heated polemics with one another. Local activists did what they could to improvise meetings, protests, and strikes, and gradually their contact with the workers improved and assumed more organized forms.

The result was a new type of workers' association, the Soviet (Council) of Workers' Deputies. First set up in the textile town of Ivanovo-Voznesensk to coordinate a general strike, the soviets were usually elected by the workers of the major enterprises in any given town, at the rate of one deputy for every 500 or so workers. They would meet in a large building, or even in the open air, where not only deputies but also their electors could attend and contribute to discussions. This was a close approach to direct democracy, since, at least in principle, any deputy could be recalled at any time if he failed to satisfy his constituents and be replaced by someone else. The members of each soviet elected an executive committee to deal with day-to-day business and to negotiate with employers, municipality, and police: often they would choose professional people, seeing them as more skillful spokesmen than they themselves could be. Through the executive committees the socialist activists gained influence over the soviets and sometimes directly organized them.[29]

The soviets were the best forum for radical intellectuals and workers to cooperate with each other at a time of political crisis. For the workers, they took a familiar form: their general meetings resembled overgrown and disorderly village assemblies, in which everyone tried to speak and mass enthusiasm welled up. On the other hand, the executive committees supplied the element of conscious policy and organization. The soviets' greatest moment came in St. Petersburg in October 1905, when they organized a general strike which disrupted normal production and communications not only in the capital city but over much of the empire. This was the decisive blow which compelled the tsar to grant the October Manifesto, promising civil liberties and an elected legislative assembly. On 18 October huge crowds thronged the streets to celebrate their triumph, while Lev Trotskii, the soviet's most brilliant orator, harangued them from the balcony of the university building. For a brief moment, *obshchestvennost* and workers were at one.[30]

367

368

The short-lived unanimity of all social classes against the autocracy grew naturally out of their previous shared impotence. Just like the workers, *obshchestvennost* had been deprived of any legal outlets for their political opinions or even for the articulation of their professional concerns and material interests. During the 1890s, following the surge of voluntary activity in the 1891 famine, consultative meetings of professional associations took on an increasingly political coloring. Doctors and teachers, for example, were frustrated at the way the low status and segregation of peasants impeded programs of education or public health. In the zemstvos, where such programs had their natural home, discontent was also mounting, especially among the "third element."

In 1901 a Union of Liberation was set up to coordinate the efforts of zemstvo and professional people. It had to hold its founding congress abroad, in Switzerland, but it soon began to campaign inside Russia, especially after reverses in the Japanese war threw doubt on the strength and competence of the autocracy. The Union issued pamphlets and held "liberation banquets," at which the demand was ever more insistently raised that the autocracy be replaced by a constitutional monarchy, with a parliament elected by universal, direct, equal, and secret ballot.

The Union was a liberal movement, but circumstances compelled it to cooperate with socialists, including those who were dedicated to the violent overthrow of the regime and its replacement by a workers' and peasants' republic. Achieving the minimal goal which they all shared—ending the autocracy and establishing an elected legislative assembly—seemed difficult enough and overshadowed more distant aspirations. Many liberals became accustomed to the sentiment that there were "no enemies to the left," since the autocracy was so repugnant that its overthrow justified all means and all alliances. When the first liberal party was set up, at the height of the revolution, in October 1905—the Constitutional Democrats, known as "Kadets" for short—it too was affected by this mood. Its program was liberal and constitutional, but it refused to condemn terrorism (when practiced by the opposition, not the regime). and it espoused the peasant demand for compulsory expropriation of landowners.[31]

This alliance across normally impermeable political and social boundaries could not last once the regime began to make real concessions. The professional and zemstvo people who found their home in the Kadet Party were largely satisfied by the October Manifesto, and so turned away from the workers' movement. For their part, the soviets possessed an inbuilt momentum which made it difficult to operate without posing ever more radical demands: moderation and routine were contrary to their nature. At the end of November, the government plucked up courage and arrested first the chairman of the St. Petersburg Soviet and then its entire executive committee. The result was an explosion in Moscow, where the soviet decided it could not sit idly by, but had no other means of expressing its indignation other than armed insurrection. As one activist said, "It was better to perish in a struggle than to be bound hand and foot without fighting. The honor of the revolution was at stake."[32]

The workers who set up barricades in the Presnia district of Moscow did not have much support from their fellow townsfolk. All the same, the government did not trust its own infantry, fearing they would be tempted to fraternize, and used artillery to crush the insurrection, destroying much of the district's housing and killing at least 1,000 people.[33]

This disaster highlighted the nature of the soviets: their strengths were also their weaknesses. They were in their element in an atmosphere of crisis and conflict, but the spontaneity which gave them birth impeded their stabilization. In no sense were they civic institutions. For a brief, heady moment workers had been able through them to dictate terms to both employers and government. What they had not been able to do was to create permanent functioning associations capable of making an effective regular input into political life. The intoxicating success of the soviets remained in the workers' minds as a fleeting dream of total liberation, which they yearned to recapture.

Peasants, though not directly affected by Bloody Sunday, were nevertheless profoundly stirred and outraged by the spectacle of the autocracy acting in a way which was both ineffective (the Japanese war) and in breach of God's law. The "little father" had proved to be not only impotent but also evil: both pravda and *vlast* (authority) had been undermined. They felt that it should be both possible and right to make the political system more responsive to them. Over the next couple of years they tried various devices: petitioning the authorities, withholding their labor from landlord estates, electing delegates first of all to a Peasant Congress, then to the State Duma, and even taking the law completely into their own hands, seizing the landlord's animals, tools, and seeds, driving him out of the manor house, and burning it down. Different tactics were employed at different times and places according to circumstance. Peasants seem to have been completely pragmatic about the means they used: their paramount concern was to put into effect their own concept of how land should be owned and villages governed.

The first stratagem, as with the workers, was to present petitions—not one giant one, but severally in their village assemblies. They were initially encouraged by the tsar's Manifesto of 18 February 1905, which invited "well-intentioned persons of every estate" to submit suggestions "concerning improvements in the political structure and the betterment of the people's existence."[34] Sometimes assisted by schoolteachers, priests, zemstvo workers, or representatives of political parties, the peasants issued *prigovory* (or *cahiers*) in three waves: one after February 1905, another following the October Manifesto, and a third during the Duma elections of spring 1906. In spite of the participation of outsiders, there is not much doubt that they reflected deeply held peasant views.

Much the most widely expressed demand was for the land to be awarded to those who cultivated it. Even the fact that a substantial minority of households now owned land privately did not weaken the general conviction that "It is essential to abolish private property in land and to put all privately owned, state, udel, monastery, and church land at the disposal of the whole people. Land should be used only by those who cultivate it"[35] Otherwise the issues peasants felt most strongly about were reforming the inequitable tax system and introducing universal free primary education, for, as a Kursk village assembly put it, "One of the main reasons we have no rights is our ignorance and lack of education."[36]

Peasants were less concerned than workers about civil rights or the empire's political structure. However, when they did express opinions on the subject—perhaps prompted by a local schoolmaster—they were similar to those of the Gapon petition. Overall, what they were demanding was that the 1861 emancipation be completed, that they be given all the land they cultivated, and be granted full citizenship on the same terms as the rest of the population.

When they felt they were not being listened to, peasants tried other strategies. One serious attempt was made to organize them above the level of the volost: that was the creation of the All-Russian Peasant Union, which held two congresses, in July and November 1905. The Socialist Revolutionary Party played a leading role in its creation, and some professional people attended its congresses. Its debates and resolutions reflected the spirit of the village petitions quite closely, though the second congress went further by calling for direct political action through a national strike and a boycott of the landowners.

Thereafter the Peasant Union suddenly fell apart, for reasons which are not wholly clear. All peasant associations above volost level were fragile, and the nonpeasant organizers had other concerns by the end of 1905. Moreover, the regime treated it as an illegal organization and arrested its members. Perhaps in any case the peasants were now putting their hopes in the upcoming elections to the First Duma.[37]

They were also trying out more forceful tactics. They organized rent strikes, felled the landlord's timber, and cut his hay. Increasingly they also stole his property, making for estate outbuildings with their carts, breaking open the padlocks, and loading grain onto their carts to trundle back home. By summertime, when another poor harvest seemed likely, they were going further, driving the landlord out and making sure he would find it difficult to return by setting fire to the manor house. Two waves of arson began in Saratov guberniia in the east and Chernigov guberniia in the west; they engulfed much of the central black-earth region, where, as we have seen, peasants were most poverty-stricken and short of land. The decision to burn the manor was usually taken in the village assembly and implemented immediately. Every householder was expected to take part in the action: "joint responsibility" was the rule in defying the regime as much as in obeying it. Over much of the affected area the night sky was red with the glow of flaming buildings: people called the spectacle the "red cockerel." Often its appearance in a neighboring village prompted the decision to burn. Nearly 3,000 manor houses, some 15 percent of the total, were destroyed during 1905–06. In addition, there was a good deal of vandalism as peasants ransacked libraries, plundering works of art and antiques which had adorned the "nests of the gentlefolk." They were destroying a milieu which they had always regarded as belonging to alien occupiers.[38]

On the other hand, they tried, not always successfully, to preserve some order in relations among themselves during the seizure of land and goods. After all, it was more important than it had ever been that they should not fight each other during this time of crisis. In Saratov guberniia, for example, the liquor shops were closed during the period of decisive action, and grain, cattle, and produce were redistributed according to strict rules. All the same, peasants often looted indiscriminately or drank themselves into a stupor, simplifying the authorities' task in dealing with them.[39]

The end of the peasant rebellion came with the return of the regime to full effectiveness during 1906–07. Once the army had been repatriated from the Far East and could be deployed in force for internal security, punitive expeditions were sent to offending villages to arrest ringleaders or, where none could be identified, to flog all the men.[40] Once again, law and order was restored through the demonstrative exercise of authority rather than through the integration of peasants into civic institutions.

The revolution of 1905–1907 demonstrated that every segment of Russian society had serious grievances which it was capable of articulating and acting on if the regime showed weakness. But it also showed that those segments could not work together or create common institutions, and that none had a vision capable of uniting the oppositional movement over the boundaries of class and ethnos, even though workers and peasants had similar aspirations. By dividing them and mobilizing its full coercive apparatus, the regime was able to overcome them.

Not, however, to restore itself in full. The gesture which had been necessary to divide the opposition, the October Manifesto, was rich in consequences, for it meant that the regime was committed to sharing power, at least in appearance, with a legislative assembly elected by all classes and most ethnic groups in the empire.

THE AMBIGUOUS CONSTITUTIONAL MONARCHY

If 1861 began the task of introducing civic institutions, then the October Manifesto renewed it. However, the new round of reforms proved to be full of contradictions, not least because of the unfinished business inherited from the first round.

Nominally an autocracy, under the "truncated Speranskii" system, the government of Russia was in fact a constellation of competing networks of personal power, with the imperial court at its center, and the ministries, the governorships, and the nobles' associations as principal arteries. The Ministry of the Interior, which controlled the provincial governors, the ordinary police, and the security police, was much the most powerful single fiefdom, and there was a tendency for it to dominate the government unless there was a strong personality among the other ministers. Sometimes there was, as when Vitte was minister of finance, and, apart from the Ministry of Finance, the Ministry of State Domains, the Ministry of the Court, and the War and Naval Ministries also had considerable wealth, coercive force, or patronage at their command.

Before 1905 the only person who could adjudicate among these powerful dominions and coordinate their activities was the emperor himself. To some extent nineteenth-century emperors had succeeded in performing these tasks, but much depended on their individual personalities. Nicholas II was poorly suited to the task: he was more interested in family gatherings than in affairs of state, as his remarkably tedious diary bears witness. Even court social occasions bored him stiff, and he curtailed them as far as he could. He aspired instead to a direct relation with the mass of loyal and true-believing Russian people, to a kind of "people's monarchy." By character he was usually yielding and hesitant, liable to agree with the last adviser he had spoken to, though he was also capable of egregious stubbornness once he had decided on a policy or a personnel appointment. He did not have the executive or secretarial staff to cope with the huge weight of work that descended on his shoulders each morning. The most able and conscientious of monarchs would not have been able to cope with all his ceremonial and substantive tasks—and Nicholas was far from being such a model ruler.[41]

373

As a result government policy became an arena for conflicting interests to jostle with one another, each working through a sympathetic minister or courtier and competing for the ear of the tsar. As A. A. Polovtsev, a member of the State Council, commented to Alexander III, "Formerly the throne was surrounded by a hereditary aristocracy, which could tell the truth to the monarchy, if not in the course of official business, then in everyday social intercourse and during entertainments. Now the aristocracy has been destroyed, and high society itself scarcely exists any more. The emperor is accessible only to servile bureaucrats who see in him a means to the achievement of their own egotistical goals."[42]

The situation in local government was equally unsatisfactory. The key figure in the guberniia was the governor, who was both the tsar's representative and the local agent of the Ministry of the Interior. He ran the local affairs of his own ministry, including the police, but also had the right to interfere in the work of other ministries, and chaired all the committees which coordinated their activities.[43]

At the next level down, in the uezd, an analogous position was occupied by the marshal of the nobility (predvoditel dvorianstva). He was an entirely different political species. Responsible for coordinating all the ministries' activities, he was also chairman of the uezd zemstvo assembly. Elected by the members of the local nobles' association, he was unpaid, in spite of the considerable range of responsibilities he had to shoulder, and he had no administrative staff to assist him. Much depended on the competence, energy, and conscientiousness of each individual holder of the office.

Below that level was a ministerial appointee, the land commandant (zemskii nachalnik), responsible for the affairs of several volosti. He was appointed from among the local gentry and, like the district commissioner in British India, had virtually unlimited authority over the peasant institutions in his area: he could veto their decisions, countermand their personnel appointments, and reverse the verdicts of their courts. There was little in practice that peasants could do if he exceeded his powers. As one land commandant remarked in his memoirs, "In his bailiwick, the land commandant is *everything*." He was the lowest rung in the ladder of personal power.[44]

At guberniia and uezd levels there were also, as we have seen, elected local government assemblies, the zemstvos. Their relationship to all the above offices was ill-defined, and the delineation of their responsibilities imperfect. Above all the zemstvos had no floor and no ceiling: they did not answer to any government office, nor did they have any jurisdiction over the volosti.

All these various institutions had grown up piecemeal, to deal with specific problems at specific times, but they had never been welded together into a system. Hence finding the right person, whether in a governor's office, a ministry, or at court, remained the key to getting things done. Only personal patronage could cut through the confusion of overlapping authorities. The memoirs of ministers and public figures at this time are full of accounts of the resulting intrigues.[45]

The October Manifesto introduced a new dimension of confusion. The Fundamental Laws of 1906 described the emperor as "autocrat" but omitted the adjective "unlimited," which had previously accompanied the term. The population was promised civil rights; the new representative assembly, the State Duma, was given substantive influence on the making of laws, including the right to veto them, as well as the right to monitor the activities of the government and its officials.

On the other hand, the emperor retained considerable powers. He nominated half the members of the legislature's upper chamber, the State Council. He still appointed the government, and he had the right to dissolve the Duma and State Council. He could also issue emergency decrees if the Duma or State Council was not in session, though he had to submit them for the deputies' approval when they reconvened.

Much of the population, moreover, still lived under emergency provisions dating from 1881, which enabled the authorities to fine, exile, or imprison individuals without a court decision, to suspend or close newspapers and journals, prohibit meetings and demonstrations, and in other ways to obstruct political life and the exercise of civil rights.[46] After the orgy of terror against officials which swept the country in 1904–1907 it is scarcely surprising that police chiefs, mayors, and governors made ample use of these powers.

Altogether we may say that Russia was at one and the same time an embryonic constitutional monarchy and a police state. Both civil society and the means of suppressing civil society were getting stronger simultaneously.

When the First Duma met in the spring of 1906, it revealed fully the potential for conflict latent in this situation. The socialist parties had boycotted the election; consequently the Kadets had done well, as the most oppositional party taking part, and emerged as the strongest single caucus. Peasants voted for them in large numbers, and also for nonparty left-wing candidates who were in effect standing in for the absent socialists. The Kadets felt bound by their mandate to emphasize the expropriation of landowners in their legislative program. The government, however, set its face against any such solution of the agrarian problem. It insisted on the inviolability of private property—the first time a Russian government had ever taken such a stance. No compromise could be found, and so Nicholas dissolved the Duma after less than three months.

375

At the same time he appointed a new prime minister, Petr Stolypin, who as governor of Saratov had marked himself out by his decisive and courageous lead in suppressing the revolutionary movement. Stolypin had a new and distinctive reform program in mind: he proposed to combine the civic and ethnic strategies which had earlier been pursued separately.

The essence of his strategy was to use the Duma to broaden the "political nation," on the one hand carrying out social reform and on the other giving new ethnic and social groups a degree of shared political responsibility. At the same time, he hoped to coordinate ministerial authority by turning the Council of Ministers into a cabinet, with collective responsibility, and to amalgamate central and local government, right down to the peasant institutions, into a single, unified system. He considered that he was not limiting the monarch's authority, but rather giving that authority a broader social base and a more consistent administrative framework within which to operate.[47]

AGRARIAN REFORMS

In the economic sense, the key to Stolypin's plans was the agrarian reform, promulgated initially under emergency provisions, to get round the Duma, on 9 November 1906. This reversed centuries of state policy and peasant practice by ending the village commune's grip on peasant land. The reform made it possible for households to leave the commune while keeping their land, which became the personal property of the head of household. Any household which demanded the title deeds on its strips of land, or their equivalent in quantity and quality, had to be satisfied by the commune. For the first time, peasant land could belong not to a kinship group or community, but to an individual. Land Settlement Commissions were set up in each guberniia and uezd to assist with the highly complex problems of land surveyance and demarcation which had to accompany the transfer.

The decree of 9 November was framed by other measures intended to help the peasants establish their status as full legal persons. "Joint responsibility" and corporal punishment had been abolished in 1903–04, and redemption payments in 1905. Now peasants were given the right to hold their own passports and to take up any occupation or employment without the permission of the volost elder.[48]

Stolypin's main requirement of the Second Duma, which convened in February 1907, was that it should pass his agrarian reform. When it became clear that, like the First Duma, it would not do so, he dissolved it. Twice pushed aside before properly establishing itself, the Duma seemed supremely irrelevant. However, Stolypin resisted pressure to abolish it altogether or even to reduce it to advisory status. Instead, he changed its electoral law to ensure that wealthier townsmen and Russian landowners would in future dominate the assembly. The electoral law of 3 June 1907 reduced the representation of peasants, less wealthy townspeople and non-Russians. Muslim representation from central Asia was abolished altogether.[49]

Stolypin succeeded in gaining the majority he wanted: the Third Duma was dominated by a solid core of landowners from the heartlands and west of Russia. The largest single bloc belonged to the Union of 17 October (or "Octobrists"), which had broken with the Kadets in 1905–06 over their support of revolutionary terrorism and the compulsory expropriation of land. They were supplemented by a large number of amorphously organized deputies calling themselves vaguely "Rightists."

In some ways, during the relatively short time it was in operation, Stolypin's land reform was quite successful. By 1916 some 2.5 million households (about a fifth of the total) had received title deeds to their land, and a further 1.3 million had gone further and enclosed their strips in a single plot. On the other hand, in the same year 61 percent of households still held their land in communal tenure, and their holdings totaled about 70 percent of allotment land. Those who left the commune tended to be at the extremes of the economic scale: the wealthy, who no longer wished to be tied by communal arrangements, and the poor, who wanted to give up trying to squeeze a living from the soil. Their departure left a solid group of "middle peasants" (as they later became known), and they remained on the whole staunchly loyal to the commune. Besides, the reform proved more successful in the west of Russia, among Ukrainian and Belorussian peasants, where hereditary land tenure was already much more popular, than in Russia, where the reform was most sorely needed.[50]

The commune was turning out, in fact, to be unexpectedly durable. General redistributions of land became more frequent between 1890 and 1910. Even smallholders who withdrew under the Stolypin provisions seldom quit the commune altogether. After all, it had jurisdiction over other things than just land, and the decisions of the village assembly, for example on roads, common land, or access to timber and water, continued to affect even those who had privatized their holdings. Withdrawal often complicated these aspects of village life and engendered bitter conflict. Perhaps for that reason, land settlement commissions increasingly encouraged commune members to privatize their land by joint action rather than individually. The remarkable growth in the number of cooperatives during these years suggests that even commercially minded peasants wanted to be collective rather than individual entrepreneurs.[51]

Stolypin had hoped that the new privatized smallholders would become full citizens and play their part in the establishment of a market economy, and that they would prove to be a reliable base for the monarchy and for the rule of law. In practice, the very peasants he hoped to see as pioneers of the new Russia proved to be the ones most attached to the commune. The progress of his reform suggested that communal institutions were still vigorous in Russia, and that breaking them up meant intensifying polarization and conflict within the village.

OTHER REFORMS

Stolypin's other reforms were intended to integrate *obshchestvennost* into the work of government, to coordinate local and central government in one network, and to end the segregation of peasant institutions. The volost was to become a zemstvo: that is, it would represent all social estates, not just the peasantry. The uezd and guberniia zemstvos were to be introduced in non-Russian areas, were to have a more democratic electoral law, and were to come under closer central control; for example, the uezd marshal of the nobility would be replaced as chairman of the zemstvo by an appointed official. The segregated volost courts were to be abolished, along with the land commandant's tutelage over them, and replaced with normal courts presided over by justices of the peace.

Stolypin also drew up draft legislation to fulfill the promises of the October Manifesto on civil liberties, for example by abolishing the discrimination against Old Believers and by defining what was meant by "inviolability of the person." Other vital proposed measures including the establishment of universal primary education, free of charge, by 1922 and compulsory insurance for workers against sickness, injury, and old age.[52]

Overall, these changes would have meant individual choice replacing joint responsibility, institutions supplanting persons as sources of authority, and ultimately perhaps the rule of law displacing arbitrary power. Such a transformation would of course have ended autocracy, as Nicholas II suspected. On the other hand, it could have strengthened *monarchy*, by giving it consistent institutions and a broader social base. Even looking back on it nearly a century later, one cannot say that a better scheme of government has ever been devised for Russia.

But the reforms fell victim both to personal intrigue and to the bitter ideological conflicts which had emerged among Russia's elites over the pace and nature of reform. The alliance which Stolypin engineered for the agrarian reform did not hold together when it came to other projects. The landowners who had supported the undermining of the commune objected strongly to losing their control of the zemstvos and to the weakening of the land commandant. The expansion of education raised deeply divisive questions about who should finance schools, and what languages and religious beliefs should be taught in them. Only workers' insurance was passed more or less in the form the government envisaged.

Especially painful to Stolypin was the blocking in 1911 of his bill to introduce zemstvos in the western provinces. This was a key measure for him, as it embodied some of his most cherished principles: democratization of local government, its integration into central government, and the Russification of a region which had been dominated by the Poles. To achieve all these aims together, he devised an extremely complicated electoral system, which made his bill vulnerable to attack. The powerful landowning bloc in the State Council suspected (rightly) that it represented a trial run for the democratization of the zemstvo elsewhere in Russia. But the decisive reason for its defeat was that Nicholas II authorized his tame members of the State Council to vote against it. Their principal motive was not so much the nature of the bill as their desire to cut Stolypin down to size, to reduce the grip of the Duma and the united Council of Ministers and restore that of the court and the autocrat.[53]

Stolypin persuaded the tsar—as ever, inconstant—to suspend both chambers for three days, so that he could pass his law under article 87, while they were "not in session." This was such a flagrant abuse of the emergency provisions that Stolypin lost most of his allies in the Duma, and he remained thereafter an isolated figure, shorn of reliable support from any quarter, even before he was assassinated in mysterious circumstances in September 1911. His fate suggested that a determined reformer was bound to create so many enemies as to make his own position untenable.

NICHOLAS II'S VISION

Like Stolypin, Nicholas realized that a dangerous gap had opened up between the mass of the population and the institutions of the empire. But his ideas about bridging it were entirely different from Stolypin's. His upbringing at court and in the Guards, under the guidance of the Orthodox Church, led him to believe that the direct link between monarch and people could be restored by reviving the customs of pre-Petrine times. He called his long-awaited heir Aleksei, after the greatest tsar of the seventeenth century, and he endeavored throughout his reign to use ceremony, and particularly religious ceremony, to recreate a sense of unity with his people. Whereas Alexander II had wanted to be a monarch in touch with the *zemlia*, with local elites, Nicholas aimed at direct contact with the *narod*, the people themselves.

In 1903, for instance, Nicholas initiated the canonization of St. Serafim of Sarov, a popular *starets* of the early nineteenth century. He insisted on a rapid procedure, against the advice of the Holy Synod, which warned that there had not been time to complete the inquiries necessary before someone could be pronounced a saint. Nicholas was too insensitive to see that this was a question the church should decide in its own way. When the ceremony took place in Tambov, it was certainly solemn and magnificent enough to satisfy many of the participants, including Nicholas himself. But the arrangements were poorly handled, so that many pilgrims from among the ordinary people were excluded, while nobles and courtiers arriving in luxurious carriages gained access. Altogether, for all its reassuring splendor, the process underlined both the subjugation of the church and the depth of social divisions.[54]

In the later years of his reign, the direct religious link to ordinary Russians was embodied for Nicholas in the person of Grigorii Rasputin, a Siberian peasant who had gained a reputation as a holy man. When his advisers expressed doubts about Rasputin's personality, Nicholas replied, "He is just a good, simple-minded, religious Russian. When in trouble or assailed by doubts, I like to have a talk with him, and invariably feel at peace with myself afterward."[55] Rasputin won the confidence of the imperial couple by his capacity to stanch the bleeding of the tsarevich, who suffered from hemophilia. In time he become one of the closest confidants to both of them, and abused his position to advance his own interests in money, power, and sexual conquest. His unpunished escapades offered an egregious example of personal protection corroding moral and legal norms, the more offensive because of the higher standards of openness and legality prevailing after 1905.

380

Nicholas regarded the Duma and State Council, together with the Council of Ministers and the growing and increasingly complex bureaucracy, as an obstacle to his communion with "holy Rus." In a sense he was right, since they were beginning (though only beginning) to embody the nation and the state as entities separate from the person of the monarch. That is why he incited members of the State Council to undermine Stolypin. For similar reasons he supported the Union of Russian People.[56]

In the end, Nicholas was the victim of processes much larger than himself. The prestige of the monarchy had begun to decline in the wake of the Crimean War, and that decline had deepened with further defeat by Japan in 1904–05 and then the loss of Poland in 1915. Nicholas' own reputation suffered further from the Bloody Sunday massacre. His association with Rasputin and with the rabble-rousing "Black Hundreds" completed the process of discrediting him. By 1914 urbanization, mass education, and revolutionary upheaval had done much to weaken the popular devotion to the distant and supposedly benevolent "little father," while the Duma had not been able to do much to integrate the mass of the people into a more institutionalized and civic style of politics.[57]

REFORM OF THE ORTHODOX CHURCH

By the early twentieth century it was widely if not universally agreed among the higher clergy that the church was failing to realize its potential because of the way in which it was run. When in April 1905 the tsar issued a manifesto promising religious tolerance, and thereby ended the Orthodox Church's privileged position among the faiths of the empire, he brought to a head the accumulating dissatisfaction. Since leaving Orthodoxy and converting to another faith was now officially permitted, it became much more urgent for the church to reform itself and renew its own spiritual health.

During the spring of 1905 all bishops were asked to give their views on the condition of the church. It transpired that almost none of them were satisfied with it. Many of them felt that the authority of the Holy Synod was uncanonical, since it violated the principle of *sobornost* and subjugated the spiritual to the secular power: one respondent denounced it as "Protestant Caesaropapism." Most held that the overprocuracy should be abolished, that the church should be governed by an elected council *(pomestnyi sobor)*, and that the synod should become merely its executive.

Reformers disagreed, however, over how the church should be run thereafter. Broadly speaking, they split into two camps: "episcopal authoritarians," who wanted the bishops, headed by a patriarch, to run the church; and "parish-centered liberals," who thought parish congregations should have the decisive say, through their elected representatives on the governing council.[58]

No one disagreed on the need to revive the parish, as a way of restoring *sobornost* from below. Many thought that its current ineffectiveness opened the way to the preaching of atheist socialism. The parish, they felt, should be granted the status of a juridical person, with the right to acquire its own property, manage its own finances, run its own schools, organize charitable work, and perhaps provide cheap credit for peasants and artisans. Some reformers also believed that parish assemblies should elect their own priests.[59]

Konstantin Pobedonostsev was opposed to all these ideas, as he had been earlier to that of a zemskii sobor. In October 1905, however, he was replaced by Aleksandr Obolenskii, who was determined to call a council and launch reform. To prepare the way, he convened a Pre-Conciliar Commission, consisting mostly of bishops and theologians, to sift through the various ideas for reform and draw up proposals for the anticipated council. The commission sat for several months in 1906 and recommended that the patriarchate should be restored and that parishes should become self-governing, should at least influence the choice of their own priests, and should have the right to manage their own funds.[60]

The stage seemed set for the most important reform in the Orthodox Church for two centuries. However, at the last moment, with the Pre-Conciliar Commission's report before him, Nicholas II decided against convening a council. After the experience of the first two Dumas, he probably did not want to create yet another forum for hostile opinions, nor did he relish the prospect of a patriarch, who might rival his own authority and detract from his religious standing. In this attitude he was supported by Stolypin.[61]

The unreformed debility of the Orthodox Church was the most fateful of the defects of late tsarist Russia. The tsars, after all, claimed to rule by divine right—Nicholas II most fervently of all. Yet they persistently humiliated and impoverished the church which should have underpinned that claim. The peasants' Orthodox belief was strong, and it was a vital part of their sense of community, but it was primitive and inflexible. The church in its unreformed state was unable to build bridges for them from low to high culture to respond adequately to the challenges posed by increasing social mobility and mass literacy.[62]

Structurally too the church, without a representative forum for clergy and laity, remained vulnerable to the intrigues of someone like the debased *starets* Rasputin. The spectacle of a debauched and semiliterate sectarian picking candidates for the Holy Synod did as much as anything else in the final years of empire to discredit the monarchy.

CIVIL SOCIETY

While the state was reforming fitfully and the church was failing to reform, society was changing very fast. The long-term consequences of Alexander II's reforms were bearing fruit. Russia was rapidly becoming a more urbanized, educated, and diverse country, and the 1905–06 political reforms meant that the various social and ethnic groups were much better able to express themselves.

One index of this evolution was the growth of the press. Between 1900 and 1914 the number of periodicals trebled, and the number of newspapers grew tenfold. Most of the expansion came after 1905 as a result of the relaxation of censorship: preliminary censorship was dropped altogether, though the authorities maintained the right to fine, suspend, and close publications which "published false information," "fostered disorder," or "provoked the population's hostility to officials, soldiers or government institutions."[63] The legalization of political and professional organizations enabled doctors, teachers, and lawyers to issue their own journals and discuss professional concerns in them frankly, even when they had political implications. Nor did the new publications reach only educated strata. Newspapers were appearing in the large cities aimed specifically at workers and lower-level employees: *Gazeta kopeika* (The Penny Paper), for example, had a circulation of 250,000 within two years of its launch.[64]

The existence of the Duma greatly simplified the task of publicity-hungry editors: they could report any words spoken during a session of the house, no matter how subversive. In 1912, for example, when the Octobrist newspaper *Golos Moskvy* (Voice of Moscow) published a letter alleging that Rasputin was a member of a discreditable religious sect, the day's issue was confiscated. But Guchkov, the Octobrist leader, evaded the prohibition by submitting an interpellation in the Duma containing the entire text of the letter, which thus became publishable copy for every newspaper in the country.[65]

After 1905, in fact, Russia abruptly became part of the modern media world, with all its dilemmas over sensationalism, responsibility, and freedom of speech. Newspapers delighted in reporting crime, violence, and scandal, and there was plenty of it to entertain readers with. Terrorism, the remarkable career of Azef, the maverick activities of Rasputin became daily press fodder. All this helped to discredit the authorities, including—perhaps especially—the emperor himself. On the other hand the attention given to cultural and intellectual matters, the reporting from abroad and from non-Russian areas, helped to give Russians a sense of their own identity and place in the world, in a sense no longer defined exclusively by tsar and Orthodox Church.[66]

383

Workers did not share fully in the flowering of civil society. In 1905–06 they were granted the right to form trade unions and to strike over economic matters. For a short time unions became the focus of working-class life, setting up mutual assistance funds, running libraries and tearooms, and issuing reports and newssheets. During the First and Second Dumas, worker deputies would address meetings organized by the unions to report on what the legislature was doing.[67]

After the coup of 3 June 1907, however, the authorities reimposed a much tighter rein on trade unions. Police kept a closer watch on them and did not hesitate to use emergency regulations to break up meetings and close down union branches. Employers consulted less with them, and membership dwindled from inactivity and discouragement. The unions which survived best were those which had a solid core of socialist activists, usually Mensheviks, though the Bolsheviks took over one or two important unions during 1912–1914.[68]

With the withering of trade unions, labor unrest once again became elemental and disorganized. In 1912 a massacre of workers agitating at the Lena goldfields in Siberia sparked off strikes and demonstrations in many cities. Led by young, skilled, and impatient workers unrestrained by socialist leaders, these protests would flare up, sometimes advance ambitious political aims, and then subside equally abruptly without achieving anything. Everything suggests that workers, especially highly skilled and literate ones, were deeply frustrated and felt they had no other way to express their demands. They received little or no support from any other social class. On the eve of war, in July 1914, there were barricades in industrial districts of St. Petersburg, while the rest of the capital went about its business.[69]

Overall, the authorities' treatment of the workers explains why they felt they had little stake in the existing order. As the workforce at the Old Lessner plant in St. Petersburg declared in September 1915, "We will stand up for our fatherland when we are given complete freedom to form labor organisations, complete freedom of speech and press, freedom to strike, equal rights for all nations of Russia, an eight-hour day, and when the landlords' lands are handed over to the poor peasants."[70]

REASSESSMENT OF THE INTELLIGENTSIA TRADITION

The creation of the Duma provided the background for a reevaluation of Russia's status as a nation and of the intelligentsia as the self-appointed guardians of her nationhood. The failure of the 1905 revolution had provoked a questioning of the assumption that the interests of intelligentsia and people were necessarily identical in the common struggle against the autocracy. The intelligentsia, as professional people, could not exist without education and some measure of property, and it was incongruous for them to be supporting political movements which assigned a low value to culture and law. This was the central charge leveled in a volume of essays, *Vekhi* (Landmarks), published in 1909, which accused the intelligentsia of being just as responsible as the regime for the political bankruptcy of post-1905 Russia.

The economist Sergei Bulgakov, a former Marxist and dissident Kadet, argued that the intelligentsia had concentrated its entire spiritual life in service to the people, idealizing the *narod*. For the intelligentsia, science, conceived in a determinist spirit, had become a faith, and the *narod* an idol, with the result that its members no longer believed in individual freedom or in the autonomous value of art, open-minded science, truth, or goodness. In their eyes truth and goodness were what served the people; art and science had value only if they raised the awareness of the people or relieved their poverty. The result, Bulgakov asserted, was that the intelligentsia worshipped human beings—*chelovekobozhestvo*—and had ceased to believe in God.[71] He, like many other Orthodox believers, held that it was essential to restore true *sobornost* to the church and to set it free from the state, as a precondition of its playing a full role in a national revival.

The leading spirit of *Vekhi* was Petr Struve, the economist who had written the Social Democrats' first program and then become a founder of the Union of Liberation and of the Kadet Party. Now he was disillusioned again, convinced that the Kadets had in effect become collaborators in the revolutionaries' attempt to destroy the Russian state. Statehood and nationhood were, he argued, no less important to Russia than to any other European people, and they required that educated people recognize the autonomous value of law and order, property and culture; both the Russian forms of socialism, Marxism and populism, preached the destruction of the state, and Marxism also aimed to dissolve the nation in an international proletariat. Impressed by the example of Germany under Bismarck, Struve preached that "The national idea of contemporary Russia is reconciliation between the authorities and the people, which is awakening to its own identity . . . State and nation must organically coalesce."[72]

Struve believed that Russian state and nation would cooperate most readily by leading the struggle of the Slavic and Orthodox peoples of the Balkans against the Ottoman and Habsburg Empires. He became the most articulate proponent of the renewed Pan-Slavism of 1908–1914, the accepted wisdom of the center-right majority in the Duma.

The message of *Vekhi* found ready listeners among the commercial and industrial bourgeoisie, who traditionally relied on a strong state, and had an obvious interest in the high valuation of property rights and of law and order. They felt that they had for too long been sidelined by the landed nobility as the leading social estate and that it was high time they claimed their heritage. In 1910 two leading Moscow commercial families, the Riabu-shinskie and the Konovalovy, founded a new political party, the Progressists, with its own newspaper, to speak for the "Lopakhins who buy up cherry orchards." The new party called for an unambiguous constitutional monar-chy, with guarantees against arbitrary violations of law or property, and a democratic educational system. In foreign policy it was outspokenly Pan-Slav.[73]

By 1914, then, *obshchestvennost* was already quite well developed and was generating its own political parties and other civic associations. But it was embedded in a society many of whose levers were still in the hands of per-sonal powerbrokers, from the tsar downward. Besides, in the increasingly unstable European great-power constellation, most of its members favored a foreign policy which risked plunging Russia into a major war.

10

WAR AND REVOLUTION

After 1906 the idea of achieving national unity through solidarity with Slavs in the Balkans had become the new orthodoxy in the broad central band of Duma politics. Actually, though, it was an extremely dangerous policy for Russia to pursue. The example of German unification was seductive, but misleading. Russia was a very different country. The multiethnic nature of the Russian Empire, as well as the continuing segregation of most peasant communities, made it far more difficult to build nationhood on the German model. The attempt to do so propelled Russia into a war in which her empire was nearly destroyed.

Russian statesmen were well aware of the dangers. But the post-1905 changes in the empire's political structure made a cautious foreign policy far more difficult to pursue. Though foreign affairs were still the prerogative of the emperor, in practice he now had to conduct them in consultation with the Council of Ministers, who in turn were exposed to the glare of comment from an uninhibited press and from Duma politicians, some of whom made them a specialty. A. P. Izvolskii as foreign minister made a point of cultivating Duma deputies, believing that their support was a vital factor in strengthening the Russian government's image abroad, especially with her detente partners, Britain and France, and in avoiding uncoordinated court intrigue of the kind which had led to the Japanese fiasco. The deputies whom he relied for public support of his policy were virtually all convinced Pan-Slavs.

To satisfy them Izvolskii was anxious to appear enterprising in the Balkans, while in fact pursuing a cautious policy because he knew Russia's military and financial condition was too weak to risk a major war. He wanted to achieve a coup by persuading Austria to agree to a revision of the 1871 Straits Convention so that Russia could send her fleet through the Straits if she was at war and Turkey was not. In return Austria was to be allowed to annex the provinces of Bosnia and Herzegovina, which had been under her nominal suzerainty since the Treaty of Berlin.

In the event Austria announced the annexation before there was any international agreement on the Straits. Izvolskii did not get the backing he had hoped for in London, and was faced with the choice of capitulating to Austria or encouraging Serbia to resist the annexation, at the risk of precipitating a general European war. The Council of Ministers under Stolypin (which had not been kept informed of Izvolskii's dealings) decided that Russia could not face a major war, and that capitulation was the only option. Serbia was even advised to submit to a peremptory Austrian demand that she undertake publicly "for the future to fulfill her obligations as a good neighbor toward the monarchy." This was a humiliating climb-down: the press lampooned it as a "diplomatic Tsushima." In government and public opinion the view now became widespread that Austria, backed by Germany, was preparing to destroy Serbia and ultimately probably the Ottoman Empire too in order to dominate the Balkans herelf.[1]

If this were the case, then even many statesmen opposed to the Pan-Slavs felt Russia could not sit idly by without forfeiting any claim to be considered a European great power. Turbulence in the Balkans tested her influence and resolve in 1912–13: the Balkan states formed a successful military alliance, which drove the Ottoman Empire from all but the tiniest foothold in Europe. The triumphant allies then fell out with one another over the resultant re-arrangement of boundaries. After Stolypin's assassination governmental unity had become more fragile. Some individual Russian diplomats had encouraged the anti-Turkish alliance more positively than N. D. Sazonov, the new foreign minister, had sanctioned, and they had the support of public demonstrations urging the government not to leave brother Slavs "in the lurch." These Pan-Slavs were enraged when Russia bowed to international pressure and acquiesced in the creation of the state of Albania, which denied Serbia a direct outlet to the Adriatic Sea.[2]

This series of diplomatic setbacks was amplified by the press and was uppermost in ministers' minds when the Austrian ultimatum of July 1914 was

delivered to Serbia following the assassination of the Archduke Franz Ferdinand. Two considerations now moved them: the desire to satisfy public opinion as articulated in the Duma and the press, and the need to stand up for
allies this time in order not to lose all credibility in the eyes of other powers.
As Minister of Agriculture A. V. Krivoshein said at a vital meeting of the
Council of Ministers, "Public and parliamentary opinion would fail to understand why, at a critical moment involving Russia's vital interests, the Imperial Government was reluctant to act boldly . . . All factors tended to prove
that the most judicious policy Russia could follow in present circumstances
was to return to a firmer and more energetic attitude towards the unreasonable claims of the Central European powers."[3]

Russia's entry into the First World War thus reflected the influence both
of a new factor, articulate public opinion, and an old one, the need to retain
great-power status in Europe. As a result, the country began the war in an
unwonted mood of national unity, at least within *obshchestvennost*, but it
was soon to become apparent that the long-term foundation of that unity
had not been secured.

THE FIRST WORLD WAR

The new mood of unity gave one last chance to bring regime, *obshchestvennost*, and the mass of the people closer together. Huge crowds appeared in
the streets of St. Petersburg to cheer the tsar and his family. The Duma voted
war credits and then agreed to indefinite prorogation on the grounds that
there were more important jobs to do than debate politics: for the moment
it did not even seem crucial to monitor the performance of the government.
Mobilization on the whole went smoothly and by December had inducted
no fewer than 6 million men into the army. Zemstvos and municipalities
offered to take over the provision of medical care and the evacuation of the
sick and wounded from the front.

Propaganda and voluntary activity reflected the newfound patriotism.
Actors and musicians went to the front to entertain the troops. Society ladies
collected money or volunteered to become nurses. Newspapers and post-
cards, as well as variety shows and nightclub routines, glorified Cossacks and
military heroes from the Russian past, as well as the devotion of nurses tending wounded soldiers in improvised field hospitals. Interestingly, the tsar
and the Orthodox Church occupied a relatively modest (and declining) place
in this propaganda, a feature which suggests that ordinary Russians were

beginning to find them a less convincing focus for loyalty than images of ordinary people and soldiers.[4]

By the spring of 1915 Russian diplomats had reached agreement with the British and French governments that after the war Constantinople and most of the Straits would become Russian territory. It began to seem possible that the ultimate goal of the Pan-Slavs, and a long-term aspiration of Russian diplomacy for centuries, might be achieved with full support from European powers and from public opinion.[5]

389

However, by the time the finishing touches were being put on the agreement, much of the public solidarity had already evaporated as a result of military defeat, the perceived inequity of war burdens, and apparent official incompetence. At the very outset the Russian army had launched an offensive into East Prussia, in keeping with its obligations under the Franco-Russian alliance. Not yet fully mobilized, beset by communications problems and poor command, it was comprehensively defeated by the Germans at Tannenberg, lost more than 100,000 prisoners, and retreated again.

In the spring of 1915 the Germans followed up their success by breaking through the Russian front at Gorlice and advancing into Poland. At this stage failure to plan for a long war meant that shortages of weapons and ammunition were becoming critical. Sometimes soldiers were sent to the front without rifles and had to wait till a comrade was killed before acquiring one. By September the Russians had had to abandon Warsaw, Vilna, and the whole "Vistula region," that is, Poland.

During the munitions crisis the zemstvos and municipalities formed a single union, Zemgor, under the chairmanship of a widely respected non-party liberal from the Tula zemstvo, Prince Georgii Lvov.[6] Zemgor offered to assist the recruitment of labor and the placing of orders for military supplies. It was set up by Moscow industrialists who wanted to shake the grip their St. Petersburg counterparts and the state ordnance factories had hitherto exercised on military production. The Moscow businessman Pavel Riabushinskii also played a leading role in the establishment of War Industry Committees to oversee the conversion of factories for military purposes. The real importance of these committees was that they represented all parties involved in the economy: the government, Zemgor, employers, and workers—the first time workers had had their own elected delegates in any official body other than the Duma.[7]

There has been much debate about the economic effectiveness of these organizations, but in the political sense they were extremely significant, for they represented the principal participants in the war effort. If they had been complemented by a government prepared to cooperate with them on a long-term basis, then civic patriotism would have had institutional embodiment at the center. In August 1915 the center parties in Duma and State Council formed a so-called Progressive Bloc, which called for the formation of a "government enjoying public confidence," including deputies from the legislature. The bloc published a reform program which recapitulated many of Stolypin's original aims: full citizenship for peasants, an end to all discrimination on ethnic or religious grounds (including against Jews), an amnesty for political prisoners, and a guarantee of workers' rights, including the full legalization of trade unions. Some ministers supported the program, and serious negotiations proceeded over the formation of a "government of public confidence."[8]

Nicholas II, however, decided otherwise. His notion of patriotism and social solidarity was entirely noncivic, based on monarchical authority and the appeal of the Orthodox Church, and he put it into practice at this juncture by personally taking command of the army. He adjourned the Duma, dismissed the ministers who had supported the Progressive Bloc, and took himself off to Stavka (military headquarters at Mogilev).

As it turned out, the army performed better under his command in 1916 than it had done before. General Brusilov's successful offensive in the Carpathians aroused hopes that Russia might take Galicia, "lost" centuries before, by military conquest. It is unlikely, though, that this success had much to do with the tsar's leadership qualities. General Alekseev, a conscientious chief of staff, directed operations, and nearly had a nervous breakdown dealing with the querulous monarch breathing down his neck. It is quite certain, however, that Nicholas' military command was disastrous for politics. He was unable to sustain even the inadequate coordinating role he had previously played, and the government, far from enjoying public confidence, became the plaything of court intrigues. Ministerial appointments were usually short-lived, and malicious commentators whispered of "ministerial leap-frog."

It matters little whether the empress and Rasputin actually determined those appointments: the point is that the public, nourished by innuendo in the press, believed it and interpreted their role in the light of the new patriotism. It had never mattered before that the empress (or any previous consort) was German: now it became all-important. "That German woman" and Rasputin were suspected of heading a court faction trying to conclude a separate and treacherous peace with Germany, though there was no serious evidence that such was the case. In December 1916 Rasputin was murdered by an incongruous conspiratorial group of grand dukes and Duma politicians, who had little in common with one another save their desire to rescue the monarchy from the monarch.

They failed. The assassination changed nothing. In a widely reported session of the Duma in November 1916 the normally highly respected leader of the Kadets, Pavel Miliukov, had made a whole series of grave accusations against the government, capping each one with the question "Is this incompetence or is it treason?" He concluded: "Does it matter, practically speaking, whether we are dealing with incompetence or with treason? . . . The government persists in claiming that organizing the country means organizing a revolution and deliberately prefers chaos and disorganization."[9] The hint of treason was completely groundless, but here Miliukov hit the nail on the head. Russia had reached the point where the old myths of autocracy could no longer hold society together, as they had done for centuries.

THE REVOLUTION OF 1917

The end of the old regime had been long predicted, yet it came very suddenly, when few people were expecting it. The discrediting of the monarchy was compounded by military incompetence, inflation, profiteering, low wages, and food shortages, which made life very difficult for ordinary townsfolk, especially women. In January 1917 the police arrested the worker members of the War Industry Committee, suspecting them of subversive activity, and thereby removed from the scene the only spokesmen able to put forward the workers' demands legitimately.

Toward the end of February 1917 rumors of imminent food shortages reached Petrograd (as the capital city had been renamed in 1914). Anxious queues of women outside the shops began to merge with demonstrations of resentful workers, some of them straight from the Putilov Works, where strikes had broken out. The movement swelled into a general strike, and placards appeared calling for an end to the war and the fall of the autocracy. Cossacks sent out to restrain the crowds did their job halfheartedly, then not at all. The insurgents stormed the arsenals and set fire to the security police headquarters.

Nicholas, cut off from the capital at Stavka and beset by contradictory reports, at first dissolved the Duma and set about imposing military rule. But he was soon persuaded that this course was hopeless, and decided, on the advice of his generals, to abdicate in order to restore internal peace for the sake of the war effort. The abdication was initially to have been in favor of his brother, Grand Duke Mikhail, but the latter declined the throne when he saw how vehement were the antimonarchist feelings of the masses in Petrograd. The imperial double eagle was torn down from public buildings, and in the Duma chamber in the Tauride Palace Repin's portrait of Nicholas II was ripped from the wall.

Unexpectedly, then, the Russian people was not only without a monarch but had overthrown monarchy as such. The Duma obeyed the tsar's order to dissolve, but its leaders set up a Provisional Government to carry out urgent reforms and keep order till Russia's future constitution might be decided by a Constituent Assembly, elected by all the adult male population. The provisional prime minister was Prince Georgii Lvov, and most of the government's members were Kadets.

In that way, by early March 1917, Russia was finally plunged into the long-awaited revolution. It turned out to be far more destructive than anyone had foreseen. In 1905–1907 the regime had managed to survive and to restore some kind of law and order, but in 1917, under the pressure of a great international war, a mere "provisional" government could not do so. The army which had defended its predecessor now disintegrated into unruly bands of armed men, intent either on seizing whatever they could or on returning to their villages. The traditional social bonds, and with them any sense of shared morality, this time fell apart completely, and Russia's peoples were delivered up to the brutality of whatever men happened to hold power, usually temporarily, in their locality. The "hooliganism" which had worried responsible observers for decades now operated without restraint.

The weakness of the old regime was not the only difference from 1905, however. In 1917 there was a political party and a leader well enough organized to take power and use it to promote their own vision of how society should be ordered. Lenin had learned much from the failure of the socialists in 1905. Above all, he knew now that peasants were a crucial part of the revolution. As a Marxist, he had been reluctant to accept this, but the evidence of land seizures and manor-house burnings had been overwhelming. He took to speaking of the "revolutionary democratic dictatorship of the proletariat and the peasantry." He had also learned that neither he nor his party could control everything, that he must allow the organizations of workers, peasants, and soldiers to do their own work in clearing away the old system. That was the motive behind his conversion to "All Power to the Soviets!" which astonished many of his own supporters when he announced it in April 1917.

In this conversion to mass spontaneity the Bolsheviks differed from the political parties which dominated politics after the fall of the monarchy, and which formed the Provisional Government. They, the Kadets, Menshe-viks, and Socialist Revolutionaries, had been on the left, even the extreme left, of tsarist politics: none of them had been accepted as fully legal. Now, however, unexpectedly catapulted to power, they took on the responsibility of holding Russia together, defending it against German invasion, curbing would-be secessionists, and preventing the collapse of civilization around them. They became, in fact, the heirs of empire and the guarantors of bour-geois society, a role none of them could have foreseen even a few months previously.

It was in the nature of Russian society that, when the monarchy fell, it was replaced not by one successor regime, but by two. The Provisional Gov-ernment drew its members mostly from the Duma and from the wartime voluntary associations, from *obshchestvennost,* and it wanted Russia to be-come a parliamentary democracy. From the very outset it was shadowed by the soviets, repositories of the workers' dreams since the heady days of 1905, and proponents of the ideal of Russia as a federation of egalitarian com-munes. As soon as the end of the monarchy seemed imminent, workers and soldiers carried out hasty elections in their factories and regiments, and sent delegates to the Tauride Palace. What they were to do there was not obvious. None of them thought they should try to run the country. On the other hand, they were an unmistakable token that the opinions of the *narod* could no longer be ignored. Soon soviets were being set up in all towns of any size, and often in villages too.

For all that it was "provisional," the new government did have an agenda of its own, which was to repudiate the heritage of the old regime. It dis-solved the tsarist security police, and along with it the ordinary police, the land captains, and every official who had exercised coercive power before February. At the same time the Provisional Government announced that Russian citizens would enjoy the full range of civil rights, while the non-Russian nationalities would be able to decide how to rule themselves. Russia was to become, as even Lenin acknowledged, "the freest country in the world."[10]

Lvov realized that his regime needed the support of the soviets, and one of his first steps was to reach an understanding with them. Its cardinal ele-ment was an agreement to continue the war on a new basis, as a defensive operation until a general peace could be negotiated "without annexations or indemnities." Both Prince Lvov and Aleksandr Kerenskii, who replaced him as prime minister in July, hoped that this agreement might adumbrate a new style of Russian patriotism, national and postimperial, which would unite *obshchestvennost* and *narod.* The two, however, proved to be too far apart in outlook and mentality: in defending this new alliance first of all the Kadets, then the Mensheviks and Socialist Revolutionaries alienated themselves from their popular base and split internally, leaving the way open for the Bolsheviks, who took over the aspirations of the *narod*, acknowledging no responsibility for law and order or for empire.

Soldiers and the Army

The breakdown of the fragile bond between *obshchestvennost* and *narod* was foreshadowed from the start, by Order no. 1, issued by the Petrograd Soviet on 1 March. It instructed soldiers to elect committees in units, at company level and above, to take charge of all aspects of military life except actual combat (when the authority of officers continued to be recognized). This fitted the soviets' ideal of working people taking responsibility for the fate of the emerging nation. Order no. 1 transformed the mood of the soldiers, who insisted that now they must have the decisive voice in military affairs. Many of them exceeded the order and actually set about electing their officers. As for the officers themselves, brought up to the unthinking hierarchy of the old army, most found this situation offensive and bewildering, not least because their disciplinary powers were fatally undermined. An officer of the Pavlovskii Regiment reflected ruefully in his diary: "When we talk about the *narod*, we mean the nation; when they talk about it, they mean the democratic lower classes . . . We can find no common language: that is the accursed heritage of the old regime."[11]

The refurbished army functioned after a fashion for much of the spring and summer of 1917. The soldiers' age-old experience of the military artel must have helped their committees to cope with the practical difficulties of assuming responsibility for the units. However, when Kerenskii tried to launch a major offensive on the Austrian front in June, he found that the new mood of the soldiers undermined it from the start. Instead of "going over the top," regimental committees debated whether to obey the command to advance. Some argued that to do so was contrary to the policy of "no annexations." One battalion decided "What's ours we won't yield, but what belongs to others we don't want," and decided to stay put.[12]

Inevitably the offensive soon petered out, leaving officers to deal with a wave of mutiny and desertion. Kerenskii's attempt to weld together *obshchestvennost* and *narod* in a surge of aggressive patriotism had failed. Comparison with the contemporary situation in the French army is illuminating. French soldiers also mutinied in 1917, declaring solidarity with striking workers, expressing concern for families at home, calling for peace without annexations or indemnities, and reaffirming their determination that "les Boches ne passeront pas." Where they differed from Russian soldiers was in their confidence that their status as "citizen-soldiers" was secure, as a result of the existence of a stable republic. They saw France as their country and themselves as part of the nation. When their commanders suspended offensive operations and gave priority to restoring morale and discipline, French *poilus* eventually returned to the front to fight. Russian soldiers, by contrast, were not confident that Kerenskii's "nation" was really theirs too; they identified more with the soviets or with their village communities, and in crisis proved ready to abandon the front and hasten back home.[13]

In Russia the attempt to restore discipline around the concept of the civic nation collapsed and plunged the army into its ultimate crisis. The new commander-in-chief, General Lavr Kornilov, appointed in July, was determined to have the soldiers' committees cut down to size and full military discipline restored, including the death penalty for desertion or insubordination in combat. Kerenskii hesitantly went along with him, not seeing any other way to revive the army's fighting capacity. But Kornilov's demands drove a horse and cart through his delicate compromises. In August Kornilov moved elite troops toward Petrograd, intending to declare martial law and install a military government, but they were halted by railway workers. Forced to come off the fence, Kerenskii dismissed Kornilov, arrested him, and charged him with treason.[14]

Therewith the ambiguities of Kerenskii's putative alliance crumbled away. Both the Provisional Government and the moderate socialist leaders of the soviets were in an untenable position, crushed between generals, who wanted to be given full powers to fight the war to the finish, and the mass of the people, who increasingly regarded the war as a pretext for perpetuating the repressive apparatus and the economic exploitation characteristic of the old empire.

Since only the Bolsheviks were promising an immediate end to the war, more and more soldiers by the autumn were turning to them and electing them to the army committees. By now many men had decided that what they really cared about was not defending someone else's Russia but getting back to their own villages to participate in the anticipated handout of the land. Soldiers were picking up their rifles and absconding from the front, commandeering trains to take them back to the interior. The newly forged patriotism was evaporating, to be replaced by crisis-stricken localism.

The Bolsheviks' seizure of power in October legitimized these aspirations. The new rulers declared a ceasefire and issued a decree transferring all land to village assemblies. Thus Lenin launched "proletarian internationalism" on the precarious and incongruous foundation of peasant paro-chialism.

Workers

The soviets of 1917 differed from those of 1905 in a number of ways. Most important was that they now had something to defend: the political settle-ment which had followed the departure of the old regime. They were local authorities and part of the postrevolutionary "establishment." This responsi-bility put pressure on the leaders of the soviets to work with the Provisional Government to keep public life going till the war was ended and a Constit-uent Assembly could decide Russia's future. As a result, executive commit-tees tended to develop into a new kind of bureaucracy, ever more remote from the soviets' plenary meetings, where the mood was tumultuous and unruly. As one observer later recalled, "The crowd of those standing became so dense that . . . those sitting in chairs abandoned them . . . The 'presidium' was also standing on a table, while around the shoulders of the chairman was a whole swarm of energetic people who had clambered onto the table and were hindering him from conducting the session."[15] It is no wonder that executive committees tended increasingly to take decisions without reference to plenary sessions.

Gradually, then, workers began to sense once more that their aspirations were being ignored. They began to transfer the focus of their political energy downward, from the town soviets to the elected factory committees which handled affairs at the workplace in individual enterprises and kept up pres-sure on employers, soviets, and government. Factory committees were in a position not merely to agitate for an eight-hour working day but actually to introduce it by direct action. At the Putilov Works (and not only there) unpopular foremen would be trundled out in a wheelbarrow to be dumped in the street or even in a nearby river.[16] This was village *samosud* in an urban setting, and it was much more satisfying for ordinary workers than bar-gaining with executive committees.

As economic conditions deteriorated during the summer, employers be-gan cutting output and laying off employees or even closing their plants altogether. These measures aroused all the old resentments at the unfair dis-tribution of wartime burdens. Workers, suspicious that their bosses were simply trying to rescue their own fortunes, demanded the right to inspect the accounts and supervise the running of the workplace: this was termed *rabochii kontrol* (workers' supervision). Workers' inherited distrust of gov-ernment meant that there was no way of restraining war profiteering through the action of the state: the workers felt they needed to see the accounts of their own employers themselves.

The Mensheviks in the Provisional Government were caught in a cruel dilemma. The workers were posing demands which at any previous juncture they would have supported wholeheartedly. But now those demands jeopardized production and therefore the further conduct of the war. M. I. Skobelev, minister of labor, himself a Menshevik, appealed to workers not to "disorganize industry and deplete the Treasury" by striking and demanding wage rises.[17] Most workers regarded such appeals as a betrayal and listened with all the more sympathy to Bolshevik exhortations to take power in the factory for themselves. A conference of factory committees in June was the first mass organization to adopt Bolshevik slogans: it called for workers to form their own militia, expropriate the industrialists and bankers, and regulate the production and distribution of goods themselves.[18]

Workers also supported the soldiers of the Petrograd garrison in refusing to be transferred to the front. In July, when the First Machine-Gun Regiment resisted transfer, workers poured into the center of the city and demanded that the soviets denounce the Provisional Government, take power themselves, and declare an end to the war. Viktor Chernov, leader of the Socialist Revolutionary Party, urged restraint, but excited demonstrators shouted at him, "Take power when it's offered you, son of a bitch!" That exclamation, and Chernov's embarrassed reaction, summed up the dilemma of the moderate socialists in the Provisional Government. In the end, appalled by the threat to public order posed by the mutinous regiment, they brought out loyal troops and dispersed the demonstrators by force, with the loss of some 300 lives. Bloody Sunday was being outstripped by the workers' own supposed leaders.[19]

The most effective workers' organizations were the Red Guards, the workers' militias which appeared piecemeal during the spring and summer. In the absence of the old police force, they soon became the only effective coercive force on the city streets. By autumn the Bolsheviks, beginning to win majorities in soviet plenaries, were setting up Military Revolutionary Committees to mobilize the Guards and coordinate them with rebellious garrison troops. This was the alliance which made possible the soviet seizure of power in Petrograd and other towns in October.[20]

Peasants

Peasants underwent the same political evolution as the soldiers and workers: at first watchful cooperation with the Provisional Government, then growing disillusion followed by the assumption of direct power over their own lives. They discovered that the Provisional Government was not about to hand all the land over to them, but was merely setting up local committees to study the land and supply problems, in order that the expected Constituent Assembly might settle them. This was a perfectly reasonable approach, since the intricate job of equitable redistribution of land could not well take place in a hurry or while so many heads of households were absent at the front. But gradualism and legality did not suit the peasants' mood. With the tsar gone, they expected to be able to take over all the land and cultivate it in their own way. They began to swamp the land committees from below, first at volost level, then increasingly at uezd and guberniia levels too, setting up elected "committees of people's power," first to articulate peasant grievances and then to set about rectifying them. Lacking its own police force, the Provisional Government was powerless to stop them.

The committees began to take charge of all the private land in their area, allowing their owners to go on farming them, but only under strict supervision, in preparation for expropriation. During the summer and autumn village and volost assemblies proceeded to direct action, in a manner reminiscent of 1905. Once more, the central black-earth provinces and the Volga basin were especially turbulent, along with Belorussia and right-bank Ukraine, which were near the front line. This time the peasant tide was swelled by soldier deserters beginning to return from the front in large numbers, armed and ready to fight if there should be any resistance.

But it was not only soldiers. All households were involved: joint responsibility ruled, as always. Typically, peasants would assemble with their carts and improvised weapons on the village square, then move off toward the manor. The squire was forced to sign a document transferring the property of the estate to the village assembly. Then the peasants would load what they could carry onto their carts and lead away the cattle, leaving behind a subsistence allowance for the landowner and his family.[21]

There was order and a certain conception of legality in the peasants' actions. Even the landowner was left with his "fair" share, provided he did not resist the new arrangements and cultivated his land without hired labor. On the other hand, peasants murdered and burned whenever they encountered resistance; even when they did not, they often simply destroyed paintings, books, furniture, sculptures—anything that suggested wealth or the alien culture the gentry had imported.[22]

Viktor Chernov, the minister of agriculture, was still leader of the Socialist Revolutionary Party, the centerpiece of whose program was that village communities should expropriate the land and divide it up among their members.

Now he had to urge them not to do so, in order to avoid disrupting food production and marketing. When he tried to half-implement his party's program by authorizing peasant committees to take over land that was "poorly used," his colleague Minister of the Interior Iraklii Tsereteli, a Menshevik, humiliated him by abruptly countermanding his circular.[23] The SRs were still the most popular party among the peasants, but under the agonizing crosspressures of revolution they were moving rapidly toward disunity and impotence.

After the expropriations, village assemblies redistributed the land as far as possible equitably, either "by eaters" (according to the number of mouths a household had to feed) or "by labor" (according to the number of working hands available in it). "Stolypin peasants" and even former landlords were drawn into the process: each was allowed his norm and no more. Everyone had the right to subsistence. In crisis the old peasant values reasserted themselves.

The Bolsheviks

Everywhere, then, the incipient alliance between *obshchestvennost* and *narod* broke down under pressure from below. The parties involved in the Provisional Government and the Petrograd Soviet were discredited for supporting the alliance and trying to make it work.

The Bolsheviks were well placed to take advantage of this breakdown. They could do so, however, only by first slaughtering a few sacred cows of their own. They had to abandon their immediate objective of reorganizing agricultural production in collective farms in face of the peasants' obvious wish to continue household farming within the framework of the village commune. Lenin's original idea that the revolution would be carried out by a tightly disciplined party of intellectuals directing the workers was pushed aside by events. Instead the Bolsheviks rode to power on the crest of a groundswell generated by the mass of the people; fulltime party members took over and steered as best they could institutions created by workers, peasants, and soldiers.

The instrument of the seizure of power in Petrograd, the Military Revolutionary Committee, was created not by the Bolsheviks, but by the Petrograd Soviet as a whole, to organize the defense of the capital against either a second military coup or a German attack. From about 20 October the MRC began taking control of strategic points in the city in order to ensure that the Provisional Government did not prevent the second All-Russian Congress of Soviets from meeting. The final operation was launched when Kerenskii tried

to close Bolshevik newspapers and arrest leading Bolsheviks. Most participants in the rising thought that they were fighting for "All Power to the
Soviets," to be embodied in the form of a coalition socialist government
which would endorse the authority of workers', soldiers', and peasants' assemblies throughout the country.

However, at the Congress of Soviets Lenin was unexpectedly able to set
up a single-party Bolshevik government (the "Council of People's Commissars," or Sovnarkom) because by then he had secured the support of a sizable
contingent of SR delegates. Fed up with the temporizing of their party's
leaders, they broke away, formed the Left Socialist Revolutionaries, and gave
Lenin vital support for several months, even joining his government for a
while. By contrast, the remaining SRs, along with most Mensheviks, walked
out of the congress, declaring that the Bolsheviks had usurped power which
belonged to the people and to all the socialist parties.[24]

In most localities the Bolsheviks were able to seize power in similar ways.
Where they were popular, they used their majority to dominate local soviets;
where they were less popular, they set up or took over an armed militia,
usually called a Military Revolutionary Committee, to coerce or replace the
soviet and enforce "All Power to the Soviets" on their own terms. Only where
a non-Russian nationality was dominant were they unable to do either.[25]

Within a few months, wherever they held power, the Bolsheviks consolidated it by closing down nonsocialist newspapers and establishing their own
security police in the form of the Cheka, or Extraordinary Commission for
Struggle against Speculation and Counterrevolution. They allowed popular
elections to the Constituent Assembly to go ahead, but when it became clear
that the SRs were to be the largest single party in it, the Bolsheviks simply
closed the Assembly down. With its destruction the form of democratization
for which *obshchestvennost* and most of the socialist parties had striven for
decades suffered inglorious shipwreck. The feeble but emerging civil institutions of late imperial Russia were destroyed, and the way was clear for the
Bolsheviks to impose their own blueprint on society.

FIRST STEPS TO A NEW SOCIETY

The Bolsheviks came to power committed to world revolution. For Lenin
Russia was merely the starting point in a worldwide chain reaction, the country where, for historical reasons, the international proletarian revolution
happened to have been launched. He anticipated that the soviets' triumph
in Russia would soon be followed by workers' risings in Germany and other

parts of Europe. That is why the Bolsheviks renamed themselves Communists, as an indication that their inspiration came not from Russia, but from the Paris Commune of 1871. When in 1919 Lenin set up a Communist International to coordinate the workers' risings he intended its founding congress to take place in Berlin; only circumstances forced him to transfer it to Moscow.[26]

But that transfer was symptomatic. Geopolitics were against him. As early as March 1918, when he signed the Treaty of Brest-Litovsk and unilaterally ended the war with imperial Germany, Lenin had to admit that the first priority for the young proletarian state must be not world revolution but the defense of what was for the time being the only fortress and homeland of socialism: Russia. He faced a challenge over this issue within the party. Nikolai Bukharin and a group of "Left Communists" urged that Russia should not sue for peace, but should continue the war on a new basis: the Germans would undoubtedly defeat and occupy Russia, but Russian workers and peasants would then carry on the struggle as partisans, arousing the morale of the people and by their example provoking a proletarian rising in the enemy's heartland. In essence this was the message of "international civil war" which Lenin had always preached. Only now that he had a state mechanism at his command, no matter how rudimentary, Lenin gave priority to defending what his party had gained at the expense of hazy broader prospects.

From that moment on, gradually and fitfully, international socialism began to coalesce with Russian imperialism. The mixture was not entirely incongruous. The idea of Russia as a millenarian people, bringing salvation to humanity as a whole, had been the basis of the national myth in the sixteenth century and had never been wholly eradicated from popular consciousness, persisting as a kind of shadow ideology in imperial Russia. Egalitarianism in the form of "joint responsibility" had characterized the life of Russian peasants and working people for centuries. Whether they liked it or not, the Bolsheviks had come to power on the wings of a largely peasant revolution imbued with that spirit. They found themselves trying to found a modern, industrialized, worldwide proletarian state on the basis of the backward, parochial Russian village community—a contradiction which haunted them, and which they later tried to overcome violently.

The fateful duality was already present in Lenin's thinking. Lenin combined in his person various strands of the Russian political tradition. He was first of all a European intellectual who appreciated the comforts and regularities of bourgeois society. His ideals were the Swiss Post Office and the British Museum Library. Like many European intellectuals of his time, he was a Marxist, who believed in the existence of scientific laws of social development and in the primacy of class struggle. But he was also a Russian populist, who believed in the leadership of a small elite over the mass revolutionary movement, who rejected compromise with bourgeois liberal parties, and who wanted to overleap the bourgeois capitalist stage of social evolution by drawing on the revolutionary potential of the Russian peasantry.

In actual fact the populists and Marxists had never been as distant from one another as the polemics of the 1890s had suggested, so perhaps one can simply conclude that Lenin represented the features which the two Russian revolutionary traditions had in common. The cardinal point is that all the elements of his outlook were subordinated to an apocalyptic vision in which a titanic revolutionary struggle would destroy the old world and create a harmonious society in which all human beings would be able to fulfill their potential because, in the words of Marx, "each would contribute according to his ability and receive according to his needs." The emotional coloring of this vision went back through Bakunin to the Old Believers and to the preachers of sixteenth- and seventeenth-century Muscovy who were torn between prophecies of ultimate doom and paeans to their country as the universal Christian realm destined to fulfill God's plan for mankind. Yet if Lenin was a visionary, he was also a pragmatic politician; the combination of the two personalities was his great strength. His intense concern with practical questions, down to the smallest detail, his domineering personality, and his capacity to persuade people of the absolute rectitude of his views recall Peter the Great and activist Russian officials of the eighteenth and nineteenth centuries.[27]

It has always been easy to overlook the visionary side of Lenin because the overwhelming majority of his writing is concerned with the tactics of the revolutionary struggle. But there was one brief moment when he felt justified in giving his vision full utterance: that was when in 1917 the revolution had started and new possibilities had opened out but the Bolsheviks had not yet come to power and Lenin was not yet engulfed by the day-to-day problems of administration. The result was *State and Revolution,* where Lenin put aside his usual obsession with tactics and for once expounded his vision of life in a future socialist society, in which the state would "wither away," because it would no longer be needed for the exploitation of the majority of the population, while its remaining "simple operations of registration, filing and checking" could be "carried out by any literate person."[28]

Many commentators have seen *State and Revolution* as an aberration. Adam Ulam, for example, declared that "no work could be more *un-*representative of its author's political philosophy."[29] In fact, however, it was

precisely the absolute nature of his vision which *justified* Lenin in his relentless elimination of any obstacles to its realization and in his constant preoccupation with tactics. The infinite desirability of the end legitimized the utter
ruthlessness of the means. It is only the totality of the vision which enables
one to explain the otherwise bewildering contradictions in Lenin's political
personality: his insistence that he had scientific, and therefore completely
certain, knowledge of social evolution combined with his constant fear that
this or that immediate opportunity might be missed and the whole enterprise
wrecked; his confidence in the complete moral rightness of his aims combined with absolute contempt for all normal standards of morality; his confidence in the long-term political creativity of the masses combined with
distrust of their propensity to be distracted by their immediate needs and
misled by the beguiling propaganda of the bourgeoisie.[30]

The split in Lenin's outlook is analogous to the tension within Marx's
writings between the sober scientific analysis of bourgeois political economy
and the prophetic vision of a future ideal society. The means by which Lenin
bridged the split was the party. The party was to lead the working masses
through the wilderness between grim, corrupted present-day reality and the
cleansed, harmonious future; and since only the party had a reliable sense
of the way ahead, the masses must accord it complete trust and obedience.
Any deviation from that line aroused Lenin's scorn and contempt. He neither
understood nor wanted to understand that the tensions within his vision
were potential contradictions which might have very destructive consequences.

The crucible in which he had the chance to realize his vision was Russia
in turmoil and upheaval in the winter of 1917–18. The objective situation
replicated the paradoxes of Lenin's outlook. Crisis is a time of opportunity,
and fundamental crisis a time of unlimited opportunity. All possibilities were
open. Lenin himself did not claim to have a precise map of the road to
socialism. Convinced of the general rightness of his direction, he expected
to lead the masses, but also to be guided by their enthusiasm and capacity
for spontaneous action.

So in the Napoleonic spirit—*on s'engage, puis on voit*—Lenin plunged
into the business of leadership, impelled by a vision of creative improvisation, supported and inspired by the mass of people, and directed in general
terms by the writings of Marx. The milieu in which he had to operate, however, was civil war, imminent or actual. That was no accident: the means
by which he had seized power made civil war almost inevitable, and Lenin
had always accepted that. But the fact itself was crucial: it meant that the
party's first practical attempt to put its ideals into practice took place in an

atmosphere of deep division and conflict, in which authoritarian solutions were virtually inevitable, and in which the gains the revolution had brought to ordinary peasants, workers, and soldiers had almost all to be nullified. The Bolsheviks seized power by promising great benefits to the people; but in order to hold on to power they had to withdraw or reverse those benefits.

They had also promised actual power to the people. In a *Pravda* article of November 1917 Lenin exhorted them: "Comrades, working people! Remember that you yourselves are now running the state . . . Get on with the job yourselves, from below. Do not wait for anyone. Observe the strictest revolutionary discipline and mercilessly suppress any attempts at anarchy by drunkards, vandals, counterrevolutionary officer cadets, Kornilovites, and so on."[31] In social upheaval and civil war, however, "discipline" and "suppression" had to be applied from above, not from below, and the new proletarian state, with its own police, soon replaced working people in that role.

The Marxist tradition had generated no blueprint for the creation of a socialist economy, but it had always been assumed that among the first steps would be the expropriation of the bourgeoisie and the socialization of the means of production. The new proletarian state would implement these measures. That is what it was for: to handle the transition. As Lenin said in *State and Revolution:* "The proletariat needs state power, a centralized organization of force, both to crush the resistance of the exploiters and to *lead* the enormous mass of the population—the peasants, the petty bourgeoisie and the semi-proletarians—in the work of organizing a socialist economy."[32]

The Second All-Russian Congress of Soviets set about accomplishing this task in October and November 1917. It abolished private landownership and handed all land over to village and volost land committees for redistribution. This was not Bolshevik policy, but it was a tribute Lenin was prepared to pay to ensure the peasants were on his side. In the towns real estate was withdrawn from the market and placed in the hands of the soviets, which began the process of *uplotnenie,* the resettlement of the poorly housed into the relatively spacious apartments of the bourgeoisie. The congress made workers' committees the owners of industrial and commercial property and gave them the power of supervision over management boards. Existing judicial institutions were replaced by new "people's courts," with judges elected by the working population. Special "revolutionary tribunals," elected by soviets, began to work alongside the Cheka to deal with speculation and counterrevolutionary activity. In the army all ranks and insignia were abolished, and units were placed under elected committees of soldiers.

The congress issued a Declaration of the Rights of the Peoples of Russia, which abolished all forms of national discrimination and established the right to self-determination for all peoples "up to and including secession and the formation of an independent state."

Seldom, if ever, has any legislature decreed such a thoroughgoing transformation of society. A hierarchical order, with discrimination according to estate, ethnos, gender, and religion, was replaced by an egalitarian one with discrimination only against formerly "privileged" classes. Centralized government yielded to a federation of elected soviets. The free market was supplanted by common ownership of real estate and the means of production. Banks were nationalized and run in such a way as to encourage the unlimited emission of money. The regime made no attempt to restrain inflation, in the expectation that it would lead to the abolition of money and make necessary the distribution of resources through the state.[33]

The logic of these measures soon asserted itself. Because of the war and because of Soviet legislation, the market could no longer deliver. On 2 December 1917 the Supreme Council of the National Economy (VSNKh) was established to "elaborate general norms and a plan for regulating the economic life of the country." The workers' committees were converted into local branches of the trade unions and all of them subordinated to VSNKh. These moves were often welcomed by the workers, even those who had fought only recently to run their own factories. As the winding down of the war and general economic disruption gathered pace in the early months of 1918, workers themselves would petition VSNKh to take over their enterprises, to forestall the employers' closing them or in the hope of ensuring continuing supplies of fuel, raw materials, and spare parts. In this way by the summer much of industry was at least nominally in the ownership of the state, and statization of all joint-stock companies was finally decreed on 28 June 1918. Making sure that VSNKh did have control over the economy, combatting "speculation" and the black market, became one of the principal functions of the Cheka, which periodically combed through the "flea markets" and stationed roadblocks at the entrance to towns, so that "bagmen," bringing in produce to sell, could be intercepted.[34]

In spite of all these measures, the workers' situation continued to deteriorate. The military ceasefire of December 1917 and the runaway inflation reduced demand for industrial goods to a minimum. When the civil war revived the need for weapons and ammunition, the workers making them were placed under military discipline. Most workers in other branches of industry were laid off and either sought poorly paid jobs elsewhere or trudged back to the villages from which they or their families had originally come. In either case their living conditions were catastrophic.

Perhaps still more demoralizing for the workers was the sense that the long struggle they had conducted, first against the tsarist regime, then against the Provisional Government, had been in vain. It must have been terribly difficult to take in what had happened during 1917 and 1918. To all appearance, workers had "won," first of all the eight-hour day and a minimum wage, then workers' control over the factories. A "dictatorship of the proletariat" had been declared in their name. In practice, however, their living conditions had become far worse and they had lost what little political influence they used to have. Their "own" revolution had given power over them to commissars in leather jackets who reacted to recalcitrance by reaching for a revolver.

The decree of 26 October 1917 abolishing all private landownership was overwhelmingly popular among the peasants, for whom it represented the achievement of centuries-old aspirations. They set about redistributing the land in the traditional way, through the village assemblies. But the process generated a good many disappointments and conflicts. It was carried out in chaotic conditions: the squabbles and feuds which go on in any village were exacerbated by demobilized soldiers newly returned from the war, and by urban workers turning up to claim plots of land in which they had long ago lost interest. Many sons wanted to break away from fathers with whom they had hitherto reluctantly lived, and claimed their own plots of land. Besides, it transpired that, even when land expropriated from landowners and church was taken into account, each peasant household could add on average only one desiatina or a little more (about two acres) to its holding. Furthermore, villages being conservative places, the older-established and wealthier families usually did better than the poor and the newcomers.[35]

All the same, the remarkable thing is that this complex restructuring was carried out at all, with a reasonable degree of consensus. The peasants had a very strong feeling that they were at last putting in place an agrarian order which was just, in accordance with God's will, and which they could run in their own way, without outside interference.

Outside interference materialized nevertheless, for the land redistribution did not solve the crucial problem of urban food supply. In fact it aggravated it, for it dispersed many of the large estates which had been the main source of large-scale provisioning. The agrarian revolution meant more primitive and less productive agricultural methods. Given the need to feed an army during the civil war, the regime decided the only way it could cope with food shortage was to declare grain a state monopoly and send requisition teams into the villages to persuade the peasants to sell grain or if necessary to take it from them by force. The authorities also endeavored to preserve some estates and turn them into collective farms, but these attempts were usually bitterly resisted by the peasants.

407

CIVIL WAR

As Lenin had foreseen, the Bolsheviks' seizure of power unleashed civil war, though not perhaps quite in the way he had expected. The cumulative effect of their early measures—the spurning of coalition socialist government, the establishment of the Cheka, the closure of the Constituent Assembly, the Treaty of Brest-Litovsk—was to push even many socialists into the ranks of the Bolsheviks' opponents. The first serious military opposition was mounted by Kadets and SRs (with the help of former Czech prisoners of war) at Omsk in Siberia, and by a Committee of the Constituent Assembly (Komuch) at Samara on the Volga: they amalgamated in September 1918 to form a "Directory."

In the end, though, it was senior officers from the old imperial armed forces—Whites, as they became known—who headed the anti-Bolshevik movement from base areas on the periphery: Admiral Aleksandr Kolchak in Siberia, having seized power from the Directory, General Anton Denikin in the Caucasus and among the Cossacks, General Nikolai Iudenich in the Baltic. They received some aid from the wartime allies, who initially were trying to bring Russia back into the war, then after November 1918 attempting rather halfheartedly to crush Bolshevism. Both in the summer and autumn of 1918 (from Siberia) and in the autumn of 1919 (from the south and the Baltic), the new Soviet state looked for a time as if it might be overrun. But on both occasions it was able to repulse the Whites. In 1920 Soviet Russia was again threatened, this time by the newly independent Poles, who were endeavoring to regain the lands they had lost in the eighteenth century: Belorussia, Ukraine, and Lithuania, beloved home of their national poet, Adam Mickiewicz. Again, the Red Army not only halted the invasion but pursued the invaders back deep into their own country.[36]

To achieve this victory the Bolsheviks had to rearm and create a new fighting force. One of their most popular policies in 1917 had been the democratization of the army and the declaration of peace. With the onset of civil war that too had to be reversed. Red Guards and units run by soldiers' committees were incapable of taking on armies properly organized and disciplined. Trotskii, as people's commissar for war, set up a new Workers' and Peasants' Red Army, which recruited its troops by conscription, and restored a command hierarchy, without the old ranks and insignia but with full military discipline, up to and including the death penalty. Soldiers' committees were abolished and replaced with "political departments," headed by "political commissars," responsible for morale and the political education of the rank and file. Unkindest cut of all, realizing that the Bolsheviks had in their ranks almost no experienced military men, Trotskii decided to invite former imperial officers to take command in the new army. True, he placed political commissars at their side, to ensure their obedience to the new regime, if necessary in extremis by shooting them.

This seldom proved to be necessary. It transpired that a good many old-regime officers were willing to serve in the Red Army. They had deeply resented the shambles to which, in their opinion, the Provisional Government had reduced a once-effective fighting force, and they now welcomed the advent of a regime which took military discipline seriously. Some of them, moreover, considered that the Reds were proving more effective in defending Russia against untrustworthy foreigners than the imperial regime, the Provisional Government, or the Whites. That sentiment intensified when Soviet Russia was invaded by the traditional enemy, Poland, in 1920. General Brusilov, the most successful of the imperial generals and a convinced enemy of socialism, appealed to his colleagues: "Forget the wrongs you have suffered. It is now your duty to defend our beloved Russia with all your strength." Otherwise "Our descendants will be right to condemn us and accuse us of letting egoistic feelings of class struggle prevent us using our military knowledge and experience. They will say we have forgotten our own Russian people and destroyed Mother Russia." His sentiment was compatible with the declaration of Karl Radek, secretary of the Communist International, that the Whites were trying to subject Russia to foreign colonization and that the Reds were leading a "national struggle of liberation."[37]

SOCIAL AND POLITICAL CONSEQUENCES OF CIVIL WAR

On a superficial level the civil war was one between two sides, the Reds and the Whites. In fact much more was involved than that: a massive breakdown of all the normal ties linking different groups of society. It is doubtful indeed whether the word "society" can be used at all: the bonds of common identity and belief had broken down almost completely and given way to a preoccupation with survival. The empire had dissolved into separate regions and disparate ethnic groups, sometimes even just individual villages, which were left to fend for themselves as best they could against an outside world which had become at best untrustworthy, at worst murderously hostile. Workers and city-dwellers, who depended most on the relatively complex ties of urban and industrial society, were reduced to isolation, poverty, and impotence, breaking up furniture for fuel they could no longer buy on the market, and bartering cherished family possessions in nearby villages in order to scrape together enough grain, potatoes, and milk to survive. The writer Evgenii Zamiatin described Petrograd as a city of "icebergs, mammoths, and wastelands" where "cavemen, swathed in hides, blankets, and wraps, retreated from cave to cave."[38] Peasants, who could (with difficulty) get by on their own, retreated from the market, trying to sow and cultivate no more than they needed for subsistence, and held on to weapons brought back from the war to resist the irruption of armed men sent by some authority or other, or even just by a predatory neighbor.

The campaigns of the Reds and Whites interacted with this underlying reality. The Reds had considerable strategic advantages, which in the long run were bound to give them victory unless they wantonly squandered them—which they nearly did. They had a base in the heartland of Russia, with most of its population and the principal industrial towns, including the main armaments works. Operating from the central strategic position, their formations could communicate with one another and move from one front to another much more easily than the Whites. The Whites, by contrast, were situated on precarious bases on the periphery of the old empire, with relatively sparse populations and meager industrial resources, and they were often reliant on mistrustful non-Russian populations. They were unable to coordinate their various offensives.

All the same, the Whites had the advantage of far more experienced officers, and also of aid from the First World War allies. Given competent leadership and some sense of common purpose, they should have been able to make better use of the occasions when they did command major strategic resources—as when Kolchak captured the Urals industrial area or when Denikin conquered the whole of the black-earth agricultural region.

But the White leaders were completely incapable of marrying the military and political aspects of their campaign, a skill essential in a civil war, where the allegiance of the population is a vital factor. The Reds did quite enough to alienate the masses, whether workers or peasants, who had once supported them. Twice their front crumbled because of mounting unrest in their rear: in the winter of 1918–19 in the Urals and Volga basin, and in the early months of 1919 as a result of their de-Cossackization program in the Don region and their brutal treatment of Ukrainian peasants. On both occasions the Whites took over a territory where the population was disposed to welcome them—

and on both occasions swiftly undermined their own support by displays of brutality less systematic but no less sickening than the Reds'.[39]

The White leaders failed utterly to take advantage of the opportunities presented to them because they had inherited from the old army a distrust of politics and of all politicians. They believed their cause—the restoration of the Russian Empire and the crushing of socialists—was self-evidently right and proper, that it required no further elaboration or presentation. Their political pronouncements were belated and confused, certainly not calculated to attract mass enthusiasm. They identified all liberal and socialist politicians, some of whom might have joined them in an anti-Bolshevik movement, as being either Jews or hangers-on of the Bolsheviks—usually both. Kadets, Right SRs, Left SRs: it was all the same to them.

They were also weakened by the fact that the monarchy was not a popular rallying cry. The Romanov dynasty had become so discredited by 1917 that White leaders, whatever their individual convictions, did not dare inscribe its restoration on their banners. Paradoxically, then, it was the Reds, the revolutionaries, rather than the Whites, the conservatives, who were defending established institutions with popular appeal—the soviets.

The Whites lacked any semblance of political organization such as might have backed up their military efforts. Individual White commanders enjoyed even more de facto freedom of action than Red commissars. Unlike Trotskii, neither Denikin nor Kolchak had a concerted program of terror; but both had to condone their subordinates' unrestrained orgies of looting, raping, flogging, and mass murder, practiced both for personal gain and to destroy supposed enemies. Kolchak's Siberia was home to the *atamanshchina*, the rule of rapacious local warlords who revived the sixteenth-century Cossack spirit of raiding and plundering sedentary populations. Under Denikin, Ukraine witnessed massive anti-Jewish pogroms, which caused more than 100,000 deaths, the worst in the whole of Russia's history.[40]

With enemies like these, the Bolsheviks did not have great need of friends—or even of mass support. For most of the time, most of the population retreated into a besieged localism, praying that governments of all political persuasions might leave them alone. This was an attitude for which history had prepared them well.

The Reds, for all the hostility they aroused, deployed both propaganda and coercion in a more purposeful way than their opponents. They also had the benefit of having on their side the true believers, the millenarians and utopians of all social classes, who were convinced that theirs was the wave of the future, that their efforts would ultimately create a better future for all humanity.

That description certainly fitted Trotskii, the one outstanding war leader produced by either side. Theorist and orator by nature rather than organization man, he nevertheless excelled at the emergency mobilization of scarce resources. Fitting himself out a special train, he would race from town to town and from front to front, enthusing his subordinates, checking up on the hesitant or incompetent, and clambering with flashing eyes onto improvised podiums to project the Communist message to workers, peasants, and soldiers.

411

The Reds' conduct during the civil war sprang not only from practical necessities but also from the nature of their ideology. Having deliberately enfeebled the normal sinews of trade, leaving the towns and army threatened by famine, they had to resort to direct food requisitioning as a substitute. To help them enforce it, they created "committees of poor peasants" in the villages: its members were supposed to provide them with intelligence about grain hoarding and also to give their operations the legitimate cover of class struggle. These committees soon proved hopelessly inefficient and corrupt, however, and had to be disbanded, after which the requisitioning became undisguised coercion. A "supplies squad" *(prodotriad)* would arrive in a village, take over the largest house, evict the "kulak" (rich peasant) who lived in it, and instruct all the villagers to deliver a pre-set quota of produce. Those who did not or could not comply were subject to searches, which might involve the ripping up of floorboards and the destruction of furniture, followed, if they proved fruitless, by beatings and arrests. Similarly, armed roadblocks were set up, and checkpoints at railway stations, where peasants taking produce to market were searched and in effect robbed.[41]

At first peasants reacted to these measures with passive rather than active resistance and attempted to seal their economy off from that of town and army. One village in Orel guberniia actually surrounded itself with trenches and barbed wire.[42] But the Reds' conscription campaigns were merciless, and resistance to them counted as desertion or mutiny, which were punishable by death. The "deserters" would flee into the forests, there to set up armed bands, known as Greens, since they opposed both Reds and Whites. Sometimes they acted independently and sometimes as an armed wing of local peasant communities. In either case, they would operate as partisan bands have done over the centuries, keeping out of the way of large enemy forces, but descending and massacring small detachments and *prodotriady*.

These disorders rumbled on throughout 1919 but became more persistent during 1920 and the first part of 1921, when in many provinces of the south and east Communist rule was effective only in the towns and intermittently on the main roads and railways. In Ukraine the peasants' antiurban mood was colored by nationalism: here several of the Green leaders called themselves "Atamans."[43] Elsewhere peasant unions were set up to coordinate civil administration with military activity, often with local SR leadership (though the SR Central Committee was hesitant about supporting all-out armed insurrection). From the autumn of 1920 partisan bands amalgamated into sizable peasant armies in much of southeast European Russia, notably Tambov, the Don and Kuban regions, and western Siberia. In the last case, Green leaders captured and for a time ran major towns, such as Tobolsk and Petropavlovsk, entirely cutting communications with the rest of Siberia. Elsewhere the Greens were confined to villages and small towns.

The peasants' political aim in 1920–21 was simple: to defend their way of life against "commissarocracy" (as they called Communist rule) and when possible to take revenge on Communist party members. Where they articulated political aims which transcended the horizons of their own provinces, these included the restoration of free trade and the right to hold free elections to their own soviets. But their uncertain grasp of politics was betrayed by the fact that some peasants, remembering with nostalgia the land seizures of 1917, seriously proclaimed the slogan "Down with the Communists! Long live the Bolsheviks!"[44]

Communists were desperately weak in the countryside, so their response to growing unrest depended on finding allies in the villages. They rewarded favored villages with improved food supplies and played on peasants' fear both of partisan violence and of official retaliation. At the same time, they drew up lists of rebels and conducted reprisals against them, if they could capture them, or against their families, if they could not. Villages which persisted in hiding partisans might be burned down.[45]

In the chaos and extremism of the civil war, there was no room for the more moderate political parties, those which did not offer brutally simple solutions to complex problems, as did both the Reds and the Whites. Even where they were popular with the population, they could not turn that popularity into a political asset.

The SRs were a genuine mass party which would probably have won any free election held during the civil war period. Not only were they unarmed, however; they were also chronically split, between those who supported the Bolsheviks as emancipators of the peasants and those who wanted to reconstitute civil society through the revival of institutions such as zemstvos and cooperatives. The former, who supported the Bolsheviks in the winter of 1917–18, later became their most bitter opponents and did what they could to sponsor peasant insurrection against them in 1920–21. As for the majority of SRs, they were paralyzed by their reluctance to fight the Bolsheviks under the leadership of tsarist generals, who had once been their bitterest enemies. They tried in vain to set up a "third force," but in the fragmented and polarized Russia of civil war, there was no place for it.[46]

The Mensheviks too were divided, between those who regarded the Bolsheviks as misguided, impetuous, but essentially progressive colleagues and those who saw them as a monstrous historical throwback, a fundamental threat to civilization and democracy. Wedded to the European vision of social democracy, which Lenin had forsaken, they were alienated by the Bolsheviks' espousal both of peasant democracy and of terror. Few Mensheviks were prepared to take up arms against their erstwhile comrades, however, and mostly they drifted helplessly, doing what they could to make contact with the increasingly alienated workers.

In places, workers responded and endeavored to mount peaceful resistance. In Petrograd dissident Mensheviks and worker activists of 1917 set up an Extraordinary Assembly of Delegates from Works and Factories, which promoted a number of protests and stoppages, though it failed to organize a general strike in Petrograd in July 1918. Already by the spring of 1918 Mensheviks and SRs had won elections in a majority of urban soviets, but were unable to make their democratic mandate effective in a setting where the man with the gun was the master of circumstances.[47]

In Tula in March 1919 and June 1920 workers in the crucial armament factories went on strike, indignant at the low rations they received while Red commissars were living in luxury. At the locomotive plant in Sormovo, workers struck, demanding abolition of Communists' privileges, the restoration of free elections, and the reconvening of the Constituent Assembly. At Tver in June 1919 workers made similar demands and also protested against the drafting of 10 percent of their labor force into the Red Army. In all these cases the Bolshevik authorities initially negotiated with the strikers, made some concessions, then, having split the workforce, arrested and deported the strike leaders. In Astrakhan in March 1919 workers actually attacked Communist Party headquarters, murdered Communists there, and temporarily disarmed a local regiment of the Red Army. Here the reprisals were much more savage: the Cheka arrested and executed hundreds of workers, some of them by drowning from barges in the Volga.[48]

In 1920 the regime tried to bring not only industry but labor itself under direct state control, by creating "labor armies"—often Red Army units not yet demobilized—recruited by conscription and held together by military discipline. In key sectors of the economy such as railways and armaments production, trade unions were replaced by "political departments," absenteeism was treated as desertion, and food supplies were handed out as

413

rations, free of charge. Bukharin argued that "militarization is nothing other than the self-organization of the working-class."[49]

When this regime had been in place a year or so, and when the worst of the war against the Whites and foreign interventionists was over, the workers' movement took on a more concerted form. The winter of 1920–21 was particularly harsh, as Communist trade policy and peasant rebellion reduced food supplies to starvation levels. Factories were closing for lack of raw materials, fuel, and spare parts. In February 1921 in Petrograd, Moscow, and many provincial towns, workers protested against these closures and a reduction in already meager rations. When the protesters in Petrograd were sacked, their colleagues went on strike, gathered on the streets, and held meetings from which Bolsheviks were forcibly expelled: "we don't see a single worker in the soviet institutions, only white-hands who sit there and destroy faith in soviet power," one worker complained. The meetings elected an Assembly of Plenipotentaries, as in 1918, which launched a general strike, declaring: "We, the representatives of plants and socialist parties in Petrograd, despite much that we disagree on, have united on the basis of the following goals: overthrow of the Bolshevik dictatorship, free elections to the soviets, freedom of speech, press and assembly for all, and the release of political prisoners."[50]

On 27 February crews of the battleships in the Baltic fleet, stationed just offshore on the island base of Kronstadt, supported this resolution and set up their own Military Revolutionary Committee, as in September 1917. Their demands coincided with those of the workers but added a few more: the abolition of political departments, the lifting of roadblocks and restoration of free trade, equalization of rations, and the convening of a nonparty conference of workers, soldiers, and sailors.[51] All this was very similar to the demands of the peasant rebels in Tambov and elsewhere. For a short time it seemed as if once more Petrograd was to be the center of a mass revolution of peasants, workers, soldiers, and sailors.

This time, however, the authorities responded with greater ruthlessness and greater skill, combining repression with concessions. Zinoviev, party leader in the city, closed most of the factories and declared martial law, bringing in *kursanty* (Red Army officer cadets) to back up arrests and dismissals among the workers. At the same time emergency supplies of food and clothing were rushed to the city to supplement rations, and Zinoviev let it be known that an end to grain requisition was being contemplated.

Just in time. Even as the workers' movement eased, the rebellion of the Baltic sailors reached its climax, with a demand for immediate free elections to the soviets. Lenin announced that this was a "White Guard" plot supported from abroad and sent in General Tukhachevskii, leading *kursanty* and special troops. They began by bombarding Kronstadt with artillery and then launched several infantry assaults across the frozen ice to take the base.

The Tenth Party Congress was starting at this very moment, and its proceedings were interrupted while some of the delegates went off to help crush the rebellion. Lenin referred to the popular anti-Communist movement as a "petty bourgeois counterrevolution" and warned delegates, rightly, that it was "undoubtedly more dangerous than Denikin, Iudenich, and Kolchak combined."[52]

The civil war permanently marked Soviet society. It completed the work, begun by the revolution, of destroying the old society, so that almost no ancien régime institutions or social classes survived in a recognizable form. The institutions of the new society could be created anew by any force which could keep control over it. That force was the Communist party, which had itself changed considerably during the civil war. From being a party of oppositional intellectuals, engaged in constant debate and open to the opinions of workers, soldiers, and peasants, it became a party of power. Its mid- and lower-level officials, whatever their social origins, were almost all Red Army veterans, who liked to be seen in their tunics and flaunted an aggressively macho image. The party no longer listened to real workers and real soldiers, whom it accused of being "déclassé" or "petty bourgeois," and it regarded genuine debate as a luxury. It saw itself as a paramilitary fraternity surrounded by a sullen and untrustworthy population which did not understand its great aims.[53]

Not all Lenin's comrades were happy with the party's metamorphosis. Some of them still hankered after the old days of free discussion and the genuine election of party officials; by the autumn of 1920 they had formed a faction calling itself the Democratic Centralists, pledged to the restoration of democracy within the party. Others were worried by the alienation of the workers from a regime which was supposed to be acting in their name: they formed the Workers' Opposition and circulated proposals for the economy to be run by the trade unions.

These matters were discussed at the Tenth Party Congress, which reassembled with delegates still preoccupied by the Kronstadt rebellion. Lenin urged that in this extreme emergency free debate was a luxury which Communists could not permit themselves. He submitted two resolutions, one condemning the Workers' Opposition as an "anarcho-syndicalist deviation," and the other "On Party Unity," ordering "the immediate dissolution, without exception, of all groups that have been formed on the basis of some platform or other . . . Failure to comply with this congress resolution is to entail unconditional and immediate expulsion from the party." Such was the siege mentality prevalent among delegates that both resolutions were passed by a huge majority. In this way the party finally substituted itself for the working class and gave its leaders the power to stifle all serious discussion.

Since other parties had virtually ceased to exist by this time, the result was to deliver into the hands of the Communist leaders a total monopoly over political life. That was the party which was now to remake Russian society in its own image. As it did so, it became clear that Russia's social memory had not perished with the institutions of the old society, that the habits of personal dependence through patron-client networks revived readily, to be given a new form by the now dominant Communists. The very completeness of the destruction probably impelled people to seek security in familiar social patterns, not only resuscitating but also reinforcing them as the only source of stability in a chaotic world.

THE BOLSHEVIKS' VIEWS ON NATIONHOOD

From the very outset the Soviet leaders were torn between the discourse of class and that of nationality. When they dissolved the Constituent Assembly, they declared that the soviets constituted a higher form of democracy, which meant asserting the primacy of class over nation. But that did not settle the issue. The Bolsheviks did not know then how events would unfold, and in building a new political system, they were torn between the ideal of an international proletarian community, still their ultimate goal, and the geopolitical imperatives of the neo-Russian state they actually controlled.

Lenin did not believe, as did the Austrian Marxist theorists Bauer and Renner, that nations were permanent features of the international order, like mountains in a landscape. On the other hand, he also did not accept Rosa Luxemburg's view that after the socialist revolution nations would simply melt into an international proletarian community, like ice floes disappearing in a springtime river. He held that nations were important, especially at the current juncture, but ultimately secondary. He was optimistic about the revolutionary potential of the nationalities colonized during the nineteenth century. In *Imperialism the Highest Stage of Capitalism* (1916) he envisaged revolution taking place not within a single country, but on an international stage, with the colonized peoples overthrowing the imperialists. The Bolsheviks' proclamation of "self-determination" for the peoples of the Russian Empire fitted into this picture.

Once they were in power, naturally enough, prospects looked a little dif-

ferent. Communists were no longer fomenting a revolution, but running—
or claiming to run—a multiethnic state. Their nationality policy now had
to satisfy conflicting priorities. Early debates on constitutional relations between the nationalities proceeded on the assumption that what was being
discussed was a world state, to include Germany, Poland, and Hungary, and
ultimately Brazil, the United States, and China. These expansive perspectives
continued to dominate discussion throughout the civil war, enlivened by
the establishment—short-lived, as it turned out—of soviet republics in Bavaria and Hungary.

The Soviet-Polish war of 1920 was a turning point, however. It began as
a defensive struggle, but as the Red Army retook Kiev and began to sweep
westward against the old enemy, Lenin tried to turn the offensive into a
campaign to liberate the proletariat of Europe, starting with Poland and
carrying on into Germany, Hungary, and Romania.[54] However, his hope that
the Polish workers would rise to greet the Red Army turned out to be wholly
illusory: they took the view that the invaders were merely familiar Russian
imperialists in unfamiliar uniform. The Red Army's headlong advance was
halted outside Warsaw and then reversed, till Russia had to accept a peace
agreement which placed western Ukraine and western Belorussia inside Poland, and gave Lithuania independence.[55]

Over the next two or three years it became clear that successful socialist
revolutions were not to be expected elsewhere in Europe. Consequently,
strengthening the new Soviet Russia itself began to seem the main priority.
If one was not to take a crudely Russifying line—something which Lenin
always rejected as repugnant—that implied drawing the non-Russian nationalities into the process of "revolutionary development," which in turn
meant modernizing their economies and encouraging their national cultures
to reach maturity.

If "self-determined" nationalities were to retain some freedom of action
within the new Russian state, though, that state would have to be federal.
The trouble was, Lenin had never envisaged a federal state, and it did not
sit well with the Bolsheviks' highly centralized system of political control.
Federalism left the unanswered question: who, in each particular case, was
to exercise the power of self-determination which had been proclaimed as
Soviet government policy? If it was to be local national leaders, did that
mean handing real power to the "bourgeoisie"?

The new regime tried to provide a forum for the settlement of these difficult issues by setting up a People's Commissariat for Nationalities—Narkomnats—with elected representatives from each recognized nationality. Its
function was to enable the non-Russians to feed their aspirations into the

emerging political system, to mediate the conflicts between them, and to make possible ultimate central control over them.

The work of Narkomnats was substantive, since all the questions of future national coexistence were wide open. Decisions still had to be taken regarding which should be the nations making up the Soviet state, where their boundaries should lie, which should be the official languages of each, what political powers each should have, and what the relations between them all should be. The recently opened archives of the Narkomnats Collegium reveal how seriously both the Bolsheviks and the members of Narkomnats took their responsibilities. They drew on censuses, historical studies, and ethnographic, geographic, and linguistic surveys to try to determine as accurately as possible the ethnic composition and degree of national development of the territories over which the Soviet state was assuming sovereignty.[56]

THE FORMATION OF THE SOVIET UNION

In confronting these issues the Soviet leaders were aware that the Russian revolution had been both a social and a national revolution, or rather a multiplicity of social and national revolutions inextricably intertwined. As we have seen, urbanization, industrialization, and the spread of the single Russian market and of Russian bureaucratic administration had proceeded unevenly in the old empire, but had drawn many non-Russian peoples into the modernizing process. Old communal, kinship, or tribal frameworks had been weakened or even burst asunder. In each different region both long tradition and immediate circumstance helped to determine whether the peoples sought horizontal (class) affiliations or vertical (national) ones. Radical politicians were divided into those who proclaimed international proletarian brotherhood and those who preached cross-class ethnic solidarity. The masses varied in their responses according to whether they felt their deepest grievances were social exploitation or the suppression of their language and culture. The outcome of these intersecting pressures then further depended on whether ethnic groups were homogeneous or intermingled, whether the Red Army was locally strong, and whether external great powers—Germany, Turkey, Britain—intervened.[57]

Different nationalities and regions asserted their new political status in different ways, then, in 1917–1922. In Finland, for example, where most social classes and political parties had become strongly anti-Russian in reaction against the tsarist Russification campaigns, the declaration of independence in December 1917 was followed by a violent anti-Red campaign, the White

Terror, since the Reds, including many Finnish urban workers, were identified as a Russian fifth column. The White Terror provoked an equally violent Red rising, involving both Russians and Finns and supported from across the border by Soviet Russia. That rising was in turn crushed after Brest-Litovsk with the help of the German Army. Thereafter Finland, though still beset by serious class conflict, finally gained its independence from Russia.[58]

Of the three Baltic peoples, the Estonians and Latvians had a well-developed working class and a lively intelligentsia (professional people, schoolteachers, clergy) in the towns. Both nationalist and socialist politicians commanded a relatively large audience, thanks to high literacy rates. The divisions between nationalism and socialism were very bitter, and the Bolsheviks polled well, especially in the large towns, in the various elections of 1917. A few months of Bolshevik rule reduced their popularity, however, especially in Estonia, and with the coming of the Germans in the spring of 1918 the local nationalists took the opportunity to declare independence. The Red Army was too preoccupied elsewhere during the following years to attempt to reverse this development, even after the Germans pulled out six months later. Estonia and Latvia thus gained their independence for a generation, and during that time became parliamentary republics.[59]

In Lithuania the peasants enjoyed a much lower level of literacy, and the Lithuanian towns were dominated by Poles, Jews, and Russians. For that reason, Lithuanian nationalism was relatively feeble as a movement until the Germans occupied the region in 1918 and created a puppet Lithuanian republic. Perhaps for the same reason, class conflict was relatively muted too. Lithuania, sometimes joined with Belorussia, sometimes separate, became a battleground contested by Germany, a resurgent Poland, and Soviet Russia. Only with the conclusion of the Polish-Soviet war could a Lithuanian Republic be established, independent of the USSR, but severely truncated, with its largest city, Vilnius, and its southwestern territories awarded to Poland.

The social and ethnic complexion of Belorussia was similar to that of Lithuania, but its fate in 1917–1921 was completely different, since the influence of Russians and of the Red Army was much stronger. Eventually in 1920 the Communists established a Belorussian Soviet Republic separate from both Lithuania and Russia, perhaps because they wanted a pliantly Russian but not obviously Muscovite republic as an ally for the Russian Republic.[60]

Ukraine was bitterly divided between national and social revolution, and the division engendered several years of chaotic violence. The Rada in Kiev, supported by professional people, rural cooperatives, and officers from the imperial army, convened a Ukrainian Military Congress, which proclaimed the existence of a Ukrainian People's Republic in November 1917. It was, however, immediately challenged by a Soviet government in Kharkov, supported in many of the industrial towns of eastern Ukraine, with their massive contingents of Russian workers. Here, then, as in the Baltic, the Soviet government and the Red Army assumed the role of Russifiers. They succeeded in capturing Kiev before the incipient civil war was interrupted by German occupation in April 1918.

During the following two and a half years at least seven different types of regime claimed at one time or another to exercise sovereignty in Ukraine— German, Russian Communist, Ukrainian Communist, White Russian, Ukrainian nationalist, anarchist, Polish. It became evident that although professional and commercial people felt strongly about Ukrainian nationhood, the same was not true of workers and peasants. Many of the workers were Russian or Jewish and supported the Soviet regime in Moscow, while the peasants were far more interested in the land question than in the national one, and looked either to the Bolsheviks or to the anarchists under leaders like Nestor Makhno to confirm their entitlement to the land. For that reason Ukrainian nationalist regimes never had enough mass support to consolidate themselves.[61]

Even if Ukrainians could not establish their nationhood separate from Russia, all the same the memory of their national independence in 1917– 1921, no matter how brief, precarious, and embattled, generated powerful myths.[62] The Ukrainian Communists were affected by it too, and in the 1920s succeeded in winning from Moscow the right to far-reaching Ukrainization of public life, including the widespread introduction of Ukrainian as the language of tuition in primary schools and insistence on knowledge of Ukrainian as a compulsory qualification for employment in any official capacity.

The Paris Peace Conference awarded Bessarabia to Romania, within whose borders it remained till 1940. As a rival, however, the Soviet authorities set up the Moldavian Autonomous Soviet Socialist Republic (SSR) in 1924, with its capital in Tiraspol, carved out of the extreme southwest of Ukraine, in the industrial regions along the eastern bank of the Dniester. The intention was to create, as it were, a Romanian Soviet "Piedmont" and to destabilize Romania itself by acting as an example of socialism to workers and peasants languishing there under "boyar" rule.[63]

In the Caucasus the situation was, as ever, extremely complex: the various nationalities were divided from one another by religion, economic interests, disagreements over borders, and relations to Russia and to other powers. The Bolsheviks sponsored a brief attempt at a federation among the three largest nationalities, the Georgians, Armenians, and Azerbaijanis, but it fell apart in May 1918, and power passed to three separate governments, each dominated by a different political force, in Georgia the Mensheviks, in Armenia the Dashnaks, and in Azerbaijan the Mussavats, a party combining socialism and nationalism, whose rule was endangered by Russian workers in Baku in their dual role as Communists and Russian colonizers. Each independent state was at least partly dependent on an outside power. The Georgians looked to Germany as protector and after 1918 to Britain, the Azerbaijanis to the Ottoman Empire, and the Armenians rather warily to their traditional defenders, the Russians, under the White General Denikin, whose unrelenting Russian imperialism, however, they distrusted.

With the end of the world war, these powers were either unable or unwilling to engage in the Caucasus wholeheartedly any more. Their hands thus freed for action, the Communists in Baku were able to exploit the Azerbaijanis' anti-Armenian feelings to promote a rebellion. Meanwhile the Armenians themselves were trying to reestablish their own independence under the worst possible conditions. They were almost overwhelmed by a Turkish invasion, which coincided with the anti-Armenian rising in Baku. Flooded with refugees and constantly threatened with blockade by its neighbors, the new state was unable to establish any kind of normal economic life. The east Anatolian provinces of Turkey were awarded to Armenia by the Paris peace conference, but the Turkish state sought the support of Soviet Russia in blocking the fulfillment of this award. In April 1920, by agreement with Turkey, the Red Army invaded Azerbaijan and imposed Soviet authority there, while in September a Turkish army invaded Armenia with Soviet support. Under the terms of the Soviet-Turkish agreement, the disputed territories of both Nakhichevan and Nagornyi Karabakh were awarded to Azerbaijan. Within its reduced boundaries Armenia became a Soviet republic.[64]

For a time Georgia seemed more of a success story: here the Mensheviks convincingly projected themselves as the bearers of Georgian all-class nationalism and embarked on a program of broad social reform. The Reds' main supporters were the non-Georgians, especially the Abkhazians and Ossetians, who feared becoming confined within a Georgian mini-empire. By this time Lenin was giving priority to securing control over the territories of the old Russian Empire, and in May 1921 he sent the Red Army into Georgia in order to reincorporate it.[65]

The relationship between Communism and Islam was ambivalent, though in the immediate sense they had much in common. Both were anticapitalist (rejecting for example usury and private property in land), and both believed in the ultimate dissolution of nations and the brotherhood of man. That was sufficient during 1917–18, since the Whites offered the Muslims nothing.

On 20 November 1917 the Soviet government issued a declaration "To all Toiling Muslims of Russia and the East," condemning religious and national oppression under the tsars and promising: "Henceforth your beliefs and customs, your national and cultural institutions are to be free and inviolate . . . Your rights, like the rights of all the peoples of Russia, are under the mighty protection of the revolution."[66] Muslim units were formed inside the Red Army, commanded by a Tatar, Mir-Said Sultan-Galiev, and they played a major role in the fighting against Kolchak on the Siberian front. A semi-autonomous Muslim Communist party was founded, and a Central Muslim Commissariat was set up inside Narkomnats, under the prominent Tatar Muslim leader Mulla-Nur Vakhitov. There were plans to create a Tatar-Bashkir Republic, which would unite the most educated and advanced Muslims of Russia.[67]

Ultimately, though, Muslims and Communists had very different visions of the universal brotherhood which was to succeed imperialism and nationalism. The *umma* bore little resemblance to "proletarian internationalism." From the beginning, moreover, there were tensions for more immediate reasons. In central Asia the workers, mostly railwaymen or textile operatives, were almost entirely Russian. As the chairman of the Tashkent Congress of Soviets explained, "It is impossible to admit Muslims to the supreme organs of revolutionary power, because the attitude of the local population towards the authority of the soviets is uncertain, and because that population does not possess any proletarian organization." When a Muslim People's Council proclaimed home rule for Turkestan in Kokand in February 1918, Red Guards were sent from Tashkent to crush them. Similarly, the Kazan Soviet arrested the leaders of the Muslim Military Council on the Volga.[68]

Muslims themselves were sharply divided in their ideals. The Jadid movement hoped that the revolution might help them to promote modernization and make conscious citizens of all Muslims by fostering literacy in local languages, emancipating women, and creating the political institutions for widespread public participation. Some of them now dreamed of a Pan-Islamic state, while others were drawn more toward Pan-Turkism. On the other hand, some Muslims rejected modernizing ideas entirely. The so-called Basmachi, like nineteenth-century anti-Russian rebels, had Sufi murids at their core, usually those of the Naqshbandi order, which gave them links with the Caucasian mountain peoples. The center of the Basmachi rebellion was the Fergana valley, and its aim was to expel all Russians and all Communists from Turkestan.[69] The rebels' hopes reached a climax when the former Ottoman war minister, Enver Pasha, came to Turkestan and proclaimed himself "Supreme Commander of the Warriors of Islam, son-in-law of the

Caliph, and emissary of Mohammed." His Basmachi troops, together with those of the emir of Bukhara, seized Dushanbe for a while and besieged Bukhara. Even after Enver's death in battle, the Basmachi movement persisted in guerrilla form for many years more.[70]

At the height of its fortunes, in 1918, the Muslim Communist Party had yet a third vision, that of an Islamic socialist state, which could become the focus of attraction for Muslims throughout Asia struggling against imperialism. Sultan-Galiev claimed that "the national liberation movement in Muslim countries has the character of a socialist revolution." They hoped to turn the Tatar-Bashkir Republic into "a hearth, from where the sparks of revolution would penetrate the heart of the East." To Lenin and Stalin a Muslim-colored world revolution was a most unwelcome rival. To forestall any such development, the Muslim Communist Party was reintegrated into the Russian Communist Party and its units brought under the Red Army. In 1923 Sultan-Galiev was arrested and accused of "nationalism" and "anti-party activity": he was the first leading Communist to be subject to criminal charges.[71]

423

In central Asia, where the Muslims were strongest, indigenous nation-building was far less advanced than elsewhere in the old Russian Empire. The coming of Russia had created a new urban environment and promoted unfamiliar production techniques, but in other ways the tenor of tribal life remained relatively undisturbed, especially in mountain, steppe, and desert regions, where each tribe spoke its own dialect. Locals had kept their distance from incoming Russians, and on occasion had tried forcibly to expel them, as we have seen. Both sides were aware of a considerable cultural distance, which they tended to articulate as being one between Islam and Christianity, or at least between Islam and an alien European way of life.[72]

Once Soviet rule was securely established, the question arose of appropriate administrative units for the region. Many local leaders were in favor of creating a single central Asian republic, a new Turkestan, perhaps as a nucleus around which one day a Pan-Turk or Pan-Islamic state might be established. Russian Communists opposed this solution, mainly because the proposed state would have been a Turkic-Muslim bloc large enough to present a potential challenge to Moscow's authority.

The alternative was to set up a number of separate republics, each of them reflecting a single nationality. The problem with that solution was the underdevelopment of nationalities in the rural areas. In the towns and oases, however, Uzbek and Tajik were already well-established literary languages, and a stronger sense of nationality had emerged during the half-century of Russian rule. Taking these areas as nuclei, Narkomnats decided that the best solution was to create ethnically based autonomous republics within the Russian Soviet Federated Socialist Republic (RSFSR). By the mid-1930s five of these had become Union Republics: Kazakhstan, Uzbekistan, Turkmeniia, Kirgiziia, and Tajikistan.

In some ways, the nationality treated worst by the new Communist rulers was the Russians. They had their own republic—the RSFSR—but a large part of it was occupied by a patchwork of non-Russian autonomous territories. This arrangement prevailed above all in Siberia, in the Volga region, and southeastward from there into central Asia. Here the Soviet government established autonomous republics (or regions, according to the size and importance of the local nationality) bearing local ethnic names, even when the local nationality was in a minority and even when local Russians objected. This is a striking indication of the extent to which, in its early days, the Soviet government was still committed to internationalism and wished to dissociate itself from the old empire and from Russian chauvinism.

The deliberations of Narkomnats resulted in a complex and minutely calibrated system of national relationships. Non-Russian leaders, even Communists, had been conditioned by their period of national independence, however brief, not to accept open subordination to Moscow. Eight republics were therefore initially recognized as independent Soviet Socialist Republics: Ukraine, Belorussia, Georgia, Armenia, Azerbaijan, Bukhara, Khorezm (formerly Khiva), and the Far Eastern Republic. Soviet Russia concluded bilateral treaties with each, though the wording of each treaty differed slightly and sometimes implied that Russia was the senior republic. In any case, there had never been any question of breaking up the Communist Party: its Central Committees in all the republics remained unambiguously subordinated to Moscow. Furthermore, during the civil war all-Russian institutions such as VSNKh, the Council for Labor and Defense (which coordinated the civilian aspects of war), and the Revolutionary Military Council (Revvoensovet: the political arm of the Red Army) exercised authority inside all of them as if the old empire had never ceased to exist. Not for the first time in Russia's history, foreign and internal affairs were not completely distinct.

A crucial turning point was reached in 1922, when all the nominally independent republics signed a Union Treaty which pooled their sovereignty in one federation. The question of what this federation was to be called proved contentious. Stalin, as the responsible commissar, thought it should be the "Russian Soviet Federated Socialist Republic." This name could, however, have implied the resumption of the old imperial relationship, dominated by Russia. Lenin, though by now he had few hopes of an early international revolution, still wanted the international character of the new state and the nominal equality of its constituent republics to be reflected in its title. He therefore argued for the nonethnic, nongeographic name "Union of Soviet Socialist Republics."

His difference with Stalin was exacerbated by a more narrowly based conflict, over Stalin's home republic of Georgia. Georgia was supposed to be absorbed into a Transcaucasian Federative Republic which would also include Armenia and Azerbaijan. Georgian Communist leaders were indignant at the proposal and claimed that they should be admitted to the Soviet Union as a separate republic, like Ukraine or Belorussia. In a heated argument over the question, Stalin's lieutenant, Sergei Ordjonikidze, physically assaulted one of his opponents. Stalin covered up for him. When Lenin found out about the incident, it confirmed his worst fears about Stalin's secretive and overbearing personality and directly influenced the terms in which he described Stalin in his testament.

In the end Lenin managed to rally support against Stalin, and the new state was called as he wished. It was nominally a federal union of equal republics, whose founding charter was the USSR constitution of 1923. In fact, however, even on the formal level, there were certain strange features about this federation. For one thing, the word "federation" was scarcely mentioned in the constitution. For another, the range of functions attributed to the center was very broad: it included not only military and diplomatic matters but also overall policy in the economy, justice, education, public health, social welfare, and other spheres normally delegated to the individual member states of a federation. Nor was there any stipulation that residual functions were to rest with member states.[73] In effect, only cultural and linguistic policy was largely left to the republics—though that was to prove extremely important, as we shall see.

THE SIGNIFICANCE OF THE REVOLUTION

What happened in 1917 broke off developments which had been going forward, if hesitantly and with setbacks, over the previous half-century toward integrating the mass of the people into the imperial Russian polity, and it relaunched that integration process in a new and completely different direction.

The emancipation of the serfs removed the peasants from the matrix of paternalism, of statized personal power in which they had been placed for some two to three centuries, but did not create institutionalized authority to fill the vacuum, except in the form of the widely resented land commandants. The peasants' new "weightless" condition was exacerbated by the rapid social changes of the following decades: urbanization, industrialization, the introduction of widespread primary education and military service—all of which brought peasants into the mainstream of Russian society without giving them institutions through which they could articulate their needs or grievances. Many of them became workers and soldiers. The church was unable to make arrangements to provide spiritual support or the possibility of spiritual growth to meet the changing life circumstances.

During the same decades a desacralization of the Russian monarchy was taking place. The tsar's aura was closely associated with the military and depended on his winning, if not battles, at least wars. The Crimean and Japanese wars shook his reputation, together with defeats in the first year of the world war, while the Bloody Sunday massacre and the corrupt dealings of Rasputin undermined his moral standing.

The outcome of these developments was that, in the crisis of 1917, once the monarchy was removed, the peasant-soldiers' burgeoning identification with "Russia" was seriously weakened and was replaced by localized joint responsibility combined with a radical and bitter rejection of the European-ized culture of the nobility and of educated and affluent townsfolk. Hence the extreme destructiveness and brutality of the revolution, its unleashing of psychopathology and criminality. All the same, the peasants were restoring a legitimate form of community and land tenure as they understood it.

Only the Bolsheviks were able to regain control over the elemental ferocity of the popular revolution—and then only by the application of savagely authoritarian methods. But they did something else too: they harnessed the primitive egalitarianism of the peasants and workers and gave it a millenial coloring in the doctrines of "world revolution" and "proletarian internation-alism." Once more there was no "nation," no "civil society," nothing between the peasant community and the dream of international brotherhood. Such were the paradoxical and fragile foundations of the new postrevolutionary society.[74]

11

SOCIAL TRANSFORMATION

AND TERROR

THE SOVIET UNION AS MULTINATIONAL STATE

If one draws back from the text of the Soviet Constitution of 1923 and considers the other realities affecting the creation of the new state, then the impression of Russian hegemony becomes overwhelming. The Russian Republic (RSFSR) contained 90 percent of the territory and 72 percent of the population of the USSR. The Communist Party was becoming ever more tightly centralized, and in 1927 65 percent of its members were Russian.[1] All-Union institutions like the Red Army, the Cheka, VSNKh, and the state planning authority, Gosplan, were all located in Moscow and were dominated by the Communist Party. It would have required ironclad guarantees to restrain Russia from dominating the Union, and those certainly did not exist. The form of the constitution may have satisfied Lenin, but in substance Stalin had achieved what he wanted.

Yet, paradoxically, the situation of the Russians as an ethnos was also unsatisfactory. Alone of the union republics, Russia had no capital city and no Communist Party of its own. In a witty and perceptive analogy, one scholar has likened the resulting setup to a communal apartment, in which each union republic had its own individual room, while the Russians occupied the hallway, corridor, kitchen, and bathroom: they ran the place and got in everyone else's way, but had no room of their own.[2] To an even greater extent than in the past, Russia's status as a potential nation-state had been dissolved in imperial institutions. The old tension between national and universal goals had reemerged in even more virulent form.

Moreover, to gain the political loyalty of local people, the regime adopted a policy of "indigenization" *(korenizatsiia)*, promoting indigenous cadres to run republics at all levels—trained, to be sure, in Moscow, but still able to speak in the name of their native peoples and to represent their interests in Narkomnats and inside the Communist Party. Locals were also encouraged to join the Communist Party during the 1920s. In Ukraine, for example, Ukrainians' membership in the Communist Party increased from 24 percent to 59 percent in 1922–1932, and in Belorussia from 21 percent to 60 percent.[3] In these ways the regime deliberately endowed non-Russian peoples, including the most backward of them, with the raw materials of nationhood and constructed for them a framework within which one day a nation-state might be created—all this within the old Russian imperial space.

The effect was deepened by the regime's socioeconomic policies. The massive urbanization and industrialization of the 1930s came when primary education in local languages had been established for a decade or so, and this meant that many locals streaming into the towns were already literate in their own language and culture. Ukrainians immigrating to Kharkov, Donetsk, and Dnepropetrovsk from the 1930s to the 1950s tended not to assimilate to the dominant Russian culture, but rather to Ukrainize those towns. Ukraine thus acquired for the first time in its history an appreciable urban mass base. Similarly Tbilisi, which had traditionally been dominated by Russians and Armenians, became for the first time a mainly Georgian city, and Baku became genuinely Azerbaijani.[4]

Since this headlong social change was not accompanied by moves to create the institutions of civil society, in some regions it had the paradoxical effect of consolidating and strengthening traditional authority, in the form of kinship or tribal structures. The nomenklatura system (discussed below) henceforth provided a monopoly framework and the backing of imperial authority for such structures, making them more rigid and durable than they had been previously. These effects were especially noticeable in central Asia and the Caucasus, where kin-based patronage systems were pervasive. In Kazakhstan, for example, *auls* (nomadic settlements) became soviets but continued to be dominated by clan leaders, now bolstered by the resources of a more powerful and interventionist state.[5]

Both as commissar for nationalities and later as the party's general secretary, Stalin insisted on the importance of *territory* for a nation. That is why every nationality, down to the smallest, was awarded its own separate territory, in the form of an "autonomous" republic, region, or even district. The

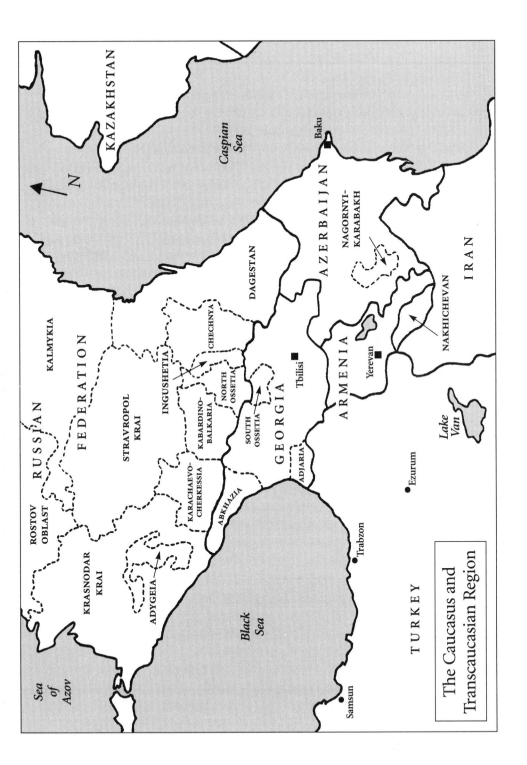

The Caucasus and Transcaucasian Region

Soviet Central Asia

RUSSIAN FEDERATION

KAZAKHSTAN

Caspian Sea

Aral Sea

Baku

5

Nukus
7
Urgench

UZBEK-
ISTAN

Tashkent
Bukhara

□Almaty
□Bishkek

KYRGYZSTAN

Namangan

CHINA

6

TURKMENISTAN

Samarkand
Khojent

*Ferghana
Valley*

Osh

Ashghabat
□

Mary (Merv)

Dushanbe
□ 1

2

IRAN

AFGHANISTAN

3   4

1 – TAJIKISTAN
2 – GORNO-BADAKHSHAN
3 – PAKISTAN
4 – INDIA (JAMMU & KASHMIR)

5 – AZERBAIJAN
6 – MONGOLIA
7 – KARAKALPAKISTAN

□ – State capital
● – Provincial
    administrative center

principle was extended to the classic homeless people, the Jews, who were offered an autonomous region, Birobidjan, on the Chinese border—where, however, very few of them actually settled. Even where the "core" nationality was outnumbered by other ethnic groups living on its territory, the administrative unit still bore its name. Thus in the Mordovian Autonomous Soviet Socialist Republic Russians made up some 60 percent of the population, and in Karelia and Buriatiia more than half.[6]

The alternative to territorial units would have been individual cultural autonomy, as recommended by the Austro-Marxists; but its application in the Soviet Union would have implied a conception of individual civil rights which the Communists had always rejected as spurious. Instead the Soviet state set about what might be called "ethnic engineering," creating nations out of the ethnic material available. This involved ethnographers being sent into the regions to collect data on language, religion, customs, economy, tribal allegiance, and other factors, and then recommending how nations might be constructed out of this raw material.

Language was a key factor. In order to draw the illiterate into their network of propaganda and political education, the Soviet regime had to make sure they acquired a written language; sometimes it even had to construct a written language for them, or at least to choose among available dialects. It then had to ensure that that language was widely used in *likbez* (the liquidation of illiteracy), the mass media, and the educational system. This dominance of local languages was often resented by Russians, who considered it insulting to have their children waste time learning "farmyard dialects" and to be compelled to use them themselves in official documents. However that may be, by the late 1920s 192 languages had been identified, most of which had to be provided with grammars and dictionaries so that they could serve this purpose.[7]

In the perspective of Marxist theory, this nation-building was expected to be a temporary phase. All the same, the fact remains that the Soviet state created a national structure which accorded ill with Marxist theory and did not reflect the reality of intermingled ethnic populations. When nation-building proved not to be temporary, the arrangements put together in the 1920s took on a new and fateful significance.

The anomaly was deepened with the introduction of internal passports in 1932. On each identity document was "entry no. 5": nationality. This meant that every Soviet citizen was ethnically identified—indeed ethnically fixed, since to change "entry no. 5" was impossible. Only young people receiving their first passport at the age of sixteen had the right to choose their ethnos—and then only if their parents were of different origins.

In practice from the mid-1930s nationality became a more important marker than "social origin" and was used for discrimination and manipulation in personnel policy. When the Soviet Constitution of 1936 was promulgated, "former" social classes were restored to full citizenship, including the right to vote. In denunciations and indictments, the designation of "class enemy" was increasingly replaced by the term "enemy of the people," unspecific as to class or nationality. On the whole, though with variations from place to place, in the Union Republics and most Autonomous Republics discrimination favored the main indigenous nationality in education, housing, and employment, and up to the 1950s also the Slavs. Each republic thus tended to become a national stronghold for its titular ethnos (although social class was not eliminated from passport entries till 1974).[8]

Non-Russians did not have everything their own way. Local republican cadres might be encouraged, but all the important decisions about their appointment and dismissal were taken in Moscow. The local economy might be developed, but along lines which were laid down by the all-Union Gosplan and which suited the Soviet Union as a whole rather than the needs of the indigenous population. With the coming of the five-year plans from 1928, more and more of the economy was controlled directly from Moscow.

Local languages and cultures were advanced, even created, but within a framework in which Russian language and culture, as well as Russian imperial values, were increasingly imposed as necessary requirements for everyone. During the 1930s, and even more after 1945, the Russian tsars were no longer merely berated as exploiters of the people, but also extolled as creators and sustainers of the great power which had anticipated the Soviet Union. From 1938 all schools had to teach at least four hours of Russian a week, whatever the native language, and during the 1930s Russian became the language of tuition in all further and higher education, except in the Transcaucasian republics. All Soviet languages, again with the exception of Armenian, Georgian, and Azerbaijani, had to adopt the Cyrillic alphabet, a measure which had the effect of cutting many peoples off from their past written culture. Russian became the sole language of command in the Red Army, and in 1938 non-Russian units were disbanded; henceforth all units had to take in recruits from a variety of nationalities. These measures were not simply imposed from above; ambitious non-Russians reckoned they would advance their careers most effectively by becoming fluent in Russian and making themselves available for employment anywhere in the USSR.[9]

Stalin hailed these changes as a triumph of "internationalism." Most people would see them as Russification. But the latter point of view is also too simple. During the 1930s some of the pillars of Russian national identity were being destroyed or suppressed as well: the village commune, the Orthodox Church, much of the finest Russian literature and culture. If what Stalin was doing was Russification, then it was imperial, neo-*rossiiskii* Russification, contemptuous of ethnic Russian *(russkii)* culture and prepared to jeopardize its very existence. For Stalin Russians were the raw material of socialist empire, and their language and culture were valuable to him only insofar as they sustained that empire, for example by helping to assimilate non-Russians and make them part of it. For the time being at least, "international" meant not the whole world, but the multinational Soviet Union, in which the "Great Russian people" was the first among equals.

The Russian nationalism which Stalin fostered was, then, *sui generis,* not of a type which would have been recognized by most pre-1917 Russian nationalists. It was internationalist, socialist, and revolutionary; it identified with science, technology, and industry, with military strength and with worship of the Great Leader himself. Yet there still remained a shadow of the old Russian ethnic culture, without which the imperial one lacked substance and the power to arouse devotion. Soviet citizens call the Second World War the Great Fatherland *(otechestvennaia)* War, yet soldiers went into battle with the cry "Za Stalina! Za rodinu!" The *rodina* to which they referred was the "motherland," the home village or town, where one's parents or family lived, celebrated by the finest of Russia's war poets, Aleksandr Tvardovskii. The fact is that the two had become inseparable: the *rodina* inspired Russians to fight, but it could not survive without the military and industrial power of the *otechestvo,* fatherland or empire. This was the substance of "Soviet patriotism."

433

Overall, then, certainly by the late 1930s, two contradictory processes were at work simultaneously. Non-Russian nationalities were being given their own territory, language, culture, and administrative structures; but at the same time, the centralized party, state economic planning, and hectic upward social mobility tended to weaken national distinctiveness and promote a generalized Soviet-Russian outlook. In essence, non-Russians were being endowed with identity but denied sovereignty—an explosive mixture.

REVOLUTIONARY CULTURE AND THE "NEW HUMAN BEING"

Lenin's apocalyptic politics were in tune with the spirit of his times. The last twenty years before the revolution, partly because of the continuing weakness of the church, had witnessed a riotous religious and cultural eclecticism, inventive but undisciplined, in which almost anyone who wanted to be treated seriously had to proclaim his own form of revelation, if not revolution.

Russian culture had moved away from realism and utilitarianism to what seemed at first like a new insistence on "art for art's sake," whose main protagonists were the Symbolists. But it soon turned out that what the Symbolists were preaching was not so much the autonomy of art as an even more ambitious project: transforming *life,* according to a new and deeper insight into reality. Rejecting the simple-minded epistemology of Chernyshevskii, they insisted that perceived material reality was merely a gateway to a deeper spiritual reality, to which it was the function of the artist to penetrate, not only as an aesthetic endeavor, but as an act of religious revelation. Vladimir Soloviev, whose ideas underlay much Symbolist writing, believed that art was meant to achieve a reconciliation of heaven and earth and bring about the ultimate transfiguration of reality. One of the leading Symbolists, Andrei Belyi, declared that "art is the creation of life" and that "creativity, carried to its conclusion, turns directly into religious creativity—theurgy."[10] For him revolution was part of this process, a tragic and ambivalent but necessary one. "The act of revolution is double-edged," he wrote. "It is violent, but it is also free. It is the death of old forms, but also the birth of new ones."[11] The Symbolist poet Aleksandr Blok specifically interpreted the Russian revolution in the light of this doctrine, proclaiming it as a new Scythian incursion from the steppes, destroying and cleansing Russian society in order then to do the same for European civilization. In his very last poem, *The Twelve*, he portrayed the Red Guards of Petrograd as apostles, with Christ himself at their head.

The Futurists, as a slightly later generation, loved to mock the Symbolists for their "mysticism," but their perspective was fundamentally the same: that the old world was undergoing a terminal crisis which would lead to great upheavals and to the birth of a new world and a new kind of human being. The poet Vladimir Maiakovskii, the best known of them and a convinced Bolshevik in his youth, believed that revolution would be a cleansing force. Steeped in the idiom of contemporary urban life, with its technology, sport, and mass communications, the Futurists agitated to "throw Pushkin, Dostoevskii, Tolstoy, and so forth" from "the ship of modernity" and to renew the language of literature with neologisms drawn from the teeming life of the city. Art would thus revitalize life and make possible the creation of a "new human being."[12]

In many ways the Communist leaders took over this project. Culture was far more important to them than it had been to the tsars. What gave the Russian revolution its impetus and the Soviet state its authority was the project of creating a new kind of human being, more harmonious, versatile, and socially conscious than people could be in a society scarred by class conflict and the division of labor. Armed with the latest technology and with a correct theory of social evolution, the "new Soviet man" would be able to transform nature and render it conformable to the needs of human beings. Trotskii proclaimed: "He will point out places for mountains and for passes. He will change the course of the rivers and he will lay down rules for the ocean." And he would combine innovatory capacity with the best qualities of Renaissance man: "Man will become immeasurably stronger, wiser, and subtler; his body will become more harmonized, his movements more rhythmic, his voice more musical . . . The average human type will rise to the heights of an Aristotle, a Goethe, or a Marx. And beyond this ridge new peaks will rise."[13]

The relationship between this supremely creative individual and the society in which he lived was conceived in different ways by different Communist thinkers. Most of them assumed the existence of a harmonious society in which the individual would be glad to subordinate personal desires to the needs of the collective, and would achieve fulfillment by doing so. Aleksei Gastev, director of the Central Institute for Labor, went much further: he actually talked of men of the future being assimilated to the world of machines. They would have "nerves of steel" and "muscles like iron rails": the mechanization of the proletarian psychology would be so far-reaching that human beings would become anonymous units, "an A, B, C, a 123,456, soulless, devoid of personality, emotion and lyricism, no longer expressing himself through screams of pain or peals of laughter, but rather through a speedometer or pressure-gauge."[14]

Gastev's Central Institute for Labor pioneered the "scientific study of labor," in which industrial processes were broken down to their minutest components and human beings slotted into them so that, by easily learned gestures and movements, they could generate a high level of productivity. This model, essentially the Taylor system imposed at the Ford Model-T works in Detroit, aroused Lenin's enthusiasm as a means of raising productivity in backward, uneducated Russia.[15]

The first experiment in recasting culture was undertaken by "Proletkult," the Proletarian Cultural-Educational Associations, which proliferated along with many other working-class organizations in 1917. Their theorist was Aleksandr Bogdanov, who believed that the working class would actually create a new culture, different in nature from that of the old aristocratic and bourgeois world, because their way of life, collectivist in its essence and governed by mechanical processes, generated a new consciousness. Art, as the "highest and least understood form of organizational activity," would play a major role in the transformation of society. Bogdanov's innovatory "organizational science" or "techtology" would combine art, science, and all fields of learning in a supreme proletarian synthesis.[16]

During 1917 there were some 150 workers' cultural and educational circles in Petrograd alone, claiming 100,000 members, mostly organized around factory committees. They included choirs, dance ensembles, drama clubs, self-education circles, political study groups, and agitational centers.[17] Like other working-class organizations, they became steadily more suspicious of the Provisional Government. Their prickly self-reliance continued after October 1917, and they kept their distance from both the Soviet government and Communist Party. In the upheavals of the following years they became probably the most numerous, independent, and enthusiastic of mass organizations. The membership of the local proletkults was mostly very young, eager to learn and to experiment.

Intellectuals and workers interacted with the proletkults on more equal terms than they had done with ordinary people at any other time in Russian history: well-known cultural figures like film director Sergei Eizenshtein, drama producer Konstantin Stanislavskii, and writers Evgenii Zamiatin and Andrei Belyi came in to give seminars. The flavor of the proletkults' creative efforts can be gauged from the titles of some of their publications: "Dawns of the Future," "The Iron Messiah," "Machine Paradise."[18] One proletarian poet called on his colleagues to "exert your mind and muscles . . . so that Russia's resurrection shall spread to the whole world," while Pavel Lebedev-Polianskii, chairman of Proletkult, prophesied that "a new science, art, literature, and morality, in short a new proletarian culture, conceived in the ranks of the industrial proletariat, is preparing a new human being, with a new system of emotions and beliefs." The organization took up "production art" to end the "bourgeois" separation of art and industry and to use industrial techniques to bring art into the everyday life of the people.[19]

The apogee of proletarian culture was reached on May Day 1920, when "The Mystery of Liberated Labor" was celebrated in Petrograd before more than 30,000 spectators by 4,000 actors, drawn from proletkults and the Red Army. The city was transformed for the occasion into a vast theater. On a dais in front of the Stock Exchange top-hatted capitalists danced to gypsy music and the can-can. Behind them a gate of gold guarded the forbidden kingdom of equality and brotherhood, and below them the downtrodden masses toiled to the heavy tread of Chopin's Funeral March. The drama consisted in an enactment of various moments of popular revolution in world history, now being erected into a canonized narrative by the impresarios of the new regime, from the Spartacus revolt in ancient Rome through to the abortive Russian revolution of 1905. Then, at last, a red star appeared in the east, and the masses swept aside their oppressors, stormed the golden gates, and threw open the promised kingdom. They finished by dancing round the Tree of Liberty, illuminated by searchlights from riverboats, while a band played the *Internationale* and factory sirens from the entire city whooped in a deafening chorus.[20]

Of course, this spectacle was far from spontaneous: it was carefully choreographed by the city's leading theater directors. All the same, more than any other postrevolutionary organizations, the proletkults embodied not only a spontaneous desire on the part of working people for self-improvement, but also a potentially universalizing messianism. As an organization, though, Proletkult could never resolve the tension between these two aims, nor its ambivalence over whether it existed mainly to teach workers the rudiments of the old culture or to experiment boldly and create a new one. Moreover, in spite of its defiant attitudes toward authority, Proletkult depended heavily on official subsidies. By the winter of 1920–21, those subsidies were drying up. In any case Lenin was unsympathetic to any association independent of the party. He insisted that Proletkult be strictly subordinated to the People's Commissariat for Enlightenment (Narkompros) and its Communist Party cells. Most of its educational and agitational functions were handed over to the party propaganda network, Agitprop, or the political education department of Narkompros, Glavpolitprosvet, under Lenin's wife, Nadezhda Krupskaia.[21]

With the loss of its independence the zest went out of Proletkult. The attempt to create a distinctive proletarian culture and to promote a mass-based utopian project was abandoned. An important source of revolutionary *élan vital* had been jettisoned. The so-called proletarian writers of the following decade, organized in RAPP (the Russian Association of Proletarian Writers) and other such groups, were neither proletarian nor innovative: their techniques looked back to the established realist writers of the nineteenth century.[22]

However, the attempt to break down the barriers between art and life, to bring art and industry together, continued among artists themselves. The First Working Group of Constructivists, formed in March 1921, preached the need for the artist "to go into the factory, where the real body of life is made," in order to "realize the communist expression of material structures." Vladimir Tatlin was commissioned by the Visual Arts Department of the Moscow Soviet to build a monument to the revolution, in line with Lenin's Plan for Monumental Propaganda, which was intended to surround workers with architectural and sculptural statements about the new society they were building. Tatlin's project became the *nec plus ultra* of the early Soviet combination of modernism, utopianism, and utilitarianism.

By the time a model of it was exhibited at the Eighth All-Russian Congress of Soviets in 1920, it had become the Monument to the Third International (that is, an organization still in the future rather than an event in the past), and its display accompanied Lenin's speech announcing the great electrification program. It was designed to span the River Neva and was to consist of three huge glass shapes in iron struts and spirals thrusting upward at an oblique angle from the ground to a height greater than the Eiffel Tower.

438

The lowest shape, a cube, was to accommodate congresses of the International and to rotate once a year; the center one, a pyramid, was to rotate once a month, and to house administrative offices; and the highest, a cylinder, was to rotate daily and serve as a center for information and agitation. The structure thus combined aesthetic and utilitarian functions in the best spirit of "production art." Tatlin himself said of it that "Iron is strong like the will of the proletariat. Glass is clear like its conscience."[23]

Significantly, the monument was never built, perhaps because it was impractical in the engineering sense, but more likely because the messianic spirit which impelled it waned during the prosaic years of the New Economic Policy.

In the theater Vsevolod Meyerhold pioneered another version of breaking down the frontiers between art and life. He wanted to break free of the "Stanislavskii theater," which used footlights and proscenium to separate audience and actors, and to bring together elements from life and art never before juxtaposed. To him theater meant circus, fairground stalls, Punch-and-Judy, strolling players, the *commedia dell'arte*, music and dance as much as verbal declamation. He cultivated a style of rhythmic bodily movement known as "biomechanics," intended to promote both harmony and dramatic effect. Far from encouraging the "willing suspension of disbelief," he deliberately "tore off the masks" and drew attention to the artificiality of dramatic performance.[24]

In their disparate areas of activity Meyerhold and Gastev had something in common: the desire to destroy old taboos and to break down old boundaries, between theater and life, between theory, aesthetics, and productivity, all in the interests of creating a new world. Their inspiration came not mainly from the Communist Party, but from a millenarian and iconoclastic mood current among intellectuals before and after the revolution.[25]

THE ORTHODOX CHURCH

The October revolution coincided with the most important event in the history of the Russian Orthodox Church for over two hundred years. Even as artillery boomed over Moscow, inside the Kremlin the long-mooted *pomestnyi sobor* was meeting and taking the decision to restore the patriarchate abolished two centuries earlier. Those assembled were also discussing how the church could take its place in a new political system no longer dominated by the tsars.

But even as they debated, the rules of the game changed abruptly for a second time. A new millenial regime was coming to power, atheist in its convictions, committed to the erosion and ultimate extirpation of all forms of theist belief. In January 1918 the Soviet government passed a decree, euphemistically entitled "On the Separation of Church and State," which was supplemented by further legislation in the 1920s. These measures expropriated all ecclesiastical land and property without compensation and stripped religious associations of their juridical status. Any congregation, consisting of at least twenty officially registered adult believers, was permitted to lease back church buildings for the purpose of worship, free of charge provided they kept it in good repair, and to hire a "servant of the cult" to perform services. Any other kind of religious activity, including education, was forbidden. The priest was now an employee, not a pastor of his flock, and charitable work, public processions, prayer meetings, and Bible study, even the ringing of church bells, were all proscribed. Outside the weekly divine service, there was little a congregation could legally do, and therewith much of the spiritual and communal significance of religion was eliminated.

Tikhon, the new patriarch, reacted vehemently to the first decrees of the new regime. He pronounced an anathema on atheists and on those who committed violence against the innocent. He did not call for physical resistance to the Soviet regime, but all the same, during the civil war, clergymen were treated as if they belonged to the enemy. By 1921 many had been arrested and confined in concentration camps, or even simply murdered, while nearly six hundred monasteries had been closed down.[26] The church was no longer a coherent organization, and Tikhon was unable to enforce his line of peaceful resistance. Some clergy in White-controlled areas and abroad preached armed resistance to the godless regime, while at Karlovtsy in Yugoslavia in 1921 an improvised émigré church council called for the overthrow of the Communists and the restoration of the monarchy.

Such disagreements within a church in upheaval gave the Communists the opportunity both to portray the Orthodox Church as an enemy and to divide and dominate it. They also encouraged schism in the church inside Russia. The divisions of 1905–1907 over ecclesiastical reform, which had never healed, now burst out with redoubled force. The renovationists, who had wanted to open the episcopate to the white clergy and to reform the liturgy by conducting it in modern Russian, formed a group called the Living Church, both to agitate for their proposed reforms and to promote a more positive relationship with the regime. Some of them even preached that Communism was a modern form of the teachings of Christ.

The famine in the Volga basin in 1921–22 gave the regime a pretext to put pressure on the church and to deepen the split. Tikhon was anxious for the church to use its remaining valuables—insofar as not needed for the liturgy—to raise funds for the relief of hunger, but he insisted that the church itself should retain control over the distribution of resources. The Communist leaders, however, encouraged the renovationists to agitate for state control of the operation, to break with those whom Trotskii called the "Black Hundred clergy," to convene a new council and elect a new hierarchy.[27]

When the GPU (as the Cheka was now called) sent in its activists to confiscate church property, some parishes mounted ferocious resistance. Clergymen who encouraged the defense of church property were arrested, and some, including Metropolitan Veniamin of Petrograd, were executed. Tikhon was placed under house arrest, and two renovationist priests, Aleksandr Vvedenskii and Vladimir Krasnitskii, went to see him to persuade him that as a result he could no longer carry out his duties. They set up a Higher Church Administration, headed by the renovationist bishop Antonin, claiming that the move had been authorized by Tikhon. With the help of the GPU, the new Administration set about gaining control of parishes, appointing their own priests to them, and implementing their planned reforms.

The disarray in the church meant that the center of gravity shifted to the parishes, which now had a freedom of maneuver they had not known for more than two hundred years. They could now, for example, elect their own priests. At the grass roots, it turned out, the renovationists' success was not to be repeated. Their reforms found little support among congregations, especially in the villages. The change which aroused the strongest misgivings was to all appearance a minor one: the adoption of the Gregorian calendar (which even Tikhon was prepared to accept). Villagers feared that it would disrupt the celebration of festivals and unjustifiably demote certain saints. Parish priests warned that such innovations would probably cause whole congregations to desert to the Old Believers.[28]

In the end, impressed by this popular opposition, the regime withdrew from its commitment to the renovationists and released Tikhon on condition that he issue a statement accommodating to the Communists. This he did not long before his death in March 1925. The Communists would not allow a sobor to elect a successor, but his *locum tenens*, Metropolitan Sergii, published an even more conciliatory declaration: "We wish to be Orthodox believers, and at the same time to acknowledge the Soviet Union as our civic homeland, whose joys and successes are our joys and successes and whose setbacks are our setbacks. Any blow directed against the Union . . . we see as a blow directed against us." The identification of the church with a "civic homeland" rather than with the state was carefully chosen, but that did not prevent further splits, as individual prelates and congregations refused to accept even such a cautious espousal of the Soviet cause.[29]

In the mid- and late 1920s the regime's challenge to the church focused on atheist propaganda and the inauguration of a secular counterculture. In 1925 a League of Godless (from 1929 Militant Godless) was set up, with its own journal, broadsheets, and agitational material. It was intended that godless agitators should be specially trained, since a good knowledge of the liturgy, scriptures, and catechism was essential to rebut the arguments of believers. Their aim was to portray the church as an oppressive and exploitative organization, deceiving ordinary people with false promises and extorting money from them for its services. In its place the agitators were to open reading rooms and "red corners," to encourage the liquidation of illiteracy and to promote discussions and disputes which would make clear the advantages of a secular and scientific worldview.[30]

Reaction to these efforts was varied, especially in the small towns and villages. Younger men, particularly those who had worked in industry, served in the Red Army, or wanted to break away from a patriarchal family to set up on their own, were often favorably disposed. In general, however, the milieu was hostile or suspicious, and the atheists themselves were too clumsy or poorly trained to make a major impact; some of them were former believers or priests themselves, still attached to religious forms in their new faith. Sometimes religious associations would mask themselves as an artel, cooperative, or collective farm, and on that basis churchwardens or even priests would participate in the village soviet.[31]

In the end the attempt to gradually establish an atheist counterculture atrophied in the midst of precipitous social change decreed from above. Most of the new industrial suburbs and settlements created during the first five-year plans had no church buildings, so that no religious alternative was on offer, while in the countryside the collectivization of agriculture often coincided with the closure of the church and the arrest of the priest. Activists would arrive to take down the church bells, needed as a source of nonferrous metal, requisition icons and utensils, seal off the building, and prepare it for some secular purpose, perhaps to become a reading room, cinema, or merely a kolkhoz store. By 1939–40 only a few hundred parish churches, five hundred at the most, were still open and active, about 1 percent of the prerevolutionary total. Only four diocesan bishops were still fully active in the patriarchal church, and a handful more in the renovationist and anti-Sergian denominations. It seems that some 25,000–30,000 priests must have been arrested and many of them executed during the 1930s.[32]

Even before the intense persecution of the 1930s the Orthodox culture of ordinary Russians had rested on tradition, community, and inherited lore rather than study, Bible reading, or personally formed conviction. The Communists came to power at a time when that was beginning to change, and a more personalized piety based on scripture was taking hold among workers and peasants. But whirlwind social change along with the atheist campaign banned scripture, uprooted communities, and interrupted tradition, and thereby undermined all three foundations for belief. For most people the result was a gradually fading religious conviction, confusion, or indifference, while for a few it meant an intense and highly conservative faith, practiced in private and largely in secret or in common with just a few fellow believers. Women were in a better position to preserve their religious faith, since far fewer of them were making careers in public life.

The cause of ecclesiastical reform was shattered by the renovationist experience, partly because of its association with the police state, but mainly because reform could not flourish in a soil saturated on the one hand by indifference and on the other by rigid traditionalism. The clergy and especially the bishops became essentially members of the nomenklatura personnel hierarchy, assessed for their contribution to the cause of the regime, or at least for the absence of religious zeal. The church became extremely hieratic and formalistic, partly for that reason and partly because it had no functions apart from weekly divine service.

THE NEW ECONOMIC POLICY

During the Tenth Party Congress, while the Kronstadt rebellion was being repressed and party discipline tightened, economic policy was eased. Few Communists welcomed this relaxation from an ideological viewpoint, but they could hardly doubt that it was necessary: the siege economy and the state monopoly had failed. Industrial production was at a fifth or less of its 1913 level, in the case of iron and steel below 5 percent. The towns were semideserted for lack of food and employment: there were less than half as many industrial workers as in 1913. The railways had come to an almost complete standstill, except for army transports. Agriculture had suffered less badly overall, but many fields had not been properly cultivated for years, cattle had starved, and horses had been requisitioned. Little of what was being grown was reaching the towns, except courtesy of "bagmen," peasants carrying sacks who evaded the roadblocks and who charged astronomical prices in improvised street markets.[33]

Production and trade had somehow to be revived and their fruits brought to ordinary people. For that purpose certain aspects of a market economy were restored. This was what was called the New Economic Policy, or NEP.

Grain requisitioning was abolished and replaced by a tax, which was both lower and more predictable than the draconian seizures of the recent past. Peasants were once more allowed to hire labor and rent land. At the same time private retail trade was legalized and rationing abolished. Peasants now had an incentive again to grow a food surplus, secure in the knowledge that they could sell it on the market for a reasonable price. So that they would have something to buy with the proceeds, the regime also abolished the state monopoly of retail trade and consumer goods manufacture. So that they would have money to buy it with, the State Bank was reopened and in November 1922 empowered to issue a new ruble, the *chervonets*, backed by gold and by a balanced state budget, though paper money continued to circulate alongside it. All this meant the revival of a money market and a stock exchange.[34]

443

The result was an immediate and dramatic material improvement, though one not to all Communists' liking. Emma Goldman, a visiting foreign socialist, later recalled that "Shops and stores sprang up overnight, mysteriously stacked with delicacies Russia had not seen for years. Large quantities of butter, cheese and meat were displayed for sale . . . Men, women and children with pinched faces and hungry eyes stood about gazing into the windows and discussing the great miracle: what was but yesterday considered a heinous offence was now flaunted before them in an open and legal manner."[35] Regular street markets appeared once more, their scruffy stalls supplied by bagmen no longer barred from the towns. All kinds of small-scale enterprise flourished: in the evenings the cafés were open again, with their bright lights and alluring aromas. So too, comrades observed with distaste, were the brothels. Private trade had many aspects.

Abundance was not universal. In the Volga-Kama basin, western Siberia, and southern Ukraine, where there was a drought, peasants faced two successive poor harvests already weakened by hunger and without any reserves. The result was famine and disease on a huge scale. The government stopped transport out of the region to prevent the spread of infection, but allowed the formation of a Public Committee to Help the Hungry (Pomgol), which distributed aid—medicine, clothes, tools, and seeds—from President Hoover's American Relief Administration. In spite of their best efforts some five million people died. The regime was intensely suspicious of the relief agents, harassed some of them and seized their supplies, and in the end arrested most of the members of Pomgol.[36]

In its immediate aims (which were all its creators had in mind) NEP was successful. In the principal industrial fields—coal, electricity, iron and steel, and machine tools—by the late 1920s the Soviet Union was approaching or had exceeded 1913 levels of production.[37] However, in the process of recovery new strains were generated. Although agricultural production reached pre-war levels by the mid-1920s, marketings did not rise above about 60 percent of them. Peasants were holding back a much larger proportion of the harvest for their own consumption, for animal feed, or for distilling into alcoholic liquor. They were discouraged from selling produce by the state of the market, where industrial wares were relatively much more expensive: since agriculture recovered more quickly than industry, its products became less scarce and so comparatively cheaper.

By the autumn of 1923 the prices of industrial goods were three times as high as in 1913 relative to agricultural ones. This was the "scissors crisis." During the civil war peasants had learned (or relearned) to become self-sufficient, and so they tended to react to this price imbalance, not by working harder and trying to earn more, but by retreating from the market altogether and doing without urban products. They distrusted both towns and Communists, and were wary of long-term economic arrangements involving either. Periodically, then, the towns were threatened by food shortages even after the famine was over.

In 1923 the government reacted to this crisis by imposing price controls on urban products commonly consumed by villagers, and in the following year it resumed grain exports, thus raising food prices. In that way it restored some equilibrium to rural-urban trade at the cost of urban consumers, and several relatively prosperous farming years followed. But no foundation had been laid for long-term growth, and party members had been given economic reasons for resentment of the NEP, to add to the political ones.

The situation of workers under the "dictatorship of the proletariat" was not easy. As the economy revived and a free labor market was restored, many who had taken refuge in the countryside streamed back to look for work. They did not always find it: there were always more seekers than jobs, and by the end of 1926 there were about a million unemployed. Even those who were more fortunate found working life harsh. "Workers' control" had completely disappeared, and one-man management had returned. With Lenin's enthusiastic support, the new bosses adopted Taylorian rationalization schemes, which dehumanized the labor process, depriving factory hands of control over their own working time. They were subject to a modified capitalism wherein price controls kept industrial goods cheap and therefore their wages low. Women workers suffered particularly. Some of them had become accustomed to responsible and skilled jobs during the war, but were now supplanted by male rivals, whom both employers and the party tended to prefer. Despite the rhetoric about equality, women were edged out into the less skilled, more insecure, and worse-paid jobs.

Trade unions were in an ambiguous situation, since they were now defending workers' interests against a self-proclaimed "workers' state." They were inhibited from launching protests, let alone all-out strikes. Furthermore, workers found that their own forms of work organization were frowned on in the new society. The artel was collectivist and egalitarian, and might have been thought to embody Communist principles. But it was also self-governing, localist in its outlook, and sometimes based on explicitly religious principles. Communist employers, like capitalists, preferred to deal with workers as individuals, whom they could discipline from above, while artels resisted the introduction of individual piece-rates as a basis for pay. After being tolerated for some years, artels were officially abolished in 1931, though some of them survived after a fashion as "brigades of Communist labor."[38]

Professional people, administrators, and managers, on the other hand, were in a relatively strong position. The regime needed them because it had few specialized people of its own to run the economy. From the very outset Sovnarkom opened a register of specialists, as a scarce resource. For their part, most "bourgeois specialists" were prepared to work with the regime, since it was evidently trying to restore law and order, accorded high priority to technical development, and was prepared to keep the workers in their place. General V. N. Ipatiev, a leading chemical engineer under the old regime, and a man of very conservative views, agreed to become director of the State Scientific Technical Institute because the Communists, whatever else one might think about them, had "saved the country from anarchy and at least temporarily preserved its intelligentsia and material wealth."[39] This did not mean that "bourgeois specialists" were Communists: as late as 1928 a survey showed that in the whole of Soviet industry only 138 engineers were members of the party.[40] But they were becoming part of the new elite, and an ideological truce was taking shape between them and the party on the basis of a modified Russian imperial patriotism. More and more this was to become the working (as distinct from theoretical) ideology of the Soviet regime.

International developments strengthened the tendency to superimpose Russian patriotism on Communism. By 1923, with the failure of a Communist rising in Hamburg, it was becoming clear that international revolution was not imminent, at least not in the advanced countries of Europe, and that for the foreseeable future socialism would have to be built, if at all, in Russia alone, without the help of more mature economies. At the Fourteenth Party Conference in 1925 Stalin gained acceptance for the idea that it was possible to build "socialism in one country," though he was roundly criticized by Trotskii for downgrading world revolution. The failure of Communist insurrections in Shanghai and Canton in 1927 seemed, though, to confirm Stalin's diagnosis.

The question remained: how should socialism be built? Lenin had always taken it for granted that the development of a modern industrial civilization in Russia would require the aid of the more advanced economies of Europe, which he expected by then to be socialist. In a hostile capitalist world, how was Russia to generate sufficient resources for the huge investment needed?

The party split over how it should answer these uncomfortable questions. One group, headed by Trotskii, proposed that the Soviet state launch a crash program of heavy industrialization, financed by very high taxes imposed on the entire private sector, the so-called nepmen. The second, whose most articulate spokesman was Bukharin, objected that this policy would open a battlefront between workers and peasants, which was foolish, even mortally dangerous, while Soviet Russia was isolated and besieged; it would make more sense to encourage the private economy, and especially the agricultural sector, to develop in its own way, and allow it to generate both savings for industrial investment and a market to which industrial goods could be sold. Bukharin admitted that his policy would be slower, but he argued that it would be much safer.[41]

Stalin initially supported Bukharin but gradually withdrew from the contest to let the two sides fight it out, while he concentrated on building up the party apparatus, which he controlled as general secretary. Most Communists had not spotted that this was where real power lay, once other political parties, institutions, and social classes had been destroyed. They were content to let Stalin assemble and classify his personnel files, not fathoming their potential. He used the information in them to appoint and advance the career of those who supported him, usually those who had joined the party during or since the civil war, and to block those who opposed him, who were not infrequently the party's old intellectuals from the days of underground struggle and early revolutionary élan.

The party rules of 1919 had stipulated that wherever there were three or more party members in any organization, they must form a party cell, "whose duty it is to increase party influence in every direction, carry out party policies in non-party milieux, and effect party supervision over the work of all organizations and institutions." In 1922 the personnel assignments office of the secretariat issued a list of 445 "central agencies and their local offices in which personnel appointments and reassignments require a resolution of the Central Committee of the RKP(b)."[42] To ensure that this could be done, the Twelfth Party Congress in 1923 instructed committees at all levels to keep up-to-date lists of employees suitable for particular kinds of work and for promotion within their field.

These lists were amalgamated with Sovnarkom's lists of specialists. Coordinated by the party secretariat, they now enabled Stalin to oversee all appointments to responsible positions, not just within the party and state but in all walks of life. This was true even where posts were supposed to be elective. The qualities expected of such appointees Stalin summed up as follows: they should be "people who can carry out directives, adopting them as a personal cause and implementing them effectively. Otherwise politics loses all sense, becomes mere gesticulation. That is why . . . we must study every appointee thoroughly." This was the start of the nomenklatura system, which in time became the most extensive and tightly controlled system of executive patronage the world had ever seen. With its help the party Central Committee became the control panel of the Soviet Union's ruling class.[43]

The core of the nomenklatura in its early days consisted of Bolsheviks of worker-peasant origin, most of whom had joined the party between 1905 and 1917 and had known some years of underground activity, prison, and exile. Typically they had taken part in the revolution and then acted as political commissars during the civil war. Such were Valerian Kiubyshev, active in the Volga region; Lazar Kaganovich, in the Volga and later central Asia; Sergei Ordjonikidze, in the Transcaucasus; and Sergei Kirov, in the Transcaucasus and later Leningrad. These men were bound by strong ties of comradeship from the shared struggles of the revolution and civil war, and when transferred or promoted they took with them their own trusted subordinates. Stalin consciously advanced the careers of these hitherto subsidiary leaders, since he felt closer to them in spirit than to the sophisticated intellectuals around Lenin and Trotskii.[44]

The Communist Party was now defining "class" in its own terms and creating a hierarchy in which its gradations could be calibrated. With the introduction of korenizatsiia, and later of internal passports and propiska (dwelling permits), it was also defining what nationality meant in the new social order. After Lenin's death, the party took in a large number of worker recruits, the so-called Lenin enrollment, who were raw material for promotion in the next decade and hence eager clients of Stalin, as head of the secretariat.[45]

The first sign of the latent power of this system was the way Stalin used it not only to defeat but also to stigmatize morally most of his rivals and potential opponents from the pioneer days under Lenin. He exploited his power of appointment to weaken Trotskii's support among the political commissars, then Zinoviev's in the Leningrad party organization and Kamenev's in Moscow. When Trotskii, Zinoviev, and Kamenev got together to form a United Opposition, he dismissed their followers and arranged for his own militants to turn up to disrupt their public meetings. He humiliated them by pinning on them the label of "Leftist Deviation," implying that they had disavowed the heritage of Lenin and the party in general. In the end the Fifteenth Party Congress of December 1927 denounced them as a "fraction" and expelled them from the Central Committee.

The reaction of those expelled was highly revealing. Kamenev remained convinced that his views were right, and recognized that in "normal" politics this would be the moment to found an opposition party. Under the "dictatorship of the proletariat," however, he felt that an opposition was inadmissible. He wrote to his colleagues, declaring that "we find it necessary to submit to the decisions of the congress, no matter how difficult they might be for us," and called on them to do the same.[46] The millenial party had a total grip even over its dissenting members.

Over the next two years Stalin applied similar techniques to Bukharin and his associates, Mikhail Tomskii, head of the trade unions, and Aleksei Rykov, chairman of the Council of People's Commissars (the inheritor of Lenin's only official position). At a Central Committee plenum of November 1929 they were condemned as Rightist Deviationists and expelled from the Politburo.

These intraparty squabbles and intrigues did not take place in a vacuum. The points at issue concerned fundamental choices over economic development. In 1928 food shortages made them urgent. State purchases of grain were running a quarter below the level of the previous year. This time the regime was not prepared to meet the problem by accommodating farmers and reducing industrial prices. Many Communists felt that quite enough concessions had been made to "kulaks" and "nepmen," whose ultimate aim anyway was to destroy the proletarian state.

The food supply crisis put wind in the sails of those numerous Communists at all levels who felt it was time to stop compromising with the class enemy and return instead to the building of socialism. Crisis revived the millenarian aspect of Communism. The party decreed a partial return to the methods of the civil war. In the Urals and Siberia markets were closed down and private trade banned. Peasants were ordered instead to sell their grain to state supply officials at fixed prices. Search teams reappeared in the villages to ferret out hoarded produce.

The initial results were quite encouraging: a good deal of grain was discovered, stored away for alcoholic distillation, feeding to livestock, or the advent of better prices. There was short-lived abundance in the state shops. But in

1929 things got much worse. Reading the signals from the Urals, peasants reduced their sowings to what was needed for subsistence. Why produce what would merely be confiscated? The state responded as in 1918, by setting up committees of poor peasants to "unleash class war in the villages" and to help requisition teams find hidden produce. Village assemblies were instructed to hold meetings at which their members were labeled "poor peasants," "middle peasants," or "kulaks": very heavy taxes and delivery targets were imposed on the latter.

This confrontation threatened the whole basis of the NEP, which is why Bukharin and his "rightist" followers objected to it so strongly. They quoted Lenin, and with some justification. Lenin had called the NEP a "breathing space," but had increasingly inclined to the view that one should draw breath "seriously and for a long time." He had not abandoned the ultimate aim of collectivizing agriculture, but toward the end of his life he was recommending that this be done gradually, through the creation of "civilized cooperatives," whose advantages over family smallholdings would be so obvious that peasants would flock to join them voluntarily.[47] Stalin's Urals-Siberian campaign of 1928–29 signaled the abandonment of this long-term perspective, and the return to emergency wartime methods.

COLLECTIVIZATION OF AGRICULTURE

The party's response to the grain shortage completely changed the concept of collectivization. Now it had to be carried out headlong, on a mass basis, both to facilitate the delivery of urgently needed grain and to reopen the road to utopia. But the party was still desperately weak in the countryside: it lacked its own agents who could be relied upon to implement policy effectively in a tricky and fast-changing situation. On the other hand, the Komsomol, the Communist youth movement, *was* relatively strong there, with roughly four times as many members in the villages as the party itself. The problem was that they were not only young and inexperienced; they were also impatient and bloody-minded. They usually came from the poorer families, and were among those most alienated by the traditional domination of the solid, well-to-do heads of households within the mir.

The only way to make use of their talents was to abandon the policy of persuasion by example, and instead to unleash class war in the countryside, sending in plenipotentiaries from the *raion* (district) to mastermind the process. Poorer peasants and Komsomols were to provide the impetus by denouncing the wealthier peasants as "kulaks" and applying a mixture of threats and cajolery to persuade others to sign up for the collective farm (*kolkhoz*). That is exactly what many local party secretaries, reading the exhortations published in the newspapers, decided to do during the winter of 1929–30. "Better to go too far than to underachieve" was the motto of the moment.[48] The simplest way to create a collective farm was not to go through a long process of persuasion but simply to call a meeting of the village *skhod* and put pressure on all its members to sign up. A collective would then exist at least on paper. Kulaks were not allowed to join, and their property was confiscated for the benefit of the collective. Plenipotentiaries would tour the village, accompanied by Komsomols and rural laborers, to "inspect" the homes of the wealthier households, puncturing mattresses, axing partitions, and ripping up floorboards to seek out hidden wealth. Furniture and clothes would be carted off, to be sold, shared out among the *kolkhozniki*, or even quietly appropriated by the searchers themselves.[49]

Some kulaks, in anticipation of such a visit, sold off their most precious belongings, slaughtered their livestock for meat, and drank their supplies of home-brewed vodka in a final bitter feast. Then they would abandon their homes, sometimes lived in for generations, and make for the towns, to seek alternative employment and elude the eyes of prying militiamen. Those who did not leave in good time were officially expropriated and rounded up. They were divided into three categories, the more fortunate receiving land in the neighborhood which was not required by a collective farm (and so was likely to be of poor quality). The kulaks deemed most "malicious" (*zlostnye*) were transported in cattle trucks to places of exile, which might be construction sites in large towns, but might equally be remote, underpopulated regions of Kazakhstan or Siberia, where they were expected to carve out new farms in the wilderness. Some of them had to start their new life in damp, drafty, half-finished barracks, others by hastily putting up some form of makeshift dwelling, living in a tent or in the open air till it was ready. The first wave of this operation, from January to April 1930, involving some 141,000 "kulaks," was coordinated by the GPU, which carried out the arrests and provided the transport.[50]

Some at least of those dubbed "kulaks" were not among the better-off peasants, but had merely shown reluctance to enter the kolkhoz. According to a schoolteacher in Kursk oblast, sent to help with the campaign, those arrested were "ordinary Russian peasant men and women," who had been roused at night and ordered to leave immediately with a minimum of equipment and clothes. Fellow villagers saw them off, weeping and wailing. They were loaded into cattle trucks, which they were forbidden to leave. "They had to relieve themselves into a bucket. Everyone together: girls, children, men."[51] So many died in the course of these transportations that one present-day Russian historian accuses the Soviet authorities of "genocide."[52]

No one had yet worked out how a collective farm should be organized, and how much of the homes, property, fields, and labor process would in fact be collectivized. But the activists did not let that stand in their way. The tone of *Pravda* editorials suggested they would not lose by taking matters to extremes, so some of them insisted that peasants hand over everything, even furniture and clothes, to collective ownership. Such zeal aroused ferocious resistance. A persistent and resourceful rumor mill—some called it the "kulak agitprop"—insinuated that all the women were to become "collective property" and sleep together under the "collective blanket," or, more realistically, that famine and devastation were imminent, and that the reign of Antichrist would soon follow. In the north Caucasus it was said that someone calling himself Jesus Christ was wandering the villages bearing a document from the Virgin Mary calling on everyone to quit the collective farms before Judgment Day. In other areas, too, warnings circulated that those who joined kolkhozy would be stamped on the forehead with the seal of the Antichrist, to mark them out for damnation at the second coming.[53]

The apocalyptic mood was encouraged by the fact that often the creation of the kolkhoz was combined with the closure of the village church and the arrest of the priest. In February 1930 the GPU reported rumors from the central black-earth region that "the kolkhozniki would be branded with a seal, and their wives would belong to everybody . . . the churches would be closed and the bells melted down to make artillery shells for a future war."[54]

Most of the Komsomols were militant atheists, and in some villages they deliberately fostered an atmosphere of antireligious carnival. First they would clamber up the belfry, take down the bells, and send them off to be recycled "for the five-year plan." Then they would parade in priests' vestments, or even dress up horses in them, and march through the village, forcibly removing icons from people's homes to build a pyre and burn them publicly in the marketplace. Sometimes there was resistance: in one village in Briansk oblast, peasants attacked and drove off Komsomol activists dismantling the church bells; later, when officials came to investigate, they too were driven back with staves and pitchforks. In Astrakhan oblast in February 1930 several hundred drunken peasants, armed with clubs, axes, and pitchforks, came running at the sound of church bells and surrounded the village soviet building, where local plenipotentiaries were discussing the dekulakization. Six Communists were killed or wounded as they came out of the building.[55]

The collectivization of livestock was the most sensitive moment in many villages. Quite often at that point women would take the initiative in re-sisting, perhaps because they were less likely to be arrested than men: they would sound the alarm bell to summon the women together to block the cowsheds or, if collectivization had already taken place, would march off to reclaim their cows from the collective byre.[56]

452

The collectivization campaign was especially destructive in Kazakhstan, where it was compounded by a campaign to end the nomadic way of life and to open up huge potentially fertile areas for arable cultivation. Most Kazakhs viewed grain-growing as an alien and unworthy activity. As soon as the program was announced, many of them gathered their flocks and emigrated from the republic, either into China or into a neighboring more mountainous Soviet republic, where nomadism was still permitted. Kazakhs who did try to adapt to agriculture found that the seeds and equipment available were insufficient and the land totally unprepared. In many areas it needed extensive irrigation and the planting of windbreaks before its po-tential could be developed. The result was a catastrophic decline in popula-tion from 1,223,000 households in 1929 to 565,000 in 1938, including perhaps 1.5 million deaths. Livestock numbers fell from 7.4 million head of cattle in 1929 to 1.6 million in 1933, and from 22 million to 1.7 million sheep. Not until the 1960s did Kazakhstan fully recoup its livestock losses.[57]

In the north Caucasus, where transhumant stockraising was common, de-kulakization provoked an immediate and ferocious reaction—not least be-cause it meant the expropriation of horses, the symbol of the mountaineers' virility and warlike standing. Armed revolts broke out in Chechnia, Ingu-shetia, Dagestan, Ossetia, Kabarda, Balkaria, and the Karachai region. The North Caucasian Military District sent in a substantial armed force, includ-ing four infantry and three artillery divisions. Restoring order proved impos-sible. In places precarious accommodations were reached on the basis that the mountaineers should keep their horses, but guerrillas controlled many of the highland regions throughout the 1930s. According to incomplete fig-ures, some 2,700 peasant insurgents lost their lives in military operations in the region.[58]

Beset by mounting chaos in the villages, the party decided that it needed to inject cadres from outside to make the new system work. In November 1929 an appeal was launched for 25,000 of the most class-conscious workers to be sent out to the villages to coordinate the collectivization campaign and to get the newly created farms working. The appeal emphasized the need to take the class war to the countryside, overcome the kulaks, modernize agriculture, and secure the food supply for the future. There was a lively response: more than 70,000 workers put forward their names in the next few weeks, and by early spring of 1930 some 27,000 had been selected, given brief training courses, and dispatched to the villages.[59]

One of them, Lev Kopelev, later recalled the ideals which motivated him: "Stalin had said 'The struggle for grain is the struggle for socialism.' I was convinced that we were warriors on an invisible front, waging war on kulak sabotage for the sake of grain that the country needed for the Five Year Plan. For grain above all, but also for the souls of peasants whose attitudes were bogged down in ignorance and low political consciousness, and who succumbed to enemy propaganda, not grasping the great truth of communism."[60]

Most of those who took part in the campaign were experienced and skilled workers, members of party or Komsomol, and some of them had grim but inspiring memories of the civil war and grain requisitions. They were determined to win the war of the "grain front" finally this time and to make sure socialism was built in the countryside. They were seen off from their home factories with bouquets and brass bands, but what greeted them as they neared their rural places of appointment was altogether less festive. They arrived at a time of maximum chaos, in the late winter of 1930. Local officials received them with indifference or ill-concealed hostility. Many newcomers found they had been assigned nowhere to live, or no ration cards for the local cooperative store. Some were told to go and milk cows or clean out ditches. Only gradually, through a mixture of determination and appeals to party authority, did the more resourceful manage to dig themselves in.

Local officials had good reason to be suspicious of the newcomers, for some of them had come to purge and replace them. The 25,000ers took over jobs on the collective farm boards, in the village soviets, in the district administration, or in the local branches of the state collectivization agency, Kolkhoztsentr. They were expected to implement the more moderate policy which was emerging from the center after the heady but destructive winter of 1929–30. They had to clean up the mess, get the spring sowing under way, convert "paper" collective farms into real ones, and discipline the peasants to new and unfamiliar work routines. Men who were used to working alone or with their families on their own plots of land, starting and stopping when they judged appropriate, now had to fall in at the summons of a bell or whistle, receive their work assignments, and troop off to work in a "brigade" on collective fields. Peasants who were used to the informality and consensus of the *skhod* would bridle at the rhetorical speeches and formalized voting on resolutions which characterized the new kolkhoz general meetings.[61]

The chaos of collectivization was compounded by a dry summer in 1931 to produce an exceptionally poor grain harvest. The following year, as information came in from the regions about disappointing grain deliveries, Stalin resisted suggestions that the Soviet Union cease exporting grain, "in order not to undermine our credit abroad," and instead sent instructions that deliveries were to be increased and policed more thoroughly. Villages failing to deliver were to have their cooperative stores closed and be cut off from retail trade. Individual households hiding grain and kolkhoz chairmen responsible for shortfalls were subject to penalties including exile, five to ten years' imprisonment, or, in the worst cases, execution by shooting. A law of 7 August 1932 went so far as to mandate the death penalty for *any* theft of "collective or cooperative property": a revival of English eighteenth-century hanging for sheep-stealing. Emissaries were sent to the principal grain-growing regions to see that these instructions were obeyed. When R. Terekhov, party secretary in Kharkov, warned that famine was taking hold in Ukraine, Stalin wrote back accusing him of "concocting fairy tales" and recommended with heavy irony that he join the Writers' Union.[62]

All the same, Terekhov was right. In the country's most productive grain-growing regions, Ukraine, the Kuban, west Siberia, and the Volga basin, people were dying of hunger. Grain had been taken away for the towns and the Red Army, while in some villages people were eating grass, bark from the trees, sparrows, cats, rats—even cannibalism was not unknown. In West Siberia a health inspector reported visiting a kolkhoz family at dinnertime and seeing "on the table . . . gnawed bones from a dead horse," while elsewhere peasants were "grinding sunflower stems, flax and hemp seeds, chaff and dried potato peelings . . . The homes are filthy; the area round them is polluted by human waste, by diarrhea caused by these substitutes. People walk around like shadows, silent, vacant . . . one rarely sees an animal on the street (apparently the last ones have been eaten)."[63]

Unlike in 1921–22 this famine remained unpublicized, in order not to disrupt the propaganda images of the success of the first five-year plan. Starving peasants who tried to make for nearby towns to find food were turned back at roadblocks, while foreign correspondents were kept out of the affected areas. It is estimated that the number of people who died as a direct result of famine was in the region of four to five million.[64]

Altogether, in the encounter between peasants and 25,000ers we can see the collision of two worlds, rural and urban, both of them the product of Russian history, now locked together in a conflict of apocalyptic proportions. Neither side could win, and the struggle therefore had to end in compromise. Neither the collective nor the individual principle triumphed unequivocally.

Peasants had to accept domination from above, but at the same time the party had to accept that it could not control all aspects of rural life. When a Kolkhoz Charter was published in 1935, it laid down that work would be organized by collective brigades, and that pay would be according to the number of "labor days" each worker had put in. On the other hand, the peasants secured the right to maintain a few domestic animals, including a cow, to cultivate small private plots, and to sell their produce on the market. Without this concession to private agriculture, the authorities could not overcome food shortages in the towns. On that basis, a modus vivendi was reached between party and peasantry.[65]

455

THE FIVE-YEAR PLANS

Communists had always believed that a socialist society should be a highly industrialized one in which the means of production were owned by the people's state. The first moves toward such a society were made soon after the revolution. VSNKh was set up in 1918 to oversee the entire economy, and in 1921 Gosplan joined it to begin collecting statistics on the operation of the economy and to plan its further development. Each year Gosplan issued "control figures," forecasting production levels a year ahead, and in due course it was a natural extension of this practice to attempt a five-year projection.

There were, however, two schools of thought within Gosplan. Some favored a scientifically meticulous plan, based on extrapolations from existing trends and attempting to achieve an overall balance among different branches of production. Others recommended planning "teleologically," that is, identifying a paramount goal and concentrating all resources on it. To create a socialist society, that paramount goal had to be heavy industry. As Stalin argued at a Central Committee plenum in 1928, heavy industry was needed by the one socialist country in a capitalist world, both to produce modern armaments and to feed basic equipment into other sectors of the economy. He spoke of the "continual beatings Russia has suffered because of her backwardness . . . We are fifty to a hundred years behind the advanced countries. We must catch up in ten years. Either we do it or we go under."

Such exhortations signaled the victory of teleological or what one might well call millennial planning. In 1931 V. G. Groman and his school of equilibrium planners were dismissed from Gosplan, and several of them were arrested to appear in a show trial, accused of having tried "criminally" to retard the country's economic development. The results of their departure can be seen in the ongoing variants of the first five-year plan, which were continually revised upward. The figures in the table are in millions of metric tons.[66]

Commodity	Actual (1927–28)	First version	Second version	Optimal	Actual results achieved (1932)
Coal	35.4	68	75	95–105	64
Oil	11.7	19	22	40–55	21.4
Iron ore	5.7	15	19	24–32	12.1
Pig iron	3.3	8	10	15–16	6.2

Even if the original—let alone the later—planned output figures proved optimistic, there is no doubt that much actually was achieved during the first two five-year plans. Output doubled or nearly doubled in all branches of heavy industry during the first plan alone, and whole new industrial areas were opened up, one around Dneproges, the hydroelectric power scheme on the lower Dnieper, another around metallurgical combines at Magnitogorsk in the Urals and in the Kuznetsk basin in western Siberia. Large tractor plants were opened at Stalingrad, Cheliabinsk, and Kharkov to provide for the mechanization of agriculture which was to accompany collectivization.

These huge production increases were achieved only by drawing very large numbers of inhabitants from the countryside into the towns to work in industry. Between 1926 and 1939 the urban population more than doubled, from 26 million to 56 million (during the first five-year plan period alone, 1928–1932, the excess of immigrants over emigrants to the towns was nearly 12 million). The number of wage and salary earners grew from 11.4 million to 23.2 million, while in Moscow alone the industrial labor force grew from 186,500 in 1928 to 614,000 in 1937. The great majority of the newcomers were former peasants. They had left the village for a variety of reasons: many of them were young men who felt restricted by the poverty and narrow-minded intimacy of rural life and yearned both for the opportunities of the city and for the chance to contribute to a great project in the making. Others smelled trouble coming to the village and decided to leave while the going was good. Some belonged to the category of dekulakized who were expropriated without being deported and made for the nearest town for lack of an alternative. Yet others were actual deportees, assigned to "special settlements" on construction sites or close to factories.[67]

One consequence of the massive peasant influx was that the towns became semipeasantized. In making the frightening transition from rural to urban life, newcomers relied heavily on relatives and on contacts from their own village or region to help them find work and housing and to give them material aid till they could stand on their own feet. Immigrants usually came from a village not far away and chose a factory where they would find familiar faces. Many of them joined an artel, as their predecessors of the 1890s had done, especially in construction and transport: this meant that an elected "elder" handled the responsible task of finding work, concluding pay agreements, and distributing wages. As we have seen, factory managers did not like to deal with the workforce this way: they wanted to impose individual wage contracts, usually on piece-rates, since they simplified discipline and in theory at least contributed to the raising of productivity. However, desperate for workers, they would often agree to an artel organization, even sometimes in heavy industry.[68]

457

The huge influx created a demand for housing such as even the most ambitious construction program could scarcely have met. As it was, the first five-year plans gave housing a relatively low priority. In the early years this downgrading was still officially justified as an aspect of social engineering: breaking down the "bourgeois family." As a Magnitogorsk newspaper explained in 1930, "The family, the basic cell of . . . capitalist society . . . loses the economic basis of its existence in the conditions of socialist society." As a result, expedients had to be devised. Families no longer fitted individual apartments. Each urban resident was assigned a small amount of notional "living space" (zhilploshchad), regardless of how that space would fit into the rooms, walls, and corridors of actual apartment buildings.

The result was that incoming workers, often recent peasants, crowded existing urban dwellers into single rooms or even parts of rooms. Families who had to share rooms would put shelves and cupboards, or even hang sheets, between themselves and their neighbors to preserve a little fragile privacy. On some of the new building sites, conditions were even worse. In Magnitogorsk workers lived in tents till more permanent dwellings could be erected, while in a ravine overlooking the railway Bashkirs and Tatars improvised mud huts roofed with scrap metal—a shantytown known to locals as "Shanghai."[69]

Other forms of extreme deprivation cropped up too. In some towns there was a typhus epidemic, while in the textile manufacturing region of Ivanovo, food supplies ran out in April 1932, and as a result there was a general strike.[70]

During the 1930s, then, we must imagine most Soviet workers living in conditions of acute deprivation and psychological strain, with little or no privacy, with much time being spent on shopping and securing basic facilities, and with everyone vulnerable to thieves, hooligans, and police informers. Life was also very unstable, with people coming and going. Finding a job was now not too difficult, since unemployment vanished early in the first five-year plan, but conditions at most workplaces were so grim that employees would quit pretty soon in order to find something less bad. Or they might leave before some infringement of labor discipline caught up with them. They would try to install their families in a room, provide food and clothing, and seek schooling for the children. Securing the simplest facilities required either bribery, sharp practice, or using "pull," the influence of a boss.[71]

Other amenities—transport, child care, medical care—were also haphazard to start with. Communal canteens were supposed to take the drudgery of daily cooking out of family life, but in many of them long queues and dubious food scared off potential customers. Communal kindergartens, baths, and laundries were in short supply, and most male workers continued to reckon that the best way to have one's clothes washed was to get married. Access to scarce amenities depended on one's standing with the employers, and that meant one's reputation in the party cell, the security police, and the local trade union branch. Those who stayed on the job and performed well, perhaps as "shock workers" or Stakhanovites, in the judgment of these all-powerful observers, could expect eventually to be allocated more favorable rations, better housing, access to daycare or kindergarten, and perhaps a month's paid holiday in a trade union sanatorium on the seaside or in the country (probably expropriated from a former nobleman). Those considered most deserving would be promoted into the administration or the party-state hierarchy.[72]

The Communists had aimed to build an egalitarian system based on plenty; instead they created a hierarchical one based on scarcity. Manipulating the means of escape from that scarcity provided the bosses with their principal instrument of social control.

One weapon which they deployed was the passport system. The Soviet authorities had tried to retain control over the migration from the villages to the towns through the system of *orgnabor,* or labor mobilization. But so torrential did the influx prove to be, most of it outside the *orgnabor* framework, that in the end they decided they would have to curb it. In December 1932 it was announced that passports would be issued to "all citizens of the USSR aged sixteen years and over, permanently living in towns and workers' settlements, working on transport, in the *sovkhozy* (state farms), and at new construction sites."[73] Absent from that list of categories were the kolkhozniki: they were not to be allowed to move into the towns without the permission of their farm chairman. To secure a passport, one now needed to obtain a propiska, which indicated one's nationality, social status, residence, and place of employment.

The passport is crucial for understanding the Soviet social structure, for the information it contained delineated a new social hierarchy and enabled individuals to be inserted into their place within it. Some towns were better provided with facilities and hence were considered more desirable to live in: first of all, Moscow, then Leningrad (as Petrograd was renamed in 1924), followed by the Union Republic capitals. In all those places a propiska was very difficult to obtain: one needed either to be a specialist in some urgently required area of work or to have the protection of a powerful patron. One's social origins, nationality, educational status, and previous work record were contributory factors in deciding where one fitted in. If in Balzac's France people had contracted marriages in order to gain money and property, in Stalin's Russia they often did so in order to secure a more desirable propiska.[74]

During 1933 the system was used to evict from the towns members of "former" social classes—people who had once been priests, nobles, merchants, or members of their families. Leningrad, as the former capital, was home to a particularly large number of such people, and it was reported that some 10,000 inhabitants had been evicted and that "huge crowds of people [were] wandering along roads out of the city searching for food and shelter . . . Some of the deported persons were taken by railway to rural districts a minimum of sixty miles from Leningrad."[75]

THE TERROR

In 1934 the Seventeenth Congress of the Communist Party met and congratulated itself on the success of the first five-year plan and of the collectivization of agriculture. It became known as the "Congress of the Victors." After the bruising battles of collectivization and the first five-year plan, the leaders wanted to give the impression that they had rallied round Lenin's great disciple and heir, Comrade Stalin. Behind the triumphalist headlines in *Pravda*, though, there were serious tensions. If there had indeed been a victory, the party leaders knew that it had been purchased at grievous cost. Millions of lives had been lost, and millions of citizens had been given reasons for hating Stalin and the party leadership. Society was in turmoil, and, even if much had been achieved, few were able yet to enjoy the benefits. On the contrary, conditions for the great majority of people had become much more squalid and harsh. The new system aroused millenial hopes, but also apocalyptic fears. It raised many new people and gave them opportunities, but it victim-ized and oppressed even more.

On top of all this, in 1933 the Nazis had come to power in Germany with the declared aim of exterminating Bolshevism and conquering the territory

of the Soviet Union as *Lebensraum* for colonization by the German people. It is scarcely surprising that, despite the "victory," the leaders felt insecure. They still saw themselves as engaged in a life-and-death battle.

The Communists had come to power a decade and a half ago with the expectation that they could transform Russia and then the world, creating a humane and prosperous society for everyone. That had obviously not hap-pened, and although one could cite all kinds of excuses for the failure, there was nevertheless intense unease and resentment, which in turn provoked the search for someone to blame. Thwarted millenarianism is a great seeker of scapegoats. Stalin's tone at the congress was triumphalist, but all the same he warned that this was a moment "not to sing lullabies to the party but to develop its vigilance."[76]

Anything like open discussion of problems had finally become impossible with the banning of the Right Deviation. But there was restiveness in the Central Committee, even a growing sense that Stalin was not leading the country toward socialism at all. In 1930 V. V. Lominadze, first party secretary of the Transcaucasian Federation, accused officials of adopting "a lordly atti-tude toward the needs and interests of workers and peasants." S. I. Syrtsov, candidate member of the Politburo, called the Stalingrad tractor plant a "Po-temkin village." Some of Stalin's colleagues were beginning to have serious misgivings about his personality and methods. Syrtsov accused him of by-passing proper party procedures and creating his own "faction" inside the Politburo. More privately, Bukharin had written him a furious letter in Octo-ber 1930, complaining of the "monstrous accusations" Stalin was spreading about him. "If I don't lick your backside, does that make me a 'preacher of terrorism?'"[77]

From lower down in the party came even more unrestrained language. In 1932 Mikhail Riutin, a district party secretary in Moscow, circulated among colleagues an "appeal to all Party Members" denouncing the "adventurist" collectivization and industrialization as a policy which was leading to mass impoverishment, demoralization, and depopulation of the countryside. He called Stalin a "dictator" and his associates "a band of unprincipled, menda-cious, and cowardly intriguers who had destroyed Leninism and brought the regime to the brink of disaster." He suggested they could be removed only by force and proposed setting up a Union of Marxist-Leninists within the Communist Party to begin the task.[78]

Riutin was expelled from the party and arrested. There was no evidence that he was preparing to act, but his language was certainly violent. Stalin, furious at his "appeal," proposed to the Politburo that he be executed as a "terrorist." This would have been the first time that such a step had been taken over a polemic within the party, and the other Politburo members, led by Kirov, resisted Stalin. In the end a ten-year prison sentence was agreed.[79]

The Congress of Victors reflected these tensions. Many of its delegates were veterans of Lenin's days, who knew that in the last months of his life Lenin, shaken by Stalin's behavior in the Georgian affair, had written a testament, subsequently suppressed, warning that Stalin had accumulated "boundless power," which he might not always know how to use with "sufficient care." He had later written a codicil, in which he called Stalin "boorish" and recommended that his comrades find some way to replace him as general secretary with someone "more tolerant, more loyal, more polite and attentive to comrades."[80]

Some of these older party leaders now approached Kirov and suggested that he challenge Stalin for the post of general secretary. Kirov declined, but Stalin heard of the approach and resented it. Later, in the elections to the Central Committee, Stalin's name was crossed off the ballot by more than one hundred delegates, while Kirov received only three or four negative votes. The figures publicized were falsified, and Stalin retained all his powers: the majority of the Central Committee was not prepared to rock the boat.[81]

At this point we enter the realm of Stalin's personal psychology. He had always been a secretive, rancorous, and vengeful person, though also one of considerable patience and political skill. Over the years he had goodhumoredly handled the organizational affairs of the party while using his control of them to amass his file cards containing information about all his colleagues and possible rivals. In 1932–1934 came the years of crisis, of famine in the countryside and chaos in the towns, and many comrades turned against him, blaming him for these disasters. Most hurtful of all, his wife Nadia committed suicide in November 1932.

Paranoia might be called the professional disease of politicians, and Stalin had it in full measure. More than that, it was shared by most leading Communists: it was fostered by the circumstances in which they had come to power and held on to it. They had all seen the world as a battleground between good and evil, the good tinged with millenial hopes, and the evil with apocalyptic forebodings. They and those entering the party from 1917 had forged their new world in the furnace of civil war. They had adopted the methods, the mentality, and the discourse of the battlefield, including intense self-sacrificing loyalty to their own comrades, murderous hatred of the enemy, and disdain for normal moral standards. By the early 1930s all party documents, the speeches and articles of the leaders, were couched in language of this kind and expressed identical sentiments. A unified rhetoric had become compulsory: anyone who failed to use it might be identified as a "deviationist" and lose any hope of further advancement. Those who had "deviated" at some time were expected now to confess their errors and swing into step with their comrades' marching columns. The rise to power of Hitler in Germany finally sealed this closing of the ranks. Rhetoric now became virtual reality, perhaps even reality itself.[82]

Stalin exemplified these tendencies to the nth degree. During the 1920s he had become persuaded that he alone was strong enough to avoid the hesitations and backslidings of his comrades and to carry forward Lenin's heritage. The apostle of moderation and compromise within the party, he always possessed the skill, the knowledge, and the manipulative power to create a central bloc of supporters within the burgeoning apparatus and to defeat opponents at either of the extremes. He had done this not just by organizational means, but by speaking to the mentality of the rank-and-file party-state officials. He had a crude but lucid mind, which sorted out people and political tendencies into unambiguous dualities, right/wrong, progressive/reactionary, for us/against us. He deployed his arguments like a seminarian his catechism, by question and answer and by accumulation of evidence, until he could sweep away the "wrong" side of each duality with overwhelming logic. There is no doubt that this style of discourse, both oral and written, was much more persuasive to ordinary party audiences than the elaborate dialectic of his more educated and cosmopolitan colleagues. It now became the only permissible party language.

This "newspeak" faithfully articulated Stalin's conviction that at the hour of both his greatest triumph and his greatest need, many of his colleagues had deserted him and thereby "objectively" played into the hands of counter-revolution and the imperialists. Sometimes this meant no more than that they were defending the interests of their huge and growing departmental empires against rival claims and against investigations and arrests. Ordjoni-kidze, for example, as people's commissar for heavy industry, fought dough-tily for his numerous employees, as well as for economic managers and spe-cialists generally, against the demands of the procuracy and the secret police. He died suddenly in February 1937; almost certainly he committed suicide after an explosive row with Stalin, perhaps foreseeing the wave of terror about to break.[83]

For Stalin, colleagues like that, building their own patronal fiefs, had, in effect, become "enemies." He resolved to defeat the challenge by rooting out all conceivable opponents within the party. In April 1933 a new commission, headed by Ian Rudzutak, was given the task, in conjunction with the GPU, of overseeing an "exchange of party cards," that is, a screening process or "purge," by which every party member would hand in his membership card and be questioned on his record and his current attitudes before receiving a new one.[84]

463

This, however, was where the drive for unanimity collided with the very nature of the ruling class the party had created. Local party bosses were not much interested in ideology and, naturally enough, exploited the "purge" to bolster their own patronage, advance their own clients, and get rid of their opponents. As a result, Stalin strongly suspected, many former "deviationists" were still safely ensconced in their posts. So he decided he would have to continue the process, this time bypassing party channels and bringing in the secret police. In 1933–34 he integrated the GPU into the NKVD (People's Commissariat of Internal Affairs), which was also put in charge of labor camps, border guards, internal security forces, and the regular police. It thus concentrated within its hands all the forces of internal coercion, and was given a Special Board with the right of passing nonjudicial sentences of up to five years. At the same time a special military collegium of the Supreme Court was established to deal with espionage, counterrevolutionary activities, and other especially serious crimes.[85]

Then, on 1 December 1934, came a dramatic and sinister development. Sergei Kirov was murdered in the party headquarters in Leningrad by a young party member, Leonid Nikolaev, who had a personal grudge against him. It has never been conclusively proved that Stalin instigated the murder, but circumstantial evidence points to the conclusion that Nikolaev, though independent of the NKVD himself, was deliberately allowed access to Kirov in the knowledge that he was a potential assassin.[86]

Stalin had ample motive for the murder. Arguably it removed his most dangerous rival, at least in the institutional sense: Kirov commanded a formidable patronage network in Leningrad, one which had already served as the basis for political opposition. Certainly the murder provided a pretext for tightening up all measures of internal security. In the unified rhetoric, "deviationism" now became equivalent to "terrorism." Stalin immediately issued a directive that in cases of suspected "terrorism" investigation and sentencing were to be carried out with maximum speed, cases were to be tried in the absence of the accused, and no appeal was to be allowed, even against the death penalty.

During 1935 the NKVD arrested all those who had been members of the Left Opposition and induced them to sign testimony that they were involved in a vast conspiracy, manipulated from abroad by Trotskii, who had organized the assassination of Kirov and was planning to do the same to Stalin and other Communist leaders, to overthrow the Soviet system and restore capitalism. The victims were also pressured to denounce others who might have been involved.

The fruit of this denunciatory frenzy was three great show trials held in Moscow during 1936–1938. At the first, in August 1936, Zinoviev, Kamenev, and others confessed to being members of a "Trotskyist-Zinovievite Center," which had murdered Kirov as the first stage in a plot to destroy the entire party leadership. They were sentenced to death and executed, probably immediately. Their confessions implicated Tomskii, who thereupon committed suicide, Rykov, and Bukharin. The state prosecutor, Andrei Vyshinskii, announced that these implications would be investigated.

At a second trial, in February 1937, Karl Radek and Grigorii Piatakov, two of Lenin's closest comrades, confessed along with others to setting up terrorist groups and conspiring to wreck and sabotage Soviet industrial projects. Piatakov was sentenced to death and Radek to ten years' imprisonment; he died a few years later in a labor camp.

Finally, in March 1938, Bukharin, Rykov, Nikolai Krestinskii, and Genrikh Iagoda (himself a former head of the NKVD) confessed to membership of an incongruously named "Trotskyist-Rightist Bloc" which was undermining Soviet military power and, together with foreign intelligence services, preparing an imperialist attack on the USSR, leading to its dismemberment. All the accused were sentenced to death, and Vyshinskii concluded his summing up by proclaiming that "Along the road cleared of the last scum and filth of the past, we, our people, with our beloved teacher and leader, the great Stalin, at our head, will march ever onward, toward communism."

Here was a primitive, manichean narrative of the revolution and the Soviet era transformed into murderous courtroom drama as a spectacle for the semieducated new elite and its followers. The speeches and confessions were reproduced in central and local newspapers, and public meetings were held at which ordinary workers were encouraged to demand death sentences for the accused. Foreign observers scarcely knew what to make of it all. The charges were highly implausible, yet it was difficult to believe that nothing lay behind them; otherwise why should the accused confess to them, and why should the NKVD go to the trouble of getting them to do so? After all, the regime could always simply murder its opponents, if it wished to.

That was not enough for Stalin, though. He wished to destroy his "enemies" not only physically but also morally. He did not want Zinoviev or Bukharin to have an afterlife as martyrs whose cause might be taken up by some future opposition. He also wanted a legal fiction: he was creating a new stable and prosperous society, not a terrorist conspiracy, or so he liked to think. The confessions were needed to create a plausible prosecution case, for there was not a scrap of any other serious evidence against the accused.

The same process was repeated a thousandfold in all regions of the country and at all levels. Denunciations bred arrests and further denunciations, until much of the population lived with a small suitcase ready packed, in dread of the midnight knock on the door which might separate them from their families forever and plunge them into senseless suffering with death as the likely outcome. Most of the arrests did not lead to show trials, for their stage-management was cumbersome and time-consuming, nor even to announcements in newspapers; but all the same, every sentence handed down by the special courts was properly formulated and recorded, and it was usually based on the confession of the accused.

465

Why did so many people who had loyally served the party for so many years suddenly confess to horrific and unlikely crimes against it? For victims from the higher echelons this was the final stage along the road Kamenev had taken when he refrained from creating a real opposition. The party had abjured compromise, treating opponents, dissenters, former allies, even in the end its own hesitant members, as enemies, to be defeated and destroyed. They could not themselves now expect to be handled differently. They had given their whole life to the party, and probably still believed in its ultimate victory. In any case, they had no alternative moral or religious conviction on the basis of which they could resist the pressures of interrogation and trial. As Bukharin said at his trial, "When you ask yourself 'If you must die, what are you dying for?', an absolutely black emptiness suddenly rises before you." Nor indeed was there anything to live for, once one was "isolated from everybody, an enemy of the people."[87]

Those lower down, who never made public confessions, were broken by the NKVD "conveyor-belt," a system of continuous interrogation for days and nights by successive relays of investigators. Cold, hungry, exhausted by sleep deprivation and in some cases by torture, and knowing that there was no end in sight to their suffering, prisoners would sign whatever was required of them.

The early stages of the 1937 terror were directed largely against members of the party who at some stage had been expelled from it; in some regions they outnumbered current party members. But the operations developed their own momentum as denunciations dragged in ever more innocent victims. The Nazi menace created an atmosphere in which people feared internal subversion and the formation of a "fifth column." As Molotov later recalled: "Take into account that after the revolution we chopped right and left. We achieved victory, but the remnants of our enemies of various tendencies survived, and in the face of the growing threat of fascist aggression they might always unite. Thanks to 1937 we had no fifth column when the war came."[88] (The last sentence of course is nonsense: large numbers of Soviet citizens fought on the German side in the second world war, as we shall see. All the same, one can understand Molotov's mentality at the time.)

The civil war practice of labeling people as enemies and then exterminating them now generated its own terrible dynamic. On 28 June 1937 a new stage was heralded by a Politburo decision "Concerning the uncovering in west Siberia of a counterrevolutionary insurrectionary organization among exiled kulaks." Thereupon the net was cast wider to trawl in everyone who had ever been labeled a kulak or a White Guardist, who belonged to a "suspect" nationality (such as Germans, Poles, Koreans), who had ever been a member of a non-Communist political party or came from a "former" social class, plus members of their families—in short, anyone who might even be suspected of harboring malign intentions toward the ruling party.

Each case was to be urgently investigated, under an abbreviated procedure, by a "troika" consisting of one representative each of the party, the NKVD, and the procuracy. The NKVD in each oblast was assigned quotas of arrests to fulfill—and some "overfulfilled" them. The treatment of high-ranking detainees was ratified personally by Stalin or by a special committee of the Politburo, which at various times included Molotov, Kaganovich, Voroshilov, Yezhov, and Mikoian. Obviously, however, they could not follow in detail the more peripheral ramifications of the sanguinary process they had unleashed. In the localities malice, ambition, intrigue, personal whim, and chance decided who was arrested and who died. Patron-client networks fought each other, using the weapons of the secret police.[89]

The question of the number of Stalin's victims has been hotly debated among historians. The recent opening of some of the relevant archive sources has reduced the margins of error involved in the controversy, but if anything rendered it even more heated.

It seems clear now that the nomenklatura elite suffered far more than ordinary workers and peasants. Of 139 members of the party Central Committee elected at the "Congress of Victors" in 1934, 110 were arrested before the Eighteenth Congress in 1939; of 1,966 congress delegates, 1,108 had disappeared by then. Among other things, this meant the liquidation of virtually all those who had fought alongside Lenin in 1917, who had known Stalin in the early stages of his career, and who might still raise the question of Lenin's testament.

Some regions and republics suffered especially severely: one of Stalin's principal aims was to disrupt ethnic patronage systems and break down local resistance to orders from Moscow. Faizulla Khodzhaev, chairman of the Uzbek Council of People's Commissars, had been an outspoken opponent of cotton monoculture, fearing that his fiefdom would be reduced to the status of Soviet "banana republic." "We cannot eat cotton," he is reported to have said. In 1937 he was arrested, charged with "bourgeois nationalism," and shot. A similar fate awaited many non-Russian republican leaderships. The party Central Committees of Armenia, Kazakhstan, Turkmenia, and the Tatar ASSR were almost totally destroyed, and Russians or Moscow-trained locals were sent in to impose a more compliant regime. Ukraine was *twice* purged, in 1933 and 1937; Nikita Khrushchev was sent to Kiev in January 1938 to complete the second purge and take over the leadership. Russian control of the all-Union Communist Party was markedly strengthened: in 1939 66 percent of its Central Committee was Russian, and by 1952 72 percent.[90]

Since the Nazi menace was often cited as a threat to the country, the purge of the armed forces leadership is particularly striking and perverse. Among those arrested were Marshal Tukhachevskii, deputy commissar for defense and the Red Army's principal strategic thinker; Marshal Egorov, chief of the General Staff; Marshal Bliukher, commander of the special Far Eastern Army, who had defeated the Japanese Manchurian Army in a major engagement at Lake Khazan only shortly before; the commanders of the Kiev and Belorussian Military Districts; the commanders of the Black Sea and Pacific fleets; and more than half the army, corps, and divisional commanders. If this was preparation for a war against Nazi Germany, it was a very strange way of going about it, and both the Germans and world opinion generally concluded that the Soviet Union was now a military weakling. Presumably to Stalin it was even more important to ensure that the one body in the country capable of massive resistance was under the control of people who owed everything to him.

The hurricane which swept through the rest of the nomenklatura elite—in diplomacy, science, industry, scholarship, the arts and culture, medicine, the law, the Comintern, even the secret police itself—was only slightly less devastating.

The labor camps to which the majority of those arrested were sent were not "death camps" in the Nazi sense of that term. No categories of the population were deliberately singled out for extermination. But the physical conditions in them and the work regime imposed there were such that premature death, disease, or lifelong disablement were highly likely outcomes. In

1929 the concentration camps of the civil war period were turned into part of the planned economy. Prisoners were henceforth required to carry out productive work. New camps were set up in remote and inhospitable regions, for logging, mining, building roads, railways, and factories, opening up and exploiting resources where wage labor was difficult to attract. The first complex was in Karelia and along the White Sea coast, where timber was the main industry. Coal mines followed in Vorkuta and the Pechora basin, then industrial development in west Siberia, the Urals, and Kazakhstan, where *zeki* (inmates) laid out the basic infrastructure. The largest complex of all was in the Far East, around Magadan and the Kolyma basin, where timber was supplemented by gold, platinum, and other precious metals. This was a whole separate frozen continent, cut off from the rest of the country by hundreds of miles of taiga; prisoners were transported there in convict ships which recalled the Atlantic slave trade.[91]

What went on in these camps was indeed slave labor. Normally, economists reckon that slave labor is relatively unproductive, since slaves have no material interest in their work. This was something the NKVD could not accept, for their camps were economic enterprises which had to meet their output norms. The "material interest" they devised was avoidance of hunger. *Zeki* received their full daily ration, enough to nourish a manual laborer, only if they fulfilled their norms. Measurement of the norm took place at the level of the work-gang, so that each member of it had an incentive to ensure that all his colleagues did their bit: this was "joint responsibility" in a new and especially malignant form.

Anything less than the norm meant an inadequate diet, which in turn meant physical weakness and further nonfulfillment. As Iurii Margolin, himself a former *zek*, remarked: "The hungrier we were, the worse we worked. The worse we worked, the hungrier we became. From that vicious circle there was no escape." It explains why so many of the inmates died, especially since so many "politicals" were unaccustomed to manual labor anyway. Unlike most slave-owners of the past, the NKVD had no particular reason to keep their slaves alive, for they could always arrest more. Even if the NKVD penal network did not consist of deliberately designed "death camps," there was every justification for Solzhenitsyn to call them "exterminatory labor camps."[92]

According to NKVD files, in the worst years of the terror, 1937–38, 1.6 million people were arrested, 87 percent of them on political charges, and the total population of prisons, labor camps, and labor colonies (where shorter sentences were served) grew from around one million in early 1937 to around 2 million at the beginning of 1939. If one adds those living in exile settlements, then the total at any time before 1939 would be up to 3.5 million, but probably not much higher. During the same years 680,000 people were sentenced to death for "counterrevolutionary and state crimes" (and 786,000 between 1930 and 1952).[93]

These are all measurable entities, and the NKVD was meticulous about its documentation, so further archival investigation is unlikely to change these figures very much. On the other hand, the archives apparently provide no unambiguous data for deaths other than executions within the penal system. The relatively recent discovery of mass graves at Kuropaty, outside Minsk, and elsewhere suggests that unknown numbers of people were killed without being processed by the GULAG (labor camp administration) system at all. So the figures we have must be set against the total background of premature mortality caused by state repression in general, by harsh conditions in labor camps, and by deportations, collectivization, and headlong industrialization, with the accompanying famine. Given the population data we now have, including the previously suppressed census figures for 1937, it seems likely that 5–6 million people, mostly peasants, died in the worst famine years of 1932 and 1933, and that excess deaths during the 1930s as a whole were in the range of 10–11 million.[94] After 1940 it becomes impossible to distinguish victims of terror from those of war.

After 1939 the population of *zeki* mushroomed, with the deportation first of Poles, Ukrainians, Belorussians, and Balts from the territories annexed in 1939–40, then of Germans, Crimean Tatars, and North Caucasian Muslims during and after the war. One must add to this prisoners captured from the Axis armies and Soviet soldiers repatriated from German captivity. A probable estimate of the number of *zeki* in January 1941 is 3.3 million and for January 1953 5.5 million.[95]

These figures are lower than the estimates many Western historians made when no archive information was available. But they are still horrifying. There must have been few families, especially among the peasantry and the intelligentsia, who did not have at least one member behind barbed wire or in barren and hopeless exile at some time between 1930 and 1953, constantly in danger of disease, disablement, and death. If one imagines the worry, grief, and physical suffering which lie behind these figures, then one has to see the Soviet peoples during those two and a half decades as a population in torment.

12

SOVIET SOCIETY TAKES SHAPE

The Bolsheviks had come to power pledged to create a worldwide egalitarian socialist community in which all people would enjoy an abundance of everything they needed to live a full life. However, the nature of the Bolsheviks' seizure of power and the civil war which followed ensured that the country's power structure would be authoritarian and hierarchical. The social revolution was carried out in such a way that it generated not abundance but chronic shortages. Those shortages became the decisive feature of the new society, which molded itself around the devices and institutions needed to overcome them. At the same time, through all the difficulties this society created its own loyalties, dramatically augmented and reinforced by the war of 1941–1945.

AGRICULTURE AND THE KOLKHOZY

The uneasy compromise concluded between regime and peasants after the upheavals of collectivization did at least enable the kolkhozy to start turning out enough produce to feed the towns and the army. Food rationing was lifted. Nevertheless, the situation was unsatisfactory. The peasants retained the conviction that they had been brutally subjugated to a "second serfdom": they rewrote the acronym of the party—VKP(b), or All-Union Communist Party (Bolshevik)—as *Vtoroe Krepostnoe Pravo (Bol'shevistskoe):* Second

Serfdom, Bolshevik.[1] They had good reason for their view: most of them were denied passports and were thus in effect fixed to the land; they were required to make deliveries of produce to the state, not only from the collective fields but also from their private plots; and from time to time they had compulsory labor and transport obligations imposed on them. The kolkhoz chairman was their new *barin* (lord). It was a restoration of "tribute-taking" and arguably of kormlenie as well. One characteristic of the old regime did not, however, survive: in spite of all propaganda, Stalin and the other Communist leaders were almost universally blamed for the famine and the "second serfdom." There was no "little father tsar" syndrome in the Soviet collectivized village.[2]

However, in spite of everything, this was a more mobile society, and there were ways out of bondage which prerevolutionary serfs had not enjoyed. Young people had the right to a passport if they were leaving for higher or specialized education or in order to perform military service. Since village primary schools were of poor quality, few of their graduates qualified for the first option, though the incentive to do so enormously enhanced the standing of education in the village. By contrast, all ablebodied young men had to report for military service, and after completing it few returned to the village; instead they used their passports to obtain an urban residence permit, with the result that there was a continuing haemorrhage of the most potentially productive males from the farms. Over the following decades the village became the habitat of children, old people, and women of all ages, many of whom were unable to find husbands.

This demographic imbalance was exacerbated by the state's investment policy, which put the overwhelming emphasis on capital industry and left the collective farms chronically short of resources. One motive for collectivization had been to create suitable units for the mechanization of agriculture. But in practice very few farms could afford to purchase combine harvesters or even tractors. Instead each kolkhoz was registered with a Machine Tractor Station, which hired out machinery and operators. The MTS also served as an outpost for the party and the security police to monitor and influence developments in the countryside, where they still remained weakly represented.

Since "labor days" were paid only after the kolkhoz had discharged all its other financial obligations—including for example to the MTS—its members were not guaranteed a proper, or indeed any, income from them. This was *barshchina* (serf labor) restored. Inevitably it meant the peasants invested most effort in their private plots, which, small though they were, produced a substantial proportion of the eggs, meat, fruit, vegetables, and dairy products on sale.

"Labor days" were, moreover, paid according to a sliding scale, under which skilled and qualified workers received more than ordinary ones. This system of pay formed the backbone of a clearly calibrated village hierarchy, with the kolkhoz chairman at the top, followed by the accountant, the business manager, the machine operators and tractor drivers, the members of the kolkhoz administrative board, the brigade leaders, and so on. Those at the upper end of the scale increasingly assumed the role of de facto owners of the farm's resources and patrons of its workers, with a responsibility to ensure their well-being but also with the right to dispose of their labor power.

In the face of continuing shortages and underpayment, kolkhozniki naturally resented these prerogatives, especially when they were abused. They had no means of redress except to write to the local newspapers, or occasionally to Stalin and Molotov. Sometimes action was taken, especially during 1936–1938, when show trials were in vogue: as in the towns, the authorities not infrequently used material from peasant denunciations to create a prosecution case against local officials they wished to remove. In that sense, rural show trials served as a kind of manipulated carnival, in which virtuous peasants castigated their evil bosses.[3]

These trials, however, changed nothing fundamental. Like carnival, they were a safety valve, not a lever to transform the system. The establishment of collective farms had solved the grain delivery crisis and enabled the towns and army to be supplied with bread. But this solution left a long-term heritage of demoralization in the villages and with it a chronically underproductive agriculture, which was one of the main causes of the eventual collapse of Communism, and which still threatens its successors.

MANAGERS AND WORKERS IN INDUSTRY

Recent Russian historians call the industrial structure created by the first five-year plans a "command-administrative system." The implication is that enterprise managers issued orders passed on from Gosplan and the workers obeyed them. Actually, things were far from being that simple. The mode of Soviet industrialization in the 1930s concealed an inbuilt tension between "Bolshevik willpower," technical rationality, and the interests of the workers themselves. Soviet industrial policy veered back and forth among the three imperatives, all of which were detrimental to the traditions of craft pride in which many older skilled workers had been brought up.

Taylorism, the system of industrial organization to which Lenin had given his blessing, entailed the meticulous and detailed study of industrial work processes, broken down into minimal units, so that each worker could be set fair and attainable norms and thereby promote the maximal efficiency of the plant. This fastidious attention to detail required a stable and well-organized labor routine. It was difficult to reconcile with a fluctuating work-force and with the work patterns of peasants, who found it difficult to adjust to industrial rhythms. They were used to doing the whole of any particular job, and to working as long as necessary to complete it. Instead, in the factory they clocked in and out at specified hours and did only tiny bits of jobs. They often lacked basic skills and found more experienced workers reluctant to teach them, for fear of creating rivals. As a result newcomers often made elementary errors which could delay a whole production line, lowering ev-eryone's piece-rate pay and provoking general resentment.[4]

Taylorism was also difficult to reconcile with millennial planning. During 1928–1931 the state hoped to replace money and the market by means of a combination of issuing commands and arousing enthusiasm. It projected an image of heroic revolutionary élan, when planned output figures took off into the realm of fantasy, and it was officially proclaimed that "there are no fortresses which Bolsheviks cannot storm." When things went wrong, drama was invoked to explain the lapses. "Bourgeois specialists" were de-nounced and in some cases, beginning with the Shakhty trial in the Donbass in 1928, arrested and subjected to show trials, which were reported in the papers as part of a struggle between good and evil. "Socialist competition" was launched: teams of enthusiastic young recruits, "shock workers," would be assigned new and difficult tasks, sharing their pay in common, and would demonstrate that the caution of the "specialists" was unfounded. This pro-duced startling results, but it also constantly threatened chaos, as people took on tasks beyond their skill and training, and qualified workers moved on in disgust to look elsewhere for better pay or the opportunity to apply their skills properly.

After 1931 it was increasingly recognized that enthusiasm and willpower could not achieve everything. Egalitarianism and scorn of expertise became unfashionable. Stalin rehabilitated the notion that skill, experience, and training were valuable, that mastering technology was crucial, and lauded inequality of pay as a positive benefit. He proclaimed: "We cannot tolerate a situation where a locomotive driver earns only as much as a copying clerk . . . We need hundreds of thousands, millions of skilled workers. But in order to create cadres of skilled workers, we must provide an incentive for unskilled workers, provide for them a prospect of advancement."[5] During this period the state paid far more attention to placing individual workers in appropriate jobs and ensuring that their skills were properly used.

In 1935 policy changed yet again, though there was no return to egalitarianism. On the contrary, the Soviet press took up the model of Aleksei Stakhanov, a Donbass coalminer reported to have hewn 102 tons of coal in a single shift, instead of the seven which was the official norm. Now technical innovation and expertise were combined with heroism: Stakhanovite workers were expected to raise output not just by hard work but also by devising better work patterns or introducing new technology. In this way the state hoped to be able to motivate workers without market stimuli, and also without giving enterprise managers any more decisionmaking powers than they already had. The focus became the fantastic *individual* achievements of ordinary workers. They received individual pay rates to match, to say nothing of access to better clothes, apartments, holidays, and medical care. Some Stakhanovites earned enough, in wages and bonuses, to be able to afford a car.[6] In this way, a new worker hierarchy began to emerge, many of whose members were later sent for political training at a party high school and became members of the party-state elite.

But this method ran counter to prevailing popular traditions of egalitarianism and "joint responsibility." Performing well on the job was a feat which depended not on one's own input alone, and other workers, envious of Stakhanovite perquisites, sometimes proved obstructive. Why should just one worker benefit from the common effort? There were other questions too about the method of pay. If materials were not delivered, if spare parts were defective, if the production line kept halting, then how could one fulfill one's norm? The workshop might be dirty or poorly ventilated. Auxiliary workers might fall short on their quotas and fail to deliver, repair, or maintain. Queues in the canteen might delay one at midday, or it might be necessary to leave early to secure scarce goods *(defitsitnye tovary)* in the shops.[7]

In short, it proved impossible to achieve high output by command from above. Instead the factory, like the old village community, became a social unit dedicated to the survival of its members. In the factory community the managers, the trade union representatives, the technicians, foremen, and fellow workers all had their place. They in turn were partly dependent on the officials of Gosplan and the industrial ministries. Because market pressures were absent, these were the decisive influences at play in deciding what product mix should be turned out, what the finished items should cost, what individual workers should be paid for their part in producing them, and in what conditions they should work. The worker was dependent on his bosses to secure him better working and living conditions and a tolerable rate of pay, while the boss was dependent on his workers for the fulfillment of norms which would enable him to avoid failure, investigation, dismissal, or even arrest. The Soviet factory, in short, was a new form of patron-client structure, in which bosses and workers often had more in common with each other than with their masters in Moscow. Their principal interests were in low output targets and absence of change.

Moscow tried from time to time to break down the mutual dependency and risk avoidance. During 1937–38 the regime deliberately reawakened the atmosphere of 1928–29, with "specialist-baiting" and show trials. Only now the victims were the managers and technicians who had taken the place of the "bourgeois specialists." Accidents and breakdowns in production were now routinely blamed on the managers' shortcomings, corruption, or even deliberate sabotage. At huge meetings they were exhorted to exercise "self-criticism" and to confess their faults before the collective. Some were arrested and subject to show trials well publicized in the local newspapers.[8]

What the Soviet regime ended by creating, then, was not a moneyless, nonmarket system, but one in which elements of the market combined with both command and motivation. The amalgam was held together by the patronage of the enterprise director, who hired and fired; dealt with the party, Gosplan, industrial ministries, and, if necessary, the police; found ways to evade the bottlenecks of fuel, spare parts, and raw materials; and in general kept his enterprise going through all the difficulties and dangers which beset it.

Workers' material interests inclined them to accept the existing hierarchy and to try to secure their place within it. But there were nonmaterial reasons for accepting it, too, which were assiduously cultivated and played up in the party's propaganda. The promise to provide universal welfare benefits was not fulfilled everywhere, but the party had made a good start with education and health care. Some workers remembered what exploitation had been like under the prerevolutionary economic system; what had replaced it had turned out no better in practice for most of them, but all the same the anticapitalist aspiration was valued, especially since the regime took every opportunity to trumpet the evils of the "final stage of capitalism" currently on display in Nazi Germany. Anticapitalism coalesced with patriotism in a mixture which party propaganda could make the most of, especially as Germany became more threatening and the danger of war more real. The image of Stalin as a leader with a simple lifestyle, friend and teacher of the workers, wise leader of progressive humanity, for all its crudity was reassuring in these circumstances. The patriotism thus bolstered was not so much Russian as *Soviet:* not that the difference was absolute—as we have seen already, Russians tend to adopt an identity which is supranational or universal and then claim to include other peoples within it.[9]

The first five-year plans succeeded in increasing industrial output considerably because they plugged so many new resources, especially former peasants, into the industrial system, and used the powers of the state to direct those resources into a few chosen areas. All other aspects of the economy were downplayed or neglected: agriculture, housing, retail trade, services, consumer industry. But the effect could not last: even industrial workers in priority sectors needed those "subsidiary" sectors of the economy, and without them were forced to disperse their effort, waste their time, or suffer ill health in a way which was damaging even to the priority sectors. Even some branches of heavy industry—chemical and electronic, for example—were relatively neglected, with damaging cumulative effects.

It was not just the lopsided nature of economic development, though, which harbored hidden dangers for the future. For the fact was that the planned economy was not actually planned at all. It was a patron-client economy, in which the workers looked to their enterprise administrators and enterprise administrators looked to the industrial ministries to guarantee them a reasonably comfortable and secure existence, all at the cost of those who were left outside heavy industry. It survived for so long because of Russia's immense resources of both human beings and natural inputs. As Moshe Lewin has commented, it "came to be hooked on waste—it could not work without it, and it built up huge constituencies that thrived on it." Industrial ministries bargained with Gosplan for resources for their clients; enterprises then bargained with the industrial ministries for resources for *their* clients. With no market forces or monetary restraints to discipline the results, maximum input was an unmitigated benefit. For that reason, construction projects were launched before anyone knew whether they could ever be completed, or would be needed when they were; expensive new machinery was imported before it was required and was left to rust in the rain and snow because there were no premises ready to house it. And so on. In a country with abundant reserves, such a system could survive for a long time. But it could not last forever: not when the resources eventually began to run out and the pressure of international competition finally made itself felt.[10]

ARCHITECTURE AND URBAN PLANNING

Nowhere did the urge to sweep away an old world and construct a new one have greater influence on everyday life than among the architects. While a few of them believed that a Russian socialist society should be antiurban, dispersed in small communities along superefficient highways, the majority held that the key to developing the new socialist man lay in redesigning cities. But there was no consensus as to how this was to be done. The most radical members of OSA (the Society of Contemporary Architects) dreamed of the *dom-kommuna*, the communal apartment block, in which cooking, laundering, and repair work would be handled centrally, so that much inefficient drudgery, especially that performed by women, would be eliminated. Each person would have a separate bed-sitting room, close to but not combined with that of a family partner. Children would live separately nearby under expert childcare and could be visited regularly, while families would be able to eat together in cafeterias and communal dining rooms.[11]

In practice, the housing crisis generated by the first five-year plan was too abrupt and severe for such comprehensive plans to be implemented. Instead, as millions of immigrants streamed into the towns, they were squeezed into existing accommodation, a whole family to a room, or even to a barricaded corner of a large room, without consideration for social or gender distinctions, everyone sharing a common kitchen, bathroom, toilet, and corridor. The wealthy and cultured were exposed to domestic violence, foul language, and lack of elementary hygiene such as they had never experienced before. They were also trapped in a milieu where any neighbor could easily spy on their most private behavior and report it to the authorities. In a way they had been rudely shoved back into the village commune, with its gossip and backbiting, but also with its need for risk avoidance and the resolution of conflict through consensus.

This was a reality far from the utopian dreams: as one former communal apartment dweller has put it, it was a "sordid romance with the collective, unfaithful both to communitarian mythologies and to traditional family values . . . Every communal apartment dweller is probably scarred for life . . . by symbolic 'joint responsibility'—a double bind of love and hatred, of envy and attachment, of secrecy and exhibitionism, of embarrassment and compromise."[12]

Immersion in this stark reality prompted a reassessment of the self-consciously crude proletarian lifestyle which many party members had adopted. Instructions on hygiene and courtesy began to appear in hallways and staircases. Communal apartment dwellers were exhorted to sweep floors regularly, to empty spittoons daily, and to refrain from washing dirty linen in the kitchen sink. Meanwhile the upper ranks of the nomenklatura began to prepare retreats for themselves: private apartments, where they could live more secluded lives, surrounded by chintz curtains and polka-dotted teacups. During the 1930s the accumulation of privileges of this kind became far more significant than monetary rewards, for there was little the latter could buy in a state-controlled economy of scarcity. Instead the calibrations of the nomenklatura hierarchy gave access to meticulously graded benefits: apartments, dachas, holiday homes, superior health care, cars—chauffeured for those at the top—so that officials did not have to struggle with late buses and crowded Metro trains. While the rest of the population endured shortages and queues at state shops or rapacious prices in the markets, good-quality produce was provided cheaply in special stores for those who had access to them.[13]

The more grandiose architectural schemes retreated from domestic life and were henceforth confined to public buildings and to projects like the Moscow Metro, the city's new underground railway network. Here, instead of the pure, straight lines and plain, somewhat sterile Bauhaus shapes beloved of the international avant-garde, structural forms gradually took on a voluptuous neoclassical air, with arches, columns, plinths, and capitals. At the First Congress of Soviet Architects in 1934, its president, Aleksei Shchusev, praised the public buildings of the Emperor Augustus and added: "In this area we alone are the direct heirs of Rome: only in socialist society and with the help of socialist technology is construction possible on a still greater scale and of still greater artistic perfection."[14]

As time went by, the proportions of those neoclassical forms gradually became distorted, more extended in size and increasingly beset with neo-baroque decorational motifs, often the hammer and sickle, banners, statues and friezes of soldiers or working people. Examples could be seen in the Gosplan building and the Moskva Hotel around the huge square cleared of traders' stalls in the center of Moscow—originally Okhotnyi Riad, now a temple cleared of moneylenders—in the towering facades along the new Gorkii Street (1936–1940), and on the Moscow Prospect running southward from the center of Leningrad. The lock-gates at either end of the Volga–Don and Moscow–Volga canals—both built by slave labor—were similarly adorned, while the Moscow Metro adapted outsize neobaroque to cavernous underground stations. In the postwar Exhibition of Economic Achievements in Moscow, local ethnic motifs were incorporated into Stalinist baroque, and set the tone for the rebuilding of the centers of Union Republican capital cities.

The climax of Stalinist neobaroque was reached in the "wedding-cake" buildings built around Moscow after the Second World War, modeled partly on Manhattan skyscrapers, but with much more extensive lower stories and often embellished around the parapets with neo-Muscovite motifs; the central complex would be topped off with a red star and a spire similar to one of the Kremlin gateways. Its largest single exemplar was the massive Moscow University building of 1953 on the hills overlooking the city—a striking tribute to the priority accorded to science and education in the Communist outlook. This was the public style of an expansive and confident empire, internationalist yet also Russian.[15]

479

LITERATURE AND THE ARTS

Stalin was doing what the avant-garde had long called for, erasing the boundaries between life and art. He was also rejecting early postrevolutionary iconoclasm, exalting empire as a fulfillment of millenarian hopes, and employing utopian rhetoric as a device of power politics. In literature the flamboyant experimentation of the early Proletkult and Maiakovskii yielded first of all to traditional realism, then to a cult of the heroic, delivered in an easily comprehensible style. In 1932 all the various competing literary groups were closed down, and a new overarching association replaced them: the Union of Soviet Writers. At its first congress in 1934 it proclaimed that the method which all its members would practice was "socialist realism," whose main features were *narodnost, partiinost,* and *ideinost,* three terms whose content was vague, but implied that writers should write about ordinary people in a language accessible to them and in a spirit which was ideologically sound and approved by the party. Writers who employed the method were published and enjoyed the modest privileges available to members of the Union: better apartments, special clinics, holiday homes.[16] Those who did not found publication difficult or impossible, endured the deprivations of ordinary Soviet citizens, and could suffer a worse fate.

The key personnel in the Writers' Union were its secretaries and the editors of its journals and publishing houses. They were the people who controlled access to publishing outlets, and they decided what did and did not satisfy the Union's criteria in each individual text. In practice it was their taste rather than party ideology which determined what should be published and in what form. Since second-rate writers were often appointed to these positions, they tended to favor a cautious, conservative, and readily comprehensible mode of writing. They were easily frightened by anything which was experimental, obscure, or critical of Soviet society. In time conformity to their taste became second nature for most Soviet writers, and was in any case inculcated in "creative seminars," public readings, and discussions of work in progress. Given these pressures, the official censorship, Glavlit, played a subsidiary role, though still a palpable one in ensuring that state secrets or narratives which jarred with the current official view of history did not reach the public.

The structure of the Writers' Union became a model for all creative unions and indeed for professional associations in general, for example, for engineers, lawyers, and doctors. Responsible officials were appointed to them through the nomenklatura system; they had to be qualified in their profession, but also to exercise it in a way approved by the party. In return for adherence to these principles, the professional association offered its members modest privileges, which shielded them from the grosser forms of the struggle for existence. It socialized its members into a way of life which combined professional competence with service to party and people.

For writers of real talent or originality, this institutionalization of literature created a troubling, even agonizing, situation. It was not just that their work was being supervised by mediocrities, though that was bad enough. Their very calling had been hijacked. Most of them believed that literature had a special, even sacred, role to play in Russian society. Now the Communists claimed to have accomplished that sacralization, but through politics rather than through art.

Most major writers tried at some stage to reorient their work in the direction indicated by the party. The poet Boris Pasternak, for example, did his best to become part of the Communist literary world, traveling on "artistic assignments," accepting official positions in the Writers' Union, and being rewarded with a splendid dacha in the writers' settlement at Peredelkino, just outside Moscow. "I have become a particle of my time and state," he wrote, "and its interests have become my own." He even composed an ode to Stalin, though one so idiosyncratic that it could not be adapted for propaganda purposes.[17]

In the end, though, he could not sustain the role he had tried to impose on himself. Traveling to the Urals with other writers during the first five-year plan, he was so horrified by the scenes of poverty and degradation he witnessed in Sverdlovsk that he returned deeply depressed and was unable to write the sketches expected of him. His works were ever more frequently rejected by Writers' Union journals because of the "unclarity of their social intentions." In the end, he stopped writing his own poetry and confined himself to translation, which did not offer the same creative dilemmas and kept him in touch with a wider world. While rendering Shakespeare, Goethe, and Georgian poets, he felt at least that he was escaping the growing claustrophobia of the Soviet literary scene and was in communuion "with the West, with the historical earth, with the face of the world."[18]

Pasternak's fate was relatively fortunate. Both Maiakovskii and the poet

Sergei Esenin committed suicide as they felt the bounds of their creative freedom narrowing. The Odessa Jewish writer Isaak Babel practiced what he called "the genre of silence" for several years, but was arrested, accused of espionage and terrorism, and sent to a labor camp, where he died.[19] Osip Mandelstam, unable to publish, attempted an ode to Stalin, but also wrote a lampoon on him, which he recited only to trusted friends; all the same he was arrested, convicted of "counterrevolutionary activities," and died in a Vladivostok transit camp in December 1938.[20] Anna Akhmatova spent countless hours in the queues outside Leningrad's prisons, hoping for news of her imprisoned husband and son and trying to deliver food parcels for them, an experience which she later commemmorated in her *Requiem,* dedicated to the memory of the women with whom she had stood in line. The novelist and dramatist Mikhail Bulgakov at least avoided arrest, but spent the 1930s in a constant and largely vain struggle to have his plays performed. Denied permission to emigrate despite a personal appeal to Stalin, he fell ill and died, not least as a result of the unending physical strain and personal frustration.

In all the arts what was sought was not so much ideological conformity as professional competence within an idiom looking back to the nineteenth century, to romanticism or realism according to circumstance. In the visual arts, preference was given to monumental forms and a celebratory manner, portraying Russian figures of the past, struggling heroes of the revolutionary and working-class movement, or cheerful collective farmers surrounded by the fruits of their labor. At the same time, it was possible for painters to practice a more modest style, provided it was easily comprehensible: portraits or scenes from everyday life, for example.

Music is a less explicit medium, but even so the composer Dmitrii Shostakovich, inspired by jazz, dance music, and industrial rhythms in the 1920s, saw his work increasingly questioned by his colleagues, until in 1936 his— mildly experimental—opera *Lady Macbeth of Mtsensk* was denounced in *Pravda* as "cacophony instead of music." Thereupon he withdrew his bold and dissonant Fourth Symphony before its first performance and simplified his style. The result was the Fifth Symphony of 1937, an extremely accomplished and successful work in a relatively orthodox sonata form. He called it "a Soviet artist's reply to just criticism," suggesting that diplomacy had become one of the most important tools of the Soviet musician's trade. Throughout these years he went about in an agony of fear that he might at any moment be arrested.[21]

All art forms thus graduated in the 1930s toward high technical competence, fostered in the thorough training programs organized by the creative unions, combined with a safe, conservative idiom favored by the usually second-rate artists who ran them.

EDUCATION AND THE NEW ELITE

Educational policy moved in a similarly hierarchical, imperial, and conservative direction. During the 1920s schoolchildren had been required to undergo a vocational and polytechnic style of education, which included manual labor. They did much of their learning "on the job," by spending periods working in a factory or a farm, or through project work, much of which was carried out not behind a desk, but in the community. Teaching of history was socioeconomic in emphasis and heavily critical of the prerevolutionary past: tsars, generals, and landowners were portrayed not as state-builders, but merely as exploiters of the people.

Employers and parents began to complain that children were approaching their first jobs without adequate basic skills. In August 1931 the Central Committee decreed that a core curriculum be laid down which would include basic training in reading, writing, and mathematics, as well as history, geography, science, Russian, and (where appropriate) the native language, as well as the fundamentals of Marxism-Leninism. Manual labor and vocational studies almost disappeared; classroom tuition was restored, backed up by officially approved textbooks and a regular regime of tests and examinations. In history, teachers were instructed to avoid "abstract sociological schemes" and to emphasize chronology. Dates, kings, and battles came back into fashion, especially battles won by Russia: Ivan the Terrible, Peter the Great, and Catherine II were once again heroes, and their conquests were "progressive" because they created the empire led by the Russian people which would one day be the Soviet Union. Anti-Russian rebels, such as Shamil, were no longer extolled for leading popular resistance movements, but were condemned for their antipatriotic attitudes.[22]

By the late 1930s school uniforms were restored, complete with compulsory pigtails for girls. Fees were reintroduced for the upper three forms of secondary school, beginning a process of conscious social stratification: the last three years were the ones required for access to higher education.

These changes reflected the fact that a new social elite was moving into the top jobs, an elite no longer moulded by prerevolutionary training but brought up entirely under the Soviet system. Anxious to disencumber itself from "bourgeois specialists," in the late 1920s the party launched a retraining program to send its promising younger people through specialist and higher education so that they could become "Red specialists." Nominated by party, Komsomol, or trade union committees from the factory bench or the tractor driving-wheel, they were given modest grants and sent to study for three to five years, many of them in technological institutes where they could train for posts of responsibility. During 1928–1932, some 110,000 party members and 40,000 nonparty people studied in this way, constituting about a third of all students in higher education.[23]

483

When they emerged, in the early 1930s, they were ideally placed for swift promotion in the expanding industries of the first five-year plans. They fitted ideally the demands of the nomenklatura filing system devised by Stalin, and rapidly became the core of the party-state elite in industry, agriculture, and the armed forces.

Gradually in the 1930s the lifestyles of "red" and "bourgeois" specialists coalesced. The new elite began to adopt the manners of traditional bourgeois society and to aspire to the material acquisitions associated with it. Dungarees and leather tunics gave way to two-piece suits and ties. Beards and long hair were spurned and a clean-shaven face became normal. Women began to use makeup and perfumes. Curtains were put up in apartments to protect privacy, lampshades ensured a discreet and cosy lighting, and meals were taken at a table covered with a tablecloth. As newspapers and journals showed, this was the way of life expected not just for managers and officials, but also for shock workers and Stakhanovites. It went along with such "professional" virtues as cleanliness, punctuality, courtesy, and devotion to public service, forming a complex of behavioral norms summed up in the word *kulturnost*. Practices which did not conform to the ideal were dismissed as *nekulturno*.[24]

The word *kultura* in Russian has a far broader meaning than its equivalent in English, combining our notion of "culture" with politeness, good work habits, and devotion to public service. Its widespread adoption reflected the fact that Soviet society was adopting the civilizing process described by Norbert Elias—a later version of the eighteenth-century campaign by Peter I to Europeanize his elite. Along with it the word *obshchestvennost* returned to Russian discourse, as a positive term, to describe educated people (who might be working-class but were likely to be skilled workers), politically aware and socially concerned. This was the image which the new "red-bourgeois" elite wished to project of itself. This was the public for which the homogeneous, heroic, and complacent products of "socialist realist" culture were designed.

The image was a long way from the reality of ordinary people's lives, however. The ideals of *kulturnost* were unattainable in a communal apartment, where one could not even protect one's privacy or hygiene. The consumer goods paraded in journals as legitimately desirable were usually not available in the state shops. To satisfy aspirations identified by the regime as legitimate, one had either to be promoted into the privileged elite, to attach oneself to a patron, or to cultivate personal acquaintances who would gain one access to high-quality consumer products, often from abroad.[25]

The propagation of the ideal, then, in the long run sharpened social stratification, highlighted the inadequacy of Soviet consumer industry, and intensified the tendency to seek patronage, protection, and the exchange of personal favors. Over the decades these became ever more prevalent features of Soviet life.

FAMILY POLICY

Marxist teaching on the family preached that in a socialist society it should be possible to emancipate women from the hypocrisy of marriages forged by the requirements of property and the division of labor. Cooking, cleaning, and childcare would be transferred to the public sphere, freeing women to take up education and paid employment on the same basis as men. Marriage and the traditional family would become superfluous; men and women would be free to form and dissolve unions on terms of equality and as mutual affection should dictate. Early Soviet legislation, culminating in the Family Code of 1926, went far to put these ideals into practice. Civil marriage was instituted, abortion was legalized and made available on demand, women's property rights were equalized with those of men, and de facto families were accorded the same status as registered unions, so that illegitimacy disappeared as a concept. Any spouse could obtain divorce merely by informing—not necessarily consulting—the partner, and alimony payments were limited to the care of children and support for the disabled.[26]

As a result of these reforms, divorce rates rose sharply. By the mid-1920s the Soviet Union had the highest in Europe; in Moscow by 1926 there was one divorce for every two marriages.[27] Similarly abortion was much more widely practiced, especially in towns, where young women were more likely to seek education and employment and where housing conditions were less suitable for large families. In Moscow the abortion rate rose from 19 per 1,000 live births in 1921 to 271 in 1934, and in other towns figures moved in a similar direction, though less sensationally. The increase in abortions was accompanied by a fall in the birthrate, from 45 births per 1,000 people in 1927 to 30.1 in 1935: all this even though the marriage rate was actually rising.[28]

Of course, the success of this legislation depended crucially on the state's replacing dissolved families in caring for children, old people, the sick, and the disabled. That it was far from being able to do. In the 1920s and early 1930s, hundreds of thousands of orphans appeared on the streets of the towns. They would hang around markets and railway stations, begging for food and clothing, and sometimes would gather in whole bands, attacking passersby and robbing traders. The main reason for their appearance in such numbers was the sheer dislocation caused first by civil war and later by collectivization and headlong urbanization, but clearly it was also linked to the legislative weakening of the family. Some of the street children were taken into orphanages, but these were poorly resourced and had a reputation for inadequate supervision and health care. Some of them became breeding grounds for crime and disease. Other orphans were fostered out to peasant households which needed working hands, but there they were often harshly exploited and deprived of the chance of getting an education.[29]

By the early 1930s, then, the Soviet leaders were faced with clear evidence that their family policy was having damaging effects. It was creating unstable families, a fall in the birthrate, and a frightening increase in the number of uncared-for children. At a time when social change was in any case undermining law and order, and when the state needed ever more young people for military service and industrial development, these effects were particularly undesirable.

Consequently, official propaganda began once more to extol the virtues of stable family life: "Marriage has a positive value for the Soviet socialist state only if the partners see in it a lifelong union. So-called 'free love' is a bourgeois invention."[30] In June 1936 abortion was outlawed except in cases of serious health risk, and a crash program of building childcare facilities was launched. Civil registry offices were spruced up and wedding ceremonies made more solemn and elaborate, to underline the importance society ascribed to the occasion. From 1944 divorce was granted only after a court hearing.

The importance of the family as an economic unit was also strengthened. The right to inherit property was restored. Although in Soviet conditions property itself was limited and so that right was less significant than in bourgeois societies, nevertheless it meant that a child could now inherit an apartment, or a dacha with a small plot of land, from its parent, by no means a triviality in conditions of scarcity. The offspring of unregistered unions had no such inheritance rights, so that de facto the concept of illegitimacy was restored.

The restoration of the bourgeois family was a tacit admission that the

Marxist ideal of family life had proved unworkable in practice. The attempt at emancipation had caused too many social problems, especially for women, who were supposed to be the main beneficiaries, and had threatened to precipitate a population decline. Instead the state offered women what Wendy Goldman has called a "tacit bargain": "it broadened both state and male responsibility for the family, but in exchange it demanded that women assume the double burden of work and motherhood." As a result, though women were entering the industrial workforce in ever greater numbers, this trend was not generating the emancipation hoped for, since pay, especially that of women, dropped sharply during the first five-year plan. Two incomes were now needed simply to sustain viable family life, and so women willynilly had to take on a "double burden," which they coped with by limiting the number of children. In that way the fruits of female emancipation became building blocks of the Stalinist neopatriarchal social system.[31]

FOREIGN AFFAIRS

The new Soviet state made its diplomatic debut by calling simultaneously for international peace and proletarian revolution. It was to pursue these two incompatible aims, somewhat uneasily, for the next seventy years. Initially at least, the Communist leaders saw no contradiction between them: they believed that proletarian revolution would lead to universal peace, and that peace was inconceivable without proletarian revolution. For them the Russian revolution was merely the flashpoint where the process had started. It remained to publish the treaties secretly concluded between Russia and her allies in 1915, and the indignant peoples of Europe would overthrow all the governments involved. Trotskii, prime apostle of international revolution, was appointed the first people's commissar for foreign affairs, and declared: "All that has to be done is to publish the secret treaties; then I will shut up shop."[32]

As we know, matters proved far more complicated than Trotskii had anticipated. Plunged into civil war for several years, Russia became an object rather than a determinant of international diplomatic and military activity. All the same, the Soviet state launched its career of revolutionary subversion by founding the Communist International, or Comintern, in March 1919. The First World War was only just over, and many European countries were torn apart by social and ethnic conflict. Hopes of world revolution did not seem unduly extravagant. Delegates denounced "reformist" and "opportunist" socialist leaders who had let their parties become "subsidiary organs of the bourgeois state," and called for the replacement of fraudulent parliamentary regimes by "a new and higher workers' democracy" in the form of soviets.[33] The second congress drew up a set of twenty-one "Conditions" on which socialist parties throughout the world might be admitted to the Comintern: they entailed breaking with social democrats and with all parties which took trade unions or parliaments seriously. Members of the Comintern were to "unmask social patriotism," denounce "the falsity and hypocrisy of socialist pacifism," and prepare for the violent seizure of power by, for example, setting up secret cells in the armed forces and using them to conduct revolutionary propaganda.[34]

These "Conditions" demonstrated vividly the incompatibility of Russian messianic socialism and European social democracy, even in its Marxist form. They excluded for a long time to come the possibility of the Communist Party's working with left-wing parties throughout Europe or condoning "separate paths to socialism," in other words embracing what would later be called a Popular Front strategy. They divided all European socialist parties into two mutually hostile factions, of which the Communists were usually much the smaller, and ensured that the revolutionary movement would not be genuinely international, but rather would be directed from Moscow. As a German Communist put it, in ironic recollection of Lord Nelson at Trafalgar, "Russia expects everyone to do his duty."[35]

The new Soviet state posed a novel problem to European diplomatic arrangements: how to integrate a power which openly aimed to subvert its diplomatic partners and to overthrow their sociopolitical systems, and which moreover sponsored organizations designed to achieve those aims, if necessary by force. Even the Vatican, using the Jesuits in its relations with Protestant states of seventeenth-century Europe, had not posed such dilemmas.

For Russia the situation was not absolutely new. It had cultivated relations with the khanate of Kazan and later with the khanate of Crimea while supporting disaffected tribal leaders within those partners' societies. But the whole structure and protocol of "diplomacy" in those days had been so different that the parallel had only limited relevance.

At any rate, the People's Commissariat of Foreign Affairs had to coexist with the Communist International. The USSR wanted to promote world revolution, yet it also desperately needed international stability in order to recover from war and revolution and to protect its own borders. Since the first socialist regime had come to power in Russia and had not immediately succeeding in spreading socialism everywhere, it had perforce to take over the traditional diplomatic concerns of Russia. Among those the most important remained the security of the empire, however transformed that empire might be. But security could only be jeopardized by the Communist desire to promote international upheavals, in the hope of seeing elsewhere the wars and revolutions with whose help they themselves had come to power in Russia. Moreover, instability had the potential to bring to power in other countries not only left-wing pro-Soviet regimes, but also right-wing, anti-Soviet ones.

Soviet diplomacy, then, had to cope not only with institutional dualism but also with genuine ambiguity about what the country's foreign policy aims were. Other European powers naturally had great difficulty in understanding those aims and hence in working out how to deal with the Soviet Union. Some foreign statesmen regarded it as an unceasing source of political subversion and therefore as a wholly unreliable regime, to be dealt with only at arm's length. Others reckoned that to all intents and purposes it had resumed the position of the Russian Empire as a great European power and was therefore a relatively stable part of any calculations about collective security or the balance of power.

These stubborn ambiguities plagued the international relations of the Soviet Union throughout the interwar years, and must be considered the basic reason for the failure to form a durable anti-Nazi alliance and to prevent the outbreak of the Second World War.

Once the Soviet Union decided that it had to seek allies, or at least nonenemies, in the international system, its most natural initial partner was Germany, a fellow outlaw of the postwar settlement. In April 1922 the two countries signed an agreement at Rapallo, restoring normal diplomatic and commercial relations. Even before it was signed, military and industrial leaders on both sides had begun discreet cooperation which was to last for more than a decade. The German army, the Reichswehr, was able to use military bases in Russia which it was forbidden by the Versailles Treaty to build in its own country. Meanwhile German industrialists clandestinely built armaments factories in Soviet territory, which enabled both countries to benefit from advanced German technology, especially in chemistry and avionics. Ironically, then, the two armies which twenty years later were to wage the most destructive war in history against each other, began by testing their strategies and manufacturing their equipment together.[36]

In 1923, when there was industrial unrest in Germany, and it seemed that there was a prospect of revolution there, the Soviets briefly changed course, gave priority to the Comintern approach, and backed an attempt to declare a general strike, obtain arms, and seize power for the workers. But when the expected coup failed to take place, normal relations resumed fairly swiftly. Neither country had an interest in prolonging hostility.[37]

With the other major powers the USSR gradually set up diplomatic relations between 1921 and 1933, each time having to pledge, tongue in cheek, not to engage in subversion inside the partner country. In fact, however, in any case by the mid-1920s the prospect of world revolution had receded. It was not that the ultimate aim had been abandoned, but rather that as a priority it had yielded to the consolidation of the Soviet Union as a great power, and to the building of a more prosperous economy there. "Building socialism" now meant strengthening and defending the Soviet Union rather than striving for world revolution.

As it happened, the major security threat for most of the 1930s came from the East, from Japan, whose invasion of Manchuria in 1931 signaled that Japan was again pursuing its continental ambitions. A tense standoff ensued on the Soviet-Manchurian border, broken by fighting near Lake Khasan in 1938 and intermittent skirmishing thereafter. Finally, in August 1939, a large Red Army force under General Georgii Zhukov deployed tanks for the first time to mount an offensive at Khalkin-Gol and drove the Japanese out of the disputed territory. This was a decisive victory, which compelled the Japanese subsequently to pursue their strategic aims elsewhere, in southeast Asia and the Pacific—just in time for the USSR to concentrate on an even greater danger looming up in Europe.[38]

The disunity which the Communists had engendered among the European socialist parties proved especially damaging in Germany, where in 1932–33 the conflicts between Communists and Social Democrats cleared the way for Hitler's Nazi party to take power. His accession radically transformed the international situation. Previous capitalist regimes had not proved implacably hostile to the USSR, but here was one whose principal declared aim was to to destroy it. Security now became not just the main but the overriding priority of Soviet foreign policy. At the same time, the repugnant nature of Nazism meant that, for the first time, the Soviet Union could hope to gain supporters in other European countries outside the marginalized extreme left. Under the cosmopolitan and pro-Western foreign commissar, Maksim Litvinov, Soviet diplomacy used its best efforts to promote cooperation with democratic parties in western Europe. It applauded the coming to power of Popular Front governments—representing Social Democrats and Communists—in Spain and France, and promoted good relations with them.[39]

Now, however, a factor which had been useful to the Soviet government in the 1920s became a hindrance: the relative weakness of the Western democracies and their inability to work together in opposing violations of international peace. The USSR signaled its arrival as a status-quo power by

490

joining the League of Nations in 1934, but it was a League of Nations already discredited by its failure to resist unprovoked aggression. At the same time, the ghost of the pre-1914 balance of power was invoked when the Soviet Union concluded an alliance with France. Only this time the alliance was not followed by general-staff consultations and shared military planning: it was an alliance intended to prevent war, not to conduct it. In any case, the arrangement lost much of its benefit when the German army occupied the Rhineland in 1936, a step which shook the Soviet leaders as much as the Western powers. They now began to work urgently toward the creation of "collective security" by an alliance of the major powers against Nazi Germany.

When one of the major Popular Front governments was threatened by military coup in Spain in July 1936, later backed by armed units despatched from Germany and Italy, the Soviet Union refrained from sending units of its own armed forces, in order not to alarm Britain and France, but instead sponsored International Brigades, in which anti-Fascist volunteers from many countries fought together. Soviet readiness to help the Popular Front contrasted with the official inaction of Britain and France and attracted considerable goodwill among European radicals and socialists, even those of decidedly non-Communist beliefs. However, the Soviet regime forfeited much of this newly gained benevolence by the obvious priority it assigned to preventing an alliance of Trotskyists and anarchists (POUM) from coming to power in Catalonia. George Orwell complained that "It was Communists above all others who prevented revolution in Spain."[40]

Besides, the Spanish Civil War coincided with the terror inside the USSR itself, a spectacle which European intellectuals and politicians watched with fascination, bewilderment, and horror. They could only regard it as a sign that the USSR was neither a desirable nor a reliable ally, especially since so many of those purged were senior officers of the armed forces. Stalin's bloodletting also raised the legitimate question whether Communist Russia was morally preferable to Nazi Germany.

All these questions underlay the hesitations with which Britain and France approached the problem of concluding an anti-Nazi alliance with the USSR, both when the Nazis occupied the Sudetenland in September 1938 and after they marched into the rest of Czechoslovakia in March 1939. The Munich agreement of September 1938 was a desperate and undignified expedient forced on British prime minister Neville Chamberlain by his loathing of the Soviet Union. When he finally abandoned appeasement and offered a guarantee against German aggression to Poland, his chiefs of staff warned him forthrightly that such a guarantee was meaningless without a Soviet alliance. Chamberlain, however, reiterated his "profound mistrust" of the Soviet Union, his skepticism about whether it could conduct an effective military campaign against Germany, and his repugnance at its idea of liberty.[41] In any case he knew that an alliance with it would mean giving the Red Army carte blanche to send troops through Romania, Poland, and the Baltic states—something none of those countries would countenance. For those reasons negotiations between the Soviet Union, Britain, and France in the summer of 1939 virtually broke down, despite the obvious common need for a defense pact.

In the end, having replaced Litvinov with the more parochial, pedestrian, and obedient Viacheslav Molotov, Stalin decided to obtain what he could from Hitler. On 23 August 1939 Molotov and his German opposite number, Ribbentrop, signed a Nazi-Soviet nonaggression pact, a secret protocol of which gave the Soviet Union a free hand in Finland, the Baltic States, eastern Poland, and Bessarabia, the areas where Stalin most wanted to strengthen his strategic presence.[42]

The pact was a desperate move on Stalin's part. It gave the Soviet Union only short-term benefits, and then on the word of a man who had never made secret his intention to destroy Communism. It eliminated the Polish "buffer" and thus, if it failed to prevent war with Nazi Germany, risked depriving the USSR of the second front in the west which was Germany's perpetual strategic nightmare.

Stalin attempted to compensate for the drawbacks of the pact by annexing the Baltic states and Bessarabia in 1940, to give the Soviet Union a stronger presence in the Baltic and Black Seas and at the mouth of the Danube. He also tried to reincorporate Finland, but the Finns resisted effectively, and after a brief, inconclusive war—the "winter war" of 1939–40—the Soviet Union had to be content with annexing a relatively small area of territory in southeast Finland.

THE GREAT PATRIOTIC WAR

It is very difficult for a Westerner to write about the Soviet-German war of 1941–1945. This is partly because of the sources. There is more material on the war than on any other period of Soviet history, but most of it is either monotonously heroic or reflects the concerns of the author and the time in which it was published. Only in recent years have historians been able to attempt a more dispassionate account of what happened.

Even more important, the war beggars the imagination. It was a war of destruction and mass extermination on an unprecedented scale. Soviet human losses were at least forty times greater than those suffered by Britain and seventy times greater than those of the United States (higher by recent estimates). Even that terrible statistic does not take into account the immeasurably greater ruthlessness with which the Germans treated their enemies in the east, and the catastrophic shortages of food, housing, and basic services which ordinary Soviet citizens had to endure for years on end.

However, the imaginative leap must be attempted, not only because of the scale and importance of the subject, but also because the war was the major formative experience in the life of most of those who lived through it, and especially the younger generations. It continues to form the outlook of ex-Soviet citizens to the present day.

When the Germans invaded at dawn on 22 June 1941 they achieved almost total surprise and a complete mastery of the air. They hit a country which in general terms was preparing for war but did not expect one at that moment, and had certainly not disposed its armed forces in optimum manner to meet one. There has been much speculation about the reason for Stalin's failure to respond even though he had been repeatedly warned by his own and others' intelligence services that invasion was imminent. According to Nikita Khrushchev, Stalin lost his nerve after the setbacks in Finland, and thereafter bent over backward to avoid provoking Hitler.[43] He was certainly aware that the Red Army, though nearly five million strong, was currently no match for the Wehrmacht. More important, he was obsessed by the danger that Germany might conclude a separate peace with Britain, in order to secure her rear for an invasion of the USSR. Without such a separate peace Stalin did not believe Hitler would dare to attack him, for fear of replaying the "two-front war" which had condemned Germany to defeat in 1918. Stalin therefore interpreted Churchill's warnings about Germany's offensive preparations as part of a provocative maneuver designed to lure the USSR into a war with Germany in which it would remain isolated and without allies. The flight of Hitler's deputy, Rudolf Hess, to Britain on 12 May 1941 naturally deepened his suspicions that Germany and Britain were about to gang up on him.[44]

In recent years some historians have suggested that in the summer of 1941 Stalin was preparing a preemptive strike against Germany, and that the reason his defensive dispositions were so inept is that he was deploying his forces to mount an early offensive.[45] No serious evidence has been found to support this contention in the numerous Soviet archives now accessible. It is true that the third five-year plan (1938–1942) made military production a priority, that in June 1940 draconian new labor laws virtually militarized the factory workforce, and that nearly a million reservists were called up in the spring of 1941. It is also true that the prevailing military doctrine of the Red Army required any war to be fought in an offensive posture and carried swiftly to the enemy's territory, in the expectation that a pro-Soviet workers' rising there would forestall widespread bloodshed. Red Army dispositions on the eve of war reflected this expectation: formations were deployed in forward position, so that in the event of an attack they could take the war swiftly on to enemy territory. The speedy success of the German Blitzkrieg in Poland and France in 1939–40 did not prompt, as it should have done, a reassessment of this thinking, a recognition that a deeper and more defensive deployment might serve better to counter the German strategy. But no serious documentary evidence has ever been adduced which goes beyond general planning under this doctrine to support the theory that Stalin was actually preparing an offensive in the summer of 1941.[46]

In 1937–38 Stalin had executed the leading theorists of the Soviet forward military doctrine, but it had not been supplanted by any alternative one, and its tenets remained in place. It was, however, now being implemented clumsily by commanders who had not properly thought it through. They were still regrouping after the frontier rectifications of 1939–40. Despite the misgivings of General Zhukov, chief of the General Staff, they had neglected to prepare a strategic defense reserve, and they had dismantled the old fortifications before erecting new ones farther forward, so that neither set was effective when the attack came.[47]

The only comfort to flow from the invasion was the immediate offer of an alliance and military aid from the United States and Great Britain. "Collective security" switched in after all, but much too late. Although it eventually played a crucial role in winning the war, its benefits took a long time to materialize. For three whole years, Stalin fretted at his new allies to open the "second front" which he had denied himself with the Nazi-Soviet Pact, and he resented their persistent failure to do so.

Stunned by the unexpected German attack, Soviet units fought piecemeal, without a defense line they could fall back on, and often without command and control as well. The generals were bewildered by the assault: their standing orders, absurdly unrealistic, were to go over to the offensive as soon as possible. In any case, they often could not contact their units, since the communications system was primitive and disrupted by the invasion. They had little air support, for most Soviet planes were destroyed where they were stationed, without camouflage, on their airfields. Nor was there any substantial defensive reserve which might be brought up to plug gaps in the front. There were instances of heroic and effective resistance, like that of the fortress at Brest, which held out till 12 July, giving a tantalizing glimpse of what could be achieved where defense had been properly prepared. But most Soviet units were cut apart or simply bypassed and later surrounded and taken captive. At all times they fought ferociously, using bayonets if they ran out of bullets. The German chief of staff remarked: "Everywhere the Russians fight to the last man. They capitulate only occasionally."[48]

The early goals of the Barbarossa invasion plan were swiftly achieved. Smolensk, halfway to Moscow, fell on 16 July, and by the end of August Army Group North directly threatened Leningrad. Soviet resistance was tougher in the south, where more troops had been stationed, but in the end this resistance served only to increase the numbers surrounded and captured. When Kiev was endangered, Stalin refused to let it be surrendered, as Zhukov advised, so that a strategic withdrawal could shorten the front line. By the time it fell on 19 September, more than half a million men had been killed or taken prisoner.

The German concentration on the northern and southern fronts delayed the advance on Moscow. When it came, at the end of September, Army Group Center achieved early successes and surrounded another five armies near Viazma. In mid-October, Moscow was in panic: files were being burned; diplomatic representatives, government offices, and specialist personnel were being hastily evacuated to Kuibyshev, on the Volga. Ordinary people were cramming themselves aboard trains, buses, and trucks—anything which would transport them out of the city.

In the end, however, Stalin decided to stay in the capital and announced his decision, to fortify morale among Muscovites. His words had a dramatic effect in stiffening the will to resist. On 7 November the traditional revolution day parade was held on Red Square, from which troops marched directly to the front, a mere forty miles away. By this time the autumn rains had turned most roads into ribbons of mud, minimizing the advantages enjoyed by German motorized formations. Even more important, an early and unusually cold winter was setting in. This was to the Soviet advantage, not because Russians suffer less in the cold—though they are more used to it—but because their communications lines were far shorter. The German army had not prepared for a winter campaign and now had great difficulty in transporting fur hats, overcoats, and antifreeze hundreds of miles through territory increasingly infested with partisans.

Zhukov was put in charge of the defense of Moscow, which at first he had to conduct with the remnants of defeated units and a hastily improvised militia of Moscow's own citizens. By December, however, Stavka brought in reinforcements from the Far East, Richard Sorge's intelligence reports from Tokyo having reassured Stalin that there was no danger of attack from Japan. Many Muscovites later recalled the relief with which they observed these fresh troops, equipped for winter combat, marching through the city.

They came just in time. The Germans had reached the outskirts of Moscow itself: visitors today can still see, on the road from Sheremetevo Airport, an outsize antitank trap marking the farthest point of their advance. On 5 December Zhukov launched a counteroffensive which drove the Germans back about eighty miles. At that point he wanted to stabilize the front to prepare for further operations in 1942. Stalin, however, insisted that the offensive be continued in an attempt to encircle Army Group Center. Such an undertaking at this juncture was far beyond the capacities of the Red Army: all that was achieved was the further loss of 400,000 men.

At least total defeat had been averted, and that itself was an extraordinary achievement. The battle before Moscow was the first occasion on which the German Blitzkrieg strategy had suffered a serious reverse. But it was only a reverse, and Stalin's attempt to overexploit it nearly caused disaster. During the late spring and summer of 1942 the Wehrmacht again advanced huge distances, this time through eastern Ukraine and the Don steppes, where the weather and terrain were perfect for Panzer divisions. The Crimea and Rostov-on-Don fell to them. German troops advanced into the Caucasus and planted the swastika on Mount Elbruz. Soviet citizens began to wonder "How much farther can we retreat?" On 28 July Order no. 227 was distributed to all units with the words *Ni shagu nazad!*—not a step backward! "Panickers" and "cowards" were threatened with summary execution or transfer to penal battalions, which were given the dirtiest and most dangerous work.[49]

The turning point came at Stalingrad. In this industrial showpiece city, named after the leader and strung out along the Volga for some forty miles, the German motorized troops came up against the most ferocious and tenacious resistance they had yet encountered, even in this "war of annihilation." If it had fallen and they had been able to cross the Volga, both Moscow and Leningrad must ultimately have fallen to an immense encircling maneuver, and the Soviet Union would have become a truncated north Asian state, on the other side of the Urals.

But it did not fall. Soviet troops stood their ground. Contesting ruined block after ruined block brought out their staunchness and their capacity to fight in small groups. At times the areas they held were so small that German aircraft and artillery were inhibited from striking them, for fear of killing large numbers of their own men. In any case, street fighting was not what the Wehrmacht did best: in that constricted environment tanks and motorized units were reduced to the level of ordinary infantry. Besides, the Germans were now fighting at the end of enormously overextended supply lines, with only one usable railway line and aircraft operating from rough airstrips.

At this juncture a major shift in power took place in the Soviet command. Unlike Hitler, Stalin was capable of learning from his mistakes. He now listened attentively to his generals, and he knew that launching offensives without sufficient preparation was suicidal, especially in this supreme emergency. In September Zhukov advised him that a strategic counteroffensive could be mounted southward from the Don basin to Rostov, cutting off the German armies in the Caucasus and around Stalingrad, but that it needed nearly two months' preparation, during which time the beleaguered armies of Generals Chuikov and Yeremenko inside the city would have to fight on without much extra reinforcement. Stalin deferred to his advice and let him go ahead.

There was also a major symbolic switch in the power hierarchy at the time of Stalingrad. Already in 1940 officers' pre-1917 ranks had been restored. Now gold braid and shoulder straps reappeared on their uniforms, and new decorations, redolent of Russia's past greatness and exclusive to officers, were instituted: the Orders of Mikhail Kutuzov and of Aleksandr Nevskii. Political commissars were downgraded to the status of "political assistants" (*zampolity*) and deprived of the right to interfere in military decisions. This change of status was permanent. Officers in the Soviet armed forces henceforth enjoyed a greater degree of autonomy than any other profession or social group.[50]

By this time the Red Army had learned to deploy its forces in the same way as the Germans, concentrating their tanks in large, fast-moving formations equipped with Katiusha mortars and anti-aircraft guns. They had formed motorized divisions of infantry, able rapidly to occupy territory opened up by the tank formations. The air force was also operating in larger squadrons, linked to ground troops by improved radio systems. Soviet industry was now turning out tanks, aircraft, and weapons of all kinds in greatly increased numbers. At all levels, command and control were becoming more effective, as Soviet officers gained experience (the hard way) in modern mechanized warfare, and as their equipment improved.[51]

Operation Uranus, launched on 19 November, was thus a far better planned and equipped strategic maneuver than anything the Red Army had attempted earlier. It achieved all its objectives. By the end of January 1943 the German Sixth Army was surrounded and destroyed in Stalingrad, while the German troops in the Caucasus were compelled to withdraw hastily.

The Soviet recovery was confirmed the following July, when the Wehrmacht launched a huge and carefully prepared Panzer attack around the town of Kursk. Here the Germans were operating in weather and on terrain that suited them ideally, but by now the Red Army was fully their equal and repulsed the attack. Therewith the force of Blitzkrieg was finally blunted. Although the Wehrmacht remained a formidable fighting force, it was no longer able to push back or even in the long run to contain the Red Army.

By this time the resources of the Soviet state and society had been mobilized as thoroughly as they could be. During the second half of 1941 and early 1942 an enormous amount of industrial equipment, in many cases whole factories, had been relocated eastward, away from the danger of being overrun by the enemy. Hundreds of thousands of workers followed their machines to the Volga basin, the Urals, Siberia, Kazakhstan, or central Asia. By a decree of February 1942 all the able-bodied population was mobilized for the war effort; time off was limited to one day a month and compulsory overtime was introduced, so that a fifty-five-hour week became the norm. Some worked even longer than that, sleeping in camp beds on the shop floor. In some industries, such as railways and munitions, workers were under military discipline, so that unauthorized absence could mean a spell in the GULAG. Such harsh authoritarianism may not have been necessary: most workers were patriotic and in any case were more dependent than ever on their employers for basic living facilities.[52]

As a result of successful mobilization, by mid-1943 Soviet industry was far outstripping its German counterpart, now severely disrupted by bombing, in the production of crucial military items. In areas where Soviet industry was weak, supplies sent from the United States and Britain under the Lend-Lease agreements helped to plug gaps: for example, trucks, rubber tires, explosive chemicals, field telephones, telephone wire, and tins of meat (Spam), which became known ironically as "second fronts." According to Khrushchev, Stalin several times acknowledged the contribution of Lend-Lease to his close associates, adding that "if we had had to deal with Germany one-to-one we could not have coped because we had lost so much of our industry."[53]

This superiority enabled the Red Army to adopt with confidence the combined-operations strategy which had brought the Germans success in the early stages of the war. A series of massive offensives in the summer of 1944 in Belorussia and Ukraine pushed the Germans finally out of the Soviet Union, including the territories annexed in 1939–40, and swept Soviet soldiers into Poland, Slovakia, Hungary, and Romania.

Soviet troops were exhausted by the campaigning of 1944, and the final stages of the war took longer than might have been expected, especially since the Wehrmacht now had to face invading Allied troops in the west as well. These difficulties may help to explain why the Red Army waited five months (August 1944 to January 1945) to mount a serious assault on Warsaw. But there were undoubtedly political motives as well for the delay. In August 1944 the non-Communist Polish Home Army launched a rising with the aim of freeing their capital city from the Germans themselves. The Red Army waited till the Germans had crushed it before resuming their advance and taking Warsaw.

Soviet casualties were very heavy in the final months of war—more than 300,000 killed and 1.1 million wounded—because of ferocious German resistance to the overrunning of their own homeland.[54] Even those Germans who did not fully realize what atrocities their own troops had inflicted on the Soviet peoples nevertheless knew that the Russians could be expected to exact a terrible revenge. Soviet commanders, for their part, restrained raping, looting, and killing among their own men only insofar as they jeopardized military discipline: they felt that the sufferings of the German population were probably deserved and certainly no concern of theirs. For them, this was a war of annihilation between the Russian and German nations. After all, Ilya Ehrenburg had written in the army newspaper: "The Germans are not human . . . If you have killed one German, kill another. There is nothing jollier than German corpses."[55]

For that reason, the Vistula-Oder operation, which began in January 1945, took four months to cover the four hundred miles to Berlin and resulted in very heavy casualties. The German troops were outnumbered three to one at the start, and later by far more, but they were still determined, well equipped, and on the whole well led until the very final days. All the same, on 30 April Hitler committed suicide and the hammer and sickle was raised over the Reichstag building. On 9 May the Germans formally surrendered unconditionally.

The Soviet Union was triumphant but devastated. The human cost had been immense. Battlefield losses probably totaled 8.5–8.7 million, and to those one must add an unknown number of civilians who emigrated, were deported, or died prematurely as a result of the war, whether from disease, hunger, or direct enemy action. Recent publication of the 1939 census makes possible the calculation that the Soviet population just before the outbreak of war was about 197 million. If one projects existing growth rates, in 1946 it should have been 212.5 million; actually it was 168.5 million. "Global losses" were therefore 44 million, though that figure includes babies not born as a result of war, perhaps 10 million, and also those who died as a result of

Soviet rather than German brutalities, for example those in labor camps and penal settlements. Accuracy is not possible, but an estimate of 25–27 million for population loss caused by war does not seem unreasonable in the light of current data.[56]

How did the Soviet leadership manage to mobilize not only the armed forces and military industry, but also the civilian population, so recently alienated through collectivization and the terror? The answer, above all, is that this was a war to defend the homeland, a war for national survival, fought against an enemy utterly ruthless and careless of human life. As a Soviet colonel remarked to a British journalist, "It's a horrible thing to say, but by ill-treating and starving our prisoners, the Germans are *helping* us."[57]

In the Baltic states and western Ukraine in 1941 the population at first welcomed the Germans as liberators from Communist oppression. But that mood very soon evaporated as it became clear that the German command had no intention of restoring nation-states or even of allowing a normal life. The Baltic region became Reichskommissariat Ostland, and Ukraine was run by Reichskommissar Erich Koch, who stated unequivocally: "There is no such thing as a free Ukraine. Our aim is to ensure that Ukrainians work for Germany."[58] Closed churches were allowed to reopen, but private farms were not restored: the kolkhozy were as useful to Nazi exploiters as they had been to Communist ones. Able-bodied men and women, including adolescents, were rounded up and deported to work as slaves in German factories and mines. Anyone who resisted was publicly hanged as an example. Several million citizens of the occupied regions worked for or collaborated with the Germans, either as soldiers or as civilians, but that was usually because the alternative was violent death.

Not always. A few became collaborators because they hoped the Germans would back a Russian anti-Communist movement. The most notable was General Andrei Vlasov, one of the heroes of the defense of Moscow in December 1941. Captured on the northern front in the summer of 1942, when Soviet fortunes were at their lowest ebb, he was persuaded by his captors to head the movement to entice Soviet prisoners of war into the Wehrmacht. In an appeal which he wrote for them in 1943, he outlined his reasons for rejecting Communism: the dekulakization (which had destroyed his own father), the mass terror, the humiliation of army officers by political commissars, and the "trampling underfoot of everything Russian."[59]

He composed a political program which accepted the October revolution and many features of the Soviet state: nationalization of public utilities, free education and health services, the provision of pensions and social security. Where Vlasov differed from the Communists was in proposing a market economy for agriculture, retail trade, services, and much of industry, and in envisaging genuine self-determination for the nationalities. Remarkably for a program composed under Nazi sponsorship, it contained no trace of anti-Semitism.[60] It probably reflected roughly what many Soviet citizens aspired to at the time, at least as revealed in the postwar Harvard interviews of Soviet citizens displaced by the war.[61]

Vlasov's crucial weakness was that Hitler had no intention of promoting Russian nationalism, and would not allow him to set up his own army or political movement until the autumn of 1944, when it was far too late to make any difference to the course of events. Many Soviet officers in captivity who sympathized with his aims refused to join him for this reason. The project of a Russian national liberation movement independent of both Stalin and Hitler was simply impractical. In the end, ironically, almost the only combat which Vlasov's army saw was *against* the Germans: his men fought to help the Czechs free their capital from the S.S. in May 1945.[62]

Many Soviet citizens, on the contrary, resisted the German occupiers on their territory by all possible means. In Belorussia and Ukraine, as well as in Russian provinces like Leningrad, Kalinin (Tver), Smolensk, and Briansk, marooned Red Army soldiers joined escaped Soviet prisoners of war, men and women sought by the Germans, and local civilians repelled by the occupiers' behavior to form armed bands, based in the forests and remote villages. They sallied out periodically to disrupt German road and rail traffic and to attack supply depots and weakly held rear positions. Stavka tried to maintain contact with them and even to direct their operations, which it was able to do only intermittently, but with increasing effectiveness. The partisans unquestionably made a major contribution to the Soviet victory by harassing the Germans' already overstretched communications and diverting formations needed for the front. On the other hand they also gave a tremendous boost to separatist sentiment in both Belorussia and especially Ukraine, where the anti-German movement became anti-Soviet after the war and survived in the forests for some years before it could be suppressed.[63]

The Communist party proved a more appropriate mechanism for running the country at war than in peacetime. This was not surprising: as we have seen, the party had been deeply affected by the spirit of the civil war, and even in peacetime couched its propaganda in military terms. It was ideally placed to effect rapid mobilization of the civilian population in an emergency. As the Germans approached a town previously thought to be safely in the rear, the party would take the lead in forming a local defense committee, recruit women, adolescents, and able-bodied elderly people to improvise defense lines and fortifications, and form up factory workers as a militia to man them until regular troops could take over. That is how Tula, with its crucial armaments industry, was saved from capture in October–November 1941.

The most famous example of the kind was Leningrad, where a Defense Council was set up by the party secretary, Zhdanov, consisting of representatives of party, city soviet, and NKVD, to coordinate military and civilian efforts to defend the city. Stalin, however, was so suspicious of its independent behavior as it became cut off by the siege that he ordered it to be disbanded.[64]

From August 1941 to January 1944 Leningrad was largely cut off from the rest of the USSR, and, especially during the first winter, its population endured conditions far worse even than those experienced elsewhere. Although no precise estimate is possible, it seems likely that one million or more people died during the siege.[65]

Party secretaries had always kept an eye on the leading industrial enterprises in their regions. That function became even more vital in wartime. Nikolai Patolichev, first party secretary in Cheliabinsk, recalled that someone from the State Defense Committee in Moscow would telephone the directors of the Magnitogorsk metal combine and the Cheliabinsk tractor factory each day to see that everything was going smoothly. The local party secretary was supposed to sort out bottlenecks and ensure that manpower, food supplies, fuel, spare parts, and so on reached the most important production units smoothly. According to Patolichev, "The working day of the obkom secretary would begin with *Pravda* and a study of the situation on the railways."[66]

As long as they coped with their jobs competently, party secretaries knew that they did not need to fear arrest at this time. Furthermore, the personal relationships they forged during the war, when working with colleagues in party, state, and military to overcome hitches and difficulties, proved to be extremely durable, and formed the backbone of the party's command network right up to the 1970s. They gave the nomenklatura hierarchy new toughness and stability and brought it the close personal ties of battle-tested comradeship.

The issue of food supplies was one of the most difficult the party-state nexus had to deal with, especially since in this field of production it had proved itself incompetent before the war. There were additional handicaps now: the German advance had deprived the country of territory on which it had grown more than a third of its grain, half of its industrial crops, and nearly all its sugar beet. On the kolkhozy most of the able-bodied men had been conscripted for the army: they were replaced by women, adolescents, older men, and even invalids. The novelist Fedor Abramov, from Arkhangel oblast, where agriculture was supplemented by logging, described the results:

> They drove out old men already clapped out by a lifetime's toil, they dragged teenagers from their school desks, and set snotty-nosed little girls to work on the fir trees. And the women, the women with children, what they went through in those years! No one made any allowances for them, not for age or anything else. You could collapse and give up the ghost there in the forest, but you didn't dare to come back without fulfilling your norm! Not on your life! Come on, let's have your cubic meters! The Front needs them! And if they could at least have eaten their rations in peace—but no, the children's hungry mouths must be stuffed first.[67]

It is not surprising, then, that food production fell catastrophically in the early part of the war. From 95.5 million tons in 1940, the grain harvest fell to a mere 30 million in 1942, while the number of pigs fell from 22.5 million to 6.1 million.[68]

The Soviet authorities did not repeat the mistakes of the civil war. They met the shortfall with a mixture of compulsion and flexibility. On the one hand, they increased the output norms of collective farmers, as Abramov implies. On the other, they abolished the restrictions on private plots and allowed free markets to operate untrammeled. Factory workers were encouraged to cultivate allotments to supplement their own diet or to make a profit on the side. Any kolkhoznik or worker who had energy to spare after fulfilling his collective norm could make unlimited money from producing and selling vegetables, fruit, eggs, and dairy products. The result was a flourishing but expensive private trade. Traveling by train from Murmansk to Moscow in the summer of 1942, Alexander Werth saw peasant women selling food of all kinds on station platforms, either for very high prices or for barter.[69]

Having such a successful sideline disinclined peasants to do collective work at all. To motivate them, some kolkhoz chairmen permitted collective work to be done on the *zveno*, or "link," system. A link was a group of a dozen or so laborers, often centered upon a family, who took complete responsibility for a plot of land for the annual cycle: they grew enough from it to make their state deliveries and were entitled to sell any surplus for whatever price they could demand. Some farms virtually broke up into family smallholdings, with kolkhoz animals, tools, and fertilizers put at their disposal. As long as food was produced and made available, no one asked searching questions.[70]

The regime also sought popular support by making concessions to the population in religion. Already in 1939 the out-and-out persecution of the Orthodox Church ceased, perhaps in the hope that a gentler policy would help the integration of Orthodox believers in western Ukraine and Belorussia. During the war Stalin undertook a more active rapprochement with the church. Priests were allowed, even encouraged, to say prayers for the triumph of Soviet arms and to raise money for a tank column; in the ceremony at which it was solemnly handed over, Metropolitan Nikolai of Moscow referred to Stalin as "our common father."[71]

In 1943 Stalin met the patriarchal *locum tenens*, Metropolitan Sergii, and gave permission for the reestablishment of the patriarchate, as well as for the reopening of a central church administration, of a theological academy and three seminaries, and for the regular publication of an ecclesiastical journal. A large number of parish churches were allowed to reopen for regular services.[72]

It would be wrong to interpret these concessions as a full concordat between church and state. All religious faiths remained under the close supervision of the Council for Church Affairs, whose chairman, G. G. Karpov, was jokingly dubbed "people's commissar for God." Priests and especially bishops were allowed to take up office only after undergoing a thorough monitoring and on condition of complete loyalty to the Soviet state. One might regard them as being members of the nomenklatura system. As before, no religious activity was tolerated other than weekly divine service, and there remained little opportunity to foster real community spirit within the parish.

DEPORTATION OF NATIONALITIES

During the 1920s Soviet leaders were trying to create areas of territorially compact ethnic settlement. To ensure this, for example, they forcibly evicted Cossacks from settlements in the Terek region to make way for Chechens to settle there. They also hoped that their country's way of life would prove attractive to co-nationals living beyond their frontiers—that, for example, Ukrainians from Poland would be attracted to immigrate and settle in Soviet Ukraine. After the upheavals of the early 1930s, however, and with the rise of international tension throughout Europe, that optimism faded. The "Piedmont principle," it was feared, might not work to the Soviet Union's advantage after all. Immigrants were regarded with suspicion, as possible enemy agents, and Soviet populations living close to the frontiers were subject to special controls as a possible security risk. Some were deported en masse, notably the Koreans from the Far East during the period of intermittent war with Japan in the late 1930s.[73]

For the same reason the Soviet Union incorporated Estonia, Latvia, Lithuania, and Bessarabia during 1940–41. The elites of those nations—teachers, doctors, scientists, political leaders, altogether some 5–10 percent of the population—were deported to permanent exile in Siberia, while Russians and Ukrainians were resettled in the homes they had left. This was still "ethnic engineering," now pursued in the interests not of socialist revolution but of territorial security.

The most drastic operation of "ethnic engineering" was the deportation of whole peoples during and after the Second World War. In 1941 Germans living in the Volga basin and in major Russian cities were deported to central Asia and Siberia. The Volga German Autonomous Republic was abolished. That operation was followed in 1944–45 by the deportation of the Crimean Tatars, and also of Greeks living in the Crimea, the Kalmyks, the Balkary, the Karachaevtsy, the Chechens, and the Ingushes. They were loaded into cattle trucks with primitive sanitation, little food and water, and no medical care, for a journey eastward which sometimes took up to a month. Typhus set in, and, as one deportee later recalled, "During brief stops in remote, deserted sidings, we buried the dead right beside the train in snow black from locomotive soot (one could be shot for moving more than five meters from the cars)."

Most of those deported were resettled in Kazakhstan or Siberia, on terrain which was unfamiliar and in a climate which was uncongenial. They were forbidden to publish newspapers or to set up schools teaching in their own languages. Meanwhile Russians and Ukrainians, especially Red Army soldiers and their families, were resettled in the villages they had been forced to abandon.

There cannot be much doubt that the main aim of these operations was imperialist: to punish and in the long run to liquidate whole peoples who had proved especially difficult to assimilate into both the Russian and the Soviet empires and also to free territory in strategically sensitive regions for settlement by more loyal peoples. With a later turn in Soviet nationality policy, however, the lasting grievances of the deported became another factor degrading and embittering relations within the USSR.[74]

PATRIOTISM AND CITIZENSHIP

The émigré historians Mikhail Geller and Aleksandr Nekrich argue that it was Russian patriotism as opposed to Communist conviction which won the war, as if they were two quite different sentiments.[75] But things are not so simple. There is no doubt that the war was won because of Russian patriotism, and that this was a surprise to many. Prewar Marxist theorists had taught that the coming confrontation would be a class war, fought "with little bloodshed" on the enemy's territory. What actually occurred was a national war, fought with huge bloodshed mostly on the Soviet Union's own territory. This fact completely changed the manner in which the Russians responded. The Soviet state and Communist party linked civilian and military, empire and local community far better than the tsars had done in their final half-century. Local communities mobilized and defended themselves— the outstanding example is Leningrad—within an overall framework of command and control which improved immeasurably as the war went on. The Russian soldiers' traditional strengths—tenacity, hardiness, the capacity to improvise and to sacrifice oneself for one's comrades—revived as never before, and now within a system which gradually made better and better use of them. During the war the regime came into its own: it was there for an obvious purpose, and it was in tune with the popular mood. Its military rhetoric for the first time had real meaning, and it supported and confirmed self-sacrificing patriotism rather than undermining it.

The Second World War did more than any other event to crystallize Russian nationhood. Of course, the fact that the young men fighting it had been through primary school and were literate was very important. But it was the war—the experience of fighting to defend one's homeland, in comradeship with others, and in situations in which one had to take decisions and fight for one's life independently of the party and the authorities—that was decisive. As Viacheslav Kondratiev, veteran and novelist, later recalled, "You felt as if you alone held the fate of Russia in your hands—it was a real, genuine feeling of *citizenship*, responsible for your fatherland. The war was for us the most *important* thing in our generation . . . It was a pure burst of love for our fatherland. That sacrificial incandescence and readiness to give one's life for it are unforgettable." Kondratiev, like many others, felt bitter that afterward this fresh-minted civic patriotism was quashed by Stalin and the Communist party.[76]

The year 1945 was a time when, briefly, propaganda and reality almost coincided. The multiethnic Soviet Union had won a great war in a sustained burst of Russian-Soviet patriotism, in which many non-Russian ethnic groups—Ukrainians, Tatars, Armenians, Jews, Kazakhs—willingly subordinated themselves to Russia and accepted its leadership. This was the closest any Russian leaders ever reached to creating a viable multiethnic state.

Even at this moment of triumph, however, serious mistakes were being made. The deportations of Crimean Tatars and other Muslim peoples sowed a legacy of hatred and resentment which weakened the Soviet Union permanently on its southern frontiers. The brutal annexation of the Baltic republics, western Ukraine, and Moldavia had similar damaging effects on the western border. In the implacable hostility of these peoples to Russia and to the Soviet Union we may see the seeds of the fragmentation and ultimate collapse of the Soviet Union.

VI

The Decline and Fall
of Utopia

13

RECOVERY AND COLD WAR

After its victory the USSR found itself in a paradoxical and frustrating situation. It had just won the greatest war in history, and might have expected to look forward to an era of peace and security. But the circumstances of the victory deprived it of many of the expected fruits. Its alliance with the United States and the other Western democracies had been at best provisional and watchful, and had degenerated amid mutual suspicions toward the end of the war. By 1945–46, with their common enemy out of the way, the prewar hostility of Communist and capitalist worlds was resuming. Now, moreover, the means by which the Soviet Union's largest ally had won the war, the atomic bomb, threatened to overturn all previous calculations, based on large land armies. As the British ambassador, Sir Archibald Clark Kerr, reported, "At a blow the balance which had seemed set and steady was rudely shaken. Russia was balked by the west when everything seemed to be within her grasp. The three hundred divisions were shorn of much of their value."[1]

Russia had always looked for security in territorial arrangements, by trying to put either strong frontiers or extensive stretches of territory between herself and a potential enemy. That is the strategy Stalin pursued in the closing stages of the war, creating a bulwark of subservient states between himself and the armies of his former allies. During 1944–45 the Red Army conquered Poland, eastern and central Germany, Czechoslovakia, Hungary, Romania, and Bulgaria from the Nazis and their allies, while Communist-led partisans freed Albania and Yugoslavia. As far as Europe was concerned, the Soviet Union had largely achieved the most ambitious Russian imperial goals by 1945. With the exception of Istanbul (Constantinople) and Greece it had absorbed all the territories and peoples once claimed by the Pan-Slavs and had established for itself a *cordon sanitaire* against attack by any European power, in particular a resurgent Germany. Alas, it was precisely at this moment that *cordons sanitaires* were losing their strategic significance.

At the international conferences of Yalta and Potsdam in 1945 the Soviet Union's allies recognized its primary interest in those countries, while attempting to stipulate that their regimes should be "democratic." The Soviet interpretation of that word, however, was very different from what Truman or Churchill had in mind. The difference was that between democracy rooted in constitutional order and democracy rooted in "joint responsibility" under authoritarian rule. For a time the difference was obscured by the fact that coalition socialist governments were broadly welcomed throughout the region, where populations welcomed the armies and political movements that had freed them from the Nazis' rule. The welcome faded, though, as it became clear that the Communists intended to dominate the coalitions and make them function on the Soviet model. After what they had gone through in 1941–1945, it was natural that the Soviet leaders should crave absolute security, and should go to any lengths to achieve it, no matter what this meant for other peoples. In the opinion of their former foreign minister, Maksim Litvinov, this was the fundamental cause of the Cold War, while a subsidiary cause was the Western powers' failure to indicate clearly where the limits must be to the Soviet craving.[2]

So in the postwar years the Soviet Union secured its grip on the emerging states of central and eastern Europe by sponsoring pliable subordinate regimes there. The Red Army, secret police, and local Communists were used to break up meetings of other parties, and the Social Democrats were persuaded to merge with the Communists. By 1948 single-party regimes had been introduced in all the countries of the region. Thereafter Soviet-style social and economic reforms were imposed. Industry was nationalized and submitted to central planning, while trade unions were centralized, brought under political control, and converted into purveyors of social security. Land reform dispossessed landowners and private farmers, and agriculture was collectivized. Education was brought under the control of the state, with an increased emphasis on practical and technical training and the introduction of compulsory Marxist-Leninist theory. Culture and the mass media were converted into propaganda devices for the Communist party.

From 1948 it would not be unreasonable to regard these countries as a kind of "outer empire," held together at first by the Cominform (Communist Information Bureau), which had replaced the Comintern after the war, later by the Council for Mutual Economic Assistance (Comecon, set up in 1949) and the Warsaw Pact (1955). However, it was never a peaceful empire. As we shall see, the conflict over models of democracy was played out in a number of crises from 1953 through 1981, in which the peoples of central and eastern Europe demanded essential features of democratic socialism such as free speech and the right to form oppositional parties and other independent associations.

One east European socialist state which did not become part of the Soviet bloc was Yugoslavia. Its leader, Marshal Tito, did not owe his victory to the Red Army and was disinclined to subordinate himself unquestioningly to Stalin. He was actually a more radical Communist: he pressed ahead with industrialization, collectivization, and the elimination of "bourgeois" political parties much faster than Stalin thought advisable. According to Milovan Djilas, Tito's colleague who accompanied him on a number of visits to Moscow, all the Yugoslav leaders were repelled by Stalin's duplicity, cynicism, and arrogance. "He knew that he was one of the cruellest, most despotic figures in human history. But this did not worry him a bit, for he was convinced that he was carrying out the will of history."[3] Personal relations between the two leaders became extremely frosty. In the end, in 1948, Stalin had Yugoslavia expelled from the Cominform.

Suddenly deprived of Soviet trade and advisers, the Yugoslav leaders decided to rethink the whole basis of their socialism, and they returned to experiments which had been tried in Russia in 1917 but subsequently abandoned or neutralized in the Soviet Union. They conceded real autonomy to their national republics, giving more genuine substance to the Leninist slogan of "national self-determination." They resurrected "workers' control" in the factories by allowing elected workers' councils to supervise the overall management of enterprises. They reorganized the collective farms as cooperatives, offering credit, marketing facilities, and bulk purchasing to smallholders, who were allowed to regain their private plots. As we can see from the fate of Yugoslavia in the 1990s, this structure turned out in the long run to encourage ethnic animosities, but in the shorter term it offered, within Europe, an alternative model of Leninist socialism.

511

NUCLEAR WEAPONS AND RELATIONS WITH THE WEST

With the explosion of the American atom bombs at Hiroshima and Nagasaki, the central European "buffer states," and even the huge Soviet army which had won the war, became far less significant. Not that Stalin believed the United States was likely in the near future to turn its nuclear weapons against the USSR. But he did anticipate that President Truman would feel he could henceforth negotiate from a position of strength, and Stalin was determined to deny him that advantage. He had concluded at an early stage that the United Nations, the new international organization which had replaced the League of Nations, could not offer effective guarantees of international peace, and that once again, therefore, war could be prevented only by a balance of power. This might entail a certain amount of playacting, to ensure that Soviet might was overestimated round the world—Gorchakov's "dressing up" over again. From time to time this meant confronting the Western powers, though never sufficiently to run a serious risk of war. It also meant that the Soviet Union had urgently to create its own atomic bomb as a counterweight.[4]

The United States did not take any more seriously the possibility that security might be achieved through the United Nations. True, the Americans did put forward a scheme, the Baruch Plan, for bringing all uses of atomic energy under a UN-sponsored body which would have the right to "control, inspect and license" all nuclear activities; the United States promised that once it was up and running it would destroy all its atomic bombs and not manufacture any more. Stalin suspected that this proposal was merely a ploy to enable the United States to freeze its temporary monopoly. In any case, the USSR was not prepared to concede to any international body, however worthy, the right to inspect its military facilities at short notice. Andrei Gromyko, the Soviet delegate to the UN, therefore put forward an alternative proposal: that all existing nuclear weapons be destroyed and their future manufacture banned. No compromise between the two positions could be found.[5]

The Soviet Union was prioritizing resources, as her political structure made possible, in order to create her own nuclear weapon. The immense economic and coercive powers of the NKVD were brought to bear on the project. Slave laborers built a nuclear reactor near Cheliabinsk and a bomb-producing plant on the site of the monastery of St. Serafim of Sarov, not far from Gorkii. This was the Soviet economic Leviathan in overdrive, achieving miracles in double-quick time, but at the same time generating human and environmental disaster on a colossal scale. The prisoners who dug out uranium in central Asian mines or who erected the nuclear installations were inadequately protected against radiation, and most of them died, even if they completed their sentences. Around the Cheliabinsk reactor radiation sickness began to appear among the population in 1949, and in 1951 it was discovered (though not of course reported in the newspapers) that extensive areas of the Tobol River system had been contaminated by nuclear waste. Ten thousand people were evacuated and a system of dams and reservoirs erected to isolate the watercourses affected.[6]

Slave labor was not enough, however. The Soviet leaders needed scientists of the highest international caliber to bring the project to fruition. True, they had at their disposal data provided by their spy in the U.S. nuclear project, Klaus Fuchs. But no amount of information about someone else's enterprise could eliminate the need to find one's own way forward. Fortunately for the Soviet leaders, their country had a great tradition in fundamental physics, going back nearly a century. Igor Kurchatov, the scientific director of the nuclear project, was an heir to this tradition: he had served his apprenticeship in the Physico-Technical Institute run by Abram Ioffe in Leningrad in the 1920s. In a sense he had been part of the international community of nuclear physicists, though only by correspondence, since he had never been able to travel abroad.

Kurchatov and his colleagues were under compulsion. They knew that they had no alternative but to do their best to create a bomb for their leaders. On the other hand, they also worked from conviction. They knew that the wartime alliance had broken down and felt that if the United States had a bomb, then they must have one too, since "one could not allow one country, especially the United States, to hold a monopoly on this weapon." Kurchatov used to call himself a "soldier," and, as Andrei Sakharov has remarked, he and his colleagues were "possessed by a true war psychology." The lure of "first-rate science" combined with patriotism to motivate them and to still their doubts.[7]

Triumph came in August 1949, when the Soviet Union successfully tested its first atomic bomb on the steppes of Kazakhstan. Stalin did not trumpet the achievement abroad. Instead, in answer to foreign press rumors on the subject, he issued a communiqué implying that the country had already had the bomb for some time. The main thing was to project an image of assured strength.[8]

The installation of dependent regimes in central and eastern Europe provoked from the Western powers the reactive strategy first formulated by the U.S. diplomat George Kennan, "containment." But Kennan intended his policy to operate through diplomatic, economic, and public relations pressure, not mainly by military means. In actuality, American policy became primarily military, partly because that was easier to present to a public which wanted to know why the United States had abandoned isolationism. And in its turn military containment became largely nuclear, since nuclear weapons, for all their expense, were cheaper than maintaining huge armies on the continent of Europe. This policy fueled Soviet/Russian feelings of insecurity and provided the perfect argument for its own proponents of massive armaments.[9]

In the confrontation with the Western powers the USSR enjoyed one major advantage and one major disadvantage. On the one hand it could threaten western Europe directly and immediately with conventional weapons, while the United States could respond to such a threat only by the use of nuclear weapons, a much bigger and more dangerous decision. On the other hand, if it came to actual all-out war with the United States, the latter was much better equipped from the late 1950s with intercontinental delivery systems to attack Soviet cities. This strategic imbalance dictated many of the terms of the Cold War.

The relationship with the United States was a rivalry of a kind Russia had never entered into before. Russia had no territorial disputes whatever with its adversary. Indeed, in some respects Russia rather resembled the United States. Both political systems had grown out of visions of the perfect society inherited from the eighteenth-century Enlightenment, and both wanted to export their vision to the entire world. Both were partly European and partly non-European, and hence had an instinctive feeling for each other's culture. Most Russians admired and envied the Americans' ability to marry advanced technology to social development. Vladimir Maiakovskii, convinced Communist and bard of the Soviet state in the 1920s, wrote one of his most enthusiastic poems about the Brooklyn Bridge. However opposed Soviet Communists might be to the rapacious capitalism they saw as characteristic of American society, they were always tempted to seek rapprochement or "détente" with the United States, as a way of limiting arms expenditure, stabilizing international relations, and acquiring Western technology which they were unable to develop at home.[10]

The nature of nuclear weapons fitted this relationship perfectly. To threaten the other party with weapons which could never be used because they would bring about mutual destruction was appropriate to a lasting confrontation without territorial dispute. The two countries might never have gone to war anyway: nuclear deterrence made certain that they did not. But it remained a highly unsatisfactory way of keeping the peace: to threaten with weapons which could not be deployed without bringing about one's own destruction always contained an element of unhinged fantasy.

Whatever the forces limiting their mutual hostility, their incompatible universalist visions and the global alliances and obligations arising from them ensured that in some respects the Soviet Union and the United States would remain deadly adversaries. If either succeeded in spreading its doctrine over most of the world, then the other would be finished as a global power and would be seriously jeopardized within its own heartland.

The U.S. bid to do so was contained in the Marshall Plan. Proposed by the U.S. secretary of state, General George Marshall, in 1947, it offered long-term American finance for a European economic program to overcome post-war poverty and unemployment, as a basis for the reestablishment of democratic political systems. All European countries were eligible to receive it, provided they accepted the requirements of a market economy. The Soviet Union declined Marshall aid, and instructed its new satellite states to do so too, because it would have required dismantling barriers to international trade and the provision of extensive information about the workings of the Soviet economy. The Soviet leaders knew that the kind of economy needed to sustain their empire was incompatible with free international markets. In any case much of the information required was either secret or not known to the Soviet leaders themselves, since their accounting systems were so different from those normally adopted elsewhere.

The rejection of the Marshall Plan did much to cement the division of Europe, since it hardened the creation of two incompatible types of economy. This process was most dangerous in Germany, where democracy and the market in the Western sense were being developed in the American, British, and French zones, while a planned economy and a Communist political monopoly were emerging in the Soviet zone. The polarity was most acute in Berlin, which, though situated within the Soviet zone, had three miniature Western zones of its own. When a new currency, the Deutschmark, was introduced in 1948, not only in West Germany but also in Berlin's Western zones, Stalin closed the city's overland access routes and thus precipitated a major international crisis. He was hoping to prevent the emergence of a Western German state, or at least to obstruct its integration into the Western bloc.

He had anticipated that the Western powers would have to let the whole of Berlin become part of the Soviet zone; instead, with the support of most of the population, the Western allies supplied their zones by air for nearly a year. Challenging the airlift would have meant shooting down planes, and Stalin was not prepared to embark on such direct military action. Instead he eventually backed down and agreed that West Berlin should become a separate political entity. The Cold War looked as if it might become a hot war, but Stalin, aware of American nuclear weapons, had left himself an escape route.[11]

516

Actually, the danger of real war between the USSR and the United States was much greater in Korea in 1950–51. Stalin evidently felt that he could risk more in Asia than in Europe, and that he needed to reassert Soviet interests against both the Americans, dominant in Japan and South Korea, and the Chinese Communists, whose successful revolution in 1949 presaged the revival of China as a great power and a challenge to Soviet leadership of the international Communist movement. Stalin supported Kim Il Sung, the North Korean leader, in a projected invasion of South Korea, anticipating that the United States would not go to war to defend it. When he found he was wrong, that the United States not only intervened but tripled its defense budget, he changed his position, allowing the Chinese to take on most of the burden of supporting the North Koreans.[12]

The early postwar years thus saw the United States and USSR testing the parameters of their cool and suspicious relationship, without allowing it to degenerate into actual fighting, whose outcome was unforeseeable and potentially very destructive. Each power gave priority to the other as the defining element in its overall foreign and military policy. The Soviet Union was coming from behind, burdened by a legacy of backwardness and a far less productive economy, further devastated by the war. There was always a danger of overreach in the Soviet attempts to claim parity with the United States. Stalin began the Berlin blockade without the determination or resources to see it through against staunch resistance. Similarly, in the Berlin crisis of 1958–1961, Khrushchev threatened to block access to West Berlin if the Western powers did not withdraw from it, but he did not have the means to implement that threat when the West stood firm. Yet again, when Khrushchev placed medium-range missiles in Cuba in the summer of 1962, he was attempting at a low cost to redress the Soviet inferiority in intercontinental delivery systems, but he lacked the conventional seaborne power in the region to defend those missiles when President Kennedy demanded that they be withdrawn. Not being prepared to risk nuclear war, he had to do as asked and pull them out.[13]

Following that humiliating climbdown, his successors took the decision to expand the production and deployment of weapons of all kinds, nuclear and conventional, landborne and seaborne, in order to be prepared for any type of future confrontation with the United States, wherever it might come. No doubt the decision was influenced by the fact that the Soviet economy was better suited to the production of military equipment than of anything else. But even there the United States could outperform it, especially in technologically sophisticated and computer-guided weapons.

Up to the early 1980s the Soviet Union hoped to compensate for its relative overall weakness by stationing medium-range SS-20 missiles aimed at west European territory but not at the United States. The aim was to take western Europe hostage: since any threatened missile strike there would not directly affect the United States, the Soviet leaders hoped the American leaders would not respond effectively, and a split would open up within NATO. They backed this weapons deployment with an intensive propaganda compaign encouraging west European peace movements to demand denuclearization of Europe and the withdrawal of NATO. Despite widespread public opposition, however, the NATO governments responded by stationing their own medium-range missiles on European territory. When in addition it emerged in the early 1980s that the United States, under Reagan, might be able to deploy computer-guided counterattacking rockets to bring down incoming intercontinental nuclear missiles, the Soviet Union realized it could not reciprocate with matching technology of its own. This perception helped to precipitate Gorbachev's "new thinking": if security could not be attained through overwhelming military power, then it was necessary to look for some other way of achieving it.[14]

The Soviet Union was very anxious to have its postwar territorial gains, and especially the division of Germany, formally acknowledged by the Western powers in a final peace treaty. Khrushchev's blustering of 1958–1961 over Berlin had been designed to achieve this goal. But until the late 1960s West German governments were disposed neither to recognize the German Democratic Republic (GDR, the former Soviet occupation zone) nor to accept the permanence of the division of their country, and they received the backing of other Western powers in this standoff, which was important for establishing the legitimacy of the West German state.

However, the election of a Social Democratic government under Chancellor Willy Brandt in 1969 signaled that the West German public was ready for a new approach, acknowledging the existence of the GDR, accepting the new territorial status quo and receiving in return guarantees of the special status of West Berlin and of Western access to it. The resulting treaty, signed in August 1971, prepared the way for a more complete European territorial settlement and an agreement on "security and cooperation" at the Helsinki conference of 1975. Here the Soviet Union in one sense achieved what it had been aiming at ever since 1945, the official ratification of the frontiers laid down de facto after the war, and the establishment of a permanent Conference on Security and Cooperation in Europe which would periodically review crises and problems in order to take joint action over them. On the other hand, the West insisted that, as part of the guarantees underpinning mutual security and cooperation, all parties pledge themselves to observe human rights as defined in the UN Charter. Soviet acceptance of this condition gave Western ideology a tiny legitimate toehold inside the Soviet Union, a circumstance which continually irritated its leaders for the following decade and a half, but which in the long run trained them in regarding international affairs through Western eyes.

The really difficult relationship was the one which should have been closest: that with China. This was precisely the opposite of the situation with the United States: Russia and China had been brothers-in-arms since the Chinese Communist revolution of 1949, but they were also the two principal powers of Eurasia, they were neighbors with a 4,500-mile common frontier, and they had territorial disputes, stemming from what the Chinese called the "unequal treaties" of the nineteenth century, over northeastern Kazakhstan and the Maritime Territory north and east of the Amur and Ussuri Rivers. Add to this the fact that most educated Russians were accustomed to regard the Asian aspect of their heritage as the source of tyranny and corruption, and therefore to look upon the largest and best-armed Asiatic people with fear and loathing. The Chinese were the only neighbor who outnumbered the Russians. Moreover from 1964 they had nuclear weapons. Most ordinary Russians unhesitatingly identified China rather than NATO or the United States as their most dangerous enemy.

China was also a direct rival in ideological ambition. For a few years after coming to power, the Chinese Communists were content to be junior partners in the international Communist movement. But after Khrushchev sought a rapprochement with Tito in 1955, began to propound "peaceful coexistence" with the West, and denounced Stalin, Mao Zedong berated him for his unrevolutionary strategy and described the United States contemptuously as a "paper tiger." Khrushchev retorted that it was "a paper tiger with nuclear teeth." From then on, China permanently challenged the Soviet Union's claim to be the custodian of Marxist-Leninist doctrine and the leader of the international Communist movement. The Great Leap Forward of 1958–59 and the Cultural Revolution of 1966–1969 exemplified the Chinese leaders' bolder style of social transformation and their determination to leap swiftly to full Communism even at huge social cost, comparable with what the Soviet population had suffered in the 1930s. China began to step up its contacts with third world countries, both selling weapons there and urging its own version of "building socialism" in preference to the Soviet one.

Various international Communist Party gatherings failed to heal the growing rift, and it was widened in 1959 when the Soviet Union withdrew its aid for the development of a Chinese nuclear weapon. The following year the Soviets pulled out more than two thousand specialist advisers engaged in Chinese economic projects, and before long each side expelled the other's students from its universities. The Soviet army placed more and more of its divisions in the Far East, until in 1980 about a quarter of them were stationed there.[15]

The climax in mutual hostility was reached in March 1969, when Chinese soldiers attacked Soviet frontier guards on Damanskii Island, in the Ussuri River, which China claimed as its own. The Soviets retaliated a couple of months later with artillery and missile attacks on Chinese territory. It appears that at this time the Soviet leadership seriously discussed the possibility of a preemptive nuclear strike against China before she could develop her delivery systems to the point of being able to respond in kind.[16]

After that both sides drew back, realizing perhaps just how destructive a war between them could become. In the early 1970s China began to commit the very sins for which it had berated the Soviet Union, seeking security in a rapprochement with the United States and moving away from "campaign socialism" toward a revival of the market economy. With the subsequent weakening of the international socialist movement, the claim to its leadership faded in importance.

During the post-Stalin period the Soviet Union launched the most ambitious attempt Russia had ever made to project its power throughout the globe. In his writings of 1914–1918 Lenin had proposed that the class struggle should be transferred from the domestic to the international scene, that colonies should rise against their imperial masters and thus decisively shift the global center of gravity in favor of socialism. The Soviet Union had, however, been too weak, beleaguered, and preoccupied with Europe to turn this vision into practical geopolitics till well after the Second World War.

From the mid-1950s this situation changed. With nuclear stalemate and the growing stabilization of the situation in Europe, it looked as if further gains could not be made there, or only at disproportionate risk, whereas in the third world opportunity seemed to beckon. There the situation was far more fluid, and the influence and economic dominance of the West could be challenged with very little danger to the Soviet Union. Setbacks could be readily accepted since Soviet security was not at stake. Khrushchev and his successors always regarded "peaceful coexistence" with the West as the continuation of struggle against imperialism by different means, not entailing the risk of direct war against imperialist powers. At the same time, with the buildup of Soviet armed power, the USSR found it useful to have naval and air facilities available to it in Asia, Africa, and Latin America.

In practice, what sponsoring third world anti-imperialist movements meant was supporting nationalism rather than socialism. This strategy was accepted, on the grounds that anticolonial "national liberation movements" and "national democratic states" were stages in the way to building socialism.

In pursuit of this policy, by the late 1950s the Soviet Union was helping to finance and support the construction of huge steel works in India and of the Aswan hydroelectric dam in Egypt, and was selling weapons to both countries. When Fidel Castro seized power in Cuba in 1959, the Soviet Union took advantage of the moment to gain a foothold in Latin America by effectively bankrolling the weak Cuban economy, buying its sugar and nickel at above world prices, while selling it oil cheaply. Cuba became a base for Soviet warships and reconnaisance aircraft, operating close to the heartland of the United States. It also supplied agents to support anticolonial movements, including terrorist organizations, in other parts of the world.[17]

When the United States intervened to protect South Vietnam from Communist revolution and external subversion in 1964, the USSR supplied weapons to North Vietnam, helping in America's eventual military defeat and taking the opportunity to discredit American policies not only in the eyes of the third world but before the public in many Western countries too. The naval and air bases gained in Vietnam enabled the USSR to project its power far more effectively throughout southeast Asia and the western Pacific.

Not all these expenditures worked out to its benefit, though. In 1972, for example, Egypt suddenly expelled all its Soviet military advisers and closed down Soviet air bases. The impotence of a superpower dealing with a client well beyond its borders was revealed: most of the investment of the preceding years was forfeited. But Moscow was always ready to write off such losses in the interests of unsettling the Western powers and extending tentacles of influence.

Where a potential ally was close to her borders, however, the Soviet Union was far more assertive. In 1979 an armed contingent was sent into Afghanistan to prevent the collapse of a Communist regime which had seized power there three years before. The Soviet troops soon got into difficulties familiar from the north Caucasus 150 years earlier. The population, scattered over extensive mountainous territory, resented the intervention and tended increasingly to support fundamentalist Islamic movements as organizers of resistance. These in turn were backed by Pakistan or the United States. Not prepared to commit genocide and unwilling to risk large numbers of troops, the Soviet leaders found themselves by the mid-1980s in a strategic stalemate.

POSTWAR SOVIET SOCIETY

The Soviet Union came out of the Second World War a victorious but devastated country. Something like a quarter of its physical assets had been destroyed: huge numbers of houses, apartment buildings, offices, and factories had to be rebuilt, roads and railways relaid, farms restored to productive capacity. To achieve this task there was a smaller, less balanced, and less healthy population: some 24–27 million people had died prematurely, and many others had been uprooted and dislocated. There was a massive deficit of able-bodied males, and a concomitant surplus of war widows and young women who would never become wives.[18]

All the same, in some ways the morale of the population was uniquely high at that moment, and the Soviet peoples felt themselves a single community as never before. A generation of military commanders and of central and local party-state cadres, relatively green and untried in 1941, had survived an initiation of fearful dimensions, and had proved themselves and their ability to organize successfully both the civilian and military aspects of mass warfare. The ordinary Soviet people, traumatized by the upheavals and terror of the 1930s, had undergone yet another terrible ordeal and had found that in the face of death they had to rely not only on the system, but on their closest comrades and immediate commanders, and also on their own courage and resourcefulness. Young men of all social strata and all ethnic origins had been brought together and forged into cohesive, mutually dependent units—albeit disrupted by the heavy casualty rate.

The legitimacy of the Soviet state had been established more satisfactorily than ever before. It had not created the perfect society, but it had saved Europe from a powerful and destructive enemy, which was a pretty good second best. The millennium was not in sight, but the apocalypse had been averted.

So the war generated a self-confident and authoritarian ruling class, and also among the population an appreciable classless, multiethnic patriotism. The old, rather artificial and insubstantial "proletarian internationalism" had given way to a new and tested Soviet-Russian imperial patriotism, especially among men of the wartime generation. What they had fought was not a class war but a national war, Russians against Germans. That was the message Ilia Erenburg had insistently repeated in his *Pravda* columns, and its truth was confirmed by the daily experience of the war. Yet the Russian patriotism was not nationalism in the usual sense, for, as we have seen, the Russians were not a nation. Rather it was a multiethnic imperial and socialist messianism given substance by victory. Creating heavy industry, "building socialism," acquired an entirely new and far more immediate meaning thanks to wartime experience. It is no accident that the symbols of the war became the dominant theme of Soviet propaganda thereafter, even more than the October revolution, for it was the war which evoked a cohesive community ruled for good reason by authoritarian means.[19]

Not all the Soviet nationalities subscribed to this neo-*rossiiskii* patriotism. The brutal incorporation of the the Baltic republics, western Belorussia, western Ukraine, and Moldavia left the majority of the population in those regions hostile and resentful toward both Russians and Communism. The Caucasian Muslims, especially the Chechens, had always felt that way, and the deportations of 1944–45 deepened their animosity toward the Soviet Union as a whole and Russians in particular. These permanently alienated peoples were to prove a grave source of weakness in future.

Even taken together, however, these peoples did not amount to more than a small minority of the population. For the rest now, if ever, was a time when a Russian nationhood might have developed in neo-*rossiiskii* form, a many-sided compound national identity, like that of Britain, only more variegated, with many more components, but with Russian language, culture, and statehood at the center. Why that did not happen we shall see.

Among the Russians, those who had reservations about Stalin or about Communist methods of rule clung to their memories of the war in order to devote themselves to their tasks. Andrei Sakharov, who was working in the secret nuclear weapons establishment at that time, later reflected: "Precisely because I had invested so much of myself in that cause and accomplished so much, I needed, as anyone might in my circumstances, to create an illusory world, to justify myself. I soon banished Stalin from that world, but the state, the nation and the ideals of communism remained intact for me."[20]

Gradual disillusionment awaited most of the young men who had survived and were demobilized in 1945–46. What they found back at home was a desperate economic situation. Disrupted families, cramped communal apartments, long queues for essential supplies, the continued wearing of bedraggled army tunics and greatcoats—this was the normal experience for soldiers and junior officers who returned from war looking for a "life fit for heroes."[21] Actually, though, most of them had expected that. What was far worse was that the qualities needed in war—boldness, the ability to think for oneself and to take risks—were highly dysfunctional in the new Soviet peace. As one returning soldier later wrote, "We did not expect a land of milk and honey. We could see for ourselves the burnt-out villages and ruined towns. But we did have some vague notions of justice, of human dignity, and of our own mission. They turned out to be depressingly at odds with what awaited us at every turn."[22]

The fact is that Stalin and the party-state apparatus, having loosened the reins of control during the war, especially over the military, were anxious to take undisputed charge once more, and believed they had proved their right to do so. The newly acquired prestige of the military was too indisputable to challenge openly, but in 1946 the right to "elect" (that is, appoint) party secretaries in military units was transferred from the armed forces command back to the party hierarchy. Although political commissars were not restored, officers were encouraged to attend special party schools set up for them, so that they could in effect become their own political commissars.[23] Marshal Zhukov, the army's hero and Stalin's postwar rival for the limelight, was demoted to take charge of the Odessa Military District, but the unprecedently high social standing of party-trained officers was underlined by the creation of the Suvorov military schools, which trained their graduates not only in military skills but also in social graces such as ballroom dancing. The party-military hierarchy was the new social elite.[24]

The party itself tightened its admissions policy: during the war, it had accepted many soldiers on the recommendation of their superiors, without checking their credentials further. The upper ranks of the party hierarchy began to professionalize themselves by opening special "party high schools," where aspirants to posts at the level of *raion* secretary and above were required to undergo a systematic course of study. Party bodies, from the Politburo downward, began to meet more regularly again, though it took them till 1952 to hold an actual party congress—the first since 1939.

With their experience of wartime solidarity, the senior members of the nomenklatura elite felt far more secure in their armchairs. Stalin had made them, but they were now conscious of their own power. They had learned to improvise, to work with each other even, if necessary, without his authorization, so they were potentially dangerous to his personal authority. Though Stalin's creatures, they could now actually survive better without him. To keep them in their place he revived terror, not on the scale of the 1930s, but selectively, in keeping with the external atmosphere, as the cold-war blocs hardened in 1947–48.

Nomenklatura solidarity and independence were most conspicuous in Leningrad, the city which had survived for more than two years almost cut off from the rest of the country. Stalin was nervous of Leningraders, and it was there that he conducted his most bloody postwar purge. Andrei Zhdanov, the wartime first party secretary in Leningrad, was now secretary of the Cominform, responsible for relations with foreign socialist parties. After the break with Marshal Tito and the Yugoslav League of Communists in 1949, Zhdanov died, probably of heart trouble caused by heavy drinking, and several other leading Leningrad politicians were arrested and executed, without charges being made public. It seems likely that this purge was connected both with the hardening of the Cold War, and with the potential nonconformity of Leningrad.[25]

Another group that had potential support abroad was the Jews, after the foundation of the state of Israel in 1948. The Jewish Anti-Fascist Committee, set up during the war to mobilize Jewish support for the war effort, was disbanded, and its chairman, Solomon Mikhoels, was murdered. The Jewish theater in Moscow was closed and many Jewish cultural figures arrested: some of them were tried and executed for allegedly conspiring to hand over the Crimea to the United States. In January 1953 it was announced that a group of doctors had been arrested: they were planning to "wipe out the leading cadres of the USSR," and the security services were reproached for "lack of vigilance" in not having detected them earlier. Everything suggests that Stalin was planning another major round of purges, perhaps on the scale of the 1930s and accompanied by the mass deportation of Jews to Siberia. However, on 5 March 1953 he died before he could take further action.

ECONOMIC RECOVERY

Postwar industrial recovery was remarkably rapid, and many indices of heavy industrial production had already reached their 1940 levels by 1947 or 1948. This success can be explained partly by the fact that factories in the western, formerly occupied territories were being restored even as their counterparts further east, relocated during the war, were continuing production. But in large part too the swift recovery reflects the fact that the principles, practices, and priorities of the 1930s were simply being reinstated without any significant change. All the distortions of the first five-year plans were reproduced: the excessive authoritarianism, the poor flows of information, the shortages, the poor-quality equipment, the "storming" at the end of each month. From wartime rigor the Soviet enterprise returned to being a mutual protection association of employers and workers.

There were now more women and undertrained males in the workforce, and far fewer skilled and experienced workers, which compounded the problems. Although workers in many branches of industry were still under military discipline, their work regime was highly disorganized, and in practice they controlled much of the labor process themselves. Employers desperate for working hands of almost any kind turned a blind eye to shoddy work and certainly did not apply the full harshness of military punishment. All the same, workers' lives were far from easy: many of them had to live in unheated, unhygienic barracks, with poor or nonexistent cooking facilities, while the workplace was often either freezing cold or overpoweringly hot, and poorly ventilated or hazardous because of dangerous unfenced machinery. They would not infrequently respond by pushing on to look for better conditions elsewhere. Labor turnover remained high, in spite of the draconian penalties for "desertion."[26]

525

The regime's long-term failure to cope with these problems meant that industry, having recovered and considerably exceeded its 1940 levels by the early 1950s, settled into a stagnant pattern of development, augmenting productive capacity by drawing in new workers from the countryside rather than by improving technology. The failure to innovate, to motivate, or to tighten work patterns meant that the Soviet Union fell behind a whole generation of development in western Europe, North America, and east Asia. By the mid-1970s the industrial economy had probably ceased to grow altogether and had begun to go into decline, becoming less and less viable except in the military field. Enterprises had become welfare benefit fortresses, with hundreds, sometimes thousands of workers and their families dependent on them for housing, childcare, social security, sport, recreation, holidays, and often health care. These functions had become at least as important as output.

Huge resources and authoritarian leadership still enabled the country to concentrate on areas of production deemed especially important, and to turn out high-quality products as needed. This was true of military and space technology, which carried high prestige and attracted the best specialists and administrators. But any branch of industry below the highest priority tended to fall into the hands of less capable and less ambitious people and therefore to stagnate.

Peasants had hoped that the collective farms would be permanently disbanded after the war, but a decree of September 1946 ordered that all land acquired by private persons during the war should be returned to the collectives, penalties for "theft of socialist property" were increased, and state delivery quotas were raised. The prices paid for those deliveries were so low that in some cases they did not even cover the cost of transporting produce into town. As a result, in 1946 the average workday in some 50 percent of kolkhozy brought in one ruble or less, that is, less than a third of the price of a kilogram of black bread.[27] Many peasants abandoned cows and took up goats—"Stalin cows," as they became known—whose milk was not subject to delivery quotas. In 1947 a currency reform sharply reduced the value of savings not held in a bank. Peasants, who tended to keep their money in a trunk under the bed, lost at a stroke most of what they had earned by private trade during the war.[28]

526

Thereafter the kolkhozy became even more poverty-stricken and demoralized than before the war. Probably most serious of all was the loss of able-bodied males. Rural lads who survived their time in the army seldom returned to the village, since they knew they would be condemning themselves and their families to a degraded, poverty-stricken existence. Instead, while they had passports, they sought jobs in transport, construction, or industry. Rural labor became virtually a female monopoly, and since draft animals were in short supply women sometimes even had to harness themselves to ploughs.[29]

In 1946 drought struck in Ukraine and Moldavia, unleashing famine and epidemics. The excessive state procurement quotas left the collective farms without enough seeds to cover their own consumption needs. Only potatoes helped to keep them going. Even so, some five million people fled the affected regions, and perhaps one million died from malnourishment and associated disease.[30]

Continuing state control and the lack of investment meant that the grain harvest recovered far more slowly than after 1921: by 1952 it had still not reached prewar levels. Rationing was ended in 1947, but even so, meat and dairy products were available in state shops only in the best-supplied cities, and then intermittently. Most people sought them in the markets, where the produce from private plots was sold. Those plots, which occupied 1–2 percent of the land, produced throughout the 1950s more than half the country's vegetables, meat, and milk, more than two-thirds of its potatoes, and more than four-fifths of its eggs.[31]

CULTURE, SCIENCE, AND EDUCATION

Wartime had seen a relaxation on the "cultural front." As cultural commissar, Zhdanov had been endeavoring to rally patriotic feelings, and for this purpose good writers and musicians were once more needed, even if they were not fully *partiinyi* in outlook. Writers long silenced, such as Anna Akhmatova, Boris Pasternak, and Mikhial Zoshchenko, were able to publish serious work again. Shostakovich was once more encouraged to compose: his "Leningrad" Symphony, with its brutal repetition of a mindless melody, became a symbol of resistance to Fascism (though Shostakovich maintained privately that its target was totalitarianism of all kinds, including the Stalinist variety).[32]

After the war the party had less need of writers and musicians. A Central Committee decree of August 1946 attacked the literary journals *Zvezda* and *Leningrad* for "servility toward everything foreign" and for basing literary policy not on "correct education of the Soviet people" but on the "interests of friendship," that is, patronage and mutual favors. Two Leningrad authors were expelled from the Writers' Union: Zoshchenko, who was accused of "vulgarity and rotten absence of moral principle"; and Akhmatova, whose verse was said to be "suffused with the spirit of pessimism, decadence . . . and bourgeois-aristocratic aestheticism."[33] Even Aleksandr Fadeev, first secretary of the Writers' Union, was criticized for his novel *The Young Guard*, which in describing the resistance movement in the German-occupied Donbass was held to have stressed inadequately the leading role of the party. Similarly, the film director Sergei Eizenshtein was attacked for an insufficiently heroic portrayal of Ivan the Terrible.

On 10 February 1948 a decree condemned "formalism" in music. Its immediate target was the Georgian opera composer, Vano Muradeli, who had "mistakenly" shown the Georgian and north Caucasian peoples as hostile to Russia during the civil war, a view which was unacceptable to neo-*rossiiskii* patriots. The activists of the Musicians' Union used the decree to veto the publication and performance of works of Shostakovich, Prokofiev, Khachaturian, and others. Shostakovich's Eighth Symphony, the "Leningrad"'s successor, had to wait several years before it reached the public.[34]

In the research institutes "cosmopolitan" tendencies were rooted out. In the Institute of Linguistics, N. Ia. Marr was dismissed for teaching that all human languages had a common root and would one day reintegrate in the proletarian internationalist society. Stalin had decided that only Russian was worthy to be the international language of the future: he implied that language was a permanent feature of a nation's culture, more or less impervious to social change.[35] In short, for Stalin proletarian internationalism and Russian imperialism had finally become indistinguishable.

In genetics a "barefoot scientist," Trofim Lysenko, with party support, gained the ascendancy over established and reputable scientists. Contrary to accepted biological theory, he taught that in living organisms characteristics derived from the environment could be passed on genetically. He deduced from his theory proposals on how plant-breeding could be improved. The academic establishment mostly resisted his ideas as poorly attested hypotheses, but he was able to gain control of the Institute of Plant Breeding, and from there to dominate genetics and much of biology for more than a decade.

In all these cases, party stooges in the institutes and creative unions were using their control of the nomenklatura personnel lists to promote their own candidates and eliminate their opponents. This was a form of clientelism against which there was no appeal. The penalty for resisting was no longer arrest and execution, as it would have been in the 1930s, but usually dismissal, with its accompanying demotion into the ranks of the unprivileged, living in communal apartments and queueing up in poorly stocked state shops. It was a price which few were prepared to pay. Most scholars and scientists reoriented their work along the lines which their bosses and ideologists expected of them, or retreated into fields free of any ideological implications. Shostakovich, for example, seriously contemplated suicide, but then withdrew into an ideologically neutral zone and composed a complete set of preludes and fugues on the model of Bach.[36]

KHRUSHCHEV AND POST-STALIN REFORM

When Stalin died, in March 1953, the Soviet leaders faced fundamental dilemmas. They had made much progress in restoring the industrial economy from the devastation of war, though in a form which tended to perpetuate the debilitating imbalances of the 1930s. In all other sectors of the economy the position was critical. Agriculture was scarcely more productive than it had been in 1913—and it now had a much larger urban population to feed. Housing was desperately inadequate and often unhygienic for all but the upper ranks of the privileged. Consumer goods and services were in short supply or unavailable. Transport was unreliable and overcrowded. These deficiencies affected even the priority sectors of the economy: workers who could not get their boots repaired, who arrived late at work, who had to queue for hours in grocery stores, and who had bronchitis because of rising damp in their flats, could not unfailingly turn out high-quality products.

The demographic situation was also threatening for a country which wished to consider itself a superpower. The war had taken a devastating toll among the young men, and a good many of those who had survived it were now in labor camps and penal settlements, where their health and their skills were prodigally misused.

In all these areas radical change was obviously and urgently needed. But it was not easy to bring about. In the few years since the war the social structure had become surprisingly stable, even rigid. By the early 1950s the postwar nomenklatura elite had settled down in their senior positions and were enjoying their power and privileges; they had also taken on all-embracing responsibilities for the workforce under their control. They were not about to relinquish any of these things lightly.

Stalin's successors had one urgent priority. That was to ensure that no one among their own number could gather into his hands the power Stalin had enjoyed. They dropped their immediate differences and united temporarily to topple Lavrentii Beria, who, as head of the security services, was the likeliest potential tyrant. He was arrested and executed under the accusation of being a "British spy." His former colleagues then drastically pruned the whole secret police system, sacking many of its operatives and informers and bringing it under strict party-state control as the KGB (Committee of State Security).

The news that Beria had been a "traitor" prompted people to write letters to the authorities requesting that sentences passed by the special courts under him be reexamined and his victims be released from detention. A few individuals were released and also rehabilitated. Actual rehabilitation was crucial: it enabled returnees to reclaim living space, jobs, and privileges lost years before, so it was a kind of reinsurance policy for the elite. It was also a sign that the courts and the procuracy were emancipating themselves from secret police control and insisting on a minimum of "socialist legality." This in its turn raised the whole question of what to do about the labor camps. Even those who took a hard-nosed view of them had to admit that they were economically wasteful and possibly a security risk. Strikes and even armed risings had begun to break out, and there was always the danger that somewhere inmates—many of whom had experience of fighting in regular or partisan units—might disarm their guards and seize a whole camp complex.

It was decided to set up a high-level commission of investigation to reexamine the sentences passed, particularly against high party-state officials, and to make recommendations about possible further releases. When that commission reported at the end of 1955 it revealed a horrifying picture of judicial lawlessness going back to the early 1930s.[37]

The revelations placed the leaders in an agonizing dilemma for the Twentieth Party Congress, scheduled for February 1956. If they suppressed the report, they would be easing the way for a future dictator, under whom they might all lose their heads. On the other hand, if they published it, they would be held at least partly responsible for the massive injustices disclosed in it. The decision to half-publish the findings was Khrushchev's own. Actually, it was a moderately courageous one, and it was opposed by some of his colleagues. He argued: "If we don't tell the truth at the congress, we'll be forced to do so some time in the future. And then we shan't be the speechmakers, but the people under investigation."[38]

In deference to his opponents, however, the official congress report made no mention of Stalin's crimes. Instead, at the end of the congress, a special closed session was held, at which Khrushchev read out Lenin's testamentary condemnation of Stalin and then reported in detail on "a whole series of exceedingly serious and grave perversions of party principles, of party democracy, and of revolutionary legality" which Stalin had committed. The delegates listened in awed silence and then dispersed, no discussion being permitted. The speech was not published in the Soviet press, but was communicated to party members at special meetings held throughout the country. Foreign Communists, who had been allowed to attend, soon leaked the text abroad, and it became widely known outside the Soviet Union.[39]

The procedure was a compromise, and so were the contents of the speech. Khrushchev concentrated on the repressions of leading party-state personnel and prominent public figures. Apart from the deportations of nationalities, he had little to say about the sufferings of ordinary people, and his catalogue of abuses began in 1934, implying that what happened before then—Stalin's crushing of the various "oppositions," the early show trials, and the mass deportation of "kulaks"—had been entirely acceptable. Furthermore, he held Stalin and a few police chiefs responsible for all the illegalities, evading the question of what share he and his colleagues in the party leadership had borne for them. All in all, this was a speech of the nomenklatura elite defending itself against Stalin's ghost.

Nevertheless, the effect was electric, for Khrushchev's revelations did raise fundamental questions about the Soviet system—without, however, settling them. On the whole, his presentation was probably what congress delegates wanted to hear. He confirmed that terror and the "cult of personality" were things of the past, that henceforth there would be "collective leadership" and "socialist legality," under which they anticipated they could hold their posts and privileges in security. That bedrock of support from lower- and medium-level party-state officials was to stand Khrushchev in good stead in the coming years.

For the mass of professional people throughout the Soviet Union and the satellite states of central and eastern Europe, though, the revelations were a profound challenge. The mixture of fear, fanaticism, naiveté, and "doublethink" with which most intelligent people had reacted to Communist rule was cut away at its very roots. Even inside the Soviet Union, meetings of students, creative unions, and professional associations raised uncomfortable questions: if this had been going on under Stalin, what guarantee was there that it had now stopped, under Stalin's closest associates? Did the revelations not imply that serious democratization was needed right now?[40] A popular anecdote related how, at a public meeting, Khrushchev received a note from the floor asking: "What were you doing while Stalin was murdering people?" Khrushchev read it out and asked: "Who sent up this note?" There was silence in the auditorium. Khrushchev waited a moment and then said, "That is your answer." He had a blunt and direct way of facing issues which his colleagues preferred to evade (all the same the story is apocryphal).

531

In central and eastern Europe, the reaction was more vehement. In Poland intellectuals demanded changes and workers went on strike until the Stalinist leadership stepped down and Władysław Gomułka (who had been arrested as a "Titoist" in 1951) took over in October 1956 with his own program of "national Communism." The Soviet leaders agreed to this change of leadership to avoid further unrest, although the Polish program rejected some aspects of the Soviet model of socialism: peasants, for example, were allowed to leave the collective farms and reestablish their smallholdings; and the Catholic Church was authorized to teach religion in schools.

Far more serious was the fallout of the "secret speech" in Hungary. Here the opposition, again intellectuals and workers, was much bolder: they demanded free speech, open elections with genuine alternative parties, and the withdrawal of Soviet occupation troops. Imre Nagy, the new prime minister, though himself a Communist, decided he had no option but to espouse this program himself. He denounced the Warsaw Pact and declared Hungary's neutrality. Soviet troops at first complied with the demand to leave, but then the Soviet leaders changed their minds: leaving the Warsaw Pact was a step too far. The army returned to crush what they now called a "counterrevolution." A more compliant government was installed under János Kádár.

The turbulence inside the Warsaw Pact naturally weakened Khrushchev's own position. In June 1957 Molotov, Malenkov, Bulganin, and Kaganovich persuaded a majority of the Presidium (as the Politburo was known at the time) to demand his resignation. Khrushchev rejoined that he had been elected to his post by the whole Central Committee and would not go without their consent. This was a shrewd move, for the republican and oblast secretaries who made up the rump of the Central Committee, as well as the military and the KGB, preferred Khrushchev to a revival of Stalinist methods. They overturned the Presidium resolution and confirmed Khrushchev as first secretary.

He turned the confrontation to his own advantage by accusing his opponents of complicity in Stalin's crimes, dubbing them the "antiparty group" and having them removed from the Central Committee. In a sense this was risky: Kaganovich asked him straight out: "Didn't you sign the orders to carry out shootings in Ukraine?"[41] But Khrushchev controlled the media by now, and could ensure that such questions were not raised there. He took over the post of prime minister himself and combined it with the first secretaryship of the party. To prove that he was no longer a Stalinist, though, he refrained from arresting his opponents. Instead Molotov was named ambassador to Mongolia, while Malenkov was sent to direct a power station in Siberia. This was a key moment in the evolution of the party-state leadership from insecure elite to stable ruling class: henceforth its members could reasonably hope that, even in the event of serious reverses, they would still enjoy a high standard of living and their relatives would not suffer.

Stability for the ruling elite did, however, pose the question of how they intended to rule without recourse to mass terror. To face this fundamental issue, Khrushchev had to find a new basis of legitimacy for the party. He took advice from Central Committee departments and from the Institute of Marxism-Leninism, custodian of the ideological heritage. These institutions, shaken by the revelations of Stalin's atrocities, were beginning to rediscover the European "bourgeois" origins of Marxism, and to see some value in concepts such as legality, civil society, and the market economy which many European Marxists took for granted as something to be perfected, not destroyed, through worker hegemony. Leading scholars from the institutes accompanied Soviet diplomats in their journeys abroad, and had an opportunity to observe how other peoples lived and to discuss problems of social development with colleagues from other countries.[42]

Khrushchev, on the other hand, was far from being a Westernized Marxist. On the contrary, he might be regarded as the last millenarian among Communist leaders. He saw the world in black-and-white terms, though without the acute malice and paranoia of Stalin. He revered Lenin and regarded him as a beacon of certainty, a source of the one true teaching, from which Stalin had diverged. Khrushchev's rhetoric indicated that, if one could get back from Stalin's dubious byways on to "Lenin's main road," then it would be possible to resume the march toward the perfect society.

There was, therefore, a duality at the heart of Khrushchev's reforms. On the one hand, they rehabilitated certain aspects of "bourgeois" legality. Yet at the same time they reverted to the utopian notion that Communist democracy should mean rule by all the people and the "withering away of the state."

His outlook was most fully summarized in the new program of the CPSU (Communist Party of the Soviet Union), submitted to its Twenty-Second Congress in 1961. It asserted that all antagonistic class relationships had ceased within Soviet society, that the state was no longer ruling in the name of any particular class and was therefore a "state of all the people." The material prerequisites needed to build Communism, the final stage of social-ism, were also in place, so that it would be possible to achieve Communism by 1980. That would mean that the "organs of state power will gradually be transformed into organs of public self-government": the distinction between state and society would lapse.[43]

533

Khrushchev, like Lenin, used the party to resolve the contradictions of his program: he announced that it would become "the leading and guiding force in Soviet society." This could only mean that the party would replace the state as the backbone of those "organs of public self-government." If that was the case, then Khrushchev could hardly continue with the party in its present form, downgraded and distorted by the malpractices for which he had criticized Stalin. He restored the regular meetings of its committees at all levels—which reassured party officials; but he also insisted on the regular rotation of office, which alarmed and unsettled them, since from their view-point the whole reason for ending terror was to give them security of tenure.

To involve the party more closely in practical economic decisionmaking, as part of its role in future self-government, Khrushchev broke up the indus-trial ministries and regrouped economic administration in about a hundred regional *sovnarkhozy* (economic councils) headed by party committees. To enable the party to sharpen its specialized economic cadres, he divided its committees at the local level into "agricultural" and "industrial" sectors, with separate hierarchies extending right up to the Central Committee. This divi-sion was regarded as an affront by those secretaries assigned to the agricul-tural departments, agriculture having lower status than industry in the politi-cal hierarchy. Furthermore, since the boundaries of some of the sovnarkhozy coincided with those of the Union Republics, they strengthened the tendency for ethnic kinship groups to run the economy.[44]

To prepare the way for greater popular involvement in politics, the legal system was reformed. Military and emergency tribunals which had been ve-hicles of terror were abolished or severely restricted in their function. The criminal code was purged of the vague and portentous concepts which had figured so frequently in justification for arrests and show trials: "counter-revolutionary activity," "terrorist intentions," and so on. Sentences were sharply reduced, and defendants were no longer to be convicted solely on the basis of their own confessions. "Comrades' courts," an experiment tried in the 1920s, were revived to deal with minor offenses, their judges to be elected at home or workplace by the collective.[45]

Khrushchev's vision was essentially populist (in the Western rather than the Russian sense of the word). In his legal reform Khrushchev betrayed a distrust of "experts" which was apparent in other fields too. In education he tried to introduce greater equality by abolishing fees for tuition in college and the upper classes of secondary school, and also by insisting that all children should leave school at fifteen and spend two years "in production," that is, gaining practical experience in factories, offices, or farms. His intention was to encourage young people to take up skilled manual labor, which the economy badly needed. Even more important, he wanted to shake up the gradually calcifying social hierarchy, in which parents bequeathed status to their children, not by means of property but through the education system. Significantly, this was the one reform he failed to persuade his colleagues to accept: consolidating and passing on their hard-won positions in the hierarchy was a paramount priority for the nomenklatura elite. The education system, and the associated diplomas and qualifications, were the equivalent of capital wealth in bourgeois society: the decisive means of building socialist kith and kin.[46]

In order to make a start toward meeting the material aspirations of the mass of people, the post-Stalin leadership embarked on a massive program of house-building, using precast reinforced concrete blocks to construct ever higher apartment blocks. By the mid-1950s most Soviet towns were surrounded by a forest of cranes and a swamp of muddy building sites which gave citizens the hope of eventual escape from the unsought intimacy of the communal apartments. Between 1955 and 1964 the housing stock nearly doubled, and progress continued long after that. This overdue rectification of a need neglected under Stalin made people's lives more comfortable, but it also intensified social hierarchies. It provided abundant opportunity for the exercise of patronage by bosses in all walks of life. Furthermore, employees who belonged to the same enterprise or professional union had the option of forming "housing cooperatives" and claiming an apartment by putting down 15–30 percent of the purchase price and then paying off the rest at a moderate interest rate. Professional people were more likely than workers to have the deposit available, and so "cooperative housing" became the badge of a kind of middle class, between the highly privileged who had no need of such housing and ordinary folk who paid a small rent to the local soviet.

RENEWED PERSECUTION OF RELIGION

After the war there was a powerful revival of religion within the borders of the USSR. It resulted partly from Stalin's accommodation with the leaders of the main Christian denominations, partly from the absorption of new western territories, but mainly from the emotional stress and the powerful patriotic feelings aroused by the experience of war. Before the war there had been perhaps a few hundred active Orthodox parishes, but by 1949 there were some 14,500. Many of the new ones were in the western territories, where there had been no prewar persecution, but a good many had reopened in the heartlands of Russia as well.[47]

The semi-concordat with the state generated dangers as well as opportunities for the churches, for it meant that their clergy no longer had an embattled freedom, but came under the direct supervision of party and state. Clerical appointments were handled through the nomenklatura system and subject to political criteria similar to those which governed secular life. Bishops belonged to the nomenklatura elite and were expected to be active in the peace movement while not displaying excessive zeal in the promotion of their faith.[48]

Khrushchev's vision of a self-governing mass socialist society made religion more dangerous to him than it had been to Stalin in his later years. Although Khrushchev's antireligious policy was launched more or less without public announcement, one can see from press articles of the late 1950s that what worried the leadership was the revival of pilgrimages to holy places, the teaching of religion to children, and the link between religion and nationalism (especially perhaps in Ukraine and Lithuania). To counteract these tendencies, Communist and Komsomol cells were instructed to encourage the celebration of secular rites of passage to replace church baptisms, weddings, and funerals. The first Palace of Weddings was opened in Leningrad in 1959.[49]

In July 1961 a council of bishops was hurriedly convened at Zagorsk. It amended the church's statutes so that priests were no longer in charge of the administrative and financial affairs of their parish. Instead they became mere "servants of the cult," hired by religious congregations purely in order to celebrate divine service for them once a week. This change made it much easier to weaken the sense of community within congregations and to infiltrate them with party activists who would agitate for the closure of church buildings and the dissolution of parishes.[50] One can explain this self-denying decision only through the pliability of hierarchs appointed under the nomenklatura system.

The result was a massive closure of churches. Between 1958 and 1964 the Russian Orthodox Church lost some 40 percent of its parishes and about three-quarters of its monasteries. Closures were especially frequent in the western territories and in regions occupied by the Germans during the war. Other denominations heavily hit by the campaign included the Armenian

Apostolic Church, the Adventists, and the Baptists, while the Jews lost about a third of their synagogues and the Muslims more than a fifth of their mosques. Unregistered groups like the Pentecostals, Jehovah's Witnesses, and the various "true Orthodox" congregations were banned outright.[51]

WORKERS AND PEASANTS

In dealing with both workers and peasants Khrushchev tried to replace coercion with material incentives. Stalin's draconian labor laws were repealed in 1956 and replaced with an arrangement under which wages remained low but bonuses were paid for fulfillment, rather than overfulfillment, of the plan. The aim was to encourage steady planned output rather than the distortions and anomalies generated by convulsive bursts of overproduction (*shturmovshchina*). The new measures failed to make much impact, because they did not eliminate the basic defects of the production system. Workers' output continued to be affected by shortages of materials and parts, inadequate repair and maintenance, and poor working conditions, so that they frequently failed to meet targets through no fault of their own. Yet managers needed to hoard labor to meet unexpected demands, so they would deliberately falsify output figures whenever possible, to cover up for their workforce. Stalin's militarized control had been removed without much improving workers' incentives.[52]

What emerged from the stalemate was a kind of informal social contract, under which workers accepted relatively low pay and the absence of the right to strike in return for cheap food, transport, and housing, social benefits, job protection, easygoing work practices, and control over much of the labor process. It was acknowledged in practice that workers might arrive late (perhaps with a hangover), take extended breaks to socialize with their colleagues, and leave early in order to queue for "deficit" goods in the shops. No penalties were normally exacted for substandard work. All these concessions were necessary to enable workers to live more or less normal lives in an economy of shortages. At the same time, of course, they perpetuated those shortages and made them a permanent fact of life.

They also consolidated the patronal power of the enterprise bosses, whose decisions determined the housing, residence permits, childcare, holiday entitlements, and many other needs of their employees. In order to be able to offset these cosy arrangements and boost production when needed, many factory managers maintained a large female workforce carrying out the less attractive and worst-paid jobs. Some also hired *limitchiki*, out-of-town workers, who obtained temporary propiski in a desirable city in return for doing short-term or unpleasant jobs shunned by regular employees.[53]

In a sense, the penurious but laidback lifestyle of the Soviet worker was an acceptable one, especially since health care, education, and housing at a basic level were guaranteed, and it left time for "moonlighting," taking secondary and much more lucrative jobs. The dissident mathematician Aleksandr Zinoviev defined the workplace as a forum where "people not only work, they spend their time in the company they know well. They swap news, amuse themselves, do all kinds of things to preserve and improve their position, have contact with people on whom their well-being depends, go to innumerable meetings, get sent on leave to rest-homes, are assigned accommodation and sometimes supplementary food-products."[54] The only trouble was that the economic and military potential of a superpower could not be sustained by a system which gave such low priority to productivity.

The field of administration which Khrushchev made peculiarly his own was agriculture, and it was one on which he was to be judged by his colleagues. At Stalin's death the whole sector suffered from chronic underinvestment and the demoralization of the population. Famine had become a thing of the past, but cheap food was provided for the towns essentially at the expense of the rural producers, the kolkhozniki and sovkhozniki, who lived in abject poverty.

There were two fundamental problems inherited from the past. One was the low priority accorded by the regime to agriculture, compared with other sectors of the economy. The other was the authoritarian and bureaucratic structure of agricultural administration, which offered the producers few incentives to improve either output or productivity.

Khrushchev tackled the first but never fully got to grips with the second. From the outset he inscribed agriculture on his personal banner by launching the "Virgin Lands" campaign in 1954. One may count this the last great movement of Communist mass mobilization; in fact it was probably also the final surge in the centuries-old European colonization of Asia. The "virgin lands" were areas of steppe in western Siberia and north Kazakhstan which had been grazed by nomads till the 1930s and had not been brought under the plough—or at least not recently: some of them had been cultivated by "Stolypin peasants" who had abandoned them during dekulakization. Khrushchev's idea was to develop them as the major grain-growing area of the future, a genuinely affluent agricultural region which would deliver produce to the towns without impoverishing its own inhabitants.

At first the campaign was a great success. By 1956 the region was already producing three times as much grain as in 1953. Tens of thousands of young people were mobilized by the Komsomol to go out there and operate thousands of new tractors and harvesters: the sight of them advancing in echelons through fields of rippling corn became a staple of propaganda films for a decade or so.

538

After initial success, however, progress became patchier. Fertile though the soil was, the region suffered from relatively low rainfall and was liable to aridity: much of it was, after all, on the edge of the central Asian desert. To ensure its long-term viability, it needed well-judged fertilization and also the planting of trees, hedges, and windbreaks to minimize soil erosion. This kind of careful preparation was not in Khrushchev's style. Like Stalin, he wanted "breakthroughs" and fast results. The high early output figures were followed by more disappointing ones, and then, after 1960, by environmental disaster. Over five years or so, in a series of windstorms, much of the unprotected topsoil was blown away, creating huge "dust bowls" where nearly half the virgin lands had been.[55]

There were human problems too. Although the nomadic way of life had been destroyed, the "virgin lands" were still extensively used for traditional livestock breeding, and many Kazakhs resented the massive influx of alien producers, both to grow grain and to mechanize livestock raising. Even some of their party secretaries were dubious about the experiment. Leonid Brezhnev was sent in to pacify them in 1954. For many of the Komsomols too, the campaign proved frustrating: they suffered from shortages of housing, supplies, and machinery, as well as the sullen suspicion of the locals, and many of them cut short the experience and returned to European Russia.[56]

Overall, even if the virgin lands campaign did not fulfill Khrushchev's extravagant expectations, it did achieve something: it plugged the gap in food supplies which was threatening to hold back urban development during the 1950s and early 1960s. When misfortune overtook it, however, Khrushchev had nowhere else to turn, since most of his other agricultural projects turned out badly. Especially unfortunate was his idea of growing maize for cattle fodder in order to increase the output of meat and milk. When visiting the United States in 1959, Khrushchev had been inspired by the sight of Iowa prairies replete with maize, and he hoped that if the virgin lands could become the granary of the Soviet Union, then European Russia could provide cattle fodder by growing maize. Apparently forgetting that nearly all of European Russia lies well to the north of Iowa, he ordered that other grain crops be curtailed and maize sown generally, to be harvested green for silage where it would not ripen fully.

Woe betide any kolkhoz chairman who declined to carry out these instructions. He would not be arrested for sabotage, as under Stalin, but he would probably be dismissed and would certainly lose face in the eyes of his superiors. At the height of the campaign, in 1962, no less than 37 million hectares were sown with maize, of which only 7 million could be harvested ripe, and much of it could not be reaped at all. Meanwhile, crops that could flourish in cool, wet summers were ignored, meadows were abandoned, and the advice of agronomists comprehensively ignored. Khrushchev compounded the problem by curtailing kolkhozniks' right to cultivate their private plots and keep their own cattle.[57]

The result was two bad harvests, in 1962 and 1963, which put all Khrushchev's policies under pressure, and particularly the crucial social contract with the workers, which depended on cheap food. In the summer of 1962 he tried to help out the farms by raising meat and dairy prices by about a third. This was the first serious food price hike since the end of the war, and it infuriated many workers. At the Budennyi locomotive works in Novocherkassk, the management foolishly raised piecework norms at the same time, effectively lowering wages. The result was an explosion. Workers downed tools, draped the factory with banners reading "Meat, milk, and a pay rise!" and blocked the nearby Moscow–Rostov main railway line. When police arrested them for obstruction, all the factories in Novocherkassk went on strike, and workers marched toward police headquarters and the party committee building to demand their release. In the turmoil which ensued, special KGB troops opened fire, and twenty-three people were killed before order was restored.[58]

There was working-class unrest in other towns too, though Novocherkassk was much the most serious flashpoint. The really important point was that here the regime was being challenged by the industrial working class in whose name it supposedly ruled, and without whose support it could survive only by reverting to terror. There were bread queues again, and black-market traders were cleaning out markets in the more prestigious cities to sell food at high prices elsewhere. Khrushchev decided to solve the problem by using precious foreign currency to buy up wheat abroad. This was a terrible humiliation for a country which had exported grain before the revolution, and for a regime which prided itself on its economic achievements.

Together with the Cuban missile crisis and the break with China, it probably sealed Khrushchev's fate. Party secretaries who had supported him in 1957 now turned against him. They also no doubt had in mind the many unsettling reforms of the party, which jeopardized the security of their posts and privileges. After all, it was for stability and in the hope of prosperity that they had backed him; now he was no longer delivering them.

At length his increasingly impatient colleagues moved against him. In October 1964, while he was on holiday on the Black Sea, they organized a Central Committee plenum, ostensibly on further agricultural reforms he was contemplating, and asked him to return for it. The actual subject of the plenum was Khrushchev himself. The indictment was read by Mikhail Suslov, who sharply criticized his rule and called for his resignation. The main points in the indictment were his mistakes in agricultural administration, his erratic conduct of foreign affairs, his increasingly rude and high-handed behavior with his colleagues, his nepotism (especially the use of son-in-law Aleksei Adzhubei as an unofficial roving ambassador), his "itch to reorganize and restructure," and "crude violations of Leninist norms of party leadership." In the event, Khrushchev, already aging and perhaps aware of his failures, decided not to resist and offered his resignation.[59]

The manner of his departure showed how much more civilized Soviet politics had become since the arrest of Beria only eleven years earlier. There were no arrests, no grotesque accusations, certainly no executions, merely newspaper editorials accusing persons unknown of "harebrained schemes" and "failure to take advantage of scientific knowledge." Khrushchev himself later commented with pride: "Perhaps the most important thing I did was just this—that they were able to get rid of me simply by voting. Stalin would have had them all arrested."[60]

In 1957, when the nomenklatura elite helped Khrushchev overcome his opponents, what they wanted from him was that he bolster their authority and their privileges while scaling down the use of terror, and consolidate the status of the USSR as a superpower equal to the United States. They supported him as long as he seemed to be making progress toward both goals. They removed him when it became clear that he was no longer advancing either.

Khrushchev was a figure symptomatic of his time. Both agent and beneficiary of Stalin's terror, he came to power disillusioned with Stalin's methods and thirsting, like most of his countrymen, for a more stable and secure existence. In his attitudes and modes of operation, however, he was a prisoner of the system which had engendered him. He saw the world in absolute terms, and in any given situation he was sure there was one "correct" solution which would solve all problems, provided it was applied by exercise of the leader's willpower. Able to establish a good rapport with ordinary people, he convinced himself that he had their support, and that therefore opposition to him was sly, elitist, and illegitimate. Scientific objections could be waved aside and political resistance overcome: the party, led by him, was always right. In essence a moderate, he approached problems like an extremist, and thus blocked his own progress.

14

SOVIET SOCIETY UNDER "DEVELOPED SOCIALISM"

BREZHNEV AS LEADER

The leaders who overthrew Khrushchev were not united in their view of the world. They included Aleksei Kosygin, who favored gradual economic reform, and Aleksandr Shelepin, who wanted to restore firmer discipline and authoritarian rule. They agreed about one thing, though: that change could be handled only by tried and trusted officials, headed by themselves. "Collective leadership" and "stability of cadres" were their watchwords. What this meant was that the party-state apparatus and the nomenklatura elite, no longer terrorized by Stalin nor inconvenienced by Khrushchev, were to be allowed to run things largely in their own interests.

Leonid Brezhnev, who became first (later general) secretary of the CPSU, was an ideal figure to lead such a team. He was in some ways a colorless personality, and certainly no theorist or orator. His colleagues probably chose him as an interim figure. In doing so they made the same mistake as their predecessors had over Stalin—though without the same disastrous results. Instinctively a consensus politician, Brezhnev preferred to avoid policy decisions rather than take steps which might alienate any of his colleagues.

His great strength was the unostentatious routine work that has to go into personnel administration. Initially quite modest, he would spend hours on the telephone each day talking to regional party secretaries and to heads of Central Committee departments, both to elicit their opinions and to knit personal relationships with them. He was a master of the art of patronage. With immense patience he eased out of the Politburo the colleagues he felt least at ease with or those who owed him least, and brought in his own former associates from his days as a party secretary in Dnepropetrovsk, Moldavia, and Kazakhstan, people like Konstantin Chernenko, who became his righthand man in the Secretariat, and Nikolai Tikhonov, who took over from Kosygin as prime minister in 1980. Malicious insiders began to joke informally about the "Dnepropetrovsk mafia."[1]

He remade the Central Committee in his own image. Or perhaps it would be more accurate to say that he survived so long because he was already in its image. Of its 1981 members, three-quarters had joined the party before 1950, gaining their first experiences of politics during the war and under Stalin. Eighty-two percent of them were workers or peasants by origin, but 78 percent had been through some kind of higher education, so most of them had risen a long way in the world. Fifty-five percent had worked either in the military or in a defense-related branch of industry. Eighty-six percent were Slavs (67 percent Russian). Virtually all (97 percent) were men. They were the core of the Soviet Union's ruling class, and their view of the world, neo-*rossiiskii*, imperialist, and militarist, dominated the party and therefore society as a whole for more than two decades.[2]

Their substantial agreement on these matters did not prevent them from dividing into cliques, each with its own boss and its own clients. Even when he became old and ill, Brezhnev remained essential as a mediator among them. When Mikhail Gorbachev became a member of the Politburo in 1978, he was horrified to discover that Brezhnev, chairing its meetings, would lose the thread of debate and even forget what was being discussed. He remarked on this privately to Andropov, who told him that Brezhnev must remain, for all his shortcomings: "It is a matter of stability within the party and the state as well as an issue of international stability." In other words, his senescent presence kept the factions among the leadership from tearing each other apart. It also suited the local party secretaries, who preferred not to have too energetic or inquisitive a leader prying into their fiefs. They had, in short, a "gentlemen's agreement" with Brezhnev which "endowed the first secretaries with almost unlimited power in their regions, and they in turn had to support the General Secretary, praising him as leader and chief."[3] This was the kind of tacit understanding which had given the tsars apparently absolute power in the sixteenth century.

When they took over, the new leaders faced exactly the same problems as had Khrushchev. Like him, they wanted to improve the living standards of ordinary people, to make the Soviet Union a model socialist society, and to increase its military and diplomatic standing as a great power, the undisputed equal of the United States. They built up all branches of the armed services, army, navy (surface and submarine), air force, and missiles, in order to be sure that in any crisis they would be able to project their power in any part of the world. This was a colossal project for a country whose economic capacity was currently so much weaker than that of the United States, and the strains it imposed affected all their other attempts to bring about improvements.

They agreed without difficulty that Khrushchev's party reforms should be abandoned, both because they were unsettling to the apparat and because they threatened to hand the economy over to amateurs. The sovnarkhozy were abolished and the centralized industrial ministries restored. The bifurcation of the party apparatus was reversed, and, even more important, the rule about regular rotation of party officials was dropped. Once again secretaries could regard their jobs as lifetime incumbencies.

In 1965 Kosygin attempted a timid reform in industrial administration, which gave enterprise directors greater freedom in deciding how to use their profits—for incentive payments to workers, for example, or for reinvestment in better equipment—and also levied modest interest charges on capital, to discourage "gigantism" and "hoarding." Plan fulfillment was to be measured not by output but by sales, which made quality a serious consideration.

The reform failed to touch the fundamentals of the economic system, though. To profit fully from it, enterprises would have needed the freedom to set their own selling prices, and this they were never granted. They were also denied the right to decide on levels and conditions of employment, for example by dismissing workers who were incompetent or were surplus to needs, for this would have violated the tacit social contract between the party and the working class.[4]

As a result, technical innovation remained sluggish. Introducing new equipment meant disrupting production lines, and within the rigid framework of the planned economy this was difficult to do, since it would have meant accepting temporary lowering of output indices and in effect reducing workers' pay. Only military and space technology on the whole kept up with the highest international standards, since they guaranteed the prestige of the country. To maintain those standards the authorities were prepared to override both the social contract and routine planning procedures.

In most fields, however, Soviet industrial output relied on materials and techniques which had proved successful during the great upswing of the late 1940s and 1950s. For the assimilation of subsequent innovations they relied on imports from western Europe and North America. In fields such as automobile and shipping construction, synthetic chemicals, food processing, and oil and gas extraction, Soviet industry came to depend more and more on partnerships with Western firms. The latter were happy to oblige, seeing the Soviet Union as a country with a docile, low-paid, and well-trained labor force and with immense potential for development. The largest scheme of this kind was the 1966 contract with the Italian automobile firm Fiat, which led to the construction of a large factory on the Volga—in a town renamed Togliatti in honor of the recently deceased Italian Communist leader. Over the next couple of decades, this factory brought the small family car within the reach of several million Soviet citizens.

Such arrangements had a direct bearing on foreign policy. The more the Soviet Union depended on the Western powers for up-to-date technology and consumer goods, the less it could afford to alienate them. In spite of the arms buildup, then, there was always a foreign-policy imperative dictating stable and peaceful relations with NATO.

Closer economic relations with the West also affected the image which ordinary citizens had of the outside world. Once rank-and-file workers and technicians had regular contact with foreigners and some of them traveled abroad, it was difficult to maintain the fiction that the Soviet Union was a country of material prosperity or social equality. Soviet citizens could see for themselves that it lagged behind many other countries in both respects.

To confront the permanent problem of agriculture the new leaders substantially increased investment in drainage, irrigation, fertilizers, and machinery, until by the early 1970s it was consuming nearly a quarter of total investment. They also fixed longer-term quotas and higher prices for deliveries of produce, so that farms could plan more effectively for the future and pay their members better for collective work. Farmers' individual freedom to trade produce grown on their private plots was restored, and much food consumed in the cities came from this source. However, it was expensive, and ordinary families could not feed themselves from the private markets on a daily basis. The output of the kolkhozy themselves remained vital, but since it was inefficiently produced, if sold at a market price it too would have been beyond the means of most workers. Staple foods were therefore sold cheaply in ordinary urban shops, and to make up the difference the regime shelled out a constantly growing subsidy, which by 1977 had reached 19,000 billion rubles a year, or what one economist has called "the most gigantic agricultural subsidy known in human history."[5] This was the price the regime was prepared to pay for its social contract with the urban worker.

Not that the result was a contented and prosperous rural population. Though actual famines were a thing of the past, and collective farmers could now make quite a lot of money from their private plots (as well as having guaranteed pensions from 1964), the village remained a depressing place. Above all, it was not an environment in which to bring up children, since a good education was impossible to obtain there. Accordingly, young men continued to leave when military service or specialized training offered them the opportunity, and young women joined them if they could. In many villages only women and elderly men were to be seen, and by the 1970s some villages were dying out altogether, with only boarded-up and slowly rotting huts bearing witness to former human habitation.

545

By the late 1960s or early 1970s, then, the society Stalin had forged in the heat of upheaval and revolution had settled down to become an intensely stable, conservative, and hierarchical network of patron-client cells, supervised and controlled through the nomenklatura system. One's life chances depended on one's position in the hierarchy and on one's patron's success in manipulating the system to ensure material and other benefits. In ordinary shops goods were cheap but in effect rationed by the queue, and, since prolonged queueing was incompatible with doing a normal day's work, enterprises of all kinds would obtain food and other everyday consumer items to sell to their employees on the premises. I recall, as a graduate student, being puzzled and somewhat irritated by the long lunchtime queues in the Lenin Library in Moscow, slowed down by people buying large quantities of milk, butter, sausage meat, candy, and the like to stuff into their string bags. I only gradually realized that these were the library's employees doing their everyday food shopping at work—which was more convenient than hunting round shops with bare shelves on the way home.

Every factory, office, farm, educational institution, transport depot—in short every place of employment—had its place in the unofficial but pervasive social hierarchy established in the 1930s and consolidated from the 1950s onward. On an institution's place in the hierarchy depended the remuneration of its staff, the perks and privileges of its directors, and the degree of urgency accorded its requests and requirements. A skillful director with good connections could improve the life chances of his employees by obtaining materials, spare parts, fuel, food deliveries, and other benefits of higher quality, more quickly or more cheaply than a rival. Most directors employed a "pusher" *(tolkach),* whose specific function it was to cultivate such connections and use them to maximum advantage to obtain benefits.[6]

Since the official economy could not produce everything that was required, it depended on a second, or "black," economy to fullfill the plan. Within and alongside state-run enterprises, employees boosted meager incomes by "moonlighting" or working "on the left," using tools and materials from the workplace to repair cars or domestic plumbing, to make clothes, consumer goods, and desperately needed spare parts, and generally to compensate for the deficiencies of planned output. The "black" operatives usually enjoyed the protection of their bosses and paid a kickback for it. Everyone treated the state economy as a common resource, to be milked for personal benefit as needed. In the later Soviet decades, in this informal but all-pervasive manner, the economy was already becoming semiprivatized. The structure of the "black" economy strengthened the ties of personal patronage and clientelism already inherent in the system.[7]

A factor which increasingly entered into the allocation of education, employment, housing, and propiski was the applicant's nationality, "entry no. five" on his passport. To be Jewish was to be disadvantaged. To be Russian was usually an advantage, but one which was being eroded: in fact, by the 1970s some Union republics, notably those in central Asia, were discreetly favoring their own indigenous nationals at the expense of outsiders, most of whom were Russians. Republican leaders knew that if they avoided gross abuses, Moscow would not interfere. "Stability of cadres" and the "black" economy encouraged ethnic exclusivism and promoted the gradual unraveling of the "multinational Soviet people."[8]

THE CZECHOSLOVAK AND POLISH CRISES

The Brezhnev consensus was disrupted by a challenge from a "separate road to socialism," quite different from the Yugoslav one, and perplexing not least because it represented a movement in the direction of Westernized, "bourgeois" Marxism such as the academic institutes in the USSR itself were beginning to cultivate.

In 1956 Czechoslovakia had been quiet, but the "thaw" eventually affected its party leadership more deeply than in either Poland or Hungary. In January 1968 a new first secretary was elected, Alexander Dubček, who gave reformist intellectuals in the party apparatus their head. The result was an Action Program, published in April, which suggested that in a developed socialist society, with the major battles of the class struggle already won, there was no danger in admitting the existence of conflicting social interests and letting those interests form their own associations and publish political programs in order to compete in the public forum. The report also recommended decentralizing decisionmaking in the economy and restoring elements of the free market in the interest of greater efficiency.

By the summer it looked as if the outcome was likely to be the abolition of censorship and the formation of non-Communist political parties. The Communist Party itself was due to hold a congress in September, at which the ban on platforms and factions (dating back to the Russian Communist Party's Tenth Congress of 1921) was to be repealed, while senior office was to be made elective, by secret ballot, and subject to regular rotation. Some of what was proposed was reminiscent of Khrushchev, but in a different context, that of pluralist democracy rather than populist socialism.

The Soviet leaders decided that this was more than they could tolerate and forestalled the planned congress by sending Warsaw Pact troops into Czechoslovakia on 21 August. The political side of the intervention was bungled—no Kadar was available—and Dubček had to be tolerated for another year before he could be replaced, the reform program wound down, and those who had supported it purged. *Pravda* followed up the invasion with a statement reiterating the legitimacy of "separate roads to socialism" but warned that parties exercising this right "must damage neither socialism in their own country nor the fundamental interests of the other socialist countries, nor the worldwide workers' movement." This statement became known as the "Brezhnev doctrine": it implied that any reform undertaken by a country within the Warsaw Pact would require the approval of the Soviet Communist Party.

The suppression of reform in Czechoslovakia had profound effects on the Soviet Communist Party. The movement back toward the European Marxist tradition—what was becoming known as "Eurocommunism"—was halted and reversed. Economic reform of even the timid Kosygin variety became taboo. In a very real sense the Soviet Communist Party became stagnant, unable to reform itself, to tolerate a lively intellectual or cultural life, or to render the economy more productive.

Whereas in Czechoslovakia the challenge came from party intellectuals reexamining the Marxist heritage, in Poland twelve years later it came from workers, enraged that the tacit social contract, which governed their life and labor as it did in the USSR, was not being observed. Polish agriculture, for different reasons, was scarcely more efficient than the Soviet variety, and food price rises in the 1970s several times provoked the workers to protest. The climax came in the summer of 1980, when the workforce of the Lenin Shipyards in Gdańsk went on strike against high prices and the dismissal of a popular workers' leader. They soon found themselves at the center of a national network of protest, supported by the country's leading intellectuals.

The Solidarity movement, which grew out of this protest, was ostensibly a trade union, but in fact became what one Western observer called "a civic crusade for national revival."[9] Lech Wałęsa, the Gdańsk electrician who led it, negotiated an agreement with the regime, which acknowledged the "lead-ing role of the party" but conceded to Poles the right to create their own associations and express their views publicly. The result was a stalemate. The party and Solidarity edged watchfully round each other, neither able to tackle the urgent issues of economic reform on its own, but neither trusting the other to cooperate in a full and open partnership. The Catholic Church tried to bring them together in a Committee of National Salvation, but mutual suspicion remained too great. In the end, fearing a Soviet invasion, the army under General Wojciech Jaruzelski intervened, declared a "state of emer-gency" in December 1981, and took over the running of the country by coer-cion. This "solution" did nothing to confront the underlying problems, and underlined the deep crisis into which state socialist societies were drifting by the 1980s.[10]

"STAGNATION" AND SOCIAL CHANGE

For a long time after the Second World War Soviet society was in a condition of convalescence. Only in the mid-1950s did the population reach again its level of 1940, and even then there was a marked shortage of males, especially in the generation born in the 1910s and 1920s. In 1959 women still formed 55 percent of the population, and not till the final years of the Soviet Union was the demographically normal proportion of 52 percent females being ap-proached. A 1965 novel about workers in Rostov-on-Don has a young man ask six of his colleagues how many have fathers. Only one raises his hand, and everyone accepts that this situation is normal.[11]

A whole generation was growing up without fathers—whatever that may have meant for their own understanding of family life—and overwhelmingly the burdens of society were being laid on the shoulders of women. During the 1920s and 1930s they had become emancipated in the sense that they had achieved equality in educational opportunities and were moving into the same professions as men. By the 1960s the USSR had the world's highest rate of female employment, and women were as well educated as men.[12]

However, inherited prejudices, demographic pressure, and financial short-ages limited the extent to which women were able to benefit from their opportunities. By and large they occupied the lower ranks of the professions, with less authority and lower pay than men. They were also taking over heavy manual jobs formerly reserved for men: it became commonplace to see women in overalls and dungarees with a pickax along the street or railway line. Furthermore, they were not being freed from the domestic responsibilities previously borne by women not taking paid employment, either because they had no husbands or because those husbands were not accustomed to housework. Childcare facilities were much better developed than in the West, but still not sufficiently to make up for the "double burden" which women now had to bear, rushing from home to bus stop to office to shops to kindergarten before arriving home to cook the supper and do the washing over a small handbasin, all in an attempt to hold family and job together. In more fortunate families the deficit was made up by the *babushka,* grandmother pitched willy-nilly into a second motherhood, whatever her age or state of health. But whoever performed the domestic chores often had to do them in competition with others in the communal kitchen.[13]

Women worked for many reasons: to fullfil themselves, to exercise their skills, to have a richer social life, to feel themselves useful in society. But in a good many cases they took paid employment not from choice but out of economic necessity. Even male pay rates were low, and for a family with children a second income was normally essential. The timid women's liberation movement which appeared in the later decades of the Soviet Union spoke out not only for the right to be properly paid for work, but also for the right *not* to work. It complained of such deficiencies as the shortage of childcare centers and the appalling conditions in maternity wards.[14]

The problems resulted in relative instability of family life and a declining birth rate. In 1940 the birth rate was 31.2 per 1,000, from where it fell to 26.7 in 1950, 24.9 in 1960, 17.4 in 1970, 18.3 in 1980, and 16.8 in 1990. The sharpest falls were in the 1940s, as a result of war, and in the 1960s, probably because of the cumulative effects of urbanization, which have lowered the birth rate in most European countries. But the heavy burden on women undoubtedly made the decline more dramatic in the Soviet Union than elsewhere, and it was most marked in those regions (Russia, Ukraine, the Baltic) where women had the highest rates of employment. Here one child per family was the norm. In the Caucasus and central Asia, where female employment was less common, birth rates remained higher.[15] By the 1970s births in Russia, Ukraine, Belorussia, and the Baltic were so reduced that the population was actually beginning to decline. In the long run, Russian dominance of the Union was under threat.

It is possible too that the return to easier availability of abortion (in 1955) and of divorce (from 1965) reduced the number of births. From 1.6 divorces per 1,000 inhabitants in 1965, the annual rate more than trebled, to 3.5, by 1979, putting the Soviet Union in the same league as the United States, traditionally a country with an exceptionally high divorce rate.[16] It is difficult to know what was responsible for this change. Shortage of housing was probably one factor: it was not getting worse during the 1960s and 1970s—the contrary was true—but individual aspirations were becoming higher, so that years of living in cramped accommodation with in-laws seemed less bearable. Drinking and domestic violence were cited among the principal reasons for divorce.

550

On the other hand, with the growth in the availability of noncommunal apartments, family and private life were growing more important. People were spending more time at home, reading, watching television, chatting with friends and relatives, and less in public meetings and probably in public life generally. So at the very time the family was becoming more important, it was also becoming less stable. This was a paradox which worried the regime, which now desperately wanted to see strong families, to promote population growth as well as social stability.

The Soviet Union was becoming an urbanized society: from the mid-1950s urban dwellers outnumbered rural ones. But it was being urbanized in a very distinctive way. Few of the civic institutions of Western urban society existed, or if they did they were usually under tight party supervision. People joined trade unions, the youth movement, women's groups, and so on to receive social benefits and to plug into the patronage network. Beyond that the still large number of communal apartments ensured that the tight but quarrelsome intimacy of rural life was reproduced in the cities. The constant queues performed the same function: while waiting to buy "deficit" products, people would exchange information, opinions, and rumors, many of them not reflected in the mass media, and some of them highly discreditable to the Soviet leaders.

SCIENCE AND EDUCATION

By the 1970s Soviet society was not only urbanized but also highly educated. In some ways raising the educational level of the population was the greatest achievement of the Soviet regime. In 1939 a mere 1.3 percent of the population had been through higher education, and 11 percent secondary education; by 1959 the figures were 3.3 percent and 40 percent, and by 1979 10 percent and 70.5 percent. In 1940–41 there were some 800,000 students at Soviet institutions of higher education, in 1950–51 1.25 million, in 1960–61 2.4 million, in 1970–71 4.6 million, and in 1980–81 5.2 million.[17]

Of course, even higher education was of many different types, some of which would qualify as vocational training in the West. All higher education required students to spend a lot of time on ideological indoctrination in subjects such as "dialectical materialism," "scientific atheism," and "the history of the CPSU." Few of them completely internalized the official ideology, but all of them were in ineluctable contact with what Aleksandr Zinoviev has called the "powerful magnetic field of ideological influence."[18] Nevertheless, the number of highly qualified people capable to some degree of independent critical thinking was high and growing. By 1988 there were 1.52 million scientists and scholars employed in higher education and research, 493,000 of them "candidates of science" (roughly: Ph.D.s) and 49,700 "doctors of science" (a much higher distinction, usually awarded in middle age for a second and more fundamental dissertation).[19]

The results showed in the achievements of Soviet science and technology. The development of nuclear weapons and delivery systems and the successful launching of a space exploration program in the 1950s showed that the Soviet Union could be a world leader in technological areas to which it deliberately devoted resources and trained manpower. Once the nuclear weapon had been created, a means of delivering it was urgently sought, and research and development concentrated on missile technology. In this area the Soviet Union achieved enough to contest by the 1970s the enormous lead which the United States had started with. The most sensational outcome of this project, however, was the Soviet space exploration program. In October 1957 a Soviet satellite was successfully launched and orbited the earth. It was followed in April 1961 by the first human journey in space, in a capsule operated by the test pilot Iurii Gagarin. These achievements, genuinely remarkable, created the illusion in the West for at least a decade to come that Soviet technology generally was at a similarly high level.

In mathematics, astronomy, and theoretical physics Soviet scholars were setting international standards till perhaps the late 1960s. But a barely perceptible decline was setting in. Among Soviet scientists themselves one could hear complaints of the effects of hidebound leadership, of official secrecy, of niggardly financing, of isolation from foreign colleagues. Computers and up-to-date equipment were often not available and foreign journals no longer subscribed to. Scholars invited to conferences abroad had to go through cumbersome and humiliating security procedures, which often resulted in their being blocked while some hack was sent in their place.[20]

The party's ideological monopoly was no less confining. This was more pernicious in the humanities and social sciences than in the natural sciences and technology, but the Lysenko affair had demonstrated how damaging it could be even there. In 1955 the physicist Petr Kapitsa wrote to Khrushchev warning that "Scientific ideas are generated and validated only in the struggle with other ideas, and only in this manner can they become truths. If that struggle ceases, then the achievements of science become dogmas . . . The most striking example of this tendency is our materialist philosophy . . . Today a meeting of our top scholars is no longer a scientific gathering concerned with solving advanced scientific problems. It reminds one more of a church service, conducted according to a set ritual."[21]

In a similar spirit Andrei Sakharov and two colleagues submitted a memorandum to the party leadership in March 1970. They criticized the "antidemocratic traditions and norms of public life established in the Stalin era, which have not been decisively eliminated to this day" and warned that "freedom of information and creative work are necessary for the intelligentsia because of the nature of its activity and its social function. The intelligentsia's attempts to increase these freedoms are legitimate and natural. The state, however, suppresses these attempts by applying all kinds of restrictions—administrative pressures, dismissals from employment and even trials."[22]

This statement highlighted a critical dilemma for the Soviet state. It needed highly qualified thinkers in all branches of science and technology, yet fostering the qualities which produced such thinkers was hazardous to the Communist party's ideological monopoly. Adopting the measures recommended by Sakharov—abolishing censorship and travel restrictions, restoring the independence of the judiciary, publishing far more information about social processes, and permitting free elections to the soviets—seemed to the authorities likely to undermine the whole system. When Gorbachev tried it two decades later, they were proved right.

Meanwhile, scientists impatient at official restrictions on their work undertook their own spontaneous countermeasures. In many research institutes, especially in Moscow, Leningrad, Tbilisi, Erevan, and the Baltic republics, scholars began to organize informal seminars to study ideas not envisaged in the official ideology or approved research programs. These were not oppositional meetings, simply gatherings of interested people anxious for greater intellectual variety than was officially tolerated.[23] In economics institutes scholars discussed Keynesianism, Hayek, and the theory and practice of the free market economy out of genuine and positive interest, not in the spirit of "knowing the enemy."[24] Sometimes they would go outside their own spheres of study: I myself recall giving a paper to a mathematics institute in Leningrad in 1973 on the Stolypin agrarian reform, at a time when tsarist reform attempts were beginning to arouse interest among intelligent Russians.

In the field of semiotics and linguistics, Soviet scholars by the 1970s were in the vanguard of international thinking. Their life experience had made them especially sensitive to the ways in which public discourse could be controlled and limited from above. Their pioneer, Mikhail Bakhtin (1895–1975), had been arrested and spent many years in exile in Mordovia, returning to Moscow only toward the end of his life. In reaction against official dogmatism, his writings, when they gradually appeared, provided good theoretical reasons for believing that statements, no matter how well attested, are never final, but always open to revision. He rehabilitated dialogue as the fundamental context of all discourse, including that which claims to be scientific. In his work on Rabelais he celebrated the subversive, grotesque, and demotic, those aspects of culture which do not submit either to aesthetic rules or to political regulation. His message went straight to the hearts of scholars in a hierarchical, censored, and controlled culture.[25]

553

During the 1960s and 1970s the Moscow-Tartu seminars in semiotics and linguistics, centered around Iurii Lotman, built on the insights of Bakhtin and of French and Czech theorists to develop a theory of the ways in which culture, religion, and other kinds of symbolic systems operate within society. These, too, proved immensely fruitful to theory in the humanities and social sciences well beyond the borders of the Soviet Union.[26]

CULTURAL LIFE

Apart from science, the other area of public life which generated nonconformist attitudes was culture, and especially literature. Just as there was a cult of science in the Soviet Union, so also there was a cult of literature. The great prerevolutionary writers—Pushkin, Turgenev, Tolstoi, Chekhov—were widely read and an integral part of the secondary school curriculum. (The less ideologically acceptable Dostoevskii was available only to the persistent, in good libraries.) They acted like ancient Greeks on the more intelligent Victorian schoolboys: as a source of ideas not provided for in the official ideology.

As in nineteenth-century Russia, the focus of literary life was in the journals and publishing houses. The journals had changed little since then: apart from publishing novels, poetry, and plays, they continued to provide an outlet for social commentators and scholars to expound their ideas, sometimes at considerable length. The editorial collective and the subscribers built up a carefully cultivated sense of common identity, marked by tolerated minor deviations from a well-defined party line.

The most celebrated example of its type was the journal *Novyi mir* (New World) from 1958 to 1970 under its principal editor, Aleksandr Tvardovskii. A member of the Communist Party and even for a time of its Central Committee, Tvardovskii was not a dissenter in the normal sense. He accepted the norms of "socialist realism." But he interpreted them in his own distinctive way. For him "realism" meant telling the truth about what had happened in Soviet society, and *narodnost* meant focusing on the lives of ordinary workers, soldiers, and peasants. He gathered around himself a group of likeminded editors and writers, prepared to work hard and take risks for the sake of what they all believed in: promoting good literature in the interests of truth. In one sense, this editorial collective was an ordinary cell of the Soviet patronage network; in another it worked to undermine that system. In the absence of indiscriminate terror, the Soviet system had started to generate its own antibodies.[27]

Tvardovskii's most famous contribution to literary history was the publication in 1962 of Aleksandr Solzhenitsyn's short novel *A Day in the Life of Ivan Denisovich*. The author had spent eight years in a Soviet labor camp before being released in the post-Stalin period. The account he gave of life there challenged the accepted literary norms in a number of ways. It was the first published exposé of the GULAG, in all its squalor, brutality, and inhumanity; it was written not in stilted official Russian, but in the language of ordinary speech, the jargon of building sites, barracks, and communal apartments; and its viewpoint was entirely subjective, not attempting any overall perspective or higher justification for the horror of what was narrated. In these respects it set the tone for much of Russian fiction in the next thirty years.[28]

It also unleashed a flood of memory and feeling, of the most diverse and contradictory kind. Ordinary Soviet citizens wrote in to the journal to congratulate or condemn its editors for having published the work. "Now I read and weep, but when I was imprisoned in Ukhta for ten years I did not shed a tear." "After reading it the only thing left to do is to knock a nail in the wall, tie a knot and hang oneself." "Although I wept when I read it, I felt myself a citizen with full rights among other people."[29] This was the "return of the repressed": feelings denied by censorship and by social pressure bursting forth with tremendous force.

In a somewhat more modest form, *Novyi mir* continued the policy of publishing revelatory but also sober and realistic works for another eight years, provoking intense controversy within the Union of Writers, till Tvardovskii was removed in 1970. Among the writers he sponsored during that period were a number who evoked with honesty, sympathy, and as much frankness as the censor would allow another "repressed" aspect of Soviet life: the village. At all stages of the modernization project, the village had suffered—the expulsion of its most productive members, the collectivization of land and most property, famine, depopulation, poverty, and demoralization. The village was what Soviet society was leaving behind, backward and despised. Tvardovskii, himself a village lad and member of a dekulakized family, gave his patronage to younger colleagues who wanted to describe rural conditions honestly. The response from literary critics—positive and negative—was very strong. So many Russians had moved from village to town during the great urbanization of the previous decades: the "village prose" writers invited them to reflect on what they had lost. This was the first articulation of a style of Russian national feeling separate from the Soviet state and even in some respects opposed to it.[30]

The theater provided another arena for nonconformist sentiments. Here players and audience were gathered together, and their interaction was even more intense than that of journal readers. Also more unpredictable: even a production passed by the censor could change its nature with each performance, the actor's gestures and intonation suggesting meanings not brought out during rehearsals. In the Sovremennik (Contemporary) Theater, founded by Oleg Efremov in 1956, the methods and spirit of the prerevolutionary Moscow Arts Theater were revived: the troupe cultivated a sober realism, authentic communication of human feeling, and the sense of the troupe as a collectivity in which director and actors shared responsibility for each production and no single player stood out as a star. The Taganka, founded by Iurii Liubimov in 1964, rehabilitated the methods of Meierhold, aiming at "total theater" by mobilizing every possible dramatic effect, including songs performed in the lobby and leaflets showered over the auditorium. The Taganka brought foreign drama to the Russian spectator, including unorthodox Communists like Bertold Brecht, and also dramatized Russian fiction on the margin of acceptability, like Dostoevskii's *Crime and Punishment* and Bulgakov's *Master and Margarita*.[31]

In the mid-1950s Boris Pasternak completed a novel, *Doctor Zhivago*, highly critical not only of Communist rule, but of all political domination of cultural and intellectual life. When Soviet journals declined to publish it, he passed it on to the Italian publisher Feltrinelli, who brought it out in Milan in 1957. This was not a deeply pondered challenge to the cultural monopoly, but the next year, when Pasternak was awarded the Nobel Prize in literature, he was subjected to a campaign of official vituperation at home and expelled from the Writers' Union.

Following his example, by the early 1960s writers impatient of official restrictions were typing out their works as one would for submission to a publishing house, only instead they would circulate them in carbon-paper copies among friends. This was *samizdat,* or "self-publishing." The first works to be "published" in this way were lyric poems—brief and easy to duplicate. Then came works previously banned in the Soviet Union, including *Doctor Zhivago,* and foreign works such as George Orwell's *1984,* Arthur Koestler's *Darkness at Noon,* and Milovan Djilas' *The New Class.* Solzhenitsyn was gradually squeezed out of Soviet journals, but his works began to circulate clandestinely. I recall reading some of his short prose poems at Moscow University in 1964, and in 1967 *Cancer Ward* and *First Circle* made their appearance, or nonappearance, in the studies of Soviet intellectuals, hidden deep in drawers or disguised in the bindings of Lenin's complete works.

Thereafter a veritable samizdat industry came into being: poems, novels, letters, petitions, protests, and memoranda, rejected or likely to be rejected by the censor, being copied and passed on in ever fainter and more illegible carbon copies. Samizdat symbolized a tacit revolt against official procedures. As Vladimir Bukovskii, human rights activist and author of a "Hymn to the Typewriter," put it, "[I] write myself, edit myself, censor myself, publish myself, distribute myself, and go to jail for it myself."[32] In a society of repression and conformism, this spontaneous assertion of the self was liberating.

It was also an assertion of a new kind of collective. Some works were in great demand, and the blurred and fading pages had to be perused and handed on within a day or two. Friends or colleagues would gather for a few hours or perhaps overnight, drink a great deal of coffee, and read each other the forbidden text. Liberated from their deadeningly predictable official contexts, words leapt to life and took on new and vivid meaning. This was collectivism and "joint responsibility" in a wholly new context. To participate in the duplication, distribution, and reading of samizdat was to know a heightened social and spiritual life.[33]

Samizdat took a directly political turn when two writers, Andrei Siniavskii and Iulii Daniel, were arrested for circulating their unpublished satirical stories. At their trial in February 1966 they were accused of spreading "anti-Soviet propaganda," and their writings were interpreted with flat-footed literalness, as political statements, and as if all their fictional characters represented the authors' viewpoints. The indictment hit writers in a sensitive spot: if any critical or satirical literary texts could be treated as straightforward political propaganda, then it would become difficult to use words in an imaginative fashion at all. Sixty-three members of the Moscow branch of the Writers' Union wrote to the forthcoming party congress warning that "the condemnation of writers for satirical works creates an extremely dangerous precedent and could impede the progress of Soviet culture."[34]

Something of a chain reaction started. Aleksandr Ginzburg, editor of a samizdat journal, compiled a record of the trial and of domestic and foreign reaction to it, which he circulated inside the country and sent abroad. He too was arrested, and his arrest sparked off further samizdat protests, calling for facts to be made known and for the Soviet authorities to observe their own laws.

The last point was an embarrassment: the authorities did not want to give up their repressive powers, but they did wish to act in an ostensibly legal manner. Stalin had shown how dangerous lawlessness could be to high-ranking officials. So they tried to restrain the wave of protests without resorting to arrests. Protesters, many of them writers, scholars, or scientists, were warned that their dissertations would not be approved, their writings would not be published, and their careers would suffer. To prove the point, some of them were dismissed and had to find odd jobs as watchmen, cloakroom attendants, or boiler-stokers. Their superiors and colleagues were warned of the importance of creating a "healthy collective" and exercising a "fruitful moral influence" over their wayward comrades. Mutual policing became the order of the day: a whole institute could suffer because of one member's signature on a protest letter. This was "joint responsibility" in yet another form, close to its Kievan origins as criminal surety.[35]

From 1968 onward, as a result, the number of professional people prepared to sign protests began to tail off. However, in their place a new and unexpected phenomenon appeared, a samizdat journal dedicated to recording the occasions when the authorities violated their own laws. Named baldly the *Chronicle of Current Events,* it bore on its front page article 19 of the UN Declaration of Human Rights (which the Soviet Union had signed), which guaranteed the "right to freedom of opinion and expression." The presentation was equally restrained. There was no editorial comment, merely a list of disciplinary actions, searches, interrogations, warnings, arrests, trials, and other official sanctions. One copy was always sent abroad, to be broadcast on Russian-language foreign radio stations, while others were typed and retyped on a distribution network which, in reverse, became a channel for the communication of information. With imperfect but still remarkable regularity, this journal continued to appear every two or three months right through to 1982.[36]

In due course the *Chronicle* spawned more limited and specialized imitations, dealing with the concerns of specific minorities, which might be national (Jewish, Georgian, Estonian), religious (Baptists, Jehovah's Witnesses, persecuted Orthodox), or social (workers, invalids). And of one majority— women. Here was a whole germinating civil society unable to push its shoots even above the level of the soil.

Groups of other kinds began to emerge, as well, not approved by the authorities but sometimes tolerated by them at least temporarily. Pop groups would perform their numbers in ill-lit cellars. In similar venues devotees of yoga would gather to practice their physical and spiritual exercises. Fan clubs would form to celebrate a particular singer or sports star. A few enterprising Komsomol organizations came forward with advice or offered them premises, but most such groups operated in a vacuum, without any social support.[37]

In this uncontrolled way, Soviet society spawned new cells, sometimes half within official structures, sometimes totally outside them, but at any rate not fully integrated. Nowhere was this process more fateful in its consequences than among the non-Russian nationalities.

NATIONAL REAWAKENING

"Stability of cadres" turned out to be a charter for ethnic particularism. "Indigenization" and the early nationalities policy of the Soviet regime had deliberately fostered the strengthening of national consciousness and of national cadres, in the expectation that this would be a necessary but temporary step on the way to "proletarian internationalism." When "indigenization" threatened to get out of hand and turn into "bourgeois nationalism," Stalin had applied terror against its exponents. Now, in the absence of mass terror, "indigenization" came to full flower. Local cadres were able to dignify and consolidate their rule. By 1985, for example, the five republican CPSU first secretaries in central Asia had all been in power for more than twelve years, and four of them for more than twenty. The result was not the creation of nations as we normally understand them, but rather the adaptation of archaic social structures—extended family, clan, or tribe—to the Soviet nomenklatura system. Since the nomenklatura worked by means of personal dependency, the transition was not too difficult to make.

In Russia and most European parts of the Soviet Union the prerevolutionary elites had been destroyed or dispersed by the revolution, and the Soviet hierarchy was a completely new one. Destruction of old elites was not so complete in central Asia and the Caucasus, at least among the nationalities not deported by Stalin. In those regions traditional elites and Soviet ruling class coalesced: the nomenklatura system offered a convenient way of maintaining and semimodernizing traditional hierarchies, for it guaranteed the competence and loyalty of their members and supported them with the full weight of party, army, and KGB authority. Collective farms often perpetuated traditional communal landownership and cooperative cultivation under a headman from a local family of notables. The low status and relative neglect of agriculture within the Soviet system encouraged villagers to fall back on their own resources for survival and whatever material benefits they could secure, but from time to time they would look beyond the farm to locally influential people to protect and help them in a crisis. Even in the towns factories, colleges, and other institutions could also mask continuing family or clan hegemony.[38]

Islam as a religion favored this preservation of social structures, for it is less dependent than Christianity on distinct buildings or a separate clergy for the celebration of its rites, and is well able to coalesce with local cults which are not necessarily Islamic in nature. Without mosques a relatively full Islamic life was still possible, as long as factory administrators were prepared to tolerate periodic obeisances toward Mecca performed alongside the workbench. (The ban on pilgrimages to Mecca, though, remained an abiding grievance.) Besides, sometimes it was possible to have a meeting hall, club, or even teahouse function de facto as a mosque. In general it was the socially integrative and ritual aspects of Islam which were to the fore, while its scriptural and theological ones were neglected. Weddings and above all funerals were the occasions which provoked the most fervent religious behavior, and even Communist Party officials were expected to participate in them.[39]

Active persecution of Islam ended by the mid-1960s, and thereafter mullahs acted as intermediaries between Muslims and the state, gaining acceptance for the faith as a pillar of social order, while discreetly rebuilding its institutions and providing a link with the past. They were not able to do much, though, to acquaint young people with the scriptures, because of continuing antireligious laws and the compulsory Cyrillic alphabet.[40]

Tribalism recovered and in some ways consolidated itself, albeit in a new form, dictated by the nomenklatura framework. Kazakhstan offers an especially striking example, since its nomadic way of life had been completely destroyed in the 1930s, and Russians had flooded into the republic in large numbers. All the same, some of the rural way of life was preserved: most collective ranches still maintained summer pastures, to which much of the community would relocate in the spring and from where they would return in the autumn in a reenactment of transhumant nomadism. Kolkhoz chairmen replaced the old *aksakaly* (village chiefs), and party obkom (oblast committee) secretaries the beys, but they often came from the same traditional powerful families.

The Kazakh birth rate was much higher than the Russian, and Kazakhs were becoming much better educated by the 1960s. Both of these factors blunted the advantage Russians initially enjoyed in the competition for good

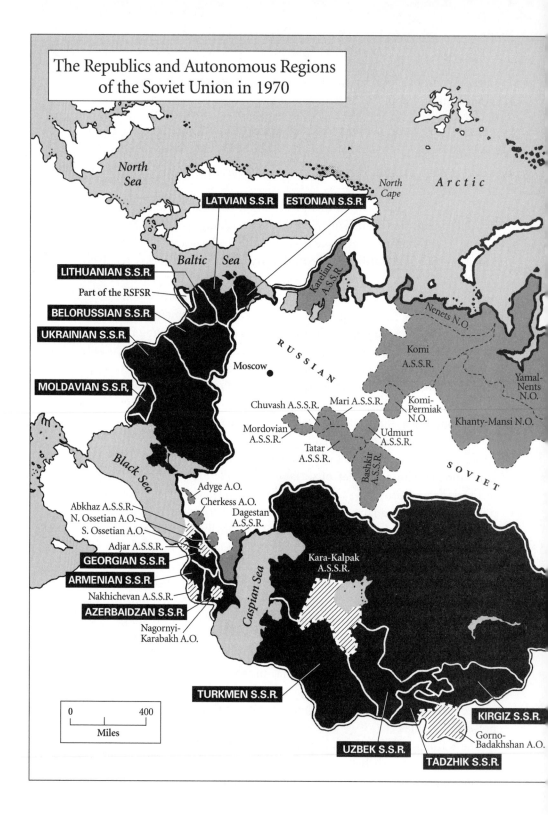

The Republics and Autonomous Regions
of the Soviet Union in 1970

*North
Sea*

North
Cape

Arctic

LATVIAN S.S.R. ESTONIAN S.S.R.

Karelian
A.S.S.R.

Nenets N.O.

Baltic Sea

LITHUANIAN S.S.R.

Part of the RSFSR

Komi
A.S.S.R.

Yamal-
Nents
N.O.

BELORUSSIAN S.S.R.

UKRAINIAN S.S.R.

R U S S I A N

Moscow

Komi-
Permiak
N.O.

Khanty-Mansi N.O.

MOLDAVIAN S.S.R.

Chuvash A.S.S.R.   Mari A.S.S.R.

Mordovian
A.S.S.R.

Udmurt
A.S.S.R.

Tatar
A.S.S.R.

Bashkir
A.S.S.R.

S O V I E T

Black Sea

Adyge A.O.

Abkhaz A.S.S.R.
N. Ossetian A.O.
S. Ossetian A.O.

Cherkess A.O.

Dagestan
A.S.S.R.

Adjar A.S.S.R.

GEORGIAN S.S.R.

Kara-Kalpak
A.S.S.R.

ARMENIAN S.S.R.

Nakhichevan A.S.S.R.

AZERBAIDZAN S.S.R.

Caspian Sea

Nagornyi-
Karabakh A.O.

TURKMEN S.S.R.

KIRGIZ S.S.R.

0   400
Miles

Gorno-
Badakhshan A.O.

UZBEK S.S.R.

TADZHIK S.S.R.

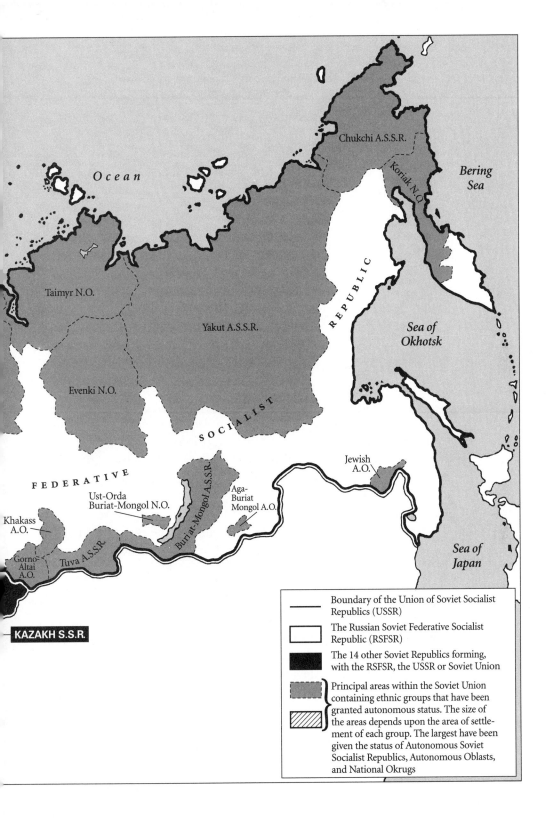

Ocean

Bering
Sea

Chukchi A.S.S.R.

Koriak N.O.

Taimyr N.O.

R E P U B L I C

Sea of
Okhotsk

Yakut A.S.S.R.

Evenki N.O.

S O C I A L I S T

Jewish
A.O.

F E D E R A T I V E

Ust-Orda
Buriat-Mongol N.O.

Buriat-Mongol A.S.S.R.

Aga-
Buriat
Mongol A.O.

Khakass
A.O.

Sea of
Japan

Gorno-
Altai
A.O.

Tuva A.S.S.R.

KAZAKH S.S.R.

Boundary of the Union of Soviet Socialist
Republics (USSR)

The Russian Soviet Federative Socialist
Republic (RSFSR)

The 14 other Soviet Republics forming,
with the RSFSR, the USSR or Soviet Union

Principal areas within the Soviet Union
containing ethnic groups that have been
granted autonomous status. The size of
the areas depends upon the area of settlement of each group. The largest have been
given the status of Autonomous Soviet
Socialist Republics, Autonomous Oblasts,
and National Okrugs

jobs. Dinmukhamed Kunaev, first secretary of the Republican Party committee from 1964 to 1986, was able to consolidate the Kazakh grip on cadre positions, systematically appointing members of his own Great Horde (one of the three major Kazakh tribes) to top nomenklatura posts, while mollifying Brezhnev by inviting him to periodic duck shoots near Alma Ata. As a member of the CPSU Politburo, Kunaev was in a uniquely favorable position to attract investment to the republic, which he did to good effect in fuel generation, space exploration, meat, and grain. In Kirgizia, likewise, political appointments were usually handled by compromise among three regional groupings, each with its own tribal backbones, the Naryn bloc in the east, the Talas bloc in the west, and the Osh bloc in the south.[41]

Often these tribal and regional networks were tied into the "black" economy. In Uzbekistan Sharif Rashidov, first secretary from 1959 to 1983, enriched himself and his associates by exploiting the readiness of Gosplan officials to believe figures showing ever higher output. For more than two decades, Uzbek cotton production figures were systematically inflated, and by the 1980s Moscow was paying out more than a billion rubles annually for nonexistent cotton. Gosplan officials from Moscow, who knew no Uzbek and found local customs baffling, failed to get to the bottom of the discrepancies. At the same time, for the cotton that *was* produced, huge amounts of water were diverted from the rivers for irrigation, and fields were treated with toxic weedkillers and defoliants. The result was the gradual drying up of the Aral Sea, a catastrophic shortage of clean drinking water, and chronic dysentery among the local population.[42]

Rashidov and those like him did not use the proceeds of these scams simply for personal enrichment. He patronized a modest resurgence of scholarship concerned with Uzbek history and culture. He made sure that his supporters and tribal associates were well treated, and he lubricated branches of the economy which could make up for official shortages, at the same time providing jobs for protégés and dependents of protégés. One of them, a certain Adylov, director of a sovkhoz, was found later to have maintained several luxurious villas, stocked with racehorses and concubines. It was said that he loved to sit by a fountain in one of his villas, sipping Napoleon brandy, issuing orders, handing out reprimands, and, if the mood took him, having a recalcitrant vassal whipped.[43] Anyone from Moscow coming down to investigate rumored abuses of power would either be perplexed by the language and local culture or disarmed by a sensational display of homemade hospitality. Besides, Rashidov had the personal protection of Brezhnev's daughter, Galina, and the minister of the interior, N. A. Shchelokov, the superior of her husband, Iurii Churbanov, who used his hospitality and payoffs to purchase jewels, foreign cars, and works of art.[44] The benefits of these shenanigans did not flow to the population of Uzbekistan, and most certainly not to the Russians, who felt increasingly excluded from access to power and wealth.

In similar manner, during the 1960s the first secretary in Azerbaijan, V. U. Akhundov, presided over a flourishing unofficial economy, in which fast cars, drugs, sex, college entry, even, it was rumored, official posts, were available to anyone with wads of rubles. (Direct sale of office has not been reported from elsewhere in the Soviet Union, so one must regard the rumors with caution.) Akhundov covered his back by cultivating his superiors in Moscow, offering them expensive gifts and luxurious holidays within his territory.

Eventually, however, these extravagances became too conspicuous: they helped to ensure that the official Azerbaijani economy was one of the worst-performing in the country. In July 1969 Ivan Kapitonov, cadres secretary of the CPSU, supervised a meeting of the Azerbaijani CP Central Committee at which Akhundov was dismissed and replaced by Gaidar Aliev. Aliev criticized "intrigues, slander, backbiting and bribery" and appointments made through "personal attachments, friendly relations, family or neighbourhood ties," but this sentiment did not prevent him promoting colleagues and subordinates who had worked with him earlier in his career in the republican KGB and in the Nakhichevan Autonomous Region.[45]

In most non-Russian republics, the consolidation of power and resources in the hands of the titular nationality's patronage networks disadvantaged immigrants, including Russians themselves. Russians who had come in to take up jobs in science, industry, or administration in the decade or two after the war began to feel that they and their children were the victims of discrimination, as jobs, housing, and educational opportunities went to the locals. By 1979 the census revealed that interethnic integration, as exemplified by such measures as migration and intermarriage, had ceased to strengthen and was going into reverse. Russians were beginning to leave non-Russian republics, especially in central Asia, and return to the RSFSR.

In European parts of the Soviet Union traditional social structures had been more thoroughly shaken up during the twentieth century, and what was emerging was a new and broader sense of identity which we can properly call national, especially after the war. It was stimulated partly by the failures and repressive policies of the regime, but also by demographic changes which had been taking place over the previous generation. The massive urbanization which had been occurring from the 1930s to the 1960s on the whole followed the liquidation of illiteracy, especially among the young. Rural immigrants came to the towns not illiterate and speaking dialects, but already literate and aware of their own written language.

The effect was most marked in Ukraine, where up till the 1930s the towns had been largely Russian, Jewish, and Polish in population. Now they became significantly Ukrainized. By the 1950s an appreciable proportion of urban young people, especially in the west of the republic, spoke and wrote in Ukrainian and were beginning to develop their own literary culture, building on the tradition of Shevchenko. They did so, however, in the face of a strong and officially supported Russian culture which, especially in the east and south, usually assimilated newcomers. Many Ukrainians in the east and south saw their nationhood as part of a Russian-speaking Soviet multiethnic state, while in the west, with its Hapsburg and Polish traditions and its still strong underground Uniate Church, Ukrainian nationhood was understood as inherently anti-Russian. Urbanization thus greatly strengthened Ukrainian national sentiment, but also split it in two different, potentially opposed directions.[46]

Petro Shelest, first secretary of the Ukrainian Communist Party from 1963 to 1972, endeavored to enhance both the status and the internal cohesion of his republic by lobbying for more investment in Ukrainian industry, by increasing the proportion of Ukrainians in the party, and by upgrading the use of Ukrainian in secondary and higher education. As in tsarist times, however, the authorities in Moscow proved particularly sensitive to any suggestion of Ukrainian separatism, and Shelest was dismissed before he could achieve very much. His dismissal was followed by a wave of arrests among young poets who had been doing much to raise the standing of modern Ukrainian as a literary language. Among those detained was a literary critic, Ivan Dziuba, who had articulated anti-Russian Ukrainian nationalism in a samizdat publication. He argued that in the Soviet Union "internationalism" in fact meant Russification. He asserted that Ukraine was being deliberately exploited economically and that its language, culture, and history were being suppressed for the benefit of a Russian-dominated Soviet Union.[47]

In Belorussia the effect of urbanization was weaker, though perceptible. Belorussia's cultural and linguistic distinctiveness was less marked than that of Ukraine, and it had no Cossack heritage to act as the focus of national mythmaking. Its greatest pride was the partisan resistance movement it had mounted against the Germans during the Second World War. It achieved a certain autonomy in running its own affairs under the leadership of a group of former wartime partisans, headed by K. T. Mazurov.[48]

Urbanization had a similar "nationalizing" effect in Georgia and Armenia, where rural immigrants to the major cities, whatever their origin, tended to absorb Georgian or Armenian language and culture. In 1965 Armenians demonstrated in Erevan to mark the fiftieth anniversary of the Ottoman massacres, and demanded the return of territory surrendered to Turkey, while in 1978 street demonstrations in Tbilisi protested against an official plan to give the Russian language equal status with Georgian in the republic. The plan was withdrawn. Two samizdat journals edited by the literary scholar Zviad Gamsakhurdia recorded human rights violations and published Georgian-language works rejected by the censor.[49]

In the Baltic republics, urbanization had quite different results, for it drew in large numbers of Russian-speakers (some of whom were Belorussians or Ukrainians), especially into Estonia and Latvia, both as managers and as manual workers. In the towns of northeastern Estonia and in Riga, the capital of Latvia, Russians were in a considerable majority. The indigenous peoples felt that their national cultures were being both manipulated from above and threatened with encroachment from below. The local party secretaries showed considerable skill in maneuvering between the demands of Moscow and the resentments of their own peoples. Estonia, whose language was incomprehensible to virtually everyone from Moscow, discreetly developed a nonconformist culture in semipublic salons and concert halls.

In Lithuania urbanizing pressures were weaker, but the Lithuanians developed their own romantic nationalist tradition, inherited from a long love-hate relationship with the Poles. It manifested itself largely through the Catholic Church, whose underground *Chronicle,* tolerated but not officially supported by the ecclesiastical hierarchy, became a rich source of information on the violation of human rights in the republic. In 1972 a student, Roman Kalanta, set fire to himself in a square in Kaunas, under a banner inscribed "Freedom for Lithuania!" His death sparked off riots in the city: people swarmed through the streets, defacing Russian street names and setting fire to party and police buildings.

Similarly in Moldavia Russian-speaking immigrants accompanied new industry into the republic, most of it concentrated in urban settlements along the River Dniester. By 1970 Moldavians, though still a majority in the republic as a whole, formed only 35 percent of the urban population, while Russians and Ukrainians totaled 47 percent, and were also disproportionately represented in party and state positions. Moldavians were gradually being edged out into subordinate and rural positions and began to feel that they were losing control of their own national life, especially since the authorities did everything possible to emphasize their separateness from Romania.[50]

The Volga Tatars were even more vulnerable, even though they numbered six million, since they did not have their own Union republic, but merely an autonomous one within the RSFSR. The development of industry in the Volga-Kama basin attracted many Russian-speaking immigrants, and they were able to dominate the educational system in such a way as to outnumber Tatars by two to one in colleges and universities by 1970. In these circumstances, familiar enough from their earlier history, the Tatars sent their sons and daughters to study and acquire jobs elsewhere in the USSR, while at home they quietly generated a minor industry in the study of their own culture, religion, folklore, and history, from the Bulgar khanate onward. They discreetly but firmly practiced Islam, like their central Asian cousins, but with the difference that Sufism was widespread in the Volga region, and fitted its brotherhoods and study circles deftly into the niches of Soviet everyday life. Pan-Turkic ideas, however, were strictly taboo and found expression only in the occasional samizdat pamphlet.[51]

The Jews were in a very distinctive position. Though downright persecution of them had ceased after Stalin's death, they remained uniquely disadvantaged. Semiofficial discrimination against them continued: although many urban Jews had assimilated entirely to Russian culture and language, "entry no. 5" on their passports often debarred them from jobs, housing, or specialist education, reminding them forcibly of their Jewish identity. The truth about the holocaust was concealed from the Soviet public: when the two best-known wartime journalists, Ilia Erenburg and Vasilii Grossman, compiled a "Black Book" enumerating Nazi atrocities against Jews on Soviet territory, they were forbidden to publish it.[52] Hebrew was a forbidden language, and Yiddish was not taught in schools.

Unlike other Soviet nationalities, however, Jews had a potential alternative homeland, the state of Israel. Some decided that they could not live a national life in the Soviet Union and began campaigning for the right to emigrate. The Jewish samizdat journal was, significantly, named *Exodus*. In February 1971 Jews organized a mass sit-in at the Supreme Soviet building in Moscow. It was broken up, but, unexpectedly, the result was that exit visas were granted to some of its participants. This was a decision taken at the highest level, and reflected the priority which the leaders were currently giving to good relations with the United States. Granting visas to some applicants but not to others also had the advantage, from the authorities' point of view, that it caused uncertainty and resentment, and sometimes thereby split Jewish families and communities. A new word entered the vocabulary of the international human rights movement to designate those who had been turned down or whose applications were left in limbo: refusenik.

In some ways the strangest situation of all was that of the Russians. They dominated the Central Committee of the Communist Party, the armed forces, and the security police. Their language was always acceptable and sometimes dominant in non-Russian republics. Their history and culture were taught in all schools and universities. Yet all the same, many Russians felt that their national identity had been decisively undermined by the Soviet authorities. Their leading spokesman was Aleksandr Solzhenitsyn. In his "Letter to the Soviet Authorities" of 1974 (published in the West but not in the USSR), he laid out Russian demographic losses from terror, alcoholism, thoughtless urbanization, industrialization, agricultural collectivization, and involvement in international terrorism and revolution. He charged that Russian culture and religion were being destroyed through censorship and persecution deployed in the name of a faceless internationalist ideology. He proposed that Russia abandon its international commitments and its hypertrophied heavy industry and withdraw into itself, taking the opportunity to develop its agriculture, crafts, and small-scale manufacture, and opening up the neglected territories of Siberia.

Although by the early 1970s Solzhenitsyn's work was prohibited, and he himself was exiled to the West in 1974, there were many professional people and intellectuals inside Russia who largely agreed with him. What they had diagnosed, of course, was the continued dominance of Russian imperial over Russian ethnic and civic priorities. As we have seen, one or two literary journals made themselves the bearers of revived Russian ethnic identity, which was embodied in the wave of "village prose," fiction focusing on the village and recalling the pre-urban solidarity of Russian peasant communities. These works were tolerated, perhaps even encouraged, by the ideological authorities; their writers were the first to reveal the realities of rural poverty, and even some of the truth about collectivization, which had so long been concealed behind official rhetoric.[53] They were widely read, an indication that many Russians were anxious to discover a way of being Russian which did not depend on empire.

During the Brezhnev era official religious policy did not change fundamentally, but was applied in a much more hesitant and even reluctant manner. Partly, this was because of the emergence of semiorganized religious dissent, which created its own networks of activists and links with foreign media. Most effective were the Baptists, who broke away from their official church, refusing to abide by the restrictions on proselytization it had accepted, and set up their own Sunday schools, summer camps, and even a printing press, as well as an action group for the support of their own imprisoned and persecuted members. There was evidence, too, that many young people were wearing crosses or collecting icons, partly as a way of flaunting their individuality, but partly perhaps as a mode of search for spiritual values not evident in life around them.

Most important of all, though, was that religion had become part of the revival of Russian patriotism which in other areas the Brezhnev regime was cautiously encouraging. Writers, especially of the "village prose" school, were permitted to write of churches and icons as symbols of continuing Russian identity, and even to permit themselves a cautious and unspecific approval of the behavior of traditional religious believers, as upholders of a stable social morality.[54]

By the 1970s ethnic conflict was beginning to affect the institution which had hitherto been the epitome of multinational solidarity: the armed forces. More and more new recruits, especially those from the Baltic, the Caucasus, or central Asia, were being deliberately victimized by their seniors in an unruly form of hazing known as *dedovshchina*. Sometimes their humiliations resulted in serious injury or even death, unleashing vengeance and inter-ethnic conflict. The armed forces were ceasing to be what Brezhnev had hailed as a "school of internationalism."[55]

As far as the nationalities are concerned, no single overall pattern of development can be discerned. Each region of the Soviet Union had its own peculiarities. But the deliberate nation-building policies of the 1920s, never completely revoked, together with the general Soviet commitment to urbanization, had very powerful long-term effects. In one form or another, most markedly in the Baltic, least so in central Asia, national consciousness was becoming stronger even where regime policies aimed to discourage or suppress it. Old national cultures were broadening out from elites to masses, and new nations were forming under conditions of extreme pressure. As a result, when crisis hit the Soviet Union, it inevitably expressed itself in inter-ethnic conflict.

The two crucial regions were Ukraine and the Baltic republics—Ukraine because it was and remained the key to Russian domination of the Union, the Baltic republics because they were the only countries whose population remembered, directly or indirectly, civil society and independent nationhood.

15

FROM PERESTROIKA TO THE
RUSSIAN FEDERATION

THE ADVENT OF GORBACHEV

By the early 1980s the long-simmering internal crisis of Soviet society was undermining the country's economic productivity, her moral standing in the world, and her great-power status. The road to utopia had long ago been lost, and claims to parity with the United States were beginning to sound hollow. The protracted and unresolved crises in Poland and Afghanistan were confusing and demoralizing. The Soviet model of socialism had ceased to be attractive to most third world countries, as Soviet leaders discovered in their travels around the world. The Soviet Union's weight in the world depended entirely on military strength, and even that was being undermined by the faltering performance of the economy.

When Brezhnev died in October 1982, his immediate successor was Iurii Andropov, who had been head of the KGB from 1967 until he moved into the party Secretariat in May 1982. An intelligent, austere, and incorruptible figure, he set about investigating corruption and tightening labor discipline. But he became fatally ill before he could have a significant impact on either problem.

His disciple and preferred successor was Mikhail Gorbachev, former first secretary in the southern Russian oblast of Stavropol, who had joined the Politburo as its agricultural overseer in 1978. He was a relatively young and energetic figure, whose arrival presaged serious and lasting change. On Andropov's death in February 1984, the Politburo at first elected Brezhnev's elderly crony, Konstantin Chernenko. He endured a mere thirteen months of ill health, however, and in March 1985 the Politburo finally took the plunge: Gorbachev became general secretary.

570   Their decision is evidence that by this time most if not all Politburo members were aware that their country faced a serious crisis and would need a relatively young man of determination and courage to solve it. Gorbachev was unusual among his colleagues in the Politburo and Secretariat not only in being younger, but also in having a law degree from Moscow University (most of them had graduated either in a technical subject or from the Party High School). He had thus been exposed in his youth to a curriculum which included the history of political thought, diplomacy, and international law, and hence to the Western "bourgeois democratic" traditions which early generations of European Marxists had taken for granted.[1] As first party secretary in Stavropol in the 1970s, he had shown some signs of a distinctive approach to agriculture when he revived the wartime "link" system, under which brigades of fifteen to thirty individuals were assigned a fixed area of land, together with seeds and equipment, and paid according to their results.

"NEW THINKING" IN FOREIGN POLICY

From his earliest days in the Politburo, Gorbachev had taken the opportunities afforded by high office to inform himself more widely on Soviet problems and to discuss frankly ideas for overcoming them. He was able to consult with experts from Central Committee departments and scholars from the policy studies institutes, whose function was to study international affairs and the social, political, and economic systems of other countries as the basis for a better-informed and more effective diplomacy. Gorbachev was naturally a warm, outgoing person, relatively unsophisticated as yet but interested in ideas and fascinated by serious debate—if rather fond of the sound of his own voice. In the institutes he found a milieu much more congenial than among his Politburo colleagues: well-informed, urbane, and cosmopolitan intellectuals whose thinking had taken them far along the road leading back to the Western roots of Marxism and even beyond, to bourgeois liberalism and social democracy. Some of his interlocutors bemoaned the intellectual impoverishment and sclerotic complacency of official Soviet Marxist dogma. As one of them said, "We have spurned the Old and New Testaments; only the Psalms remain."[2]

The first policy studies institute had been established as early as 1957, in the first era of "peaceful coexistence." The most influential of them were the Institute for the Study of the United States and Canada, under Georgii Arbatov, and the Institute of the World Economy and International Relations (IMEMO), which in 1983 passed under the leadership of Aleksandr Iakovlev, former head of the Central Committee Propaganda Department, who had been dismissed in 1972 for criticizing Russian nationalism.

Their members published articles in the media and in scholarly journals, but also wrote much franker memoranda for circulation to the political leaders, sometimes making recommendations for reform drawn from foreign experience. During the 1960s and 1970s they reported positively on Keynesian economics, the welfare state, and the formation of the European Economic Community. They argued that capitalism was proving able to adapt itself to the modern world and that its governments, not necessarily merely the tools of greedy industrial bosses, saw advantages in cooperating with socialist powers on matters such as disarmament, trade, and environmental policy. Mikhail Suslov, the party's chief ideologist, was worried by their approach: he grumbled about "oppositional platforms," and in 1981 tried to have IMEMO closed down, but there was sufficient support for it among members of the Politburo for him to be overruled.[3]

What restrained party leaders from suppressing the irritant missives was partly the need for ideological ammunition in the long ideological conflict with China, which made "Westernizing" perspectives more acceptable, and partly the imperative of good relationships with European Communist parties, especially those of the Warsaw Pact. In addition to this, for instrumental reasons, the Soviet Union had long been supporting Western peace movements, and some in the foreign policy establishment longed to do so for genuine rather than manipulative reasons, and to observe some of the restraint which those peace movements urged on their own governments.[4] The journal *Problemy mira i sotsializma* (Problems of Peace and Socialism), edited in Prague by A. M. Rumiantsev, had been deeply affected by the "Prague spring" of 1968, and adopted a discourse close to that of Western socialists: from it came such later Gorbachev advisers as Anatolii Cherniaev, Georgii Shakhnazarov, and Vadim Zagladin. Similarly, the Central Committee Department for Relations with Socialist Parties, headed in the 1960s by Iurii Andropov, was well versed in the possibilities offered by alternative models of socialism: from it Gorbachev drew on the advice of Shakhnazarov, Fedor Burlatskii, Aleksandr Bovin, and Oleg Bogomolov.[5]

By the mid-1980s, even before Gorbachev's accession, Soviet leaders had come to the conclusion that fomenting revolution in the third world was too expensive and did not really enhance the security of their country. In a way, they had already been pursuing an alternative policy for decades, since alongside the attempts to provoke and sustain anti-imperialist revolutions in the third world the pursuit of "peaceful coexistence" had never been entirely abandoned. Indeed during the 1970s and 1980s, even as the USSR was expanding its arsenal of armaments almost without restraint, it was also meeting and concluding agreements with the major Western powers on "security and cooperation," such as the one in Helsinki in 1975. The needs of an increasingly decrepit economic system compelled it more and more to rely on imports of Western equipment to ensure that at least in certain key sectors it remained abreast of the latest technology. By the late 1970s, moreover, up to 40 percent of hard currency in foreign trade was being spent on agricultural produce, in order to maintain the informal "social contract" with the townsfolk (low pay in return for cheap food).[6]

In many ways, then, the Soviet Union already depended on friendly, or at least cooperative, ties with the West even while it was deploying a rhetoric of confrontation. Advances made by the United States in computer-guided weapons compelled the Soviet leaders by the mid-1980s to try to eliminate this contradiction and to forge a coherent strategy. This is what became known as the "new thinking," already largely formulated by autumn 1984. The Soviet Union had reached the condition which Paul Kennedy dubbed "imperial overstretch," when an imperial power is devoting so much of its economy to military preparedness that other sectors of the economy are drained, overall economic efficiency is impaired, and eventually military production suffers too. A vicious circle is set up which renders retreat from excessive ambition imperative.[7]

Gorbachev and his foreign minister, Eduard Shevardnadze, had come to the conclusion that the Soviet Union was overstretched, and moreover that it was counterproductive to seek security by relentlessly accumulating armaments, since they nourished "enemy images" of the Soviet Union in the populations and governments of other countries and impelled them to rearm as well, to the mutual insecurity of everyone.

Nor was it just a matter of dismantling weaponry. Gorbachev and Shevardnadze had a broader vision, both political and geopolitical, of a "common European home," a Europe united by diverse variants of socialism and democracy—something like an idealized version of 1944–1947, when the Soviet Union had been at its most powerful in the military, diplomatic, and moral senses, when Communists had been welcomed by populations overjoyed to see the end of the Nazis, and when neo–Popular Front coalitions had been in power in several east European countries. Gorbachev was supported by some of the west European Communist Parties, notably the Italian one, and he was prepared to make concessions to Europeans to realize his vision. "The time had come for us to acknowledge that, even by Cold War logic, Soviet superiority in conventional weaponry in Europe stopped making political sense the moment we had reached nuclear parity with the USA. On the contrary, this situation helped to maintain the image of the Soviet Union as the enemy, thus creating ever new threats to our own security."[8]

Gorbachev's enthusiastic, at times almost reckless pursuit of this vision was in a thoroughly Russian tradition of peacemaking tsars and foreign ministers, conscious of their country's poverty and vulnerability, trying to build pan-European structures of peace. In some ways he reminds one of Alexander I, preaching a universal gospel of peace and brotherly love and trying to embody it in the Holy Alliance. Only Gorbachev was operating from a posture of perceived near-defeat rather than victory.

He took his first step by trying to bounce Reagan into a mutual and complete renunciation of nuclear weapons at Reykjavik in 1986. Having failed there, he pressed ahead by another route: in December 1987 in Washington the United States and the USSR signed an agreement phasing out all intermediate-range missiles. Then in a speech to the United Nations General Assembly in December 1988 Gorbachev explicitly renounced the "primacy of the class struggle" and the notion of the superiority of socialism as cardinal components of Soviet foreign policy doctrine. "The vital imperative which faces mankind is the priority of all-human values, a world without violence and wars, diversity of social progress, dialogue and cooperation for the sake of development and the preservation of civilization, and movement toward a new world order."[9]

By this time there was a veritable "Gorbachev cult" in western Europe and even in the United States. Wherever he went on official visits, to Milan, to London, to Bonn, to New York, his motorcade had to edge its way through cheering crowds, and he would leap impatiently out of his car to shake hands with delighted onlookers. Nor were his declarations mere empty words. They were part of a policy which during 1988–89 withdrew Soviet troops from Afghanistan, accepted the scrapping of medium-range nuclear missiles and a reduction in conventional arms, ceased to support terrorist and Communist movements throughout the world, cut the number of troops on the Chinese border, and eventually accommodated itself to the abolition of Comecon and the Warsaw Pact, that is, the dismantling of Communist domination of central and eastern Europe.

THE FALL OF COMMUNISM IN CENTRAL EUROPE

The renunciation of central Europe was the most painful sacrifice: it meant loss of the dominions which the Soviet Union had conquered as the result of the most destructive war in history. Gorbachev and his advisers had come to the conclusion that forcing the central and east European peoples to live under regimes they found profoundly distasteful—forcefully "saddling cows," as Stalin might have put it—was not reinforcing the Soviet Union's security but rather was jeopardizing it.

For their part, most of the Warsaw Pact leaders were dubious about Gorbachev and uneasy about his *perestroika* reform program, fearing that any weakening of one-party authority could lead to their own overthrow. When Gorbachev visited East Berlin in October 1989, his host, Erich Honecker, was horrified to be confronted by demonstrators from the party youth movement parading with the slogan "Perestroika! Gorbachev! Help us!"[10]

The Hungarian Communists formed the major exception. The threat of the Romanian leader, Nicolae Ceaușescu, to raze several thousand Hungarian villages in Transylvania prompted them to take a super-Gorbachevian reformist line: in January 1989 they permitted alternative political parties, and in May Imre Nagy was reburied with honors. The Communists sought to recreate the 1944–1947 alliance with the Social Democrats, as Nagy had proposed in 1956. Soviet diplomats, hesitantly at first, let it be known that the Brezhnev doctrine would not be enforced. Gennadii Gerasimov, foreign ministry spokesman, spoke jocularly of its being replaced by a "Sinatra doctrine": "Do it your way!" In Poland Solidarity was relegalized and then carried the day in free elections, so that in August 1989 a non-Communist prime minister, Tadeusz Mazowiecki, took office for the first time in central Europe in more than forty years.

About the same time, the Hungarian leaders opened their border with Austria. This step had decisive effects not in their own country but in the German Democratic Republic (GDR): by October more than thirty thousand of its citizens had exploited the opening to emigrate to West Germany. In the course of the debate on how to stem this process, Honecker was overthrown, and a reform Communist leadership raised the possibility of allowing limited travel across the Berlin Wall. The mere posing of the question transformed the situation. On 9 November huge East Berlin crowds gathered to demonstrate alongside the wall. Some demonstrators began to scale it—and no one was prepared to use machine guns to prevent them.

The GDR leaders knew by this time that they would receive no Soviet support for a policy of violent repression. Their decision to refrain doomed their own state, the Warsaw Pact, Communism in central and eastern Europe, and arguably the Soviet Union itself. Nothing would be the same again once it was demonstrated that an unarmed peaceful crowd could dismantle the front line of the Communist system.

Not that this was immediately apparent. Gorbachev undoubtedly hoped that the collapse of the Berlin Wall would be followed by far-reaching democratic reforms in the GDR, so that the two Germanies could form a closer relationship, as harbinger of a rapprochement between NATO and the Warsaw Pact and the establishment of stable and peaceful international relations throughout Europe.[11]

This was a diplomat's vision, and it was a humane and generous one. What Gorbachev had not taken into account was the influence ordinary people have in a genuine democracy. (It was the same partial blindness which led him to ignore the importance of being popularly elected in the USSR—the trump card which Yeltsin held against him.) Fundamentally it was the mood of the German people which thwarted him, filtered through the energetic diplomacy of the Federal Republic's chancellor, Helmut Kohl. The latter's espousal of reunification on the West's terms at first upset and dismayed Gorbachev.[12] But he had to yield to plain evidence that Germans overwhelmingly supported Kohl: East Germans were leaving their country in droves, and their economy was disintegrating. In March 1990 Kohl's Christian Democratic Union won 40 percent of the vote in GDR elections and was able to form a government, after which it was merely a matter of time before the country was absorbed by the Federal Republic.

Gorbachev tried to save what he could from this debacle. In return for conceding a united Germany inside NATO, he insisted that the West Germans sign a nonaggression pact with the USSR, reduce their armed forces, finance the withdrawal of Warsaw Pact troops from the territory of the former GDR, and renounce nuclear and chemical weapons. He also stipulated that the Conference on Security and Cooperation in Europe (guarantor of the Helsinki process) should be strengthened so that it could intervene to warn of and prevent or curtail violent conflicts. The result of this was the Paris "Charter for a New Europe" of November 1990, which reaffirmed that the two European military pacts were now working together as partners, and created for the Council for Security and Cooperation in Europe a permanent secretariat, consultative committee, and conflict prevention center.[13]

ECONOMIC AND POLITICAL REFORM

In internal affairs Gorbachev's advisers had no coherent alternative program ready for implementation. His early thinking flowed from the advice he had inherited from the KGB and from Andropov: that the economy and the party-state apparatus were riddled with corruption and embroiled with the unofficial and criminal economy, and that the time had come to clean things up. This was the policy Andropov pursued during his brief tenure of office in 1982–1984.

It was also Gorbachev's during his first year or two. He set about the dismissal and in some cases criminal investigation of officials who had grossly abused their office for personal gain. He set up a state inspectorate (Gospriemka) to examine products leaving factories, reject those unfit for sale or use, and dock the pay of workers and managers responsible. He called for "acceleration" (*uskorenie*) of work processes, tightened labor discipline, and invoked the feats of the legendary overproducing Donbass miner of the 1930s, Aleksei Stakhanov. He restricted the sale of alcoholic liquor and banned it at official receptions, thus affronting traditional Russian notions of hospitality and celebration. Two of the people whom Gorbachev helped into top positions, Egor Ligachev and Boris Yeltsin, were "authoritarian puritans" who supported determined measures to root out privilege, corruption, and slovenliness. Later they were to become bitter opponents as their recipes for achieving this diverged sharply.

It is probably also in this spirit that we should understand the promulgation of Gorbachev's policy of *glasnost*—frankness or openness—which figured in his very earliest speeches. Initially it meant exposing instances of official corruption or incompetence, so that the socialist economy could function properly. Stalin too had pursued such a policy as part of his purges, encouraging ordinary workers or collective farmers to denounce their bosses, in order to eradicate the cosy cliques obstructing the lines of command.

The extent of the malpractices which glasnost disclosed surprised, even horrified Gorbachev. Party leaders often did not know much about them, since they were shielded from the difficulties experienced by ordinary people, and knew well only the areas of their departmental concern. Meeting workers in Kuibyshev and Toliatti, two typical large industrial towns, he found the workers enthusiastic about his proposed reforms, but the party-state officials cool and reserved. As he remarked later, "My desire to learn the true state of affairs clearly did not suit the local bosses. My talking directly to the people so upset some of them that they tactlessly tried to break in." Even in his own former bailiwick, Stavropol, he had the impression that "No one was against perestroika. Everyone was 'for it.' But nothing was changing."[14] In 1986 at a meeting of writers he spoke of being up against "a managerial stratum, a ministerial and party apparatus which . . . does not want to give up . . . its privileges." He even began to speak of the virtues of having a political opposition.[15] Once he began to mobilize writers and members of the intelligentsia to back him in this struggle, glasnost broadened its boundaries in a way which eventually proved to be uncontrollable, for by now its proponents had a rich and semisuppressed reservoir of information and ideas to draw upon.

The Chernobyl explosion of April 1986 probably did more than any other single event to dramatize the dangers to which the population was exposed by irresponsible and incompetent officials. In Gorbachev's own words, it "shed light on many of the sicknesses of our system as a whole. Everything that had built up over the years converged in this drama: the concealing or hushing up of accidents and other bad news, irresponsibility and carelessness, slipshod work, wholesale drunkenness."[16]

While for the first few days the official response to the explosion was the traditional one of denial and coverup—probably because Gorbachev himself did not realize how serious it was—it was reversed within a fortnight, and thereafter perestroika moved in new and unexpected directions.[17] Gorbachev approved personnel changes designed to encourage a freer flow of information and ideas: the appointments of Vitalii Korotich and Egor Iakovlev as editors of two popular weeklies, *Ogonek* (The Beacon) and *Moskovskie novosti* (Moscow News), and of Sergei Zalygin and Grigorii Baklanov as editors of the literary monthlies *Novyi mir* and *Znamia* (The Banner). The climax of this stage of "personified glasnost" was reached in December 1986, when Andrei Sakharov was permitted to return from Gorkii to Moscow and given carte blanche to express his opinions in public. Gorbachev welcomed his support for "new thinking" in international affairs, and was prepared to accept some criticism in return. Thereafter many "prisoners of conscience," confined for their espousal of human rights, were released from prisons and labor camps.

Over the next year or two the revitalized periodicals, and others inspired by their example, began at first tentatively, then with increasing self-confidence, to publish works of literature which had been banned for most of the decades of Soviet rule, from Pasternak's *Doctor Zhivago* to Solzhenitsyn's *Gulag Archipelago* and Vasilii Grossman's *Forever Flowing*, works which indicted Lenin as the ultimate progenitor of the horrors of Communist rule.[18]

Glasnost was the first and in a sense the easiest stage. In launching the economic and political reforms, Gorbachev was up against a fundamental dilemma. His principal enemies were the patron-client networks whose influence he wished to eradicate in the economic and political systems. Yet he depended for his power on the supreme patron-client network, the one run by the Secretariat of the CPSU, of which he was the head. The process of reform thus compelled him to saw away at the branch which held him aloft. It is scarcely surprising that in the process he had to adopt some undignified postures.

Apart from glasnost, his first priority was economic reform, since the malfunctioning of the economy was the most obvious threat both to "building socialism" and to the great-power status of the Soviet Union. His economic reform of 1986–1988 had three main lines. The Law on Individual Labor Activity legalized individual and family enterprise of the kind which had long flourished on the black market, providing small-scale services which the state economy was too inflexible to offer. The Law on the State Enterprise freed enterprises from ministerial directives, democratized their internal structure, gave them greater control over their own budgets, including the prices they charged for their wares, and required them to be "self-financing," that is, to make a profit. The Law on Cooperatives made it legal to open joint-stock companies, provided all the shareholders were employees of the company.

The problem with all these reforms was that they operated within the confines of an economic system still mainly run by the state and still plagued by shortages. The new private firms could and did raise their prices to take advantage of lively demand and short supply. State firms clamored for permission to do the same, to exploit their dominant position in a stunted market. Moreover, all firms continued to rely on state supply allocation for most of the goods and tools they required to carry on their businesses. Often they used the same "pushers" and informal suppliers, linking them with the old unofficial economy and its rough-and-ready semilegal devices. Only now, the greater freedom of the private firms gave them greater clout.

As a result, the private sector sucked goods out of the state sector, aggravating already serious shortages. As someone from Saratov complained in *Pravda,* "In the shops everything has vanished, but in the private markets there is more and more. How does it get there? You have to pay 250 to 300 rubles for a pair of women's boots. My daughter needs some, but she earns only 115 rubles a month."[19] During 1989 inflation—hitherto an evil unknown to Soviet citizens—was beginning to take hold, while certain categories of goods became so scarce that they were for sale only to customers who could show their passports to prove that they lived in the same town or oblast as the shop in which they were making their purchases. Ordinary Soviet citizens had begun by welcoming the new cooperative restaurants, boutiques, and car-repair shops, where they could find goods and services previously available only on the black market. They soon began to grumble, though, at the high prices charged there and to suspect profiteering. And they started to feel nervous that further market reform would deprive them of many of the public services—housing, transport, education, health care—which they had hitherto enjoyed free of charge or at minimal cost.[20]

579

The workers, who were supposed to benefit both from economic modernization and from the democratization of enterprises, actually suffered from the changes. Gorbachev resurrected memories of "workers' control", 1917 style, by establishing Councils of Labor Collectives, elected by the workforce, to take key decisions on production plans, disposal of profits, and social funds. In practice these councils were usually dominated by management, since workers had no experience of organizing themselves to run meaningful election campaigns, and soon found themselves operating in a deteriorating climate which severely circumscribed their freedom of action. In 1989–90 the councils were phased out as perestroika entered a new stage.[21]

By now workers and other ordinary consumers were losing out heavily as economic reform disrupted the patronage networks and personal arrangements through which they had previously secured scarce goods and services. The pressures of economic reform prompted workers to take strike action, at first to demand the improvement in pay and conditions they had long been promised, then at a later stage to reverse the erosion of the modest but tangible social benefits they derived from the old regime. However, because their immediate bosses were constrained by the demands of "self-financing," their demands were soon fed upward and became overtly political, woven into the fabric of an increasingly complicated political struggle in the republican capitals and in Moscow.

The first major strike movement, in the coalmining regions of Donbass, Kuzbass, Vorkuta, and Karaganda in July 1989, grew out of long-pent-up demands for better pay, housing, social facilities, and working conditions. When the first strikers, from Mezhdurechensk in the Kuzbass, had their demands rejected by the local bosses *and trade unions,* they paraded in front of the Communist Party headquarters. Within two days M. I. Shchadov, minister of the coal industry, came down from Moscow to negotiate with them. Deprived of support from the party-run trade unions, miners here and in other towns set up their own local strike committees, which improvised social services during the stoppage. Blocked by the bureaucracy, they began to demand political changes, including the abolition of the Communist Party's "leading role" in government.

These and later strikes eventually crumbled. The workers' position was simply too weak; anyway fundamentally they were appealing for the restoration of benevolent patronage. At a time when the economic climate was becoming harsher, they were more dependent than ever on the benefits handed out by the management and administered by the trade unions. Most workers were reluctant to be seen defying both. Alternatively, they could be persuaded that the sovereignty of their republic or its transfer to a full market economy would solve all their problems—both serious delusions. As a result, time and again strikes fizzled out with their leaders accepting promises which could never be fulfilled. Either that or they were bought off by one party or the other in the many-sided struggle engulfing the USSR in its last years.[22]

Even brief experience of economic reform was enough to convince Gorbachev that the Soviet Union's main internal problem was political. He decided he needed to mobilize public opinion at large against the party-state apparatus, which was either obstructing or perverting reform. In the summer of 1988 he called a special conference of the CPSU to discuss reform of the electoral and legislative systems. He persuaded the conference to accept the idea of a move toward genuine parliamentarism by allowing real elections to take place, with alternative candidates, to a new Congress of People's Deputies, of 2,250 members, which would be the supreme legislature, delegating day-to-day representative duties to a revamped Supreme Soviet of 450 deputies chosen from among the Congress's own members. This was still some way from representative democracy as that is normally understood. For one thing, one-third of the Congress was to be chosen from candidates nominated by "social organizations," all of which had Communist Party cells at their center. All candidates nominated had to be confirmed at public meetings where one could expect the local apparat to throw its weight around. Still, the new system was a great advance on the meaningless elections of the past.

It certainly enabled informal political movements to mobilize for the first time. Until 1986 the Soviet Union's lively unofficial culture was allowed no expression on the streets or in the public media. But in that year unofficial human rights journals with names like *Ekspress-khronika* and *Glasnost* began to be sold openly in places like Moscow's Gogol Boulevard. Initiative groups were set up to defend historical buildings from demolition (such as the Hotel Angleterre in Leningrad, where the poet Sergei Esenin had committed suicide) or to protest against environmental pollution. In Latvia 30,000 people signed a petition against the construction of a hydroelectric power station on the Daugava River; in Erevan 2,000 demonstrated on the streets against the construction of a nuclear power station, and in Ufa a similar number marched with banners warning against a planned chemical factory and demanding "Clean Air for Ufa!" In Moscow's Gorkii Park an unofficial "Group for Establishing Trust between the USSR and the USA" distributed leaflets explaining the dangers of nuclear fallout and recommending precautions members of the public could take.[23]

581

These early initiatives focused on matters of "motherhood and apple pie": no one could argue that historic buildings, the environment, and nuclear power were not issues of legitimate public concern. The experience of taking action on them brought people together, encouraged them to seek solutions to wider problems, and propelled them into the arena of political conflict. Seminars were held, some of them in academy institutes, with members of the public admitted, to make policy recommendations. An ongoing seminar at the Central Economic-Mathematical Institute in Moscow turned itself in 1987 into the Klub Perestroika, which drew up proposals for the forthcoming enterprise reform, then turned to other questions of social reform. One of its offshoots was the society Memorial, set up to agitate for a public memorial to Stalin's victims and to conduct thorough research into the illegal repressions of the past. During the summer and autumn of 1988 Memorial collected signatures on the street for a petition, and in November it held a "week of conscience" in a number of Russian cities. In Moscow a "wall of memory" was erected, where photographs of the repressed and "disappeared" were exhibited behind a convict's wheelbarrow where visitors could place their donations toward a memorial.[24]

By now these informal movements were moving on from "safe" issues to raise fundamental questions about the past, and by implication about the right of the Communist Party to continue its monopoly of the political system. As the historian Iurii Afanasiev said at the founding congress of Memorial in January 1989: "The most important task of Memorial is to restore to the country its past. But the past is alive in the present. Therefore Memorial is a political movement, for today has not settled accounts with yesterday."[25] It was also a forum which linked young and unknown people with renowned public figures like Sakharov and Solzhenitsyn, literary scholars like Dmitrii Likhachev, writers like Evgenii Evtushenko and Bulat Okudzhava, and journal editors like Vitalii Korotich, in the pursuit of aims which till recently would have provoked immediate political repression. Broad ranks of the urban population began to become accustomed to the idea that they could confront the party-state apparatus over fundamental civic issues.

The first elections to the Congress of People's Deputies, held under the new procedure in March 1989, returned a safe majority of traditional nomenklatura nominees. All the same there were a few sensational upsets in which official candidates were defeated for the first time in seventy years. In some big cities, and in the more rebellious republics, informal and independent public associations organized themselves effectively enough to get their candidates nominated and confirmed, and then to campaign for them. Their most sensational triumph was in Moscow, where Boris Yeltsin garnered 90 percent of the vote to trounce the apparat candidate, the director of the ZIL automobile works. Apparat nominees were also defeated in a few other Russian towns, but the most telling losses were in the Baltic republics, where most seats were won by the Popular Fronts.

The first meeting of the new Congress, in May 1989, represented a climax of glasnost. It was televised live, and many citizens took time off work to watch delegates mount the rostrum one after another to denounce the apparat's abuses of power. Generals were grilled on their crowd control methods, ministers on their probity and competence, and the government as a whole on the consequences of its reform policies. It was a feast of public debate, the last and greatest "return of the repressed," adorned by the quiet but insistent presence of Andrei Sakharov, and presided over by Gorbachev in a sometimes brusque but not wholly intolerant manner.

NATIONALITIES

If public opinion could manifest itself in this way in Russia, then the effect was even more powerful in the non-Russian republics. The process caught on most rapidly in the Baltic, with its interwar constitutional traditions. In Estonia, Latvia, and Lithuania, activists began by demanding better protection of the environment, a more secure status for their languages in publication and education, and defense of the rights of religious believers. With remarkable speed they moved on to the fundamental question of whether their incorporation in the Soviet Union had been legal at all. Huge demonstrations took place to mark national anniversaries, and speakers demanded publication of the secret protocols of the Nazi-Soviet pact of 1939. Since that pact had subsequently been repudiated, they argued, it followed that the incorporation of the Baltic states into the USSR had been illegal in the eyes of international law. Arguments of this kind united former dissident nationalists with reformist figures from the local Communist parties. Together they set up Popular Fronts in the Baltic republics and Moldavia to agitate publicly and conduct election campaigns: they proved remarkably successful at focusing disparate strands of political opinion, whose only common feature was opposition to Russian domination and the Communist political monopoly.

In Ukraine a Popular Front came much later, but from 1987 the unofficial Culturological Club claimed that the Ukrainian language was being gradually squeezed out by Russian in publishing and in the educational system. Activists also called for disclosure of full evidence about the Ukrainian famine of 1932–1934 and the filling in of other "blank pages" in Ukraine's history. In Belorussia the discovery of mass graves outside the capital city, Minsk, provoked the setting up of an informal association called "Martyrology," which proposed the building of a memorial to Stalin's victims and a thorough investigation of his crimes. In both Ukraine and Belorussia oppositionists blamed Russians as much as Communists for their sufferings, even in cases such as the Chernobyl disaster, which had no ethnic dimension whatever.

Similarly, when in December 1986 Gorbachev, as part of his anticorruption drive, dismissed Kunaev as first party secretary in Kazakhstan and sent in a Russian, Gennadii Kolbin, to take over as the clean broom, Kazakhs reacted to his appointment as an ethnic slight, and anti-Russian riots broke out in the capital, Alma Ata. The perpetuation of patron-client networks as a system of political control both personalized and ethnicized conflict once that control was weakened. Ethnic patronage, as practiced for so long in the Soviet Union, encouraged the view that all ills resulted from the evil behavior of another ethnos and generated the tendency to subsume all problems in nationalist agitation.

We can observe the same process in the Caucasus. In Armenia the issues were even more explosive. Protests soon focused on the problem of Nagornyi Karabakh, the pastoral and mountainous region to the east of the Armenian SSR, which had been awarded to Azerbaijan in 1921. A Karabakh Committee was set up, the rough equivalent of the Baltic Popular Fronts. The way in which patronage worked within the Azerbaijani Republic ensured that Armenians were disadvantaged in Karabakh even though they formed three-quarters of the population. In January 1988 a petition with tens of thousands of names was sent to Moscow, demanding a referendum within Karabakh on the region's future, and this was followed by massive demonstrations both in Erevan and in Karabakh itself. Gorbachev appealed for calm while the party considered the issue. The demonstrations ceased, but calm did not ensue: on 28 February riots broke out in Sumgait, an Azerbaijani industrial town where many Armenians lived. For two days thugs roamed the streets before the army restored order, and some thirty people, mostly Armenians, were killed.

The Azerbaijanis were suspicious of Armenians, not only as Christians but also as influential people who looked as if they were close to the centers of power. That the authorities had unprecedentedly permitted demonstrations demanding Azerbaijani territory confirmed them in the view that there was a concerted anti-Azerbaijani conspiracy in high places, to which they reacted with blind fury.[26]

584

In Georgia a number of nationalist groups emerged in 1987–88, divided by personal conflicts but agreeing on the need to promote Georgian culture and language, defend their environment, and prevent Moscow from using the Abkhaz and Ossetian national movements to fragment the republic. In April 1989 massive public demonstrations took place in Tbilisi; they began as a protest against plans for Abkhazian secession from Georgia, but rapidly moved on to demand Georgian independence from the Soviet Union. The Georgian Communist authorities appealed to Moscow for help, and on 9 April Soviet Army and Interior Ministry troops forcibly cleared the crowds off the streets and squares of central Tbilisi. In the process they killed at least twenty people with poison gas and sharpened trenching tools.[27]

This was a major turning point, partly because it was the first time massive state violence had been used against demonstrators, but also because it brought to a critical level tensions which had been building up inside the armed forces. This was the moment when the military found themselves thrust into explosive conflict situations by politicians who had lost control. The experience was repeated in January 1990, when the Azerbaijani Popular Front launched a pogrom against Armenians living in Baku and seemed on the point of seizing political power in the republic. Some of the Front's members tore down guardposts on the Soviet-Iranian border in order to reunite the two halves of their people. The Soviet army was ordered in, not to stop the pogrom, which had already run its course, but to reestablish the border, secure key facilities in the city, and assist in the restoration of Communist power. In doing so, they killed at least 130 people.[28]

This was not just a crisis in civilian-military relations. The Communist Party and the "coercive forces" (including the armed services, KGB, and Interior Ministry troops) had been so closely intertwined that a crisis in one automatically became a crisis in the other. In February 1990 an army division refused to move into Dushanbe, the capital of Tajikistan, to suppress rioting, because the officers feared that if they obeyed orders, they might subsequently be disavowed and held responsible for the inevitable violence.[29]

THE END OF THE USSR

From the autumn of 1989 Soviet citizens could see, daily on their television sets, what happened when Communist rule was no longer maintained by force. They saw First Secretary Miloš Jakeš removed in Prague by a "velvet" revolution and Ceauşescu in Bucharest by a bloody one. Some of them liked it, some of them did not. Their differences now mattered. Previously, imperial authorities, Russian and Soviet, had always been able to make concessions to foreign "enemies" whenever they held it expedient, without provoking domestic political protest. Now, however, democratization generated an extra dimension to foreign policy: the loss of empire and the degradation of the USSR's status as great power called forth outspoken public opposition at home. The effect was to create an explicit alliance of two political tendencies which had previously been at arm's length from each other, the Russian nationalists (really imperialists) and the imperial Marxist-Leninists. In new-found unanimity, they denounced Gorbachev and Shevardnadze as traitors and declared their intention of saving the Russian-Soviet empire. They created first of all a "Bolshevik platform" within the CPSU, and then during 1990 a Russian Communist Party, nominally within the CPSU but actually in opposition to it, or at any rate to Gorbachev's leadership of it.

In 1990 Gorbachev loosened the electoral procedure one stage further by amending article 6 of the Soviet constitution to end the Communist Party's monopoly and legalize the formation of alternative political parties. At the time elections to the Supreme Soviets of the union republics were imminent, and for the most part new political parties did not have time to organize themselves and participate effectively. All the same, those elections transformed the political scene yet again. For one thing, they fatally weakened the Communist Party's executive power: more or less since 1917 it had been the effective focus of state authority, coordinating and directing whatever was undertaken by public bodies of all kinds. Its abdication of this function left a great vacuum at the center of politics. Gorbachev attempted to fill it by creating the post of President of the USSR and having himself elected to it by the Congress of People's Deputies. But the new presidency had no real executive chain of command of its own. In any case, Gorbachev, never having been confirmed by popular election, lacked the legitimacy of, say, a U.S. president. This want of either symbolic or substantive authority undermined him fatally over the next year and a half as economic crisis and interethnic conflict engulfed his reform program.

Even more important, the new elections, together with the demonstration effect from central Europe, undermined the Soviet Union itself. During 1990 several Union republic leaders, fortified by the voting figures, declared themselves sovereign states and insisted that their laws took precedence over those of the USSR. In March 1990 Lithuania went even further and declared its secession from the USSR. Latvia and Estonia soon followed suit with somewhat greater caution, announcing the start of a transition period toward independence. Gorbachev reacted with an economic blockade of Lithuania, which proved largely ineffective.

This was the point of no return. If a Union republic could declare itself independent of the USSR and get away with it, then the future of the whole Union was open to question. The Baltic republics, with their memories of national independence, democracy, and civil society, were the pioneers, and in 1988–1990 they played their hand with what looked like reckless boldness in seeking exit from the Soviet Union rather than reform.[30]

The most threatening challenger to the Union, however, was its largest but hitherto most docile member, the Russian Republic itself. By the spring of 1990 it had a formidable political leader: Boris Yeltsin, speaker of the Russian Supreme Soviet. In June 1991 he became president of Russia in the first election ever held to choose a Russian leader. He now not only led the largest republic, but enjoyed the legitimacy conferred by a popular mandate.

Yeltsin had gained a strong following because he had stood up to a system generally seen as hopelessly corrupt, and because he seemed to embody the one aspect of Communism which had remained popular, its aspiration to social justice. In his party secretaryships in Sverdlovsk and Moscow, he had demonstratively declined to avail himself of the privileges most senior appointees took for granted. Instead he traveled on public transport and occasionally appeared in grocery stores, where he would ask ordinary shoppers about their lives and sometimes expose assistants hiding superior produce for their bosses. In October 1987 he was dismissed from his Moscow post because he attacked Gorbachev for taking perestroika too slowly, and in pique he resigned from the Politburo. No party figure had ever come back from such a reverse before, but democratization made Yeltsin the exception: in his campaigning he managed to give ordinary voters the impression that he cared about their everyday problems over shopping, transport, housing, corruption, and crime. In August 1990, for example, he told a rapt audience of coalminers in Kemerevo that their housing and work conditions were so appalling because they were being robbed by the party-state elite.[31]

However, he still needed a political movement to organize his campaigns. This was Democratic Russia, formed in January 1990 by delegates from a number of informal prodemocratic associations. Its stated aim was to propagate "the ideas of Andrei Sakharov," meaning a commitment to "liberty, democracy, the rights of man, a multiparty system, free elections, and a market economy."[32] But Sakharov had died the previous month, and the new organization actually began the erosion of some of his ideas. Its very name was a challenge to received ideas: democrats, including Sakharov, had always assumed that their concepts applied to the Soviet Union as a whole. The two words "democratic" and "Russia" had hardly ever been used together before, and it had not occurred to many people that, if they were, they implied the dissolution of the Soviet Union, as an empire held together by nondemocratic means.

587

As a result of the efforts of Democratic Russia, democrats did much better in the March 1990 RSFSR elections than they had the previous year in the all-Union ones. They won absolute majorities in the city soviets of Moscow and Leningrad, as well as in a number of other industrial towns. They used this victory to demand that all power within the RSFSR, including the military and the KGB, pass to the Russian Congress of People's Deputies.[33]

This platform gave Yeltsin the perfect means to outflank Gorbachev and formed the basis of his campaign to become Russian president in 1991. In adopting it, he was turning to his personal advantage Russia's deepest historical problem: its anomalous situation inside its own empire. He was using Russia to challenge the Soviet Union. It is not clear that he saw the logic of his personal vendetta, and he was certainly embarking on a dangerous game, for it exposed the whole ambiguity and frailty of Russia as a political concept. He distanced himself from traditional Russian nationalists, proponents of ethnic Russian domination of the Soviet Union, and instead espoused the concept of Russia as a democratic state, in the Western sense, as one among a confederation. Pointedly, he used the civic term *rossiiskie* rather than the ethnic *russkie*. But he had no solution to the dual problem of what was to happen to *russkie* living outside the Russian republic or to the autonomous territories named after non-Russian ethnic groups within the Russian republic. To the latter he gave a hostage to fortune with his promise that they could "take as much independence as you can handle."[34]

Together, Gorbachev's foreign policy and Yeltsin's Russian challenge provoked the newly allied imperial Communists and Russian nationalists to active resistance. They struck first in the decisive region, the Baltic. In January 1991 anonymous "National Salvation Committees" issued statements in Latvia and Lithuania saying that they were ready to assume power to "avert an economic collapse" and prevent the establishment of a "bourgeois dictatorship." Paratroopers and special Interior Ministry riot troops seized press and television buildings in Vilnius and Riga. When they advanced on the Lithuanian Supreme Soviet building, thousands of people gathered and linked arms to bar their way. In the resultant fighting fourteen people were killed in Vilnius and six in Riga. Yeltsin condemned the assaults, and they were not pressed home. Gorbachev, whether or not he initiated the offensive, called them off.

Unable or unwilling to bolster the Union by force, Gorbachev decided instead to forestall the threatened disintegration by a negotiated renewal of the Union Treaty of 1922. The proposed new treaty, agreed in advance with Yeltsin, would end the "war of sovereignties" by devolving most powers to the constituent republics while leaving the Union in charge of military affairs, foreign policy, and the currency. In March 1991 an outline of the new treaty was approved in a popular referendum throughout the Soviet Union.

Most republican leaders outside the Baltic indicated their readiness to sign up to the new arrangements. But on 19 August, the day before the ratification ceremony was due to take place, a self-styled Emergency Committee, led by the vice-president, Gennadii Ianaev, announced that Gorbachev was ill and declared a state of emergency "with the aim of overcoming the profound and comprehensive crisis, political, ethnic, and civil strife, chaos and anarchy which threaten the lives and security of the citizens of the Soviet Union."[35] Apart from Ianaev, the leading members of the Emergency Committee were Interior Minister Boris Pugo, Defense Minister Dmitrii Iazov, and head of the KGB Vladimir Kriuchkov—all Gorbachev appointees. They brought troops and tanks into Moscow and prepared to assault the White House, the Russian Supreme Soviet building.

Their coup had been planned long before, but all the same it was poorly managed. It suffered from an inner contradiction, summed up aptly by General Aleksandr Lebed, deputy commander of the paratroops: "How could these people seize power? They were already the very embodiment of authority!"[36] Hitherto the forces of coercion and the CPSU leadership had been identical; now the two were deeply divided from one another. The Emergency Committee was trying to restore a concept of law and authority whose foundations had already been undermined—undermined moreover by the party leadership itself. It was relying on a military chain of command which had been fatally disrupted. It was expecting passive compliance from a population thoroughly stirred up by two years of genuine politics.

Above all, the nominally federal structure of the USSR (which Lenin had insisted on in 1921–22) gave republican leaders both the right and the incentive to assert themselves once it became clear that the center's control had slackened. The ambiguous arrangement which had held together the various nationalities for decades now became a fatal weakness. That logic applied with redoubled force to Russia. When tanks were sent to surround the White House, the Russian parliament building, Yeltsin was able to clamber onto one of them and to disarm the coup morally by declaring it "a state crime" against the "legally elected authority of the Russian Republic."[37] Those who obeyed the coup leaders would, he promised, be punished under the Russian criminal code. By this time thousands of people of all kinds had come to surround the White House as a symbol of freedom, and their presence ensured that if the Russian president and parliament were to be stormed, it could be done only at the cost of heavy bloodshed.

This prospect was quite sufficient to provoke fatal hesitation in the minds of officers and soldiers sent to crush resistance to the Emergency Committee. If they were going to fire on unarmed crowds, they wanted to be quite certain that the order to do so was legal. But legality was now divided, between the Russian and Soviet authorities, and some commanders hedged their bets. Why no assault was launched on the White House from 19 through 21 August remains uncertain. According to some accounts, the Alpha Group special unit sat down, in a spirit reminiscent of 1917, debated whether or not to do so, and in the end decided that an attack was probably illegal. According to other accounts, no order was in fact ever given, because of confused planning and fear of taking responsibility for bloodshed.

589

Instead, the Emergency Committee behaved with characteristic ambivalence and made for the Crimea to attempt a deal with Gorbachev. Whether or not he had given them any grounds for hoping that a deal was possible, he now waved them aside. After some hesitation which suggests ambivalence on his side too, they were arrested.[38]

This was the real end of the Soviet Union. The political system to which Gorbachev returned the next day was transformed, though it took him a little while to realize it. Within a few days Yeltsin had suspended the legality of the CPSU while its complicity in the coup was investigated, Ukraine had declared itself independent, and most other republics had followed suit, some willingly, others with trepidation. All the nomenklatura leaders at republican level had understood by now that they could no longer rely on Moscow to back them up, and that they must create a new power base at home in alliance with nationalist intellectuals and their own elites.

Over the next few months Gorbachev tried to revive the project of a Union Treaty, even more decentralized, with only a vague coordinating role for the center in military and foreign policy. But republican leaders were evasive, and when on 1 December a popular referendum endorsed the independence of Ukraine, the efforts were finally abandoned. As Gorbachev had warned voters in March, "There can be no Union without Ukraine." Yeltsin met Leonid Kravchuk and Stanislav Shushkevich, leaders of Ukraine and Belorussia, in the Belovezh forest outside Minsk. Together they declared that "the USSR, as a subject of international law and a geopolitical reality, has ceased to exist."[39] In its place they established a "Commonwealth of Independent States" and invited other republics to join it. As envisaged, it would maintain unified strategic armed forces and constitute a single economic space; but it would have no president, and its central institutions, to be located in Minsk rather than Moscow, would be purely advisory.

Gorbachev, characteristically, at first protested that the Belovezh resolution was illegal, then more realistically warned that the end of the USSR would mean economic breakdown and interethnic conflict. Finally he bowed to the inevitable. On 25 December he announced on television that he was resigning the post of USSR president. On the Kremlin roof the hammer and sickle was lowered and replaced by the pre-1917 Russian tricolor, without the double-headed eagle. The Soviet Union and its indwelling spirit, the CPSU, had passed into history.

It was not clear what was to replace either. The new Commonwealth was vague and intangible in its conception, and none of the other republics had been consulted about its establishment. All the same, most of them accepted the invitation to join it, except Estonia, Latvia, Lithuania, and Georgia, where anti-Russian feeling remained very strong.

PRESIDENT VERSUS LEGISLATURE

Even within Russia itself the demise of the CPSU left a huge gap in the authority structure. Without its coordinating executive role, the institutions of state succumbed almost completely to their own clannish networks, competing for control over material wealth and the means of coercion. Heading the struggle were on the one side the president and on the other the chairman of the Supreme Soviet, Ruslan Khasbulatov, a wily Chechen who had begun as a follower of Yeltsin but spotted the chance to break loose and form his own clientele, using the bran-tub of goodies available to the Supreme Soviet—Moscow flats, cars, foreign trips—and backed up by the armed parliamentary guards. The Soviet constitution, which survived *faute de mieux* until it could be replaced, had always in theory accorded supreme power to the legislature, though in practice the Communist Party had always exercised it. Now, however, real authority devolved on the Supreme Soviet, loosening the cement which had previously ensured stability, and opening the way for a naked confrontation between executive and legislature—reminiscent in some ways of that which convulsed England in the mid-seventeenth century.

The only way to avoid open conflict would have been to essay the arts of compromise and to draw up a new, agreed constitution as soon as possible. Both sides were unwilling to do this. Yeltsin, though a maverick in recent years, was also a well-tried apparatchik accustomed to Soviet-style authoritarian clannishness, and he did not see it as part of his duties to mollify demanding and refractory deputies (as any U.S. president has to spend much of his time doing). Khasbulatov, for his part, knew that a new constitution would probably deprive his domain of much of its standing, and he managed to attract to his side Aleksandr Rutskoi, the vice-president, for whom Yeltsin had neglected to provide functions consistent with his dignity.

Some commentators afterward reproached Yeltsin for not dissolving the Supreme Soviet and calling new elections in the autumn of 1991, so as to clear away the remains of the Soviet era and lay a fresh and stable foundation for the new politics. Actually, it was almost inconceivable that he should do so: he had just won a joint victory in solidarity with the deputies, and in any case in October 1991 they granted him special powers to carry through his reforms. A year later, however, his powers expired, competition over the spoils of office was starting to take its toll, and many deputies were beginning to act as spokesmen—their proper function, after all—for the very large number of people doing badly out of economic reform and the collapse of the Soviet Union: the old, the sick, the disadvantaged, the managers and workers of heavy industry, the refugees, and the Russians living outside the Russian Federation. In the absence of a disciplined cohort of party caucuses, fortuitous majorities could be assembled for irresponsible resolutions, such as declaring Sevastopol (base of the Black Sea fleet in the Crimea and therefore part of newly independent Ukraine) to be Russian territory or providing for a budget deficit amounting to 25 percent of gross domestic product.

In March 1993 Yeltsin decided that the continuing standoff and the failure to pass a new constitution were damaging Russia's stability. He made a television address in which he appeared to initiate the process of reviving rule by decree. But in the face of opposition even from some of his own supporters, he backed down. The opposition in the Supreme Soviet then launched a campaign for his impeachment which only just failed to muster the necessary number of votes. Instead the Soviet insisted that a referendum be held, in which voters would be asked whether (i) they had confidence in the president, (ii) they approved of his socioeconomic policies, (iii) they wanted preterm presidential elections, (iv) they wanted pre-term parliamentary elections.

The result on 25 April was a qualified victory for Yeltsin. Fifty-eight percent of those who voted expressed confidence in him, and 53 percent (to most people's surprise) approved his policies; 50 percent called for presidential elections, and 67 percent for parliamentary ones.[40]

This was the moment when, if ever, Yeltsin could have claimed explicit popular support for exceeding his powers under the creaking ex-Soviet constitution, dissolving parliament and announcing fresh elections. He chose not to do so, but instead to steer round the Supreme Soviet by putting up his own version of the new constitution, and then trying to persuade the heads of republics and regions to support it at a special constitutional conference. This was a far more risky course, since not all the local bosses supported Yeltsin's proposals, and some of them—the heads of the titular non-Russian republics, notably Tatarstan, Bashkortostan, and Sakha-Iakutia (Chechnia pointedly boycotted the whole process)—were seeking special concessions for their own fiefdoms. A constitutional conference in June–July 1993 agreed on a draft close to the president's but ended without settling the issue of the regions, and it became clear during the late summer that not enough "subjects of the Federation" (regions and republics) would accept the draft to give it legitimacy.

Accordingly, on 21 September, Yeltsin appeared again on television, this time to declare that his attempts to reach a compromise with the deputies had failed. The existing constitution offered no way out of the deadlock, and "the security of Russia and its people was of higher value than formal compliance with the contradictory norms created by a legislative power which has utterly discredited itself." He announced that he was therefore issuing Decree no. 1400, dissolving the Supreme Soviet and setting elections for a new legislature to take place in mid-December. They would be followed six months later by presidential elections.[41]

The Supreme Soviet, forewarned, was already in session in the White House. It declared Yeltsin's decree unconstitutional, deposed him as president, swore in Rutskoi in his place, and appointed its own ministers of defense, security, and the interior—two of them men recently dismissed by Yeltsin for corruption. As the parliamentarians had their own armed guards, and could summon the paramilitaries of people like Aleksandr Barkashov, leader of the fascist Russian National Unity movement, the stage was set for violent confrontation from the outset. All the same, Yeltsin was slow to impose a blockade on the White House, and by the time he did many armed men and weapons were inside, ready to defend it or to break out and assault strategic points in the capital. A lot of deputies, finding their company distasteful, quit the White House, leaving behind a rump of about two hundred. These appealed for nationwide strikes and for support from the armed forces and the regions. Workers and soldiers did not respond, but some regional leaders did, if equivocally: a gathering of sixty-two (out of eighty-eight) leaders of "subjects of the Federation" called on Yeltsin to rescind Decree no. 1400 and return to the status quo before 21 September, then declare simultaneous presidential and parliamentary elections.

Attempts were made to mediate between the two sides, notably by Patriarch Aleksii of the Russian Orthodox Church. But on 3 October, before negotiations could get anywhere, thousands of opposition demonstrators gathered in October Square, under the statue of Lenin, and then marched down the ring road to the White House. They broke the blockade, and Rutskoi came out on the balcony to address them. He called on them to attack the office of the Moscow mayor and the Ostankino television station. Armed formations left the White House to storm both buildings, taking the mayor's office and occupying part of Ostankino for some six hours, during which time most television channels stopped transmission.

A state of emergency was declared, and Yeltsin flew to the Kremlin by helicopter. He spent most of the night persuading Pavel Grachev, the minister of defense, and the generals to send in army units to storm the White House. He found them extremely reluctant to take responsibility in a political conflict, perhaps because of their post-1989 experiences, or perhaps because it was not yet obvious who would win. As Yeltsin subsequently recalled, "They looked gloomy, and many of them lowered their gaze. Even they could understand the absurdity of the situation: legitimate authority hung by a single hair, and the army could not defend it, because some units were away digging potatoes and others did not want to fight." Eventually Aleksandr Korzhakov, head of the president's bodyguard, produced an assault plan, ironically prepared by the putschists in August 1991 but not put into action then. The generals reluctantly agreed to implement it, but Grachev demanded written confirmation from Yeltsin that he was authorized to use tanks in the middle of Moscow.[42]

At seven in the morning of 4 October those tanks rumbled onto the New Arbat bridge, opposite the White House. For the next few hours they fired high-explosive shells into the parliament building, before the cameras of CNN, which brought the spectacle straight to the world, as if it were a Wimbledon tennis final. By midafternoon, white flags were displayed from the windows, and Khasbulatov, Rutskoi, and their followers emerged, white-faced and shaken, to surrender and be taken off to Lefortovo Prison. According to official figures, 144 people had been killed in the fighting; according to unofficial ones, several times that number.

Many Russian commentators, and a few Western ones, have suggested that the whole affair of 3–4 October was deliberately staged by Yeltsin in order to have an excuse to overwhelm his opponents while retaining the support of the Western powers.[43] This seems to be one of those paranoid fantasies which is bred by tribal politics. No serious evidence for it has ever emerged, and it is inherently improbable that Yeltsin, impulsive though he was, would have taken such huge risks without even lining up the necessary armed units for his planned counterattack. Much more likely, and wholly in character, is that his contingency plans were vague and that he simply neglected to prepare adequately for a possible armed confrontation. That failure could have been extremely serious, for the seizure of Ostankino very nearly succeeded. Had it done so, and opposition politicians had begun broadcasting their version of events throughout Russia, it is quite possible that local politicians and military leaders would have joined them. In short, on the night of 3–4 October 1993 Russia was on the brink of civil war between executive and legislature.

In one sense the defeat of the White House occupants was the final end of the Soviet era. The last Russian politicians elected in a still more or less Soviet system were sent packing, and the way was opened for Yeltsin to complete his reforms. Yet in another sense, it was Yeltsin's greatest failure to date. The whole world, and of course many Russians, had watched his troops reduce the White House, the home of their parliament, to a blackened and smoking shell, with terrible bloodshed. The lingering idealism of the democrats was finally shattered.

Certainly, when the election results of December 1993 were declared, it became obvious that Yeltsin had suffered a serious reverse. The democratic politicians, gathered at a televised banquet in the Kremlin, arranged to celebrate their triumph, fell silent as the bulletins began to come in from the first regions to declare their results. The real victors, it transpired, were the so-called Liberal Democrats, headed by Vladimir Zhirinovskii, who consistently outpolled the government party, Russia's Choice, in the party lists. The effect was partly deceptive, for once the constituency results were also declared, Russia's Choice finished with slightly more seats than the Liberal Democrats. All the same, since Russia's Choice expected a comfortable victory, the publicity effect of their relatively modest performance was stunning. In the flurry, it passed almost unnoticed that Yeltsin's constitution had received 58 percent of votes cast, enough to legitimate it.

In retrospect it is a little clearer why Zhirinovskii did so well. He had run an effective if mendacious television campaign, offering the Russian people simple solutions to complex problems: free vodka, huge profits from increased arms sales, a restored Soviet Union (nay Russian Empire, including Finland and Alaska), hegemony over Persia and India, and to hell with the West. His style and image were almost a caricature of Yeltsin's, and they had their roots in Russian realities as perceived by ordinary people. Like Yeltsin, he posed both as victim and as dominating man of power—and in truth Russians had found themselves in both roles over the centuries, especially within living memory. In his autobiography, Zhirinovskii recounted his childhood in Kazakhstan as a hungry, ill-clothed lad, living in a cramped communal apartment because the Kazakhs received all the more spacious ones, and neglected by his mother because she had to work so hard. Generalizing from his experience, he commented: "We smashed the Germans and sent man into space, but in the process destroyed families and our sense of history . . . We mutilated our country. We turned it into a backward place, compelling the Russian nation, which had at one time occupied the vanguard, to retreat."[44] He was a buffoon—but a dangerous buffoon—pirouetting between nation and empire, and offering Russians alluring images of both.

595

Zhirinovskii had the advantage of being neither a Communist nor a democrat—both now hated for different reasons by most of the electorate. Moreover, since the proposed constitution allotted only modest powers to the new parliament, the State Duma, voters were free to treat the elections to it in the way British voters treat by-elections: as an opportunity to kick the government in the teeth without overthrowing it. A vote for Zhirinovskii was both a warning to Yeltsin and a subliminal, if backhanded, confirmation of support for him (Zhirinovskii was the only opposition politician who had backed Yeltsin throughout the crisis).

The December 1993 elections also marked the beginning of the return of the Communist Party, restored to legality after being banned in August 1991, but much changed by its sojourn in the wilderness. It had emerged not from the CPSU, but from the *Russian* Communist Party, set up in opposition to Gorbachev in the last year of Soviet power. It had completely jettisoned the Western "bourgeois" element (and most of the Marxism too) in the Soviet Communist synthesis, leaving Russian imperial nationalism as the main content of the revised ideology. This change was summed up in the person and thought of the party's new leader, Gennadii Ziuganov.

To anyone who had observed the bitter antireligious campaigns of Lenin, Stalin, and Khrushchev, the greatest surprise must have been the new reconciliation between Communism and Orthodox Christianity. The demise of empire had removed the final barriers between the two belief systems. Ziuganov preached that the Russians were still a peculiarly egalitarian and communal people, and maintained that Russian socialism had its origins as much in the teachings of Jesus Christ as in those of Karl Marx. Besides, according to him, Orthodoxy had played the leading role in creating Russian statehood and reviving it when it was under pressure; it had acted as the main conduit of literacy, enlightenment, and culture. Now that culture was being threatened by debased Western imports, such as pornography and pop music, while the great Russian tradition in science and education was being allowed to wither away for lack of state funding. Gorbachev and Yeltsin had jointly betrayed Russia to the Western powers, which were now preparing to turn their erstwhile rival into an impoverished provider of raw materials, and to weaken it by both military and spiritual means.[45] By the time of the elections of December 1995, this message had even greater resonance, NATO having meanwhile announced that it intended to expand eastward to take in some of the members of the former Warsaw Pact, and the Communists were returned as much the largest party in the Duma.

ECONOMIC REFORM AND ITS RESULTS

Gorbachev had never found a way out of the crisis of shortages and inflation unleashed by his reforms. Some advisers felt he should move much more boldly toward a free market, but he never committed himself fully. With Yeltsin in power there were to be no further equivocations over reform, and no more talk of a "third way" between socialism and laissez-faire capitalism. He was determined to move unambiguously toward the market, and to do so in the manner already adopted in Poland, described by some as "shock therapy." In a speech of 28 October 1991 he announced that privatization of state property would be accelerated, prices would no longer be controlled, the currency would be stabilized, state subsidies would be drastically cut, and the budget would be balanced.

To carry out this program Yeltsin appointed a team of bright and arrogant young economists mostly in their thirties from the Central Economic-Mathematical Institute, headed by Egor Gaidar, who had recently set up a think-tank called the Institute for Market Reform. They were disciples of Hayek, Friedman, and Thatcher, and also of the Polish reformer Leszek Balcerowicz. They asserted that Russia was not "special," that it was subject to the same economic laws as any other country, that it must abandon the pernicious practices of state socialism—indeed socialism of any kind—and do so as quickly as possible, for to delay would be to prolong the inevitable agony of the transition.

They believed that swift marketization was the right way not only to restore productivity to the economy, but also to secure political freedoms. As Anatolii Chubais liked to say, quoting his mentor, Hayek, "A market economy is the guarantee not just of the effective use of financial and natural resources . . . but also of a free society and of the independence of the citizen."[46]

The strategic situation of these "boys in pink pants" (as their opponents soon dubbed them) was paradoxical. Till recently their economic models had been purely academic, so distant from reality as to seem little more than an entertaining and defiant game. Furthermore, though democrats by conviction, they had received their mandate to reform not from parliament, political parties, or the institutions of civil society, but from a president ruling by decree. Even though Gaidar was appointed deputy prime minister, they scarcely regarded themselves as politicians, rather as technicians hired to do a job which the previous discredited "experts" had bungled. They had few illusions about the resistance they would face: Gaidar termed his team a "kamikaze" administration and half-expected to end in prison. What perhaps they did not foresee was that their measures would actually *strengthen* some of the more unruly and archaic features of the Soviet system. Once again, in the Russian context, the attempt to leap "from darkness into light" reinforced much of what was being repudiated.

The reformers would have liked to have more time at their disposal, to carry out their measures in a planned and coordinated way. But the crisis of the old system compelled them to act immediately. There was a looming shortage of food supplies in the cities, region was ceasing to trade with region, the official debt was swelling out of control. Action needed to be taken urgently to restore some equilibrium to a market economy which actually already existed, in a highly distorted form.

Gaidar decided to begin with the freeing of prices, on 2 January 1992. They rose by about 400 percent during the first month, and continued upward thereafter. In any other European country, this would have caused immediate massive demonstrations, probably riots, and the fall of the government.

Russia was different. First of all, many people had plenty of savings, accumulated through years of not having much to buy in the shops, and they hastened to spend them, while they were still worth something, to purchase survival for a few more months. Second, people in a productive part of the economy could now sell goods at much higher prices and make a decent profit; indeed, with the opening up of international trade, they could sometimes sell it abroad at an indecent profit. Third, not all prices were actually freed: gas, electricity, housing, public transport, and some foodstuffs remained controlled. These concessions enabled ordinary people to survive, but created massive problems for municipal councils, many of whose expenses had risen, while their income remained low.

There is no doubt, however, that the price rises inaugurated a period of poverty and acute uncertainty for many, especially since they were soon accompanied by the first efforts to balance the state budget by cutting welfare expenditure. Accumulated savings were soon wiped out—faster than in Germany after the First World War. Pensioners saw the accumulations of decades vanish in a few weeks. Many people had to find new ways of making money. The least fortunate could soon be found lined up outside city markets or Metro stations, selling pathetic bundles of flowers, matches, kittens, old clothes, whatever they thought someone might be willing to buy. The slightly more fortunate put up makeshift booths or kiosks from which to conduct a somewhat more regular trade. Beggars appeared on the streets, some of them old people or invalids. Others simply spent more time on their allotments, growing food which previously they would have bought, or they called on the resources of *blat* (informal exchange), relying on a network of family, workmates, and friends to keep them afloat.

The health service, always underfunded and subsisting on bribery, now became more or less overtly a paid service, which meant that many ceased to use it. Illness and mortality rates increased appreciably, especially among small children and middle-aged men—the latter caused partly by increased stress, as people tried to find new ways of making ends meet. Alcoholism and suicide rates rose sharply, especially among men.

Yet during the following years anyone visiting Russia regularly could not help being aware that a substantial minority of people were better off than before. As shops began to fill with imported goods—food, clothes, consumer durables—customers appeared to buy them, not just in a few exclusive shops, but in provincial towns all over the country. Wealth was being generated somewhere, and was trickling down to an appreciable proportion of the population.

One does not have to look far to see where it was coming from. Already in the Gorbachev years state and party officials had begun to convert their de facto control over the means of production into a *de jure* ownership. They had used funds and property available to the party and the ministries to set up joint ventures with foreign firms, to acquire export businesses, to lease premises, or to redevelop urban property. The earliest organization to take advantage of these possibilities was the Komsomol, which, to combat falling enrollments, began in the mid-1980s to decentralize and diversify into nonpolitical activities of interest to young people. It set up "centers for scientific-technical creativity," where they could convert ideas into commercial ventures, and backed them with a "Commercial Youth Bank." Soon the nomenklatura elite as a whole were imitating the process, with the much greater resources at their disposal. They would convert their assets into cash, use their position to obtain cheap credits, and trade abroad, profiting from unbalanced exchange rates, or within the Soviet Union, exploiting the differential between the subsidized and nonsubsidized sectors of the economy. In such ways huge sums of money could be made in a short time.[47]

The post-Soviet privatization program impelled the process further. The law of June 1992 under which it was accomplished allowed managers and workforce to acquire a 51 percent stake in any enterprise being privatized, usually very cheaply. This became the normal route to privatization, and since the managers were nearly always able to buy out the workers afterward, the old nomenklatura bosses were soon firmly in the driving seat at shareholders' meetings. By 1994 about half of Russia's workforce was in the private sector, but usually in firms being run by very familiar faces.[48]

To portray them completely cynically would be unfair. They wanted to line their own pockets, certainly, but most of them also felt a responsibility for their employees, who looked to them not just for an income, but also usually for a whole range of social benefits. Some managers were running factories so large that whole towns depended on them. Like feudal lords, the new-old entrepreneurs enjoyed their personal power and wealth, but wanted to see their retainers do well too.

Their struggle to achieve these aims constitutes one of the main political and economic battles of the early post-Soviet years. For in the brave new world of free trade their firms were mostly terribly vulnerable. Some of them, especially in military industry, were producing high-quality items which the state was no longer purchasing. For the rest, decades of state protection, underinvestment, and outmoded technology had left them incapable of producing goods that any customer outside a siege economy would want to buy. In any case, they were unused to looking for customers: previously the purchasers of their products had had nowhere else to turn, and marketing skills had been superfluous. Now all that abruptly changed. The word "marketing," a more than usually graceless neologism, entered the Russian language, and consultancies specializing in it began to spring up in many towns.

For most of the industrial dinosaurs, however, there was no option but to turn to the familiar source of income, the state, either as customer or as provider of subsidies and cheap credits. Formerly money had followed the plan, as a mere accounting unit which enabled it to be implemented and did not cost anything. Few could adjust to the idea that things had changed, that money had a real cost, that issuing too much of it meant inflation, and that that in turn was equivalent to grossly inequitable taxation, robbing the poor to enrich the rich.

But what was the alternative? To let whole cities go bankrupt, when there was not even a bankruptcy law to cope with the consequences? That is what was argued by Viktor Gerashchenko, the chairman of the State Bank, echoed by many deputies in the Supreme Soviet (and after 1993 in the State Duma). With the tacit agreement of Egor Gaidar, and later of the next prime minister, Viktor Chernomyrdin, he minted money in huge quantities to tide ailing enterprises over difficulties to which no end was visible. Many of those enterprises survived after a fashion for years, partly on subsidy, partly by not settling their debts, partly by paying their workers very late in inflated rubles, and partly by laying them off. For their part, workers were willing to continue their attachment to the enterprises at almost any price, since it meant their housing and other benefits were secure. If they were not paid, they simply spent more time on their allotments or in moonlighting. After all, this was merely a blunter version of the old Soviet social contract: "They pretend to pay us, and we pretend to work." Unemployment figures thus stayed relatively low. Inflation, however, continued to soar: in 1992 it was 2,323 percent, and in 1993 still 844 percent.[49]

One of the firms which was most successful in operating this system was Gazprom, formed in 1989 from the installations run by the Soviet Ministry of Gas, headed by Viktor Chernomyrdin. Converted into a joint-stock company in 1992 and privatized in 1994, it negotiated for itself a series of tax breaks and used its huge size to buy up ailing and therefore cheap enterprises: shipping companies, airlines, hotels, farms, and food-processing plants. It thus became a huge conglomerate, employing 360,000 people and with at least five million more wholly or partly dependent on it. Its size, and protection from Chernomyrdin, who was prime minister from 1992 to 1998, gave it enviable bargaining power, for who would want to reduce five million people to sudden penury? It continued to withhold taxes, claiming that firms and municipalities were not paying for the energy it provided; it kept its accounts closed and refused to undertake serious restructuring.[50]

No other firm had quite the clout of Gazprom, but its conduct was not untypical and showed why Russia was largely unsuccessful in obtaining what it vitally needed, foreign investment to enable it to restructure its industries and bring them up to international standards of technology, design, marketing, and servicing. Foreign businessmen who made the pilgrimage to Russia often found that their counterparts there regarded investment not as an opportunity to transform their enterprises, but as a new kind of subsidy to enable them to continue shouldering their social responsibilities. It scarcely needs adding that affluent Russians avoided investment in their own industries for the same reason, and instead exported their funds to foreign stock exchanges or bank accounts, or used them to buy speedboats, sports cars, luxury country houses, and other forms of ostentatious wealth.

In the meantime, the state, having sold much of the productive economy to the revivified nomenklatura and the "new Russians" at knockdown prices, was itself bankrupt. It tried to keep going by decreeing very high rates of taxation, which were a disincentive both to investment and to honest business. Those firms—a large number—which did most of their business by barter or by accumulating debt were in any case impossible to tax effectively. Business life became a grueling story of systematic tax evasion punctuated by unannounced tax inspectors' visits to examine accounts and assets. By 1996 the treasury was so desperate that the government set up a Temporary Extraordinary Commission with special powers to raid and investigate suspected evaders; its initials (VChK) recalled, presumably deliberately, the dreaded Soviet security police of the civil war years.[51]

A second stage of privatization, in 1995–96, brought many of the more profitable privatized companies into large conglomerates. The government accepted arrangements whereby, to cover its mounting deficit, private firms offered loans in return for receiving shares at very low prices. At this juncture the new capitalists extended and rounded off their holdings. Vladimir Gusinskii, for example, who first made money in perestroika days by selling computer equipment, headed the Most financial group, built originally on the shoulders of Mosstroi-1, the capital's main construction agency in Soviet times. By 1995 Most, in close alliance with the mayor of Moscow, Yurii Luzhkov, controlled a major bank, the newspaper *Segodnia,* and the television channel NTV; it had some 2,500 armed security personnel to protect its affairs. Boris Berezovskii, director of the Logovaz automobile distributor, took over the newspaper *Nezavisimaia gazeta* (The Independent) and bought a large tranche of shares in the Ostankino television channel (now renamed ORT), which he used, together with other shareholders, such as National Credit Bank, Stolichnyi Bank, Gazprom, and the news agency Itar-Tass, to support the president and the "party of power." Together Gusinskii, Berezovskii, and other corporate magnates clubbed together to finance President Yeltsin's reelection campaign in 1996. Berezovskii was rewarded with a senior government post.[52]

By 1996, then, a full-scale corporate economy had emerged, that is, one in which a few huge conglomerates controlled most of the market and worked in close alliance with government officials. Ironically, international financial organizations reinforced the cliquishness of Russian business by channeling their input through a tight circle of entrepreneurs and consultants around the privatization chief, Anatolii Chubais.[53] To police their own rivalry and to keep outsiders at bay, each of the conglomerates employed sizable armed security forces. Small and medium firms, which lacked the means to do this, often instead paid money to criminal gangs, who protected them while they paid up, or wrecked their premises and murdered their managers if they did not. This was a world in which the shady operators and underground entrepreneurs of the Soviet-period "black" economy were in their element. So-called mafia killings were frequently reported in the newspapers, and fear of criminal violence became part of everyday life on Russian city streets.[54]

To cover its persistent deficits the treasury issued bonds (GKOs) at attractive rates of interest, which found a ready market both at home and abroad. They kept the government afloat, and also enabled it to persuade the International Monetary Fund that it was solvent and deserved generous loans to finance its economic reform program. In August 1998, however, the elaborate balancing act came to an inglorious end. Unable to fund its soaring GKO obligations despite a large recent IMF loan, the government declared that Russia was defaulting on its debts. Overnight most of Moscow's large banks became technically insolvent, the wealth of the "oligarchs" was sharply reduced, and the new middle class lost much of its savings. Real wages fell by 40 percent over the next six months, the ruble declined to less than a third of its previous exchange rate, and the proportion of the population living below the official poverty line leapt from around 20 percent to more than 35 percent.[55]

The devaluation gave Russia's producers the chance to set about supplanting the imports of food and consumer goods which had been flooding the country at artificially cheap prices. Over the following months, the tins and packets in grocery stores began to show Russian names instead of foreign ones. The future may suggest that what ended in August 1998 was a "soap-bubble" economy sustained by short-term international loans. Whether a more healthy one can replace it remains to be seen. The legacy of rust-belt factories, rent-seeking attitudes, environmental pollution, and an unhealthy and often inappropriately trained population remains highly discouraging.

THE CHECHEN PROBLEM

The weakness of the state gave the "subjects of the federation" more power to negotiate their own arrangements, including the taxes they would pay and the subsidies they would receive. But a problem of a different order was presented by Chechnia. Two centuries of bitter hostility to Russia had been exacerbated by economic decline as well as the resentments stirred up by the Chechens' return from deportation during and after the late 1950s, when they were amalgamated in a joint republic with Ingushetiia.

In 1990 the All-National Congress of the Chechen People broke away from the Chechen-Ingush Supreme Soviet, claiming thirteen of the fifteen districts of the old Chechen-Ingush Republic. In November 1990 the Congress elected an air force general, Dzhokhar Dudaev, as its chairman. He challenged the legitimacy of the Supreme Soviet and in September 1991 closed it down. He then announced presidential elections in the framework of an independent Chechen state, separate from Ingushetiia, which he proceeded to win with 85 percent of the vote.

Yeltsin, who had hitherto supported Dudaev as a thorn in Gorbachev's flesh, was determined not to allow Russia to begin going the way of the Soviet Union. He declared Dudaev's acts unconstitutional, called a state of emergency, and sent in Interior Ministry troops to restore order. These were soon surrounded by Chechen guerrillas and were allowed to leave in ignominy only after the Russian Supreme Soviet had defied the president and revoked the state of emergency. Thereafter Dudaev expelled Russian troops from Chechnia and, as they went, either seized or bought from them much of their equipment, including aircraft, tanks, and artillery.

That incident warned of the poor condition of Russia's means of coercion even before the collapse of the Soviet Union. It initiated a conflict soon complicated by other factors which were not peculiar to Chechnia, but merely represented an intense version of problems common to all regions. The term "clan," something of a metaphor when applied in many other regions, was the literal and basic social unit in Chechnia, certainly in the villages, and with tentacles in the towns. The clan formed a secure nucleus within which economic activities could develop independent of the state, even the Chechen state, let alone the Soviet or Russian one. It provided a channel for trade in drugs and arms, and a means by which oil flowing in a pipeline through the republic could be diverted to finance operations of all kinds. Though the Muscovite popular rumor mill exaggerated their potential, there is no doubt that Chechens controlled much organized crime, not only in post-Soviet territory, but in Europe and the United States as well. In February 1993 two Chechens traveling on diplomatic passports were murdered in Britain by Armenians, to prevent them from selling missiles to Azerbaijan.[56]

The clan was also an effective nucleus for the organization of a popular army. As the break with Russia disrupted or criminalized most of the republic's oil and gas trade, thousands of unemployed became part-time or full-time fighters, armed with weapons recently belonging to Russia and available for service when needed.

Chechnia was a real problem, then: of that there is no doubt. For two years Yeltsin negotiated with Dudaev in a desultory way, but refused to meet him personally and could achieve no settlement short of full independence for the refractory republic, which he was not prepared to concede. In the end, he decided instead to try to dislodge Dudaev by other means: by exploiting the clan rivalries within Chechnia to back his opponents. This was classical Russian borderlands diplomacy. By autumn 1994 (by which time an international oil deal on the Caspian made the matter urgent) the Federal Counter-Intelligence Service (FSK) was providing anti-Dudaev armed formations covertly with tanks, helicopters, and "volunteer" troops from the Kantemirov Guards Division (unbeknownst to their commanding officer). In November they launched a strike against the capital, Groznyi, itself. It failed, the Russian soldiers were captured, and the whole undercover operation was disclosed in the most humiliating manner.

Thereupon Yeltsin decided he could face no further indignity at the hands of Dudaev and invaded Chechnia in all seriousness. The decision was taken by a small circle of senior politicians and commanders, each of whom had his own sectoral interests to protect. The defense minister, Pavel Grachev, was said by some to be reluctant to intervene, but felt that he could not go on being overshadowed by the Interior Ministry and Counter-Intelligence. In the army as a whole, the decision was greeted with consternation. Two senior officers, Boris Gromov, the last Soviet commander in Afghanistan, and Aleksandr Lebed, currently commanding the 14th Army in Moldavia, publicly condemned it. Several other commanders reacted more discreetly, but refused to have their units involved. Grachev, Sergei Stepashin (head of the FSK), and Viktor Erin (minister of the interior) thus had to cobble together a motley intervention force consisting of Cossacks, border troops, Interior Ministry troops, local and central army units—anyone whose officers were willing to undertake the enterprise, many of them raw and barely trained conscripts.

The result was further humiliation. Forty thousand Russian regular troops faced a smaller number of Chechens, mostly irregulars, but had the greatest difficulty in taking Groznyi. Thereafter, poorly equipped and motivated, they never controlled much of the countryside, especially the southern, more mountainous territory, ideal for guerrilla operations. The Chechens, by contrast, fought superbly with their Russian weapons. They were operating on familiar terrain, they enjoyed the support of the population, and they were spurred on by the clannish sense of honor and the desire to defeat a national enemy. Internal opposition to Dudaev evaporated for the duration of the campaign as nearly all Chechens united to repel the Russian invaders.[57]

In the end Yeltsin had to face the reality that his armed forces could not defeat the Chechens. He instructed Aleksandr Lebed, who in the meantime had become his national security chief, to negotiate with the Chechen chief of staff, Aslan Maskhadov. The result was a deal, concluded in August 1996, by which Russia withdrew its troops in return for a five-year moratorium on the question of the republic's status. In practice, Chechnia had become an independent state in all but name, and forthwith set about turning itself into an Islamic republic. Russia had shown that, only a few years after being a superpower claiming equality with the United States, it could not prevent secession by a tiny constituent territory.

The Chechen debacle demonstrated how an ambitious individual politician could exploit the logic of the ethnic-administrative divisions of the old USSR, set up his own semicriminal rule claiming legitimacy as "leader of the people," and successfully challenge the might of Russia. It posed in acute form the problem of Russia's relationship with its own constituent republics after the breakup of the Soviet Union.

RUSSIA AND ITS NEIGHBORS

Soon after the failure of the August 1991 coup, Yeltsin declared that "The Russian state has chosen freedom and democracy, and will never be an empire, nor an older or younger brother. It will be an equal among equals."[58] In fact, however, it has never played that role consistently, and perhaps cannot do so. It may no longer be the core of an empire and global superpower, but it is still a regional great power, and its neighbors have been destabilized by the collapse of the Soviet Union. The mildest conception of its interests, even of its stability, would require that it try to influence those neighbors. Since Russia still has not arrived at a stable concept of its "national interest," and since governmental coordination is weak, it is inevitable that some Russian institutions have, from time to time, gone far beyond mere "influence" in the affairs of its neighbors. Many Russians have difficulty in acknowledging that Minsk, Donetsk, and Pavlodar are now in foreign countries; hence the ambivalent term adopted to designate the former Soviet Union, the "near abroad." The distinction between domestic and foreign policy is still not absolutely clear.

The proposal to establish a Commonwealth of Independent States, put forward at Minsk in December 1991, at first included only Russia, Belorussia, and Ukraine, implying an "East Slav" concept of post-Soviet Nationhood. The central Asian leaders, especially President Nazarbaev of Kazakhstan, reacted swiftly and vehemently to the proposal, since it would imply losing most of the northern half of his territory, with its compact population of Russians. They demanded that Kazakhstan and the other central Asian republics be included too. The CIS therewith lost any coherent rationale. It was seen by some as a way of gradually and peacefully reassembling the Soviet Union, without the Baltic republics, by others as a mechanism for finally winding it up. But it has always been too loose and fluctuating in its structures to be capable of fulfilling either function consistently.

In any case, its members soon discovered that they had diverging interests which were stronger than the converging ones. The centrifugal drive was manifested most strongly in Russia itself, which had no desire to continue supplying its neighbors with fuel and raw materials at a tiny fraction of world prices, nor to allow its currency to be debauched by neigboring central banks issuing rubles without observing the disciplines of tight monetary policy. By 1993 the ruble zone was wound up, and interrepublican trade on the old Soviet pattern diminished sharply. In reaction, and even in anticipation, the other states started to look for lucrative commercial contacts elsewhere in the world, each in accordance with its own potentialities and geographical position.

In some republics, moreover, anti-Russian nationalism was an important factor in loosening ties with Russia. That was especially true in the Baltic states (which kept out of the CIS as a result), western Ukraine, Moldavia, Georgia, and to some extent Azerbaijan. In Estonia and Latvia (though not Lithuania) citizenship was made automatically available to anyone who had lived in the republics before 1940 and their direct descendants. This provision excluded most Russians, who had immigrated since 1945, and hence deprived them of the vote and the right to stand for public office, as well as making it more difficult for them to participate in privatization. They did not mobilize effectively to demand a better deal, and the Russian Federation did not help them, though occasionally sounding off against Estonian and Latvian discrimination. Some local Russians were in any case no doubt content simply to enjoy their modest share of growing Baltic prosperity.

In Moldavia by contrast Russian-speakers defended themselves. As Moldavia gained its independence from the USSR and began to gravitate toward Romania, Russians and Ukrainians set up a breakaway ministate of their own on the left bank of the River Dniester, the "Trans-Dniester Republic." Moldavian irregulars attacked it in the spring of 1992, and it was defended by units of the Soviet 14th Army, still stationed in the area. From June 1992 its commander was General Aleksandr Lebed, who proved more astute than his predecessor: he negotiated a ceasefire which left Transdniestria provisionally in charge of its own affairs, under observation from a trilateral peacekeeping commission, Russian, Moldavian, and Transdniestrian.[59]

On the whole, however, national feeling, when it arose, was directed not against Russians but against other neighboring ethnic groups.

607

By late 1991 the conflict in Nagornyi Karabakh had degenerated into full-scale war, in spite of efforts by the Soviet Union, and later the CSCE, to mediate. Karabakh had always been the main focus of the Armenian democratic movement, and self-defense militias gradually became units in an Armenian army whose aim was the conquest of Karabakh from Azerbaijan. By 1993 they had achieved their aim, and also captured the corridor separating Karabakh from the Armenian republic, together with abutting Azerbaijani territory. Whether or not they had received Russian aid in this operation, as was widely rumored, the Armenians consented to the establishment of Russian bases in their republic.

Abkhazia declared its secession from Georgia in 1990, and in 1992–93 most Georgians fled the territory. Fighting broke out, and, in a flagrant example of the disunity in Russia's government, the Defense Ministry backed Abkhazia with weapons and aircraft, while the Foreign Ministry under Andrei Kozyrev sought international mediation through the United Nations. The UN was so slow to respond that the war was over by the time its first observers reached the scene. This was a glaring example of the international community's failure to respond to the desire of at least part of the Russian government to submit its security affairs to international law. To regain Russian support, Georgia agreed to enter the CIS and to permit Russian bases on her territory.

In Tajikistan civil war broke out among regional political clans, the old Communist leadership finding its support in the Khodjent and Kuliab oblasts, while a loose alliance of opposition groups based itself in Kurgan Tiube oblast. Among the latter was the Islamic Renaissance Party, which received arms and fighters from across the border in Afghanistan. Citing the danger of Muslim fundamentalism and drug-smuggling, Russia headed a CIS force to seal off the border and attempt to hold the ring while the warring parties sought a lasting peace.[60]

In all three cases, Russia had a legitimate interest in securing stability on her borders and in strategically sensitive regions adjacent to them, and it could argue that international organizations had proved ineffective in that role. On the other hand, it was also clear that Russia was making use of these border conflicts to make its military and political influence felt in its former empire, and to retain some influence in regions like the Caucasus, vital for its strategic security and because of international rivalry over lucrative new sources of oil.

The age-old blind drive for territory had slackened, however. President Aleksandr Lukashenka of Belorussia was patently anxious to merge his republic with Russia, and in April 1997 an agreement between the two countries stopped only just short of outright union. Russia remained unwilling to go the full distance, being reluctant to assume the burden of reviving Belorussia's devastated economy. No longer was empire pursued regardless of cost.

Similarly, Russia signed a treaty of friendship with Ukraine in May 1997 which recognized the inviolability of the two states' frontiers and divided the Black Sea fleet and naval base between them. Russia refrained from capitalizing on widespread support within the Ukrainian population for reunion; nor did she exploit the separatist movement in the Crimea which sought to become a Russian exclave.

FOREIGN POLICY

The collapse of the Soviet Union left Russia in a paradoxical situation. The Cold War had ended, and with it the greatest strategic threat to Russia. Yet on the other hand it had ended in a manner which many people interpreted as Russia's defeat: its population had been halved and its territory had shrunk so that it no longer had a common frontier with any central European nations (except in the anomalous enclave of Kaliningrad, on the Baltic). It had lost direct control of some of the vital approaches to its own heartland, such as the Baltic and the Caucasus, for whose dominance Russia had struggled over centuries. From being at the heart of a superpower which proclaimed itself the equal of the United States, Russia had become no more than a north Eurasian regional power, comparable with, say, Brazil or Indonesia— except that it still possessed the dubious heritage of a superpower, a massive nuclear arsenal.

Approaches to international relations were polarized. The "Atlanticists," the heirs to Gorbachev and Shevardnadze, hoped to guarantee Russia's security through continued disarmament, cooperation with the West and with international institutions to resolve conflicts and to obtain investments for the development of Russia's economy. The "Eurasians," on the contrary, believed that the West merely intended to co-opt Russia as a new colony, a peripheral supplier of raw materials, and to enforce its own domination over the former Warsaw Pact, including perhaps even the non-Russian republics of the USSR; they recommended cultivating good relations with

608

Asiatic powers, including those frowned on by the United States, such as Iran and Iraq, and using every means, including military, to emphasize Russia's continuing influence in the "near abroad."

At an early stage, the foreign policy establishment began to move from an "Atlantic" to a "Eurasian" perspective. It is true that Andrei Kozyrev, foreign minister from 1991 to 1996, remained temperamentally inclined to a strongly pro-Western policy, and as late as the summer of 1992 Yeltsin was still talking of a "democratic zone of trust, cooperation and security . . . across the northern hemisphere."[61] Agreements to remove Russian troops from central Europe and the Baltic were implemented in full.

Yet the very fact of having "national interests"—a category which Soviet politicians had eschewed as outmoded and "bourgeois"—inclined their Russian successors to a more robust egoism. Added to that was disappointment that the West and the international financial institutions did not extend more help to Russia. The G7 states invited Russia to become a member of their political consultations—the "G8" for those purposes—and in 1992 they assembled a package totaling $24 billion. They transferred the task of disbursing it, however, to the International Monetary Fund, whose conditions were stringent and which was wary of handing large sums of money over to mafiosi politicians and crooked businessmen. Actual receipts, then, were meager compared with expectations, and this opened Russia's democratic politicians to the accusation that they had sold their country's birthright, including intermediate-range nuclear weapons and a military presence in central Europe, for insubstantial promises. By October 1992 Yeltsin was warning that "Russia is not a country that can be kept waiting in the anteroom."[62] This anticlimax was the first sign of how difficult it was going to be to integrate Russia's commercial and financial institutions into an international economy ever more globalized and interdependent.

The West's policy of expanding NATO eastward to include Poland, the Czech Republic, and Hungary intensified the disillusion with the West, even among democratic politicians, and *a fortiori* among the nationalist and Communist opposition. All the same, the Russian reaction was never extreme or ill-considered. In 1994 Russia joined the Partnership for Peace, a kind of indefinite anteroom to NATO designed to increase cooperation, common training, and consultation over all threats to international peace. In May 1997 Yeltsin signed a Russia-NATO Charter, under which Russia accepted expansion in return for a permanent presence at NATO headquarters, the right to be consulted on all matters of importance, and an assurance that NATO would not move troops or missiles into the new members' territories.

However, in the spring of 1999 NATO intervened in Yugoslavia without a direct United Nations mandate, and against Russian objections, to protect Albanians against "ethnic cleansing" in Kosovo. Its air bombing campaign in Serbia revived and intensified the fears aroused by its enlargement. Perhaps for the first time ever, most Russians genuinely began to regard NATO as their principal enemy, and saw the Kosovo campaign as a dress rehearsal for what it subsequently planned to do within the borders of the ex-USSR.

In the autumn of 1999 Prime Minister Vladimir Putin was able to capitalize on this growing resentment. Reacting to the seizure of Dagestani villages by Chechen irregulars, and to two very destructive (and unexplained) explosions in apartment blocks inside Russia, he gave the military the go-ahead for a renewed invasion of Chechnia, in the hope of crushing the rebellion there once and for all. In that way he reasserted Russia's great-power status and its determination to control its own sovereign territory. This stance earned him strong support among the Russian public and ensured good results for the bloc Unity, which he supported in the December 1999 Duma election campaign. Yeltsin resigned his presidency six months early, enabling Putin to take over and win the presidential elections of March 2000 from the position of incumbent.

RUSSIA AT THE TURN OF THE CENTURY

Russia entered the new millennium with fundamental questions about her identity still unsettled. At the same time several shadow identities, inherited from the past, still hung over the country and hampered her adjustment to the twenty-first century. They raised fundamental questions, for Russian nationhood, as this book has suggested, has never existed outside the framework of empire, which has left it stunted and underdeveloped. It followed that to build a Russian nation-state out of the ruins of the Soviet Union was by no means an automatic process. Who were the Russians? What were the appropriate borders of their state? What kind of state best answered their needs? There are broadly five ways in which the "Russian nation" might be defined today:

1. By Russia's imperial mission, as the creator and sustainer of a great multiethnic empire in northern Eurasia; this is the view which has the firmest basis in history, and it would imply borders similar to those of the USSR.

2. As a nation of East Slavs; this would imply some kind of formal union between Russia, Ukraine, and Belorussia.

3. As a community of Russian speakers, regardless of ethnic origin or current civic status. Since Russian-speakers are so scattered, this would imply some concept of civic status independent of frontiers.

4. As the Russian Federation, with citizenship independent of ethnic origin.

5. As the Russian Federation, with preferential status for ethnic Russians.[63]

The one which corresponds most closely to current reality is the fourth, but in practice few Russians would be prepared to concede that the present-day Russian Federation embodies what they understand as "Russia." The fifth beckons as a temptation to which Russians may resort if they are unable to solve their geopolitical problems in any other way.

After the fall of the Soviet Union, the Orthodox Church should have been in a strong position to benefit from the newly released patriotism and spiritual freedom of ordinary Russians and to act as a focus for emerging Russian nationhood. In practice, however, its long-held close relationship with the state and the stunted congregational life which it inherited from the Soviet decades inhibited its development. Nervous of other religious movements, especially those which came with foreign subsidies and the latest information technology, it requested and obtained from the Duma statutory restrictions on some of its rivals. Far from uniting Russians, there seemed a danger the church might divide them further.

For centuries, amid the dangers and temptations of northern Eurasia, Russia has had to improvise the mobilization of her resources, using whatever means were immediately to hand, usually local personal power networks, without creating lasting laws or institutions. That is a habit which has now far outlived its usefulness, but it has left a malignant legacy in the form of an enfeebled state and a chronically underproductive economy. Of all the world's economies, Russia's may be the most difficult to integrate into the global network, since it has many of the characteristics of an underdeveloped country, but also the distortions of misplaced heavy industrial and military investment undertaken to sustain great-power status.

All the same, nearly ten years after the fall of the Soviet Union, Russian society seems to have acquired a certain stability. The way in which the country withstood the default of August 1998, and arguably even fared better as a result of it, showed that tough and lively socioeconomic institutions were at work. The Communist Party of the Soviet Union has disappeared, but the nomenklatura elite has survived and has adapted itself to new social circumstances by co-optation from among young people and from the former underground economy. In effect, it has completed its second self-emancipation: in the 1950s it freed itself from Stalin's terror, in the 1990s it threw off the CPSU, Gosplan, and the KGB. Directly or indirectly, it controls the lion's share of the country's economy, having acquired it from the state at negligible cost.

The result is a society held together largely by personal ties of a patron-clientelistic type, and by the authority of a president who holds an overriding position in the constitution. Political parties and autonomous social institutions exist but are weakly developed and usually depend on either personal bonds or presidential authority for their survival. The transmission of power from Yeltsin to Putin in 1999–2000 was handled in characteristically patrimonial fashion; the second Chechen war accompanying it was conducted as if by a new tribal chieftain anxious to demonstrate his authority. It remains to be seen whether Putin can use this authority to restrain the "oligarchs" who control the new financial-industrial-media conglomerates and the provincial governors, who dominate their own territories in sometimes highly authoritarian fashion.

In the meantime the Russian people have little confidence in those who govern them. Those who can do so seek protection from powerful and wealthy individuals; the rest get by through exchanging goods and services as they used to in Soviet times. But today such devices do not always work: money is much more important, while health and education are no longer universal services which can be taken for granted. The result is a sharp decline in the health and life expectancy of the population.

All the same, some democratic institutions have withstood the crises of the post-Soviet years. Newspapers, radio, and television are distorted by the pressure of their oligarchic owners but remain lively, while their sheer variety ensures that members of the public who wish to be well informed can usually find what they want. Parliamentary and local elections have become part of the fabric of political life, even if it remains to be proved that a government can hand over power peacefully to an opposition. The two legislative chambers remain serious assemblies, patchy in achievement, but capable at times of criticizing and monitoring government performance, rejecting or amending its draft laws, and airing matters of public concern

It is difficult to tell at the moment whether the strong presidency backed by patronal networks is likely to prove a permanent feature of Russian society, or represents simply a temporary scaffolding under the shelter of which more lasting democratic political institutions can come to maturity.

The problems are serious, but the future is by no means hopeless. Russia's paradoxical geopolitical situation, which has brought so many handicaps, is today almost entirely an advantage. For the first time in centuries, it faces no serious strategic threat across its borders and does not have to devote a crippling proportion of its resources to defense. At the same time, twenty-first-century technology renders the exploitation of its scattered and remote natural resources much easier than before. In the last decade of the twentieth century, poor leadership and the legacy of Soviet attitudes and practices made these advantages difficult to mobilize or even to perceive, but later generations could well be better placed to capitalize on them.

This is more especially the case since Russia's cultural and intellectual life remains lively, in spite of the state's failure to invest in it. Its science and technology, though eroded in recent decades, remain at a high international level. Probably the image of "Russia" which has the broadest appeal among Russians themselves is of a linguistic and cultural community, of a nation which speaks Russian and has been brought up in the culture of Pushkin and Tolstoi, Musorgskii and Shostakovich, Repin and Chagall. The major achievement of the Soviet educational system is that this heritage is no longer confined to an elite. Russian culture is lively, humane, and has very widespread appeal, both in and outside the country. It is, moreover, unmistakably European, and counteracts the political and economic proclivities which tend to alienate Russia from Europe.

Russia, in its various forms, is one of world history's great survivors. As this book has shown, it has been in desperate situations before, some of them to all appearance far worse than its current one—and it has recovered from them, even in some respects thrived. Its society and culture are extraordinarily resilient. It will, though, need statesmen of unusual ability and vision, not only to bring about change but also to rescue what was valuable in its past and remold it in a form viable for the twenty-first century.

CHRONOLOGY

860	First recorded appearance of the Rus (Varangians) in Constantinople
ca. 880–912	Prince Oleg, who unites Novgorod and Kiev
911	The Rus raid Constantinople and gain trade concessions from the Byzantine emperor
965	Prince Sviatoslav defeats the Khazars on the lower Volga
978–1015	Prince Vladimir, during whose reign (ca. 988) Kievan Rus accepts Orthodox Christianity
1019–1054	Prince Iaroslav (the Wise)
1054	Split between Byzantine and Roman churches
1097	Liubech agreement among the princes of Rus
1103, 1111	Successful Kievan military campaigns against the Kipchaks
1113–1125	Prince Vladimir Monomakh
1136	First election of *posadnik* in Novgorod
1147	First mention of Moscow in chronicles
1157–1174	Andrei Bogoliubskii rules in Suzdal-Vladimir
1165	Novgorod becomes full archbishopric
1169	Andrei Bogoliubskii conquers Kiev
1199	Roman Mstislavich unites Galicia and Volynia
1201–02	Foundation of Riga and the German Order of Swordbearers (later amalgamated with the Teutonic Knights)
1221–1264	Daniil rules in Volynia
1223	Battle of Kalka River

616

1236–1263	Aleksandr Nevskii rules in Novgorod, and from 1252 in Vladimir
1237–1242	Mongol armies under Batu conquer most of Rus; capital of the Kipchak khanate (Golden Horde) established at Sarai, on the lower Volga
ca. 1238–1263	Mindaugas rules in Lithuania
1240–1242	Aleksandr Nevskii defeats the Swedes on the Neva River and the Teutonic Knights on Lake Peipus
1257–58	Aleksandr Nevskii suppresses serious rebellion in Novgorod with aid of Mongols
ca. 1276–1303	Daniil, son of Aleksandr Nevskii, rules in the new principality of Moscow
1299	Metropolitanate transferred from Kiev to Vladimir
1303–1325	Iurii Danilovich rules in Moscow
1316–1341	Gediminas rules in Lithuania and expands his territory southward and eastward
1325–1341	Ivan I (Kalita) rules Moscow, from 1328 as grand prince
1326	Metropolitanate transferred from Vladimir to Moscow
1327	Anti-Mongol rising in Tver, suppressed with the help of Ivan I of Moscow
1341–1353	Semen I rules in Moscow
1341–1377	Algirdas rules in Lithuania, which attains its greatest territorial extent
1359	Assassination of Khan Berdi-bek starts fragmentation of the Golden Horde
1359–1389	Dmitrii (Donskoi) rules in Moscow
1360s–1370s	Dynastic conflict in Golden Horde
1362	Lithuania defeats the Golden Horde at the Battle of Blue Waters
1377–1398	Jogaila rules in Lithuania, marries Jadwiga of Poland (1386), and inaugurates personal union of Lithuania and Poland
1380	September 8: at the Battle of Kulikovo Field, Dmitrii Donskoi defeats Mamai, a claimant to authority in the Golden Horde
1382	Moscow sacked by Tokhtamysh, khan of the Golden Horde
1385–86	Union of Krewo, between the Polish and Lithuanian crowns
1389–1425	Vasilii I rules in Moscow
1391	Timur (Tamerlane), from the Chagatai khanate, defeats Tokhtamysh and sacks Sarai
1392–1430	Vitautas rules in Lithuania
1398	Nizhnii Novgorod annexed to Moscow
1399	Golden Horde defeats Lithuania at Battle of Vorskla River

1403–04	Lithuania conquers and annexes Smolensk
1410	Polish-Lithuanian army defeats Teutonic Knights at Battle of Tannenberg
1413	Agreement of Horodlo unites the Polish and Lithuanian nobilities
1425–1462	Vasilii II's reign in Moscow is marked by long civil war among rival members of the dynasty
1438–39	Council of Ferrara-Florence briefly reunites Catholic and Orthodox Churches but is never accepted in Moscow
1448	Iona, an opponent of the Council of Florence, is consecrated as metropolitan of Moscow
1453	Byzantium falls to the Ottoman Turks
1462–1505	Ivan III
1471	Moscow defeats Novgorod, forcing it to renounce its alliance with Lithuania and pay tribute to Moscow
1472	Marriage of Ivan III with Zoe Paleologue, niece of the last Byzantine emperor
1478	Novgorod acknowledges Moscow's sovereignty
1480	After an indecisive battle on the River Ugra against the Golden Horde, Moscow no longer acknowledges the Horde's overlordship
1480s–1490s	Breakup of Golden Horde into smaller khanates
1485	Tver annexed to Moscow
1497	Law Code (*Sudebnik*)
1505–1533 Vasilii III	
1510	Pskov annexed to Moscow
1533–1584 Ivan IV	
1533–1538	Regency under Ivan's mother, Elena Glinskaia
1547	Ivan assumes the throne and is crowned tsar
1549–1556	Meeting of Reconciliation Council, followed by meetings of zemskii sobor (1550) and period of attempted reforms
1551	Stoglavyi sobor (church council)
1552	Conquest and annexation of khanate of Kazan
1553	Richard Chancellor is shipwrecked in the White Sea and comes to Moscow; opening of Russo-English trading relations
1556	Conquest and annexation of khanate of Astrakhan
1558–1582	War in Livonia (Zemskii sobor convened in 1566 to discuss the war)
1564	First printed book, the Acts of the Apostles, is published in Moscow; flight of Prince Andrei Kurbskii to Lithuania
1564–1572	Muscovy divided into *oprichnina* and *zemshchina*

617

618

1569	Union of Liublin, creating Commonwealth of Poland-Lithuania
1570	Muscovite punitive expedition carries out massacre in Novgorod
1571	Crimean Tatars raid and sack Moscow
1581	Ivan IV kills his eldest son and heir
1581	The first "forbidden year," when peasants are not allowed to leave their lord on St. George's Day; the first printed Slavonic Bible is published

1584–1598 Fedor I

| 1589 | Creation of Moscow patriarchate |
| 1596 | Union of Brest, creating Greek Orthodox or Uniate Church in Poland-Lithuania |

1598–1605 Boris Godunov

1604–1613 Time of Troubles

1605	False Dmitrii is crowned tsar in Moscow
1606	Dmitrii overthrown; Shuiskii crowned tsar; Bolotnikov rising
1608	Another False Dmitrii establishes a court at Tushino, outside Moscow
1610	Shuiskii deposed; Polish troops occupy Moscow
1611–12	Minin and Pozharskii put together a national militia, which drives the Poles out of Moscow
1613	Zemskii sobor elects Mikhail Romanov as tsar

1613–1645 Mikhail Fedorovich

1617	Peace of Stolbovo with Sweden
1618	Fourteen-year truce with Poland begins; Filaret Romanov, Mikhail's father, is freed from Polish captivity, is elected patriarch, and becomes in effect co-ruler till his death in 1633
1632–1634	Unsuccessful war against Poland
1632	Establishment of Iakutsk, on the River Lena
1637	Don Cossacks seize Azov
1639	The first Cossacks reach the Pacific coast

1645–1676 Aleksei Mikhailovich

1648	First Pacific settlement established, on the Bay of Okhotsk; riots in Moscow; Bogdan Khmelnitskii leads a Cossack rebellion against Poland
1649	A zemskii sobor adopts a Law Code (*Ulozhenie*)
1649–1652	Expedition of Khabarov in Amur basin and first clash with Chinese troops
1652	Nikon becomes patriarch
1653	Nikon's first reforms of the liturgy and scriptures
1654–1667	War with Poland, ending in the Treaty of Andrusovo

1658	Nikon resigns the patriarchate
1666–67	A church council anathematizes those who refuse to accept liturgical and scriptural reforms
1668–1676	Rebellion of the Solovki Monastery
1670–71	Major rebellion in southeast, led by Stepan Razin

1676–1682 Fedor Alekseevich

1682–1725 Peter I (until 1696 jointly with Ivan V)

1682	*Streltsy* rebellion in Moscow; abolition of *mestnichestvo*
1685	"Slav-Greek-Latin" Academy opens in Moscow
1686	"Permanent Peace" with Poland; Russia joins the Holy League
1687, 1689	Abortive military expeditions, led by Golitsyn, against the Crimean Tatar khanate
1689	Treaty of Nerchinsk marks border with China; regent Sophia overthrown
1695–96	Two military expeditions to capture Azov, the second of which is successful
1697–98	Peter's "special embassy" visits much of northern Europe
1698	Final revolt and abolition of streltsy
1700	Russian army defeated by Sweden at Narva
1703	Establishment of new capital city of St. Petersburg
1705	Establishment of permanent standing army based on obligatory conscription of the taxpaying population
1708	Mazepa, Ukrainian hetman, joins the Swedes; Bulavin rebellion in the Don region
1709	Defeat of Swedish army at Poltava
1711	Establishment of Ruling Senate
1718	Establishment of colleges
1721	Abolition of patriarchate and establishment of Spiritual College, later Holy Synod; Treaty of Nystadt ends the Great Northern War, and Russia gains the Baltic provinces
1722	Institution of Table of Ranks; Ukraine is deprived of autonomy and of elective hetmanate
1723	Introduction of poll tax

1725–1727 Catherine I

| 1725–27 | Bering's expedition discovers the straits dividing Siberia from Alaska |
| 1726 | Opening of Academy of Sciences |

1727–1730 Peter II

1730–1740 Anna

| 1730 | On accession, Anna at first accepts "Conditions" presented by powerful court factions, then disavows them |

620

1731	Kazakhs of the Little Horde acknowledge Russian sovereignty
1736	Unsuccessful campaign, led by Münnich, against the Crimean Tatars

1740–41 Ivan VI

1741–1761 Elizabeth

1753	Abolition of internal customs duties
1754	Establishment of first law codification commission, under Petr Shuvalov
1755	Establishment of Moscow University
1756–1763	Seven Years' War

1761–62 Peter III

1762	Emancipation of nobility from compulsory state service
1762–1764	Secularization of church land and property

1762–1796 Catherine II

1765	Creation of Free Economic Society
1767–68	Law Code Commission
1768–1774	War with the Ottoman Empire, ending with the Treaty of Kuchuk Kainardji
1769	Introduction of paper money *(assignaty)*
1772, 1793, 1795	Partitions of Poland
1773–1775	Pugachev rebellion
1775	Reform of provincial administration: creation of *gubernii* and *uezdy*
1783	Establishment of Russian Academy; Georgia becomes a Russian protectorate; Russia incorporates the Crimea
1785	Sheikh Mansur declares "holy war" and calls on north Caucasian tribes to repel the Russian invaders; Charter of the Nobility; Charter of the Cities
1786	National Statute of Education promulgated
1787–1791	War with the Ottoman Empire, ending with the Treaty of Jassy
1791	Establishment of the Jewish Pale of Settlement
1792	Foundation of city of Odessa

1796–1801 Paul

1797	Serf forced labor is limited to three days a week and prohibited on Sundays

1801–1825 Alexander I

1801	Russia annexes Georgia
1802	Establishment of ministries to replace the colleges
1804–1813	War with Persia
1805–1807	War of the Third Coalition against France, ending with the Treaty of Tilsit

1806–1809	War with the Ottoman Empire, ending with the Treaty of Bucharest, by which Russia acquires Bessarabia
1808–09	War with Sweden, ending with the incorporation of Finland
1809	Foundation of Grand Duchy of Finland
1810	Establishment of State Council
1812	Napoleon's Grande Armée invades Russia, is defeated and expelled from the country
1815	Congress of Vienna; establishment of Holy Alliance; creation of Congress Kingdom of Poland, under Russian rule
1816	Creation of combined Ministry of Spiritual Affairs; foundation of Union of Salvation (first of the secret societies which will lead to the Decembrist revolt)
1818	New Testament published in modern Russian
1822	All secret societies and Masonic lodges prohibited
1824	Dismissal of Golitsyn and reestablishment of Holy Synod
1825	Decembrist revolt

1825–1855 Nicholas I

1826–1828	War with Persia, ending with Treaty of Turkmanchai
1827–1829	War with Ottoman Empire, ending with Treaty of Adrianople
1830–31	Polish revolt
1832	Publication of new law code
1833	Publication of Pushkin's *Evgenii Onegin*
1836	Chaadaev's "First Philosophical Letter" appears; Pushkin founds the journal *Sovremennik*
1842	Publication of the first part of Gogol's *Dead Souls*
1845	Foundation of Russian Geographical Society
1846	Beginning of publication of *Complete Collection of Russian Chronicles*
1851	Completion of railway line from St. Petersburg to Moscow
1853–1856	Crimean War, ending with Treaty of Paris

1855–1881 Alexander II

1857	Foundation of Society of Russian Railways
1858	Treaty of Aigun settles the Russo-Chinese border
1859	Capture of Shamil, leader of the north Caucasian resistance
1860	Foundation of State Bank
1861	Emancipation of the serfs
1863	University Statute
1863–64	Polish revolt
1864	Establishment of zemstvos; judicial reform; statutes on primary and secondary education
1865	New censorship regulations

1865–1869	Publication of Tolstoi's *War and Peace*
1865–1876	Russian conquest of the khanates of Kokand and Khiva and the emirate of Bukhara
1866	Attempt by Karakozov on life of tsar; closure of *Sovremennik*
1870	Reform of municipal government
1871	Abrogation of Black Sea clauses of Treaty of Paris
1873	League of Three Emperors
1873–74	High point of "going to the people" movement
1874	Introduction of universal military service; first performance of Musorgskii's *Boris Godunov*
1875–76	Risings against Ottoman rule in Bosnia, Herzegovina, and Bulgaria
1876	Formation of *Zemlia i volia;* first performance of Chaikovskii's *Swan Lake*
1877–78	War against Ottoman Empire, ending with Treaty of San Stefano, revised at Congress of Berlin
1878	Vera Zasulich affair
1879	Formation of *Narodnaia volia*
1879–80	Publication of Dostoevskii's *Brothers Karamazov*
1880	Formation of Supreme Executive Committee under General Loris-Melikov
1881	Assassination of Alexander II

1881–1894 Alexander III

1881	Establishment of Okhrana; "Temporary Regulations" place many provinces under emergency rule
1882	Anti-Jewish discrimination formulated in May Laws
1884	New University Statute; closure of *Otechestvennye Zapiski*
1889	Introduction of *zemskie nachalniki* (land commandants)
1890	New Zemstvo Statute
1891–92	Famine in the Volga basin, followed by cholera epidemic
1891–1894	Formation of Franco-Russian alliance

1894–1917 Nicholas II

1898	Formation of Russian Social Democratic Workers' Party (RSDRP); first issue of the journal *Mir iskusstva*
1899	Imperial manifesto on Finland; appointment of Bobrikov as governor-general
1901	Foundation of Socialist Revolutionary Party; formation of Zubatov police trade unions
1903	Formation of Union of Liberation; completion of Trans-Siberian Railway
1904	Assassination of Pleve

1904–05	War with Japan, ending with Treaty of Portsmouth
1905	January: Bloody Sunday massacre in St. Petersburg
	May: formation of first Soviet of Workers' Deputies in Ivanovo-Voznesensk
	August: formation of All-Russian Muslim League
	October: general strike; formation of St. Petersburg Soviet; October Manifesto; formation of Council of Ministers; huge anti-Jewish pogrom in Odessa
	December: arrest of all members of St. Petersburg Soviet; workers' rising in Moscow
1906	January: appointment of Pre-Conciliar Commission to prepare reform of Orthodox Church
	March: legalization of professional associations and trade unions
	April: convening of First Duma
	July: dissolution of First Duma; Vyborg Manifesto; appointment of Stolypin as prime minister
	August: assassination attempt on Stolypin; summary courts-martial introduced
	November: Stolypin's main agrarian reform
1907	February: convening of Second Duma
	June: dissolution of Second Duma; new electoral law
	November: convening of Third Duma
1908	Azef exposed as double agent; Austria annexes Bosnia-Herzegovina
1909	Publication of *Vekhi*
1911	Student disorders in universities; western zemstvo crisis; assassination of Stolypin
1912	Convening of Fourth Duma; First Balkan War
1913	Celebration of tricentennial of Romanov dynasty; Second Balkan War; first performance, in Paris, of Stravinskii's *Rite of Spring*
1914	Outbreak of First World War; defeat at Tannenberg
1915	May: defeat in Galicia
	July: foundation of *Zemgor*
	July–August: loss of Poland
	August–September: formation of Progressive Bloc; attempt to set up a Progressive Bloc government fails; Nicholas assumes command of army
1916	May–July: Brusilov offensive in Galicia
	December: murder of Rasputin
1917	February: rising in Petrograd; formation of Petrograd Soviet

624

March: abdication of Nicholas II; formation of Provisional Government; Order no. 1

April: Lenin returns to Russia; demonstrations over Miliukov note

June: First All-Russian Congress of Soviets; Ukrainian Rada proclaims autonomy of Ukraine; Kerenskii offensive in Galicia

July: "July Days" in Petrograd; Kerenskii becomes prime minister

August: Kornilov affair

August–November: council of the Orthodox Church, meeting in Moscow, reestablishes the patriarchate and elects Tikhon patriarch

October: Bolsheviks seize power in the name of the soviets; Second All-Russian Congress of Soviets

December: armistice on German front; Finland declares independence

1918   January: dissolution of Constituent Assembly; Ukrainian Rada declares independence

March: Treaty of Brest-Litovsk

May: Armenia, Azerbaijan, and Georgia declare independence; Czech Legion rebels against Soviet rule

June: anti-Bolshevik governments set up in Samara and Omsk

July: Fifth All-Russian Congress of Soviets ratifies first Soviet constitution; imperial family murdered in Ekaterinburg

August: White army captures Kazan

September: declaration of Red Terror

November: Kolchak seizes power in Omsk

1919   March: First Congress of Comintern; Eighth Congress of Communist Party creates Politburo and Orgburo

May–October: major White offensives, led by Denikin in the south and Iudenich in the Baltic

October–January 1920: Red counterattacks defeat both Denikin and Iudenich

1920   April: Poland invades Soviet Russia; Soviet power installed in Azerbaijan

June–August: Red Army repels the Poles, invades Poland, and tries unsuccessfully to capture Warsaw

August: Second Congress of Comintern adopts the "21 Points"

October: Polish-Soviet armistice

	November: Soviet power installed in Armenia
	December: Central Committee directive on Proletkult
1921	February: creation of Gosplan; Soviet power installed in Georgia
	February–March: general strike in Petrograd; Kronstadt rebellion
	March–May: Tenth Communist Party Congress bans factions and declares New Economic Policy
1921–22	Famine in the Volga basin
1922	February: decree authorizes seizure of church valuables for famine relief
	March–April: at Eleventh Communist Party Congress, Stalin becomes general secretary
	April: Treaty of Rapallo; house arrest of Patriarch Tikhon
	May: Lenin's first stroke
	August: capture of Enver Pasha
	December: formation of Union of Soviet Socialist Republics
1923	"Scissors crisis"; first council of Living Church; release of Patriarch Tikhon
1924	Death of Lenin
1925	Trotskii resigns as commissar of war; Fourteenth Party Conference accepts doctrine of "socialism in one country"; foundation of League of Godless
1926	Trotskii expelled from Politburo; new Family Code
1927	April: Chinese Communists massacred in Shanghai by Kuomintang
	December: Fifteenth Communist Party Congress expels "Trotskyites" and "Zinovievites" from the party and decides on collectivization of agriculture
1928	May: Shakhty trial
	October: beginning of first five-year plan
1929	Start of forced collectivization of agriculture and dekulakization; Right Opposition defeated and Bukharin expelled from Politburo
1930	March: Stalin's article "Dizzy with Success" appears in *Pravda*
	April: suicide of Maiakovskii; establishment of GULAG administration under OGPU
1932	April: Central Committee resolution closes all literary groups and creates Union of Soviet Writers
	October: opening of Dneproges hydroelectric power project
	November: suicide of Stalin's wife, Nadezhda Allilueva
	December: introduction of internal passport and *propiska*

626

1932–1934	Major famine, especially in Ukraine, Kuban, Volga basin, and west Siberia
1933–1937	Second five-year plan
1934	January: Seventeenth Communist Party Congress
	July: security functions of OGPU transferred to NKVD
	August: First Congress of Union of Soviet Writers
	September: USSR enters League of Nations
	December: assassination of Kirov
1935	Model collective farm statute; introduction of "Stakhanovite" labor
1936	January: exchange of party cards is ordered; Shostakovich's *Lady Macbeth of Mtsensk* is denounced in *Pravda*
	June: new decree on family, restricting abortion and divorce
	August: show trial of Zinoviev, Kamenev, and others; suicide of Tomskii
	September: Yezhov becomes head of NKVD
	December: promulgation of "Stalin Constitution"
1937	January: show trial of Radek, Piatakov, and others
	February: suicide of Ordjonikidze
	June: arrest and execution of eight military leaders, including Tukhachevskii
1938	March: show trial of Bukharin, Rykov, and others; decree requires teaching of Russian in all non-Russian schools
	October: Stalin's *Short Course* published
	December: Beria succeeds Yezhov as head of NKVD
1939	August: Nazi-Soviet pact; Red Army defeats Japanese at Khalkin-Gol in Mongolia
	September: Red Army occupies eastern Poland (western Belorussia and western Ukraine)
	November: Red Army invades Finland
1940	March: peace concluded with Finland
	June: annexation of Baltic states and Bessarabia; unjustifiable absence from work is made a criminal offense
	August: assassination of Trotskii in Mexico
	October: fees introduced for higher and upper secondary education
1941	22 June: German army invades the USSR
	September: siege of Leningrad begins; fall of Kiev; United States and Great Britain agree to deliver war supplies to USSR
	October: Moscow is threatened and partially evacuated
	December–January 1942: German army thrown back from Moscow

1942	May–June: USSR, United States, and Great Britain conclude alliance on basis of Atlantic Charter
	June: German Army launches major offensive in Ukraine
	August–February 1943: Battle of Stalingrad
	October: political commissars downgraded in army
	November: Operation Uranus encircles German Sixth Army in Stalingrad
1943	May: dissolution of Comintern
	July: Battle of Kursk
	September: Stalin receives Metropolitan Sergii and gives permission for a church council
	November: Stalin, Roosevelt, and Churchill meet at Teheran Conference
1943–44	Deportation of peoples from the north Caucasus and Crimea
1944	August–October: Warsaw rising
1945	February: Yalta Conference; Church council elects Aleksii patriarch
	9 May: unconditional surrender of Nazi Germany
	July–August: Potsdam Conference
1946	August: Central Committee statement attacking Akhmatova and Zoshchenko
	September: decree on "measures to liquidate breaches of the kolkhoz statute"
1946–47	Famine in Ukraine
1947	United States launches Marshall Plan; establishment of Cominform; currency reform
1948	January: murder of Mikhoels, head of Jewish Anti-Fascist Committee
	February: Central Committee statement criticizing "decadent tendencies in music"; Prague coup completes Communist domination of central and eastern Europe
	June–May 1949: Berlin blockade
	June: Cominform expels Yugoslavia
	August: Lysenko triumphs at Agricultural Academy
	November: dissolution of Jewish Anti-Fascist Committee
1949	Major purge in Leningrad
	January: formation of Comecon
	April: formation of NATO
	August: successful test of first Soviet atomic bomb
1950	Outbreak of Korean War; Stalin's *Pravda* article on linguistics

627

628

1953	January: discovery of "doctors' plot" announced
	5 March: death of Stalin
	June: arrest of Beria
	July: armistice ends Korean War
	summer: risings in labor camps at Vorkuta and Norilsk
	September: Khrushchev confirmed as first secretary of CPSU
1954	February: launch of "virgin lands" campaign
	March: security services reformed and reconstituted as KGB
	April–June: rising in Kengir labor camp
1955	Formation of Warsaw Pact; publication of *The Thaw,* by Ilia Erenburg
1956	February: at Twentieth Communist Party Congress, Khrushchev delivers "secret speech"
	April: dissolution of Cominform
	June: fees for higher and upper secondary education abolished
	October: Gomulka elected first secretary of Polish United Workers' Party
	October–November: insurrection in Hungary, suppressed by Soviet military intervention
1957	June: Central Committee plenum backs Khrushchev against "antiparty group"
	October: launch of first man-made space satellite (*sputnik*); Zhukov dismissed as defense minister
	November: Pasternak's *Doctor Zhivago* is published in Italy
1958	Tvardovskii returns as chief editor of *Novyi mir;* Pasternak is awarded the Nobel Prize for literature; promulgation of new criminal code; publication of proposed educational reforms; Khrushchev proposes that Berlin become a free, demilitarized city
1959	Khrushchev visits United States, launches maize-growing campaign
1959–60	USSR ends all nuclear cooperation with China and recalls all technicians and specialists stationed there
1960–61	*Sovnarkhozy* are established
1961	April: first manned space flight, by Iurii Gagarin
	July: church council acknowledges reduced ecclesiastical control over parishes
	August: closing of Berlin sector borders and construction of Berlin Wall

1962	June: workers' riots in Novocherkassk
	October: Cuban missile crisis; Twenty-second Communist Party Congress issues new program and mandates Stalin's removal from the Lenin Mausoleum
	November: Solzhenitsyn's *A Day in the Life of Ivan Denisovich* is published in *Novyi mir;* CPSU is divided into industrial and agricultural sectors
1963	Soil erosion in "virgin lands" and low production elsewhere generate serious agricultural crisis; nuclear test ban treaty signed
1964	Fall of Khrushchev; Brezhnev becomes first secretary of CPSU
1965	March: Central Committee plenum approves agricultural reforms
	April: demonstrations in Erevan commemorating Ottoman massacre of Armenians
	September: Central Committee plenum abolishes *sovnarkhozy* and relaxes state control over enterprises
	December: demonstration in Pushkin Square calling for observance of Soviet constitution
1966	Trial of Siniavskii and Daniel
1967	Andropov becomes head of KGB
1968	January: Dubcek becomes first secretary of Czechoslovak Communist Party; launching of "Prague spring"
	April: first issue of *Chronicle of Current Events*
	August: Warsaw Pact invasion of Czechoslovakia
	September: "Brezhnev doctrine" published in *Pravda*
1969	Armed clashes on Soviet-Chinese border; Solzhenitsyn expelled from Union of Soviet Writers
1970	First issue of Ukrainian samizdat journal *Ukrainskii visnik*
	February: Tvardovskii resigns as chief editor of *Novyi mir*
	April: first issue of Jewish samizdat journal *Exodus*
	August: West Germany under Chancellor Brandt agrees to respect postwar European borders
	October: Solzhenitsyn is awarded Nobel Prize for literature
	December: workers' riots in Poland; Gierek replaces Gomulka as first secretary of Polish United Workers' Party
1971	February: Jewish demonstrations in Moscow; beginning of permitted Jewish emigration
	September: international agreement on status of Berlin, guaranteeing unhindered access to the city

629

630

1972	First issue of samizdat *Chronicle of Lithuanian Catholic Church* January: widespread searches and arrests among Ukrainian intellectuals May: riots in Kaunas following self-immolation of Roman Kalanta; Shcherbitskii replaces Shelest as first secretary of Ukrainian Communist Party May: Nixon and Brezhnev sign SALT I agreements July: Egypt expels all Soviet advisers
1973	Solzhenitsyn's *Gulag Archipelago* is published in Paris
1974	February: Solzhenitsyn is expelled from the USSR
1975	August: Final Act of the Conference on Security and Cooperation in Europe (CSCE) is signed in Helsinki by 35 countries, including USSR October: Sakharov is awarded the Nobel Peace Prize
1977	New Soviet constitution
1978	Khalq seizure of power in Afghanistan; street demonstrations defending Georgian language in Tbilisi
1979	June: Carter and Brezhnev sign SALT II agreements December: Soviet military intervention in Afghanistan
1980	January: Sakharov exiled to Gorkii August: workers' unrest in Poland; formation of Solidarity
1981	Jaruzelski declares martial law in Poland
1982	Death of Brezhnev; Andropov becomes general secretary of CPSU
1984	Death of Andropov; Chernenko becomes general secretary of CPSU
1985	Death of Chernenko; Gorbachev becomes general secretary of CPSU
1986	April: explosion at Chernobyl nuclear power station June: Eighth Congress of Union of Soviet Writers October: Gorbachev meets Reagan at summit in Reykjavik November: law permitting private economic activity December: rioting in Alma Ata, capital of Kazakhstan; Sakharov is released from administrative exile and returns to Moscow
1987	February: law permitting cooperatives June: law reforming state enterprises August: demonstrations in Baltic republics mark anniversary of Nazi-Soviet pact October: Yeltsin resigns from Politburo

1988	Pasternak's *Doctor Zhivago* and Grossman's *Life and Fate* are published February: Armenian demonstrators call for incorporation of Nagornyi Karabakh in Armenian Republic; anti-Armenian pogrom in Sumgait April: Gorbachev receives Patriarch Pimen in the Kremlin; first "Popular Front" formed in Estonia July: Nagornyi Karabakh unilaterally withdraws from Azerbaijan October: Gorbachev becomes president of USSR December: Gorbachev visits United States, addresses United Nations
1989	February: Soviet troops complete withdrawal from Afghanistan March: elections for Congress of People's Deputies produce some non-Communist victories April: demonstration in Tbilisi is violently suppressed June–July: Nineteenth Conference of CPSU July: coalminers' strike in Kuzbass spreads to other regions August: *Novyi mir* begins publishing Solzhenitsyn's *Gulag Archipelago* September: foundation of Ukrainian Popular Front (Rukh) September: formation of first non-Communist government in Poland November: fall of Berlin Wall; fall of Communist regimes in Czechoslovakia and Bulgaria December: Lithuanian Communist Party breaks away from CPSU; fall of Ceaușescu regime in Romania December: death of Sakharov
1990	January: violent suppression of Azerbaijani nationalist rising in Baku March: abolition of "leading role" of CPSU in constitution; in republican elections many nomenklatura nominees are defeated; Lithuania secedes from USSR; Estonian parliament votes for gradual secession May: Yeltsin is elected president of Russian Supreme Soviet June: formation of Russian Communist Party June: abolition of media censorship July: Gorbachev meets Chancellor Kohl of West Germany and agrees that a reunified Germany can become a member of NATO

631

632

July: Ukrainian parliament declares sovereignty

August: Armenia secedes from USSR and asserts sovereignty over Nagornyi Karabakh; Abkhazia secedes from Georgia

October: First Congress of Democratic Russia; reunification of Germany

November: Conventional Forces in Europe Treaty (CFE) and Paris Charter for a New Europe

1991   January: paratroopers acting in the name of a "National Salvation Committee" storm public buildings in Vilnius and Riga

April–May: Georgia secedes from USSR; and Gamsakhurdia is elected president of Georgia

June: Yeltsin is elected president of Russia by public ballot

June–July: dissolution of Warsaw Pact and Comecon

July: Gorbachev attends G-7 summit; Strategic Arms Reduction Treaty (START) signed

August: Attempted coup in Moscow by "Emergency Committee"; Ukraine, Belorussia, and Moldavia secede from USSR; Gorbachev resigns as general secretary of CPSU and disbands its Central Committee; Supreme Soviet suspends legality of CPSU

October–November: Yeltsin announces radical economic reform program for Russia and is given emergency powers to implement it

November: Dudaev declares Chechnia a sovereign state

December: dissolution of USSR and formation of Commonwealth of Independent States

1992   Russia becomes member of enlarged G-7 (G-8)

January: abolition of most state subsidies in Russia causes huge price rises; war breaks out between Armenia and Azerbaijan over Nagornyi Karabakh

March: Chechen parliament issues declaration of independence

March–June: clashes between Moldavian forces and secessionists in Dniester Republic

June: Russian privatization law

October: outbreak of civil war in Tajikistan

1993   End of ruble zone

March–April: conflict between Yeltsin and Russian Supreme Soviet; public referendum on both

June–July: Russian constitutional conference

September–October: Yeltsin reimposes rule by decree and suppresses an armed rising by Supreme Soviet

December: election for Russian State Duma and new constitution

1994 July: Russia becomes member of NATO Partnership for Peace

December: Russian armed forces invade Chechnia

1995 December: elections for Russian State Duma

1996 June: Yeltsin is reelected president of Russia

August: ceasefire in Chechnia; Russia begins withdrawal of its troops

October: Temporary Extraordinary Commission set up to raid and investigate suspected tax evaders

1997 April: Russo-Belorussian agreement

May: Russo-Ukrainian friendship treaty; Russia-NATO Charter

1998 August: Russian government defaults on its debts

1999 March–June: Kosovo crisis: NATO bombs Yugoslavia

September: new Russian invasion of Chechnia

December: elections for Russian State Duma; Yeltsin resigns as president

2000 March: Putin is elected president of Russia

NOTES

INTRODUCTION

1. Carsten Goehrke, "Geographische Grundlagen der russischen Geschichte," *Jahrbücher der osteuropäischen Geschichte* 18 (1970), 161–204; A. M Khazanov, *Nomads and the Outside World* (Cambridge: Cambridge University Press, 1984); Robert N. Taaffe, "The Geographic Setting," in Denis Sinor, ed., *The Cambridge History of Early Inner Asia* (Cambridge: Cambridge University Press, 1990), 19–40; David Christian, "Inner Eurasia as a Unit of World History," *Journal of World History* 5 (1994), 173–211.

2. Alfred Rieber, "Persistent Factors in Russian Foreign Policy: An Interpretative Essay," in Hugh Ragsdale, ed., *Imperial Russian Foreign Policy* (Cambridge: Cambridge University Press, 1993), 347.

3. Rieber, "Persistent Factors."

4. P. A. Brunt, *Social Conflicts in the Roman Republic* (London: Chatto & Windus, 1971), 48–50.

5. M. N. Afanas'ev, *Klientelizm i rossiiskaia gosudarstvennost'* (Moscow: Tsentr konstitutsionnykh issledovanii, 1997).

6. These general observations are based partly on John P. LeDonne, *The Russian Empire and the World, 1700–1917: The Geopolitics of Expansion and Containment* (New York: Oxford University Press, 1997), 1–20.

7. Robin Milner-Gulland, *The Russians* (Oxford: Blackwell, 1997), 28–36; Basile Kerblay, *L'Isba d'hier et d'aujourdhui* (Lausanne: L'Age d'Homme, 1973), chaps. 2–3.

8. Kerblay, *L'Isba,* 38–41; Friedrich Christian Weber, *The Present State of Russia,* vol. 1 (1722; reprint, New York: Da Capo Press, 1968), 118.

9. David Moon, *The Russian Peasantry, 1600–1930: The World the Peasants Made* (London: Longman, 1999), chap. 4.

10. Arcadius Kahan, "Natural Calamities and Their Effect upon the Food Supply in Russia," *Jahrbücher für Geschichte Osteuropas* 16 (1968), 353–377; idem, "Social Aspects of Plague Epidemics in 18th Century Russia," *Economic Development and Cultural Change* 27 (1978–79), 255–266; Roderick McGrew, *Russia and the Cholera, 1823–1832* (Madison: University of Wisconsin Press, 1965); John T. Alexander, *Bubonic Plague in Early Modern Russia: Public Health and Urban Disaster* (Baltimore: Johns Hopkins University Press, 1980), 229–238. In its active measures for confronting epidemics, as in other ways, the Russian state was becoming more "European" in the eighteenth century: see E. L. Jones, *The European Miracle: Environments, Economies and Geopolitics in the History of Europe and Asia,* 2d ed. (Cambridge: Cambridge University Press, 1987), 139–149.

11. This argument is developed at length in Colin White, *Russia and America: The Roots of Economic Divergence* (London: Croom Helm, 1987), especially part 2; see also Peter Gatrell, "Poor Russia: Environment and Government in the Long-Run Economic History of Russia," in Geoffrey Hosking and Robert Service, eds., *Reinterpreting Russia* (London: Edward Arnold, 1999), 89–106.

12. R. E. F. Smith and David Christian, *Bread and Salt: A Social and Economic History of Food and Drink in Russia* (Cambridge: Cambridge University Press, 1984), 129–133, 194–197; Moon, *Russian Peasantry,* 94–95, 139–142.

13. Moon, *Russian Peasantry,* 295–298.

14. Ibid., 280–283.

15. Ibid., 284–287.

16. Quoted in Smith and Christian, *Bread and Salt,* 8.

17. V. V. Pokhlebkin, *Istoriia vazhneishikh pishchevykh produktov* (Moscow: Tsentrpoligraf, 1996), 136–140, 150–156.

18. "Povest' vremennykh let," in *Pamiatniki literatury drevnei Rusi: nachalo russkoi literatury xi—nachalo xii veka* (Moscow: Khudozhestvennaia literatura, 1978), 98–99.

19. Smith and Christian, *Bread and Salt,* 81.

20. Ermolai Erazm, quoted in ibid., 92.

21. Ibid., 323–326.

22. Ibid., 225, 301–303, 305; S. M. Troitskii, *Finansovaia politika russkogo absoliutizma v 18-om veke* (Moscow: Nauka, 1966), 219.

23. Smith and Christian, *Bread and Salt,* 140–149, 305–307.

24. Pokhlebkin, *Istoriia,* 216–228.

25. Ibid., 300–305.

26. Quoted in Smith and Christian, *Bread and Salt,* 59.

27. V. O. Kliuchevskii, *Sochineniia,* vol. 1 (Moscow: Gospolitizdat, 1956), 314.

28. M. M. Gromyko, *Mir russkoi derevni* (Moscow: Molodaia Gvardiia, 1991), 74–76; L. V. Milov, *Velikorusskii pakhar' i osobennosti rossiiskogo istoricheskogo protsessa* (Moscow: Rosspen, 1998), 429–30.

29. Horace W. Dewey, "Russia's Debt to the Mongols in Suretyship and Collective Responsibility," *Comparative Studies in Society and History* 30 (1988), 249–270.

30. B. N. Mironov, *Sotsial'naia istoriia Rossii perioda imperii,* vol. 1 (St. Petersburg: Dmitrii Bulanin, 1999), 330. Even today, opinion polls show that Russians cherish equality above freedom as the paramount social value; *Vlast' i obshchestvo: resul'taty representa-*

tivnogo oprosa zhitelei Rossii (Moscow: Vserossiiskii tsentr izucheniia obshchestvennogo mneniia, 1998).

31. Milov, *Velikorusskii pakhar'*, 418–423; L. V. Danilova and V. P. Danilov, "Krest'ianskaia mental'nost' i obshchina," in V. P. Danilov and L. V. Milov, eds., *Mentalitet i agrarnoe razvitie v Rossii (xix–xx vv)* (Moscow: Rosspen, 1996), 22–39.

32. Eve Levin, *Sex and Society in the World of the Orthodox Slavs, 900–1700* (Ithaca: Cornell University Press, 1989), esp. introduction and chap. 1.

33. Maureen Perrie, *Pretenders and Popular Monarchism in Early Modern Russia: The False Tsars of the Time of Troubles* (Cambridge: Cambridge University Press, 1995); D. S. Likhachev, A. M. Panchenko, and N. V. Ponyrko, *Smekh v drevnei Rusi* (Leningrad: Nauka, 1984), 7–59.

34. D. S. Likhachev, "Zametki o russkom," *Novyi mir*, no. 3 (1980), 12; John Givens, "Siberia as *Volia*: Vasilii Shukshin's Search for Freedom," in Galya Diment and Yuri Slezkine, eds., *Between Heaven and Hell: The Myth of Siberia in Russian Culture* (New York: St. Martin's Press, 1993), 171–184.

35. Milov, *Velikorusskii pakhar'*, 433–482; Steven L. Hoch, *Serfdom and Social Control in Russia: Petrovskoe, a Village in Tambov* (Chicago: University of Chicago Press, 1986), chaps. 3–4.

36. Kliuchevskii, *Sochineniia*, 1: 32.

37. V. K. Iatsunskii, "Osnovnye momenty istorii sel'skogo-khoziaistvennogo proizvodstva v Rossii s XVII veka do 1917g," in *Ezhegodnik po agrarnoi istorii vostochnoi Evropy 1964g* (Kishinev: Karta moldoveniaske, 1966), 44–64; David Moon, "Peasant Migration and the Settlement of Russia's Frontiers, 1550–1897," *Historical Journal* 40 (1997), 859–893.

38. D. J. B. Shaw, "The Southern Frontiers of Muscovy, 1550–1700," in James H. Bater and R. A. French, eds., *Studies in Russian Historical Geography* (London: Academic Press, 1983), 117–142.

39. Yuri Slezkine, *Arctic Mirrors: Russia and the Small Peoples of the North* (Ithaca: Cornell University Press, 1994), 97–98; Willard Sunderland, "Russians into Yakuts? 'Going Native' and Problems of Russian National Identity in the Siberian North, 1870s–1914," *Slavic Review* 55 (1996), 806–825.

40. Alton Donnelly, "The Mobile Steppe Frontier: The Russian Conquest and Colonisation of Bashkiria and Kazakhstan to 1850," in M. Rywkin, ed., *Russian Colonial Expansion* (London: Mansell, 1988), 189–207.

41. Michael Khodarkovsky, *Where Two Worlds Met: The Russian State and the Kalmyk Nomads, 1600–1771* (Ithaca: Cornell University Press, 1992), 229–235.

42. Moon, "Peasant Migration," 893.

43. I. V. Kondakov, *Vvedenie v russkuiu kul'turu* (Moscow: Aspekt-press, 1997), 59–68.

44. Iu. M. Lotman and B. A. Uspenskii, "The Role of Dual Models in the Dynamics of Russian Culture (up to the End of the Eighteenth Century)," in Lotman and Uspenskii, *The Semiotics of Russian Culture*, ed. Ann Shukman, Michigan Slavic Contributions, no. 11 (Ann Arbor: Department of Slavic Studies, University of Michigan, 1984), 5.

45. This is the basic thesis of A. S. Akhiezer, *Ot proshlogo k budushchemu* (Moscow: PIK, 1994); and idem, *Rossiia: kritika istoricheskogo opyta* (Moscow: Filosofskoe obshchestvo SSSR, 1991), vol. 1.

637

46. Quoted in Leonid Ouspensky, *Theology of the Icon,* trans. Anthony Gythiel, vol. 2 (Crestwood, N.Y.: St. Vladimir's Seminary Press, 1992), 266.

47. P. Florenskii, "Ikonostas," in *Izbrannye trudy po iskusstvu* (Moscow: Izobrazitel'noe iskusstvo, 1996), 98; for a detailed description of the various elements of the iconostasis, see Ouspensky, *Theology of the Icon,* 2: 275–285.

48. Linda J. Ivanits, *Russian Folk Belief* (Armonk, N.Y.: M. E. Sharpe, 1992), esp. chap. 3.

49. Likhachev, Panchenko, and Ponyrko, *Smekh v drevnei Rusi,* 7–59; Russell Zguta, *Russian Minstrels: A History of the Skomorokhi* (Oxford: Clarendon Press, 1978).

50. Likhachev, Panchenko, and Ponyrko, *Smekh v drevnei Rusi,* 72–153.

51. Eva M. Thompson, *Understanding Russia: The Holy Fool in Russian Culture* (Lanham, Md.: University Press of America, 1987).

52. B. F. Egorov, "Ocherki po istorii russkoi kul'tury xix veka," in *Iz istorii russkoi kul'tury,* vol. 5: *xix vek* (Moscow: Iazyk Russkoi Kul'tury, 1996), 51–79. On the prevalence of utopias and antiutopias, see Leonid Heller and Michel Niqueux, *Histoire de l'Utopie en Russie* (Paris: Presses Universitaires de France, 1995).

1. KIEVAN RUS, THE MONGOLS, AND THE RISE OF MUSCOVY

1. Carsten Goehrke, *Frühzeit des Ostslaventums* (Darmstadt: Wissenschaftliche Buchgesellschaft, 1992), 170–172; Pavel M. Dolukhanov, *The Early Slavs: Eastern Europe from the Initial Settlement to the Kievan Rus* (London: Longman, 1996), chap. 8; Peter B. Golden, "The Peoples of the South Russian Steppes," in D. Sinor, ed., *The Cambridge History of Early Inner Asia* (Cambridge: Cambridge University Press, 1990), 256–284; David Christian, *A History of Russia, Central Asia and Mongolia,* vol. 1: *Inner Eurasia from Prehistory to the Mongol Empire* (Oxford: Blackwell, 1998), 287–297, 327–333.

2. Gwyn Jones, *A History of the Vikings,* 2d ed. (London: Oxford University Press, 1984), 255.

3. Golden, "Peoples of South Russian Steppes"; Thomas Noonan, "Why the Vikings First Came to Russia," *Jahrbücher für Geschichte Osteuropas* 34 (1986), 321–348; Janet Martin, *Treasure of the Land of Darkness: The Fur Trade and Its Significance for Medieval Russia* (Cambridge: Cambridge University Press, 1986), 5–14.

4. Serge A. Zenkovsky, ed., *Medieval Russia's Epics, Chronicles, and Tales,* rev. ed. (New York: E. P. Dutton, 1974), 49–50.

5. Christian, *History,* 1: 338.

6. Gottfried Schramm, "Fernhandel und frühe Reichsbildungen am Ostrand Europas: zur historischen Einordnung der Kiever Rus," in K. Colberg, ed., *Staat und Gesellschaft im Mittelalter und Früher Neuzeit* (Göttingen: Vandenhoeck & Ruprecht, 1983), 15–39; Noonan, "Why the Vikings First Came."

7. Horace W. Dewey and Ann M. Kleimola, "From the Kinship Group to Every Man His Brother's Keeper: Collective Responsibility in Pre-Petrine Russia," *Jahrbücher für Geschichte Osteuropas* 30 (1982), 321–335; Horace W. Dewey, "Russia's Debt to the Mongols in Suretyship and Collective Responsibility," *Comparative Studies in Society and History* 30 (1988), 249–270.

8. On local communities, see the excellent work by some historians of the late Soviet and post-Soviet period: I. Ia. Froianov and A. Iu. Dvornichenko, *Goroda-gosudarstva*

drevnei Rusi (Leningrad: Izdatel'stvo Leningradskogo Universiteta, 1988); I. Ia. Froia-nov, *Kievskaia Rus': ocherki sotsial'no-politicheskoi istorii* (Leningrad: Izdatel'stvo Le-ningradskogo Universiteta, 1980); L. V. Danilova, *Sel'skaia obshchina v srednevekovoi Rusi* (Moscow: Nauka, 1994).

9. Froianov and Dvornichenko, *Goroda-gosudarstva*, 63–64; V. I. Sergeevich, *Veche i kniaz': russkoe gosudarstvennoe upravlenie vo vremena kniazei riurikovichei* (Moscow, 1867), 51–80.

10. Froianov, *Kievskaia Rus'*, 185–215.

11. Simon Franklin and Jonathan Shepard, *The Emergence of Rus, 750–1200* (London: Longman, 1996), 142.

12. *Pamiatniki literatury drevnei Rusi: nachalo russkoi literatury, xi—nachalo xii veka* (Moscow: Khudozhestvennaia Literatura, 1978) (hereafter *PLDR*), 122–123.

13. Franklin and Shepard, *Emergence of Rus*, 163–164.

14. Iu. M. Lotman and B. A. Uspenskii, "The Role of Dual Models in the Dynamics of Russian Culture (up to the End of the Eighteenth Century)," in Lotman and Uspenskii, *The Semiotics of Russian Culture*, ed. Ann Shukman, Michigan Slavic Contributions, no. 11 (Ann Arbor: Department of Slavic Studies, University of Michigan, 1984), 3–35, esp. 6–7.

15. Franklin and Shepard, *Emergence of Rus*, 241.

16. Zenkovsky, *Medieval Russia's Epics*, 87–91; George P. Fedotov, *The Russian Religious Mind*, 2 vols. (Cambridge, Mass.: Harvard University Press, 1966), 1: 94–100.

17. Zenkovsky, *Medieval Russia's Epics*, 101–105; W. K. Medlin, *Moscow and East Rome: A Political Study of the Relations of Church and State in Muscovite Russia* (Geneva: E. Droz, 1952), 47; Franklin and Shepard, *Emergence of Rus*, 246–249.

18. Igor Smolitsch, *Russisches Mönchtum: Entstehung, Entwicklung, und Wesen* (Amster-dam: Verlag Adolf M. Hakkert, 1978), 55–58; Zenkovsky, *Medieval Russia's Epics*, 92–98.

19. Zenkovsky, *Medieval Russia's Epics*, 47.

20. There has been much speculation as to why Prince Iaroslav flouted the normal conven-tion and sanctioned the appointment of a local prelate. The most authoritative exami-nation of the issue concludes that he did so not as a challenge to the ecclesiastical authority of the Byzantine patriarch, but as an assertion of canon law, which required that a bishop be appointed by a gathering of the clergy and laity of his own diocese; Andrzej Poppe, "La tentative de réforme ecclésiastique en Russia au milieu du xième siècle," in *The Rise of Christian Russia* (London: Variorum Reprints, 1982), item V.

21. Simon Franklin, trans. and ed., *Sermons and Rhetoric of Kievan Rus'*, Harvard Library of Early Ukrainian Literature, no. 5 (Cambridge, Mass.: Harvard University Press, 1991), 23–24.

22. All existing texts of *Russkaia Pravda* are later compilations, and there is some doubt about whether Iaroslav actually wrote a connected code, or merely compiled and added to existing princely rulings. See Franklin and Shepard, *Emergence of Rus*, 217.

23. George Vernadsky, *Medieval Russian Laws* (New York: W. W. Norton, 1969), 26–56; Daniel Kaiser, *The Growth of the Law in Medieval Russia* (Princeton: Princeton Univer-sity Press, 1980), 3–17.

24. George Vernadsky, *Kievan Russia* (New Haven: Yale University Press, 1948), 83.

25. T. S. Noonan, "The Flourishing of Kiev's International and Domestic Trade, 1100–ca. 1240," in I. S. Koropecky, ed., *Ukrainian Economic History: Interpretive Essays* (Cambridge, Mass.: Harvard University Press, 1991), 102–146; I. Ia. Froianov, *Drevniaia Rus': opyt issledovaniia istorii sotsial'noi i politicheskoi bor'by* (Moscow: Zlatoust, 1995), chap. 5. Froianov discusses the parallel with Athens under Solon on pp. 248–254.

26. *PLDR*, 392–413; quotation p. 396.

27. Noonan, "The Flourishing."

28. Danilova, *Sel'skaia obshchina*, chap. 4.

29. The English text is *The Lay of Warfare Waged by Igor*, trans. Irina Petrova (Moscow: Progress, 1981). For discussion of the *Lay's* authenticity, see John Fennell and Anthony Stokes, *Early Russian Literature* (London: Faber & Faber, 1974), 191–206.

30. Christian, *History*, 1: 395.

31. David Morgan, "Who Ran the Mongol Empire?" *Journal of the Royal Asiatic Society*, no. 2 (1982), 124–136.

32. George Vernadsky, *The Mongols and Russia* (New Haven: Yale University Press, 1953), 10–32; David Morgan, *The Mongols* (Oxford: Blackwell, 1986); Thomas T. Allsen, *Mongol Imperialism: The Policies of the Grand Qan Möngke in China, Russia, and the Islamic Lands, 1251–1259* (Berkeley: University of California Press, 1987); E. Kara-Davan, *Chingiz-Khan kak polkovodets i ego nasledie* (Belgrade, 1930), reprinted in I. B. Muslimov, ed., *Na styke kontinentov i tsivilizatsii* (Moscow: Insan, 1996), esp. 95–162.

33. The Lavrent'ev Chronicle says of the Mongols' first appearance in 1223: "People came of whom nobody knows for certain who they were, where they had come from, or what was their language, their tribe, their faith"; *Pamiatniki literatury drevnei Rusi: XIII vek* (Moscow: Khudozhestvennaia Literatura, 1981), 132.

34. Morgan, *Mongols*, 61–73; Allsen, *Mongol Imperialism*, chap. 7 and 224–225.

35. John Fennell, *The Crisis of Medieval Russia, 1200–1304* (London: Longman, 1983), 66–69. The Mongol appeal enabled the Russian ethnographer Lev Gumilev to claim that the Mongols had no intention of making war on Rus, but that they changed their minds because under their law the killing of envoys was a crime which demanded vengeance. See his *Ot Rusi k Rossii: ocherki etnicheskoi istorii* (Moscow: Ekopros, 1992), 116.

36. *PLDR: XIII vek*, 136.

37. Thomas Noonan, "Rus, Pechenegs, and Polovtsy: Economic Interaction along the Steppe Frontier in the Pre-Mongol Era," *Russian History* 19 (1992), 301–327; Charles J. Halperin, *Russia and the Golden Horde* (Bloomington: Indiana University Press, 1985), chap. 2.

38. Allsen, *Mongol Imperialism*, chap. 2.

39. Christian, *History*, 1: 416, 425–427.

40. Fennell, *Crisis of Medieval Russia*, 118–119.

41. Thomas T. Allsen, "Mongol Census Taking in Rus, 1245–1275," *Harvard Ukrainian Studies* 5 (1981), 32–53.

42. Donald Ostrowski, *Muscovy and the Mongols: Cross-Cultural Influences on the Steppe Frontier* (Cambridge: Cambridge University Press, 1998), 42–43.

43. Anatoly M. Khazanov, "Muhammad and Jenghis Khan Compared: The Religious Factor in World Empire-Building," *Comparative Studies in Society and History* 35 (1993), 461–479.

641

44. V. O. Kliuchevskii, *Sochineniia*, vol. 2 (Moscow: Gospolitizdat, 1957), 244–262.

45. N. S. Trubetskoi, "Nasledie Chingiskhana: vzgliad na russkuiu istoriiu ne s Zapada, a s Vostoka," in *Istoriia. Kul'tura. Iazyk* (Moscow: Univers, 1995), 223.

46. Günther Stökl, "Die politische Religiosität und die Entstehung des Moskauer Staates," in *Der russische Staat in Mittelalter und früher Neuzeit* (Wiesbaden: Franz Steiner Verlag, 1981), 411.

47. P. R. Magocsi, *A History of Ukraine* (Toronto: University of Toronto Press, 1996), chap. 9.

48. The section on Lithuania-Poland is based on Magocsi, *A History of Ukraine*, chaps. 10–12; S. C. Rowell, *Lithuania Ascending: A Pagan Empire within East-Central Europe, 1295–1345* (Cambridge: Cambridge University Press, 1994); A. E. Presniakov, *Lektsii po russkoi istorii*, vol. 2, part 1: *Zapadnaia Rus' i litovsko-russkoe gosudarstvo* (Moscow: Gosudarstvennoe sotsial'no-ekonomicheskoe izdatel'stvo, 1939); Norman Davies, *God's Playground: A History of Poland*, vol. 1 (Oxford: Clarendon Press, 1981), chap. 5.

49. Martin, *Treasure*, 49–68.

50. Eric Christiansen, *The Northern Crusaders*, 2d ed. (Harmondsworth: Penguin Books, 1997), 113–117.

51. William Urban, *The Baltic Crusade*, 2d ed. (Chicago: Lithuanian Research and Studies Center, 1994), 189–201.

52. Allsen, *Mongol Imperialism*, 139–140; Fennell, *Crisis of Medieval Russia*, 106–116.

53. This is the main contention of Gumilev, *Ot Rusi k Rossii*.

54. Iu. A. Limonov, *Vladimir-suzdal'skaia Rus': ocherki sotsial'no-politicheskoi zhizni* (Leningrad: Nauka, 1987), 54–62.

55. Research on the local communities of medieval Rus is scarce. I have relied here on the work of the early twentieth-century historian N. P. Pavlov-Sil'vanskii, who described in detail the papers of the volost of Volochek Slovenskii, a portage on the route from Beloe Ozero to Vologda, on one of the principal northern trading routes. His documents date mostly from the fifteenth century but suggest an order which was already quite stable or evolving only slowly. In any case there are much earlier chronicle references to *starosty, sotskie,* and *volosti*. See his *Feodalizm v drevnei Rusi* (Moscow: Nauka, 1988), 152–168, 184–186, 194–196, 204–207, 217–233.

56. Danilova, *Sel'skaia obshchina*, esp. 191–194.

57. Richard Pipes, *Russia under the Old Regime* (Harmondsworth: Peregrine Books, 1977), 50–52.

58. S. G. Pushkarev, *Dictionary of Russian Historical Terms from the Eleventh Century to 1917* (New Haven: Yale University Press, 1970), 167; Alexandre Eck, *Le Moyen Age Russe*, 2d ed., ed. Marc Szeftel (1933; reprint, The Hague: Mouton, 1968), 43–49.

59. Danilova, *Sel'skaia obshchina*, chap. 5; Pavlov-Sil'vanskii, *Feodalizm v drevnei Rusi*, 79–125, 178–207.

60. Brian Davies, "The Politics of Give and Take: Kormlenie as Service Remuneration and Generalized Exchange, 1488–1726," in A. M. Kleimola and G. D. Lenhoff, eds., *Culture and Identity in Muscovy, 1359–1584*, UCLA Slavic Studies, New Series, vol. 3 (Moscow: ITZ-Garant, 1997), 39–67.

61. On the udel principalities and their interrelations, see V. I. Sergeevich, *Veche i kniaz':*

russkoe gosudarstvennoe upravlenie vo vremena kniazei riurikovichei (Moscow: Tipografiia A. I. Mamontova, 1867); and Eck, *Le Moyen Age Russe*, 61–121.

62. J. L. I. Fennell, *The Emergence of Moscow, 1304–1359* (London: Secker & Warburg, 1968), 186–190, 290–291; R. C. Howes, ed., *The Testaments of the Grand Princes of Moscow* (Ithaca: Cornell University Press, 1967), 212.

63. Donald Ostrowski, "Why Did the Metropolitan Move from Kiev to Vladimir in the Thirteenth Century?" *California Slavic Studies* 16 (1993), 83–101; John Fennell, *A History of the Russian Church to 1448* (London: Longman, 1995), 134–136.

64. On the church's functions, rights, and immunities, see Eck, *Le Moyen Age Russe*, 122–184.

65. John Meyendorff, *St. Gregory Palamas and Orthodox Spirituality* (Crestwood, N.Y.: St. Vladimir's Seminary Press, 1998); idem, *Byzantium and the Rise of Russia: A Study of Byzantine-Russian Relations in the Fourteenth Century* (Cambridge: Cambridge University Press, 1981), chap. 5.

66. Meyendorff, *Byzantium*, 224.

67. Ibid., 254–255.

68. Smolitsch, *Russisches Mönchtum*, 79–100; Pierre Gonneau, "Monachisme et diffusion de la foi dans la Russie moscovite (14–16ème siècle)," *Annales ESC* 51 (1996), 463–489.

69. This ideal biography is set out in Smolitsch, *Russisches Mönchtum*, 82–85.

70. Ibid., 86–93; V. A. Kuchkin, "Sergii Radonezhskii," *Voprosy istorii*, no. 10 (1992), 75–92; Pierre Gonneau, "The Trinity-Sergius Brotherhood in State and Society," in Kleimola and Lenhoff, *Culture and Identity*, 116–145.

71. A. I. Klibanov, "K kharakteristike mirovozzreniia Andreia Rubleva," in M. V. Alpatov, ed., *Andrei Rublev i ego epokha* (Moscow: Iskusstvo, 1971), 62–102.

72. Meyendorff, *Byzantium*, 136–138; Fedotov, *The Russian Religious Mind*, 2: 230–245.

73. P. Florenskii, "Ikonostas," in *Izbrannye trudy po iskusstvu* (Moscow: Izobrazitel'noe iskusstvo, 1996), 122.

74. Leonid Ouspensky, *The Theology of the Icon*, trans. Anthony Gythiel, vol. 2 (Crestwood, N.Y.: St. Vladimir's Seminary Press, 1992), chap. 13.

75. Klibanov, "K kharakteristike mirovozzreviia Andreia Rubleva."

76. D. S. Likhachev, *Kul'tura Rusi vremeni Andreia Rubleva i Epifaniia Premudrogo* (Moscow: Izdatel'stvo Akademii Nauk SSSR, 1962), 116–132.

77. Robert O. Crummey, *The Formation of Muscovy*, 1304–1613 (London: Longman, 1987), 49.

78. V. A. Kuchkin, "Pobeda na Kulikovom Pole," *Voprosy istorii*, no. 8 (1980), 3–21.

79. Fennell, *History of the Russian Church*, 170–183.

80. Marc Szeftel, "The Title of the Muscovite Monarch up to the End of the Seventeenth Century," *Canadian-American Slavic Studies* 13 (1979), 59–81, esp. 62–65.

81. R. G. Landa, *Islam v istorii Rossii* (Moscow: Vostochnaia Literatura RAN, 1995), 63–64, 71–72.

2. IVAN IV AND THE EXPANSION OF MUSCOVY

1. Marc Szeftel, "The Title of the Muscovite Monarch up to the End of the Seventeenth Century," *Canadian-American Slavic Studies* 13 (1979), 59–81; Gustav Alef, "The Adoption of the Muscovite Two-Headed Eagle: A Discordant View," in *Rulers and Nobles*

in Fifteenth-Century Muscovy (London: Variorum Reprints, 1983), item IX; Donald Ostrowski, *Muscovy and the Mongols: Cross-Cultural Influences on the Steppe Frontier, 1304–1589* (Cambridge: Cambridge University Press, 1998), 176–187.

2. Joel Raba, "The Fate of the Novgorodian Republic," *Slavonic and East European Review* 45 (1967), 311–323.

3. Henrik Birnbaum, *Lord Novgorod the Great: Essays in the History and Culture of a Medieval City-State* (Columbus, Ohio: Slavic Publishers, 1981); idem, "Medieval Novgorod: Political, Social, and Cultural Life in an Old Russian Community," *California Slavic Studies* 14 (1992), 1–43; R. G. Skrynnikov, *Tragediia Novgoroda* (Moscow: Izdatel'stvo imeni Sabashnikovykh, 1994), chaps. 1–2.

4. Leslie Collins, "On the Alleged 'Destruction' of the Great Horde in 1502," in Anthony Bryer and Michael Ursinus, eds., *From Manzikert to Lepanto: The Byzantine World and the Turks, 1071–1571*, Byzantinische Forschungen, no. 16 (Amsterdam: Adolf M. Hakkert Verlag, 1991), 361–399.

5. Gustav Alef, "The Origins of the Muscovite Autocracy: The Age of Ivan III," *Forschungen zur osteuropäischen Geschichte* 39 (1986); A. A. Zimin, *Rossiia na rubezhe xv–xvi stoletii* (Moscow: Mysl', 1986), 233–262.

6. Sigismund Freiherr von Herberstein, *Notes upon Russia*, vol. 1 (London, 1851), 106; Gustav Alef, "The Origin and Development of the Muscovite Postal Service," in *Rulers and Nobles*, item VIII.

7. Gustav Alef, "The Crisis of the Muscovite Aristocracy: A Factor in the Growth of Monarchical Power," in *Rulers and Nobles*, item V; idem, "The Boyar Duma under Ivan III," ibid., item VI. According to Kollmann, the Patrikeevy supported Dmitrii as successor to the throne even after Ivan had made his preference for Vasilii clear; Nancy Shields Kollmann, *Kinship and Politics: The Making of the Muscovite Political System, 1345–1547* (Stanford: Stanford University Press, 1987), 138–140.

8. Donald Ostrowski, "The Military Land-Grant along the Muslim-Christian Frontier," *Russian History* 19 (1992), 327–359.

9. V. B. Kobrin, "Stanovlenie pomestnoi sistemy," *Istoricheskie zapiski* 105 (1980), 150–195; V. B. Kobrin, *Vlast' i sobstvennost' v srednevekovoi Rossii* (Moscow: Mysl', 1985), 133–135; Ostrowski, "The Military Land-Grant."

10. Gustav Alef, "Muscovite Military Reforms in the Second Half of the Fifteenth Century," in *Rulers and Nobles*, item VII.

11. A. V. Chernov, *Vooruzhennye sily russkogo gosudarstva v xv–xvii vekakh* (Moscow: Voennoe Izdatel'stvo, 1954), 27–33.

12. Herberstein, *Notes upon Russia*, 1: 30.

13. Richard Pipes, *Russia under the Old Regime* (Harmondsworth: Peregrine Books, 1977), esp. 64–79.

14. Ibid., 64.

15. Marc Szeftel pointed this out in a review of Pipes's book: "Two Negative Appraisals of Russian Pre-Revolutionary Development," *Canadian-American Slavic Studies* 14 (1980), 74–76.

16. Robert Craig Howes, trans. and ed., *The Testaments of the Grand Princes of Moscow* (Ithaca: Cornell University Press, 1967), 241–261, 271.

17. I borrow the term from M. N. Afanas'ev, *Klientelizm i rossiiskaia gosudarstvennost'*

643

(Moscow: Tsentr konstitutsionnykh issledovanii moskovskogo obshchestvennogo nauchnogo fonda, 1997), 85.

18. Afanas'ev, *Klientelizm;* Marshall Poe, "What Did Russians Mean When They Called Themselves 'Slaves of the Tsar'?" *Slavic Review* 57 (1998), 585–608; Ernest Gellner, *Nations and Nationalism* (Oxford: Blackwell, 1983).

644

19. Claudio Sergio Ingerflom, "Oublier l'état pour comprendre la Russie? (xvi–xixème siècle)," *Revue des études Slaves* 66 (1994), 125–134.

20. Max Vasmer, *Russisches Ethymologisches Wörterbuch,* vol. 1 (Heidelberg: C. Winter, 1953), 114–115.

21. Kollmann, *Kinship and Politics,* esp. chap. 1.

22. Strictly speaking a *namestnik* was assigned to an *uezd* (district), while the lower-level unit, the volost (township or canton), received a *volostel'*. In fact, however, there were many inconsistencies in the structure and the associated nomenclature.

23. O. I. Chistiakov and I. D. Martysevich, *Istoriia gosudarstva i prava SSSR,* vol. 1 (Moscow: Izdatel'stvo Moskovskogo Universiteta, 1985), 89–90; Brian Davies, "The Politics of Give and Take: Kormlenie as Service Remuneration and Generalized Exchange, 1488–1726," in A. M. Kleimola and G. D. Lenhoff, eds., *Culture and Identity in Muscovy, 1359–1584,* UCLA Slavic Studies, New Series, vol. 3 (Moscow: ITZ-Garant, 1997), 39–67.

24. N. P. Pavlov-Sil'vanskii, *Feodalizm v Rossii* (Moscow: Nauka, 1988), 209–215; Horace W. Dewey and Ann M. Kleimola, "From the Kinship Group to Every Man His Brother's Keeper: Collective Responsibility in Pre-Petrine Russia," *Jahrbücher für Geschichte Osteuropas* 30 (1982), 321–335.

25. M. F. Vladimirskii-Budanov, *Obzor istorii russkogo prava,* 6th ed. (St. Petersburg: N. Ia. Ogloblin, 1909), 215–217; Horace W. Dewey, "The 1497 *Sudebnik*—Muscovite Russia's First National Law Code," *American Slavonic and East European Review* 15 (1956), 325–338.

26. In outlining the political culture of Muscovy, I draw especially upon Edward L. Keenan, "Muscovite Political Folkways," *Russian Review* 45 (1986), 115–181.

27. Ibid., 132.

28. Nancy Shields Kollmann, *By Honor Bound: State and Society in Early Modern Russia* (Ithaca: Cornell University Press, 1999).

29. Natalia Pushkareva, *Women in Russian History,* trans. and ed. Eve Levin (Armonk, N.Y.: M. E. Sharpe, 1997), 44–50; quotation p. 49.

30. Ibid., 105–108.

31. Ibid., 91.

32. Ostrowski, *Muscovy and the Mongols,* chap. 3.

33. Nancy Shields Kollmann, "Woman's Honor in Early Modern Russia," in Barbara Evan Clements, Barbara Alpern Engel, and Christine D. Worobec, eds., *Russia's Women: Accommodation, Resistance, Transformation* (Berkeley: University of California Press, 1991), 60–73.

34. Vladimir Ivanitskii, "Russkaia zhenshchina i epokha Domostroia," *Obshchestvennye nauki i sovremennost',* no. 3 (1995), 161–173.

35. Carolyn Johnston Pouncy, trans. and ed., *The Domostroi: Rules for Russian Households in the Time of Ivan the Terrible* (Ithaca: Cornell University Press, 1994), 124.

36. Janet Martin, "Muscovy's Northeastern Expansion: The Context and a Cause," *Cahiers du monde Russe et Soviétique* 24 (1983), 459–470.

37. Otto Brunner, "Stadt und Bürgertum in der europäischen Geschichte," in *Neue Wege der Verfassungs- und Sozialgeschichte*, 2d ed. (Göttingen: Vandenhoek & Ruprecht, 1968), 214, 225–241.

38. Jaroslaw Pelenski, "The Origins of the Official Muscovite Claims to the 'Kievan Inheritance,'" *Harvard Ukrainian Studies* 1 (1977), 29–52; quotation p. 40.

39. Ostrowski, *Muscovy and the Mongols*, 137.

40. B. A. Rybakov, *Strigol'niki: russkie gumanisty 14-ogo veka* (Moscow: Nauka, 1993), esp. 218–222, 328–335.

41. Ia. S. Lur'e, *Ideologicheskaia bor'ba v russkoi publitsistike kontsa xv–nachala xvi veka* (Moscow: Izdatel'stvo AN SSSR, 1960), 154–203; John D. Klier, "Judaizing without Jews? Moscow-Novgorod, 1470–1504," in Kleimola and Lenhoff, *Culture and Identity*, 336–349.

42. Joseph L. Wieczynski, "Archbishop Gennadius and the West: The Impact of Catholic Ideas upon the Church of Novgorod," *Canadian-American Slavic Studies* 6 (1972), 372–389.

43. Serge A. Zenkovsky, ed., *Medieval Russia's Epics, Chronicles, and Tales*, rev. ed. (New York: E. P. Dutton, 1974), 328–329; G. Kushelev-Bezborodko, ed., *Pamiatniki starinnoi russkoi literatury*, vol. 1 (St. Petersburg, 1860), 296; see also V. Malinin, *Starets Eleazarova Monastyria Filofei i ego poslaniia* (Kiev, 1901), 492 ff. Some scholars, however, believe the *Legend* was written only in the later sixteenth century: see Ostrowski, *Muscovy and the Mongols*, 236.

44. The original text is in Malinin, *Starets Eleazarova Monastyria Filofei*, appendix, 54–55. On the background to the letter, see N. Andreyev, "Filofei and His Epistle to Ivan Vasilievich," *Slavonic and East European Review* 38 (1959), 1–31.

45. Daniel Rowland, "Did Muscovite Literary Ideology Place Limits on the Power of the Tsar (1540s–1660s)?" *Russian Review* 49 (1990), 152–153.

46. Donald Ostrowski, "Church Polemics and Monastic Land Acquisition in Sixteenth-Century Muscovy," *Slavonic and East European Review* 64 (1986), 355–379. An intelligent statement of the traditional view, resting on close examination of the sources, can be found in N. A. Kazakova, *Ocherki po istorii russkoi obshchestvennoi mysli: pervaia tret' xvi veka* (Leningrad: Nauka, 1970), 68–86.

47. Kazakova, *Ocherki*, 60–65; Marc Szeftel, "Joseph Volotsky's Political Ideas in a New Historical Perspective," *Jahrbücher für Geschichte Osteuropas* 13 (1965), 19–29; quotation p. 20.

48. Kazakova, *Ocherki*, 65–68; George A. Maloney, *Russian Hesychasm: The Spirituality of Nil Sorskii* (The Hague: Mouton, 1973), chap. 3.

49. Jack V. Haney, *From Italy to Muscovy: The Life and Works of Maxim the Greek* (Munich: Wilhelm Fink Verlag, 1973), 175.

50. On Maksim's life and ideas, see ibid.; and Kazakova, *Ocherki*, chap. 4.

51. Michael Cherniavsky, *Tsar and People: Studies in Russian Myths* (New Haven: Yale University Press, 1961), 41–42; David B. Miller, "The Velikie Minei-Chetii and the Stepennaia Kniga of Metropolitan Makarii and the Origins of Russian National Consciousness," *Forschungen zur osteuropäischen Geschichte* 26 (1979), 263–382; Geoffrey Hosking, *Russia: People and Empire, 1552–1917* (Cambridge, Mass.: Harvard University Press, 1997), 6.

52. For recent reappraisals of "Moscow the Third Rome," see Edgar Hösch, "Zur Rezep-

tion der Rom-Idee im Russland des 16 Jahrhunderts," *Forschungen zur osteuropäischen Geschichte* 25 (1978), 136–145; Peter Nitsche, "Translatio Imperii? Beobachtungen zum historischen Selbstverständnis im Moskauer Zartum um die Mitte des 16 Jahrhunderts," *Jahrbücher für Geschichte Osteuropas* 35 (1987), 321–338; Daniel Rowland, "Moscow—Third Rome or New Israel?" *Russian Review* 55 (1996), 59–88.

53. Alexander Dvorkin, *Ivan the Terrible as a Religious Type*, Quellen und Studien zur orthodoxen Theologie, no. 31 (Erlangen: Oikonomia, 1992), 78.

54. Michael Cherniavsky, "Ivan the Terrible and the Iconography of the Kremlin Cathedral of Archangel Michael," *Russian History* 2 (1975), 3–28; David B. Miller, "Creating Legitimacy: Ritual, Ideology, and Power in Sixteenth-Century Russia," *Russian History* 21 (1994), 289–315.

55. Dvorkin, *Ivan the Terrible*, 40, 58.

56. Robert O. Crummey, "Court Spectacles in Seventeenth-Century Russia: Illusion and Reality," in Daniel Waugh, ed., *Essays in Honor of A. A. Zimin* (Columbus, Ohio: Slavica Publications, 1985), 130–146; Paul A. Bushkovitch, "The Epiphany Ceremony of the Russian Court in the Sixteenth and Seventeenth Centuries," *Russian Review* 49 (1990), 1–17; Michael S. Flier, "Breaking the Code: The Image of the Tsar in the Muscovite Palm Sunday Ritual," *California Slavic Studies* 19 (1994), 213–242.

57. Dvorkin, *Ivan the Terrible*, 86–87, 92.

58. A. A. Zimin, ed., *Sochineniia I. Peresvetova* (Moscow: Izdatel'stvo AN SSSR, 1956), 224–232; quotation p. 226.

59. Michael Cherniavsky, "Ivan the Terrible as Renaissance Prince," *Slavic Review* 27 (1968), 195–211.

60. Werner Philipp, *Ivan Peresvetov und seine Schriften zur Erneuerung des Moskauer Reiches* (Königsberg: Ost-Europa Verlag, 1935), 1–10.

61. A. A. Zimin, *Reformy Ivana Groznogo: ocherki sotsial'no-ekonomicheskoi i politicheskoi istorii Rossii serediny xvi veka* (Moscow: Izdatel'stvo Sotsial'no-ekonomicheskoi Literatury, 1960).

62. A. A. Kizevetter, *Mestnoe samoupravlenie v Rossii IX–XIX stoletii* (1917; reprint, The Hague: Mouton, 1974), 40–69.

63. L. V. Cherepnin, *Zemskie sobory russkogo gosudarstva v xvi–xvii vv* (Moscow: Nauka, 1978), 55–115.

64. R. G. Skrynnikov, *Velikii gosudar' Ioan Vasil'evich Groznyi*, 2 vols. (Smolensk: Rusich, 1996), 1: 157–159

65. A. V. Kartashev, *Ocherki po istorii russkoi tserkvi*, vol. 1 (Moscow: Terra, 1993), 433–442; Hosking, *Russia: People and Empire*, 51.

66. Chernov, *Vooruzhennye sily russkogo*, 55–57.

67. Ibid., 57–59; Skrynnikov, *Velikii Gosudar'*, 1: 166–167, 265–267.

68. Chernov, *Vooruzhennye sily russkogo*, 82–86, 89–91, 100–104.

69. Günther Stökl, *Die Entstehung des Kosakentums*, Veröffentlichungen des Osteuropa-Instituts München, no. III (Munich: Isar Verlag, 1953); Philip Longworth, *The Cossacks* (London: Constable, 1969), chap. 1.

70. A. P. Skorik, ed., *Kazachii Don: ocherki istorii*, vol. 1 (Rostov-on-Don: Izdatel'stvo rostovskogo oblIUU, 1995), 140–144.

71. Skorik, *Kazachii Don*, 1: 67–79.

72. Edward Keenan, "Muscovy and Kazan: Some Introductory Remarks on the Patterns of Steppe Diplomacy," *Slavic Review* 26 (1967), 548–558.

73. These arguments are examined in Jaroslaw Pelenski, *Russia and Kazan: Conquest and Imperial Ideology (1438–1560s)* (The Hague: Mouton, 1974).

74. N. Andreyev, "O dele d'iaka Viskovatogo," in his *Studies in Muscovy: Western Influence and Byzantine Inheritance* (London: Variorum Reprints, 1970), item III; David B. Miller, "The Viskovatyi Affair of 1553–4: Official Art, the Emergence of Autocracy, and the Disintegration of Medieval Russian Culture," *Russian History* 8 (1981), 293–332.

75. Skrynnikov, *Velikii Gosudar'*, 1: 227–231.

76. M. S. Anderson, *Britain's Discovery of Russia, 1553–1815* (London: Macmillan, 1958), chap. 1.

77. Eric Christiansen, *The Northern Crusades*, 2d ed. (Harmondsworth: Penguin Books, 1997), 248–258; David Kirby, *Northern Europe in the Early Modern Period: The Baltic World, 1492–1772* (London: Longman, 1990), 66–73.

78. Skrynnikov, *Velikii Gosudar'*, 2: 146–150.

79. The best text of this correspondence is *Perepiska Ivana Groznogo s Andreem Kurbskim* (Leningrad: Nauka, 1979); there is an English translation in J. L. I. Fennell, ed., *The Correspondence between Prince A. M. Kurbsky and Tsar Ivan IV of Russia, 1564–1579* (Cambridge: Cambridge University Press, 1955).

80. A. A. Zimin, *Oprichnina Ivana Groznogo* (Moscow: Mysl', 1964), 249–257.

81. A. I. Klibanov, *Reformatsionnye dvizheniia v Rossii v xiv—pervoi polovine xvi vv* (Moscow: Izdatel'stvo AN SSSR, 1960), 265–266.

82. A. I. Klibanov, *Narodnaia sotsial'naia utopiia v Rossii: period feodalizma* (Moscow: Nauka, 1977), 55–83.

83. Skrynnikov, *Velikii Gosudar'*, 2: 311–326.

84. Zimin, *Oprichnina Ivana Groznogo*, 342–343; Skrynnikov, *Velikii Gosudar'*, 1: 365–371.

85. Skrynnikov, *Velikii Gosudar'*, 1: 375–407, 417–421.

86. Ibid., 2: 70–87, 97.

87. Ibid., 87–90.

88. G. P. Fedotov, *The Russian Religious Mind*, vol. 2 (Cambridge, Mass.: Harvard University Press, 1966), chap. 12; D. S. Likhachev, A. M. Panchenko, and N. V. Ponyrko, *Smekh v drevnei Rusi* (Leningrad: Nauka, 1984), 81–153.

89. The notion of a steppe khanate is suggested by Ostrowski, *Muscovy and the Mongols*, 191–197.

90. Skrynnikov, *Velikii Gosudar'*, 2: 226–231, 240–241.

91. Ibid., 273–275.

647

3. THE TURBULENT SEVENTEENTH CENTURY

1. Donald Ostrowski, *Muscovy and the Mongols: Cross-Cultural Influences on the Steppe Frontier, 1304–1589* (Cambridge: Cambridge University Press, 1998), 239.

2. N. F. Kapterev, *Kharakter otnoshenii Rossii k pravoslavnomu vostoku v xvi i xvii stoletiiakh*, 2d ed. (Sergiev Posad: M. S. Elov, 1914), 34–60; B. A. Uspenskii, *Tsar' i Patriarkh: kharizma vlasti v Rossii* (Moscow: Iazyki Russkoi Kul'tury, 1998), 495–517.

648

3. Paul Bushkovich, "The Formation of National Consciousness in Early Modern Russia," *Harvard Ukrainian Studies* 10, nos. 3/4 (1986), 355–376; Michael Cherniavsky, "Russia," in Orest Ranum, ed., *National Consciousness, History, and Political Culture in Early Modern Europe* (Baltimore: Johns Hopkins Press, 1975), 118–143.

4. L. A. Dmitriev and D. S. Likhachev, eds., *Pamiatniki literatury drevnei Rusi: xii vek* (Moscow: Khudozhestvennaia Literatura, 1980), 130.

5. A. S. Lur'e, "Perepiska Ivana Groznogo s Kurbskim v obshchestvennoi mysli drevnei Rusi," in A. S. Lur'e and Iu. D. Rykov, eds., *Perepiska Ivana Groznogo s Andreem Kurbskim* (Moscow: Nauka, 1993), 214–249.

6. A. P. Pavlov, *Gosudarev dvor i politicheskaia bor'ba pri Borise Godunove (1584–1605gg)* (St. Petersburg: Nauka, 1992), chap. 2.

7. On the growing tax burden: Marc D. Zlotnik, "Muscovite Fiscal Policy, 1462–1584," *Russian History* 6 (1979), 243–258.

8. R. G. Skrynnikov, *Rossiia nakanune smutnogo vremeni* (Moscow: Mysl', 1980), 55–56.

9. Richard Hellie, *Enserfment and Military Change in Muscovy* (Chicago: University of Chicago Press, 1971), 93–103. Even today Russians sometimes say: "There's St. George's Day for you!" (*Vot tebe i Iur'ev den'!*) when an eagerly awaited occasion turns out a complete flop.

10. Skrynnikov, *Rossiia nakanune*, chaps. 9 and 12.

11. Richard Pipes, *Russia under the Old Regime* (Harmondsworth: Peregrine Books, 1977), 78.

12. B. A. Uspenskii, "Tsar and Pretender: *Samozvanchestvo* or Royal Imposture in Russia as a Cultural-Historical Phenomenon," in Iu. M. Lotman and B. A. Uspenskii, *The Semiotics of Russian Culture*, ed. Ann Shukman, Michigan Slavic Contributions, no. 11 (Ann Arbor: Department of Slavic Studies, University of Michigan, 1984), 259–292; Maureen Perrie, *Pretenders and Popular Monarchism in Early Modern Russia* (Cambridge: Cambridge University Press, 1995).

13. V. O. Kliuchevskii, *Sochineniia*, vol. 3 (Moscow: Gospolitizdat, 1957), 41–43.

14. P. G. Liubomirov, *Ocherki istorii nizhegorodskogo opolcheniia, 1611–13gg* (Moscow, 1939), 72–77.

15. G. Edward Orchard, "The Election of Michael Romanov," *Slavonic and East European Review* 67 (1989), 378–402.

16. L. V. Cherepnin, ed., *Skazanie Avraama Palitsyna* (Moscow: Izdatel'stvo Akademii Nauk, 1955), 231–233; quotation p. 232.

17. S. M. Solov'ev, *Sochineniia*, vol. 5 (Moscow: Mysl', 1990), 7–16.

18. My account of the Time of Troubles rests primarily on the classic work by S. F. Platonov, *The Time of Troubles* (Lawrence: University of Kansas Press, 1970); and the modern account by R. G. Skrynnikov, *The Time of Troubles: Russia in Crisis, 1604–1618* (Gulf Breeze, Fla.: Academic International Press, 1988). See also the important revisionist challenge of Chester Dunning, "Crisis, Conjuncture, and the Causes of the Time of Troubles," *Harvard Ukrainian Studies* 19 (1995), 97–119; and his review of Skrynnikov in *Russian Review* 50 (1991), 71–81.

19. Andreas Kappeler, *Russlands erste Nationalitäten: das Zarenreich und die Völker der mittleren Wolga vom 16ten bis zum 19ten Jahrhundert* (Cologne: Böhlau Verlag, 1982), 217–218.

20. Ibid., 238–243.

21. George V. Lantzeff and Richard A. Pierce, *Eastward to Empire: Exploration and Conquest on the Russian Open Frontier, to 1750* (Montreal: McGill–Queen's University Press, 1973), 84–91.

22. James Forsyth, *A History of the Siberian Peoples: Russia's North Asian Colony, 1581–1990* (Cambridge: Cambridge University Press, 1992), 28–33. R. G. Skrynnikov, "Ermak's Siberian Expedition," *Russian History* 13 (1986), 1–40, argues convincingly for a date of 1582 against the more usual assumption of 1581. He also asserts that the Siberian troops had firearms and cannon, which makes Ermak's victory against overwhelming numerical odds very difficult to explain.

23. R. H. Fisher, *The Russian Fur Trade, 1550–1700* (Berkeley: University of California Press, 1943), 29–34.

24. Yuri Slezkine, *Arctic Mirrors: Russia and the Small Peoples of the North* (Ithaca: Cornell University Press, 1994), 13–17.

25. Alan Wood, "Russia's 'Wild East': Exile, Vagrancy and Crime in Nineteenth Century Siberia," in Alan Wood, ed., *The History of Siberia: From Russian Conquest to Revolution* (London: Routledge, 1991), 117–139.

26. Lantzeff and Pierce, *Eastward to Empire,* chap. 10; John J. Stephan, *The Russian Far East: A History* (Stanford: Stanford University Press, 1994), chap. 4.

27. Henry L. Eaton, "Decline and Recovery of Russian Cities from 1500 to 1700," *Canadian-American Slavic Studies* 11 (1977), 220–252.

28. Anne Lincoln Fitzpatrick, *The Great Russian Fair: Nizhnii Novgorod, 1840–1890* (London: Macmillan, 1990), chap. 1.

29. Samuel H. Baron, "The *Gosti* Revisited," in *Explorations in Muscovite History* (London: Variorum Press, 1991), item II.

30. Richard Hellie, "The Stratification of Muscovite Society: The Townsmen," *Russian History* 5 (1978), 119–175; Samuel H. Baron, "Who Were the *Gosti?*" *California Slavic Studies* 7 (1973), 1–40; idem, "Vasilii Shorin: 17th Century Russian Merchant Extraordinary," *Canadian-American Slavic Studies* 6 (1972), 503–548.

31. Baron, "Vasilii Shorin."

32. L. Langer, "The Historiography of the Pre-Industrial Russian City," *Journal of Urban History* 5 (1978–79), 209–240; Samuel H. Baron, "Entrepreneurs and Entrepreneurship in 16th and 17th Century Russia," in Gregory Guroff and Fred V. Carstensen, eds., *Entrepreneurship in Imperial Russia and the Soviet Union* (Princeton: Princeton University Press, 1983), 27–58.

33. A. A. Kizevetter, "Posadsksia obshchina v 18-om veke," in *Istoricheskie ocherki* (Moscow, 1912), 242–263; J. Michael Hittle, *The Service City: State and Townsmen in Russia, 1600–1800* (Cambridge, Mass.: Harvard University Press, 1979), chap. 6.

34. Richard Hellie, *Slavery in Russia, 1450–1725* (Chicago: University of Chicago Press, 1982); see also idem, "Muscovite Slavery in Comparative Perspective," *Russian History* 6, pt. 2 (1979), 133–209.

35. J. L. H. Keep, "The Regime of Filaret, 1619–1633," *Slavonic and East European Review* 38 (1959–60), 334–360.

36. William C. Fuller Jr., *Strategy and Power in Russia, 1600–1914* (New York: Free Press, 1992), 6–14, 33–34.

649

37. John L. H. Keep, *Soldiers of the Tsar: Army and Society in Russia, 1462–1874* (Oxford: Clarendon Press, 1985), 80–83, 88–90.

38. Quoted in R. E. F. Smith and David Christian, *Bread and Salt: A Social and Economic History of Food and Drink in Russia* (Cambridge: Cambridge University Press, 1984), 71.

39. Keep, *Soldiers of the Tsar,* chaps. 3–4.

40. Another polity turning itself into a "fiscal-military state" at about the same time was England. Since after 1689 she was a parliamentary monarchy, whose Parliament was dominated by landowners and wealthy City men, her creditworthiness was much higher, and war finance accordingly much easier to borrow. See John Brewer, *Sinews of Power: War, Money and the English State, 1688–1783* (London: Unwin Hyman, 1989); and, for broader European comparisons, Marshall Poe, "The Consequences of the Military Revolution in Muscovy in Comparative Perspective," *Comparative Studies in Society and History* 38 (1996), 603–618; and Brian M. Downing, *The Military Revolution and Political Change: Origins of Democracy and Autocracy in Early Modern Europe* (Princeton: Princeton University Press, 1991).

41. Peter B. Brown, "Muscovite Government Bureaus," *Russian History* 10 (1983), 269–330.

42. N. F. Demidova, "Gosudarstvennyi apparat Rossii v 17-om veke," *Istoricheskie zapiski* 108 (1982), 109–155.

43. L. V. Cherepnin, *Zemskie sobory russkogo gosudarstva v xvi–xvii vv* (Moscow: Nauka, 1978), 55–115; John L. H. Keep, "The Decline of the Zemskii Sobor," in *Power and the People: Essays on Russian History* (Boulder, Colo.: East European Monographs, 1995), 51–86.

44. Hans-Joachim Torke, *Die Staatsbedingte Gesellschaft im Moskauer Reich: Zar und Zemlja in der altrussischen Herrschaftsverfassung, 1613–1689* (Leiden: E. J. Brill, 1974), 100–116, 213–224; Valerie Kivelson, "The Devil Stole His Mind: The Tsar and the 1648 Moscow Rising," *American Historical Review* 98 (1993), 733–756.

45. Valerie A. Kivelson, *Autocracy in the Provinces: The Muscovite Gentry and Political Culture in the Seventeenth Century* (Stanford: Stanford University Press, 1996), chap. 8.

46. Carol Belkin Stevens, *Soldiers on the Steppe: Army Reform and Social Change in Early Modern Russia* (De Kalb: Northern Illinois University Press, 1995), 163.

47. Hellie, *Enserfment and Military Change,* 130–131.

48. Chapter 11, article 2, in M. N. Tikhomirov and P. P. Epifanov, eds., *Sobornoe Ulozhenie 1649g* (Moscow: Izdatel'stvo moskovskogo universiteta, 1961), 160–161.

49. The relevant articles of the *Ulozhenie* are given in English translation in R. E. F. Smith, *The Enserfment of the Russian Peasantry* (Cambridge: Cambridge University Press, 1968), 141–152.

50. Hellie, *Enserfment and Military Change,* 137–138, 241; Tikhomirov and Epifanov, *Sobornoe Ulozhenie,* 228–236; Hittle, *The Service City,* chap. 6.

51. See B. N. Mironov, *Sotsial'naia istoriia Rossii perioda imperii (xviii–nachalo xx veka)* (St. Petersburg: Dmitrii Bulanin, 1999), 413–415.

52. The term "Ruthenian" is used to describe East Slavic peoples not of Great Russian nationality, that is, those of what later became Belorussia and Ukraine. "Ukraine" originally meant "borderland." The term was used by the Polish state to denote the southeastern border palatinate of Kiev-Bratslav-Chernigov, and by the Zaporozhian

Cossacks to evoke their homeland. It was first used to describe a potential nation by early nineteenth-century writers and ethnographers. See Andrzej Sulima Kaminskij, "Ruthenia, Cossackdom, the Ukraine, and the Commonwealth of Two Nations," *Polish Review* 32 (1987), 93–110.

53. B. Gudziak, *Crisis and Reform: The Kyivan Metropolitanate, the Patriarchate of Constantinople, and the Genesis of the Union of Brest* (Cambridge, Mass.: Harvard University Press, 1998).

54. Paul Robert Magocsi, *A History of Ukraine* (Toronto: University of Toronto Press, 1996), 188.

55. N. I. Kostomarov, "Kievskii mitropolit Petr Mogila," in *Istoricheskie proizvedeniia* (Kiev: Izdatel'stvo kievskogo gosudarstvennogo universiteta, 1989), 282–312.

56. Magocsi, *History of Ukraine,* chaps. 12–16; Orest Subtelny, *Ukraine: A History* (Toronto: University of Toronto Press, 1988), chap. 8.

57. V. S. Shul'gin, "'Kapitonovshchina' i ee mesto v raskole XVII veka," *Istoriia SSSR* 4 (1969), 130–139; V. S. Rumiantseva, *Narodnoe antitserkovnoe dvizhenie v Rossii v 17-om veke* (Moscow: Nauka, 1986), 66–81; Gabriele Scheidegger, "'Die Kirche ist keine Kirche mehr.' Der 'Raskol': alte Quellen neu betrachtet," *Jahrbücher für Geschichte Osteuropas* 46 (1998), 177–194.

58. N. F. Kapterev, *Patriarkh Nikon i Tsar' Aleksei Mikhailovich,* 2 vols. (Sergiev Posad, 1909, 1912), 1: chaps. 1–2; Sergei Zen'kovskii, *Russkoe staroobriadchestvo: dukhovnye dvizheniia 17-ogo veka* (Munich: Wilhelm Fink Verlag, 1970), chap. 7; Rumiantseva, *Narodnoe antitserkovnoe dvizhenie,* 45–53.

59. Georg Michels, "The First Old Believers in Tradition and Historical Reality," *Jahrbücher für Geschichte Osteuropas* 41 (1993), 481–508.

60. Zen'kovskii, *Russkoe staroobriadchestvo,* 302–303.

61. V. V. Andreev, *Raskol i ego znachenie v narodnoi russkoi istorii* (St. Petersburg, 1870), 68; Pierre Pascal, *Avvakum et les Débuts du Raskol: la crise religieuse du 17ème siècle en Russie* (Paris: Librairie ancienne Honoré Champion, 1938), 407–408, 411, 511.

62. A. M. Panchenko, *Russkaia kul'tura v kanun petrovskikh reform* (Leningrad: Nauka, 1984), 42–45.

63. For my account of Nikon's reforms and the schism, I have relied mainly on Pascal, *Avvakum;* Zen'kovskii, *Russkoe staroobriadchestvo;* and Kapterev, *Patriarkh Nikon i Tsar' Aleksei Mikhailovich.*

64. Georg Michels, "The Solovki Uprising: Religion and Revolt in Northern Russia," *Russian Review* 51 (1992), 1–15.

65. Robert O. Crummey, *The Old Believers and the World of Antichrist: The Vyg Community and the Russian State, 1694–1855* (Madison: University of Wisconsin Press, 1970), 19.

66. V. M. Soloviev, *Anatomiia russkogo bunta: Stepan Razin—mify i real'nost'* (Moscow: TIMP, 1994); C. S. Ingerflom, "Entre le mythe et la parole: l'action. Naissance de la conception politique de pouvoir en Russie," *Annales* 51 (1996), 733–757; Michael Khodarkovsky, "The Stepan Razin Uprising: Was It a Peasant War?" *Jahrbücher für Geschichte Osteuropas* 42 (1994), 1–19.

67. Serge A. Zenkovsky, "The Ideological World of the Denisov Brothers," *Harvard Slavic Studies* 3 (1957), 49–66; quotations pp. 57–58.

68. Ibid., 60.

651

69. A. S. Prugavin, *Staroobriadchestvo vo vtoroi polovine XIX veka* (Moscow, 1904), 7–23; N. S. Gur'ianova, "Monarkh i obshchestvo: k voprosu o narodnom variante monarkhizma," in E. M. Iukhimenko, ed., *Staroobriadchestvo v Rossii (xvii–xx vv)* (Moscow: Iazyki russkoi kul'tury, 1999), 126–148; Geoffrey Hosking, *Russia: People and Empire, 1552–1917* (Cambridge, Mass.: Harvard University Press, 1997), 70–74.

4. PETER THE GREAT AND EUROPEANIZATION

1. Gerhard Oestreich, *Neostoicism and the Early Modern State* (Cambridge: Cambridge University Press, 1982); Richard L. Gawthrop, *Pietism and the Making of Eighteenth-Century Prussia* (Cambridge: Cambridge University Press, 1993).

2. Philip Longworth, *Alexei: Tsar of All the Russias* (London: Secker & Warburg, 1984), 37, 108–109, 156–161, 204–205.

3. N. I. Kostomarov, "Epifanii Slavinetskii, Simeon Polotskii i ikh preemniki," in *Istoricheskie proizvedeniia* (Kiev: Izdatel'stvo pri kievskom gosudarstvennom universitete, 1989), 313–349; N. F. Kapterev, *Kharakter otnoshenii Rossii k pravoslavnomu vostoku v xvi i xvii stoletiiakh*, 2d ed. (Sergiev Posad: M. S. Elov, 1914), 477–480, 495–498, 505.

4. A. V. Kartashev, *Ocherki po istorii russkoi tserkvi*, vol. 2 (Moscow: Terra, 1992), 291–297.

5. Nancy Shields Kollmann, "Concepts of Society and Social Identity in Early Modern Russia," in Samuel H. Baron and Nancy Shields Kollmann, eds., *Religion and Culture in Early Modern Russia and Ukraine* (De Kalb: Northern Illinois University Press, 1997), 34–51.

6. S. F. Platonov, *Moscow and the West*, trans. Joseph L. Wieczynski (Hattiesburg, Miss.: Academic International, 1972), 115–124.

7. Ibid., 106–111; V. S. Ikonnikov, "Blizhnii boiarin Afanasii Lavrent'evich Ordin-Nashchokin," *Russkaia starina* 40 (1883), 17–66, 273–308.

8. Platonov, *Moscow and the West*, 111–115; A. S. Lavrov, "Vasilii Vasilievich Golitsyn," *Voprosy istorii*, no. 5 (1998), 61–72.

9. William C. Fuller Jr., *Strategy and Power in Russia, 1600–1914* (New York: Free Press, 1992), 17–21; Carol B. Stevens, "Why Seventeenth Century Muscovite Campaigns against Crimea Fell Short of What Counted," *Russian History* 19 (1992), 487–504.

10. Lindsey Hughes, *Sophia, Regent of Russia, 1657–1704* (New Haven: Yale University Press, 1990), chap. 3.

11. F. H. Hinsley, *Power and the Pursuit of Peace: Theory and Practice in the Pursuit of Relations between States* (Cambridge: Cambridge University Press, 1963), 25–26, 34.

12. Paul W. Schroeder, *The Transformation of European Politics, 1763–1848* (Oxford: Clarendon Press, 1994), 8.

13. D. McKay and H. M. Scott, *The Rise of the Great Powers, 1648–1815* (London: Longman, 1982), chap. 7.

14. M. S. Anderson, *The Rise of Modern Diplomacy, 1450–1919* (London: Longman, 1993).

15. Ibid., 71, 89–90, 95.

16. Quoted in Simon Dixon, *The Modernisation of Russia, 1676–1825* (Cambridge: Cambridge University Press, 1999), 45.

17. Anderson, *The Rise of Modern Diplomacy*, 185.

18. Reinhard Wittram, *Peter I: Czar und Kaiser,* vol. 1 (Göttingen: Vandenhoek & Ruprecht, 1964), 129–167.

19. Michael Roberts, *The Swedish Imperial Experience, 1560–1718* (Cambridge: Cambridge University Press, 1979); for Swedish influence on Peter I's reforms, see Claes Peterson, *Peter the Great's Administrative and Judicial Reforms,* Rättshistoriskt Bibliothek no. 29 (Stockholm: Nordiska Bokhandeln, 1979).

20. Lindsey Hughes, *Russia in the Age of Peter the Great* (New Haven: Yale University Press, 1998), 80–89.

21. John P. LeDonne, *The Russian Empire and the World, 1700–1917: The Geopolitics of Expansion and Containment* (New York: Oxford University Press, 1997), chaps. 1–3.

22. Walter M. Pintner, "Russia's Military Style, Russian Society, and Russian Power in the Eighteenth Century," in A. G. Cross, ed., *Russia and the West in the Eighteenth Century* (Newtonville, Mass.: Oriental Research Partners, 1983), 262–270; quotation p. 265.

23. Christopher Duffy, *Russia's Military Way to the West: The Origins and Nature of Russian Military Power, 1700–1800* (London: Routledge, 1981), chap. 4.

24. Schroeder, *Transformation of European Politics,* 11–19, 46–52; Norman Davies, *Heart of Europe: A Short History of Poland* (Oxford: Clarendon Press, 1984), 296–311.

25. Quoted in Hughes, *Russia in the Age of Peter the Great,* 56.

26. Justin McCarthy, *The Ottoman Turks: An Introductory History to 1923* (London: Longman, 1997), 185–190.

27. Artur Attman, "The Russian Market in World Trade, 1500–1860," *Scandinavian Economic History Review* 29 (1981), 177–202; McCarthy, *Ottoman Turks,* 132–143, 202–204; for an account which emphasizes the superiority of Russia's administration in the late eighteenth century, see William H. McNeill, *Europe's Steppe Frontier, 1500–1800* (Chicago: University of Chicago Press, 1964).

28. Kapterev, *Kharakter otnoshenii Rossii,* 362–379.

29. Fuller, *Strategy and Power in Russia,* 17–21.

30. John L. H. Keep, *Soldiers of the Tsar: Army and Society in Russia, 1462–1874* (Oxford: Clarendon Press, 1985), 103–108; Hughes, *Russia in the Age of Peter the Great,* 65–71, 115, 137–138.

31. Elise Kimerling Wirtschafter, *From Serf to Russian Soldier* (Princeton: Princeton University Press, 1990), chap. 5.

32. Ibid., 87–88; John Bushnell, "Peasants in Uniform: The Tsarist Army as a Peasant Society," *Journal of Social History* 13 (1979–80), 565–576.

33. John Keegan and Richard Holmes, *Soldiers: A History of Men in Battle* (London: Hamish Hamilton, 1985), chap. 2.

34. Philip Longworth, *The Art of Victory: The Life and Achievements of Generalissimo Suvorov* (London: Constable, 1965).

35. On neo-Stoicism and cameralism, see Oestreich, *Neostoicism and the Early Modern State;* also Marc Raeff, *The Well-Ordered Police State: Social and Institutional Change through Law in the Germanies and Russia, 1600–1800* (New Haven: Yale University Press, 1983). For parallels with contemporary European societies, see Gawthrop, *Pietism and the Making of Eighteenth-Century Prussia;* and Peterson, *Peter the Great's Administrative Reforms.*

654

36. Richard S. Wortman, *Scenarios of Power: Myth and Ceremony in Russian Monarchy*, vol. 1 (Princeton: Princeton University Press, 1995), chap. 2; Hughes, *Russia in the Age of Peter the Great*, 271–275.

37. On Peter's ecclesiastical reforms in general, see James Cracraft, *The Church Reform of Peter the Great* (London: Macmillan, 1971); on the establishment of the Holy Synod and its functioning, see Igor Smolitsch, *Geschichte der russischen Kirche, 1700–1917* (Leiden: E. J. Brill, 1964), 99–120.

38. A. V. Muller, ed., *The Spiritual Regulation of Peter the Great* (Seattle: University of Washington Press, 1972), 10.

39. V. M. Zhivov and B. M. Uspenskii, "Tsar' i bog: semioticheskie aspekty sakralizatsii monarkha v Rossii," in B. A. Uspenskii, ed., *Iazyki kul'tury i problemy perevodimosti* (Moscow: Nauka, 1987), 47–153.

40. *Polnoe sobranie zakonov Rossiiskoi Imperii*, vol. 6, no. 4012, 685–689.

41. P. V. Znamenskii, *Prikhodskoe dukhovenstvo v Rossii so vremeni reformy Petra* (Kazan, 1873), chap. 1; Gregory Freeze, "The Disintegration of Traditional Communities: The Parish in Eighteenth Century Russia," *Journal of Modern History* 48 (1976), 32–50.

42. Cracraft, *Church Reform*, 86–87, 251–261; Igor Smolitsch, *Russisches Mönchtum: Entstehung, Entwicklung, and Wesen* (Amsterdam: Verlag Adolf M. Hakkert, 1978), 390–395.

43. G. V. Florovskii, *Puti russkogo bogosloviia* (Paris: YMCA, 1937), 84; Kartashev, *Ocherki po istorii russkoi tserkvi*, 2: 323–330.

44. Aleksandr Shmeman, *Istoricheskii put' pravoslaviia* (New York: Izdatel'stvo imeni Chekhova, 1954), 380–381; Florovskii, *Puti russkogo bogosloviia*, 82–83.

45. Zhivov and Uspenskii, "Tsar' i bog," 142.

46. Hughes, *Russia in the Age of Peter the Great*, 378–389.

47. Iu. M. Lotman and B. A. Uspenskii, "Echoes of the Notion 'Moscow the Third Rome' in Peter the Great's Ideology," in Lotman and Uspenskii, *The Semiotics of Russian Culture*, ed. Ann Shukman, Michigan Slavic Contributions, no. 11 (Ann Arbor: Department of Slavic Studies, University of Michigan, 1984), 53–67; Christoph Schmidt, "Aufstieg und Fall der Fortschrittsidee in Russland," *Historische Zeitschrift* 263 (1996), 1–30.

48. *Polnoe sobranie zakonov Rossiiskoi Imperii*, vol. 6, no. 3534, 28 February 1720.

49. The dichotomy is well examined in Raeff, *The Well-Ordered Police State*.

50. Hughes, *Russia in the Age of Peter the Great*, 249–257.

51. George L. Yaney, *The Systematization of Russian Government: Social Evolution in the Domestic Administration of Imperial Russia, 1711–1905* (Urbana: University of Illinois Press, 1973), esp. 81–100.

52. On the naming of the nobility, see Brenda Meehan-Waters, *Autocracy and Aristocracy: The Russian Service Elite of 1730* (New Brunswick, N.J.: Rutgers University Press, 1982), 18, 208.

53. Ibid., chap. 1; A. Romanovich-Slavatinskii, *Dvorianstvo v Rossii ot nachala xviii-ogo veka do otmeny krepostnogo prava* (St. Petersburg, 1870), 11–22; Lee Farrow, "Peter the Great's Law of Single Inheritance: State Imperatives and Noble Resistance," *Russian Review* 55 (1996), 430–447.

54. Meehan-Waters, *Autocracy and Aristocracy*, 31; Ia. E. Vodarskii, "Praviashchaia gruppa

svetskikh feodalov v Rossii v xvii-om veke," in N. I. Pavlenko, ed., *Dvorianstvo i krepostnoi stroi Rossii 16–18vv: sbornik statei posviashchennykh pamiati Alekseia Andreevicha Novosel'skogo* (Moscow: Nauka, 1975), 105–107.

55. John LeDonne, *Absolutism and Ruling Class: The Formation of the Russian Political Order, 1700–1825* (New York: Oxford University Press, 1991), 3.

56. Evgenii Anisimov, *Vremia petrovskikh reform* (Leningrad: Lenizdat, 1989), 385–393; Hughes, *Russia in the Age of Peter the Great*, 210–228.

57. Hughes, *Russia in the Age of Peter the Great*, 301–304.

58. Romanovich-Slavatinskii, *Dvorianstvo v Rossii*, 82–83; *Modern Encyclopedia of Russian and Soviet History*, vol. 6, 86–89.

59. Hughes, *Russia in the Age of Peter the Great*, 307–308; Alexander Vucinich, *Science in Russian Culture: A History to 1860* (London: Peter Owen, 1963), chaps. 2–3.

60. Vucinich, *Science in Russian Culture*, 105–116; Ilya Z. Serman, *Mikhail Lomonosov: Life and Poetry* (Jerusalem: Center of Slavic and Russian Studies of the Hebrew University, 1988), chap. 1.

5. STATE AND SOCIETY IN THE EIGHTEENTH CENTURY

1. Iu. M. Lotman and B. A. Uspenskii, "The Role of Dual Models in the Dynamics of Russian Culture (up to the End of the Eighteenth Century)," in Lotman and Uspenskii, *The Semiotics of Russian Culture*, ed. Ann Shukman, Michigan Slavic Contributions, no. 11 (Ann Arbor: Department of Slavic Studies, University of Michigan, 1984), 5.

2. Valerie A. Kivelson, "Kinship Politics/Autocratic Politics: A Reconsideration of Early Eighteenth Century Political Culture," in Jane Burbank and David L. Ransel, eds., *Imperial Russia: New Histories for the Empire* (Bloomington: Indiana University Press, 1998), 5–31; the essential documents on the events of 1730 are translated in Marc Raeff, ed., *Plans for Political Reform in Russia* (Englewood Cliffs, N.J.: Prentice-Hall, 1966), 41–52.

3. B. V. Anan'ich, ed., *Vlast' i reformy: ot samoderzhavnoi k sovetskoi Rossii* (St. Petersburg: Dmitrii Bulanin, 1996), 158–159; O. A. Omel'chenko, *"Zakonnaia monarkhiia" Ekateriny II: prosveshchennyi absoliutizm v Rossii* (Moscow: Iurist, 1993), 39–45.

4. David L. Ransel, *The Politics of Catherinian Russia: The Panin Party* (New Haven: Yale University Press, 1975), 76–98; 136–137.

5. Article 37, in P. Dukes, ed., *Russia under Catherine the Great*, vol. 2: *Nakaz to the Legislative Commission* (Newtonville, Mass.: Oriental Research Partners, 1977), 46; Omel'chenko, *"Zakonnaia monarkhiia,"* 100–102.

6. Omel'chenko, *"Zakonnaia monarkhiia,"* 112–126.

7. R. E. Jones, *The Emancipation of the Russian Nobility, 1762–1785* (Princeton: Princeton University Press, 1973), 267–283; an English text of the charter can be found in David Griffiths and George E. Munro, eds., *Catherine II's Charters of 1785 to the Nobility and the Towns* (Bakersfield, Calif.: Charles Schlacks, 1991), 1–21.

8. John P. LeDonne, *Ruling Russia: Politics and Administration in the Age of Absolutism, 1762–1796* (Princeton: Princeton University Press, 1984), 343.

9. Elise Kimerling Wirtschafter, "Legal Identity and the Possession of Serfs in Imperial Russia," *Journal of Modern History* 70 (1998), 561–587.

10. R. P. Bartlett, "Catherine II's Draft Charter to the State Peasants," *Canadian-American Slavic Studies* 23 (1989), 36–57.

11. John LeDonne, *Absolutism and Ruling Class: The Formation of the Russian Political Order, 1700–1825* (New York: Oxford University Press, 1991), 297–301.

12. LeDonne, *Ruling Russia*, 5, 343.

13. A. Romanovich-Slavatinskii, *Dvorianstvo v Rossii ot nachala xviii-ogo veka do otmeny krepostnogo prava* (St. Petersburg, 1870), 82–83; S. M. Troitskii, *Russkii absoliutizm i dvorianstvo v xviii-om veke* (Moscow: Nauka, 1974), 269–271.

14. V. O. Kliuchevskii, "Kurs russkoi istorii," in *Sochineniia*, vol. 5 (Moscow: Gospolitizdat, 1958), 183; Marc Raeff, *Origins of the Russian Intelligentsia: The Eighteenth Century Nobility* (New York: Harcourt, Brace, 1966), 75.

15. Michel Confino, "Histoire et psychologie: à propos de la noblesse russe au dix-huitième siècle," in *Société et mentalités collectives en Russie sous l'Ancien Régime* (Paris: Institut d'Etudes Slaves, 1991), 345–387.

16. Anan'ich, *Vlast' i reformy*, 147; Arcadius Kahan, *The Plow, the Hammer, and the Knout: An Economic History of Eighteenth-Century Russia* (Chicago: University of Chicago Press, 1985), 319–321, minimizes the additional burden represented by the poll tax. P. N. Miliukov, *Gosudarstvennoe khoziaistvo Rossii v pervoi chetverti xviii stoletiia i reforma Petra I* (St. Petersburg, 1895), 727–728, estimated that the burden rose by some 42 percent.

17. Lindsey Hughes, *Russia in the Age of Peter the Great* (New Haven: Yale University Press, 1998), 137–138.

18. Kahan, *Plow, Hammer, and Knout*, chap. 3; Mikhail I. Tugan-Baranovsky, *The Russian Factory in the Nineteenth Century* (Homewood, Ill.: Irwin, 1970), chap. 1.

19. V. A. Aleksandrov, *Sel'skaia obshchina v Rossii xvii–nachalo xix veka* (Moscow: Nauka, 1976), 111–115; Confino, "Histoire et psychologie," 51–62, 80–86, 117–126.

20. Arcadius Kahan, "The Costs of 'Westernization' in Russia: The Gentry and the Economy in the Eighteenth Century," *Slavic Review* 25 (1966), 40–66.

21. LeDonne, *Absolutism and Ruling Class*, 269–275.

22. Jerome Blum, *Lord and Peasant in Russia from the Ninth to the Nineteenth Century* (New York: Atheneum, 1964), 380–385.

23. A. A. Kizevetter, "Posadskaia obshchina v 18-om veke," in *Istoricheskie ocherki* (Moscow, 1912), 242–263; P. G. Ryndziunskii, *Gorodskoe grazhdanstvo doreformennoi Rossii* (Moscow: Izdatel'stvo Akademii Nauk SSSR, 1958), 40–51; J. Michael Hittle, *The Service City: State and Townsmen in Russia, 1600–1800* (Cambridge, Mass.: Harvard University Press, 1979), chap. 6.

24. Hittle, *Service City*, chap. 10; Manfred Hildermeier, *Bürgertum und Stadt in Russland, 1760–1870: Rechtliche Lage und soziale Struktur* (Cologne: Böhlau Verlag, 1986), 81–90.

25. B. N. Mironov, *Russkii gorod v 1740–1860-ye gody: demograficheskoe, sotsial'noe i ekonomicheskoe razvitie* (Leningrad: Nauka, 1990); David Moon, "Reassessing Russian Serfdom," *European History Quarterly* 26 (1996), 483–526.

26. Richard L. Rudolph, "Family Structure and Proto-Industrialization in Russia," *Journal of Economic History* 40 (1980), 111–118; Steven L. Hoch, "Serfs in Imperial Russia: Demographic Insights," *Journal of Interdisciplinary History* 13 (1982), 221–246.

27. The only full-scale study of the artel is Georg Staehr, *Ursprung, Geschichte, und Bedeutung des russischen Artels,* 2 vols. (Dorpat, 1890–1891).

28. Richard L. Rudolph, "Agricultural Structure and Proto-Industrialization in Russia: Economic Development with Unfree Labor," *Journal of Economic History* 45 (1985), 47–69; Edgar Melton, "Proto-Industrialization, Serf Agriculture, and Agrarian Social Structure: Two Estates in Nineteenth-Century Russia," *Past and Present,* no. 115 (1987), 69–106; Henry Rosovsky, "The Serf Entrepreneur in Russia," *Explorations in Entrepreneurial History* 6 (1953–54), 207–229.

29. Geoffrey Hosking, *Russia: People and Empire, 1552–1917* (Cambridge, Mass.: Harvard University Press, 1997), 104–105; E. V. Anisimov, *Rossiia v seredine xviii veka: bor'ba za nasledie Petra* (Moscow: Mysl', 1986), 54–56, 61–62; S. M. Troitskii, *Finansovaia politika russkogo absoliutizma v xviii veke* (Moscow: Nauka, 1966), 214; David Christian, *Living Water: Vodka and Russian Society on the Eve of Emancipation* (Oxford: Clarendon Press, 1990), 42–43, 142–151.

30. Steven L. Hoch, *Serfdom and Social Control in Russia: Petrovskoe, a Village in Tambov* (Chicago: University of Chicago Press, 1986), chap. 1; quotation p. 64; Moon, "Reassessing Russian Serfdom," 500–508.

31. B. N. Mironov, *Sotsial'naia istoriia Rossii perioda imperii (xviii–nachalo xx veka)* (St. Petersburg: Dmitrii Bulanin, 1999), 429–435.

32. Aleksandrov, *Sel'skaia obshchina,* chaps. 2–3.

33. A. I. Novikov, *Zapiski zemskogo nachal'nika* (Newtonville, Mass.: Oriental Research Partners, 1980) 39–42; *Byt velikorusskikh krest'ian-zemlepashtse,* (SPB: Izdatel'stvo Evropeiskogo Doma, 1993), 45–50. Both of these studies treat peasant life in the 1890s, but the practices they describe go back at least a century and probably far more.

34. Aleksandrov, *Sel'skaia obshchina,* chap. 4; Dorothy Atkinson, "Egalitarianism and the Commune," in Roger Bartlett, ed., *Land Commune and Peasant Community in Russia* (London: Macmillan, 1990), 7–20.

35. R. D. Bohac, "Peasant Inheritance Strategies in Russia," *Journal of Interdisciplinary History* 16 (1985), 23–42; C. A. Frierson, "*Razdel:* The Peasant Family Divided," *Russian Review* 46 (1987), 35–51.

36. P. A. Kropotkin, *Zapiski revoliutsionera* (Moscow: Moskovskii rabochii, 1988), 218.

37. I. D. Iakushkin, *Memuary, stat'i, dokumenty* (Irkutsk: Vostochno-Sibirskoe Knizhnoe Izdatel'stvo, 1993), 99.

38. P. Ia. Miroshnichenko, "Narodnye istoki utopicheskogo sotsializma v Rossii," in *Istoriia obshchestvennoi mysli: sovremennye problemy* (Moscow: Nauka, 1972), 480.

39. Hughes, *Russia in the Age of Peter the Great,* 454–455.

40. Ibid., 456–457; Maureen Perrie, "Popular Monarchism: The Myth of the Ruler from Ivan the Terrible to Stalin," in Robert Service and Geoffrey Hosking, eds., *Reinterpreting Russia* (London: Edward Arnold, 1999), 156–169.

41. *Pugachevshchina,* vol. 1: *Iz arkhiva Pugacheva* (Moscow: Gosudarstvennoe Izdatel'stvo, 1926), 40–42.

42. For good narratives of the Pugachev rebellion, see Marc Raeff, "Pugachev's Rebellion," in Robert Foster and Jack P. Greene, eds., *Preconditions of Revolution in Early Modern Europe* (Baltimore: Johns Hopkins Press, 1970), 161–201; and Philip Longworth, "The Pugachev Revolt: The Last Great Cossack-Peasant Rising," in H. A. Landsberger, ed.,

657

658

Rural Protest: Peasant Movements and Social Change (London: Macmillan, 1974), 194–256.

43. See Raeff, "Pugachev's Rebellion," 161–201.

44. John P. LeDonne, *The Russian Empire and the World, 1700–1917: The Geopolitics of Expansion and Containment* (New York: Oxford University Press, 1997), 105; Bernard Lewis, *The Middle East: 2000 Years of History from the Rise of Christianity to the Present Day* (London: Weidenfeld & Nicolson, 1995), 279.

45. LeDonne, *Russian Empire,* 106.

46. J. Black, *British Foreign Policy in an Age of Revolutions, 1783–1793* (Cambridge: Cambridge University Press, 1994), 288.

47. LeDonne, *Russian Empire,* 107–108; E. Hösch, "Das sogenannte 'griechische Projekt' Katharinas II," *Jahrbücher für Geschichte Osteuropas* 12 (1964), 168–206.

48. Barbara Jelavich, *Russia and the Formation of the Romanian National State, 1821–1878* (Cambridge: Cambridge University Press, 1984), chap. 1.

49. Barbara Jelavich, *Russia's Balkan Entanglements, 1806–1914* (Cambridge: Cambridge University Press, 1991), 86.

50. LeDonne, *Russian Empire,* 137.

51. R. A. Fadeev, *Shestdesiat let kavkazskoi voiny* (Tiflis, 1860), 8–9.

52. Ronald Grigor Suny, *The Making of the Georgian Nation* (London: I. B. Tauris, 1989), chap. 2.

53. Muriel Atkin, *Russia and Iran, 1780–1828* (Minneapolis: University of Minnesota Press, 1980), chap. 1.

54. LeDonne, *Russian Empire,* 115–119; George G. Bournoutian, "The Ethnic Composition and Socio-Economic Condition of Eastern Armenia in the First Half of the Nineteenth Century," in Ronald Grigor Suny, ed., *Transcaucasia: Nationalism and Social Change,* rev. ed. (Ann Arbor: University of Michigan Press, 1996), 69–86; Ronald Grigor Suny, "Eastern Armenians under Tsarist Rule," in Richard G. Hovannisian, ed., *The Armenian People from Ancient to Modern Times,* vol. 2 (London: Macmillan, 1997), 109–134.

55. Uwe Halbach, "'Heiliger Krieg' gegen den Zarismus," in A. Kappeler, G. Simon, and G. Brunner, eds., *Die Muslime in der Sowjetunion und in Jugoslawien* (Cologne: Markus Verlag, 1989), 213–214.

56. Paul B. Henze, "Circassian Resistance to Russia," in Marie Bennigsen Broxup, ed., *The North Caucasus Barrier: The Russian Advance towards the Muslim World* (London: Hurst, 1992), 75–76.

57. Moshe Gammer, "Russian Strategies in the Conquest of Chechnia and Dagestan, 1825–1859," in Broxup, *North Caucasus Barrier,* 45–61.

58. Gammer, "Russian Strategies," 47.

59. Henze, "Circassian Resistance," 98–105.

60. For the long-term results of this policy, see Anatol Lieven, *Chechnya: Tombstone of Russian Power* (New Haven: Yale University Press, 1998).

61. For a comparative perspective on tax collection, monetarization of the economy, and the capacity of the state, see Charles Tilly, *Coercion, Capital and European States, A.D. 990–1992* (Oxford: Blackwell, 1992), 74–75, 87–89.

62. The appearance was partly illusion, as historians have shown, but contemporaries were

impressed. See M. Lyons, *Napoleon Bonaparte and the Legacy of the French Revolution* (London: Macmillan, 1994).

63. A. Pypin, *Masonstvo v Rossii: xviii i pervaia chast' xix veka* (1916; reprint, Moscow: Bek, 1997), chap. 4; G. V. Vernadskii, *Russkoe masonstvo v tsarstvovanie Ekateriny II* (St. Petersburg: Izdatel'stvo imeni N. I. Novikova, 1999), 83–90, 109.

64. Gareth W. Jones, *Nikolai Novikov: Enlightener of Russia* (Cambridge: Cambridge University Press, 1984), 145.

65. Ibid., 206–215; Isabel de Madariaga, *Russia in the Age of Catherine the Great* (London: Weidenfeld & Nicolson, 1991), 524–531; K. A. Papmehl, "The Empress and 'un Fanatique': A Review of the Circumstances Leading to Government Action against Novikov in 1792," *Slavonic and East European Review* 68 (1990), 665–691.

66. A. N. Radishchev, "Beseda o tom, chto est' syn otechestva," in *Polnoe sobranie sochinenii*, vol. 1 (Moscow: Izdatel'stvo Akademii Nauk SSSR, 1938), 215–223.

67. Allen McConnell, *A Russian Philosophe: Alexander Radishchev, 1749–1802* (The Hague: Nijhoff, 1964).

6. THE REIGNS OF PAUL, ALEXANDER I, AND NICHOLAS I

1. The best study of Paul is Roderick McGrew, *Emperor Paul I of Russia, 1754–1801* (Oxford: Clarendon Press, 1992).

2. George L. Yaney, *The Systematization of Russian Government* (Urbana: University of Illinois Press, 1973), 118–128.

3. *Correspondance de Frédéric César de la Harpe et Alexandre Ier*, vol. 1 (Neuchâtel: Editions de la Baconnière, 1978), 216; N. Berdiaev, *Russkaia ideia* (Paris: YMCA, 1946), 23.

4. Perhaps unintentionally: see Yaney, *Systematization*, 95–100.

5. Ibid., 194–205; Marc Raeff, *Mikhail Speransky: Statesman of Imperial Russia, 1772–1839* (The Hague: Nijhoff, 1957), 105–169. Speranskii was not just an advocate of a Rechtstaat, as was thought till recently. The publication of his papers in the 1960s showed that his thinking was based on Anglo-American doctrines of the separation of powers; John Gooding, "The Liberalism of Mikhail Speransky," *Slavonic and East European Review* 64 (1986), 401–424.

6. Yaney, *Systematization*, 212–219.

7. This view of Napoleon is set out in Paul W. Schroeder, *The Transformation of European Politics, 1763–1848* (Oxford: Clarendon Press, 1994).

8. N. A. Troitskii, *Aleksandr I i Napoleon* (Moscow: Vysshaia Shkola, 1994), 120–128, 178–183.

9. Schroeder, *Transformation*, 416–425.

10. Risti Alapuro, *State and Revolution in Finland* (Berkeley: University of California Press, 1988), 23–25.

11. E. V. Tarle, *1812 god* (Moscow: Izdatel'stvo Akademii Nauk SSSR, 1959), 585.

12. Ibid., 613.

13. V. I. Semevskii, "Volneniia krest'ian v 1812g i sviazannye s otechestvennoi voinoi," in A. K. Dzhivelegov et al., eds., *Otechestvennaia voina i russkoe obshchestvo*, vol. 5 (Moscow: I. D. Sytin, 1912), 76–77, 81, 92–93.

659

14. Tarle, *1812 god*, 674–675.

15. A. K. Kabanov, "Opolcheniia 1812-ogo goda," in Dzhivelegov et al., *Otechestvennaia voina*, 5: 49.

16. Ibid., 98–100.

17. M. Florinsky, *Russia: A History and an Interpretation*, vol. 2 (New York: Macmillan, 1960), 644.

18. G. V. Florovskii, *Puti russkogo bogosloviia* (Paris: YMCA, 1937), 132.

19. A. N. Pypin, "Rossiiskoe bibleiskoe obshchestvo," *Vestnik Evropy*, no. 8 (1868), 665–667; Stephen K. Batalden, "Printing the Bible in the Reign of Alexander I: Towards a Reinterpretation of the Imperial Russian Bible Society," in G. A. Hosking, ed., *Church, Nation and State in Russia and Ukraine* (London: Macmillan, 1991), 65–78.

20. Pypin, "Bibleiskoe obshchestvo," 262–264.

21. Igor Smolitsch, "Die Geschichte der russischen Kirche, 1700–1917," part 2, *Forschungen zur osteuropäischen Geschichte* 45 (1991), 19.

22. *Dictionnaire de Théologie Catholique* (Paris, 1932–1934), vol. 12, col. 1386.

23. Smolitsch, "Geschichte der russischen Kirche," 21–23, 29; Geoffrey Hosking, *Russia: People and Empire, 1552–1917* (Cambridge, Mass.: Harvard University Press, 1997), 138–142. As far as I can discover, there is no serious study of Filaret in any language: a remarkable lacuna for one of the most important figures in nineteenth-century Russia.

24. William H. E. Johnson, *Russia's Educational Heritage* (New York: Octagon Books, 1969), 49–57; Isabel de Madariaga, *Russia in the Age of Catherine the Great* (London: Weidenfeld & Nicolson, 1991), 497–498.

25. Isabel de Madariaga, "The Foundation of the Russian Educational System by Catherine II," *Slavonic and East European Review* 57 (1979), 369–395.

26. James T. Flynn, *The University Reform of Tsar Alexander I, 1802–1835* (Washington, D.C.: Catholic University of America Press, 1988).

27. Alexander Vucinich, *Science in Russian Culture: A History to 1860* (London: Peter Owen, 1963), 351–360; A. N. Pypin, *Istoriia russkoi etnografii*, 2 vols. (St. Petersburg, 1890–1892), 2: 110–132.

28. Hans Rogger, *National Consciousness in Eighteenth-Century Russia* (Cambridge, Mass.: Harvard University Press, 1960); Yuri Slezkine, "Naturalists versus Nations: Eighteenth-Century Russian Scholars Confront Ethnic Diversity," in Daniel R. Brower and Edward J. Lazzerini, eds., *Russia's Orient: Imperial Borderlands and Peoples, 1700–1917* (Bloomington: Indiana University Press, 1997), 27–57.

29. M. Kukiel, *Czartoryski and European Unity, 1770–1861* (Princeton: Princeton University Press, 1955).

30. The best account of the 1830–31 rebellion is R. F. Leslie, *Polish Politics and the Revolution of 1830* (London: Athlone Press, 1956).

31. Piotr Wandycz, *The Lands of Partitioned Poland, 1795–1918* (Seattle: University of Washington Press, 1974), 122–125.

32. John Doyle Klier, *Russia Gathers Her Jews: The Origins of the "Jewish Question" in Russia, 1772–1825* (De Kalb: Northern Illinois University Press, 1986); *Polnoe sobranie zakonov Rossiiskoi Imperii*, vol. 28, no. 21547, 731–737.

33. Louis Greenberg, *The Jews in Russia: The Struggle for Emancipation*, vol. 1 (New York: Schocken Books, 1976), chap. 4.

34. Quoted in M. V. Nechkina, *Dvizhenie dekabristov,* vol. 1 (Moscow: Izdatel'stvo Akademii Nauk SSSR, 1955), 100.

35. I. D. Iakushkin, *Memuary, stat'i, dokumenty* (Irkutsk: Vostochno-Sibirskoe Krizhnoe Izdatel'stvo, 1993), 77.

36. A. Murav'ev, "Moi zhurnal," in *Memuary dekabristov: severnoe obshchestvo* (Moscow: Izdatel'stvo Moskovskogo Universiteta, 1981), 124.

37. Nechkina, *Dvizhenie dekabristov,* 1: 152–157.

38. "Zakonopolozhenie Soiuza Blagodenstviia," in Iu. G. Oksman, ed., *Dekabristy: otryvki iz istochnikov* (Moscow: Gosudarstvennoe Izdatel'stvo, 1926), 84–85.

39. Oksman, *Dekabristy,* 84–102; quotation p. 92.

40. Iurii Lotman, "The Decembrist in Everyday Life: Everyday Behavior as a Psychological Category," in Iu. M. Lotman and B. A. Uspenskii, *The Semiotics of Russian Culture,* ed. Ann Shukman, Michigan Slavic Contributions, no. 11 (Ann Arbor: Department of Slavic Studies, University of Michigan, 1984), 71–123: Hosking, *Russia: People and Empire,* 176.

41. Substantial excerpts from the two drafts of *Russkaia pravda* can be found in Marc Raeff, ed., *The Decembrist Movement* (Englewood Cliffs, N.J.: Prentice-Hall, 1966), 124–156; quotation p. 130.

42. Raeff, *Decembrist Movement,* 146–147.

43. Ibid., 153–156.

44. Hans Lemberg, *Die nationale Gedankenwelt der Dekabristen* (Cologne: Böhlau Verlag, 1963), 133–138.

45. Extensive extracts from the Northern Society constitution can be found in Raeff, *Decembrist Movement,* 100–118; the full text is in Oksman, *Dekabristy,* 236–249.

46. Franklin A. Walker, "K. F. Ryleev: Self-Sacrifice for Revolution?" *Slavonic and East European Review* 47 (1969), 436–446.

47. Hugh Seton-Watson, *The Russian Empire, 1801–1917* (Oxford: Clarendon Press, 1967), 185.

48. "Aleksandr Dmitrievich Borovkov i ego avtobiograficheskie zapiski," *Russkaia starina* 29 (November 1898), 353–362.

49. N. K. Shil'der, *Imperator Nikolai I: ego zhizn' i tsarstvovanie,* vol. 1 (St. Petersburg, 1903), 468–470.

50. Richard Wortman, *The Development of a Russian Legal Consciousness* (Chicago: University of Chicago Press, 1976).

51. Olga Crisp, "The State Peasants under Nicholas I," in *Studies in the Russian Economy before 1914* (London: Macmillan, 1976), 84–95. On the potato campaign: N. M. Druzhinin, *Gosudarstvennye krest'iane i reforma P. D. Kiseleva,* vol. 2 (Moscow: Isdatel'stvo Akademii Nauk SSSR, 1958), 465–498.

52. M. Polievktov, *Nikolai I: biografiia i obzor tsarstvovaniia* (Moscow: Izdatel'stvo M. i S. Sabashnikovykh, 1918), 312.

53. N. Riasanovsky, *Nicholas I and Official Nationality in Russia* (Berkeley: University of California Press, 1959), 74.

54. Shil'der, *Nikolai I,* 1: 147; John L. H. Keep, "The Military Style of the Romanov Rulers," in *Power and the People: Essays on Russian History* (Boulder, Colo.: East European Monographs, 1995), 189–209.

55. Richard Pipes, "The Russian Military Colonies, 1810–1831," *Journal of Modern History* 22 (1950), 205–219.

56. John L. H. Keep, "The Russian Army's Response to the French Revolution," in *Power and the People,* 211–235.

57. Lina Bernstein, "Women on the Verge of a New Language: Russian Salon Hostesses in the First Half of the Nineteenth Century," in Helena Goscilo and Beth Holmgren, eds., *Russia—Women—Culture* (Bloomington: Indiana University Press, 1996), 209–224.

58. Rogger, *National Consciousness in Eighteenth-Century Russia,* 117–119; V. D. Levin, *Ocherk stilistiki russkogo literaturnogo iazyka kontsa xviii–nachala xix vekov* (Moscow: Nauka, 1964), 115–153.

59. A. G. Cross, *N. M. Karamzin: A Study of His Literary Career, 1783–1803* (Carbondale: Southern Illinois University Press, 1971), 222.

60. On "imagined communities" and the role of language and print technology in creating them, see Benedict Anderson, *Imagined Communities: Reflections on the Origin and Spread of Nationalism* (London: Verso, 1983).

61. A good recent biography of Pushkin is Iu. M. Lotman, "Biografiia pisatelia," in *Pushkin* (St. Peterburg: Iskusstvo SPB, 1995), 21–184.

62. Deborah A. Martinsen, ed., *Literary Journals in Imperial Russia* (Cambridge: Cambridge University Press, 1997).

63. P. V. Annenkov, *Literaturnye vospominaniia* (Leningrad: Akademia, 1928), 306.

64. Aleksandr Gertsen, *Byloe i dumy,* vol. 1 (Moscow: Goslitizdat, 1963), 347.

65. Chester M. Rzadkiewicz, "Polevoi's *Moscow Telegraph* and the Journal Wars of 1825–34," in Martinsen, *Literary Journals,* 64–87.

66. Victor Terras, *Belinskij and Russian Literary Criticism: The Heritage of Organic Aesthetics* (Madison: University of Wisconsin Press, 1974); and idem, "Belinsky the Journalist and Russian Literature," in Martinsen, *Literary Journals,* 117–128.

67. Raymond T. McNally, ed., *The Major Works of Peter Chaadaev* (Notre Dame: University of Notre Dame Press, 1969), 28, 37.

68. See Chaadaev's "Apology of a Madman," ibid., 199–218.

69. N. Riasanovsky, "Khomiakov on *Sobornost,*" in E. J. Simmons, ed., *Continuity and Change in Russian and Soviet Thought* (Cambridge, Mass.: Harvard University Press, 1955), 183–184.

70. N. Riasanovsky, *Russia and the West in the Teaching of the Slavophiles: A Study of Romantic Ideology* (Cambridge, Mass.: Harvard University Press, 1952), 135.

71. N. L. Brodskii, ed., *Rannie slavianofily* (Moscow, 1910), 85–86.

72. The best overall study of the Slavophiles is Andrzej Walicki, *The Slavophile Controversy: A History of Conservative Utopia in Nineteenth Century Russia* (Oxford: Clarendon Press, 1975).

73. Leah Greenfeld, *Nationalism: Five Roads to Modernity* (Cambridge, Mass.: Harvard University Press, 1992), 265; Gertsen, *Byloe i Dumy,* 1: 445.

74. V. G. Belinskii, *Polnoe sobranie sochinenii,* vol. 7 (Moscow: Isdatel'stvo Akademii Nauk SSSR, 1955), 435.

75. Ibid., 8: 472; 10 (1956): 9, 19–21.

76. Derek Offord, *Early Russian Liberals* (Cambridge: Cambridge University Press, 1985), 178–186. My own view, as can be seen elsewhere, is that the kinship principle was

replaced not by the individual principle but by that of communal or joint responsibility.

77. Aleksandr Herzen, "Russkii narod i sotsializm" (letter to Jules Michelet), in A. I. Gertsen, *Polnoe sobranie sochinenii i pisem*, vol. 6 (Petrograd, 1919), 447. On Gertsen's intellectual evolution the best works are Martin Malia, *Herzen and the Birth of Russian Socialism, 1812–1855* (Cambridge, Mass.: Harvard University Press, 1961); and Edward Acton, *Alexander Herzen and the Role of the Intellectual Revolutionary* (Cambridge: Cambridge University Press, 1979). On Westernism in general and its evolution toward socialism, see A. I. Volodin, "'Chto vy Evropoi nam kolete glaz?' (Shtrikhi k portretu russkogo 'zapadnichestva')," in E. L. Rudnitskaia, ed., *V razdum'iakh o Rossii* (Moscow: Arkheograficheskii Tsentr, 1996), 189–212.

78. John P. LeDonne, *The Russian Empire and the World, 1700–1917: The Geopolitics of Expansion and Containment* (New York: Oxford University Press, 1997), 121–122.

79. M. S. Anderson, *The Eastern Question, 1774–1923: A Study in International Relations* (London: Macmillan, 1966), 84–85; N. S. Kiniapina, *Vneshniaia politika Rossii pervoi poloviny XIX veka* (Moscow: Vysshaia shkola, 1963), 189–190.

80. LeDonne, *Russian Empire*, 123–125.

81. G. Bolsover, "Nicholas I and the Partition of Turkey," *Slavonic and East European Review* 27 (1948), 115–145.

7. ALEXANDER II'S UNCERTAIN REFORMS

1. John Sheldon Curtiss, *Russia's Crimean War* (Durham, N.C.: Duke University Press, 1979), 535–548; quotation p. 545.

2. William C. Fuller Jr., *Strategy and Power in Russia, 1600–1914* (New York: Free Press, 1992), 278–281.

3. P. A. Zaionchkovskii, *Voennye reformy 1860–1870-kh godov v Rossii* (Moscow: Izdatel'stvo Moskovskogo Universiteta, 1952), 284.

4. D. C. B. Lieven, *Russia and the Origins of the First World War* (London: Macmillan, 1983), 23–24.

5. M. Polievktov, *Nikolai I: biografiia i obzor tsarstvovaniia* (Moscow: Izdatel'stvo M. i S. Sabashnikovykh, 1918), 312.

6. Iu. Samarin, *Sochineniia*, vol. 2 (Moscow, 1878), 17–20.

7. B. N. Chicherin, "O krepostnom sostoianii," *Golosa iz Rossii*, vol. 1, part 2 (1856; reprint, Moscow: Nauka, 1974), 131, 170.

8. K. D. Kavelin, *Sobrannye sochineniia*, vol. 2 (St. Petersburg, 1889), 33–34.

9. Steven L. Hoch, "The Banking Crisis, Peasant Reform, and Economic Development in Russia, 1857–61," *American Historical Review* 96 (1991), 795–820.

10. Ibid.; B. V. Anan'ich, ed., *Vlast' i reforma: ot samoderzhavnoi k sovetskoi Rossii* (St. Petersburg: Dmitrii Bulanin, 1996), 319–320, 323–324.

11. A. V. Gordon, "Khoziaistvovanie na zemle—osnova krest'ianskogo samosoznaniia," in V. P. Danilov and L. V. Milov, eds., *Mentalitet i agrarnoe razvitie Rossii (xix–xx vv)* (Moscow: Rosspen, 1996), 57–74, esp. 67–68.

12. Daniel Field, *Rebels in the Name of the Tsar* (Boston: Houghton Mifflin, 1976), 31–112.

663

664

13. Anan'ich, *Vlast' i reforma*, 321–322; V. V. Garmiza, "Predlozheniia i proekty P. A. Valueva po voprosam vnutrennei politiki (1862–66gg.)," *Istoricheskii Arkhiv*, no. 1 (1958), 141–144.

14. Terence Emmons, *The Russian Landed Gentry and the Peasant Emancipation of 1861* (Cambridge: Cambridge University Press, 1969), 343–344.

15. *Dnevnik P. A. Valueva, ministra vnutrennikh del*, vol. 1 (Moscow: Izdatel'stvo Akademii Nauk SSSR, 1961), 181.

16. Emmons, *Russian Landed Gentry*, chaps. 9–10.

17. George Yaney, *The Systematization of Russian Government: Social Evolution in the Domestic Administration of Imperial Russia, 1711–1905* (Urbana: University of Illinois Press, 1973), 187–192.

18. For evidence on their landholdings, see Andreas Grenzer, *Adel und Landbesitz im ausgehenden Zarenreich* (Stuttgart: Franz Steiner Verlag, 1995); on their own self-image, see Geoffrey Hosking and Roberta Thompson Manning, "What Was the United Nobility?" in Leopold H. Haimson, ed., *The Politics of Rural Russia, 1905–1914* (Bloomington: Indiana University Press, 1979), 142–183.

19. Charles E. Timberlake, "The Zemstvo and the Development of a Russian Middle Class," in Edith W. Clowes, Samuel D. Kassow, and James L. West, eds., *Between Tsar and People: Educated Society and the Quest for Public Identity in Late Imperial Russia* (Princeton: Princeton University Press, 1991), 164–179.

20. Nancy M. Frieden, *Russian Physicians in an Era of Reform and Revolution, 1856–1905* (Princeton: Princeton University Press, 1981), 192–195, 242–261; Christine Ruane, *Gender, Class, and the Professionalization of Russian City Teachers, 1860–1914* (Pittsburgh: Pittsburgh University Press, 1994), chap. 4.

21. Richard G. Robbins Jr., *Famine in Russia: The Imperial Government Responds to a Crisis* (New York: Columbia University Press, 1975), esp. chaps. 7, 10; Geoffrey Hosking, *Russia: People and Empire, 1552–1917* (Cambridge, Mass.: Harvard University Press, 1997), 322–326.

22. Anan'ich, *Vlast' i reforma*, 291.

23. Samuel Kucherov, *Courts, Lawyers, and Trials under the Last Three Tsars* (Westport, Conn.: Greenwood Press, 1974), 130, 269, 274–275; William E. Pomeranz, "Justice from Below: The History of the Underground *Advokatura*," *Russian Review* 52 (1993), 321–340.

24. William G. Wagner, *Marriage, Property and Law in Late Imperial Russia* (Oxford: Clarendon Press, 1994).

25. Samuel D. Kassow, "The University Statute of 1863: A Reconsideration," in Ben Eklof, John Bushnell, and Larissa Zakharova, eds., *Russia's Great Reforms, 1855–1881* (Bloomington: Indiana University Press, 1994), 247–263.

26. V. R. Leikina-Svirskaia, *Intelligentsiia v Rossii vo vtoroi polovine xix veka* (Moscow: Mysl', 1971), 56, 62–63.

27. Pavel Miliukov, "Moi universitetskie gody," in *Moskovskii universitet, 1755–1930: iubileinyi sbornik* (Paris: Izdatel'stvo "Sovremennye Zapiski," 1930), 262.

28. Daniel R. Brower, *Training the Nihilists: Education and Radicalism in Tsarist Russia* (Ithaca: Cornell University Press, 1975); Susan K. Morrissey, *Heralds of Revolution: Russian Students and the Myth of Radicalism* (New York: Oxford University Press, 1998), chaps. 1–2.

29. Garmiza, "Predlozheniia i proekty," 151–152.

30. Charles Ruud, *Fighting Words: Imperial Censorship and the Russian Press, 1804–1906* (Toronto: Toronto University Press, 1982), 198–199.

31. Dietrich Geyer, *Russian Imperialism: The Interaction of Domestic and Foreign Policy, 1860–1914* (Leamington Spa: Berg, 1987), 110–112, 118–121.

32. Louise McReynolds, *The News under Russia's Old Regime: The Development of a Mass-Circulation Press* (Princeton: Princeton University Press, 1991); Daniel R. Brower, "The Penny Press and Its Readers," in Stephen P. Frank and Mark D. Steinberg, eds., *Cultures in Flux: Lower-Class Values, Practices, and Resistance in Late Imperial Russia* (Princeton: Princeton University Press, 1994), 147–167.

33. Dietrich Beyrau, *Militär und Gesellschaft im vorrevolutionären Russland* (Cologne: Böhlau Verlag, 1984), 269.

34. Miliutin's struggle is described in Zaionchkovskii, *Voennye reformy*, esp. chaps. 6–7.

35. Peter Kenez, "A Profile of the Pre-Revolutionary Russian Officers Corps," *California Slavic Studies* 7 (1973), 121–158. Alexander Solzhenitsyn dramatized this contrast in his novel *August 1914.* On the restoration of the Cadet Corps, see P. A. Zaionchkovskii, *Samoderzhavie i russkaia armiia na rubezhe xix–xx stoletii* (Moscow: Mysl', 1973), 295–299.

36. Gregory Freeze, *The Parish Clergy in Nineteenth-Century Russia: Crisis, Reform, Counter-Reform* (Princeton: Princeton University Press, 1983), 188.

37. Ibid., 81–101, 311–319, 363–372; S. V. Rimskii, "Tserkovnaia reforma 60–70kh godov xix veka," *Otechestvennaia istoriia*, no. 2 (1995), 166–175.

38. Roy R. Robson, *Old Believers in Modern Russia* (De Kalb: Northern Illinois University Press, 1995), chaps. 3 and 7.

39. Adele Lindenmeyr, *Poverty Is Not a Vice: Charity, Society, and the State in Imperial Russia* (Princeton: Princeton University Press, 1996), 10–12, 18–25.

40. Ibid., 132–135, 169–173.

41. Father Sergii Chetverikov, *Starets Paisii Velichkovskii: His Life, Teachings, and Influence on Orthodox Monasticism* (Belmont, Mass.: Nordland, 1980); a useful summary of the revival of hesychasm is Robert L. Nichols, "The Orthodox Elders of Imperial Russia," *Modern Greek Studies Yearbook* 1 (1985), 1–30.

42. Valentin Zander, *Father Serafim of Sarov* (Crestwood, N.Y.: St. Vladimir's Seminary Press, 1975), 24.

43. Nichols, "Orthodox Elders."

44. K. Mochul'skii, *Dukhovnyi put' Gogolia* (Paris: YMCA Press, 1976), 131; D. P. Bogdanov, "Optina pustyn' i palomnichestvo v nee russkikh pisatelei," *Istoricheskii vestnik*, no. 10 (1910), 327–339; N. A. Pavlovich, "Optina pustyn': pochemu tuda ezdili velikie?" *Prometei* 12 (1980), 84–92.

45. A. G. Dostoevskaia, *Vospominaniia* (Moscow: Pravda, 1987), 347.

46. F. M. Dostoevskii, *Brat'ia Karamazovy*, in *Polnoe sobranie sochinenii*, vol. 14 (Leningrad: Nauka, 1976), 26–29 (my translation).

47. R. F. Leslie, *Reform and Insurrection in Poland, 1856–1865* (London: Athlone Press, 1956).

48. Quoted in Adam Michnik, "1863: Poland in Russian Eyes," in *Letters from Prison and Other Essays* (Berkeley: University of California Press, 1985), 249–274; quotation p. 257.

49. Leslie, *Reform and Insurrection*, chap. 9.

665

50. Norman Davies, *God's Playground: A History of Poland,* vol. 2 (Oxford: Clarendon Press, 1981), 364–365.

51. M. A. Bakunin, *Sobranie sochinenii i pisem, 1828–1876,* ed. Iu. M. Steklov, vol. 3 (Moscow: Izdatel'stvo vsesoiuznogo obshchestva politkatorzhan i ssyl'no-poselentsev, 1935), 148; Aileen Kelly, *Mikhail Bakunin: A Study in the Psychology and Politics of Utopianism* (Oxford: Clarendon Press, 1982), 52–60.

52. M. A. Bakunin, *Statism and Anarchy,* trans. and ed. Marshall S. Shatz (Cambridge: Cambridge University Press, 1990), 38–39.

53. Kelly, *Mikhail Bakunin,* 131.

54. Hosking, *Russia: People and Empire,* 281–284.

55. Nikolai Valentinov, *The Early Years of Lenin* (Ann Arbor: University of Michigan Press, 1969), 135–136.

56. Barbara Alpern Engel, *Mothers and Daughters: Women of the Intelligentsia in Nineteenth Century Russia* (Cambridge: Cambridge University Press, 1983), chaps. 2–3.

57. Quoted in Franco Venturi, *Roots of Revolution: A History of the Populist and Socialist Movements in Nineteenth-Century Russia* (New York: Universal Library, 1966), 345–346.

58. Ibid., 365.

59. Ibid., chap. 15.

60. James Billington, *Mikhailovsky and Russian Populism* (Oxford: Clarendon Press, 1958), chap. 8; an attempt to draw Old Believers into revolutionary work is recounted in "'Ispoved' V. I. Kel'sieva," *Literaturnoe nasledstvo* 41–42 (1941), 297–335.

61. Billington, *Mikhailovsky,* 126–127; A. A. Titov, ed., *Nikolai Vasil'evich Chaikovskii: religioznye i obshchestvennye iskaniia* (Paris, 1929), 53–55; quotation p. 55.

62. Venturi, *Roots of Revolution,* chap. 19.

63. O. V. Aptekman, *Obshchestvo "Zemlia i volia" 70-kh godov po lichnym vospominaniiam* (Petrograd: Kolos, 1924), 133.

64. Hosking, *Russia: People and Empire,* 350–353.

65. Aptekman, *Obshchestvo "Zemlia i volia,"* 152. For a discussion of recent research see Daniel Field, "Peasants and Propagandists in the Russian Movement to the People of 1874," *Journal of Modern History* 59 (1987), 415–438.

66. Aptekman, *Obshchestvo "Zemlia i volia,"* 168–177; Vera Figner, *Zapechatlennyi trud* (Moscow: Mysl', 1964), 162–165; quotation pp. 164–165.

67. V. Debagorii-Mokrievich, *Vospominaniia* (St. Petersburg, 1904), 277–282.

68. Kucherov, *Courts, Lawyers, and Trials,* 217–225; quotation p. 220.

69. A. S. Suvorin, *Dnevnik* (Moscow: Izdatel'stvo L. D. Frenkel, 1923), 15–16.

70. F. I. Tiutchev, "Russkaia geografiia," in *Lirika,* vol. 2 (Moscow: Nauka, 1965), 118.

71. N. Ia. Danilevskii, *Rossiia i Evropa* (New York: Johnson Reprint, 1966), 556–557; Hosking, *Russia: People and Empire,* 369.

72. F. M. Dostoevskii, "Dnevnik pisatelia," April 1877, in *Polnoe sobranie sochinenii,* vol. 25 (Leningrad: Nauka, 1983), 100.

73. P. A. Zaionchkovskii, *Krizis samoderzhaviia na rubezhe 1870–1880-kh godov* (Moscow: Izdatel'stvo Moskovskogo Universiteta, 1964), 451–460.

74. Hans Kohn, *Panslavism: Its History and Ideology* (New York: Vintage Books, 1960), 184–186.

75. "Un grand état compact slave": B. H. Sumner, *Russia and the Balkans, 1870–1880* (Oxford: Clarendon Press, 1937), 601.

76. Ivan Aksakov, *Sochineniia*, vol. 1 (Moscow, 1886), 271.

77. A. V. Buganov, *Russkaia istoriia v pamiati krest'ian xix veka i natsional'noe samosoznanie* (Moscow: Institut etnologii i antropologii, 1992), 179.

78. George F. Kennan, *The Fateful Alliance: France, Russia and the Coming of the First World War* (Manchester: Manchester University Press, 1984).

79. Zaionchkovskii, *Krizis samoderzhaviia*, 217.

80. Ibid., 287–290; Daniel Orlovsky, *The Limits of Reform: The Ministry of Internal Affairs in Imperial Russia, 1802–1881* (Cambridge, Mass.: Harvard University Press, 1981), chap. 6.

81. E. A. Peretts, *Dnevnik E. A. Perettsa, 1880–1883* (Moscow: Gosudarstvennoe Izdatel'stvo, 1927), 38–39.

82. Zaionchkovskii, *Krizis samoderzhaviia*, 451–460; *Pis'ma K. P. Pobedonostseva k Aleksandru III-emu*, vol. 1 (Moscow, 1925), 381.

83. Zaionchkovskii, *Krizis samoderzhaviia*, 400–410.

84. Thomas S. Pearson, *Russian Officialdom in Crisis: Autocracy and Local Self-Government, 1861–1900* (Cambridge: Cambridge University Press, 1989), chap. 5; A. I. Novikov, *Zapiski zemskogo nachal'nika* (1899; reprint, Newtonville, Mass.: Oriental Research Partners, 1980), 38–39.

85. Pearson, *Russian Officialdom*, chap. 6; L. G. Zakharova, *Zemskaia kontrreforma 1890g* (Moscow: Izdatel'stvo Moskovskogo Universiteta, 1968); Kermit E. McKenzie, "Zemstvo Organisation and Role within the Administrative Structure," in Terence Emmons and Wayne S. Vucinich, eds., *The Zemstvo in Russia: An Experiment in Local Self-Government* (Cambridge: Cambridge University Press, 1982), 31–78.

8. THE RISE OF NATIONALISM

1. Beatrice F. Manz, "Historical Background," in Manz, ed., *Central Asia in Historical Perspective* (Boulder, Colo.: Westview Press, 1994), 4–22; Maria Eva Subtelny, "The Symbiosis of Turk and Tajik," ibid., 45–61; S. A. M. Adshead, *Central Asia in World History* (London: Macmillan, 1993). In the nineteenth century the Kazakh and Kirgiz peoples were known indiscriminately as Kirgiz.

2. Shirin Akiner, "Islam, the State, and Ethnicity in Central Asia in Historical Perspective," *Religion, State, and Society* 24, no. 2 (1996), 91–94.

3. Ibid., 94–99.

4. Quoted in David Gillard, *The Struggle for Asia, 1828–1914: A Study in British and Russian Imperialism* (London: Methuen, 1977), 72–73.

5. S. S. Tatishchev, *Imperator Aleksandr II: ego zhizn' i tsarstvovanie*, vol. 2 (St. Petersburg: Izdatel'stvo A. S. Suvorina, 1903), 115–116.

6. A. J. Rieber, *The Politics of Autocracy: Letters of Alexander II to Prince A. I. Bariatinskii, 1857–1864* (Paris: Mouton, 1966), 72.

7. David Mackenzie, "Expansion in Central Asia: St. Petersburg vs. the Turkestan Generals, 1863–1866," *Canadian Slavic Studies* 3 (1969), 286–311; quotation p. 303.

8. Ibid., 305.

9. Quoted in Akiner, "Islam," 100.

10. Andreas Kappeler, *Russland als Vielvölkerreich: Entstehung, Geschichte, Zerfall* (Munich: C. H. Beck Verlag, 1992), 160–168.

11. Richard A. Pierce, *Russian Central Asia, 1867–1917: A Study in Colonial Rule* (Berkeley: University of California Press, 1960), 147–149, 156–162.

12. Beatrice F. Manz, "Central Asian Uprisings in the Nineteenth Century: Fergana under the Russians," *Russian Review* 46 (1987), 267–281.

13. Serge A. Zenkovsky, *Panturkism and Islam in Russia* (Cambridge, Mass.: Harvard University Press, 1960), chap. 3; R. G. Landa, *Islam v istorii Rossii* (Moscow: Vostochnaia Literatura, 1995), 142–145; S. A. Dudoignon, "Djadidisme, mirasisme, islamisme," *Cahiers du monde Russe et Soviétique* 37 (1996), 13–40.

14. Hugh Seton-Watson, *The Russian Empire, 1801–1917* (Oxford: Clarendon Press, 1967), 612; Zenkovsky, *Panturkism and Islam,* chap. 4.

15. Landa, *Islam,* 145–150.

16. Pierce, *Russian Central Asia,* chaps. 7 and 14.

17. John J. Stephan, *The Russian Far East: A History* (Stanford: Stanford University Press, 1994), 40–50; Mark Bassin, *Imperial Visions: Nationalist Imagination and Geographical Expansion in the Russian Far East* (Cambridge: Cambridge University Press, 1999), chaps. 2–4.

18. Quoted in V. P. Semennikov, *Za kulisami tsarizma: arkhiv tibetskogo vracha Badmaeva* (Leningrad, 1925), 80.

19. Ian Nish, *The Origins of the Russo-Japanese War* (London: Longman, 1985).

20. V. A. Tvardovskaia, *Ideologiia poreformennogo samoderzhaviia* (Moscow: Nauka, 1978), 26; Martin Katz, *Mikhail Katkov: A Political Biography, 1818–1887* (The Hague: Mouton, 1966), 83; M. N. Katkov, *Sobranie peredovykh statei Moskovskikh Vedomostei 1867g* (Moscow, 1897), 265.

21. M. N. Katkov, *1863 god: sobranie statei po pol'skomu voprosu,* vol. 1 (Moscow, 1887), 100–101.

22. David Saunders, "Russia's Ukrainian Policy (1847–1905): A Demographic Approach," *European History Quarterly* 25 (1995), 181–205.

23. Orest Subtelny, *Ukraine: A History* (Toronto: University of Toronto Press, 1988), 234.

24. Ibid., chaps. 13, 16, 17.

25. Saunders, "Russia's Ukrainian Policy," 187; see also his "Russia and Ukraine under Alexander II: The Valuev Edict of 1863," *International History Review* 57 (1995), 23–50.

26. Wolfdieter Bihl, "Die Ruthenen," in Adam Wandruszka and Peter Urbanitsch, eds., *Die Hapsburger Monarchie, 1848–1918* (Vienna: Verlag der Österreichischen Akademie, 1980), 555–584; for the Uniate Church, see above, Chapter 2.

27. Risto Alapuro, *State and Revolution in Finland* (Berkeley: University of California Press, 1988), 19–40.

28. Ibid., 92–98; on the significance of literary activity in Finland, see Miroslav Hroch, *Social Conditions of National Revival in Europe* (Cambridge: Cambridge University Press, 1985), 62–75.

29. Edward C. Thaden, ed., *Russification in the Baltic Provinces and Finland, 1855–1914* (Princeton: Princeton University Press, 1981), 76–83; D. G. Kirby, *Russia and Finland,*

1808–1920: From Autonomy to Independence (London: Macmillan, 1975), 76–81; Fred Singleton, *A Short History of Finland* (Cambridge: Cambridge University Press, 1989), 96–99.

30. Michael H. Haltzel, "The Baltic Germans," in Thaden, *Russification*, 134–178; Gert von Pistohlkors, *Deutsche Geschichte im Osten Europas: Baltische Länder* (Siedler Verlag, 1994), 397–416.

31. A. Plakans, "Peasants, Intellectuals, and Nationalism in the Russian Baltic Provinces," *Journal of Modern History* 46 (1974), 445–475.

32. A. Ascher, *The Russian Revolution of 1905: Russia in Disarray* (Stanford: Stanford University Press, 1988), 94, 159–160; Toivo O. Raun, "The Revolution of 1905 in the Baltic Provinces and Finland," *Slavic Review* 43 (1984), 453–467.

33. C. Leonard Lundin, "The Road from Tsar to Kaiser: Changing Loyalties of the Baltic Germans, 1905–1914," *Journal of Central European Affairs* 10 (1950), 222–254.

34. R. G. Suny, "The Emergence of Political Society in Georgia," in Suny, ed., *Transcaucasia: Nationalism and Social Change*, rev. ed. (Ann Arbor: University of Michigan Press, 1996), 109–140.

35. Richard G. Hovanissian, "The Armenian Question in the Ottoman Empire, 1876–1914," in Hovanissian, ed., *The Armenian People from Ancient to Modern Times* (London: Macmillan, 1997), 203–238.

36. See the report of the viceroy, Count Vorontsov-Dashkov, to Prime Minister Stolypin in "Bor'ba s revoliutsionnym dvizheniem na Kavkaze," *Krasnyi Arkhiv* 34 (1920), 202–218.

37. Kappeler, *Russland als Vielvölkerreich*, 225.

38. Ivan Aksakov, leading article in *Rus'*, 10 October 1881, in his *Sochineniia*, vol. 3 (Moscow, 1886), 751–752.

39. Stephen Lukashevich, *Ivan Aksakov, 1823–1886* (Cambridge, Mass.: Harvard University Press, 1965), 167–168; Geoffrey Hosking, *Russia: People and Empire, 1552–1917* (Cambridge, Mass.: Harvard University Press, 1997), 390–392.

40. Louis Greenberg, *The Jews in Russia: The Struggle for Emancipation*, vol. 2 (New York: Schocken, 1976), 30–47.

41. S. Nilus, *Bliz griadushchii Antikhrist* (Moscow, 1911); Norman Cohn, *Warrant for Genocide: The Myth of the Jewish World Conspiracy and the "Protocols of the Elders of Zion"* (London: Eyre & Spottiswoode, 1967).

42. "Perepiska Nikolaia II i Marii Fedorovny," *Krasnyi arkhiv* 22 (1927), 169.

43. Heinz-Dietrich Löwe, *The Tsars and the Jews: Reform, Reaction and Anti-Semitism in Imperial Russia, 1772–1917* (Chur: Harwood Academic Publishers, 1993), 221–228.

44. Shlomo Lambroza, "The Pogroms of 1903–6," in John Klier and Shlomo Lambroza, eds., *Pogroms: Anti-Jewish Violence in Modern Russian History* (Cambridge: Cambridge University Press, 1992), 195–207; quotation p. 205.

45. *Znamennyi* meant "written down in the form of symbols."

46. Alfred J. Swan, *Russian Music and Its Sources in Chant and Folk-song* (London: John Baker, 1973), 60.

47. Nikolai Rimskii-Korsakov, *My Musical Life* (London: Eulenburg Books, 1974), 117.

48. On the textual history of *Boris Godunov* see Caryl Emerson and Robert William Oldani, *Modest Musorgskii and Boris Godunov: Myths, Realities, Reconsiderations* (Cambridge: Cambridge University Press, 1994), chap. 2.

669

49. Quoted in Richard Taruskin, *Musorgsky: Eight Essays and an Epilogue* (Princeton: Princeton University Press, 1993), 314.

50. The political and social implications of these musical developments are examined in Robert C. Ridenour, *Nationalism, Modernism, and Personal Rivalry in Nineteenth-Century Russian Music* (Ann Arbor: UMI Research Press, 1981).

51. Catriona Kelly, *Petrushka: The Russian Carnival Puppet Theatre* (Cambridge: Cambridge University Press, 1990), 167–172.

52. Richard Taruskin, "Stravinsky and the Subhuman," in *Defining Russia Musically: Historical and Hermeneutical Essays* (Princeton: Princeton University Press, 1997), 360–388.

53. Elizabeth Valkenier, *Russian Realist Art: The Peredvizhniki and Their Tradition* (Ann Arbor: Ardis, 1977); John O. Norman, "Pavel Tretiakov and Merchant Art Patronage, 1850–1900," in E. W. Clowes, S. D. Kassow, and J. L. West, eds., *Between Tsar and People: Educated Society and the Quest for Public Identity in Late Imperial Russia* (Princeton: Princeton University Press, 1991), 93–101.

54. Camilla Gray, *The Russian Experiment in Art, 1863–1922,* 2d ed. (London: Thames & Hudson, 1986), chap. 2; A. N. Bokhanov, "Savva Mamontov," *Voprosy istorii,* no. 11 (1990), 48–67.

55. Marc Slonim, *Russian Theater from Empire to Soviets* (Cleveland: World Publishing, 1961), 102–118; Laurence Senelick, "Theatre," in Nicholas Rzhevsky, ed., *The Cambridge Companion to Modern Russian Culture* (Cambridge: Cambridge University Press, 1998), 268–271.

56. Jo Ann Ruckman, *The Moscow Business Elite: A Social and Cultural Portrait of Two Generations, 1840–1915* (De Kalb: Northern Illinois University Press, 1984), 88–108.

57. Count Sollogub, quoted in Donald Fanger, *The Creation of Nikolai Gogol* (Cambridge, Mass.: Harvard University Press, 1979), 225.

58. *War and Peace,* vol. III, part 2, chap. 39.

59. F. M. Dostoevskii, *Polnoe sobranie sochinenii,* vol. 14 (Leningrad: Nauka, 1978), 285.

60. Aleksandr Blok, *Sobranie sochinenii,* vol. 5 (Moscow: Gosizdat Khudozhestvennoi Literatury, 1962), 327–328; Avril Pyman, *The Life of Aleksandr Blok,* vol. 2: *The Release of Harmony* (New York: Oxford University Press, 1980), 26.

9. SOCIAL CHANGE AND REVOLUTION

1. I. F. Gindin, *Gosudarstvennyi bank i ekonomicheskaia politika tsarskogo pravitel'stva, 1861–1892gg* (Moscow: Gosfinizdat, 1960), 30–32.

2. Thomas C. Owen, *The Corporation under Russian Law, 1800–1917: A Study in Tsarist Economic Policy* (Cambridge: Cambridge University Press, 1991); Olga Crisp, "Banking in the Industrialisation of Tsarist Russia," in *Studies in the Russian Economy before 1914* (London: Macmillan, 1976), 111–158; David Christian, *Living Water: Vodka and Russian Society on the Eve of Emancipation* (Oxford: Clarendon Press, 1990), 371–374.

3. Alfred J. Rieber, "The Formation of La Grande Société des Chemins de Fer Russes," *Jahrbücher für Geschichte Osteuropas* 21 (1973), 375–391; A. M. Solov'eva, *Zheleznodorozhnyi transport Rossii vo vtoroi polovine XIX veka* (Moscow: Nauka, 1975), chaps. 2–

4; Stephen Marks, *Road to Power: The Trans-Siberian Railroad and the Colonization of Asian Russia* (London: Tauris, 1991).

4. Peter Gatrell, *The Tsarist Economy, 1850–1917* (London: Batsford, 1986), chap. 5.

5. See for example Robert Eugene Johnson, *Peasant and Proletarian: The Working Class of Moscow in the Late Nineteenth Century* (Leicester: Leicester University Press, 1979).

6. Olga Crisp, "Russian Financial Policy and the Gold Standard at the End of the Nineteenth Century," in *Studies*, 96–110.

7. Vitte's policies and the opposition to them are examined in T. H. von Laue, *Sergei Witte and the Industrialization of Russia* (New York: Columbia University Press, 1963); Heinz-Dietrich Löwe, *The Tsars and the Jews: Reform, Reaction and Anti-Semitism in Imperial Russia, 1772–1917* (Chur: Harwood, 1993), 115–116.

8. Alexander Gerschenkron, *Economic Backwardness in Historical Perspective* (Cambridge, Mass.: Harvard University Press, 1962); the argument has been amplified and brought up to date by Theodor Shanin in *Russia as a Developing Society* (London: Macmillan, 1985).

9. Heinz-Dietrich Löwe, *Die Lage der Bauern in Russland, 1880–1905* (St. Katharinen: Scripta Mercaturae Verlag, 1987); Paul Gregory, *Russian National Income, 1885–1913* (Cambridge: Cambridge University Press, 1982); Olga Crisp, "Russia," in Richard Sylla and Gianni Toniolo, eds., *Patterns of European Industrialisation* (London: Routledge, 1991), 248–268. There is a good summary of the controversy in Gatrell, *Tsarist Economy*, chap. 1; he examines the development of cottage industry on pp. 154–157.

10. A. I. Shingarev, *Vymiraiushchaia derevnia* (St. Petersburg, 1907), offers a vivid picture of conditions in such rural areas.

11. Robert J. Kaiser, *The Geography of Nationalism in Russia and the USSR* (Princeton: Princeton University Press, 1994), 43–83.

12. D. C. B. Lieven, "The Security Police, Civil Rights and the Fate of the Russian Empire," in Olga Crisp and Linda Edmondson, eds., *Civil Rights in Imperial Russia* (Oxford: Clarendon Press, 1989), 235–262; Jonathan Daly, "The Security Police and Politics in Late Imperial Russia," in Anna Geifman, ed., *Russia under the Last Tsar: Opposition and Subversion, 1894–1917* (Oxford: Blackwell, 1999), 217–240. The Lenin quote is from "Chto delat'?" in *Polnoe sobranie sochinenii*, 5th ed., vol. 6 (Moscow: Politizdat, 1959), 126.

13. Nurit Schleifman, *Undercover Agents in the Russian Revolutionary Movement: The SR Party, 1902–1914* (London: Macmillan, 1988); Geoffrey Hosking, *Russia: People and Empire, 1552–1917* (Cambridge, Mass.: Harvard University Press, 1997), 358–359.

14. Anna Geifman, *Thou Shalt Kill: Revolutionary Terrorism in Russia, 1894–1917* (Princeton: Princeton University Press, 1993), 20–21; Richard Pipes, *The Russian Revolution, 1899–1919* (London: Harvill, 1990), 146–149, 169–171; the career of Azef is examined in Boris Nicolaevsky, *Azeff: The Russian Judas* (London: Hurst & Blackett, 1934).

15. Richard Pipes, "*Narodnichestvo*: A Semantic Inquiry," *Slavic Review* 23 (1964), 441–458; J. L. H. Keep, *The Rise of Social Democracy in Russia* (Oxford: Clarendon Press, 1963), 15–24; Robert Service, "Russian Populism and Russian Marxism: Two Skeins Entangled," in Roger Bartlett, ed., *Russian Thought and Society, 1800–1917: Essays in Honour of Eugene Lampert* (Keele: University of Keele, 1984), 220–246.

671

16. Essentially this was the founding congress: there had been an earlier one in Minsk in 1898, but nearly all its delegates had been arrested shortly afterward.

17. Robert Service, *Lenin: A Political Life*, vol. 1 (London: Macmillan, 1985), 100–105.

18. This view of Lenin is most fully expounded in Rolf Theen, *Lenin: Genesis and Development of a Revolutionary* (London: Quartet Books, 1974).

19. Jeffrey Brooks, *When Russia Learned to Read: Literacy and Popular Literature, 1861–1917* (Princeton: Princeton University Press, 1985).

20. Steve Smith and Catriona Kelly, "Commercial Culture and Consumerism," in Catriona Kelly and David Shepherd, eds., *Constructing Russian Culture in the Age of Revolution, 1881–1940* (Oxford: Oxford University Press, 1998), 106–164.

21. Lucian Hölscher, "Secularization and Urbanization in the Nineteenth Century: An Interpretive Model," in Hugh McLeod, ed., *European Religion in the Age of Great Cities, 1830–1930* (London: Routledge, 1995), 263–288; Simon Dixon, "The Orthodox Church and the Workers of St. Petersburg, 1880–1914," ibid., 119–141.

22. Joan Neuberger, *Hooliganism: Crime, Culture, and Power in St. Petersburg, 1900–1914* (Berkeley: University of California Press, 1993); S. A. Smith, "The Social Meanings of Swearing: Workers and Bad Language in Late Imperial and Early Soviet Russia," *Past and Present*, no. 160 (1998), 167–202.

23. Stephen P. Frank, "Confronting the Domestic Other: Rural Popular Culture and Its Enemies in Fin-de-Siècle Russia," in Stephen P. Frank and Mark D. Steinberg, eds., *Cultures in Flux: Lower-Class Values, Practices, and Resistance in Late Imperial Russia* (Princeton: Princeton University Press, 1994), 74–107.

24. Daniel Brower, "Labor Violence in Russia in the Late Nineteenth Century," *Slavic Review* 41 (1982), 417–431.

25. Tim McDaniel, *Autocracy, Capitalism, and Revolution in Russia* (Berkeley: University of California Press, 1987).

26. Georgii Gapon, *Istoriia moei zhizni* (Moscow: Kniga, 1990), 17, 22; Walter Sablinsky, *The Road to Bloody Sunday: Father Gapon and the St. Petersburg Massacre of 1905* (Princeton: Princeton University Press, 1976), 85.

27. A text of the petition can be found in Sablinsky, *Road to Bloody Sunday*, 344–349.

28. Gerald Surh, *1905 in St. Petersburg: Labor, Society, and Revolution* (Stanford: Stanford University Press, 1989), 11–12.

29. Oskar Anweiler, *The Soviets: The Russian Workers', Soldiers', and Peasants' Councils, 1905–1921* (New York: Pantheon Books, 1974), 40–43, 51–55.

30. Surh, *1905 in St. Petersburg*, 337–341.

31. Shmuel Galai, *The Liberation Movement in Russia, 1900–1905* (Cambridge: Cambridge University Press, 1973).

32. V. Zenzinov, *Perezhitoe* (New York: Izdatel'stvo imeni Chekhova, 1953), 225.

33. In similar manner, in 1994–95 and 1999–2000, uncertain of the population's loyalty, the Russian army in Chechnia used artillery to eradicate terrorism, causing many civilian casualties in the process.

34. G. G. Savich, *Novyi gosudarstvennyi stroi* (St. Petersburg, 1907), 12.

35. A typical resolution, from Volokolamsk uezd, Moscow guberniia: L. T. Senchakova, *Prigovory i nakazy rossiiskogo krest'ianstva 1905–1907gg: po materialam tsentral'nykh gubernii*, vol. 1 (Moscow: Institut Rossiiskoi Istorii, 1994), 132–138.

36. Ibid., 196.

37. E. I. Kiriukhina, "Vserossiiskii krest'ianskii soiuz v 1905g," *Istoricheskie zapiski*, no. 50 (1955), 95−141; Maureen Perrie, *The Agrarian Policy of the Socialist Revolutionary Party from Its Origins to the Revolution of 1905−7* (Cambridge: Cambridge University Press, 1976), 108−110.

38. Maureen Perrie, "The Russian Peasant Movement of 1905−7," *Past and Present* 57 (1972), 123−155; Theodor Shanin, *Russia, 1905−7: Revolution as a Moment of Truth* (London: Macmillan, 1986), 83−84, 94−98; Orlando Figes, *A People's Tragedy: The Russian Revolution, 1891−1924* (London: Jonathan Cape, 1996), 182−184.

39. Shanin, *Russia, 1905−7*, 101; A. Shestakov, *Krest'ianskaia revoliutsiia, 1905−7gg* (Moscow, 1926), 38−39.

40. L. Martov, P. Maslov, and A. Potresov, eds., *Obshchestvennoe dvizhenie v Rossii v nachale xx-ogo veka* (St. Petersburg, 1909−1914), vol. 2, part 1, 119−120.

41. Dominic Lieven, *Nicholas II: Emperor of all the Russias* (London: John Murray, 1993), esp. chap. 5.

42. *Dnevnik Gosudarstvennogo Sekretaria A. A. Polovtseva*, vol. 2 (Moscow, 1966), 109.

43. Richard G. Robbins, *The Tsar's Viceroys: Russian Provincial Governors in the Last Years of the Empire* (Ithaca: Cornell University Press, 1987).

44. A. A. Novikov, *Zapiski zemskogo nachal'nika* (1899; reprint, Newtonville, Mass.: Oriental Research Partners, 1980), 39. For the legislation setting up the post and the motives of those who planned it, see Thomas S. Pearson, *Russian Officialdom in Crisis: Autocracy and Local Self-Government, 1861−1900* (Cambridge: Cambridge University Press, 1989), chap. 5.

45. See for example V. I. Gurko, *Features and Figures of the Past: Government and Opinion in the Reign of Nicholas II* (Stanford, Calif.: Hoover Institution, 1939); V. N. Kokovtsev, *Out of My Past* (Stanford, Calif.: Hoover Institution, 1935); and above all S. Iu. Vitte, *Vospominaniia*, 3 vols. (Moscow: Izdatel'stvo Sotsial'no-ekonomicheskoi Literatury, 1960), available in English as *The Memoirs of Count Witte*, trans. and ed. Sidney Harcave (Armonk, N.Y.: M. E. Sharpe, 1990).

46. P. Waldron, "States of Emergency: Autocracy and Extraordinary Legislation, 1881−1917," *Revolutionary Russia* 8 (1995), 1−25.

47. Roberta Manning, *The Crisis of the Old Order in Russia: Gentry and Government* (Princeton: Princeton University Press, 1982), 260−271.

48. Dorothy Atkinson, *The End of the Russian Land Commune, 1905−1930* (Stanford: Stanford University Press, 1983), 61−70.

49. Alfred Levin, *The Third Duma: Election and Profile* (Hamden, Conn.: Archon Books, 1973), chap. 1.

50. Atkinson, *End of Russian Land Commune*, 89−91; W. E. Mosse, "Stolypin's Villages," *Slavonic and East European Review* 43 (1964−65), 257−274; Judith Pallot, "Open Fields and Individual Farms: Land Reform in Pre-Revolutionary Russia," *Tijdschrift voor economische en sociale geografie* 75 (1984), 46−60.

51. Judith Pallot, "Did the Stolypin Land Reform Destroy the Peasant Commune?" in R. B. McKean, ed., *New Perspectives in Modern Russian History* (London: Macmillan, 1992), 117−132; George L. Yaney, "The Concept of the Stolypin Land Reform," *Slavic Review* 23 (1964), 275−293.

674

52. G. A. Hosking, *The Russian Constitutional Experiment: Government and Duma, 1907–1914* (Cambridge: Cambridge University Press, 1973), chap. 6; Peter Waldron, *Between Two Revolutions: Stolypin and the Politics of Renewal in Russia* (London: UCL Press, 1998), chap. 2.

53. Hosking, *Russian Constitutional Experiment*, 116–134.

54. G. Freeze, "Tserkov', religiia i politicheskaia kul'tura na zakate starogo rezhima," in *Reforma ili revoliutsiia? Rossiia, 1861–1917gg* (St. Petersburg: Nauka, 1992), 32–35; idem, "Subversive Piety: Religion and the Political Crisis in Late Imperial Russia," *Journal of Modern History* 68 (1996), 308–350.

55. V. I. Rodzianko, "Krushenie imperii: zapiski predsedatelia Russkoi Gosudarstvennoi Dumy," *Arkhiv Russkoi Revoliutsii* 17 (1926), 37–38.

56. S. A. Stepanov, *Chernaia sotnia v Rossii, 1905–1907* (Moscow: Rosvuznauka, 1992); Don C. Rawson, *Russian Rightists and the Revolution of 1905* (Cambridge: Cambridge University Press, 1995), chap. 11.

57. Orlando Figes and Boris Kolonitskii, *Interpreting the Russian Revolution: The Language and Symbols of 1917* (New Haven: Yale University Press, 1999), chap. 1.

58. N. K. Gordienko and P. K. Kurochkin, "Liberal'no-obnovlencheskoe dvizhenie v russkom pravoslavii nachala XX veka," *Voprosy nauchnogo ateizma* 7 (1969), 313–340; J. Y. Cunningham, *A Vanquished Hope: The Movement for Church Renewal in Russia, 1905–1906* (Crestwood, N.Y.: St. Vladimir's Seminary Press, 1981), 133–162.

59. Cunningham, *Vanquished Hope*, chap. 4.

60. Ibid., chaps. 6–7.

61. A. V. Zen'kovskii, *Pravda o Stolypine* (New York: Vseslavianskoe Izdatel'stvo, 1956), 81–84; Episkop Nikon (Rklitskii), *Zhizneopisanie blazhennogo Antoniia, Mitropolita Kievskogo i Galitskogo*, vol. 3 (New York, 1957), 159–160.

62. Simon Dixon, "The Orthodox Church and the Workers of St. Petersburg, 1880–1914," in McLeod, *European Religion in the Age of Great Cities*, 244–245.

63. Caspar Ferenczi, "Freedom of the Press under the Old Regime, 1905–1914," in Crisp and Edmondson, *Civil Rights in Imperial Russia*, 191–214; Benjamin Rigberg, "The Efficacy of Tsarist Censorship Operations, 1894–1917," *Jahrbücher für Geschichte Osteuropas* 14 (1966), 327–346.

64. Louise McReynolds, *The News under Russia's Old Regime: The Development of a Mass-Circulation Press* (Princeton: Princeton University Press, 1991), 225–226; Manfred Hagen, *Die Entfaltung der politischen Öffentlichkeit in Russland, 1906–1914* (Wiesbaden: Steiner Verlag, 1982), 144–149.

65. Hosking, *Russian Constitutional Experiment*, 211–212.

66. McReynolds, *News*, chap. 10. Having spent many months myself reading the Russian press of 1907–1914, I can testify to the liveliness and frankness, but also the very high quality, of the best newspapers.

67. Victoria E. Bonnell, *Roots of Rebellion: Workers' Politics and Organizations in St. Petersburg and Moscow, 1900–1914* (Berkeley: University of California Press, 1983), 195–209, 260–262, 312–315.

68. Ibid., chap. 8.

69. Ibid., chap. 10; Leopold Haimson, "Labor Unrest in Imperial Russia on the Eve of the First World War," in Leopold Haimson and Charles Tilly, eds., *Wars and Revolu-*

tions in International Perspective (Cambridge: Cambridge University Press, 1989), 500–511.

70. Quoted in S. A. Smith, "Workers and Civil Rights, 1899–1917," in Crisp and Edmondson, *Civil Rights in Imperial Russia,* 163.

71. Sergei Bulgakov, "Geroizm i podvizhnichestvo," in *Vekhi: sbornik statei o russkoi intelligentsii* (Moscow, 1909), 23–69; quotations pp. 30, 36.

72. P. B. Struve, "Velikaia Rossiia," in *Patriotica: sbornik statei za piat' let, 1905–1910gg* (St. Petersburg: Izdatel'stvo D. E. Zhukovskago, 1911), 93–94.

73. P. A. Berlin, *Russkaia burzhuaziia v staroe i novoe vremia* (Moscow, 1922), 286–293; V. Ia. Laverychev, *Po tu storonu barrikad: iz istorii bor'by moskovskoi burzhuazii s revoliutsiei* (Moscow: Mysl', 1967), 78–95; Richard Pipes, *Struve: Liberal on the Right, 1905–1944* (Cambridge, Mass.: Harvard University Press, 1980), 176–186.

10. WAR AND REVOLUTION

1. I. V. Bestuzhev, *Bor'ba v Rossii po voprosam vneshnei politiki, 1906–1910* (Moscow: Izdatel'stvo Akademii Nauk, 1961), 222–251; Barbara Jelavich, *Russia's Balkan Entanglements, 1806–1914* (Cambridge: Cambridge University Press, 1991), 217–225; Caspar Ferenczi, *Aussenpolitik und Öffentlichkeit in Russland, 1906–1912* (Husum: Matthiessen Verlag, 1982), 180–193.

2. David M. McDonald, "A Lever without a Fulcrum: Domestic Factors and Russian Foreign Policy, 1905–1914," in Hugh Ragsdale, ed., *Imperial Russian Foreign Policy* (Cambridge: Cambridge University Press, 1993), 268–311; Ernst Christian Helmreich, *The Diplomacy of the Balkan Wars, 1912–1913* (New York: Russell & Russell, 1969).

3. D. C. B. Lieven, *Russia and the Origins of the First World War* (London: Macmillan, 1983), 142–143.

4. Hubertus F. Jahn, *Patriotic Culture in Russia during World War I* (Ithaca: Cornell University Press, 1995).

5. The documents are in E. A. Adamov, ed., *Konstantinopol' i prolivy: po sekretnym dokumentam byvshego ministerstva vneshnikh del* (Moscow: Litizdat NKID, 1926).

6. There is an excellent verbal portrait of him in Orlando Figes, *A People's Tragedy: The Russian Revolution, 1891–1924* (London: Jonathan Cape, 1996), 49–51.

7. Lewis Siegelbaum, *The Politics of Industrial Mobilisation in Russia, 1914–1917: A Study of the War Industry Committees* (London: Macmillan, 1983), chap. 3.

8. Michael F. Hamm, "Liberal Politics in Wartime Russia: An Analysis of the Progressive Bloc," *Slavic Review* 33 (1974), 453–456; Raymond Pearson, *Russian Moderates and the Crisis of Tsarism, 1914–1917* (London: Macmillan, 1977), chap. 3.

9. Pearson, *Russian Moderates,* 115.

10. Leonard Schapiro, "The Political Thought of the First Provisional Government," in Richard Pipes, ed., *Revolutionary Russia* (Cambridge, Mass.: Harvard University Press, 1968), 97–113.

11. "Iz ofitserskikh pisem s fronta v 1917g," *Krasnyi arkhiv* 50 (1932), 200.

12. Allan Wildman, *The End of the Russian Imperial Army,* vol. 2 (Princeton: Princeton University Press, 1987), 92.

13. For the attitudes of French soldiers during the mutinies, see Leonard V. Smith, *Between*

Mutiny and Obedience: The Case of the French Fifth Infantry Division during World War I (Princeton: Princeton University Press, 1994), 189–195, 252–258; and David Moon, "Peasants into Russian Citizens? A Comparative Perspective," *Revolutionary Russia* 9 (1996): 43–81.

14. George Katkov, *The Kornilov Affair: Kerensky and the Break-up of the Russian Army* (London: Longman, 1980).

15. A description of a debate in the Petrograd Soviet by one of the most acute chroniclers of the revolution; N. N. Sukhanov, *Zapiski o revoliutsii*, vol. 1 (Moscow: Izdatel'stvo Politicheskoi Literatury), 116. On the increasing remoteness of executive committees, see Marc Ferro, *October 1917: A Social History of the Russian Revolution* (London: Routledge, 1980), chap. 7.

16. David Mandel, *Petrograd Workers and the Fall of the Old Regime*, vol. 1 (London: Macmillan, 1983), 97–100. Factory committees also acted as a depository of worker radicalism in Moscow and elsewhere; see for example Diane Koenker, *Moscow Workers and the 1917 Revolution* (Princeton: Princeton University Press, 1981), chap. 4.

17. R. P. Browder and A. F. Kerenskii, eds., *The Russian Provisional Government, 1917: Documents*, vol. 2 (Stanford: Stanford University Press, 1961), 731–732.

18. John L. H. Keep, *The Russian Revolution: A Study in Mass Mobilisation* (London: Weidenfeld & Nicolson, 1976), 83–84.

19. Alexander Rabinowitch, *Prelude to Revolution: The Petrograd Bolsheviks and the July Uprising* (Bloomington: Indiana University Press, 1968), chaps. 5–6.

20. Rex A. Wade, "The Red Guards: Spontaneity and the October Revolution," in Edith Rogovin Frankel et al., eds., *Reassessments of 1917* (Cambridge: Cambridge University Press, 1992), 54–75.

21. This is a summary of the peasant mode of action, based on numerous archival sources, by Orlando Figes, *Peasant Russia, Civil War: The Volga Countryside in Revolution, 1917–1921* (Oxford: Clarendon Press, 1989), 52–53, 56.

22. V. V. Kabanov, "Oktiabr'skaia revoliutsiia i krest'ianskaia obshchina," *Istoricheskie zapiski*, no. 111 (1984), 100–150; John Channon, "The Peasantry in the Revolutions of 1917," in Frankel et al., *Reassessments of 1917*, 119; Figes, *A People's Tragedy*, 362–367.

23. Browder and Kerenskii, *Russian Provisional Government*, 2: 558–563.

24. Alexander Rabinowitch, *The Bolsheviks Come to Power* (Bloomington: Indiana University Press, 1968), chaps. 14–15; Oliver Radkey, *The Sickle under the Hammer: The Russian Socialist Revolutionaries in the Early Months of Bolshevik Rule* (New York: Columbia University Press, 1963), chap. 3.

25. An excellent brief account of provincial events is given in John Keep, "October in the Provinces," in Pipes, *Revolutionary Russia*, 180–223.

26. Robert Service, *Lenin: A Political Life*, vol. 3 (London: Macmillan, 1995), 46–49.

27. Ibid., especially the introduction to vol. 3.

28. V. I. Lenin, *Collected Works*, 4th ed., vol. 25 (London: Lawrence & Wishart, 1965), 420–421.

29. Adam Ulam, *The Bolsheviks* (New York: Macmillan, 1965), 353.

30. Andrzej Walicki, *Marxism and the Leap to the Kingdom of Freedom: The Rise and Fall of the Communist Utopia* (Stanford: Stanford University Press, 1995), chap. 4.

676

31. V. I. Lenin, *Polnoe sobranie sochinenii*, 5th ed., vol. 35 (Moscow: Gospolitizdat, 1962), 67.

32. Lenin, *Collected Works*, 25: 404.

33. Silvana Malle, *The Economic Organisation of War Communism, 1918–1921* (Cambridge: Cambridge University Press, 1985), chap. 4.

34. Malle, *Economic Organisation*, 46–67; George Leggett, *The Cheka: Lenin's Political Police* (Oxford: Oxford University Press, 1981), 214–217.

35. Keep, *The Russian Revolution*, chaps. 29–30.

36. A good summary of the civil war is Evan Mawdsley, *The Russian Civil War* (London: Allen & Unwin, 1987).

37. Figes, *A People's Tragedy*, 696–699; M. Agurskii, *Ideologiia natsional-bol'shevizma* (Paris: YMCA Press, 1980), 56.

38. Evgenii Zamiatin, *Sochineniia* (Moscow: Kniga, 1988), 207.

39. Vladimir N. Brovkin, *Behind the Front Lines of the Civil War: Political Parties and Social Movements in Russia, 1918–1922* (Princeton: Princeton University Press, 1994), chap. 3.

40. Elias Heifetz, *The Slaughter of Jews in the Ukraine in 1919,* Report of the All-Ukrainian Committee for the Victims of Pogroms, submitted to the International Red Cross (New York, 1921); Jonathan D. Smele, *Civil War in Siberia: The Anti-Bolshevik Government of Admiral Kolchak, 1918–1920* (Cambridge: Cambridge University Press, 1996), 385–387.

41. Brovkin, *Behind the Front Lines*, 132–134; Jan Meijer, "Town and Country in the Civil War," in Pipes, *Revolutionary Russia*, 259–281.

42. Lars T. Lih, *Bread and Authority in Russia, 1914–1921* (Berkeley: University of California Press, 1990), 135.

43. Michael Palij, *The Anarchism of Nestor Makhno, 1918–1921: An Aspect of the Ukrainian Revolution* (Seattle: University of Washington Press, 1976).

44. Figes, *Peasant Russia, Civil War*, 209.

45. Brovkin, *Behind the Front Lines*, chap. 11.

46. V. Chernov, "Istoriia PSR," in Marc Jansen, ed., *The Socialist Revolutionary Party after October 1917: Documents from the PSR Archive* (Amsterdam: Stichting Beheer IISG, 1989), 5–12; Oliver H. Radkey, *The Unknown Civil War in Soviet Russia: A Study of the Green Movement in Tambov Region, 1920–1921* (Stanford, Calif.: Hoover Institution Press, 1976), chap. 3.

47. M. S. Bernshtam, *Nezavisimoe rabochee dvizhenie v 1918g: dokumenty i materialy* (Paris: YMCA Press, 1981); Vladimir N. Brovkin, *Mensheviks after October: Socialist Opposition and the Rise of the Bolshevik Dictatorship* (Ithaca: Cornell University Press, 1987), 159–160; Orlando Figes, "The Village and Volost Soviet Elections of 1919," *Soviet Studies* 40 (1988), 21–46.

48. Brovkin, *Behind the Front Lines*, 73–77, 82–85, 292–297; Jonathan Aves, *Workers against Lenin: Labor Protest and Bolshevik Dictatorship* (London: Tauris, 1996), 50–56.

49. Aves, *Workers against Lenin*, 11–17.

50. Brovkin, *Behind the Front Lines*, 389–393; Mary McAuley, *Bread and Justice: State and Society in Petrograd, 1917–1922* (Oxford: Clarendon Press, 1991), 398–411; Aves, *Workers against Lenin*, 112–130.

51. Israel Getzler, *Kronstadt, 1917–1921: The Fate of a Soviet Democracy* (Cambridge: Cambridge University Press, 1983), 213–214; *Rossiia XX vek: Kronstadt 1921* (Moscow: Mezhdunarodnyi Fond "Demokratiia," 1997), 50–51.

52. *Desiatyi s'ezd RKP(b), mart 1921: stenograficheskii otchet* (Moscow: Politizdat, 1963), 34.

53. Robert Service, *The Bolshevik Party in Revolution: A Study in Organisational Change, 1917–1923* (London: Macmillan, 1979); Sheila Fitzpatrick, "The Legacy of the Civil War," in Diane Koenker et al., eds., *Party, State, and Society in the Russian Civil War: Explorations in Social History* (Bloomington: Indiana University Press, 1989), 375–388.

54. See document in *Izvestiia*, 27 April 1992, p. 3, quoted in Robert Service, *A History of Twentieth Century Russia* (London: Allen Lane, 1997), 564.

55. Norman Davies, *White Eagle, Red Star: The Polish-Soviet War, 1919–1920* (London: McDonald, 1972); Service, *Lenin*, 3: 117–121, 135–137.

56. Service, *Twentieth Century Russia*, 114; V. Tishkov, *Ethnicity, Nationalism and Conflict in and after the Soviet Union: The Mind Aflame* (London: Sage, 1997), 15–21.

57. Very helpful in conceptualizing these issues are Ronald Grigor Suny, *The Revenge of the Past: Nationalism, Revolution, and the Collapse of the Soviet Union* (Stanford: Stanford University Press, 1993), chap. 1; and Andreas Kappeler, *Russland als Vielvölkerreich: Entstehung, Geschichte, Zerfall* (Munich: Verlag C. H. Beck, 1992), chap. 9.

58. Anthony F. Upton, *The Finnish Revolution, 1917–1918* (Minneapolis: University of Minnesota Press, 1980); Risto Alapuro, *State and Revolution in Finland* (Berkeley: University of California Press, 1988), chap. 9.

59. Stanley Page, *The Formation of the Baltic States* (Cambridge, Mass.: Harvard University Press, 1959); Toivo Raun and Andrejs Plakans, "The Estonian and Latvian National Movements: An Assessment of Miroslav Hroch's Model," *Journal of Baltic Studies* 21 (1990), 131–144.

60. This is suggested by a secret Central Committee instruction of January 1919 to the Belorussian Bolsheviks; Service, *Lenin*, 3: 93.

61. Steven L. Guthier, "The Popular Base of Ukrainian Nationalism," *Slavic Review* 38 (1979), 30–47; Bohdan Krawchenko, *Social Change and National Consciousness in Twentieth-Century Ukraine* (London: Macmillan, 1985), 57–63.

62. Andrew Wilson, "Myths of National History in Belarus and Ukraine," in Geoffrey Hosking and George Schöpflin, eds., *Myths and Nationhood* (London: Hurst, 1997), 194–197.

63. Hannes Hofbauer and Viorel Roman, *Bukowina, Bessarabien, Moldawien* (Vienna: Promedia, 1993), 89–98.

64. Richard G. Hovannisian, "Caucasian Armenia between Imperial and Soviet Rule: The Interlude of National Independence," in R. G. Suny, ed., *Transcaucasia, Nationalism, and Social Change: Essays in the History of Armenia, Azerbaijan, and Georgia*, rev. ed. (Ann Arbor: University of Michigan Press, 1996), 261–294; Tadeusz Swietochowski, *Russian Azerbaijan, 1905–1920: The Shaping of National Identity in a Muslim Community* (Cambridge: Cambridge University Press, 1985), chaps. 5–7; Richard G. Hovannisian, "Armenia's Road to Independence," in Hovannisian, ed., *The Armenian*

People from Ancient to Modern Times, vol. 2 (London: Macmillan, 1997), 275–302.

65. R. G. Suny, *The Making of the Georgian Nation,* 2d ed. (Bloomington: Indiana University Press, 1994), 185–212.

66. A. Bennigsen and C. Lemercier-Quelquejay, *Islam in the Soviet Union* (London: Pall Mall Press, 1967), 82.

67. A. Bennigsen and S. Wimbush, *Muslim National Communism in the Soviet Union* (Chicago: University of Chicago Press, 1979), 28, 60–65; R. G. Landa, *Islam v istorii Rossii* (Moscow: Vostochnaia Literatura, 1995), 207–210; idem, "Mirsaid Sultan-Galiev," *Voprosy istorii,* no. 8 (1999), 53–70.

68. Bennigsen and Lemercier-Quelquejay, *Islam,* 84–87.

69. A. Bennigsen and S. Enders Wimbush, *Muslims of the Soviet Empire: A Guide* (London: Hurst, 1985), 21, 85.

70. Landa, *Islam,* 200–204; Suhnaz Yilmaz, "An Ottoman Warrior Abroad: Enver Pasha as an Expatriate," *Middle Eastern Studies* 35, no. 4 (October 1999), 40–69.

71. Landa, *Islam,* 208, 216–217; Landa, "Mirsaid Sultan-Galiev."

72. Jeremy Smith, *The Bolsheviks and the National Question, 1917–1923* (London: Macmillan, 1999), 94–101.

73. Hélène Carrère d'Encausse, *The Great Challenge: Nationalities and the Bolshevik State, 1917–1930,* trans. Nancy Festinger (New York: Holmes & Meier, 1992), 133–138.

74. For a recent Russian interpretation of the revolution which develops some of these ideas, see V. Buldakov, *Krasnaia smuta: priroda i posledstviia revoliutsionnogo nasiliia* (Moscow: Rosspen, 1997).

11. SOCIAL TRANSFORMATION AND TERROR

1. Gerhard Simon, *Nationalism and Policy toward the Nationalities in the Soviet Union* (Boulder, Colo.: Westview Press, 1991), 415.

2. Yurii Slezkine, "The USSR as Communal Apartment, or How a Socialist State Promoted Ethnic Particularism," *Slavic Review* 53 (1994), 414–452.

3. Simon, *Nationalism,* 32.

4. Ronald Grigor Suny, *The Revenge of the Past: Nationalism, Revolution, and the Collapse of the Soviet Union* (Stanford: Stanford University Press, 1993), 111; George Liber, "Urban Growth and Ethnic Change in the Ukrainian SSR, 1922–32," *Soviet Studies* 41 (1989), 574–591.

5. Martha Brill Olcott, *The Kazakhs* (Stanford, Calif.: Hoover Institution Press, 1987), 170–175.

6. V. Kabuzan, *Russkie v mire* (St. Petersburg: Blits, 1996), 249–250; Robert Kaiser, *The Geography of Nationalism in Russia and the USSR* (Princeton: Princeton University Press, 1994), 118.

7. V. Tishkov, *Ethnicity, Nationalism and Conflict in and after the Soviet Union: The Mind Aflame* (London: Sage, 1997), 15–21 and chap. 2; Slezkine, "The USSR as Communal Apartment."

8. Suny, *Revenge,* 121.

9. Simon, *Nationalism,* 138–155.

10. Irina Paperno, "The Meaning of Art: Symbolist Theories," in Irina Paperno and Joan

680

Delaney Grossman, eds., *Creating Life: The Aesthetic Utopia of Russian Modernism* (Stanford: Stanford University Press, 1994), 13–23; quotations pp. 16–17.

11. Andrei Belyi, *Revoliutsiia i kul'tura,* quoted in I. V. Kondakov, *Vvedenie v istoriiu russkoi kul'tury* (Moscow: Aktsent Press, 1997), 340.

12. "A Slap in the Face of Public Taste," in Ellendea Proffer and Carl Proffer, eds., *The Ardis Anthology of Russian Futurism* (Ann Arbor: Ardis Press, 1980), 179; Irina Gutman, "The Legacy of the Symbolist Aesthetic Utopia: From Futurism to Socialist Realism," in Paperno and Grossman, *Creating Life,* 167–196.

13. Leon Trotsky, *Literature and Revolution,* trans. Rose Strunsky (Ann Arbor: University of Michigan Press, 1960), 251, 254–256.

14. A. Gastev, "Tendentsii proletarskoi kul'tury," *Proletarskaia kultura,* no. 9–10 (1919).

15. Zenovia A. Sochor, "Soviet Taylorism Revisited," *Soviet Studies* 33 (1980–81), 246–264; Jay Bergman, "The Idea of Individual Liberation in Bolshevik Visions of the New Soviet Man," *European History Quarterly* 27 (1997), 57–92.

16. Gutman, "Legacy," 172–173.

17. Lynn Mally, *Culture of the Future: The Proletkult Movement in Revolutionary Russia* (Berkeley: University of California Press, 1990), 21–25.

18. Ibid., chaps. 2–5; titles on pp. 99, 139.

19. Ibid., 160–161.

20. Richard Stites, *Revolutionary Dreams: Utopian Vision and Experimental Life in the Russian Revolution* (New York: Oxford University Press, 1989), 94–95; Katerina Clark, *Petersburg, Crucible of Cultural Revolution* (Cambridge, Mass.: Harvard University Press, 1995), 126–131.

21. Peter Kenez, *The Birth of the Propaganda State: Soviet Methods of Mass Mobilization, 1917–1929* (Cambridge: Cambridge University Press, 1985), chap. 6.

22. Edward Brown, *The Proletarian Episode in Russian Literature, 1928–1932* (New York: Columbia University Press, 1953).

23. Christina Lodder, *Russian Constructivism* (New Haven: Yale University Press, 1983), 55–67; quotations p. 65.

24. Clark, *Petersburg,* 87–98.

25. Boris Grois, *The Total Art of Stalinism: Avant-Garde, Aesthetic Dictatorship, and Beyond* (Princeton: Princeton University Press, 1992).

26. Dimitry V. Pospielovsky, *Soviet Anti-Religious Campaigns and Persecutions: A History of Soviet Atheism in Theory and Practice and the Believer,* vol. 2: *Soviet Anti-Religious Campaigns and Persecutions* (London: Macmillan, 1988), 14–16.

27. Trotskii's memorandum on the subject is reproduced in N. N. Pokrovskii, "Politbiuro i tserkov', 1922–1923," *Novyi mir,* no. 8 (1994), 189–190.

28. Gregory Freeze, "Counter-Reformation in Russian Orthodoxy: Popular Response to Religious Innovation, 1922–1925," *Slavic Review* 54 (1995), 305–339.

29. O. Iu. Vasil'eva, "Russkaia pravoslavnaia tserkov' i sovetskaia vlast' v 1917–1927gg," *Voprosy istorii,* no. 8 (1993), 40–54.

30. Glennys Young, *Power and the Sacred in Revolutionary Russia: Religious Activists in the Village* (University Park: Pennsylvania State University Press, 1997), 92–100, 135–146.

31. Young, *Power and the Sacred,* esp. chap. 5.

32. Pospielovsky, *Soviet Anti-Religious Campaigns and Persecutions,* 65–68.
33. Roger A. Clarke and Dubravko J. Matko, *Soviet Economic Facts, 1917–1981,* 2d ed. (London: Macmillan, 1983), 34, 90, 91; R. W. Davies and S. G. Wheatcroft, eds., *The Economic Transformation of the Soviet Union, 1913–1945* (Cambridge: Cambridge University Press, 1994), 135, 321.
34. E. H. Carr, *The Bolshevik Revolution, 1917–1923,* vol. 2 (London: Macmillan, 1952), chap. 19; idem, *The Interregnum, 1923–24* (London: Macmillan, 1954), 27–38.
35. Emma Goldman, *My Further Disillusionment in Russia* (London, 1925), 201–202.
36. Orlando Figes, *A People's Tragedy: The Russian Revolution, 1891–1924* (London: Jonathan Cape, 1996), 775–780.
37. Clarke and Matko, *Soviet Economic Facts,* 83, 86, 89, 91, 101; Davies and Wheatcroft, *Economic Transformation,* 110–112, 296–297.
38. Sheila Fitzpatrick et al., eds., *Russia in the Era of NEP* (Bloomington: Indiana University Press, 1991), chaps. 3–5.
39. Quoted in Kendall Bailes, *Technology and Society under Lenin and Stalin* (Princeton: Princeton University Press, 1978), 24.
40. Ibid., 197.
41. Stephen F. Cohen, *Bukharin and the Bolshevik Revolution* (New York: Alfred A. Knopf, 1973), chap. 6.
42. Diane P. Koenker and Ronald D. Bachman, eds., *Revelations from the Russian Archives: Documents in English Translation* (Washington, D.C.: Library of Congress, 1997), 352–359.
43. M. S. Voslensky, *Nomenklatura: Anatomy of the Soviet Ruling Class* (London: Bodley Head, 1984), chaps. 2–3; T. P. Korzhikhina and Iu. Iu. Figatner, "Sovetskaia nomenklatura: stanovlenie, mekhanizmy deistviia," *Voprosy istorii,* no. 7 (1993), 25–38, quotation p. 29; Geoffrey Hosking, *The First Socialist Society: A History of the Soviet Union from Within,* 3d ed. (Cambridge, Mass.: Harvard University Press, 1992), 88–89.
44. Gerald M. Easter, *Reconstructing the State: Personal Networks and Elite Identity in Soviet Russia* (Cambridge: Cambridge University Press, 2000), chaps. 2–4.
45. Sheila Fitzpatrick, "Ascribing Class: The Construction of Social Identity in Soviet Russia," *Journal of Modern History* 65 (1993), 745–770; T. H. Rigby, *Party Membership in the USSR, 1917–1967* (Princeton: Princeton University Press, 1968), chap. 3.
46. Koenker and Bachman, *Revelations,* 100–101.
47. V. I. Lenin, "On Cooperation," in *Collected Works,* 4th ed., vol. 33 (Moscow: Progress, 1966), 467–471.
48. N. A. Ivnitskii, *Kollektivizatsiia i raskulachivanie: nachalo 30-kh godov* (Moscow: Magistr, 1996), 88.
49. Sheila Fitzpatrick, *Stalin's Peasants: Resistance and Survival in the Russian Village after Collectivization* (New York: Oxford University Press, 1994), 34–37, 42–45, 60–62. On "kulak resistance," see Koenker and Bachman, *Revelations,* 376–379. Numerous reports on the grain procurement campaign can be found in V. P. Danilov et al., eds., *Tragediia sovetskoi derevni: kollektivizatsiia i raskulachivanie (dokumenty i materialy),* vol. 1: *mai 1927–noiabr' 1929g* (Moscow: Rosspen, 1999); this is the first volume of what promises to be a major documentary collection on collectivization.
50. Ivnitskii, *Kollektivizatsiia,* 102–123; see the experiences of the family of the later literary

681

682

editor, Aleksandr Tvardovskii, described in Ivan Tvardovskii, "Stranitsy perezhitogo," *Iunost'*, no. 3 (1988), 10–32.

51. Ivnitskii, *Kollektivizatsiia*, 139–140.

52. Ibid., 203. For an OGPU progress report of July 1931 on dekulakization, see Koenker and Bachman, *Revelations*, 384–387.

53. Lynne Viola, "The Peasant Nightmare: Visions of Apocalypse in the Soviet Countryside," *Journal of Modern History* 62 (1990), 747–770; see also idem, "*Bab'i bunty* and Peasant Women's Protest during Collectivisation," *Russian Review* 45 (1986), 23–42.

54. Nicolas Werth and Gael Moullec, eds., *Rapports secrets Soviétiques, 1921–1991* (Paris: Gallimard, 1994), 125–126.

55. Fitzpatrick, *Stalin's Peasants*, 60–62, 65.

56. Lynne Viola, *Peasant Rebels under Stalin: Collectivisation and the Culture of Peasant Resistance* (New York: Oxford University Press, 1996), chap. 6.

57. Martha Brill Olcott, "The Collectivization Drive in Kazakhstan," *Russian Review* 40 (1981), 122–142; Zh. B. Abylkhozhin, "Kazakhstanskaia tragediia," *Voprosy istorii*, no. 7 (1989), 55–71.

58. Ivnitskii, *Kollektivizatsiia*, 159–160; Abdurahman Avtorkhanov, "The Chechens and the Ingush during the Soviet Period and Its Antecedents," in Marie Bennigsen Broxup, ed., *The North Caucasus Barrier: The Russian Advance toward the Muslim World* (New York: St. Martin's Press, 1992), 157–184.

59. Lynn Viola, *The Best Sons of the Fatherland: Workers in the Vanguard of Soviet Collectivization* (New York: Oxford University Press, 1987), 37–46.

60. Lev Kopelev, *The Education of a True Believer*, trans. Gary Kern (London: Wildwood House, 1981), 226.

61. Viola, *Best Sons of the Fatherland*.

62. N. A. Ivnitskii, "Golod 1932–33gg. Kto vinovat?" in *Golod 1932–1933 godov* (Moscow: Rossiiskii gosudarstvennyi gumanitarnyi universitet, 1995), 43–66; quotations pp. 44, 58.

63. Koenker and Bachman, *Revelations*, 393.

64. Ivnitskii, *Kollektivizatsiia*, 203–225; D. N. Khubova, "Chernye doski: tabula rasa—Golod 1932–33gg v ustnykh svidetel'stvakh," in *Golod 1932–1933 godov*, 67–88; Robert Conquest, *Harvest of Sorrow: Soviet Collectivization and the Terror Famine* (London: Hutchinson, 1986); Davies and Harrison, *Economic Transformation*, 74–76.

65. "Primernyi ustav sel'skokhoziaistvennoi arteli," in *Resheniia partii i pravitel'stva po khoziaistvennym voprosam*, vol. 2: *1929–1940* (Moscow: Izdatel'stvo Politicheskoi Literatury, 1967), 519–530.

66. Alec Nove, *Economic History of the USSR, 1917–1991*, 2d ed. (Harmondsworth: Penguin Books, 1991), 146, 188; table in Hosking, *First Socialist Society*, 151–152.

67. Sheila Fitzpatrick, "The Great Departure: Rural-Urban Migration in the Soviet Union, 1929–33," in William G. Rosenberg and Lewis H. Siegelbaum, eds., *Social Dimensions of Soviet Industrialization* (Bloomington: Indiana University Press, 1993), 21–27; David L. Hoffmann, *Peasant Metropolis: Social Identities in Moscow, 1929–1941* (Ithaca: Cornell University Press, 1994), 32–41, 73–74.

68. Hoffmann, *Peasant Metropolis*, 86–91, 109–112.

69. Stephen Kotkin, *Magnetic Mountain: Stalinism as a Civilization* (Berkeley: University of California Press, 1995), 157–159, 174–177.

70. Werth and Moullec, *Rapports secrets,* 209–216.

71. Moshe Lewin, "Society, State and Ideology during the First Five-Year Plan," in *The Making of the Soviet System: Essays in the Social History of Interwar Russia* (London: Methuen, 1985), 209–240.

72. Kotkin, *Magnetic Mountain,* 201–215, 242–247; V. Andrle, *Workers in Stalin's Russia: Industrialization and Social Change in a Planned Economy* (Hemel Hempstead: Harvester Press, 1988), 106–107.

73. Mervyn Matthews, ed., *Soviet Government: A Selection of Official Documents on Internal Policy* (London: Cape, 1974), 74.

74. Fitzpatrick, "Ascribing Class"; the most thorough study of the Soviet passport system is Mervyn Matthews, *The Passport Society: Controlling Movement in Russia and the USSR* (Boulder, Colo.: Westview Press, 1993), esp. chaps. 3–4.

75. Fitzpatrick, "The Great Departure," 28–31.

79. Hoffmann, *Peasant Metropolis,* 89–91.

76. I. V. Stalin, "Report to Seventeenth Party Congress," in *Works,* vol. 13 (Moscow: Foreign Languages Publishing House, 1955), 385.

77. Quoted in O. V. Khlevniuk, *Politbiuro: mekhanizmy politicheskoi vlasti v 1930-ye gody* (Moscow: Rosspen, 1996), 38.

78. *Iunost',* no. 11 (1988), 22–25.

79. Robert C. Tucker, *Stalin in Power: The Revolution from Above, 1928–1941* (New York: W. W. Norton, 1990), 209–212. Oleg Khlevniuk, who has made a thorough study of the Politbuiro papers, says there is no evidence that the Politburo even discussed Riutin or that Kirov opposed the sentence. In view of the unprecedented nature of the discussion, though, it is quite conceivable that it was not minuted.

80. Quoted in Robert Service, *Lenin: A Political Life,* vol. 3 (London: Macmillan, 1995), 284, 297.

81. Tucker, *Stalin in Power,* 247–252, 260–264. Once again, Khlevniuk objects that there is no documentary evidence for this story; but, had there been any, Stalin would certainly have destroyed it.

82. J. Arch Getty and Oleg V. Naumov, *The Road to Terror: Stalin and the Self-Destruction of the Bolsheviks, 1932–1939* (New Haven: Yale University Press, 1999), introduction.

83. Khlevniuk, *Politbiuro,* 166–186.

84. Tucker, *Stalin in Power,* 217–222.

85. Getty and Naumov, *The Road to Terror,* 119–134.

86. The evidence in favor of this version is deployed in Tucker, *Stalin in Power,* 288–296; and more fully in Amy Knight, *Who Killed Kirov? The Kremlin's Greatest Mystery* (New York: Hill & Wang, 1999). For a more skeptical view, see Adam Ulam, *Stalin: The Man and His Era* (London: Allen Lane, 1973), 381–388. In the late Soviet years Politburo member Aleksandr Iakovlev headed an official investigation into the Kirov murder. It came to the conclusion that Nikolaev had acted on his own and that Stalin was not implicated. Iakovlev, however, felt there were still many questions unanswered and recommended reopening the investigation; Koenker and Bachman, *Revelations,* 70–71.

683

87. Robert C. Tucker and Stephen F. Cohen, eds., *The Great Purge Trial* (New York: Grosset & Dunlap, 1965), 666.

88. *Sto sorok besed s Molotovym: iz dnevnika F. Chueva* (Moscow: Terra, 1991), 390.

89. Khlevniuk, *Politburo*, 137–139, 189–190; Oleg Khlevniuk, "The Objectives of the Great Terror, 1937–38," in Julian Cooper, Maureen Perrie, and E. A. Rees, eds., *Soviet History, 1917–53: Essays in Honour of R. W. Davies* (Basingstoke: Macmillan, 1995), 158–176; Roberta T. Manning, "Terror in the Belyi Raion, 1937–38," in J. Arch Getty and Roberta T. Manning, eds., *Stalinist Terror: New Perspectives* (Cambridge: Cambridge University Press, 1993).

90. Simon, *Nationalism,* 155–166; Robert Conquest, *The Great Terror: A Reassessment* (London: Hutchinson, 1990), 223–224, 356–359.

91. Robert Conquest, *Kolyma: The Arctic Death Camps* (London: Macmillan, 1983).

92. Iurii Margolin, *Puteshestvie v stranu ze-ka* (New York: Izdatel'stvo imeni Chekhova, 1952), 33 ff.; quotation p. 48. The term "exterminatory labor camps" is the title of part three of Alexander Solzhenitsyn, *The Gulag Archipelago, 1918–1956: An Experiment in Literary Investigation,* trans. H. T. Willetts (London: Collins-Harvill, 1978); Hosking, *First Socialist Society,* 200–201.

93. Alec Nove, "Victims of Stalinism—How Many?" in Getty and Manning, *Stalinist Terror,* 261–274; J. Arch Getty, Gabor T. Ritterspoorn, and Viktor N. Zemskov, "Victims of the Soviet Penal System in the Pre-War Years: A First Approach on the Basis of Archival Evidence," *American Historical Review* 98 (1993), 1017–49.

94. Nove, "Victims of Stalinism," 268.

95. R. W. Davies, "Forced Labour under Stalin: The Archive Revelations," *New Left Review,* no. 214 (1995), 67.

12. SOVIET SOCIETY TAKES SHAPE

1. N. A. Ivnitskii, *Kollektivizatsiia i raskulachivanie: nachalo 30-kh godov* (Moscow: Magistr, 1996), 150.

2. According to Sheila Fitzpatrick, *Stalin's Peasants: Resistance and Survival in the Russian Village after Collectivization* (New York: Oxford University Press, 1994), 287–293.

3. Ibid., 296–312.

4. David L. Hoffmann, *Peasant Metropolis: Social Identities in Moscow, 1929–1941* (Ithaca: Cornell University Press, 1994), 89–91.

5. Hiroaki Kuromiya, *Stalin's Industrial Revolution: Politics and Workers, 1928–32* (Cambridge: Cambridge University Press, 1988), parts III and IV; quotation pp. 283–284.

6. Lewis H. Siegelbaum, *Stakhanovism and the Politics of Productivity in the USSR, 1935–1941* (Cambridge: Cambridge University Press, 1988).

7. V. Andrle, *Workers in Stalin's Russia: Industrialization and Social Change in a Planned Economy* (Hemel Hempstead: Harvester Press, 1988), 135, 144–146.

8. Sheila Fitzpatrick, "Workers against Bosses: The Impact of the Great Purges on Labour-Management Relations," in Lewis H. Siegelbaum and Ronald Grigor Suny, eds., *Making Workers Soviet: Power, Class, and Identity* (Ithaca: Cornell University Press, 1995), 311–340.

9. Stephen Kotkin, *Magnetic Mountain: Stalinism as a Civilization* (Berkeley: University of California Press, 1995), 225–230.

10. M. Lewin, "On Soviet Industrialization," in William G. Rosenberg and Lewis H. Siegelbaum, eds., *Social Dimensions of Soviet Industrialization* (Bloomington: Indiana University Press, 1993), 278.

11. Richard Stites, *Revolutionary Dreams: Utopian Vision and Experimental Life in the Russian Revolution* (New York: Oxford University Press, 1989), chap. 9.

12. Svetlana Boym, *Common Places: Mythologies of Everyday Life in Russia* (Cambridge, Mass.: Harvard University Press, 1994), 123–124.

13. M. S. Voslensky, *Nomenklatura: Anatomy of the Soviet Ruling Class* (London: Bodley Head, 1984), chap. 6.

14. Quoted in Igor Golomstock, *Totalitarian Art* (London: Collins Harvill, 1990), 278.

15. William Croft Brumfield, *A History of Russian Architecture* (Cambridge: Cambridge University Press, 1993), 485–492.

16. Geoffrey Hosking, "The Institutionalisation of Literature," in G. F. Cushing and G. A. Hosking, eds., *Perspectives on Literature and Society in Eastern and Western Europe* (London: Macmillan, 1989), 55–75.

17. Christopher Barnes, *Boris Pasternak: A Literary Biography*, vol. 2: *1928–1960* (Cambridge: Cambridge University Press, 1998), 100; Evgenii Gromov, *Stalin: Vlast' i iskusstvo* (Moscow: Respublika, 1998), 224–227.

18. Barnes, *Pasternak*, 2: 23, 50, 132.

19. Vitaly Shestalinsky, *The KGB's Literary Archive* (London: Harvill Press, 1995), chap. 2.

20. Ibid., chap. 9.

21. Elizabeth Wilson, ed., *Shostakovich: A Life Remembered* (London: Faber & Faber, 1994), chap. 3.

22. Nicholas S. Timasheff, *The Great Retreat: The Growth and Decline of Communism in Russia* (New York: Arno Press, 1972).

23. Sheila Fitzpatrick, *Education and Social Mobility in the Soviet Union, 1921–34* (Cambridge: Cambridge University Press, 1979), 92.

24. Catriona Kelly and Vadim Volkov, "Directed Desires: *Kulturnost* and Consumption," in Catriona Kelly and David Shepherd, eds., *Constructing Russian Culture in the Age of Revolution, 1881–1940* (Oxford: Oxford University Press, 1998), 291–313.

25. Catriona Kelly, "*Kul'turnost'* in the Soviet Union: Ideal and Reality," in Geoffrey Hosking and Robert Service, eds., *Reinterpreting Russia* (London: Edward Arnold, 1999), 198–213.

26. Wendy Z. Goldman, *Women, the State and Revolution: Soviet Family Policy and Social Life, 1917–1936* (Cambridge: Cambridge University Press, 1993), chaps. 1, 6.

27. Ibid., 105–109.

28. Ibid., 288–291.

29. Ibid., chap. 2 and 307–308.

30. Timasheff, *The Great Retreat*, 198.

31. Goldman, *Women, the State and Revolution*, 336.

32. Quoted in Adam B. Ulam, *Expansion and Coexistence: The History of Soviet Foreign Policy, 1917–1967* (New York: Praeger, 1968), 54.

33. Jane Degras, ed., *The Communist International, 1919–1943: Documents,* vol. 1 (London: Oxford University Press, 1956), 43, 46.

34. Ulam, *Expansion and Coexistence,* 115–116.

35. Ibid., 115.

686

36. Hans W. Gatzke, "Russo-German Military Collaboration during the Weimar Republic," *American Historical Review* 63 (1958), 565–597; John Erickson, *The Soviet High Command: A Military-Political History, 1918–1941* (Boulder, Colo.: Westview Press, 1984), chap. 9.

37. E. H. Carr, *A History of Soviet Russia: The Interregnum, 1923–4* (London: Macmillan, 1954), 201–226.

38. Erickson, *Soviet High Command,* 495–498, 517–521, 532–537.

39. Jonathan Haslam, *The Soviet Union and the Struggle for Collective Security in Europe, 1933–1939* (London: Macmillan, 1984), chaps. 6–7.

40. George Orwell, *Homage to Catalonia* (Harmondsworth: Penguin Books, 1962), 57.

41. Haslam, *Soviet Union and Collective Security,* 206–207.

42. For a thorough account of the dual-track negotiations with the West and Germany, see ibid., chap. 10.

43. *Khrushchev Remembers: The Glasnost Tapes,* trans. Jerrold L. Shecter (Boston: Little, Brown, 1990), 55.

44. Gabriel Gorodetsky, "Stalin and Hitler's Attack on the Soviet Union," in Bernd Wegner, ed., *From Peace to War: Germany, Soviet Russia and the World, 1939–1941* (Oxford: Berghahn Books, 1997), 343–359.

45. The case was first argued in detail by Viktor Suvorov, in *Icebreaker: Who Started the Second World War?* trans. Thomas R. Beattie (London: Hamish Hamilton, 1990).

46. Cynthia A. Roberts, "Planning for War: The Red Army and the Catastrophe of 1941," *Europe-Asia Studies* 47 (1995), 1293–1326; R. Raack, "Stalin's Plans for World War II," *Journal of Contemporary History* 26 (1991), 215–227; William J. Spahr, *Zhukov: The Rise and Fall of a Great Captain* (Novato, Calif.: Presidio, 1993), 47–49; David M. Glantz, *Stumbling Colossus: The Red Army on the Eve of World War* (Lawrence: University of Kansas Press, 1998), 102–107. The controversy and the evidence are exhaustively examined in Gabriel Gorodetsky, *Grand Delusion: Stalin and the German Invasion of Russia* (New Haven: Yale University Press, 1999).

47. Robert E. Tarleton, "What Really Happened to the Stalin Line?" *Journal of Soviet Military Studies* 5 (1992), 187–219; 6 (1993), 21–61; Spahr, *Zhukov,* 38–39.

48. Richard Overy, *Russia's War* (London: Allen Lane, 1998), 87.

49. David M. Glantz and Jonathan House, *When Titans Clashed: How the Red Army Stopped Hitler* (Lawrence: University of Kansas Press, 1995), 121.

50. Political commissars had been downgraded once already before the war, but then reinstated; Alexander Werth, *Russia at War, 1941–1945* (New York: Carroll and Graff, 1964), 414–416; John Erickson, *The Road to Stalingrad,* vol. 1: *Stalin's War with Germany* (London: Weidenfeld & Nicolson, 1975), 22–24, 371–372.

51. Overy, *Russia's War,* 187–193.

52. John Barber and Mark Harrison, *The Soviet Home Front, 1941–1945: A Social and Economic History of the USSR in World War Two* (London: Longman, 1991), 127–132, 163–167.

53. B. Sokolov, "Lend-Lease in Soviet Military Efforts, 1941–1954," *Journal of Slavic Military Studies* 7 (1994), 567–586; *Khrushchev Remembers*, 84.

54. Calculated from John Erickson, "Soviet War Losses: Calculations and Controversies," in John Erickson and David Dilks, eds., *Barbarossa: The Axis and the Allies* (Edinburgh: Edinburgh University Press, 1994), 265–266.

55. Werth, *Russia at War*, 414.

56. The most detailed picture of battlefield casualties is in G. F. Krivosheev, ed., *Grif sekretnosti sniat: poteri vooruzhennykh sil SSSR v voinakh, boevykh deistviiakh i voennykh konfliktakh* (Moscow: Voenizdat, 1993); for broader figures, see L. E. Poliakov, *Tsena pobedy: demograficheskii aspekt* (Moscow: Finansy i statistika, 1985). There is an analysis of the 1939 census in V. S. Kozhurin, "O chislennosti naseleniia SSSR nakanune velikoi otechestvennoi voiny," *Voenno-istoricheskii zhurnal*, no. 2 (1991), 21–26. The overall issues are examined in Erickson, "Soviet War Losses."

57. Werth, *Russia at War*, 388–389.

58. David Marples, *Stalinism in Ukraine in the 1940s* (Basingstoke: Macmillan, 1992), 50.

59. V. Shtrik-Shtrikfel't, *Protiv Stalina i Gitlera: General Vlasov i russkoe osvoboditel'noe dvizhenie* (Frankfurt am Main: Posev, 1975), 423.

60. The program is reproduced in Catherine Andreyev, *Vlasov and the Russian Liberation Movement: Soviet Reality and Emigré Theories* (Cambridge: Cambridge University Press, 1987), 206–209.

61. Alex Inkeles and Raymond A. Bauer, *The Soviet Citizen: Daily Life in a Totalitarian Society* (New York: Atheneum, 1968), chap. 10.

62. Sergej Fröhlich, *General Wlasow: Russen und Deutsche zwischen Hitler und Stalin* (Cologne: Markus, 1987).

63. Leonid D. Grenkevich, *The Soviet Partisan Movement, 1941–44: A Critical Historiographical Analysis* (London: Frank Cass, 1999).

64. Harrison E. Salisbury, *The Siege of Leningrad* (London: Secker & Warburg, 1969), 217–220.

65. Ibid., 514–518.

66. N. S. Patolichev, *Ispytanie na zrelost'* (Moscow: Politizdat, 1977), 171, 213.

67. Fedor Abramov, *Izbrannoe*, vol. 1 (Moscow: Izvestiia, 1976), 344.

68. Alec Nove, *Economic History of the USSR, 1917–1991*, 2d ed. (Harmondsworth: Penguin Books, 1991), 282; Geoffrey Hosking, *The First Socialist Society: A History of the Soviet Union from Within*, 3d ed. (Cambridge, Mass.: Harvard University Press, 1992), 286–287.

69. W. Moskoff, *The Bread of Affliction: The Food Supply in the USSR during World War II* (Cambridge: Cambridge University Press, 1990), chap. 8; Alexander Werth, *The Year of Stalingrad* (London: Hamish Hamilton, 1946), chap. 3.

70. Richard Lorenz, *Sozialgeschichte der Sowjetunion* (Frankfurt am Main: Suhrkamp, 1976), 290.

71. Walter Kolarz, *Religion in the Soviet Union* (London: Macmillan, 1961), 49–51.

72. Felix Corley, *Religion in the Soviet Union: An Archival Reader* (Basingstoke: Macmillan, 1996), 139–147.

73. Terry Martin, "The Origins of Soviet Ethnic Cleansing," *Journal of Modern History* 70 (1998), 813–861.

687

74. Alexander Nekrich, *The Punished Peoples: The Deportation and Fate of Soviet Minorities at the End of the Second World War* (New York: W. W. Norton, 1978); N. F. Bugai, "K voprosu o deportatsii narodov SSSR," *Istoriia SSSR*, no. 6 (1989), 135–144; and idem, "Pravda o deportatsii chechenskogo i ingushskogo narodov," *Voprosy istorii*, no. 7 (1990), 32–44.

75. Mikhail Geller and Aleksandr Nekrich, *Utopiia u vlasti: istoriia Sovetskogo Soiuza s 1917g do nashikh dnei* (London: Overseas Publications Interchange, 1986), 492–496.

76. Viacheslav Kondrat'ev, "Paradoks frontovoi nostal'gii," *Literaturnaia gazeta*, 9 May 1990, 9.

13. RECOVERY AND COLD WAR

1. David Holloway, *Stalin and the Bomb: The Soviet Union and Atomic Energy, 1939–1956* (New Haven: Yale University Press, 1994), 154.

2. Vojtech Mastny, *The Cold War and Soviet Insecurity: The Stalin Years* (New York: Oxford University Press, 1996), 23.

3. Milovan Djilas, *Conversations with Stalin* (London: Hart-Davis, 1962), 94–108; quotation p. 98.

4. N. I. Egorova, "NATO i evropeiskaia bezopasnost': vospriiatie sovetskogo rukovodstva," in A. O. Chubarian, ed., *Stalin i kholodnaia voina* (Moscow: Institut vseobshchei istorii RAN, 1998), 291–314.

5. Holloway, *Stalin and the Bomb*, 161–166.

6. Ibid., 184–201.

7. Ibid., 203–206; Andrei Sakharov, *Memoirs*, trans. Richard Lourie (London: Hutchinson, 1990), 96–98.

8. Holloway, *Stalin and the Bomb*, 265–268.

9. John L. Gaddis, *Strategies of Containment: A Critical Appraisal of Postwar American National Security Policy* (Oxford: Oxford University Press, 1982).

10. Adam Ulam, *The Rivals: America and Russia since World War Two* (London: Allen Lane, 1973).

11. Mikhail M. Narinskii, "The Soviet Union and the Berlin Crisis, 1948–49," in Francesca Gori and Silvio Pons, eds., *The Soviet Union and Europe in the Cold War* (Basingstoke: Macmillan, 1996), 57–75.

12. Sergei N. Goncharov, John W. Lewis, and Xue Litai, *Uncertain Partners: Stalin, Mao, and the Korean War* (Stanford: Stanford University Press, 1993).

13. The fullest account of the Cuban crisis, using recently released Russian archive sources, is Aleksandr Fursenko and Timothy Naftali, *One Hell of a Gamble: The Secret History of the Cuban Missile Crisis* (New York: W. W. Norton, 1997).

14. Alvin Z. Rubinstein, *Soviet Foreign Policy since World War II: Imperial and Global*, 4th ed. (London: HarperCollins, 1992), 240–248, 315–328.

15. Ibid., 157.

16. Joseph L. Nogee and Robert H. Donaldson, *Soviet Foreign Policy since World War II*, 3d ed. (New York: Pergamon Press, 1988), 229–239.

17. Vladimir Boukovsky, *Jugement à Moscou* (Paris: Robert Laffont, 1995), chap. 1.

18. L. E. Poliakov, *Tsena pobedy: demograficheskii aspekt* (Moscow: Finansy i Statistika,

1985); G. F. Krivosheev, *Grif sekretnosti sniat: poteri vooruzhennykh sil SSSR v voinakh, boevykh deistviiakh i voennykh konfliktakh* (Moscow: Voenizdat, 1993); John Erickson, "Soviet War Losses: Calculations and Controversies," in John Erickson and David Dilks, eds., *Barbarossa: The Axis and the Allies* (Edinburgh: Edinburgh University Press, 1994), 255–277; Mark Harrison, *Accounting for War: Soviet Production, Employment and the Defence Burden, 1940–1945* (Cambridge: Cambridge University Press, 1996), 159–164.

19. Nina Tumarkin, *The Living and the Dead: The Rise and Fall of the Cult of World War II in Russia* (New York: Basic Books, 1994).

20. Sakharov, *Memoirs*, 164.

21. E. Iu. Zubkova, *Obshchestvo i reformy, 1945–1964* (Moscow: Rossiia Molodaia, 1993), 33–44.

22. V. Kardin, "Lushchie gody nashei zhizni, ili pochemu ia ravnodushen k antiutopiiam," *Ogonek* 19 (1990), 17; quoted in E. S. Seniavskaia, *1941–1945 Frontovoe pokolenie: istoriko-psikhologicheskoe issledovanie* (Moscow: Institut Rossiiskoi Istorii RAN, 1995), 164–165. See also Seniavskaia, 71–93.

23. Iu. P. Petrov, *Stroitel'stvo politorganov, partiinykh i komsomol'skikh organizatsii armii i flota, 1918–1968gg* (Moscow: Voennoe Izdatel'stvo, 1968), 336, 393–394, 397.

24. Timothy J. Colton, *Commissars, Commanders, and Civilian Authority: The Structure of Soviet Military Politics* (Cambridge, Mass.: Harvard University Press, 1979), esp. chap. 11.

25. Werner G. Hahn, *Postwar Soviet Politics: The Fall of Zhdanov and the Defeat of Moderation* (Ithaca: Cornell University Press, 1982), 94–113, 118–129; B. Bonwetsch, "Die Leningrad-Affäre," *Deutsche Studien* 28 (1990), 306–322.

26. Donald Filtzer, *Soviet Workers and Stalinist Industrialisation: The Formation of Modern Soviet Production Relations, 1928–1941* (London: Pluto, 1986), chap. 9; also his "Soviet Economy and Society in the Postwar Period," in Stefan Plaggenborg, ed., *Handbuch der Geschichte Russlands*, vol. 4 (Stuttgart: Hiersemann Verlag, forthcoming).

27. I. M. Volkov, ed., *Sovetskaia derevnia v pervye poslevoennye gody, 1946–1951* (Moscow: Nauka, 1978), 456–457.

28. Alec Nove, *Economic History of the USSR, 1917–1991*, 2d ed. (Harmondsworth: Penguin Books, 1989), 303–311, 316.

29. John Barber and Mark Harrison, *The Soviet Home Front, 1941–1945: A Social and Economic History of the USSR in World War II* (London: Longman, 1991), 104; V. F. Zima, *Golod v SSSR, 1946–47gg: proiskhozhdenie i posledstviia* (Moscow: Institut Rossiiskoi Istorii RAN, 1996), 12–18.

30. Zima, *Golod*, 65–75, 164–171.

31. E. Strauss, *Soviet Agriculture in Perspective: A Study of Its Successes and Failures* (London: Allen & Unwin, 1969), 307; Karl Wädekin, *Privatproduzenten in der sowjetischen Landwirtschaft* (Cologne: Verlag Wissenschaft und Politik, 1967), 24.

32. Elizabeth Wilson, *Shostakovich: A Life Remembered* (London: Faber & Faber, 1994), 158–159.

33. Gleb Struve, *Russian Literature under Lenin and Stalin, 1917–1953* (London: Routledge & Kegan Paul, 1972), 350–357; Robert H. McNeal, ed., *Resolutions and Decisions of the CPSU*, vol. 3: *The Stalin Years, 1929–1953* (Toronto: University of Toronto Press, 1974), 240–243.

689

34. Wilson, *Shostakovich*, 207–215.

35. Wolfgang Girke and Helmut Jachnow, *Sowjetische Soziolinguistik: Probleme und Genese* (Kronberg: Scriptor Verlag, 1974), 50–68.

36. Wilson, *Shostakovich*, 210–211.

37. Nikita Khrushchev, *Khrushchev Remembers,* trans. and ed. Strobe Talbott (Boston: Little, Brown, 1970), 345; V. P. Naumov, "Bor'ba N. S. Khrushcheva za edinolichnuiu vlast," *Novaia i noveishaia istoriia,* no. 2 (1996), 15.

38. Khrushchev, *Khrushchev Remembers,* 346–351; Fedor Burlatskii, *Khrushchev and the First Russian Spring,* trans. Daphne Skillen (London: Weidenfeld & Nicolson, 1991), 39–40; Robert Service, *A History of Twentieth Century Russia* (London: Allen Lane, 1997), 338.

39. Naumov, "Bor'ba N. S. Khrushcheva," 15–16.

40. Ibid., 16.

41. Ibid., 23.

42. Georgii Arbatov, *Zatianuvsheesia vyzdorovlenie, 1953–1985* (Moscow: Mezhdunarodnye Otnosheniia, 1991), 64–79.

43. L. Schapiro, ed., *The USSR and the Future: An Analysis of the New Program of the CPSU* (New York: Praeger, 1963), 297.

44. Roy Medvedev and Zhores Medvedev, *Khrushchev: The Years in Power* (New York: Oxford University Press, 1977), 104–105, 152–155.

45. P. H. Juviler, *Revolutionary Law and Order: Politics and Social Change in the USSR* (London, Collier-Macmillan, 1976), 78–79.

46. Medvedev and Medvedev, *Khrushchev,* 143–145, 181–182.

47. John Anderson, *Religion, State and Politics in the Soviet Union and Successor States* (Cambridge: Cambridge University Press, 1994), 9.

48. Evidence of the criteria adopted in appointments and promotions is contained in a report to the CPSU by the deputy chairman of the Council for Religious Affairs, V. Furov, leaked to the West in the 1970s: "Iz otcheta po delam religii—chlenam KPSS," *Vestnik Russkogo Khristianskogo Dvizheniia,* no. 130 (1979), 275–344.

49. Anderson, *Religion, State and Politics,* 30–34; Christel Lane, *The Rites of Rulers: Ritual in Industrial Society—the Soviet Case* (Cambridge: Cambridge University Press, 1981).

50. Jane Ellis, *The Russian Orthodox Church: A Contemporary History* (London: Croom Helm, 1986), 53–69.

51. Anderson, *Religion, State and Politics,* 55–59.

52. Donald Filtzer, *Soviet Workers and De-Stalinization: The Consolidation of the Modern System of Soviet Production Relations, 1953–1964* (Cambridge: Cambridge University Press, 1992).

53. Ibid., chaps. 7–8.

54. Alexander Zinoviev, *The Reality of Communism* (London: Victor Gollancz, 1984), 114.

55. Strauss, *Soviet Agriculture,* 170–175; Martin McCauley, *Khrushchev and the Development of Soviet Agriculture: The Virgin Land Programme, 1953–1964* (Basingstoke: Macmillan, 1976), chaps. 4, 6.

56. Martha Brill Olcott, *The Kazakhs* (Stanford, Calif.: Hoover Institution Press, 1987), chap. 10.

57. Strauss, *Soviet Agriculture,* 175–178.

58. See the KGB report in *Istoricheskii arkhiv*, no. 1 (1993), 122–129.

59. William J. Tompson, *Khrushchev: A Political Life* (Basingstoke: Macmillan, 1995), 270–276; Suslov's speech is in *Istoricheskii arkhiv*, no. 1 (1993), 7–15.

60. Medvedev and Medvedev, *Khrushchev*, 245.

14. SOVIET SOCIETY UNDER "DEVELOPED SOCIALISM"

1. Roy Medvedev, *Lichnost' i epokha: politicheskii portret L. I. Brezhneva* (Moscow: Novosti, 1991), esp. chap. 3.

2. Mark R. Beissinger, "The Political Elite," in James Cracraft, ed., *The Soviet Union Today: An Interpretive Guide* (Chicago: Bulletin of the Atomic Scientists, 1983), 35–51; Geoffrey Hosking, *The First Socialist Society: A History of the Soviet Union from Within*, 3d ed. (Cambridge, Mass.: Harvard University Press, 1992), 377–378.

3. Mikhail Gorbachev, *Memoirs* (London: Doubleday, 1996), 112, 114.

4. Alec Nove, *Economic History of the USSR, 1917–1991*, 2d ed. (Harmondsworth: Penguin Books, 1989), 367–368.

5. Alec Nove, "Agriculture," in Archie Brown and Michael Kaser, eds., *The Soviet Union since the Fall of Khrushchev*, 2d ed. (Basingstoke: Macmillan, 1975), 9–11.

6. Victor Zaslavsky, *The Neo-Stalinist State: Class, Ethnicity, and Consensus in Soviet Society* (Armonk, N.Y.: M. E. Sharpe, 1982), chaps. 4–5.

7. Gregory Grossman, "The 'Second Economy' of the USSR," *Problems of Communism* 26, no. 5 (September 1977), 25–40; Hedrick Smith, *The Russians* (New York: Quadrangle Books, 1976), chap. 3; Alena Ledeneva, *Russia's Economy of Favours: Blat, Networking and Informal Exchange* (Cambridge: Cambridge University Press, 1998).

8. R. Kaiser, *The Geography of Nationalism in Russia and the Soviet Union* (Princeton: Princeton University Press, 1994), chap. 4, esp. 166–170.

9. Timothy Garton Ash, *The Polish Revolution: Solidarity, 1980–82* (London: Jonathan Cape, 1983), 78.

10. Ibid.; Neal Ascherson, *The Polish August: The Self-Limiting Revolution* (Harmondsworth: Penguin Books, 1982).

11. This scene comes at the beginning and end of Vitalii Semin, "Semero v odnom dome," *Novyi mir*, no. 6 (1965), 62–144; Basile Kerblay, *Modern Soviet Society*, trans. Rupert Swyer (London: Methuen, 1983), 24–38.

12. Gail W. Lapidus, ed., *Women, Work, and Family in the Soviet Union* (Armonk, N.Y.: M. E. Sharpe, 1982), 253.

13. Norton T. Dodge, "Women in the Professions," and Janet G. Chapman, "Equal Pay for Equal Work?" in Dorothy Atkinson, Alexander Dallin, and Gail Warshofsky Lapidus, eds., *Women in Russia* (Hassocks: Harvester Press, 1978), 205–224, 225–239.

14. Alix Holt, "The First Soviet Feminists," in Barbara Holland, ed., *Soviet Sisterhood* (London: Fourth Estate, 1985), 237–265.

15. Kerblay, *Modern Soviet Society*, 34–38; Manfred Hildermeier, *Geschichte der Sowjetunion, 1917–1991* (Munich: C. H. Beck Verlag, 1998), 948–950.

16. Kerblay, *Modern Soviet Society*, 123–124.

17. Dietrich Beyrau, *Intelligenz und Dissens: die russischen Bildungsschichten in der Sowjetunion, 1917–1985* (Göttingen: Vandenhoek & Ruprecht, 1993), 312.

18. Aleksandr Zinov'ev, *Zheltyi dom,* vol. 1 (Lausanne: L'Age d'Homme, 1980), 48.

19. Beyrau, *Intelligenz und Dissens,* 314.

20. Peter Kneen, *Soviet Scientists and the State* (London: Macmillan, 1984), chap. 4; Stephen Fortescue, *Science Policy in the Soviet Union* (London: Routledge, 1990), chap. 1.

21. P. L. Kapitsa, *Pis'ma o nauke, 1930–1980* (Moscow: Moskovskii Rabochii, 1989), 316–317.

22. A. D. Sakhartov, V. F. Turchin, and R. A. Medvedev, "Appeal of Soviet Scientists to the Party-Government Leaders of the USSR," *Survey,* no. 76 (Summer 1970), 160–170.

23. Beyrau, *Intelligenz und Dissens,* 210.

24. See the description of work in the late 1970s and early 1980s in the Institute of Systematic Research and the Economic-Mathematical Institute in Egor Gaidar, *Dni porazhenii i pobed* (Moscow: Vagrius, 1996), 29–31.

25. Katerina Clark and Michael Holquist, *Mikhail Bakhtin* (Cambridge, Mass.: The Belknap Press of Harvard University Press, 1984); Tsvetan Todorov, *Mikhail Bakhtin: The Dialogic Principle,* trans. Wlad Godzich (Manchester: Manchester University Press, 1984).

26. Ann Shukman, *Literature and Semiotics: A Study of the Writings of Yu. M. Lotman* (Amsterdam: North Holland Publishing, 1977).

27. For an account of its early years, see Edith Rogovin Frankel, *Novy Mir: A Case Study in the Politics of Literature, 1952–58* (Cambridge: Cambridge University Press, 1981).

28. Geoffrey Hosking, *Beyond Socialist Realism: Soviet Fiction since Ivan Denisovich* (London: Granada Books, 1980).

29. L. Labedz, ed., *Solzhenitsyn: A Documentary Record* (London: Allen Lane, 1970), 15–16.

30. Hosking, *Beyond Socialist Realism,* chap. 3; Kathleen Parthé, *Russian Village Prose: The Radiant Past* (Princeton: Princeton University Press, 1992).

31. Maia A. Kipp, "Soviet Theater from 1953 to the Demise of the Soviet Union," in *A Concise Encyclopedia of Soviet Civilization* (Austin, Texas: Holt, Rinehart, forthcoming).

32. Vladimir Bukovsky, *To Build a Castle: My Life as a Dissenter* (London: Andre Deutsch, 1978), 115.

33. Beyrau, *Intelligenz und Dissens,* 229–234.

34. L. Labedz and M. Hayward, eds., *On Trial: The Case of Sinyavsky (Tertz) and Daniel (Arzhak)* (London: Collins & Harvill Press, 1967), 290–291.

35. Beyrau, *Intelligenz und Dissens,* 222–225; Oleg Kharkhordin, *The Collective and the Individual in Russia: A Study of Practices* (Berkeley: University of California Press, 1999), chap. 7.

36. Mark Hopkins, *Russia's Underground Press: The Chronicle of Current Events* (New York: Praeger, 1983).

37. I. Iu. Sundiev, "Neformal'nye molodezhnye ob"edineniia: opyt ekspozitsii," *Sotsiologicheskie issledovaniia,* no. 5 (1987), 56–62.

38. Tamara Dragadze, *Rural Families in Soviet Georgia: A Case Study in Ratcha Province* (London: Routledge, 1988); Akbar Rashidov, "Family and Tribal Structure and Social Conflicts in Soviet Central Asia," in Marco Buttino, ed., *In a Collapsing Empire: Under-*

development, Ethnic Conflicts and Nationalism in the Soviet Union (Milan: Feltrinelli, 1993), 291–299.

39. R. G. Landa, *Islam v istorii Rossii* (Moscow: Vostochnaia Literatura RAN, 1995), 240–242; Shirin Akiner, "Islam, the State, and Ethnicity in Central Asia in Historical Perspective," *Religion, State, and Society* 24 (1996), 114–116.

40. Akiner, "Islam," 110–113.

41. Landa, *Islam*, 244–245; Martha Brill Olcott, *The Kazakhs* (Stanford, Calif.: Hoover Institution Press, 1987), 240–246; Ahmed Rashid, *The Resurgence of Central Asia: Islam or Nationalism?* (London: Zed Books, 1994), 116, 145.

42. Rashid, *Resurgence of Central Asia*, 91–92; J. Critchlow, *Nationalism in Uzbekistan: A Soviet Republic's Road to Sovereignty* (Boulder, Colo.: Westview Press, 1991), 64–69, 78–91.

43. *Literaturnaia gazeta*, 20 January 1988, 13.

44. John L. H. Keep, *Last of the Empires: A History of the Soviet Union, 1945–1991* (Oxford: Oxford University Press, 1995), 211, 221.

45. John P. Willerton, *Patronage and Politics in the USSR* (Cambridge: Cambridge University Press, 1992), chap. 6; I. Zemtsov, *Partiia ili mafiia? Razvorovannaia respublika* (Paris: Editeurs Réunis, 1976).

46. Bohdan Krawchenko, *Social Change and National Consciousness in Twentieth-Century Ukraine* (Basingstoke: Macmillan, 1985), 119–120, 178–186; Paul S. Pirie, "National Identity and Politics in Southern and Eastern Ukraine," *Europe-Asia Studies* 48 (1996), 1079–1104.

47. Ivan Dzyuba, *Internationalism or Russification? A Study in the Soviet Nationalities Problem* (London: Weidenfeld & Nicolson, 1968); Michael Browne, ed., *Ferment in the Ukraine: Documents by V. Chornovil and Others* (London: Macmillan, 1971).

48. V. P. Kozlov, *The Peoples of the Soviet Union* (London: Hutchinson, 1988), 58–59; Jan Zaprudnik and Michael Urban, "Belarus: From Statehood to Empire?" in Ian Bremmer and Ray Taras, eds., *New States, New Politics: Building the Post-Soviet Nations* (Cambridge: Cambridge University Press, 1997), 284–285.

49. Nora Dudwick, "Armenia: The Nation Awakes," in I. Bremmer and R. Taras, eds., *Nations and Politics in the Soviet Successor States* (Cambridge: Cambridge University Press, 1993), 272; Stephen Jones, "Georgia: A Failed Democratic Transition," ibid., 292–294.

50. William Crowther, "Moldova: Caught between Nation and Empire," in Bremmer and Taras, *Nations and Politics*, 318–319.

51. Azade-Ayse Rorlich, *The Volga Tatars: A Profile in National Resilience* (Stanford, Calif.: Hoover Institution Press, 1986), chap. 11.

52. John Garrard and Carol Garrard, *The Bones of Berdichev: The Life and Fate of Vasilii Grossman* (New York: Free Press, 1996), 199–214.

53. Yitzhak M. Brudny, *Reinventing Russia: Russian Nationalism and the Soviet State, 1953–1991* (Cambridge, Mass.: Harvard University Press, 1998), chaps. 4–6.

54. Anderson, *Religion, State and Politics*, chap. 4; Brudny, *Reinventing Russia*, chaps. 3–4.

55. William E. Odom, *The Collapse of the Soviet Military* (New Haven: Yale University Press, 1998), 286–289.

693

15. FROM PERESTROIKA TO THE RUSSIAN FEDERATION

1. Mikhail Gorbachev, *Memoirs* (London: Doubleday, 1996) 43–46.

2. G. A. Arbatov, *Zatianuvsheesia vyzdorovlenie: svidetel'stvo sovremennika, 1953–1985* (Moscow: Mezhdunarodnye otnosheniia, 1991), 15–16.

3. Ibid., 67–72, 282–287, 381–399.

4. Neil Malcolm, "De-Stalinization and Soviet Foreign Policy: The Roots of 'New Thinking,'" in Tsuyoshi Hasegawa and Alex Pravda, eds., *Perestroika: Soviet Domestic and Foreign Policies* (London: Royal Institute of International Affairs, 1990), 178–205.

5. Arbatov, *Zatianuvsheesia vyzdorovlenie,* 75–85; Archie Brown, *The Gorbachev Factor* (Oxford: Oxford University Press, 1996), 98–103.

6. Malcolm, "De-Stalinization and Soviet Foreign Policy," esp. 192.

7. Paul Kennedy, *The Rise and Fall of the Great Powers: Economic Change and Military Conflict from 1500 to 2000* (London: Unwin Hyman, 1988). Curiously, Kennedy applied the concept of "overstretch" more consistently to the United States at the time he was writing than to the USSR, which seemed already then a classic example of it; see, for example, 514–515.

8. Gorbachev, *Memoirs,* 502; Anthony D'Agostino, *Gorbachev's Revolution, 1985–1991* (London: Macmillan, 1998), 14–25.

9. *Pravda,* 8 January 1989.

10. Gorbachev, *Memoirs,* 524.

11. In his *Memoirs* (526), Gobachev calls this hope "brief" and "faint," but the evidence suggests that it was his strategic priority in first of all pressuring Honecker and then accepting the fall of the Berlin Wall.

12. A. S. Cherniaev, *Shest' let s Gorbachevym: po dnevnikovym zapisiam* (Moscow: Kultura, 1993), 305–306.

13. Timothy Garton Ash, *In Europe's Name: Germany and the Divided Continent* (London: Jonathan Cape, 1993), chap. 7.

14. Cherniaev, *Shest' let s Gorbachevym,* 83–93; Gorbachev, *Memoirs,* 188, 194–195.

15. *Materialy samizdata,* AS 5785, 1–3.

16. Gorbachev, *Memoirs,* 193.

17. Cherniaev, *Shest' let s Gorbachevym,* 85–87.

18. Alec Nove, *Glasnost in Action: Cultural Renaissance in Russia* (London: Unwin Hyman, 1989); R. W. Davies, *Soviet History in the Gorbachev Revolution* (Basingstoke: Macmillan, 1989).

19. *Pravda,* 16 January 1989, 1.

20. William Moskoff, *Hard Times: Impoverishment and Protest in the Perestroika Years—the Soviet Union, 1985–1991* (Armonk, N.Y.: M. E. Sharpe, 1993), esp. chap. 2.

21. Donald Filtzer, *Soviet Workers and the Collapse of Perestroika: The Soviet Labour Process and Gorbachev's Reforms* (Cambridge: Cambridge University Press, 1994), 82–93.

22. Ibid., 94–122.

23. Geoffrey Hosking, "The Beginnings of Independent Political Activity", in G. A. Hosking, J. Aves, and P. J. S. Duncan, *The Road to Post-Communism: Independent Political Movements in the Soviet Union, 1985–1991* (London: Pinter, 1992), 1–28.

24. Ibid., 13, 17–19; Kathleen E. Smith, *Remembering Stalin's Victims: Popular Memory and the End of the USSR* (Ithaca: Cornell University Press, 1996), chap. 5.

25. A. V. Gromov and O. S. Kuzin, *Neformaly: kto est' kto?* (Moscow: Mysl', 1990), 107.

26. Ronald Grigor Suny, *Looking toward Ararat: Armenia in Modern History* (Bloomington: Indiana University Press, 1993), 196–200.

27. J. Aves, "The Rise and Fall of the Georgian National Movement, 1987–1991," in Hosking, Aves, and Duncan, *Road to Post-Communism*, 157–179.

28. William E. Odom, *The Collapse of the Soviet Military* (New Haven: Yale University Press, 1998), 260–268.

29. Ibid., 267–268.

30. For their contribution to the breakup of the USSR, see Kristian Gerner and Stefan Hedlund, *The Baltic States and the End of the Soviet Empire* (London: Routledge, 1993).

31. John B. Dunlop, *The Rise of Russia and the Fall of the Soviet Empire* (Princeton: Princeton University Press, 1993), 50.

32. Ibid., 93.

33. Ibid., 92–95.

34. Ibid., 62.

35. Geoffrey Hosking, *The First Socialist Society: A History of the Soviet Union from Within*, 3d ed. (Cambridge, Mass.: Harvard University Press, 1992), 491.

36. Aleksandr Lebed', *Za derzhavu obidno* (Moscow: Moskovskaia Pravda, 1995), 390.

37. Dunlop, *Rise of Russia*, 214.

38. For good accounts of the coup, which draw on evidence from a variety of sources, see Odom, *Collapse of the Soviet Military*, chap. 14; and Dunlop, *Rise of Russia*, chap. 5. For evidence that Gorbachev was playing it both ways, see Dunlop, 202–206; for counterarguments, see Brown, *Gorbachev Factor*, 294–300.

39. Hosking, *First Socialist Society*, 497–498.

40. G. D. G. Murrell, *Russia's Transition to Democracy: An Internal Political History, 1989–1996* (Brighton: Sussex Academic Press, 1997), chap. 9.

41. Ibid., 157–177.

42. Boris El'tsin, *Zapiski Prezidenta* (Moscow: Ogonek, 1994), 423–426.

43. For example, Bruce Clark, *An Empire's New Clothes: The End of Russia's Liberal Dream* (London: Vintage, 1995), 253–255.

44. Vladimir Zhirinovsky, *My Struggle* (New York: Barricade Books, 1996), 15, 17.

45. *My Russia: The Political Autobiography of Gennadii Ziuganov*, ed. Vadim Medish (Armonk, N.Y.: M. E. Sharpe, 1997), 9–15.

46. John Lloyd, *Rebirth of a Nation: An Anatomy of Russia* (London: Michael Joseph, 1998), 212–218; Chubais quoted p. 218.

47. Olga Kryshtanovskaya and Stephen White, "From Soviet Nomenklatura to Russian Elite", *Europe-Asia Studies* 46 (1996), 711–733; Steven L. Solnick, *Stealing the State: Control and Collapse in Soviet Institutions* (Cambridge, Mass.: Harvard University Press, 1998), chap. 4.

48. Joseph R. Blasi, Maya Kroumova, and Douglas Kruse, *Kremlin Capitalism: Privatizing the Russian Economy* (Ithaca: Cornell University Press, 1997), 39–49.

49. Ibid., 190.

50. Lloyd, *Rebirth of a Nation*, 277–279.

695

51. Thane Gustafson, *Capitalism Russian-Style* (Cambridge: Cambridge University Press, 1999), chap. 9.

52. Lloyd, *Rebirth of a Nation,* 288, 303, 306–307; Mark Galeotti, *The Kremlin's Agenda: The New Russia and Its Armed Forces* (Coulsdon, U.K.: Jane's Intelligence Review, 1995), 37.

53. Janine Wedel, *Collision and Collusion: The Strange Case of Western Aid to Eastern Europe* (Basingstoke: Macmillan, 1998), chap. 4 and 188–190.

54. Gustafson, *Capitalism Russian-Style,* chap. 6.

55. Ibid., 104–107, 175.

56. Galeotti, *The Kremlin's Agenda,* 67.

57. Anatol Lieven, *Chechnya: Tombstone of Russian Power* (New Haven: Yale University Press, 1998), chaps. 2–3; for the background to the Chechen conflict, see Valery Tishkov, *Ethnicity, Nationalism and Conflict in and after the Soviet Union: The Mind Aflame* (London: Sage, 1997), chaps. 9–10.

58. Quoted in Lloyd, *Rebirth of a Nation,* 335.

59. Neil Melvin, *Russians beyond Russia: The Politics of National Identity* (London: Royal Institute of International Affairs, 1995), 61–65.

60. Muriel Atkin, "Tajikistan: Reform, Reaction and Civil War," in Ian Bremmer and Ray Taras, eds., *New States, New Politics: Building the Post-Soviet Nations* (Cambridge: Cambridge University Press, 1997), 603–634; Ahmed Rashid, *The Resurgence of Central Asia: Islam or Nationalism?* (London: Zed Books, 1994), chaps. 7, 9.

61. Lloyd, *Rebirth of a Nation,* 356.

62. Ibid.

63. Vera Tolz, "Conflicting 'Homeland Myths' and Nation-State Building in Postcommunist Russia," *Slavic Review* 57 (1998), 267–294.

INDEX

Abkhazia/Abkhazians, 238, 315, 584, 607
Abramov, Fedor, 502
Abramtsevo, 348
Academy of Sciences, 208, 581
Adrianople, 316
Adriatic Sea, 387
Adventists, 536
Adzhubei, Aleksei, 540
Afanasiev, Iurii, 581
Afghanistan, 520, 569, 573, 607
Africa, 520
Agitprop, 437, 451
Agriculture, 3, 7–15, 19, 21; pre-imperial, 29–30, 34, 35; productivity, 194, 256, 358; under Peter I, 220–222; central Asian, 325; mechanization of, 357, 456, 460, 471; agrarian reform, 375–377, 406–407; collectivization of, 399, 407, 441, 449–455, 456, 470–472, 499, 501–502, 510, 525–526, 544, 558–559, 567; New Economic Policy and, 442, 443, 444; labor days, 471–472; in World War II, 501–502; cooperatives, 511; postwar, 528; under Khrushchev, 533, 536–540; mechanization of, 538; under Brezhnev, 544–545; Polish, 547; Kazakhstan, 559; foreign currency spent on, 572
Akhmat Khan, 87–88, 125
Akhmatova, Anna, 481, 526, 527
Akhundov, V. U., 563
Aksakov, Ivan, 316, 341–342

Aksakov, Konstantin, 276
Aksakov, Sergei, 348
Albania/Albanians, 387, 510, 610
Alcohol/alcoholism, 11–14, 25, 166, 299, 363–364, 516, 550, 598; distilling liquor, 149, 155, 448; liquor monopoly, 194, 224; Jews barred from liquor trade, 258–259
Aleksandr Nevskii Monastery, 206
Aleksandrovskaia Sloboda, 122–123
Alekseev, General M. V., 390
Aleksei Alekseevich (tsarevich), 172
Aleksei Mikhailovich (tsar), 15, 154, 157–158, 164, 166, 168, 169, 170, 176, 379
Aleksii (metropolitan), 73
Aleksii (patriarch), 593
Alexander I, 12, 241, 246–264, 255, 573
Alexander II, 266, 279, 285–319, 333–334, 341, 359, 379, 382
Alexander III, 300, 317–319, 334, 338–339, 373
Alexandra (empress), 390–391
Algirdas, 59
Aliev, Gaidar, 563
All-Russian Congress of Soviets, 399–400, 404, 437, 442
All-Russian Muslim League, 326
All-Russian Peasant Union, 370
Alma Ata, 322, 583
Amu Darya River, 320
Amur River/basin, 147–148, 328, 518–519

Amvrosii, 303–304

Anarchism, 227, 420

Anatolia, 38, 193–194, 315, 341

Andizhan, 326

Andropov, Iurii, 542, 569–570, 571, 576

Anna (empress), 213

Anna (princess), 38

Annenkov, P. V., 273

Anti-Semitism, 61, 341–344, 358, 390, 410

Antonii, 41

Antonin (bishop), 440

Aptekman, Osip, 311

Arakcheev, Aleksandr, 248

Aral Sea, 321, 562

Araxes River, 236

Arbatov, Georgii, 571

Archangel Cathedral, 109

Architecture, 8, 23–24, 39, 42, 206, 339, 476–479

Arkhangelsk, 206

Armenia/Armenians, 236, 279, 424, 425, 467, 506, 564–565, 583–584, 607; nationalism, 340–341, 420–421; language, 432

Armenian Apostolic Church, 535–536

Army: in Muscovy, 89–91, 94–98; under Peter I, 185–186, 190, 195–197, 207, 217; Pugachev rebellion, 230; and tsars, 268; under Alexander II, 285, 287; military reform, 300; in World War, I, 388–391; Revolution of 1917, 392, 393, 394–396, 398–400, 407–408, 414; and Communist party, 415; purges, 467; under Stalin, 523; post-Stalin, 531, 567; hazing, 568

Arsenii (metropolitan of Rostov), 201

Artel, 197, 222, 445, 457

Arts/visual arts, 26, 40, 77–78, 109, 223, 344–352, 433–438, 481–482

Assembly of Russian Factory and Mill Workers, 365–366

Astrakhan, 14, 85, 108, 115, 142, 171, 228, 413; oblast, 451

Aswan dam, 520

Atamanshchina, 410, 411

Atheism, 351, 364, 438–439, 441, 442, 451

Austria, 190, 191, 281, 316, 387, 574

Autocracy, 4, 5; pre-imperial, 34, 40–41, 70; and Orthodox Church, 85, 148, 174, 193; under Peter I, 205; under Alexander I, 247; under Nicholas I, 267–268; under Alexander II, 292; under Alexander III, 318; under Nicholas II, 343, 368, 372, 374, 378, 384

Avvakum (archpriest), 166, 168, 169

Azef, Evno, 360, 382

Azerbaijan/Azerbaijanis, 424, 425, 563, 583–584, 606, 607; nationalism, 321, 420–421, 428; language, 432

Azeris, 236

Azeri Turks, 341

Azov, Sea of, 33, 194, 195, 279

Babel, Isaak, 481

Baikal, Lake, 143

Bakhtin, Mikhail, 553

Baklanov, Grigorii, 577

Baku, 236, 341, 421, 428, 584

Bakunin, Mikhail, 306–307, 309, 402

Balakirev, Milyi, 345–346

Balcerowicz, Leszek, 596

Balkans, 193–194, 233, 387; crisis of 1875–1878, 299

Balkaria/Balkars, 238, 452, 504

Baltic region, 357, 407

Baltic republics, 552, 565, 586, 606; and Russification, 338–339, 522, 582; in World War II, 491, 499, 506; and armed forces, 568

Baltic Sea, 184–190

Baltic Wars, 119–122, 134

Banks/banking, 356, 405, 443, 598, 601, 602, 606

Baptists, 536, 567

Bariatinskii, Prince A. I., 239–240, 324

Bariatinskii, Iu. N., 172

Barkashov, Aleksandr, 592

Baruch Plan, 512

Bashkin, Matvei, 121–122

Bashkirs/Bashkortostan, 4, 20, 230, 592

Basil (emperor), 38

Basmachi, 422, 423

Basmanov, A. D., 120

Batu, 52–53, 54

Batum, 315

Bekbulatovich, Simeon, 125

Belevskii family, 90

Belinskii, Vissarion, 274, 277

Beloozero, 78

Belorussia: serfs in, 305; religion in, 306; agrarian reform in, 375–377; in World War I, 398; civil war in, 407, 419; independence of, 424, 589, 605–608, 610; indigenization in, 428; in World War II, 497, 500; and Russian nationalism, 522, 583; urbanization, 564

Belovezh resolution, 589–590

Belskii family, 90, 108

Belyi, Andrei, 434, 436
Benkendorf, Aleksandr, 271
Berdiaev, Nikolai, 247
Berdi-bek, 79
Berezovskii, Boris, 601
Beria, Lavrentii, 529
Berlin, Congress of (1878), 299, 316, 337
Berlin Wall, 574–575
Bessarabia, 234, 316, 337, 420, 491, 504
Bezobrazov, A. M., 329, 332
Bible/gospels, 37, 113, 124–125, 162–163, 166,
    168, 200, 303, 439
Bible Society, 253–255, 256
Birobidjan, 430
Black Hundreds, 380, 440
Black-market trade, 539, 545–546, 562, 578,
    602
Black Sea, 31, 32, 235, 279, 281, 286, 608
Blanc, Louis, 310
Bliukher, Marshal, 467
Blok, Aleksandr, 352, 434
Bloody Sunday, 338, 366, 368, 380, 397
Blumentrost, Lavrentii, 208
Bobrikov, Nikolai, 338
Bogdanov, Aleksandr, 435
Bogoliubskii, Andrei, 66–67, 71
Bogomolov, Oleg, 571
Bojarai, 61
Bolotnikov, Ivan, 137
Bolsheviks, 361, 362; and trade unions, 383; and
    Provisional Government, 392–393, 394, 399–
    401; and army, 395, 397; in civil war, 407,
    408–416, 426, on nationhood, 416–418; in no-
    menklatura system, 447
Borderlands/frontiers, 3–4, 6, 20, 21–26, 29–31,
    42, 134, 136, 143, 146–148, 158, 190, 463, 489,
    506, 509, 604, 607–608
Boretskii, Iov, 162
Boris (khan), 37
Boris, Saint, 40–41
Borovkov, A. D., 264–265
Bosnia, 387
Bothnia, Gulf of, 63, 187
Bovin, Aleksandr, 571
Boyars: pre-imperial, 34–35, 48, 67–68, 70, 72–
    73; in Muscovy, 86, 87, 89–91, 92–93, 95, 96,
    112–113, 121–122; under Boris Godunov, 134;
    in Time of Troubles, 137, 139; and Romanov
    dynasty, 141; under Peter I, 205
Brandt, Willy, 517
Brecht, Bertold, 555

Brest, 494; Union of, 162
Brezhnev, Leonid, 538, 541–568, 569
Brezhnev doctrine, 547, 574
Briansk oblast, 59, 451, 500
Bribery, 13, 458, 562–563, 598
Brigandry, 18, 20, 33, 46, 115, 116, 124, 146, 147,
    170–171, 238
Britain, 187, 235, 280, 322–324, 334, 360, 386;
    trade with, 120; relations with, 126, 490–491;
    and Crimean War, 281; and Turkish war of
    1877–78, 316; in World War I, 389; military
    aid from, 493, 497
Brusilov, Aleksei Alekseevich, 390, 408
Bug River, 29, 58, 233–234
Bukhara, 320, 321, 322, 324, 327, 423, 424
Bukharin, Nikolai, 401, 414, 446, 448, 449, 460,
    464, 465
Bukovskii, Vladimir, 556
Bulavin, Kondratii, 228–229
Bulgakov, Mikhail, 481, 555
Bulgakov, Sergei, 384
Bulganin, N. A., 531
Bulgaria, 37, 52, 53, 234, 316, 510; revolt of
    1875–76, 315
Bulgarin, Faddei, 272
Bulgar khanate, 566
Bulgars, 30
Bureaucracy, 12–13, 153, 155–156, 158, 265, 380,
    396; in Muscovy, 88–99, 113; under Peter I,
    202
Buriatiia/Buriats, 146, 430
Burlatskii, Fedor, 571
Buturlin, Vasilii, 164
Buturlin family, 205
Byzantium, 30, 31, 33, 34, 37, 38, 39, 40, 45, 47,
    73–74, 81, 82, 85, 100

Cadet Corps, 207, 217, 242, 300
Capitalism, 340, 360–361, 402, 513–514, 571
Carpathians, 1
Casimir, Jan, 164
Casimir IV, 86
Caspian Sea, 2, 3, 30, 31, 61–62, 117, 235
Castro, Fidel, 520
Cathedral of St. Peter and St. Paul, 206
Catherine II, 201, 214–218, 221, 233, 242, 243,
    244, 255
Catholic Church, 4, 5, 37–38, 39, 165, 176; in
    Lithuania, 59, 565; in Poland, 60, 531, 548; in
    Novgorod, 65; in Byzantium, 81, 100; Greek,
    161–162

Caucasus/Caucasians, 117, 231, 235–240, 316, 357, 407, 428, 558, 583, 607–608; tribal kingdoms, 115; and Russification, 340–341; nationalism, 420–421; and collectivization of agriculture, 452

Caves Monastery, 162

Ceauşescu, Nicolae, 574, 585

Censorship, 271, 273, 276, 318–319, 382–383, 400, 479–480, 552, 554, 555, 556–557, 567; under Alexander II, 298–300; in Poland, 305

Census, 21, 65, 219, 498–499, 563

Central Asia, 320, 321, 325, 341, 356, 423, 424, 428, 558, 605–606

Central Committee: party rules of 1919, 446–447; expulsions from, 448; and Stalin, 455, 460, 461, 466, 482, 527; and Khrushchev, 531, 532, 540; and Brezhnev, 541, 542, 567; Department for Relations with Socialist Parties, 571

Central Economic-Mathematical Institute, 581, 596

Central Institute for Labor, 435

Central Muslim Commissariat, 422

Chaadaev, Petr, 274–275

Chaikovskii, Petr, 347

Chamberlain, Neville, 490–491

Chancellor, Richard, 120

Charitable associations, 301–302, 364, 381, 443

Charles XII, 185–187

Charter for a New Europe, 575

Chechnia/Chechens, 20, 237, 238, 315, 452, 503, 504, 522, 592, 602–605, 610, 612

Cheka, 400, 404, 405, 407, 413, 427. See also GPU; KGB

Chekhov, Anton, 327–333, 349, 553

Cheliabinsk, 456, 512, 513

Cheliadnin family, 90

Cheremis, 117, 142

Cherkasskii family, 205

Chernenko, Konstantin, 542, 570

Cherniaev, Anatolii, 571

Cherniaev, Mikhail, 299, 315, 324

Chernigov, 59, 153, 262

Chernigov guberniia, 371

Chernobyl explosion, 577, 583

Chernomyrdin, Viktor, 600

Chernov, Viktor, 397, 398–399

Chernyshevskii, Nikolai, 307–308, 310, 348, 433

Chesme Bay, 231

Chicherin, Boris, 288

Chimkent, 324

China, 6, 147, 327–328; trade with, 14, 148, 329, 356; and Mongols, 50–51, 54; as world power, 417, 516, 518–519, 571; Cultural Revolution, 518–519; Great Leap Forward, 518–519

Chinese Eastern Railway, 333

Chingizid line, 101

Chingiz Khan, 321

Christianity. See specific denominations, e.g., Russian Orthodox Church

Chronicles, 42, 44, 50, 53, 70, 106–107, 110, 256

Chubais, Anatolii, 596, 601

Chuikov, Vasilii Ivanovich, 496

Churbanov, Iurii, 562–563

Churbanova, Galina, 562

Churchill, Winston, 492, 510

Chuvash, 142

Circassians, 238, 240

Citizenship, 342, 370, 390, 393, 505–506, 606

Civil Cassation Court, 296

Civil war, 403–404, 407–416, 408–416

Clergy: pre-imperial, 39, 41, 42, 53, 57, 72–78; in Muscovy, 102–107, 126; under Peter I, 199–200, 201; education of, 301; and peasants, 370; and Communists, 439, 440, 535

Cold War, 608; society, 509–540

Collectivization. See Agriculture: collectivization of

Colleges and universities, 177, 249, 255–256, 266, 296–297, 308, 335, 339, 534

Collins, Samuel, 176

Colonization, 19–21, 21–22, 32, 57, 143, 146–147, 416, 421, 460, 608

Comecon, 511, 573

Cominform, 511

Comintern, 4, 401, 408, 486–487, 511

Commissariat of External Affairs, 4, 486

Committee of State Security. See KGB

Committee of the Constituent Assembly (Komuch), 407

Commonwealth of Independent States, 589–590, 605–608

Communications, 3, 16, 21, 23, 50, 54, 140, 285–286, 355; in Muscovy, 89, 112; and railways, 356

Communist Party, 401, 590, 611; and civil war, 415–416; centralization, 427, 523; ethnic membership, 427–428; and Orthodox Church, 441–442; congresses, 446–448, 459, 461, 529, 532–533; personnel appointments, 446–447; purges, 459–469, 490, 523–524, 576; international influence of, 519; and Khrushchev, 532–533; reform of, 547, 579–581, 585, 595

Communist youth movement. *See* Komsomol
Community values. *See Pravda*
Comrades' courts, 533
Conference on Security and Cooperation in Europe, 517–518, 575
Confino, Michel, 218
Congress of People's Deputies, 580, 581–582, 585, 587
Constantinople, 100, 280–281, 316, 389
Constitution, 247, 257–258, 585, 590, 591; Soviet, of 1923, 425, 427; Soviet, of 1936, 431
Constitutional monarchy, 372–375, 385
Constructivists, 437
Consumer goods, 357, 363, 364, 443, 474, 477–478, 484, 522, 528, 545, 578–579, 598, 602
Cooperatives, 578
Cossacks, 4, 18, 20, 21, 115–117, 134, 136–141, 143, 146, 225–228, 328; registered, 160–163; Ukrainian rebellion, 163–165; Razin rebellion, 170–172; and Westernizers, 228–229; and Napoleon, 251; and Revolution of 1917, 391, 407, 409; deportation of, 503; in Chechnia, 604
Cottage industry, 222–223, 357, 358
Council for Church Affairs, 503
Council for Labor and Defense (Vesenkha), 424
Council for Mutual Economic Assistance (Comecon), 511, 573
Council of Ministers, 375, 378, 380, 386, 387, 388
Council of People's Commissars (Sovnarkom), 400, 448
Council of Reconciliation, 112–113
Councils of Labor Collectives, 579
Crimea, 30, 85, 231, 233, 495, 524
Crimean Horde, 119
Crimean khanate, 108, 115, 175, 487
Crimean Tatars, 20, 115, 119, 121, 142, 163, 192, 231, 326, 504, 506
Crimean War, 279–281, 285, 289, 300, 328, 337, 380
Criminal law, 35, 44, 67, 155, 156, 294, 312–313, 318, 454, 533
Cuba, 516, 520
Culture, 20, 21–26; pre-imperial, 34, 40–41, 60, 65; under Peter I, 175–209; and Russian identity, 218, 330–334, 344–352, 384, 432, 430–438, 612; and language, 269, 567; and urbanization, 362–363; bourgeois, 483; Cold War, 511; postwar, 526–528; under Brezhnev, 553–558
Cyril, 37
Czaplinski, Daniel, 163
Czartoryski, Adam, 257–258

Czechoslovakia, 490, 500, 546–547, 571, 585; conquest by Red Army, 510
Czech Republic, 609

Dagestan/Dagestanis, 237, 239, 315, 452, 610
Dal, Vladimir, 256
Damanskii Island, 519
Daniel, Iulii, 556
Daniil of Moscow, 71
Daniil of Volynia, 58
Danilevskii, Nikolai, 313–314
Danilovichi, 71, 80, 95, 100
Danube principalities, 234
Danube River, 58, 279, 286
Dardanelles, 280–281
Dashnaks, 340–341, 421
Daugava River, 580
Decembrists, 259–264, 271
Declaration of the Rights of the Peoples of Russia, 404–405
Dekulakization, 451, 452, 456, 499, 537
Democratic Centralists, 415
Denikin, Anton, 407, 409, 410, 421
Denisov, Semen, 173–174
Denmark, 6, 85, 107, 120, 185, 187
Denunciations and indictments, 431, 464–465, 477, 556–557
Derbysh-Ali (khan), 119
Derpt/Dorpat, 120, 121, 255, 256; University, 339
Diagilev, Sergei, 348
Diaki/state secretaries, 88–89
Diet/nutrition, 7–15, 20
Diplomacy, 608–610; and Ottoman Empire, 178–179, 315; European alliances, 181–184, 386–387, 389; under Peter I, 207; and isolationism, 246; with Japan, 332; Stalinist, 486–491; and economic relations, 544; under Gorbachev, 570–573; under Yeltsin, 605–608
Djilas, Milovan, 511, 556
Dmitrii (Donskoi), 72, 73, 74, 79, 80, 100
Dmitrii I of Moscow, 78
Dmitrii Shemiaka, 80
Dnepropetrovsk, 428, 542
Dnieper River, 29, 31, 32, 119, 184, 456
Dniester River, 58, 234, 337, 565, 606
Dolgorukii, Iurii, 171
Dolgorukii family, 205, 214
Donetsk, 428, 605
Don River, 33, 79, 119, 411
Dostoevskii, Fedor, 303–304, 312–313, 314, 350–351, 553, 555

Drug trafficking, 603, 607
Druzhina/retainers, 5, 34, 36, 42, 69
Dubček, Alexander, 546–547
Dudaev, Dzhokhar, 603, 604
Duma, 17, 610, 611; Boyar, 93–94, 113, 121, 123, 138, 150, 202, 205; State, 368, 374, 595, 600; First, 370, 374–375, 383; Second, 376, 383; Third, 376; under Nicholas II, 378, 380–382, 385, 386, 388, 391; Progressive Bloc in, 390; and Revolution of 1917, 391, 392, 393
Durnovo, P. N., 344
Dushanbe, 423, 584
Dvina River, 14, 29, 31, 184
Dvoretskii/majordomo, 88
Dvorianstvo/nobility, 69, 90, 204, 207, 216, 335

Eastern Rumelia, 316
Ecology/environment, 1–4, 71, 147, 513, 562, 571, 580, 581
Economic councils, 533
Edigei, 80
Education, 426, 612; Orthodox influences, 177; Europeanized system, 206–209, 217–218, 241–242, 255–257; teachers, 207, 293, 368, 370, 382, 504; and civil service, 249; under Peter I, 269; under Alexander II, 296–297; for women, 308; of peasants, 311, 370, 471; in central Asia, 327; ministerial schools, 339; universal, 377, 378, 385, 475; Stalinist, 482–484; Cold War, 510–511; party schools, 523; post-Stalin, 533–534; under Brezhnev, 550–553
Efremov, Oleg, 555
Egorov, Marshal A. I., 467
Egypt, 193–194, 279–280, 520
Ehrenburg, Ilya, 498, 566
Eizenshtein, Sergei, 436, 527
Elbruz, Mount, 495
Electrification, 437, 456, 580
Elgin, Lord, 233
Elias, Norbert, 483
Elizabeth (empress), 207, 214
Elizabeth I of England, 120, 126
Emergency Committee, 588–589
Emergency rule, 318–319
Emigrés, 359, 439
Engineers, 445, 480, 513
Enlightenment, 243, 247, 250, 255, 272, 308, 513–514
Entrepreneurism, 342, 536, 578, 599, 601
Enver Pasha, 422–423
Epidemics, 9, 20, 55, 124, 268, 294, 358, 443, 457, 526

Erevan, 236, 552, 565, 580
Erfurt, 250
Erin, Viktor, 604
Ermolov, General A. P., 239
Esenin, Sergei, 480–481, 580
Estonia, 187, 338, 339, 419, 504, 565, 582, 585–586, 590, 606
Eugene IV (pope), 81
Eurocommunism, 547
Evtushenko, Evgenii, 581

Factories. *See* Industrialization
Factory committees, 396, 397
Fadeev, Aleksandr, 527
Fadeev, General Rostislav, 235, 314–315
Family/kinship: church jurisdiction over, 295; divorce, 295–296, 484–485, 549–550; and urbanization, 362–363, 548; and agrarian reform, 375; and nationalities, 418, 428; 558, 559; childcare, 458, 477, 484–486, 525, 536, 549; abortion, 484, 549; Stalinist policy, 484–486
Famine, 8–9, 10, 15, 18, 124, 134, 537; in Volga basin, 294, 358; post-Revolution, 414; in Volga basin/Siberia, 439, 443, 444, 454; in labor camps, 469; in Ukraine and Moldavia, 526
Far East, 327–333
Federal Counter-Intelligence Service (FSK), 604
Fedor Alekseevich (tsar), 172, 178, 180
Fedor Ivanovich (tsar), 127, 131
Fedorov, Ivan, 122
Feodosii, 41
Feofan the Greek, 77–78
Fergana valley, 320, 326, 327, 422
Ferrara-Florence, Council of, 81, 100, 173
Figner, Evgeniia, 311
Figner, Vera, 311
Filaret (metropolitan), 303
Filaret (patriarch), 153
Filipp (metropolitan), 121
Filofei (abbot of Eleazarov Monastery), 103
Finance, 71, 219–231, 329, 342, 355–358, 405, 443, 471, 473, 526, 572, 579, 598–599, 600, 601, 602, 606
Finland, 63, 187, 248, 250, 337–340, 491; Gulf of, 30, 121, 138; nationalism in, 418–419
Fishing industry, 11, 63, 66, 94, 99, 150, 226
Fiskaly, 202–203, 242

Fitrat, Abdalrauf, 327
Five-year plans, 432, 451, 453, 455–459, 472–476, 492–493
Florenskii, Pavel, 24, 77
Folk culture, 25, 344–346, 347–348, 349
Food rationing, 413–414, 470
Food shortages, 391, 457
Fools in Christ, 25–26, 124–125, 134
Foreign policy. *See* Diplomacy
Fotii (archimandrite), 254
France, 187, 190, 218, 316–317, 329, 386, 493; claims to Holy Land, 280; and Crimean War, 281; socialism in, 307; and World War I, 389; and Revolution of 1917, 394–395; diplomatic relations with, 489, 490–491
Franz Ferdinand (archduke), 388
Frederick the Great, 190
Freedom of speech, 292, 295, 511, 531, 557
Free Economic Society, 256
Freemasonry, 242–244, 254, 263
Free Russian Press, 279
French Revolution, 241, 243, 246, 343
Frontiers. *See* Borderlands/frontiers
Fuchs, Klaus, 513
Fur trade, 59, 62, 63, 66, 99, 146, 150

Gagarin, Iurii, 551
Gaidar, Egor, 596, 597, 600
Galich, 78
Galicia, 58–61, 73, 192, 336, 390
Gamsakhurdia, Zviad, 565
Gapon, Father Grigorii, 365–366
Gaspirali, Ismail Bey, 326
Gastev, Aleksei, 435, 438
Gavriil (metropolitan), 302–303
Gazprom, 600, 601
Gdańsk, 547
Gediminas, 58, 59
Geller, Mikhail, 505
Gennadii (archbishop), 102
Geopolitics, 3–4, 5, 15, 22, 34, 38, 85, 147, 175, 192, 313, 320–321, 401, 423, 519, 611–612
Georgia/Georgians, 14; and Peter I, 236, 237; Georgian Military Highway, 237; nationalism, 340, 420–421, 428, 584, 590, 606, 607; independence of, 424, 425; language, 432; urbanization, 564–565
Gerashchenko, Viktor, 599–600
Gerasimov, Dmitrii, 102–103
Gerasimov, Gennadii, 574
German settlers, 336, 338, 339, 340, 504

Germany, 62, 218, 254, 316, 329, 357, 384, 387; unification of, 286, 299, 314, 386; Nazi, 343, 460, 462, 475, 489, 491–506, 566; bourgeois capitalism in, 360; Social Democratic party, 361; in World War I, 388–391; and Revolution of 1917, 400–401; and Soviet-Polish war of 1920, 417; and Finnish independence, 419; in Lithuania, 419; in Ukraine, 420; in Georgia, 421; diplomatic relations with, 488–489; Nazi-Soviet nonaggression pact, 491, 582; conquest by Red Army, 510; Berlin airlift, 515–516; postwar, 515–516, 517; Berlin crisis of 1958–1961, 516, 517; German Democratic Republic, 517, 574–575; and *perestroika*, 574–575
Germogen (patriarch), 138–139
Ginzburg, Aleksandr, 556–557
Glasnost, 298, 576, 577, 578, 582
Glavlit, 479–480. *See also* Censorship
Glavpolitprosvet, 437
Gleb, Saint, 40, 41
Gleb Iurevich (Kievan prince), 66
Glinka, Mikhail, 345
Glinskii, Iurii, 111
Glinskii family, 108, 111
God-building, 46–47, 351–352
Godunov, Boris, 131, 134–136, 137
Gogol, Nikolai, 274, 335, 349–350
"Going to the people" movement, 297, 312
Gok Tepe, 324
Golden Horde, 86, 87, 88, 99, 101, 115, 117
Goldman, Emma, 443
Goldman, Wendy, 486
Golitsyn, Aleksandr, 253–255
Golitsyn, Vasilii, 179–180, 194
Golitsyn family, 205, 214
Golovin family, 205
Gomułka, Władysław, 531
Goncharova, Larissa, 348
Gorbachev, Mikhail, 517, 542, 552, 569–590, 596, 598, 608, 611
Gorchakov, Aleksandr, 287, 305, 323–324, 512
Gorkii, Maksim, 349
Gorkii Street, 478
Gosplan, 427, 432, 455, 472, 476, 562, 611; building, 478
Gospriemka, 576
Gosudar/lord, 90
Gosudar vseia Rusi, 85
Governors. *See* Local government
GPU, 440, 450, 463. *See also* Cheka; KGB
Grachev, Pavel, 593, 604

Grain, 9, 10, 18, 19, 42; trade, 61, 150, 160, 222, 356, 358; for serfs, 225; nomad-raised, 325; as state monopoly, 406–407; and New Economic Policy, 443, 444, 448, 449; and five-year plans, 454; in World War II, 502, 526; priority under Khrushchev, 537

Greater Khingan range, 1

Greece/Greeks, 234, 504

Greek Catholic Church, 5, 162

Greek Orthodox Church, 37, 39, 81, 131–133, 167

Greenfeld, Leah, 277

Greens, 411–412

Grodno, 186

Groman, V. G., 455

Gromov, Boris, 604

Gromyko, Andrei, 512

Grossman, Vasilii, 566, 577

Groznyi, 604

Gubernii, 216, 255

Guby, 112, 156

Guchkov, Aleksandr, 382

GULAG, 469, 497, 554

Gumilev, Lev, 66

Gumilevskii, Aleksandr, 302

Guria, 236

Gusinskii, Vladimir, 601

Habsburg Empire, 179, 286, 313, 336, 385

Hanover, Union of, 187

Hanseatic League, 62

Health care, 458, 475, 485, 525, 537, 598; and doctors, 178, 368, 382, 467, 480, 504, 524; and public hygiene, 291, 299, 458, 477, 484

Hegel, G. W. F., 306

Helsinki conference (1975), 517–518, 572

Heraclius (king of Georgia), 237

Herberstein, Sigismund von, 89, 91

Herder, Johann, 339

Hermits/hermitage, 302–303

Herzegovina, 387

Herzen, Aleksandr, 273, 277, 278–279, 307, 310

Hesychasm, 74, 76–77, 78, 106, 122, 124, 302, 303, 304

Hitler, Adolf, 462, 492, 496, 498, 500

Hobbes, Thomas, 199

Hoch, Steven, 225

Holy Alliance, 253–255, 286, 316, 573

Holy League, 181–182

Holy Synod, 379, 380, 382

Honecker, Erich, 574

Hooliganism, 364–365, 392, 457

Hoover, Herbert, 443

Horodlo, Agreement of, 61

Housing, 7–9, 20, 25; Cossack, 115; military, 268; *uplotnenie*, 404; of indigenous nationalities, 431; and five-year plans, 457, 477; and *kulturnost*, 483–484; postwar, 522, 525, 528; cooperative, 534; post-Stalin, 534, 536, 537, 549–550; strikes for, 579

Hungary, 53, 497, 531, 574, 609; and Soviet-Polish war of 1920, 417; conquest by Red Army, 510

Iablonoi mountains, 147–148

Iagoda, Genrikh, 464

Iakovlev, Aleksandr, 571

Iakovlev, Egor, 577

Iakushkin, I. D., 228, 259

Iakutsk/Iakuts, 143, 146

Ianaev, Gennadii, 588

Iarlyk, 71

Iaropolk (Kievan prince), 37

Iaroslav (grand prince of Kiev), 42, 45, 62

Iaroslavkii family, 90

Iaroslavl, 86, 140, 166

Iasak, 142, 146

Iazov, Dmitrii, 588

Ibn Rusta, 33

Ibn Sinna (Avicenna), 321

Icons, 23–24, 40, 66, 77–78, 119, 223, 567

Ieremei (patriarch), 132

Ignatiev, N. P., 318

Igor (Kievan prince), 48

Ilarion, 44

Ilmen, Lake, 31

Imeretia, 236

Immigrants, 17, 35, 41, 178, 325, 364, 365, 457, 477, 503–504, 565

Imperial Academy of Art, 348

Imperial Archaeographic Commission, 256

Imperial Chancellery: Second Department, 265; Third Department, 265, 271, 273

Imperial Lyceum, 271

Imperial School of Jurisprudence, 266

India, 520, 594

Indigenization, 428, 447, 558–559

Industrialization, 219–220, 285–286, 352, 355–357, 360, 426, 428, 433; New Economic Policy, 442–449; five-year plans, 455–459, 472–

476; postwar, 521–522, 524–526; under Brezhnev, 543–544; under Gorbachev, 576–582; under Yeltsin, 602
Inflation, 405, 578–579, 600; in Crimean War, 287, 289
Ingria, 153, 186, 187
Ingush/Ingushetiia, 237, 452, 504, 602
Inheritance laws, 68–69, 96
Inorodtsy, 341
Institute for Market Reform, 596
Institute for the Study of the United States and Canada, 571
Institute of Linguistics, 527
Institute of Marxism-Leninism, 532
Institute of Plant Breeding, 527
Institute of the World Economy and International Relations, 571
Intelligentsia, 247, 296–297, 335, 342, 362, 367, 384, 401–402, 552; and proletkults, 436; post-Stalin, 531
International Monetary Fund, 602, 609
Ioachim (patriarch), 177, 180
Ioffe, Abraham, 513
Iona (metropolitan), 81, 100
Ipatiev, V. N., 445
Iqta, 90
Iran, 609
Iraq, 609
Isidor (metropolitan), 81, 100
Islam, 12, 21, 108; Vladimir and, 37–38; and empire building, 147, 192; and Armenia, 236; insurrections, 238; among nomads, 321–322, 325–326; Shiite Muslims, 341; and Communists, 421–424; fundamentalists, 520; repression of, 536, 559; among Tatars, 566
Islamic Renaissance Party, 607
Israel, 524, 566
Italy, 254, 544, 573; socialism in, 307
Itar-Tass, 601
Itil, 33
Iudenich, Nikolai, 407
Iugra (Khanty) people, 99
Iuriev University, 339
Iurii Dmitrievich (of Muscovy), 80
Iurii Vladimirovich (Kievan prince), 66
Ivan I, 71
Ivan III, 85–86, 86–88, 89, 90, 91, 94–95
Ivan IV, 5, 25, 82, 106, 107–127, 131, 149, 152, 180–181, 267
Ivangorod, 121

Ivan Iurievich (prince), 90
Ivanovo-Voznesensk/Ivanovo, 223, 367, 457
Izborsk, 65
Iziaslav (Kievan prince), 41, 42
Izmail, 197
Izvolskii, A. P., 386, 387

Jadidism, 326
Jadwiga, 60
Jakeš, Miloš, 585
Japan, 328, 329, 332–333, 357, 366, 386, 489, 516
Jaruzelski, Wojciech, 548
Jehovah's Witnesses, 536
Jerusalem, Latin patriarchate of, 280
Jewish Anti-Fascist Committee, 524
Jewish Bund, 361
Jewish Statute of 1804, 258
Jews, 506; in Poland and Lithuania, 61, 163, 192, 258–259, 419; *advokat*, 295; Ukrainian, 336, 420, 564; and Russification, 341–344, 546; and Whites, 410; offered autonomous region, 430; and purges, 524; synagogues of, 536; and Israel, 566
Jogaila, 60
John of Kronstadt, Father, 302
Joint responsibility, 9, 16, 21, 34–35, 510, 556, 557
Journals, 246, 271–279, 298–300, 307–308, 348, 364, 441, 527, 553–555, 556, 557, 565, 566, 571, 580
Judaism, 37, 38
Judaizers, 101–102

Kabarda, 117, 231, 237–238, 452
Kádár, János, 531
Kadets, 368, 374–375, 376, 384, 392, 393, 394, 407
Kaganovich, Lazar, 447, 466, 531
Kahal, 61, 258, 259
Kaiochow crisis, 329
Kakhetia, 236
Kalanta, Roman, 565
Kaliningrad, 608
Kalinin (Tver), 71, 86, 90, 500
Kalka River, 52
Kalmyks, 21, 171, 230, 504
Kama River, 14, 99, 143
Kamenev, Lev, 447–448, 464
Kandinskii, Vasilii, 348
Kapiton, 165–166
Kapitonov, Ivan, 563
Kapitsa, Petr, 551–552
Karachai region/Karachais, 238, 452, 504

Karaganda, 579
Karakalpaks, 321
Karakozov, D. V., 308
Karamzin, Nikolai, 270
Karelia/Karelians, 121, 153, 187, 337–338, 430, 468
Karlovtsy Church Council, 439
Karl Philipp, 140–141
Karpov, G. G., 503
Kars, 315
Kartli, 236
Katkov, Mikhail, 262, 299, 333–334
Kaufman, K. P., 325
Kavelin, Konstantin, 277, 288
Kazakhstan/Kazakhs, 21, 321, 322, 424, 428, 452, 467, 504, 506, 518–519, 542, 559, 562, 583, 605–606; industrialization, 468; and nuclear weapons testing, 513; and Virgin Lands campaign, 537–538
Kazan, 85, 89, 99, 108, 115, 117, 119, 123, 142, 230, 255; Cathedral, 312; Soviet, 422; khanate, 487
Keenan, Edward, 95–96
Kemerovo, 586
Kennan, George F., 513–514
Kennedy, John F., 516
Kennedy, Paul, 572
Kerenskii, Aleksandr, 295, 393–394, 395, 399–400
Kerr, Archibald Clark, 509
Kestutis, 59
Kettler, Gustav, 120
KGB, 529, 531, 558, 569, 576, 611. See also Cheka; GPU
Khabarov, Erofei, 147–148
Khachaturian, Aram, 527
Khalkin-Gol, 489
Khanty, 143
Kharkov, 255, 335, 420, 428, 456
Khasan, Lake, 489
Khasbulatov, Ruslan, 590, 591, 593
Khazaria/Khazars, 30, 37
Kherson, 231
Khiva, 320, 324, 327
Khmelnitskii, Bogdan, 163–165
Khodjent oblast, 607
Khodzhaev, Faizulla, 467
Kholmskii family, 90
Khomiakov, Aleksei, 275–276
Khorezm, 424
Khovrin family, 90
Khrushchev, Nikita, 467, 492, 497, 516, 517, 518–519, 528–534

Kiev, 2, 7, 85; pre-imperial, 30, 32, 34, 36, 38, 41, 42, 45, 46, 47, 59; intelligentsia in, 335; in Soviet-Polish war of 1920, 417; Rada in, 419–420; in World War II, 467, 494
Kim Il Sung, 516
Kipchaks, 45–46, 51, 52, 54
Kiprian (metropolitan), 73–75, 80
Kireevskii, Ivan, 303
Kirgiz/Kirgiziia, 321, 424, 562
Kirov, Sergei, 447, 461, 463, 464
Kiselev, P. D., 234, 266
Kizhi, 8
Kizliar, 238
Kliazma River, 7
Kliuchevskii, Vasilii, 15, 19, 218
Klub Perestroika, 581
Koch, Erich, 499
Koestler, Arthur, 556
Kohl, Helmut, 575
Kokand, 322, 324, 422
Kolbin, Gennadii, 583
Kolchak, Admiral Aleksandr, 407, 409, 410, 422
Kolkhoz. See Agriculture: collectivization of
Kolomna, 52, 71
Kolyma basin, 468
Komsomol, 449, 450, 451, 453, 483, 535, 538, 558, 598
Kondratiev, Viacheslav, 505
Konovalov family, 385
Konstantin, Nikolaevich (grand duke), 304
Konstantin, Pavlovich (grand duke), 257, 263
Kopelev, Lev, 453
Korea, 328, 329, 332, 356, 504
Korean War, 516
Kormchaia Kniga, 40
Kormlenie, 5, 34, 42, 67–68, 69, 94, 112, 221
Kornilov, Lavr, 395
Korotich, Vitalii, 577, 581
Korzhakov, Aleksandr, 593
Koshelev, Aleksandr, 305
Koshkin family, 90
Kosoi, Feodosii, 122
Kosovo, 610
Kostroma, 78, 141, 166, 222–223
Kosygin, Aleksei, 541, 542, 543
Kotliarevskii, Ivan, 335
Kozelsk, 53, 303
Kozyrev, Andrei, 607, 609
Krasnitskii, Vladimir, 440
Krasnoiarsk, 143

Kremlin, 109, 590, 593, 594
Krestinskii, Nikolai, 464
Krewo, Union of, 60
Kriuchkov, Vladimir, 588
Krivoshein, A. V., 388
Kronstadt, 62, 186, 187, 414–415, 442
Kropotkin, Petr, 227
Krugovaia poruka. See Joint responsibility
Krupskaia, Nadezhda, 437
Kruzhok, 273, 275, 278, 279, 288, 335
Kryzhanovskii, N. A., 324
Kuban region, 233, 411, 454
Kuchum (khan), 143
Kuibyshev, Valerian, 447, 494, 576
Kulak, 411, 448, 449–451, 452, 453, 466, 530
Kuliab oblast, 607
Kulikovo, Battle of, 74, 79–80, 133
Kunaev, Dinmukhamed, 562, 583
Kura/Araxes River, 235
Kurakin family, 205
Kurbskii, Andrei, 110, 121, 133
Kurchatov, Igor, 513
Kurds, 340
Kurgan Tiube oblast, 607
Kuritsyn, Feodor, 102
Kuropatkin, A. K., 329
Kuropaty, 469
Kursanty, 415
Kursk, 497
Kuzbass, 456, 579
Kvas, 12, 13–14

Labor armies, 413–414
Labor camps, 463, 464, 467–469, 481, 497, 528, 529, 554, 577
Ladoga, Lake, 31, 54, 62
La Harpe, Frédéric-César, 247
Lamsdorf, Vladimir Nikolaevich, 329
Land, 10, 16–17, 61, 67, 70, 156, 216, 226, 266, 276, 325–326; transfers, 87; registers, 90–91; census, 134–135; tenure, 228; commandants, 319, 373, 378, 393, 425–426; agrarian reform, 375–377, 406–407; redistribution, 398–399, 404, 406, 450, 510, 525; communal owner-ship of, 558–559
Land and Freedom, 312
Landowners, 5, 10, 48, 67; liquor production by, 13; in Muscovy, 99–107, 114; and agrarian reform, 220–223, 225; independence of, 240; and Napoleon, 251; ban on Jewish, 259; Sla-

vophile, 275; and emancipation of serfs, 292, 356; and *zemstvos,* 319, 378; Ukrainian, 336; and industrialization, 357; expropriation of, 368, 370, 371, 375, 392, 398–399, 404, 406, 510
Land Settlement Commissions, 375
Languages, 20, 34, 37, 39, 64; written, 50, 431; Ruthenian, 60; French, 183, 269–270; Bible translations, 253–254; Russian, 306; of Mon-gols, 321; and Russification, 333–337, 339, 432, 527; and Narkomnats, 418, 423; Ukrainian, 420, 583; and urbanization, 565–566
Lapps, 337–338
Larionov, Mikhail, 348
Latin America, 520
Latvia, 338, 339, 419, 504, 565, 580, 582, 585–586, 587, 590, 606
Lavrov, Petr, 309, 310
Law Code Commission, 201, 214–215, 242
Law codes, 44–45, 50, 94–95, 112, 158, 159, 201, 265; Fundamental Laws of 1906, 374; lawyers, 382, 467, 480; Family Code of 1926, 484
Law courts, 339, 377, 404, 463, 533; under Alex-ander II, 294–296
League of Godless, 441
League of Nations, 490
Lebed, Aleksandr, 588, 604, 605, 606–607
Lebedev-Polianskii, Pavel, 436
LeDonne, John, 205, 216, 234, 280
Lefortovo Prison, 593
Left Communists, 401
Left Opposition, 463–464
Left Socialist Revolutionaries, 400
Leibniz, Gottfried, 207–208
Leipzig, Battle of, 253
Lena River, 143
Lend-Lease agreements, 497
Lenin, V. I., 400–407, 414–417, as *advokat,* 295; influences on, 307; on revolution, 359, 361, 362, 392, 393, 395–396, 399, 433, 519; support for, 400; on social democracy, 413; and Geor-gia, 421; and Stalin, 424–425, 427, 461; Plan for Monumental Propaganda, 437; and indus-trialization, 444, 446; on collectivizing agri-culture, 449; Khrushchev on, 532; writers on, 577
Leningrad, 459, 478, 494, 500, 501, 523–524, 552, 587. *See also* Petrograd; St. Petersburg
Leo IX (pope), 39
Leontiev, Konstantin, 303
Lewin, Moshe, 476

Liapunov, Prokopii, 139
Liberal Democrats, 594
Liberalism, 343, 361, 368
Lieven, Count Kh., 253
Ligachev, Egor, 576
Likhachev, Dmitrii, 18, 581
Literacy, 208, 338, 339, 383, 419, 422, 431
Literature, 26, 48; and aristocratic culture, 246,
    261; and Russian identity, 269–279, 344–352,
    433–438, 567, 568, 612; socialist ideas in,
    307–308; Ukrainian, 335–336, 564; Stalinist
    era, 479–482; during World War II, 526,
    527; under Brezhnev, 553–558; and *glasnost,*
    577
Lithuania: and pre-imperial Rus, 58–61, 71, 73;
    and Muscovy, 85, 86, 88, 90, 107–108, 124,
    164; union with Poland, 120, 160–163, 191,
    304; religion in, 306; and Bolsheviks, 407; in-
    dependence of, 417, 419, 582, 585, 586, 587,
    590; Soviet-Polish war of 1920, 417; national-
    ism in, 419, 535
Litvinov, Maksim, 489, 510
Liubech, 46
Liubimov, Iurii, 555
Living Church, 439
Livonia, 112, 187, 338
Livonian Order, 120
Local government, 94, 95, 111–112, 156, 216, 240,
    292, 338–339, 373, 377, 378, 453; under Alexan-
    der II, 293–294
Lominadze, V. V., 460
Lönnrot, Elias, 337–338
Loris-Melikov, M. T., 315, 317–318
Lotman, Iurii, 22, 38, 213, 261, 553
Lovat River, 30
Löwenhaupt, General, 186
Lukashenka, Aleksandr, 608
Lutheran Church, 337, 338
Luzhkov, Iurii, 601
Lvov, Georgii, 389, 392, 393–394
Lysenko, Trofim, 527

Macartney, George, 183
Macedonia, 316
Machiavelli, Niccolò, 111
Magadan, 468
Magnitogorsk, 456
Maiakovskii, Vladimir, 434, 480–481, 513–514
Makarii (metropolitan), 106, 108, 122, 139, 173
Makhno, Nestor, 420
Maksim the Greek, 105–106

Malenkov, 531
Malevich, Kasimir, 348
Mamai, 79
Mamontov, Savva, 348, 349
Manchuria, 329, 332, 333, 356, 489
Mandelstam, Osip, 481
Mansi (Voguly) people, 99, 143
Mansur, Sheikh, 238
Mao Zedong, 518–519
Margolin, Iurii, 468
Mari, 142
Maritime Territory, 328, 333, 518–519
Marr, N. Ia., 527
Marshall Plan, 515
Martov, Iulii, 361
Marx, Karl, 310, 360, 402
Marxism, 360–361, 362, 384, 392, 402, 404, 431,
    487
Maskhadov, Aslan, 605
Mazepa, Hetman Ivan, 186
Mazowiecki, Tadeusz, 574
Medvedev, Silvestr, 177
Mehmet Ali, 234, 279–280
Mehmet II, 110
Memorial, 581
Mengli Girei (khan), 88
Mensheviks, 361, 362, 383, 393, 394, 397, 400,
    413, 421
Menshikov, A. S., 280, 285
Merchants, 72–73, 137, 149–151, 179, 206, 221,
    258, 341
Merv, 320
Messianism, 313
Mestnichestvo, 94, 111, 177, 179, 204
Methodius, 37
Meyerhold, Vsevolod, 438, 555
Mezetskii family, 90
Mickiewicz, Adam, 407
Middle East, trade with, 117
Migration, 18, 19–22, 32, 59, 61
Mikhail (grand duke), 392
Mikhoels, Solomon, 524
Mikoian, A. I., 466
Military equipment, 285, 389, 405, 497, 501, 517,
    603
Military Revolutionary Committees, 397, 399–
    400, 414
Military service, 16, 19, 21, 49–50, 54, 55, 69–
    70, 426; in Muscovy, 89–90, 91, 94, 95–97,
    98, 101, 113–115; recruitment, 153–155, 291,
    338, 388, 411, 471, 545; European-style re-

forms, 175–176; under Peter I, 219; exemptions, 221, 259
Miliukov, Pavel, 297, 391
Miliutin, Dmitrii, 300, 305, 324, 355
Miloradovich, General, 264
Mindaugas, 58
Mingrelia, 236
Minin, Kuzma, 139–140
Mining/minerals, 223, 329, 356, 357, 443, 456, 468, 474, 579
Ministry of Education, 253–255
Ministry of Finance, 372
Ministry of Spiritual Affairs and Popular Enlightenment, 253–255
Ministry of State Domains, 266, 372
Ministry of the Court, 372
Ministry of the Interior, 249, 291, 342–343, 344, 372, 373, 587, 603, 604
Ministry of War/Defense, 372, 607
Minsk, 583, 589–590, 605
Mir. See Village communes
Mogila, Petr, 162–163
Moldavia, 53, 164, 234, 302, 506, 522, 526, 542, 565, 582, 606–607
Moldavian Autonomous Soviet Socialist Republic, 420
Molotov, Viacheslav, 465–466, 491, 531, 532
Monasteries, 11, 67; and Slavic Christianity, 41; chronicles, 42, 44; colonization, 57; tribute paid by, 69; as landowners, 73, 75–76, 77; in Muscovy, 99–107, 113, 114, 123, 124; as colleges, 162; reform of, 200; charitable work of, 301–302; closure of, 439
Money/monetary policy. See Finance
Mongolia/Mongols, 21, 48–58, 63, 65, 99–101, 320, 532
Moon, David, 21
Mordvins/Mordovia, 142, 430
Morozov, Boris, 156–157
Morozov family, 90
Moscow, 2, 70–72, 79, 318, 427, 459, 552, 587; epidemics, 9; expansion of Muscovy, 83–127; patriarchate, 131–133; industrialization, 357, 456; police, 359; insurrection in, 369–370; in World War I, 389; in Revolution of 1917, 414; Soviet, 437; architecture, 478; German advance on, 494–495
Moscow Arts Theater, 349
Moscow River, 71
Moscow Society for the Study of Russian History and Antiquity, 256

Moscow University, 242, 259, 297, 479, 570
Mosstroi-1, 601
Most financial group, 601
Mozhaisk, 71, 89
Mstera, 223
Mstislav (prince), 52
Mukden, 333
Munekhin, Misiur, 103
Municipal government, 221–222, 367, 388, 389
Münnich, General B. Kh., 195
Muradeli, Vano, 527
Muraviev, Aleksandr, 260
Muraviev, Nikita, 263
Muraviev, Nikolai, 328
Murom, 89
Muscovy, 19, 83–127, 402
Music, 24, 25, 344–352, 363, 436, 481, 526–527, 558
Muslim Communist Party, 422, 423
Musorgskii, Modest, 346–347
Mussavats, 421

Nagornyi Karabakh, 421, 583, 607
Nagy, Imre, 531, 574
Nakhichevan, 421
Namestniki/vice-regents, 69, 94, 112
Napoleon, 249–252
Napoleonic wars, 241
Narkomnats, 417–418, 422, 423–424, 428
Narkompros, 437
Narodnaia Volia, 313, 317, 359
Narodnost, 554
Narva, 121, 185
Narva River, 30, 65
Naryshkin, Captain, 251–252
Natanson, Mark, 310
Nationalism, 267, 288, 320–352, 334, 412, 511, 520, 535, 606–607
Nationalities, 416–418, 427–433, 466, 546, 557, 558–568, 582–584, 585–586, 610–612; deportations, 503–504, 522, 530
National Salvation Committees, 587
NATO, 517, 518–519, 544, 575, 609–610; Partnership for Peace, 609
Navy, 186, 194, 195, 233, 280, 328, 329, 332, 333, 414, 608; in Crimean War, 281, 286; Ministry, 372
Nazarbaev, President Nursultan, 605–606
Nechaev, Sergei, 309
Nekrasov, Nikolai, 298
Nekrich, Aleksandr, 505

Neman River, 29
Nepmen, 446, 448
Nepravda, 18, 24–25
Nesselrode, Count Karl Robert, 234
Neva River, 54, 63, 437
Nevelskoi, Gennadii, 328
Nevskii, Aleksandr, 54, 63, 65, 71, 86
New Economic Policy, 438, 442–449
New Russia, 258
Newspapers/press, 364, 571, 577, 601; introduction of, 205; censorship of, 298–300, 318, 327; growth of, 382–383; Progressist, 385; in World War I, 388, 390; under Bolsheviks, 400, 404; and collectivization of agriculture, 451
Nicholas I, 259, 263, 264–281, 296
Nicholas II, 329, 332, 334, 338, 343, 344, 369–370, 372–375, 378, 379–380, 381, 383; and World War I, 390; and Revolution of 1917, 391–400
Nicodemus the Hagiorite, 302
Nietzsche, Friedrich, 352
Nikolaev, Leonid, 463
Nikolaevskii Post, 328
Nikolai (metropolitan), 503
Nikon (monk), 44
Nikon (patriarch), 164, 165–174
Nizhnii Novgorod, 89, 139, 140, 149, 172, 223
NKVD, 463–464, 465, 466, 468, 469, 501, 512
Nogai Horde, 108, 115, 117, 171
Nomads, 18, 20, 21, 33, 42, 71; Kipchaks, 45; Mongols, 48–49; Golden Horde, 78–79; Cossacks as, 115; in Caucasus, 238; Turkic, 320–322; and Russian colonization, 325, 327; as inorodtsy, 341; in soviets, 428; in Kazakhstan, 452, 537
Nomenklatura system, 5, 428, 447–448, 467, 477–478, 503, 523, 528, 530, 534, 535, 540, 541, 545, 558, 581
Nomocanon (Byzantine law code), 40
Novgorod, 35–36, 38, 42, 53, 54, 58, 71, 78, 80, 86, 87, 89, 99–101, 153; Lord Novgorod the Great, 61–65
Novgorod-Severskii, 59
Novikov, Nikolai, 242–243
Novocherkassk, 539
Novosilskii family, 90
Nuclear reactors, 512–513, 577, 580
Nuclear weapons, 512–520, 551, 571, 572, 573, 575, 609

Obolenskii, Aleksandr, 381
Obolenskii, Evgenii, 263
Obolenskii family, 90
Obruchev, N. N., 287
Obshchestvennost, 294, 296, 367, 368, 377, 388, 393, 394–396, 399, 400, 483
Obshchina. See Village communes
Ochakov, 197
October Manifesto, 367, 369–370, 372, 374, 377
Octobrists, 340, 376, 382
Odessa, 234, 343, 365; Military District, 523
Ogarev, Nikolai, 273
Ögödei (great khan), 52, 53
Oil and gas industry, 357, 544, 600, 603, 604
Oka River, 66, 71, 89
Okhotsk, 143
Okudzhava, Bulat, 581
Old Believers, 170, 172–174, 181, 254, 301, 377; and Peter I, 200, 346; and peasants, 228, 290; and Cossacks, 229; and agrarian reform, 266; and socialism, 310, 402; artists, 349
Olearius, Adam, 11, 14
Olga (Kievan princess), 37–38
Omsk, 407
Onega, Lake, 8, 62
Oprichnina, 122–127
Optyna Pustyn, 303
Ordjonikidze, Sergei, 425, 447, 462
Ordyn-Nashchokin, Afanasii, 178–179
Orel guberniia, 411
Orenburg, 230
Orgnabor, 458–459
Orthodox Christianity, 5. See also Greek Orthodox Church; Russian Orthodox Church
Orwell, George, 490, 556
Ossetia/Ossetians, 237, 421, 452; national movement, 584
Ostankino, 593, 594, 601
Otrepev, Grigorii, 136–137
Otto I, 38
Ottoman Empire, 6, 115, 175, 314, 385; and Muscovy, 85, 90, 99, 108, 110–111; and Peter I, 192–195; partition of, 231–235, 236; and Crimean War, 279–281, 286, 313; and Armenia, 340–341; trade with, 356; and Balkan states, 387; and Azerbaijanis, 421

Paganism, 15, 20, 21, 22, 37, 38, 48, 60, 143, 147, 347
Pakistan, 520

Palamas, Gregory, 76–77
Palen, Count Petr, 246
Pale of Settlement, 258, 341, 342, 343
Palitsyn, Avraamii, 139, 141
Pamir Mountains, 320
Panin, Count Nikita, 214
Pan-Slavism, 313–317, 318, 341, 385, 387, 389
Paris Peace Conference, 420
Passports, 376, 431, 432, 447, 458–459, 471, 526, 546, 566
Pasternak, Boris, 480, 526, 555, 556, 577
Patolichev, Nikolai, 501
Patrikeev family, 90
Patrimonial monarchy, 91, 92
Patrimony (votchina), 48, 67, 72
Paul (emperor), 241, 243, 245–246
Pavlodar, 605
Pay/wages, 444, 457, 474, 536, 539, 549, 600
Peaceful coexistence, 519–520, 571, 572
Peasant Congress, 369
Peasants, 7–20, 68; in local assemblies, 35, 48; Polish-Lithuanian, 61; in Muscovy, 90–91, 96, 98, 126; under Boris Godunov, 134, 135; fugitive, 158; under Catherine, 217; and Westernization, 220–221, 222; and joint responsibility, 224–228; and Napoleon, 251, 252; and agrarian reform, 266; and Crimean War, 286; and socialism, 310–311; under Alexander III, 317, 318–319; and Russification, 338–339; literary views of, 350, 351; and industrialization, 356, 357, 358, 368–370, 371; as potential revolutionaries, 362; middle, 375–377, 449; and Revolution of 1917, 392, 395–399, 401, 406, 411–412, 414, 425–426; and New Economic Policy, 443, 444, 449; and collectivization of agriculture, 449–455, 470–472; poor, 449; and five-year plans, 456–457; under Khrushchev, 536–540; under Brezhnev, 544–545
Pechenegs, 33, 34, 42, 54
Pechora River/basin, 62, 468
Peipus, Lake, 65
Pentecostals, 536
People's Commissariat for Enlightenment (Narkompros), 437
People's Commissariat for Nationalities (Narkomnats), 417–418, 422, 423–424, 428
People's Commissariat of Foreign Affairs, 487–488
People's Commissariat of Internal Affairs. See NKVD
Peredvizhniki/wanderers, 348
Pereiaslav, 59, 71
Perestroika, 574, 577, 579, 586
Peresvetov, Ivan, 110
Permiaki people, 99
Persia, 6, 21, 37, 235–236, 356, 594
Pestel, Pavel, 261–262
Peterhof, 206
Peter I, 22, 25, 180–209, 213, 214, 219, 234, 236, 269, 276, 346, 402
Peter III, 190, 201
Petitions, 155, 157–159, 472
Petrograd, 391, 392, 395, 409, 413, 414, 436; Soviet, 394, 399; garrison, 397; and Revolution of 1917, 399–400. See also Leningrad; St. Petersburg
Petropavlovsk, 411
Petrov, Anton, 290
Piatakov, Grigorii, 464
Piatigorsk, 117
Pietism, 254
Pinsk, 58
Pipes, Richard, 91
Pitt, William, 233
Platon (metropolitan), 303
Plekhanov, Georgii, 313, 360–361, 362
Pleshcheev family, 205
Pleve, Viacheslav, 262, 342–343, 360
Plevna, 315–316
Pobedonostsev, K. P., 318, 381
Podolia, 59
Pogroms, 340, 341, 343, 344, 410, 584
Poland/Poles, 4, 5, 6, 58–61, 190–192, 287, 564; nobility, 60–61; and Muscovy, 85, 108, 115, 179; union with Lithuania, 120, 160–163; in Time of Troubles, 136–137, 138; in Thirty Years' War, 153–154; and European culture, 176, 248; and Baltic region, 184; and Napoleon, 250; Jews in, 258–259; rebellion in, 304–306, 333; and Russification, 333; industrialization, 357; independence of, 380; in World War I, 389; and Revolution of 1917, 407; Soviet-Polish war of 1920, 417, 419; in world state, 417; in World War II, 490–491, 493, 497, 498; conquest by Red Army, 509–510; post-Stalin, 531; Solidarity movement in, 547–548, 569, 574; in NATO, 609
Polevoi, Nikolai, 272–273

Police/security police, 216, 240, 249, 342–343, 344, 359, 360, 365, 367, 374, 383, 457–458, 510, 567. See also Cheka; GPU; KGB
Politburo, 448, 460, 461, 466, 542, 569, 570, 611
Polotsk, 42, 58, 120, 121
Polotskii, Simeon, 177
Polovtsev, A. A., 373
Poltava, 186–187
Pomestie system, 87, 90, 96–97, 99–101, 114, 204, 289
Pomestnyi sobor, 276, 380–381, 438
Pomochi, 16
Pontic steppes, 51
Populism, 343, 357, 360–361, 362, 384, 402, 533–534
Port Arthur, 329, 332, 366
Posad, 151, 159, 179, 221
Pososhkov, Ivan, 355
Postal system, 50, 54, 89, 150
Potatoes, 10, 11, 266, 526
Potemkin, Grigorii, 233
Poti, 279
Potsdam conference, 510
Pozharskii, Dmitrii, 140
Pravda, 17–18, 24–25, 44, 290
Pre-Conciliar Commission, 381
Premudryi, Epifanii, 77
Pretenderism, 136–139
Prices, 10, 444, 478, 539, 544, 545, 578–579, 597–598
Prikaz system, 113, 115, 155, 178, 183, 249
Pripet River, 29
Privacy, 363, 457, 484, 550
Privatization, 602, 606
Professional strata, 293, 295, 342, 367, 368, 382, 445, 467, 480, 483, 504, 530–531, 548
Progressists, 385
Prokofiev, Sergei, 527
Prokopovich, Feofan, 199
Proletarian Cultural-Educational Associations (Proletkult), 435–437
Property, 151, 217, 384, 385, 485; laws, 96–97
Propiska/dwelling permit, 447, 536
Prostitution, 299, 364
Protestantism, 4, 24, 122, 140, 161, 165, 176, 178, 200, 337, 338, 380
Provisional Government, 392, 393, 395, 396, 397, 398, 399, 406, 408, 435
Prozorovskii, Ivan, 171
Prussia, 175, 176, 187, 190, 191, 243; East, 389
Prut River, 337

Pskov, 65, 87, 89, 99–101, 124, 178
Publishing, 279, 298–300, 553–556. See also Newspapers/press
Pugachev, Emelian, 229–231
Pugachev revolt, 271
Pugo, Boris, 588
Pusher/tolkach, 545, 578
Pushkin, Aleksandr, 261, 264, 271–272, 274, 346, 349, 553
Putilov Works, 357, 366, 391, 396
Putin, Vladimir, 610, 612

Radek, Karl, 408, 464
Radishchev, Aleksandr, 243–244
Raeff, Marc, 218
Railways, 325, 355–356, 442
Rashidov, Sharif, 562–563
Rasputin, Grigorii, 379, 381–382, 390–391
Rasputin, Valentin, 18
Razin, Stepan, 171–172, 229
Reagan, Ronald, 517, 573
Red Army, 407–408, 417, 421, 427, 432, 489, 492, 496, 497, 498, 504, 509–510
Red Guards, 397
Reds, 408–416
Red Square, 494
Refusenik, 566
Reitern, M. Kh., 355
Repnin, Nikolai, 233
Representative assemblies, 247, 248, 260, 263, 292, 317, 366, 367, 368, 374, 407, 413
Research institutes, 208, 256–257, 527–528, 552
Revolutionary Military Council (Revvoensovet), 424
Revolutionary tribunals, 404
Revolution: of 1905, 366–372, 384, 392, 396; of 1917, 22, 391–400, 393, 400–416, 425–426
Reykjavik conference, 573
Riabushinskii, Pavel, 389
Riabushinskii family, 385
Riazan, 52, 86
Ribbentrop, Joachim von, 491
Riga, 187, 339, 565, 587
Right Deviationists, 448, 460
Rightists (in Duma), 376
Rimskii-Korsakov, Nikolai, 345
Rion River, 235
Riurik, 31
Riurikovich dynasty, 131, 133
Riutin, Mikhail, 460–461

Romania, 497, 585, 606–607; Soviet-Polish war of 1920, 417; conquest by Red Army, 510

Roman Mstislavich (prince of Volynia), 58

Romanov, Fedor Nikitich, 141

Romanov, Mikhail, 140, 141, 152–153, 155

Romanov family, 136, 286, 410

Romodanovskii family, 205

Roosevelt, Theodore, 333

Rostov, 42, 58, 62, 65–67, 78, 86

Rostov-on-Don, 495

Rtishchev, Fedor, 177

Rubinstein, Anton, 347

Rublev, Andrei, 78

Rudzutak, Ian, 463

Rumiantsev, A. M., 571

Rumiantsev, General Petr, 231

Russian Academy, 270

Russian Association of Proletarian Writers, 437

Russian Federation, 606, 611

Russian Geographical Society, 256

Russian nationalism, 274; under Alexander II, 299; Bakunin on, 306–307; artistic expression of, 344–352; under Provisional Government, 393–394; under Stalin, 432–433; during World War II, 500, 505; in postwar society, 521; under Brezhnev, 566–568; under Gorbachev, 571, 585; under Yeltsin, 587; and Orthodox Church, 595, 610–612. *See also* Slavophiles

Russian National Unity movement, 592

Russian Orthodox Church, 17, 22–24, 37–40, 41, 57, 148, 611; fasting laws, 11, 17; and alcohol, 12, 14; and Catholic Church, 65, 161–163; in pre-imperial Rus, 72–78, 81, 82; and Muscovy, 85, 97–98, 99–107, 108–110, 113, 119, 121–122; and Cossacks, 115; Moscow patriarchate, 131–133; conversion to, 143, 306, 380; reform of, 165–174, 380–382, 383; under Peter I, 198–199; and Napoleon, 250; and Bible Society, 253–255; under Nicholas I, 267; under Alexander II, 301–304; and Pan-Slavism, 314; Dostoevskii on, 351; and urbanization, 364; in World War I, 388–389; under Stalin, 432, 503; and Soviet government, 438–442; and collectivization of agriculture, 451; postwar persecutions, 534–536; and Communist Party, 595–596

Russian Soviet Federated Socialist Republic, 424, 427, 586

Russia's Choice, 594

Russification, 288–289, 333–341, 378, 417, 420, 432–433, 564

Russo-Japanese War, 332–333, 380

Ruthenia, 166, 169, 336

Rutskoi, Aleksandr, 592, 593

Rykov, Aleksei, 448, 464

Ryleev, Kondratii, 263

Saburov family, 90

St. Basil's Cathedral, 119, 124

St. Petersburg, 186, 206, 242, 255, 262, 302, 318, 344; police, 359; industrialization, 364, 366, 367, 368; in World War I, 389. *See also* Leningrad; Petrograd

St. Pierre, Abbé, 181

Saint-Simon, 278

Sakha-Iakutia, 592

Sakhalin, 328

Sakharov, Andrei, 513, 522, 552, 577, 581, 582, 586

Salons, 273, 275

Salt, 14, 143, 150, 154, 155

Saltykov family, 205

Samara, 13, 407

Samarin, Iurii, 277, 288

Samarkand, 79, 320, 321

Samizdat, 555–557, 565, 566

Samoderzhets, title of, 85

Samogitia, 60

Samoieds, 146

Samosud, 343

Sarai, 72, 79

Saratov, 172, 230, 371, 375

Sarov, 303

Sartak (khan), 54

Sazonov, N. D., 387

Schools. *See* Education

Science and technology, 180, 184–185, 198, 206–209, 217, 256, 433, 467, 513, 525; postwar, 526–528, 543, 550–553, 612

Scissors crisis, 444

Second Department of Imperial Chancellery, 265

Secret societies, 260–264

Sectarianism, 350, 364

Security police. *See* Police

Semiotics and linguistics, 552–553

Serafim, Saint, of Sarov, 303 379, 512

Serafim (metropolitan), 254

Serbia, 234, 387, 388; revolt of 1875–76, 315

Serfdom, 5, 10, 18–19, 135, 152, 276; alcohol production, 13; in Poland-Lithuania, 61, 160, 305, 334; in Volga region, 142; effect of, 159; under Catherine, 216; industrial, 219–220, 230; under Peter I, 220–222; abolition of, 245, 260, 262, 263, 279, 287, 288–292, 307, 425–426; under Paul, 246; and Napoleon, 251; under Nicholas I, 267; second, 470–471
Sergiev, Ioann, 302
Sergii (metropolitan), 441, 503
Sergii of Radonezh, 76–77, 79
Service ethic, 196, 241, 242, 268, 291, 362, 483
Sevastopol, 281, 285, 591
Seven Years' War, 190, 223–224
Shakhnazarov, Georgii, 571
Shakhty trial, 473
Shamanism, 20, 21, 26, 321–322
Shamil, Imam, 239–240
Shanghai, 446
Shchadov, M. I., 579
Shchelokov, N. A., 562–563
Shcherbatov family, 205
Shchusev, Aleksei, 478
Shein, General M. B., 154
Shelepin, Aleksandr, 541
Shelest, Petro, 564
Sheremetev, Ivan, 119
Sheremetev family, 205
Shevardnadze, Eduard, 572, 585, 608
Shevchenko, Taras, 335–336
Shipka Pass, 315
Shlisselburg fortress, 243
Shorin, Vasilii, 150
Shostakovich, Dmitrii, 481, 526–527, 528
Shuiskii, Vasilii Ivanovich, 137, 138
Shuiskii family, 108
Shushkevich, Stanislav, 589
Shuvalov, Ivan, 208, 214
Shuvalov, P. I., 10, 214, 355
Siberia, 18, 19, 328; khanates of, 85, 108, 117, 143; Chancellery, 146; exile to, 244, 258, 305, 504, 532; civil war in, 407, 410, 411; under Soviet government, 424; and New Economic Policy, 443; collectivization of agriculture in, 454; industrialization, 468; Virgin Lands campaign, 537–538
Silvestr, 97
Simbirsk, 172
Simeon (khan), 37

Siniavskii, Andrei, 556
Sipiagin, Dmitrii, 360
Skhod. See Village assemblies
Skobelev, General Mikhail, 299, 324–325
Skobelev, M. I., 397
Skrynnikov, R. G., 113
Slavery, 31, 35, 41, 42, 46, 55, 69, 115, 134, 137, 151–152, 468, 499, 512. See also Serfdom
Slav-Greek-Latin Academy, 208
Slavinetskii, Epifanii, 167
Slavophiles, 275–278, 288, 303, 306–307, 342
Slavs, 29–30, 31, 33–34, 37, 66, 115, 385, 386, 431, 542, 610
Slovakia, 497
Smolensk, 53, 59, 87, 89, 138, 153–154, 164, 494, 500
Sobornost, 275–276, 380, 384
Social Democratic Workers' Party/Social Democrats, 361, 365, 367, 384, 510, 574
Socialism, 278, 306–311, 312–313, 340, 344, 352, 360–361, 362, 368, 384, 392, 596; international, 400–407, 416–418, 445–446, 487–488, 518–519; developed, 541–568
Socialist Revolutionaries, 359, 360, 367, 370, 393, 394, 398–399, 400, 407, 411, 413
Sokhozy/state farms, 458
Solidarity movement, 547–548
Soloviev, Sergei, 256
Soloviev, Vladimir, 303, 351, 352, 434
Solvychegodsk, 143
Solzhenitsyn, Aleksandr, 554, 556, 567, 577, 581
Sophia Miloslavskaia, 180–181
Sorge, Richard, 494–495
Sormovo, 413
Sorskii, Nil, 104, 105
Soslovie, 292, 293, 362
Soviet (Council) of Workers' Deputies, 367, 368–369
Soviet-Polish war of 1920, 417, 419
Soviets, 22, 393, 394, 396, 397, 399, 400, 404, 405, 416, 453, 552, 587
Soviet Union, formation of, 418–425
Sovnarkom, 445, 447
Space technology, 525, 543, 551
Spain, 254, 489
Spanish Civil War, 490
Speranskii, Mikhail, 248, 249, 265, 355
Stakhanov, Aleksei, 474, 576
Stakhanovites, 458, 483

Stalin, I. V., 5, 424–425, 427, 428, 432–433, 445–448, 454, 511, 527; and five-year plans, 455–459, 473; purges, 459–469, 490, 523–524, 530, 532, 576; Nazi-Soviet nonaggression pact, 491; Soviet-German war, 491–506

Stalina, Nadia, 461

Stalingrad, 456, 495–496

Stanislavskii, Konstantin, 349, 436, 438

Stanovoi mountains, 147–148

Starets/holy man, 351, 379, 381

Starodub, 78

Starosta/village elder, 19, 67, 94, 112, 156, 222, 225–226

Stasov, Vladimir, 346–347

State Bank, 356

State Council, 248–249, 317, 374, 378, 380, 390

State farms/*sokhozy*, 458

Stavka, 390, 391

Stavropol, 569, 570, 576–577

Stefan of Perm, 77

Stepashin, Sergei, 604

Stoglav Council, 114

Stolypin, Petr, 375, 376, 377, 378, 379, 380, 381, 387, 390

Straits Convention of 1871, 387

Stravinskii, Igor, 347–348

Streltsy/musketeers, 228

Strikes, 365–367, 370, 383, 391, 413, 457, 529, 536, 539, 579, 580

Stroganov, Grigorii, 143

Stroganov, Pavel, 248

Stroganov family, 141

Struve, Petr, 384, 385

Students, 296–297, 310, 312–313, 344, 530

Sufism, 238

Sukhona River, 14

Sultan-Galiev, Mir-Said, 422, 423

Sumarokov, Aleksandr, 207

Sumgait, 583

Supreme Council of the National Economy (VSNKh), 405, 427, 455

Supreme Soviet, 566, 580, 588, 590, 591, 592, 600, 603

Suslov, Mikhail, 540, 571

Suvorin, A. S., 299

Suvorov, Aleksandr, 197, 231

Suzdal, 53, 58, 65–67, 78

Sviatopolk (Kievan prince), 40–41, 42, 46

Sviatoslav (Kievan prince), 33, 36, 37

Sviatoslav (grand prince of Kiev), 41, 45–46

Sviazhsk, 117

Sweden, 6, 62, 63, 85, 107, 120, 138, 153, 175, 337; and Baltic Sea, 184–190

Syria, 193–194

Syrtsov, S. I., 460

Sytin, I. D., 299

Szlachta, 61. *See* Polish nobility

Table of Ranks, 204, 205, 216, 227, 249

Taganrog, 195

Tajiks/Tajikistan, 320–321, 423, 424, 584, 607

Tallinn, 339

Taman penninsula, 233

Tamara (queen of Georgia), 235

Tambov, 379, 411

Tannenberg, 389; Battle of, 60

Tariffs, 219, 223, 357

Tashkent, 324; Congress of Soviets, 422

Tatar ASSR, 467

Tatar-Bashkir Republic, 423

Tatarstan, 592

Tatlin, Vladimir, 437–438

Tauride Palace, 393

Taxation, 12–13, 16, 17, 19, 21, 292, 599; by Mongols, 55; by princes, 69; in Muscovy, 90–91, 94, 98, 112, 126; under Boris Godunov, 135; excise tax, 150, 151, 156, 224, 356, 357; for military expansion, 154–155; poll tax, 194, 219, 221, 223–224, 357; by local government, 240–241; under Alexander II, 291; evasion, 601; Temporary Extraordinary Commission, 601

Tbilisi, 428, 552, 565, 584

Television, 23, 593, 594, 601

Temuchin (Chingiz Khan), 49

Terekhov, R., 454

Terrorism, 359, 360, 368, 371, 374, 382–383, 410, 411, 413

Teutonic Knights, 63, 65, 85, 107, 120

Theater, 25, 166, 344–352, 363, 436, 438, 481, 524, 555

Third Department of Imperial Chancellery, 265, 271, 273

Thirty Years' War, 153–154, 175

Three Emperors' League, 316

Thurn, Jörg von, 102

Tien Shan Mountains, 321

Tiflis, 236, 237, 341

Tikhon (patriarch), 439–440, 441

Tikhonov, Nikolai, 542

Tilsit, 250

Timber, 16, 19, 66, 94, 99, 226, 329, 377, 468

Time of Troubles, 95, 136–142, 149, 152, 165

Timofeevich, Ermak, 143

Timur (Tamerlane), 79, 80, 321

Tiraspol, 420

Tito, Marshal (Josip Broz), 511, 518–519, 524

Tiumen, 143

Tiutchev, Fedor, 313

Tobol River, 513

Tobolsk, 143, 322, 411

Tokhtamysh, 79, 80

Toliatti, 576

Tolstoi, Dmitrii, 318–319

Tolstoi, Lev, 299, 303, 350, 553

Tomskii, Mikhail, 448, 464

Towns/urbanization, 35, 36, 47, 317, 364–365, 550; in Muscovy, 75, 90–91, 92, 94, 149; under Boris Godunov, 135; under Catherine, 217, 221–222; nationalities in, 358–359, 563–564; and New Economic Policy, 442; and five-year plans, 456; dwelling permits, 459; urban planning, 476–479

Trade/commerce, 14–15, 20, 30–31, 33, 35, 571; in Kievan Rus, 42, 45, 47, 48; and Mongol conquest, 53–54, 55; Novgorod, 61, 62; under Golden Horde, 78; by Muscovy, 117, 120; Nizhnii Novgorod, 140; Siberia, 147–148; and urbanization, 149–151, 178; joint companies, 179; with Europe, 194; under Catherine II, 221–222, 223; under Peter I, 236; with central Asia, 322; with Georgia, 340; and railways, 356; under Bolsheviks, 405, 414; New Economic Policy, 442–443; under Stalin, 448, 515

Trade unions, 364, 365, 383, 390, 405, 413–414, 445, 448, 458, 483, 550, 579, 580

Transcaucasian Republics, 425, 432, 460

Transcaucasus, 287

Trans-Dniester Republic, 606–607

Transportation, 16, 54, 223, 285–286, 327–333, 377, 458, 478, 528, 536

Trans-Siberian Railway, 328, 329, 332, 356

Trans-Volga Elders, 104–105

Transylvania, 53, 574

Treaties: Adrianople, 279; Aigun, 328; Andrusovo, 184; Beijing, 328; Berlin, 387; Brest-Litovsk, 401, 407; Gulistan, 236; Kuchuk-Kainardji, 231, 280; Lublin, 160; Nerchinsk, 148; Nystad, 187; Paris, 286; Pereiaslavl, 164; Stolbovo, 153; Tilsit, 187; Turkmanchai, 236;

Union, of 1922, 424–425, 588, 589; Unkiar Skelessi, 279–280; Westphalia, 182

Trepov, General F. F., 312

Tretiakov, Pavel, 348, 349

Tribes/tribalism, 2, 4, 6, 29–31, 34, 35, 45, 49, 66, 146, 237, 418, 428, 558, 559, 562

Tribute, 21, 34, 35, 42, 48, 50, 54, 55, 57, 63, 65, 67–68, 69, 71, 80, 142, 146, 148

Trinity Monastery, 181, 303

Trotskii, Lev, 362, 367, 407–408, 410, 411, 434–435, 440, 446, 447, 448, 464, 486

Trubetskoi, Nikolai, 57–58

Trubetskoi, Sergei, 259, 263, 264

Truman, Harry, 510, 512

Tsar: as God's anointed, 18; title of, 85, 108, 109–110, 131, 164

Tselovalniki, 12

Tsereteli, Iraklii, 399

Tsushima, Battle of, 333

Tsyiatskii, 70

Tukhachevskii, Mikhail N., 415, 467

Tula, 154, 413

Tulchin, 262

Tungus, 146

Tura River, 143

Turgenev, Ivan, 553

Turkestan, 325, 326–327, 422–423

Turkey, 6, 21, 30, 73–74, 82, 190, 215, 233, 234, 236, 280, 387, 421, 565

Turkish War: of 1768–1774, 224; of 1877–78, 313–317

Turkmenia/Turkmens, 321, 324, 424, 467

Turov, 42, 58

Tushino, 138

Tvardovskii, Aleksandr, 433, 553–555

Tver (Kalinin), 71, 86, 90, 500

Udel principalities, 68–69, 89, 94, 123, 125

Udmurts, 142

Uezdy, 216, 255, 373, 377, 398

Ufa, 580–581

Uglich, 78

Ugra River, 87

Ukraine, 20, 258, 305, 375–377, 398, 407, 409, 424, 522, 526, 568, 605–608, 610; Cossack rebellion, 163–165; Russification in, 335–337; industrialization, 357; and Soviet-Polish war of 1920, 417; nationalism in, 419–420, 428, 506, 535, 564, 583; Communist Party membership, 428; and New Economic Policy, 443; purges

in, 467; German advances in, 497, 499, 500; religion in, 535; urbanization, 564; independence, 589; treaty of friendship with, 608
Ukrainian Military Congress, 419–420
Ulam, Adam, 402–403
Uniate Church, 136, 162, 191, 258, 306, 336, 564
Union of Brest, 162
Union of Hanover, 187
Union of Krewo, 60
Union of Liberation, 365, 368, 384
Union of 17 October. *See* Octobrists
Union of Salvation, 260–261
Union of Soviet Socialist Republics, 425
Union of the Russian People, 343–344, 380
Union of Welfare, 260–261
Union Treaty of 1922, 424–425, 588, 589
United Nations, 512, 518, 607, 610
United States, 357; bourgeois capitalism in, 360; in world state, 417; American Relief Administration, 443; military aid from, 493, 497; diplomatic relations with, 509, 519; and nuclear weapons, 512–520, 513–514, 516
Urals, 1, 3, 7, 19, 62, 322, 409; industrialization, 468
Urals-Siberian campaign of 1928–29, 449
Urbanization. *See* Towns/urbanization
Uspenskii, B. A., 22, 38, 201
Uspenskii Cathedral, 108, 137
Ussuri River, 328, 518–519
Uvarov, Count S. S., 267
Uzbekistan, 321, 423, 424, 467, 562–563

Vakhitov, Mulla-Nur, 422
Valdai Hills, 2
Valuev, Petr, 291, 292, 300, 305, 336
Vasiliev Island, 366
Vasilii I, 74–75, 80
Vasilii II, 80, 82, 91–92
Vasilii III, 86, 87, 89, 105, 106
Vasilii Kosoi, 80
Veche, 35–36, 55, 57
Veliaminov family, 205
Velichkovskii, Paisii, 302
Veniamin (metropolitan), 440
Verv, 35
Viatichi, 66
Viatka River, 99
Viazma, 89
Vienna, Congress of (1815), 253
Vietnam, 520

Vikings, 6, 30, 31, 32, 34
Village assemblies, 17, 197, 225–226, 369, 395–396, 398, 399, 406, 449, 450, 453
Village chiefs, 559
Village communes, 15–19, 35, 48, 67, 69, 94, 112, 148, 156, 222, 225–228, 273, 358, 375, 376–377, 378, 399, 432
Village elder. *See Starosta*
Vilna/Vilnius, 59, 255, 256, 389, 587
Virgin Lands campaign, 537–538
Viskovatyi, Ivan, 119
Vistula region, 305
Vitte, Count S. Iu., 328–329, 332, 342, 343, 344, 357–358
Vladimir (grand prince of Kiev), 2, 12, 37–38, 42, 45
Vladimir (city and region), 11, 52, 58, 65–67, 80, 166, 222–223
Vladimir Monomakh, 46–47, 100, 109
Vladivostok, 328
Vlasov, General Andrei, 499–500
Vodka, 11, 13–14, 16, 150, 450, 594
Voevody, 69, 73
Voguly (Mansi) people, 99, 143
Volga German Autonomous Republic, 504
Volga-Kama basin, 443, 566
Volga River/basin, 2, 7, 14, 19, 31, 61–62, 66, 89, 119, 326, 398, 409, 424, 439, 454
Volga Tatars, 565–566
Volia, 18, 115, 139, 225–228, 251, 252, 290, 336
Volkhov River, 29, 30, 62
Vologda Province, 8
Volokolamsk Monastery, 122
Volosteli, 69
Volosti, 67, 94, 156, 290, 291, 376, 377, 398, 404
Volotskii, Iosif, 23, 104–105, 109, 124, 173
Volynia, 58–61
Volynskii family, 205
Vorkuta, 468, 579
Voroshilov, K. E., 466
Vorotynskii family, 90
Vorskla River, Battle of, 60
Votchina/patrimony, 48, 67, 72, 90, 91–92, 114, 121, 204
Vozha River, 79
Vsevolod (prince of Vladimir), 66, 67
Vvedenskii, Aleksandr, 440
Vychegda River, 14, 99
Vysheslav (prince), 42
Vyshinskii, Andrei, 464

Vyshnegradskii, I. Ia., 357
Vytautas, 60

Wałęsa, Lech, 547–548
Wallachia, 164, 234
War Industry Committees, 389, 391
Warsaw, 257, 389, 498
Warsaw Pact, 531, 547, 571, 573, 574, 575, 608
Werth, Alexander, 502
Westernizers, 169–170, 175–209, 216, 218, 228–229, 275, 276–277, 278–279, 288, 295–296, 571
Whites, 407, 408–416, 421–422, 439, 466
White Sea, 62, 63, 468
White Terror, 418
Wielopolski, Alexander, 304
Winter Palace, 206
Władysław (king), 138, 139, 163
Władysław Jagiello, 60
Women, 17, 35, 48, 550, 557; and property, 96–98, 295; and salons, 269–279; education of, 297, 308; Muslim, 422; wages for, 444; and collectivization of agriculture, 452; family policy, 484–486; in workforce, 524, 536, 548–549; rural labor, 526
Workers/industrial workers, 310, 357–366, 383; and Revolution of 1905, 366–372; compulsory insurance for, 377, 378; and World War I, 389; and Revolution of 1917, 391–400, 405, 409, 413–414; and Communist Party, 415; and proletkults, 436, 437; and New Economic Policy, 444–445; five-year plans, 472–476, 492–493; in postwar economy, 524–526; post-Stalin, 531; under Khrushchev, 536–540; under Gorbachev, 576–582; under Yeltsin, 602
Workers' and Peasants' Red Army. See Red Army
World War I, 388–391, 392
World War II, 433, 488, 490–491, 491–506, 521
Writers, 269–279
Writers' Union, 479–480, 527, 555

Xinjiang, 1

Yalta conference, 510
Yalu River, 329
Yeltsin, Boris, 575, 576, 582, 586–596, 611, 612; and Chechnia, 602–605
Yeremenko, General A. I., 496
Yezhov, N. I., 466
Young Turk movement, 326
Youth movement, 550
Yugoslavia, 439, 510, 511, 524, 609–610

Zagladin, Vadim, 571
Zagorsk, 535
Zaikonospasskii Monastery, 177
Zalygin, Sergei, 577
Zamiatin, Evgenii, 409, 436
Zasulich, Vera, 312
Zeki, 468–469
Zemgor, 389
Zemlia, 111–112, 379
Zemlia i Volia, 313
Zemshchina, 123–127
Zemskie nachalniki/land commandants, 319, 373, 378, 393, 425–426
Zemskie sobory, 112–113, 133–134, 138, 148, 152, 156–158, 381
Zemstvo, 112, 293, 317, 318, 368, 370, 373–374, 377, 378, 388, 389
Zeravshan valley, 320
Zhdanov, Andrei, 501, 523–524, 526
Zhirinovskii, Vladimir, 594–595
Zhivov, V. M., 201
Zhukov, General Georgii Konstantinovich, 489, 493, 494–495, 496, 523
Zinoviev, Aleksandr, 414, 447, 448, 464, 537, 551
Ziuganov, Gennadii, 595
Zizanii, Lavrentii, 166
Zoshchenko, Mikhail, 526, 527
Zubatov, Sergei, 359, 365
Zveno/link system, 502–503
Zygmunt III, 138, 139
Zyriane people, 99